Life's Pilgrimage Through the Gītā

Rediscovering Indian Literary Classics
(ISSN - 0972-0111)

1. Taittirīya Upaniṣad: With the Original Text in Sanskrit and Roman Transliteration. Translation with an Exhaustive Commentary; by Muni Narayana Prasad. (ISBN 81-246-0014-7)

2,4-5. Bṛhadāraṇyaka Upaniṣad: With Original Text in Roman Transliteration. English Translation and Appendices; by Nitya Chaitanya Yati; Vol. 1: Madhu Kāṇḍa; Vol. 2: Muni Kāṇḍa; Vol. 3: Khila Kāṇḍa. (ISBN 81-246-0008-2)

3. Kena Upaniṣad: With the Original Text in Sanskrit and Roman Transliteration. Translation with an Extensive Commentary; by Muni Narayana Prasad. (ISBN 81-246-0034-1)

6. Muṇḍaka Upaniṣad: With the Original Text in Sanskrit and Roman Transliteration. Translation with an Exhaustive Commentary; by Muni Narayana Prasad. (ISBN 81-246-0105-4)

7. Kaṭha Upaniṣad: With the Original Text in Sanskrit and Roman transliteration. Translation with an Exhaustive Commentary; by Muni Narayana Prasad. (ISBN 81-246-0110-0)

8. Praśna Upaniṣad: With the Original Text in Sanskrit and Roman transliteration. Translation with an Extensive Commentary; by Muni Narayana Prasad. (ISBN 81-246-0129-1)

9. Aitareya Upaniṣad: With the Original Text in Sanskrit and Roman transliteration. Translation with an Extensive Commentary; by Muni Narayana Prasad. (ISBN 81-246-0142-9)

10. Śrī Dakṣiṇāmūrti Stotram of Śrī Śaṅkarācārya; with the commentary Tattvaprakāśikā; by Swami Tattvavidananda Saraswati; Edited by Puppala B. (ISBN 81-246-0210-7)

11. Āditya Hṛdayam: With the Commentary Tattvaprakāśikā; by Swami Tattvavidananda Saraswati (ISBN 81-246-0231-X)

12. Vāstuśāstra: Ancient Indian Architecture and Civil Engineering — Retrospects and Prospects; by Rahul Kumar Altekar (ISBN 81-246-0246-8)

13. Gaṇapati Upaniṣad: With the Commentary Tattvaprakāśikā; by Swami Tattvavidananda Saraswati (ISBN 81-246-0265-4)

Rediscovering Indian Literary Classics, no. 14

Life's Pilgrimage Through The Gītā

A Commentary on the Bhagavad Gītā

Swami Muni Narayana Prasad

D. K. Printworld (P) Ltd.
New Delhi

Cataloging in Publication Data — DK
[Courtesy: D.K. Agencies (P) Ltd. <docinfo@dkagencies.com>]

Narayana Prasad, *Muni,* 1938 -

Life's pilgrimage through the Gītā : commentary on the Bhagavad Gītā / Swami Muni Narayana Prasad.

p. 23 cm.
(Rediscovering Indian literary classics, no. 14)
Includes text of Bhagvadgītā in Sanskrit (Devanagari and Roman).
ISBN 13: 9788124603109
ISBN 10: 8124603103

1. Bhagavadgītā. — Commentaries. I. Bhagavadgītā. English & Sanskrit. II. Title. III. Series : Rediscovering Indian literary classics, no. 14.

294. 592 404 7 21

ISBN13: 978-81-246-0310-9 (HB) ISBN10: 81-246-0310-3
ISBN13: 978-81-246-0355-0 (PB) ISBN10: 81-246-0355-3

First published in India in 2005
Second impression in 2008

Published and printed by:
D. K. Printworld (P) Ltd.
Regd. office : *'Sri Kunj'*, F-52, Bali Nagar
Ramesh Nagar Metro Stn., New Delhi - 110 015
Phones : (011) 2545-3975; 2546-6019; *Fax* : (011) 2546-5926
E-mail: dkprintworld@vsnl.net
Web: www.dkprintworld.com

Preface

It might appear odd if the founder of a spiritual movement and two of his immediate successors wrote separate commentaries on the same Vedāntic text, as has happened in the Narayana Gurukula.

Nataraja Guru, our founder, wrote his famous *Gītā* commentary, which was first published in 1961. Here the parallels of ideas were mainly from the West.

Guru Nitya Chaitanya Yati, his successor, wrote a condensed commentary in English and an elaborate one in Malayālam. While following the line of thought of his Guru, the parallels used by Guru Nitya, were from the East.

The present commentary written by Guru Nitya's successor, rather than going into parallel streams of thought, prefers to try and explore what is directly evident in the verses and chapters of the text.

Way back in 1951, while I was seventeen years old, I happened to participate in a thirtytwo-day-long discourse on the *Gītā* by a renowned scholar. Though at that time I understood little, then, it aroused in me an enthusiasm to undertake the learning of the *Gītā*. Afterwards, when I became a disciple of Nataraja Guru, his commentary on the *Gītā*, along with the philosophy of Narayana Guru, marked the guidelines of my disciplehood. During all these years and for almost two decades the longing to arrive at a clear understanding of the *Gītā* constantly welled up in my being.

It was only after the *samādhi* of Nataraja Guru, that I felt fully satisfied in this regard. Nataraja Guru himself had nudged me towards the core of the *Gītā* not only through direct teaching, but also by asking penetrating questions. These questions, which he himself never answered, required long contemplation (in my case, two decades!) to finally get answered.

I also had the opportunity to take down more than half of Guru Nitya Chaitanya Yati's commentary in Malayālam. The *Gītā* contains a number of apparently paradoxical positions that require solution before all the several details can be put together into a coherant philosophical vision, and this was made easier with the help of hints in Guru Nitya's commentary.

Thus I was aided in many ways in my attempt to understand the *Gītā*, and by way of further preparing myself to gain an overall perspective, I gave a series of discourses on the *Gītā* at different places. Whenever I felt a lack of clarity or became unsure how to proceed, the philosophy of Narayana Guru came to my rescue. The present book is thus an outcome of the efforts I have described earlier.

It may be recalled here that Ādi Śaṅkara's immediate succeessors had made further commentaries on those of their Guru. Such successive commentaries are known as *vārttikas* (explanatory supplements) and *ṭīkās* (glosses), and the present commentary can be treated as a *vārtika*, though it can be read and understood independently also.

The commentary for each verse was written after discussions with a group of senior research students of the Narayana Gurukula, who also took down the commentry. This dictation was given in Malayālam, while I prepared the English version myself. The Malayālam version was published in 2000 and was well received by readers, and well reviewed by the press. Mrs. Kala of Bangalore helped me with the editing of the book.

Messrs D.K. Printworld of New Delhi are rendering great services to the cause of promoting the wisdom heritage of India. They had always shown willingness to publish such commentaries by including them in their series, "Rediscovering Indian Literary Classics." Those who love wisdom will remain grateful to D.K. Printworld.

I offer this *Life's Pilgrimage Through the Gītā*, as a guide to spiritual aspirants who look for guidance in the *Gītā*.

Prostrations at the feet of my two direct *gurus*, and the long line of previous *gurus*!

Varkala **Swami Muni Narayana Prasad**
Feb. 13, 2005
Vasant Pañcamī

Contents

Introduction

INDIA has always been glorified for her wisdom tradition. The Sanskrit name of India, 'Bhārata,' itself means "one who delights in effulgence" (*bhā* meaning effulgence, and *rata,* the one who delights in). What is the essential content of this wisdom? It is necessary to know that which is essentially real in one's being; only then will one be able to lead a happy life. One should know that one's existence is inseparable from the existence of the whole, and one's life is inseparable from the life of the whole. This awareness makes life meaningful and free of fetters. This is the essential content of wisdom, and the ultimate goal of life.

The Bhagavad-Gītā

This wisdom, more a vision than a systematized philosophy, first found expression in the Upaniṣads. The gems of this vision, scattered all through the various Upaniṣads, were collected, collated and systematized as a critically appreciable school of thought by Bādarāyaṇa in his *Vedānta-Sūtras,* also known as *Brahma-Sūtras, Uttara-Mīmāṁsā-Sūtras* or *Śārīraka-Mīmāṁsā-Sūtras.* Bādarāyaṇa's goal was to ensure logical plausibility to the philosophical problems, directly and indirectly resolved in the Upaniṣads. The *Bhagavad-Gītā,* on the other hand, re-presents the same philosophy of life — the Advaita Philosophy — as the one and final absolute solution to all conflicting life situations. One's own life, its peculiarities, and dilemmas are all perceived as part of the overall wheel of life — *prakṛti* or nature — which rolls on moving by its inherent creative urge. This perception brings about a peaceful life, and gives one the boldness to face dilemmas with undeterred firmness, and an absolute sense of freedom and detachment. The *Gītā,* in enabling its student to transform a non-dual vision of Reality into this kind of life, gives an experience far different from any kind of certainty through intellectual acumen.

Universal Appeal

The *Gītā* fulfils the need for universality. National, religious and other barriers are rendered irrelevant under the force of its vision, and this has gained the *Gītā* universal acceptance. It cuts across all boundaries, even as the Hindus continue to treat it as their most sacred scripture.

The *Gītā* has been translated into almost all the world languages, sometimes many translations appearing in the same language. Each new translation hopes to be closer to the original. Countless commentaries on the *Gītā* have appeared through the ages. Though not much is known about the commentaries prior to Śaṅkara, a large collection of varying nature, emerging after Śaṅkara, is now available. However, often, though the insights are profound, the feeling still continues that something more remains hidden, and this is what urges people into creating new commentaries. Some of these commentaries appeared to support particular ideologies or ideals, with proponents of certain schools of thought choosing to interpret it in ways that supported their philosophy. What the commentators often find difficult or even forget, is being true to the vision and intention of the original author, Vyāsa. This point was underscored by Nataraja Guru in his commentary on the *Gītā*.

Dialectics

Nataraja Guru's guiding principle in his work was to be fully true to the spirit of Vyāsa's intentions. He kept as a central point the fact that the *Gītā* calls itself a *yoga śātsra* (the science of *yoga*). Kṛṣṇa himself off and on points out that he relies on *yoga-buddhi* (the method of *yoga*). *Yogī, yukta, yogārūḍha, yogayukta, yogayuktātmā* are some of the terms he uses to identify those who understand his teaching. Nataraja Guru pointed out that this *yoga-buddhi* is, in essence, not different from the "dialectics" of Western thought, used from the time of Socrates. Plato characterized "dialectics" as the coping stone of wisdom. The *Gītā*, in the same tone, declares that its ultimate teaching is "that wisdom, attaining which, nothing more remains to be known."

The characteristic of having opposing facets is, in general, present in all life situations, e.g., pain and pleasure, heat and cold, success and failure, gain and loss. It is comparable to the two poles of a magnet, one defining the other. Like a magnet, life situations too have their own polar opposites. In real life, this creates a number of dilemmas; the way out is realizing the one Reality underlying such opposites. This has the advantage that the opposite poles became means to know the one neutral Reality. Not only do we then discover what Reality is, but we also become aware that the dilemma was, in the first place, caused by our wrongly judging apparent facets for reality. Moreover, this intuitive awareness enables us to face all conflicting situations with a firmness hitherto unknown. This is the vision that the *Īśa Upaniṣad* is pointing to, when it says,

> Enlightened on the secret of wisdom and ignorance together, one crosses over death through knowing ignorance, and attains immortality resorting to wisdom.
>
> — 11

Again,

> Enlightened on the secret of becoming and destruction together, one crosses over death through knowing destruction, and attains immortality tthrough knowing what becoming is.
>
> — 14

The best example citable from the *Gītā* is Verse II. 16, which reads,

> The unreal cannot manifest itself. The real never ceases to manifest itself. The inherent Truth of these two has thus been perceived by seers of the ultimate Reality.

Why Another New Commentary?

Nataraja Guru's commentary on the *Gītā* was based on the awareness that the dialectics of Plato and the *yoga-buddhi* or *buddhi-yoga* of the *Gītā*, are essentially one. Following the same trail, this commentator has been meditating on both the original and Nataraja Guru's commentary. On this journey was found that a number of references of dialectical import presented themselves and it was felt that tracking and explicating these would render Nataraja Guru's comments even more meaningful and closer to life's problems. Ādi Śaṅkara, referred to in the history of Indian thought as "the commentator" (*bhāṣyakāra*), had pressed some of his disciples to elucidate further on his own commentaries. Sureśvara's *Vārttika* on the *Bṛhadāraṇyaka Upaniṣad* is one of the best outcomes of this. Such *vārttikas* (glossarial elucidations) are meant to further clarify points that may not have been made sufficiently clear by an earlier commentary, by adding more supporting points and clearing points of doubt, etc. This book, *Life's Pilgrimage through the Gītā,* is really meant more as a *vārttika* to Nataraja Guru's commentary.

The Overall Scheme of the Gītā

The philosophy of life portrayed in the *Gītā* has a structural coherence and perfection, and Nataraja Guru compares it to the structure of an arched doorway— an arch made of the eighteen well-shaped stones of each chapter. The first and the last stones rest on *terra firma,* and the other stones, each with its specific shape and position, one over another, meet at a central neutral point touching the heights of wisdom. The *Gītā* begins with Arjuna's very down-to-earth-dilemma. Rising from there, Kṛṣṇa's discourse takes Arjuna and the readers with him, step by step, to the zenith of wisdom's secret, revealed in Chapter IX. Then begins the reverse process, of descending to the actualities of life as it concerns the individual. Arjuna is finally seen to be rid of all doubts and purposefully holding up his bow and arrow in the battle field. So too, as a result of this teaching we will find overselves standing on the firm ground of life, with a sense of purpose — aware of our place and role in the overall scheme of life.

The Importance of Chapters III and XI

As this writer dwelt at length on the original text of the *Gītā,* aided by Nataraja Guru's commentary, the overall plan of teaching slowly became clearer with each reading, more particularly in the light of

Chapters III and XI, dealing with *karma* and the cosmic form of the Real. Arjuna's conflict originated from his judgment that he was about to commit the unpardonable sin by killing his *gurus* and siblings. It takes him a while to see that the doer of all actions that take place in *prakṛti* (nature) is *prakṛti* itself, not an individual. As part of *prakṛti*, we too remain active, yet all such *karmas* are always nature's and not ours. Since we are not the doers, there is no question of our committing sin or gaining any merit. Perceiving ourselves, our life, and our activities as part of *prakṛti*, sublimates those actions (*karmas*) as *niṣkāma-karmas* (non-motivated actions). And *karma* becomes transformed as *karma-yoga*.

The wheel of *karma*, of *prakṛti*, is eternally rolling on and our *karmas* are a part of this. Ignorant of this simple fact, we think, "I am the doer of this *karma*," and this results in our falling into the mire of a deep sense of sinfulness. Chapter III highlights this aspect; Verse 27 underscores it thus:

> Actions in every way do take place owing to the *guṇas* of *prakṛti*. Deluded by I-sense, one holds, "I am their doer."

Narayana Guru confirms this perception at the very beginning of the Chapter *Karma-Darśana* (Vision by Action) of his *Darśana-Mālā* (Garland of Visions), thus:

> *Ātmā* alone, owing to its own *māyā*, does *karmas*, assuming numerous forms.

This *karma*-perspective is the overall teaching of the *Gītā*, which helps to gain a hitherto unknown clarity.

Chapter XI, Yoga of Cosmic Form (*Viśvarūpa-Darśana-Yoga*), in unravelling the applied aspect of wisdom, gives further clarity to the overall scheme of the *Gītā*. "All the multiplicities are really I alone" is what Kṛṣṇa ultimately reveals in Chapter IX, and, as though flipping the coin, in the next chapter, he teaches, "I manifest as everything." Arjuna *understands* that it is the Absolute alone that exists, that it is the Absolute alone that appears as everything. Now the desire wells up in his (Arjuna's) mind to *perceive* directly what he has *understood* clearly — a desire to transmute philosophical understanding into a vision of life. Kṛṣṇa, in order to fulfil this desire, shows him his cosmic form in which Arjuna actually sees all the manifestations referred to in Chapter X. Every person in the battlefield, including Arjuna, is also seen in this cosmic form of Kṛṣṇa, appearing as part of the cosmos. The suggestion is that each of us, while living, must view ourselves as part of and one with the cosmic system, the form in which the one ever-existing Reality manifests.

Every individual, even as living in unity with the cosmic system, has personal characteristics. These should also be known to oneself while living as part of the whole, and should be given full consideration, while choosing a way of life or opting for a field of activity. Only then does one live as oneself, happy with oneself. This requires an advance preparation on our part, the most important of which is submitting onself to a self-examination to identify what peculiarities and potentials are hidden in one's own inner nature. In Chapters XII to XVIII, the *Gītā* seeks to enable each of us to make such a self-examination and decisively know for oneself what one is. And therefore, it is in the light of the *Viśvarūpa* of Chapter XI that one should view the rest of the chapters. This writer feels, clarifying this point would make the structural scheme, which Nataraja Guru brought out, more discernible.

The Problem of the Hereafter

One of the intriguing beliefs that lingers in the religious mind of Indians is concerning the state after death — that souls are reborn in later birth according to the merits of their *karma*s in the present birth. This writer has dwelt at length on how this problem is dealt with in the *Gītā* and Upaniṣads and, in the light of the philosophy of Advaita, has gained some insights with the passage of time.

The only Reality is immortal, and individual entities are transitory appearances that emerge and re-merge in that one Reality. Hence, what is real in each being is that one Substance alone, apparent individual beings having no existence of their own. If individual's identity is with the one Substance, then the individual too is immortal, and being deathless, no question of the after-death arises. The problem arises only when one considers oneself a mortal being, which is a sure sign of ignorance (*avidyā*) or mistaking appearance for reality. Any statement in a basic scripture like the *Gītā* concerning the effects of ignorance, should never be treated as forming part of its basic teaching. Such statements are meant to correct the notions brought about by ignorance and to lead on to the path of the Real, the Immortal. To treat such aspects as part of the core-teaching is to do an injustice to the spirit of the scripture and to the original author, here Vyāsa. The *Gītā* is no exception in this respect. Such interpretations mostly are in total disregard for the theme the context deals with. This often happens when some ideas already gathered from such secondary scriptures like *Itihāsa*s and *Purāṇas*, based again on misinterpretations, are projected as the basic texts of the *Gītā*. One such glaring example is Verse II.22 which reads when translated thus:

> As a person casts off his worn-out garments and changes into other new ones, so too the embodied (Reality) casts off worn-out bodies and assumes new ones.

In the same chapter appear the lines:

> The born, for sure, have to die,
> and the dead, for sure, have to be born again. — II.27

Such statements do not profess the basic tenet of the *Gītā*. In a few verses prior to this verse, the basic stand of the *Gītā* is categorically stated:

> That (Reality) is never born, nor does
> It die. Once having been,
> It never ceases to be either. — II.20

Given these two alternatives, now it is our turn to adjudge ourselves either as the unborn and deathless *ātmā,* or as mortal individual entities. The former is the *jñānin*'s perception, and the latter, the *ajñānin*'s. The former takes *sat* (the all-underlying substance) as real, and the latter, transitory appearance (*bhāva*) as real. Even after so discriminating, if you continue to identify yourself with mere appearance, then the conceived appearance will die and some new one will emerge again. Verse II.27 portrays simply an ignorant's perception of life, not what the *Gītā* intends to teach.

The insight thus gained on the *Gītā* was further strengthened by contemplation on the *Ātmopadeśa Śatakam* (One Hundred Verses of Self-Instruction) of Narayana Guru. Essentially what the two texts teach is the same philosophy, and on subtle points the two are complementary to each other.

A Bird's Eye-View

Let us now take an overview of the way the *Gītā* develops its philosophy, following its own unique method.

CHAPTER I

The *Gītā* opens with Arjuna facing a dilemma at the very outset of the Battle of Mahabhārata. He feels weighed down by the feeling that he will have to kill his teachers and close relatives, thus incurring sin beyond measure, as a result of which he will go to hell after death. It is not as if Arjuna is certain of all this, it is merely something that has been heard from others, just a belief. Fleeing from the battlefield was also unthinkable at that juncture. In the middle of this dilemma he asks Kṛṣṇa to teach him about what is the best to follow (*śreyas*) in life.

CHAPTER II

That he would have to kill his own kith and kin was Arjuna's main worry. Kṛṣṇa, at the very outset of his teaching, discloses the most fundamental secret of life: What is Real in each of us does not come into being; nor does it cease to exist. That Reality is akin to indestructible gold in destructible ornaments. He who has realized the Reality, not in the apparent individual form, will feel, "I was never born; I will never die."

This secret of life frees one from all death-related fears and worries. This secret was unfolded by Kṛṣṇa in the first half of Chapter II, which he calls *sāṁkhya-buddhi* (basic understanding).

The second half of Chapter II clarifies *yoga-buddhi* (dialectical understanding) — the intuitive awakening by which we realize ourselves to be one with the Substance that one really is, and by which one sees the many in one and the one in many. This perception of oneness is called *vyavasāyātmika-buddhi* (fully convincing and resolute knowledge), and it finds expression in Vedānta. Seeing the many as real is the opposite of such a perception, and the Vedas are its best representations. The *vyavasāyātmitkā-buddhi* attained, one perceives oneself engaging in life's normal activities as part of the one Reality manifesting itself in different forms. One's *karma*s are thus transmuted to *niṣkāma-karma*s (non-motivated actions). The one Reality thus perceived is *Brahman,* and the finding of one's own active existence in *Brahman* is *brāhmī-sthiti.* With this awakening one finds oneself engaged in one's natural activities with no sense of sin or guilt.

CHAPTER III

Having made clear that knowledge is more important than doing *karmas,* why did Kṛṣṇa ask Arjuna to engage in this ghastly *karma* of fighting? With this question of the latter begins Chapter III.

The one Substance underlying everything is not inert, but rather always assumes new apparent forms. This process is what we call *prakṛti,* loosely rendered as "nature" in English. There is *kṛti* in the word *prakṛti;* and there is *kṛti* (action) everywhere in nature. Emerging and re-merging of apparent forms, are simply part of that cosmic *karma* of *prakṛti.* As part of *prakṛti,* we too are filled with *kṛti* and so must remain active. To try to escape is unthinkable. What is possible and advisable is to realize that all our actions are but part of this never ending process on the wheel of *prakṛti,* that no *karma* is ours, and thus being engaged in activities with no sense of attachment. Those ignorant of this *karma*-related reality, maintain a sense of attachment towards what they do, thinking, "This *karma* is mine; its fruits too are mine." After realization, we see that all we do is, just offering our oblation in the fire of *prakṛti,* making a *yajña* (fire sacrifice) of all that we do. Actions performed as *yajña* neither make one bound, nor become sinful.

Why is it that we do wrong, even though we are unwilling, as though under the compulsion of some unknown force? Desire and anger, Kṛṣṇa says, originating from *rajo-guṇa*, a part of *prakṛti*, are the culprits. They are to be treated as enemies by a true seeker, and are to be subjugated. Then alone can one realize one's inseparable oneness with *prakṛti*, and become a *karma-yogī*.

CHAPTER IV

Prakṛti's karma and our *karma* are really one. This *yoga*-secret constitutes wisdom and is preserved and handed down through a long line of wise men. At times when this secret is temporarily lost, as if a historical necessity, there arises a master of original vision who recovers this lost clarity, and restores a firm foundation for human life. The *Gītā* undertakes just such a mission.

It is indeed difficult to treat all the activities that take place in nature and all voluntary and involuntary actions of life, as one *karma* variously manifested. Once illumined with wisdom, we realize that this oneness or *yoga* applies not only to *karma*s but also to the existence *in toto*. The substance that underlies *prakṛti*, also underlies our being. This oneness-in-essence of individual and the whole, is a new experience of *yoga* — a *yoga* that has significance beyond the bounds of *karma*. It is *jñāna-yoga*. Various paths can be adopted for attaining this goal, each means treated as a *yajña* in which the oblation is the individual being and the sacrificial fire, total existence. Of such *yajñas*, *jñāna-yajña* is considered the best. This *yajña*, in essence, means to perceive the existence of all beings in onself and oneself in the Absolute or *Brahman*. Kṛṣṇa, identified with *Brahman*, thus says, "I am That."

Our existence is one with the existence of *Brahman*, just as an ornament is one with gold. We remain oblivious of this oneness due to our own ignorance (*ajñāna*) that draws a veil over our understanding. This has to be cut away with the sword of wisdom (*jñāna*), a need that dawns on us only when pointed out by an enlightened master (*guru*). Finding such a master and approaching him with proper questions is thus the only way to attain enlightenment of this *yoga*-secret.

CHAPTER V

Being aware of the oneness of the *karma* of *prakṛti* and the *karma* of oneself, is *karma-yoga;* and being aware that what appears as the world and what appears as oneself is one *ātmā,* is *jñāna-yoga.* The two in essence are not two but one *yoga.* Living the life of a *karma-yogī* is not possible without *jñāna,* and a *jñānin*'s life will always be that of a *karma-yogī.* A *yogī, yoga-yukta* or *yukta,* as understood by the *Gītā* from Chapter V onwards, will thus be the one who constanty experiences in life the onenes of *karma-yoga* and *jñāna-yoga.* Certain peculiarities seen in the life of such are also described in this chapter.

CHAPTER VI

Life has been perceived till now as a unity, but always having two seemingly opposite facets — *sat* against *bhāva,* one against many, the whole against individual, and so on. The *yoga*-secret is not meant merely to be understood philosophically, but is to be directly perceived in actual life-involving activities. One has to practise seeing the one Reality manifesting as everything, no matter what the vicissitudes of life may be. Such is the practising of meditation that the *Gītā* teaches in this chapter, *Dhyāna-yoga.* Meditation, in other words, is not simply something to be practised for a while sitting alone. We may choose to sit alone and experience a sense of merger as a part of transmuting our life into a practice of meditation. How to go about such a practice is also suggested. Such a meditation ultimately leads to the realization of oneself to be always existing in *Brahman* as one with *Brahman,* here presonified by *Bhagavān* or Kṛṣṇa.

CHAPTER VII

A real *yogī* sees one alone everywhere in the world, everywhere in life, in each and every specific aspect of appearance and experience. *Jñāna* thus reaching down to the specifics is *vijñāna;* the prefix *vi* standing for *viśeṣa* or specificity. The one in whom *jñāna* and *vijñāna* are mutually inclusive, is a *jñāna-vijñāna tṛptātmā* (one fully content with *jñāna* together with *vijñāna*), an ideal state which this chapter highlights. And the chapter also is therefore named *Jñāna-vijñāna-yoga,* in the sense that *jñāna* and *vijnana* are here in a state of *yoga* or union.

CHAPTER VIII

Taking into account all that we have covered so far, we now go back to where we left Chapter II, with the eternal *sat* and transient *bhāva* being perceived unitively. *Sat* is termed here *akṣara* (the indestructible), and *bhāva, kṣara* (the destructible). The indestructible, is *Brahman*, all the destructibles emerging from and merging back with It, Itself serving as the causal Substance. The indomitable creative urge in the Indestructible to ceaselessly produce from Itself all these destructibles, is called *karma*. Each one of us is an evanescent appearance, the emerging of which we call birth and the merging, death. A real *yogī* lives seeing his own specific apparent form and all its peculiarities as existing not apart from the one Indestructible, and so sees himself also as Indestructible. One who does not see himself so is ignorant (*ajñānin*), and treats the evanescent appearance as real, and considers that birth marks his real beginning and death his end. It is therefore that the question of what will happen after death, worries him. A *jñānin*, on the other hand, seeing himself as immortal, remains unconcerned about what happens to the appearance. The ignorant one also has heard of the immortality attained by the *jñānin*, but thinks himself incompetent to reach that state. The mind of the ignorant being already filled with stories of the hereafter, he believes, his soul, after death, will go to *pitṛ-loka* (the world of manes) and will return to this world to be reborn in another form, depending on the merits he has acquired through doing good deeds. He calls this path of the soul *pitṛ-yāna* (*yāna* meaning path) or *kṛṣṇa-gati* (the black path). A *jñānin*'s soul, according to ignorant belief, following a brighter path called *deva-yāna* or *śukla gati*, reaches the world of *Brahman*. Both the paths, mere constructions of ignorant minds, are of no concern for a *jñānin* or *yogī*, and thus do not form part of the core-teaching of the *Gītā*.

CHAPTER IX

All worldly phenomena — birth and death not excluded — are nothing but manifestations of the Indestructible, personified as Kṛṣṇa the *guru* of the *Gītā*. Seeing Kṛṣṇa or *Bhagavān* alone in everything thus marks the acme of wisdom, and is the *Rājavidyā-rāja-guhya-yoga* the *Gītā* teaches. This zenith of wisdom attained, one begins to live as *Bhagavān* does; one's mind becomes *Bhagavān*'s; one's thinking become's *Bhagavān*'s; problems, if any, also become *Bhagavān*'s. Asserting this point marks the middle (and the highest), point of the arch of wisdom-teaching of the *Gītā*.

CHAPTER X

Chapter X reverses what was stated in the last chapter. The stance of the teaching in Chapter IX is "Everything is I indeed in essence," whereas Chapter X says: "I become manifested as every specific entity," the former looking upwards at the One from the world of the many, and the latter looking downwards at the world of the many from the height of the One. Each specific form the one Reality assumes, is a *vibhūti* (that which has specifically (*vi*) come into being (*bhūti*)). Kṛṣṇa, after pointing out some such *vibhūti*s that can be easily meditated upon as the manifestation of the One, concludes with the words, "It is merely a minute part of My being that appears as all these worlds."

CHAPTER XI

Arjuna — and we too along with him — now finds himself at the highest point of clarity. He is now fully convinced of the truth that all the worlds, he himself, the battlefield upon which he stands, all the warriors arrayed there, the entire cosmos — are all but Kṛṣṇa (the Absolute) manifesting variously. At this juncture a desire wells up in Arjuna to see with his own eyes, Kṛṣṇa having assumed the form of the cosmos. Kṛṣṇa willingly grants his wish and shows his *Viśvarūpa* (Cosmic Form). All the *vibhūtis* mentioned in Chapter X are now directly seen in Kṛṣṇa's cosmic body. All the temperamental modes of life (*bhāvas*), from the most gentle and peaceful (*śānta*) to the most ghastly and terrible (*ghora*), are also seen appearing and disappearing in that ever changing form. The Kurukṣetra Battlefield and all the great warriors are also seen there. We too, it is suggested, have to see ourselves as forming part of this form as having our own place somewhere in that body like a leaf upon a giant banyan tree; just as a leaf is one with the tree, and the shedding of old leaves and the sprouting of new ones are part of the natural life of the tree, so too do all things have their existence in this cosmic form. The remaining chapters of the *Gītā,* in a systemic way, help us to find our places in the Cosmic Form of Kṛṣṇa.

CHAPTER XII

What we need first, in order to see ourselves as part of the Cosmic Form of Kṛṣṇa, is to meditatively and adoringly perceive (*upāsanā*) Kṛṣṇa as being the Reality most close to us, like a tree is to the leaf. A close rapport with *Bhagavān* thus becomes a direct experience. Trying to establish such a closeness is known as *bhajana,* those who practice it are *bhaktas,* and such a mind-set is known as *bhakti.* It will be easier for us, already seeing ourselves as part of the Cosmic Form, to establish this *bhakti* than if we were to conceive of *Bhagavān* as an abstract Substance. The lives of those endowed with such a *bhakti* will always be tranquil

CHAPTER XIII

We, as part of the Cosmic Form, are destined to live our own lives, to live another's would be disastrous and fearful. Living one's own life requires the knowledge of latent propensities in oneself, as well as one's personal characteristics. As the next step towards this end, there comes a discrimination of the *kṣetra* (field) and *kṣetrajña* (knower of the field) aspects in our being. *Kṣetra* is our bodily being or *śarīra,* literally that which perishes. The *śarīra* as understood by the *Gītā* is more than the physical body. All that which is changing — from the most subtle animating principle (*cetanā*) to the grossest aspect of our being — together constitutes the *kṣetra*. *Kṣetrajña* is the knowing faculty in us, always conscious of all that is changing. The two, thus discriminated, are to be perceived of course as forming part of the Cosmic Form. In order to help us to have a detailed understanding of both the aspects, *kṣetra* and *kṣetrajña* are equated to *prakṛti* and *puruṣa,* the two basic concepts of the Sāṁkhya School, both without beginning and without end, constituting the Cosmic Form.

CHAPTER XIV

This chapter goes into the details of the *prakṛti* aspect in each of us. *Prakṛti* has inherent in it the three *guṇas* (nature modalities): *sattva* (pure and clear), *rajas* (active) and *tamas* (dark and inert). What the defining characteristics of these *guṇa*s are and how they reflect in the being of each of us differently, are all detailed, helping us discern how and in what proportion these *guṇa*s find place in us as part of the Cosmic Form.

CHAPTER XV

Having examined the *prakṛti* aspect in us, we now proceed to deal with the *puruṣa* aspect. Inconceivable as such, it is the consciousness that knows all that happens in *prakṛti,* and therefore studying it is no easy task. *Puruṣa* is the knowledge aspect of our existence. It is one unconditioned consciousness that unfolds itself as the various conditioned forms in which knowledge finds expression in practical life. Negating all such conditionings is the only way to realize it. Vedas here represent all such conditioned forms of *puruṣa.* The original source of consciousness remaining unknown, and how it branches out only being known, it is comparable to a giant fig tree with roots on high and branches growing downwards. This tree is to be cut down with one's own sense of detachment towards conditionings for weapon. The *puruṣa* thus realized, transcending both the *kṣara purusa* and *akṣara puruṣa* as it is, is named *puruṣottama* (the Supreme Person), which in essence is none other than *Bhagavān* (Kṛṣṇa) Himself.

CHAPTER XVI

Going one step down to actual personal traits, Chapter XVI helps us find out whether we are of divine or of demonic qualities. A detailed portrayal of the external signs of these qualities is also made. This self-examination is made easier by the concept of the three *guṇa*s seen earlier. It is reiterated that whatever be our qualities, we are part of the Cosmic Form.

CHAPTER XVII

The personal life-interests of each of us also vary, and how they do, is examined in Chapter XVII, again on the basis of the three *guṇa*s. Such interests, called *śraddhā*, can be *sāttvika, rājasa* or *tāmasa.* The range or field in which *śraddhā* varies are represented by the three conventional Vedic disciplines: *yajña* (fire sacrifice), *tapas* (austere self-discipline) and *dāna* (offering gifts). Each of us, in view of this, has to find out, on our own, our natural field of interest, again forming part of the Cosmic Form.

CHAPTER XVIII

On the basis of the general outline given so far, one has to look at certain aspects of oneself and conclude, of what nature they are. Our willingness to give up (*tyāga*), the deeds we do (*karma*), the basis of such deeds (*athiṣṭhāna*), the knowledge that urges one to do something (*jñāna*), our own knowerhood (*parijñātṛ*), the known (*jñeya*), our being the doer (*kartṛtva*), and many such factors are to be assessed as to whether they are *sāttvika, rājasa* or *tāmasa*. So too are our understanding (*buddhi*) and firmness of mind (*dhṛti*). Finally one has to appraise for oneself whether one's yearning for happiness (*sukha*), the one goal of all, is *sāttvika, rājasa* or *tāmasa*. All this done, each of us has to explore the nature of our character. Such character-variations, though inconceivable, in a general way are classifiable as brāhmaṇa, kṣatriya, vaiśya and śūdra, as forming part of the Cosmic Form. Anticipating all these was the statement in Chapter IV: "The four-fold colouration of human character (*cāturvarṇya*) was created by Myself."

Now we have to decide how we are to live as ourselves as parts of the Cosmic Form. If I find myself a brāhmaṇa by character, then I should live the life of a brāhmaṇa. Only then will I be happy, and the happiness thus experienced is but that of realizing my self-content and thus Self-Happiness. In this respect, brāhmaṇa, kṣatriya, vaiśya and śūdra are equal, as the *Gītā* puts emphasis thus: "By becoming joyful in one's own *karma,* each one gains the final attainment." If I find that I am a kṣatriya by nature, then I should adopt the way of life of a kṣatriya. Arjuna, we know, is a down-to-earth kṣatriya. Adopting a way of life and action, which fits with one's natural temperament is known as *svadharma,* and this transforms one's life into the happiness of realizing oneself. Resorting to a pattern of life foreign to one's nature, known as *paradharma,* is disastrous and fearful. Doing one's *svadharma,* in effect, is to realize oneness with the Cosmic Form. Experiencing the actualization of this oneness with the Cosmic Form is where the teaching of the *Bhagavad-Gītā* becomes fully meaningful as a *yoga-śāstra* (science of *yoga* or of dialectics). When this state of *yoga* is attained, one becomes absolutely free of all sin. One then attains the best in life (*śreyas*). Arjuna's request at the very beginning was to teach him how to attain this *śreyas*.

For Whom is This Science Meant?

Exhortations like, "Therefore you do fight" are at times heard from Kṛṣṇa, especially at the beginning stage of his teaching. In the later chapters it changes to "Do as you like (*yathechasi tathā kuru*)," meaning, "you are free to do what you think good in view of what I have been teaching." There is of course an addition of "scrutinizing everything, omitting nothing (*vimṛsyaitad aśeṣeṇa*)." The Arjuna we see thereafter is not the one boggled down by confusion, but a resolute one, holding up his bow and arrow.

The wheel-like nature of life that the *Gītā* depicts may not be evident to everyone. Only a real seeker with a yearning for wisdom, accompanied by unrelenting austere sternness, who dedicates himself to attaining this one goal, can perceive it clearly. And it is to be taught only to one who has the humility and openness to seek a *guru*, serve him and ask proper questions at the proper time. This is the warning with which Kṛṣṇa's instruction ends.

We are all Arjunas seeking to tranform our lives as well-established in the Real and to see the individual life of each of us as forming part of the Cosmic Form. This we do in order to make our lives free while being engaged in activities, and to become free of sin and merit as well. And this is the ultimate benefit we gain from the *Gītā*.

Chāndogya Upaniṣad and the Gītā

The *Gītā*, as it states at the end of each of its eighteen chapters, imparts the essential content of Upaniṣadic wisdom. As we know, this wisdom is an outgrowth of Vedism and its rituals. The major Upaniṣads used revaluing and restating the significance of these brute rituals as a method of revealing the essential content of wisdom. The *Chāndogya Upaniṣad* is a classic example; it attributes wisdom and significance first to the *udgītha* rite, and then to *soma-yāga* of which the *udgītha* rite is a part. The *yajña* (fire-sacrifice) in general is seen as a symbolic representation of the life system in its entirety, *brahma-yajña* forming its cosmic aspect and *puruṣa-yajña* the individual aspect. After all this, the Upaniṣad discloses the famous dictum *"sarvam khalvidam brahma"* (Everything here indeed is *Brahman*, III.14.1). This is followed by the statement, *"taddhaitad ghora aṅgirasaḥ kṛṣṇāya devakīputrāya uktvā"* (III.17.6) (Ghora Aṅgirasa, after having imparted this wisdom to Kṛṣṇa, the son of Devakī, said).

It becomes evident, on relating this reference with the *Gītā* context, that Śrī Kṛṣṇa handed down this wisdom to Arjuna. The wisdom taught in the *Gītā*, in other words, is a thorough elaboration on the Upaniṣadic dictum, "Everything here indeed is *Brahman*."

The first nine chapters show how the existence of everything, including individuals and their *karma*s, total nature and the events taking place in it, are inseparably one with *Brahman* as the all-underlying abstract (*avyakta*) Reality.

The latter half portrays the entire cosmic system, in its concrete form, as a *vibhūti* or apparent manifest form of the same *Brahman*; everyone of us has a place and a role in it. Even an individual's personal traits and the occupation that fits in with them (*svadharma*) are visualized as forming part of the cosmic form of *Brahman*.

The seeker is expected to perceive the non-dual oneness of the abstract and concrete aspects of *Brahman*, like the inseparability of gold-substance from an ornament. The finale of the seeker's pilgrimage is when she/he finds her/his being in the non-dual *Brahman*.

About this Pilgrimage

On uncovering such a structural perfection, it was felt that there was the need to reintroduce the entire gamut of the divine song that the *Gītā* is, in its light. How each chapter leads to the next, how each verse shows the way to the next, also got cleared as the "Pilgrimage" progressed. Not even a single verse was found out of place interrupting the smooth flow of thought or in discord with the overall message of the *Gītā*. The attempt made in this book is to clarify the import of each verse, with no other commentator quoted and no other scriptural support referred to.

The source of inspiration with regard to the way of presentation, of course, was the *Jñāneśvarī*, Arjuna interpreting his words himseslf, Sañjaya interpreting his and Kṛṣṇa elaborating on his. Some background aspects, for example, those of historical import, are not presentable in such a mode; they are introduced as told by Vyāsa to Janamejaya, the former being the original author, and the latter the one to whom the entire *Mahābhārata* story, of which the *Gītā* forms a part, was narrated.

Commenting comprehensively on the basic scriptures like the *Gītā* that deal with the *yoga*-secret of life, is a task humanly impossible, as life is not fully comprehensible in every detail. The present "Pilgrim" will therefore feel fully satisfied if this "Pilgrimage" helps anyone perceive a new ray of light, enlightening the great mystery that life is, thereby enabling him/her to find his/her own sound basis of existence.

I

Arjuna-Viṣāda-Yoga

—The Yoga of Arjuna's Dilemma—

धृतराष्ट्र उवाच —

धर्मक्षेत्रे कुरुक्षेत्रे समवेता युयुत्सवः।
मामकाः पाण्डवाश्चैव किमकुर्वत सञ्जय ॥१॥

dhṛtarāṣṭra uvāca —

dharma-kṣetre kurukṣetre samavetā yuyutsavaḥ,
māmakāḥ pāṇḍavāś caiva kim akurvata sañjaya ॥1॥

Dhṛtarāṣṭra said —

At Kurukṣetra, the field of *dharma*, my people and the sons of Pāṇḍu, having come together, eager to fight, what did they do?

Dhṛtarāṣṭra:

O Sañjaya, you know I am Dhṛtarāṣṭra, literally, the one who upholds the nation — its king. And you are well aware what my state is. I am blind, not only in my external eyes, but internally also. I am blind to truth; I am blind to justice! That is why, even though I know that my sons are on the wrong path, I am on their side. It is really nothing more than a father's attachment to his children. Incapable as I am of stabilizing myself in truth and justice, how is it possible for me to make others do so? A king's (*rājā*'s) duty is to keep the entire nation pleased and satisfied (*rañj*). I am the king; Duryodhana; my son, is reigning only as my proxy. In treating the people of my nation as "my people" and "others," I am being unjust. Truth and justice will not prevail in the country ruled by a king like me. Though aware of all this, so overwhelming is my fatherly attachment that I am unable to help it.

A country ruled by such a monarch will surely feel the lack of proper political leadership, and the people, being denied their civil rights, instead of approaching king or court, will fight among themselves. What is happening at Kurukṣetra now is just a replica of this.

I am eager to hear what is happening in the battlefield. You are assigned with the duty of describing to me everything that is happening there, which you can see with the divine sight given to you by Vyāsa.

Vyāsa:

O Janmejaya, *dharmakṣetre kurukṣetre* (at Kurukṣetra, the field of *dharma*) are the words, the *Gītā* begins with. *Kṣetra* means "farmland." *Dharma,* deriving from the verb root *dhṛ*, meaning "to support," means that basic principle which sustains everything as belonging to a functional system. The world as a whole, life *in toto*, has a functional order of its own; each entity in it ensures the existence and happiness of all others. Humans are also part of it. Realizing this and living as part of that total system makes man's life in accordance with *dharma*. The opposite of this is the path of *adharma.* Both *dharma* and *adharma* are relevant only where actions (*karma*s) of some sort are involved. Kurukṣetra, the name of the locality where the Battle of Mahābhārata takes place, literally means, "the field of actions," symbolizing our life — a field of activities. In the farmland where *karma*s thrive, *dharma* also prevails taking cognizance of all actions. Human actions in accordance with the activities of total life system are righteous.

Arjuna will be seen shortly, unable to distinguish what is righteous in a conflicting life-situation, and thus totally confounded. The real teaching of the *Gītā* stems from this situation. Yet what Kṛṣṇa is going to teach Arjuna ultimately is not how to avoid *adharma* and stick to *dharma,* but how to go beyond both *dharma* and *adharma* by taking refuge in the Absolute.

During the usual course of life, social conventions, customary behaviour patterns, mental pre-conditionings, fixed ideas, other man-made laws, regulations etc., are the deciding factors in what is considered "righteous" or "unrighteous." Since such factors are not permanent, it is not possible to determine any fixed content to righteousness. Following rules and regulations in life needs no basic understanding of life; one just has to obey them. All such laws and moral codes are relative, with no absolute criterion. On the other hand, one, fully aware of the basic reality of life, needs no directives from anyone, society, religion or state, in determining how he should live, or how he should act and react. He, fully aware of his oneness with the total, with the Absolute, is never worried about either *dharma* or *adharma*. He finds himself beyond the relative limitations of both. Life, for him, is simply the spontaneous unfoldment of the ever existing one Reality. Whatever happens as part of that unfoldment is amoral. Caught in between as to what is *dharma* and *adharma* in a conflicting situation, Arjuna, in the *Bhagavad-Gītā*, is being led by Kṛṣṇa, to find himself standing beyond both. Serious *Gītā* students, those who consider the *Gītā* as a reassuring guide in life, have to use it for the same purpose. An implicit suggestion of this conclusive teaching of the *Gītā* could be seen in its opening words *dharmakṣetre kurukṣetre*.

You should keep in mind that the *Gītā* is not a textbook of moral codes (*dharma-śāstra* or *smṛti*). What it teaches is *brahma-vidyā* (the Science of the Absolute), the essential wisdom that all the Upaniṣads expound. To the extent that it does not directly lay down the do's and don't-s of life, it is a *śruti*, though the *Mahābhārata*, the epic into whose fabric the *Gītā* is woven and presented, is considered a *smṛti* or *dharma śāstra*.

The basic scriptures of India are grouped into two — *śrutis* and *smṛtis*. *Śruti* means "that which is heard"; they are the compendium of the words of wisdom heard from seers of the past. *Smṛti*, meaning "that which is remembered," mainly contains moral instructions to ensure a well ordered social and personal life. The do's and don'ts of life taught in the *smṛtis* are codified remembering the wisdom of the *śrutis*, and hence their name *smṛtis*. The teaching of the *śrutis* has eternal and universal validity, whereas the moral instruction of the *smṛtis* has to change in accordance with the exigencies of time and place. Unlike the dharma-śāstras like *Manu-Smṛti*, the *Gītā* contains an eternally valid wisdom and therefore is to be considered a *śruti* text.

सञ्जय उवाच —

दृष्ट्वा तु पाण्डवानीकं व्यूढं दुर्योधनस्तदा ।
आचार्यमुपसङ्गम्य राजा वचनमब्रवीत् ॥२॥

sañjaya uvāca —

dṛṣtvā tu pāṇḍavānīkaṁ vyūḍhaṁ duryodhanas tadā ।
ācāryam upasaṅgamya rājā vacanam abravīt ॥2॥

Sañjaya said —

Duryodhana, the Prince, seeing the armies of the Pāṇḍavas arrayed, approached his master (Droṇa) with these words:

Vyāsa:

O Janamejaya, you know, Sañjaya, with the divine eyes I gave him, became capable of directly seeing everything that happens on the battlefield, so that he could describe the battle in detail to Dhṛtarāṣṭra. Literally, Sañjaya means, "one who has conquered all," connoting that he is a person who has overcome the temptations of desires, sentiments and emotions, a quality lacking in Dhṛtarāṣṭra. The fact that Sañjaya discribes all this to Dhṛtarāṣṭra is thus highly suggestive.

पश्यैतां पाण्डुपुत्राणामाचार्य महतीं चमूम् ।
व्यूढां द्रुपदपुत्रेण तव शिष्येण धीमता ॥३॥
अत्र शूरा महेष्वासा भीमार्जुनसमा युधि ।
युयुधानो विराटश्च द्रुपदश्च महारथः ॥४॥
धृष्टकेतुश्चेकितानः काशिराजश्च वीर्यवान् ।

पुरुजित्कुन्तिभोजश्च शैब्यश्च नरपुङ्गवः ॥५॥
युधामन्युश्च विक्रान्त उत्तमौजाश्च वीर्यवान्।
सौभद्रो द्रौपदेयाश्च सर्व एव महारथाः ॥६॥

paśyaitāṁ pāṇḍu-putrāṇām ācārya mahatīṁ camūm ।
vyūḍhāṁ drupada-putreṇa tava śiṣyeṇa dhīmatā ॥3॥

atra śūrā maheṣvāsā bhīmārjunasamā yudhi ।
yuyudhāno virāṭaś ca drupadaś ca mahārathaḥ ॥4॥

dhṛṣṭaketuś cekitānaḥ kāśirājaś ca vīryavān ।
purujit kuntibhojaś ca śaibyaś ca narapuṅgavaḥ ॥5॥

yudhāmanyuś ca vikrānta uttamaujāś ca vīryavān ।
saubhadro draupadeyāś ca sarva eva mahārathāḥ ॥6॥

Behold, O Master, this grand army of the sons of Pāṇḍu, arrayed by your own talented disciple, the son of Drupada.

Here are the valorous, mighty archers, equals to Bhīma and Arjuna in battle: Yuyudhāna, Virāṭa and Drupada, the great chariot-men.

Dhṛṣṭaketu, Cekitāna the valiant king of Kāśī, Purujit and Kuntībhoja, and Śaibya the pre-eminent.

Yudhāmanyu the chivalrous, the heroic Uttamaujas, the son of Subhadrā as well as the sons of Draupadī — all great chariot-men.

अस्माकं तु विशिष्टा ये तान्निबोध द्विजोत्तम।
नायका मम सैन्यस्य संज्ञार्थं तान्ब्रवीमि ते ॥७॥

asmākaṁ tu viśiṣṭā ye tān nibodha dvijottama ।
nāyakā mama sainyasya saṁjñārthaṁ tān bravīmi te ॥7॥

Know well now, O best of the twice-born, the pre-eminent amongst us. Who the leaders of my army are, I tell you, so as to be on the alert.

Duryodhana:

O Droṇa, my Master, you now know who lead our enemies. Now look at those who are at the helm of affairs on our own side. On comparing the two sides alone will we be able to keep ourselves on the alert. These are our leaders:

भवान्भीष्मश्च कर्णश्च कृपश्च समितिञ्जयः।
अश्वत्थामा विकर्णश्च सौमदत्तिस्तथैव च ॥८॥
अन्ये च बहवः शूरा मदर्थे त्यक्तजीविताः।
नानाशस्त्रप्रहरणाः सर्वे युद्धविशारदाः ॥९॥

bhavān bhīṣmaś ca karṇaś ca kṛpaś ca samitiñjayaḥ ।
aśvatthāmā vikarṇaś ca saumadattis tathaiva ca ॥8॥

anye ca bahavaḥ śūrā mad-arthe tyakta-jīvitāḥ ।
nānā-śastra-praharanāḥ sarve yuddha-viśāradāḥ ॥9॥

They are yourself, Bhīṣma, Karṇa and Kṛpa, Aśvatthāmā ever victorious in battle, Vikarna and likewise the son of Somadatta;

And many other heroes armed with weaponries of all sorts, and all skilled in warfare, are risking their own lives for me.

My Master, all these heroes, skilled in warfare, are on our side; still I feel something morally lacking with us. *Dharma* prevailing is what the Pāṇḍavas fight for. Our case is different. It is for me personally that all these men of valour are willing to risk their lives. An unbridgeable gulf, therefore, seems to exist between the two armies.

अपर्याप्तं तदस्माकं बलं भीष्माभिरक्षितम्।
पर्याप्तं त्विदमेतेषां बलं भीमाभिरक्षितम् ॥१०॥

aparyāptaṁ tad asmākaṁ balaṁ bhīṣmābhirakṣitam ।
paryāptaṁ tvidam eteṣāṁ balaṁ bhīmābhirakṣitam ॥10॥

Inadequate is that army of ours under Bhīṣma's safekeeping, yet adequate is this army of theirs under Bhīma's safekeeping.

Vyāsa:

Janmejaya, what Duryodhana fights for, you know, is not righteousness. Nevertheless, he is not to be considered insensitive to righteousness. He knows what is righteousness and who is righteous, but stronger is his passion for power. It is this passion that unconsciously compels him to make a comparison of the two armies. Yet his unconscious desire for righteousness and abhorrence of unrighteousness slip out in his words in this verse. He should naturally have referred to his own army as "this army of ours" and to the enemy's as, "that army of theirs" but what actually slipped out of his mouth are the words: "that army of ours" and "this army of theirs." Unconsciously he seems to want to distance himself from the side of unrighteousness. His lack of confidence is apparent in the next verse as well.

अयनेषु च सर्वेषु यथाभागमवस्थिताः ।
भीष्ममेवाभिरक्षन्तु भवन्तः सर्व एव हि ॥११ ॥

ayaneṣu ca sarveṣu yathā-bhāgam avasthitāḥ ।
bhīṣmam evābhirakṣantu bhavantaḥ sarva eva hi ॥11 ॥

Stationed in your respective positions in all fronts, all of you, therefore, do safeguard Bhīṣma alone at any cost.

Duryodhana:

Our sole moral strength is in Bhīṣma, the grandfather of the princes on both sides. He will die only when he wants to, and cannot be vanquished in battle. As long as he is with us, we don't have to fear defeat. Therefore, at any cost, he is to be safeguarded by all of us.

I know, what I ask you to do is aganist the rules of battle. Bhīṣma is our Commander-in-Chief. His is the duty to lead the battle to its successful end, safeguarding the entire army. To ask those who are to be safeguarded to safeguard their own protector is apparently meaningless, however the need of the moment demands it.

तस्य सञ्जनयन्हर्षं कुरुवृद्धः पितामहः ।
सिंहनादं विनद्योच्चैः शङ्खं दध्मौ प्रतापवान् ॥१२॥

tasya sañjanayan harṣaṁ kuru-vṛddhaḥ pitāmahaḥ ।
siṁha nādaṁ vinadyoccaiḥ śaṅkhaṁ dadhmau pratāpavān ॥12॥

To cheer him (Duryodhana) up, the mighty old Kuru-patriarch blew his conch roaringly, loud like a lion.

Sañjaya:

O King, Bhīṣma sensed the feeling of defeat that overcame Duryodhana's mind, and saw that it was crucial to instill Duryodhana with the valour customary to him, and with this intention Bhīṣma blew his conch roaring like a lion. Here too we see a crucial deviation — it is the offender, not the aggrieved, that blows the conch marking the start of battle and indicating a challenge. Here the aggrieved are the Pāṇḍavas, they are the ones who need the battle. Duryodhana is already in power and does not need confrontation. The first call of challenge, therefore, had to come from Pāṇḍavas' side. Bhīṣma's mistake may be seen as either stemming from his desire to shake-up Duryodhana, or as an indication of the general orderlessness on their side.

ततः शङ्खाश्च भेर्यश्च पणवानकगोमुखाः ।
सहसैवाभ्यहन्यन्त स शब्दस्तुमुलो ऽभवत् ॥१३॥

tataḥ śaṅkhāś ca bheryaś ca paṇavānaka-gomukhāḥ ।
sahasaivābhyahanyanta sa śabdas tumulo 'bhavat ॥13॥

Then quite suddenly were played conches and drums and gongs, kettle-drums and horns — all together, creating a tumultous sound.

Following Bhīṣma's blowing his conch, others on their side too began to blow their conches and play instruments of war music, all together and quite suddenly, creating a sort of confused cacophony. On the side of the Pāṇḍavas we are to see quite the opposite — they will blow their conches one by one in perfect order.

The nature of Duryodhana's worry having been made clear, we now proceed to see Arjuna's affliction. The two are far apart in nature. What afflicts Duryodhana is a moral depression and foreboding of defeat. He therefore compares his own army with the enemy's. Arjuna, on the other hand, places himself at the mid-point between the two armies and, with a neutral mind, looks at both sides. Instead of noticing the sufficiency or insufficiency of his own army, as Duryodhana did, what he does perceive are his own *gurus*, relatives and friends arrayed on either side of him in mutual enmity. His mind is filled with a new distress that assumes the colours of a definite, fundamental problem of life, and paves way for the *Gītā*-teaching, the *yoga-śāstra* (science of dialectics). His *viṣāda* (dilemma) thus assumes the sublimity of a yogic dilemma; hence the name of this chapter; *Arjuna-Viṣāda-Yoga* (The Yoga of Arjuna's Dilemma).

ततः श्वेतैर्हयैर्युक्ते महति स्यन्दने स्थितौ ।
माधवः पाण्डवश्चैव दिव्यौ शङ्खौ प्रदध्मतुः ॥१४॥

tataḥ śvetair hayair yukte mahati syandane sthitau ।
mādhavaḥ pāṇḍavaś caiva divyau śaṅkhau pradadhmatuḥ ॥14॥

Then, seated in the illustrious chariot yoked to white horses, Kṛṣṇa and Arjuna blew their splendid conches.

When a side is challenged on the battlefield, what one expects is that the Commander-in-Chief of the other side will take on the challenge and blow his own conch. The Commander-in-Chief of the

Pāṇḍavas is Dhṛṣṭadyumna, but it was neither he nor Dharmaputra, the eldest of the Pāṇḍavas, who responded to the challenge. Instead, Kṛṣṇa and Arjuna together came forward and blew their conches disregarding all war etiquettes. As a charioteer, having no direct involvement in the battle, Kṛṣṇa had no right to blow his conch. These are all indications that certain concessions and alterations will be made when a battlefield and a war are the scene of a wisdom dialogue. The main characters of the *Gītā*-dialogue are Kṛṣṇa and Arjuna and it is therefore that they are brought to the front first, marking the superseding of the battle by the wisdom teaching. Just as the calf should be nearby when milking a cow, so too is the presence of Arjuna beside Kṛṣṇa in the *Gītā*. The conches they blew are divine and splendid (*divya*). *Divya* literally means, "of the essence of effulgence." What is always effulgent is the essential content of consciousness, and it is this Reality that is about to be revealed in the *Gītā*. The glory of this effulgence is suggested further by the pure white of the horses yoked to the illustrious (*mahat*) chariot. *Mahat* literally means, "that which is worthy of worship."

पाञ्चजन्यं हृषीकेशो देवदत्तं धनञ्जयः ।
पौण्ड्रं दध्मौ महाशङ्खं भीमकर्मा वृकोदरः ॥१५ ॥
अनन्तविजयं राजा कुन्तीपुत्रो युधिष्ठिरः ।
नकुलः सहदेवश्च सुघोषमणिपुष्पकौ ॥१६ ॥
काश्यश्च परमेष्वासः शिखण्डी च महारथः ।
धृष्टद्युम्नो विराटश्च सात्यकिश्चापराजितः ॥१७ ॥
द्रुपदो द्रौपदेयाश्च सर्वशः पृथिवीपते ।
सौभद्रश्च महाबाहुः शङ्खान्दध्मुः पृथक्पृथक् ॥१८ ॥
स घोषो धार्तराष्ट्राणां हृदयानि व्यदारयत् ।
नभश्च पृथिवीं चैव तुमुलो व्यनुनादयन् ॥१९ ॥
अथ व्यवस्थितान्दृष्ट्वा धार्तराष्ट्रान्कपिध्वजः ।
प्रवृत्ते शस्त्रसंपाते धनुरुद्यम्य पाण्डवः ॥२० ॥
हृषीकेशं तदा वाक्यमिदमाह महीपते ।

अर्जुन उवाच —
सेनयोरुभयोर्मध्ये रथं स्थापय मे ऽच्युत ॥२१॥

pāñcajanyaṁ hṛṣīkeśo devadattaṁ dhanañjayaḥ ।
pauṇḍraṁ dadhmau mahā-śaṅkhaṁ bhīma-karmā vṛkodaraḥ ॥15॥

anantavijayaṁ rājā kuntī-putro yudhiṣṭhiraḥ ।
nakulaḥ sahadevaś ca sughoṣa-maṇipuṣpakau ॥16॥

kāśyaś ca parameṣvāsaḥ śikhaṇḍī ca mahārathaḥ ।
dhṛṣṭadyumno virāṭaś ca sātyakiś cāparājitaḥ ॥17॥

drupado draupadeyāś ca sarvaśaḥ pṛthivīpate ।
saubhadraś ca mahābāhuḥ śaṅkhān dadhmuḥ pṛthak pṛthak ॥18॥

sa ghoṣo dhārtarāṣṭrāṇāṁ hṛdayāni vyadārayat ।
nabhaś ca pṛthivīṁ caiva tumulo vyanunādayan ॥19॥

atha vyavasthitān dṛṣṭvā dhārtarāṣṭrān kapidhvajaḥ ।
pravṛtte śastra-sampāte dhanur udyamya pāṇḍavaḥ ॥20॥

hṛṣīkeśaṁ tadā vākyam idam āha mahīpate ।

arjuna uvāca —
senayor ubhayor madhye rathaṁ sthāpaya me 'cyuta ॥21॥

Kṛṣṇa blew Pāñcajanya, and Arjuna, Devadatta; Bhīma of enormous deeds blew his great conch Pauṇḍra.

Prince Yudhiṣṭhira, the son of Kuntī, blew Anantavijaya; and Nakula and Sahadeva, Sughoṣa and Maṇipuṣpaka.

The King of Kāśī, excellent in archery, Śikhaṇḍī, the great chariot-man, Dhṛṣṭadyumna, Virāṭa and the unbeatable Sātyaki.

Drupada as well as the sons of Draupadī, the mighty armed son of Subhadra, O Lord of earth, all blew their conches one by one.

This resonant high sound of announcement rent the hearts of the sons of Dhṛtarāṣṭra, while re-echoing through earth and sky.

Arjuna of monkey-ensign, seeing then the sons of Dhṛtarāṣṭra marshalled, took up his bow, as arrows were just taking to the air.

O King (Dhṛtarāṣṭra), he at that moment asked Kṛṣṇa thus:

Arjuna said —

O Acyuta, position my chariot right in the middle of the two armies,

The mutual challenging over, arrows have just started flying. At this critical moment, Arjuna abruptly asks Kṛṣṇa to position his chariot midway between the two armies. That such a thing is impossible in an actual battlefield everyone knows, but since it is not the battle, but the wisdom-teaching that is important here, Arjuna's action is significant. He is about to be caught in a dilemma, from the horns of which he will be led by Kṛṣṇa to a realm beyond, to enlightenment and wisdom. Arjuna's asking Kṛṣṇa to place his chariot at the middle of the two armies is suggestive of the state of Arjuna's mind.

यावदेतान्निरीक्षे ऽहं योद्धुकामानवस्थितान् ।
कैर्मया सह योद्धव्यमस्मिन्रणसमुद्यमे ॥२२॥
योत्स्यमानानवेक्षे ऽहं य एते ऽत्र समागताः ।
धार्तराष्ट्रस्य दुर्बुद्धेर्युद्धे प्रियचिकीर्षवः ॥२३॥

yāvad etān nirīkṣe 'haṁ yoddhu-kāmān avasthitān ।
kair mayā saha yoddhavyam asmin raṇa-samudyame ॥22॥

yotsyamānān avekṣe 'haṁ ya ete 'tra samāgatāḥ ।
dhārtarāṣṭrasya durbuddher yuddhe priyacikīrṣavaḥ ॥23॥

So that I may behold those who stand here eager to fight, and also with whom I should fight in this encounter.

Let me look on the warmongers gathered here, anxious for pleasing the evil-minded son of Dhṛtarāṣṭra in this war.

सञ्जय उवाच —

एवमुक्तो हृषीकेशो गुडाकेशेन भारत।
सेनयोरुभयोर्मध्ये स्थापयित्वा रथोत्तमम् ॥२४॥
भीष्मद्रोणप्रमुखतः सर्वेषां च महीक्षिताम्।
उवाच पार्थ पश्यैतान् समवेतान्कुरूनिति ॥२५॥

sañjaya uvāca —

evam ukto hṛṣīkeśo guḍākeśena bhārata ।
senayor ubhayor madhye sthāpayitvā rathottamam ॥24॥

bhīṣma-droṇa pramukhataḥ sarveṣāṁ ca mahīkṣitām ।
uvāca pārtha paśyaitān samavetān kurūn iti ॥25॥

Sañjaya said —

O Bhārata (Dhṛtarāṣṭra), Guḍākeśa (Kṛṣṇa), thus appealed to, stationed the magnificent chariot midway between the two armies,

Facing Bhīṣma and Droṇa and all such rulers of the earth, and he said: O Pārtha, behold these Kurus marshalled here.

Sañjaya:

O King Dhṛtarāṣṭra, Kṛṣṇa notices Arjuna's mind beginning to falter. Arjuna asks Kṛṣṇa to station his chariot between the two armies, so that he could look on both sides. Such a neutral position was bound to dampen the war-vigour Arjuna was feeling, but obeying the master being the bounden duty of the charioteer, Kṛṣṇa stops the chariot facing the enemy-ranks. The words uttered by Kṛṣṇa are also energizing: "Behold these Kurus marshalled here." Seeing the enemy army ready for war would make the warriors' blood boil.

The *Gītā* is in the form of a rather long dialogue in which three layers are discernible. First is the dialogue that forms part of the narration of the epic story; this is between you and me. The second is between Kṛṣṇa and Arjuna as friends and brothers-in-law, and as charioteer and master, in which stage we are seeing them now. A charioteer is expected to always be ready to extend all manner of timely help to his master and this includes keeping up the master's vigour and morale high as well. At the third level Kṛṣṇa and Arjuna are related as *guru* and disciple. The real teaching takes place at this level. Unless these levels are discriminated, we may make the mistake of treating all the *Gītā* verses on par and misquoting in support of our own ideas.

The third level further separates into different strata. Kṛṣṇa will say many things to set the stage for unveiling the wisdom-secret and to revalue some existing concepts. These words which are meant to portray the state of mind of the ignorant, though uttered by Kṛṣṇa, do not form part of the real teaching. At times Kṛṣṇa dwells approvingly on certain already prevailing ideas; this too does not form part of the core teaching. Kṛṣṇa puts his seal, with such words as, "my well thought-out conclusion" (*niścitaṁ matam uttamam* — XVIII.6), 'this well thought-out conclusion of mine'(*ye me matam idaṁ* — III.31), whenever he touches the core of the lessons of his wisdom-teaching.

Sañjaya continues:

तत्रापश्यत्स्थितान् पार्थः पितृनथ पितामहान्।
आचार्यान्मातुलान्भ्रातृन्पुत्रान्पौत्रान्सखींस्तथा ॥२६ ॥
श्वशुरान् सुहृदश्चैव सेनयोरुभयोरपि।
तान्समीक्ष्य स कौन्तेयः सर्वान्बन्धूनवस्थितान् ॥२७ ॥
कृपया परयाविष्टो विषीदन्निदमब्रवीत्।

tatrāpaśyat sthitān pārthaḥ pitṝn atha pitāmahān ।
ācāryān mātulān bhrātṝn putrān pautrān sakhīṁs tathā ॥26 ॥

śvaśurān suhṛdaś caiva senayor ubhayor api ।
tān samīkṣya sa kaunteyaḥ sarvān bandhūn avasthitān ॥27 ॥

kṛpayā parayāviṣṭo viṣīdann idam abravīt ।

Then, Pārtha (Arjuna) saw before him fathers and grandfathers, teachers and uncles, brothers and sons, grandsons and friends as well as

Fathers-in-law and companions in both the armies. The son of Kuntī (Arjuna), saw all are close relatives standing firm.

He, possessed by a transcendental compassion, spoke thus in grief:

अर्जुन उवाच —

दृष्ट्वेमान्स्वजनं कृष्ण युयुत्सूं समुपस्थितम् ।२८ ॥
सीदन्ति मम गात्राणि मुखं च परिशुष्यति ।
वेपथुश्च शरीरे मे रोमहर्षश्च जायते ॥२९ ॥
गाण्डीवं स्रंसते हस्तात्त्वक्चैव परिदह्यते ।
न च शक्नोम्यवस्थातुं भ्रमतीव च मे मनः ॥३० ॥

arjuna uvāca —

dṛṣṭvemān svajanaṁ kṛṣṇa yuyutsūṁ samupasthitam ॥28 ॥

sīdanti mama gātrāṇi mukhaṁ ca pariśuṣyati ।
vepathuś ca śarīre me roma-harṣaś ca jāyate ॥29 ॥

gāṇḍīvaṁ sraṁsate hastāt tvak caiva paridahyate ।
na ca śaknomy avasthātuṁ bhramatīva ca me manaḥ ॥30 ॥

Arjuna said —

Seeing these kinsmen of ours, O Kṛṣṇa, gathered here intent to fight,

My limbs fail, my mouth gets parched, my body quivers, my hair stands on end.

Gāṇḍīva (the bow) slides down from my hand, I feel as though my skin burns all over, unable am I even to stand up firm, my mind seems to whirl round.

Vyāsa:

Arjuna now begins to detail his present state of being. Starting with a description of bodily sensation, he proceeds to delineate his mental state. When the body is fatigued, the mind too becomes bogged down. As the mind gets weak, the body too begins to feel exhausted. The body is the grossest aspect of the individual, and mind, the subtlest. Whatever the individual experiences is naturally reflected in both aspects.

निमित्तानि च पश्यामि विपरीतानि केशव ।
न च श्रेयो ऽनुपश्यामि हत्वा स्वजनमाहवे ॥३१॥

nimittāni ca paśyāmi viparītāni keśava ।
na ca śreyo 'nupaśyāmi hatvā svajanam āhave ॥31॥

I do see portents opposite in nature, O Keśava (Kṛṣṇa); I do not see anything of higher value to ensue killing our own kinsmen in the battle, either.

Arjuna:

Kṛṣṇa, it is common among us to believe in omens; certain portents seen now seem to indicate that things are going to be favourable; certain others show the opposite. This makes me all the more uncertain. Our intention, I know, is to win the war and thus glorify ourselves. But is it not inhuman and unrighteous to kill our own kith and kin for mere worldly gains? Thinking of it, my mind is saddled with grief and am hesitant to fight.

न काङ्क्षे विजयं कृष्ण न च राज्यं सुखानि च।
किं नो राज्येन गोविन्द किं भोगैर्जीवितेन वा॥३२॥

na kāṅkṣe vijayaṁ kṛṣṇa na ca rājyaṁ sukhāni ca ।
kiṁ no rājyena govinda kiṁ bhogair jīvitena vā ॥32॥

I do not aspire for victory, O Kṛṣṇa, nor want kingdom and pleasures; of what avail is kingdom or enjoyments, or even life, for us, O Govinda?

Vyāsa:

Further clarifying his state of mind, Arjuna comes to reflecting on the meaning of life. This, however, comes to an abrupt end in the next verse where he is concerned with the well-being of his kinsmen and conventional morality. It is from these relativistic notions of the ethical that Kṛṣṇa, through his teaching, leads Arjuna to Absolutist wisdom wherein all relativistic concerns are subsumed.

येषामर्थे काङ्क्षितं नो राज्यं भोगाः सुखानि च।
त इमेऽवस्थिता युद्धे प्राणांस्त्यक्त्वा धनानि च॥३३॥
आचार्याः पितरः पुत्रास्तथैव च पितामहाः।
मातुलाः श्वसुराः पौत्राः स्यालाः सम्बन्धिनस्तथा॥३४॥
एतान्न हन्तुमिच्छामि घ्नतोऽपि मधुसूदन।
अपि त्रैलोक्यराज्यस्य हेतोः किं नु महीकृते॥३५॥
निहत्य धार्तराष्ट्रान्नः का प्रीतिः स्याज्जनार्दन।
पापमेवाश्रयेदस्मान्हत्वैतानाततायिनः॥३६॥

yeṣām arthe kāṅkṣitaṁ no rājyaṁ bhogāḥ sukhāni ca ।
ta ime 'vasthitā yuddhe prāṇāṁs tyaktvā dhanāni ca ॥33॥

ācāryāḥ pitaraḥ putrās tathaiva ca pitāmahāḥ ।
mātulāḥ śvasurāḥ pautrāḥ syālāḥ sambandhinas tathā ॥34॥

etān na hantum icchāmi ghnato 'pi madhusūdana ।
api trailokya-rājyasya hetoḥ kiṁ nu mahīkṛte ॥35॥

nihatya dhārtarāṣṭrān naḥ kā prītiḥ syāj janārdana ।
pāpam evāśrayed asmān hatvaitān ātatāyinaḥ ॥36 ॥

Those for whose sake we aspire after kingdom, pleasures and comforts, are arrayed here in the battlefield, resigned to their own lives and riches:

Teachers and fathers, sons and likewise, grandfathers, maternal uncles, fathers-in-law, grandsons, brothers-in-law, and other close kinsmen.

Them I do not wish to kill, O Madhusūdana (Kṛṣṇa) — though myself killed by them — even for the sake of the sovereignty of the three worlds, let alone for the sake of the earth.

By killing the sons of Dhṛtarāṣṭra, what happiness could we achieve, O Janārdana? Sin alone would come upon us through killing them, desperadoes though they are.

Vyāsa:

Thinking of the sinfulness of what he was about to do, Arjuna's mind is evidently weighed down. Kṛṣṇa rescues Arjuna from all such concepts, as we will see in due course.

तस्मान्नार्हा वयं हन्तुं धार्तराष्ट्रान् स्वबान्धवान्।
स्वजनं हि कथं हत्वा सुखिनः स्याम माधव ॥३७॥
यद्यप्येते न पश्यन्ति लोभोपहतचेतसः
कुलक्षयकृतं दोषं मित्रद्रोहे च पातकम् ॥३८॥
कथं न ज्ञेयमस्माभिः पापादस्मान्निवर्तितुम्।
कुलक्षयकृतं दोषं प्रपश्यद्भिर्जनार्दन ॥३९॥
कुलक्षये प्रणश्यन्ति कुलधर्माः सनातनाः।

धर्मे नष्टे कुलं कृत्स्नमधर्मोऽभिभवत्युत ॥४०॥
अधर्माभिभवात्कृष्ण प्रदुष्यन्ति कुलस्त्रियः।
स्त्रीषु दुष्टासु वार्ष्णेय जायते वर्णसङ्करः॥४१॥
सङ्करो नरकायैव कुलघ्नानां कुलस्य च।
पतन्ति पितरो ह्येषां लुप्तपिण्डोदकक्रियाः॥४२॥
दोषैरेतैः कुलघ्नानां वर्णसङ्करकारकैः।
उत्साद्यन्ते जातिधर्माः कुलधर्माश्च शाश्वताः॥४३॥
उत्सन्नकुलधर्माणां मनुष्याणां जनार्दन।
नरके नियतं वासो भवतीत्यनुशुश्रुम॥४४॥

tasmān nārhā vayaṁ hantuṁ dhārtarāṣṭrān svabāndhavān ।
svajanaṁ hi kathaṁ hatvā sukhinaḥ syāma mādhava ॥37॥

yady apy ete na paśyanti lobhopahata-cetasaḥ ।
kula-kṣaya-kṛtaṁ doṣaṁ mitra-drohe ca pātakam ॥38॥

kathaṁ na jñeyam asmābhiḥ pāpād asmān nivartitum ।
kula-kṣaya-kṛtaṁ doṣaṁ prapaśyadbhir janārdana ॥39॥

kula-kṣaye praṇaśyanti kula-dharmāḥ sanātanāḥ ।
dharme naṣṭe kulaṁ kṛtsnam adharmo 'bhibhavaty uta ॥40॥

adharmābhibhavāt kṛṣṇa praduṣyanti kula-striyaḥ ।
strīṣu duṣṭāsu vārṣṇeya jāyate varṇa-saṁkaraḥ ॥41॥

saṁkaro narakāyaiva kulaghnānāṁ kulasya ca ।
patanti pitaro hy eṣāṁ lupta-piṇḍodaka-kriyāḥ ॥42॥

doṣair etaiḥ kulaghnānāṁ varṇa-saṁkara-kārakaiḥ ।
utsādyante jāti-dharmāḥ kula-dharmāś ca śāśvatāḥ ॥43॥

utsanna-kula-dharmāṇāṁ manuṣyāṇāṁ janārdana ।
narake niyataṁ vāso bhavatīty anuśuśruma ॥44॥

We, therefore, are not to kill the sons of Dhṛtarāṣṭra, our own kinsmen; how can we remain happy after killing our own people, O Madhusūdana?

Although they, with minds clouded by greed, do see no wrong in causing the destruction of the entire clan and plotting against well-wishers;

How should we, who clearly see the wrong in bringing destruction upon the entire clan, not turn away from that sin, O Janārdana?

Destruction of the clan means destruction of its righteous tradition; righteous tradition lost, chaos overtakes the entire clan.

Chaos prevails, O Kṛṣṇa, if women of the clan go corrupt; with corrupt women, O Vārṣṇeya (Kṛṣṇa), caste-intermixing occurs.

This intermixing leads the clan, its desroyers as well, to hell; the ancestors' souls, the offerings due to them thus deprived, happen to fall.

Caused by the wrongs done by clan-destroyers is brought about caste-intermixing, and thus extinction of the immemorial morality-traditions of caste and clan.

With clan-traditions lapsed, members of the clan are destined to live in hell — so do we hear, O Janārdana (Kṛṣṇa).

Vyāsa:

Arjuna is worrying about a number of things: the decline of the tradition of the Kuru clan, its destruction, women becoming corrupt, the resultant intermixing of castes, the likelihood of ancestors' souls being deprived of offerings, and the possibility of going to hell. However, he is not really sure of these eventualities; they are merely part of what is in the air, the ideas that have got fixed in people's minds, and he makes this clear himself when he says, "so do we hear."

When facing severe mental conflicts and finding no clear solution, or when a clear sense of the meaning of life is lacking, looking for solace in popular beliefs is not an uncommon practice. Problems of the individual would then be examined in the light of such notions. Yet a solution may not be forthcoming. Instead of clarifying the nature of the problems and finding a suitable solution, at such junctures, people are often to be seen concentrating on the validity of these beliefs. It is thus that people, on meeting holy men or *saṁnyāsins*, may ask, "What do you think of the belief that the destroyers of a clan and its tradition will go to hell after death?"

What Arjuna is doing here, though he describes in detail his feelings and thoughts, is simply a restatement of certain prevailing religious notions. The *Gītā* does not say whether such notions are right or wrong, instead, Arjuna will gradually be led to a conviction of the overall meaning of life, where all such notions are seen to be of no relevance.

अहो बत महत्पापं कर्तुं व्यवसिता वयम्।
यद्राज्यसुखलोभेन हन्तुं स्वजनमुद्यताः ॥४५॥
यदि मामप्रतीकारमशस्त्रं शस्त्रपाणयः।
धार्तराष्ट्रा रणे हन्युस्तन्मे क्षेमतरं भवेत् ॥४६॥

aho bata mahat pāpaṁ kartuṁ vyavasitā vayam ।
yad rājya-sukha-lobhena hantuṁ svajanam udyatāḥ ॥45॥

yadi mām apratīkāram aśastraṁ śastra-pāṇayaḥ ।
dhārtarāṣṭrā raṇe hanyus tan me kṣemataraṁ bhavet ॥46॥

Alas! Resolved are we to commit great sin in that we are endeavouring to kill our own kinsmen out of greed for the pleasures of kingdom.

It would be better for me if the sons of Dhṛtarāṣṭra, fully armed, kill me unresisting and unarmed in the battle.

सञ्जय उवाच —

एवमुक्त्वार्जुनः सङ्ख्ये रथोपस्थ उपाविशत् ।
विसृज्य सशरं चापं शोकसंविग्नमानसः ॥४७॥

sañjaya uvāca —

evam uktvārjunaḥ saṁkhye rathopastha upāviśat ।
visṛjya saśaraṁ cāpaṁ śoka-saṁvigna-mānasaḥ ॥47॥

Sañjaya said —

Having spoken thus, Arjuna sat down in his chariot in the battlefield casting away his bow and arrow, with mind weighed down with sorrow.

O King Dhṛtarāṣṭra, Gāṇḍīva, the bow, first slipped down from the hands of Arjuna in his undecided state of mind. Now it seems he is more decided. He casts away his arms. This decision too is not final. His mind is totally unstable. How a precise philosophical problem touching the fundamentals of life arises from this state of mind is to be seen at the beginning of the next chapter.

Thus ends Chapter One entitled Arjuna-Viṣāda-Yoga of the Bhagavad-Gītā, the essence of the Upaniṣads, that embodies the yoga-śāstra of brahma-vidyā in the form of a dialogue between Śrī Kṛṣṇa and Arjuna.

II

Sāṁkhya-Yoga

— The Yoga of Disclosure —

Vyāsa:

O Janmejaya, now we enter the second chapter, *Sāṁkhya-Yoga*. Though Sāṁkhya is the name of one of the Indian schools of thought, its philosophy is not being taught here. *Khyā* means "to tell," "to declare," "to communicate." The prefix *saṁ* stands for "properly" and thus *saṁkhya* means "properly disclosed knowledge," and *sāṁkhya*, "that which is related to this disclosure." Disclosing the overall nature of life, along with outlining the general way of approach of the *Gītā*, is what this chapter deals with.

सञ्जय उवाच —

तं तथा कृपयाविष्टमश्रुपूर्णाकुलेक्षणम् ।
विषीदन्तमिदं वाक्यमुवाच मधुसूदनः ॥१॥

sañjaya uvāca —

taṁ tathā kṛpayāviṣṭam aśrupūrṇākulekṣaṇam ।
viṣīdantam idaṁ vākyam uvāca madhusūdanaḥ ॥1॥

Sañjaya said —

To him thus overcome by tenderness, with tearful distressed look, and grieving, Madhusūdana (Kṛṣṇa) spoke these words.

श्री भगवानुवाच —

कुतस्त्वा कश्मलमिदं विषमे समुपस्थितम् ।
अनार्यजुष्टमस्वर्ग्यमकीर्तिकरमर्जुन ॥२॥

क्लैब्यं मा स्म गमः पार्थ नैतत्त्वय्युपपद्यते ।
क्षुद्रं हृदयदौर्बल्यं त्यक्त्वोत्तिष्ठ परन्तप ॥३॥

śrī bhagavān uvāca —

kutas tvā kaśmalam idaṁ viṣame sam upasthitam ।
anārya-juṣṭam asvargyam akīrtikaram arjuna ॥2॥

klaibyaṁ mā sma gamaḥ pārtha naitat tvayy upapadyate ।
kṣudraṁ hṛdaya-daurbalyaṁ tyaktvottiṣṭha parantapa ॥3॥

Śrī Kṛṣṇa said —

Whence has come upon you this dispiritedness, typical of a non-Āryan, opposed to heaven-reaching and disgraceful, at this untimely hour, O Arjuna?

O Pārtha, yield not to eunuch-like impotence; it is quite unbecoming of you. Shake off this mean faint-heartedness and stand up, O Conqueror!

Vyāsa:

O Janmejaya, Arjuna arrived at the battlefield intending to fight his enemies, and that fight has just started. Right at this critical moment Arjuna is overcome by tenderness, and becomes dispirited. At such a juncture, Kṛṣṇa speaks in a manner intended to arouse Arjuna's self-confidence.

Kṛṣṇa points out to Arjuna that such dejection is not helpful in reaching heaven, the goal considered the highest by Vedism. The idea that he would go to hell torments Arjuna's mind, suggesting that he considered reaching heaven the goal of life. Kṛṣṇa, at the same time, does not mean that the wisdom he is to reveal shortly is aimed at attaining heaven; its goal rather is attaining *mukti*, final liberation from all bondages and conditionings.

Kṛṣṇa, arousing Arjuna's spirit, asks him to discard his present eunuch-like impotence and to stand up vigorously to fight. This call might well be misconstrued as forming the crux of the teaching of the *Gītā*, or at least as one of its most important aspects. As a matter of fact, the actual teaching has not even begun at this point. The present words, belong not to the *guru* Kṛṣṇa, but to the friend, brother-in-law and good charioteer, all of which Kṛṣṇa is to Arjuna. Self-confidence is necessary to face up to hardships, and that is what Kṛṣṇa tries to arouse in Arjuna. His wisdom teaching begins only after Arjuna declares himself a disciple and openly accepting Kṛṣṇa as his *guru*, which he will do in a moment.

अर्जुन उवाच —

कथं भीष्ममहं सङ्ख्ये द्रोणं च मधुसूदन।
इषुभिः प्रतियोत्स्यामि पूजार्हावरिसूदन ॥४॥
गुरूनहत्वा हि महानुभावान् श्रेयो भोक्तुं भैक्ष्यमपीह लोके।
हत्वार्थकामांस्तु गुरूनिहैव भुञ्जीय भोगान् रुधिरप्रदिग्धान् ॥५॥

arjuna uvāca —

kathaṁ bhīṣmam aham saṁkhye droṇaṁ ca madhusūdana ।
iṣubhiḥ pratiyotsyāmi pujārhāvarisūdana ॥4॥

gurūn ahatvā hi mahānubhāvān śreyo bhoktuṁ bhaikṣyam apīha loke ।

hatvārtha-kāmāṁs tu gurūn ihaiva bhuñjīya bhogān rudhira-pradigdhān ॥5॥

Arjuna said —

In this battle, O Madhusūdana, how can I dare fight Bhīṣma and Droṇa with arrows, worthy as both are of reverence, O slayer of enemies (Kṛṣṇa)?

To be sure, it is better to live on alms in this world than to kill these noble-minded masters; killing them (on the other hand), gain-desiring as they are, I should enjoy only blood-stained pleasures in this world.

Vyāsa:

O Janmejaya, Bhīṣma is the grandfather of the entire clan, and Droṇa, the teacher who taught Arjuna and all else the art of warfare. How can Arjuna dare to take up arms against them? Is not Arjuna's mind noble that it should consider living on alms far superior to enjoying these pleasures gained after killing his own masters! Living on alms is the way of life of a *saṁnyāsin*. Immersed in *gurubhakti* (devotion to one's masters), Arjuna overlooks his incompetence in being a *saṁnyāsin*.

Bhīṣma and Droṇa chose to be on Duryodhana's side of *adharma*, not because they were unmindful of the truth or *dharma*. They are both aware of who is in the right and who is wrong, but they chose to be on the Kauravas' side because of the obligation to Duryodhana as the king. In that context it would not be wrong to say that they too desire gain and in that way are deserving of death. However, the pleasures that Arjuna might enjoy after defeating them, would be tainted with blood.

Arjuna sees two opposing alternatives — to refrain from killing his elders and teachers and so live a beggar's life, or to go ahead, fight and kill all enemies and so enjoy a life of pleasures which would be stained with the blood of loved and respected ones.

न चैतद्विद्मः कतरन्नो गरीयो यद्वा जयेम यदि वा नो जयेयुः।
यानेव हत्वा न जिजीविषामस्ते ऽवस्थिताः प्रमुखे धार्तराष्ट्राः ॥६॥
कार्पण्यदोषोपहतस्वभावः पृच्छामि त्वां धर्मसम्मूढचेताः।
यच्छ्रेयः स्यान्निश्चितं ब्रूहि तन्मे शिष्यस्ते ऽहं शाधि मां त्वां प्रपन्नम् ॥७॥
न हि प्रपश्यामि ममापनुद्याद् यच्छोकमुच्छोषणमिन्द्रियाणाम्।
अवाप्य भूमावसपत्नमृद्धं राज्यं सुराणामपि चाधिपत्यम् ॥८॥

na caitad vidmaḥ kataran no garīyo yad vā jayema yadi vā no jayeyuḥ ।
yān eva hatvā na jijīviṣāmas te 'vasthitāḥ pramukhe dhārtarāṣṭrāḥ ॥6॥

kārpaṇya-doṣopahata-svabhāvaḥ pṛcchāmi tvāṁ dharma-saṁmūḍhacetāḥ ।
yac chreyaḥ syān niścitaṁ brūhi tan me śiṣyas te 'haṁ śādhi māṁ tvāṁ prapannam ॥7॥

na hi prapaśyāmi mamāpanudyād yac chokam ucchoṣaṇam indriyāṇām ।
avāpya bhūmāv asapatnam ṛddhaṁ rājyaṁ surāṇām api cādhipatyam ॥8 ॥

Neither do we know which is better for us: whether we conquering them or they conquering us. The sons of Dhṛtarāṣṭra, killing whom we should not wish to live, are standing here as enemies facing us.

Smitten with a fickleness as is my inner being, and confounded in mind about *dharma*, I ask you: tell me decisively what is best for me; I am your disciple; please teach me who takes refuge in you.

I do not see what could dispel this grief that dries up my senses, though should I gain unrivalled, prosperous kingdom on earth or even lordship of gods.

Vyāsa:

O Janmejaya, Arjuna is by now fully aware of the indisposed state he is in — a state he calls *kārpaṇya-doṣa*, fickleness arising from ignorance. The irony is that this fickleness arises from a tenderness of heart and unworldliness.

Caught between this tenderness of heart and his sense of duty as a warrior, he finds himself wavering, unable to decide what actions would be *dharma* for him and what could turn out to be *adharma*. He is fully aware how serious the problem is, and this is why he feels that his senses are being dried up. He feels that as long as this problem remains unresolved, even gaining the overlordship of the entire earth and heaven, would be meaningless. Only those who desire to find solutions to such fundamental problems, as a pre-condition to make life meaningful, will be ready to imbibe wisdom. All worldly gains would seem irrelevant to them until the problem is solved. Only such persons would seek a *guru* and become seeker-disciples (*śiṣyas*). Arjuna, therefore, prays to Kṛṣṇa: "Tell me decisively what is best for me." He declares himself a *śiṣya* (disciple) accepting Kṛṣṇa as *guru*.

The seeking mind of Arjuna is now ready to grasp Kṛṣṇa's wisdom.

सञ्जय उवाच —

एवमुक्त्वा हृषीकेशं गुडाकेशः परन्तप ।
न योत्स्य इति गोविन्दमुक्त्वा तूष्णीं बभूव ह ॥९॥

sañjaya uvāca —

evam uktvā hṛṣīkeśaṁ guḍākeśaḥ parantapa ।
na yotsya iti govindam uktvā tūṣṇīṁ babhūva ha ॥9॥

Sañjaya said —

Guḍākeśa (Arjuna), having spoken thus to Hṛṣīkeśa (Kṛṣṇa), decidedly told Govinda, "I will not fight" and then became silent.

O King Dhṛtarāṣṭra, Arjuna is passing through a critical stage in his life. To retreat from the battlefield is unbecoming of him, and really impossible. So he must fight. Yet at this moment, more pressing is the need to find a solution to his problem, and thus to free himself. This is the reason why he, unmindful of the battle that has already begun, falls into a silence, after declaring, "I will not fight."

तमुवाच हृषीकेशः प्रहसन्निव भारत ।
सेनयोरुभयोर्मध्ये विषीदन्तमिदं वचः ॥१०॥

tam uvāca hṛṣīkeśaḥ prahasann iva bhārata ।
senayor ubhayor madhye viṣīdan tam idaṁ vacaḥ ॥10॥

To him, O Bhārata (Dhṛtarāṣṭra), sitting afflicted between the two armies, Hṛṣīkesā (Kṛṣṇa), as though smiling, spoke these words:

Don't you notice Kṛṣṇa's equanimous reaction to Arjuna's affliction? A smile even appears on his face, in contrast to the distressed face of Arjuna. What worries Arjuna now is not the prospect of having to go to hell after killing his own *gurus*; neither is it the fear of the impending destruction of his entire clan. Now his mind is afflame with the desire for knowledge. Such would normally be the state of mind of all true seekers, when they are in the presence of a *guru*; others will not feel the need to approach a *guru* either.

Just as a flaming fire needs water to put it out, the *guru*'s soothing and assuring attitude puts out the fire of the seeker's quest. Kṛṣṇa's silent smile says, "I know what you are worried about. I know the solution. Listen to me calmly."

Vyāsa referring to what Kṛṣṇa is about to elaborate at length in the following seventeen chapters as "this word" in singular, is deliberate. It suggests that all that is detailed could very well be summarized in one word: *auṁ*. The entire *Gītā* text, in other words, is a form of elaboration on *auṁ*. Kṛṣṇa, in the course of his teaching, will refer to it himself.

श्रीभगवानुवाच —

अशोच्यानन्वशोचस्त्वं प्रज्ञावादांश्च भाषसे ।
गतासूनगतासूंश्च नानुशोचन्ति पण्डिताः ॥११ ॥

śrī bhagavān uvāca —

aśocyān anvaśocas tvaṁ prajñā-vādāṁś ca bhāṣase ।
gatāsūn agatāsūṁś ca nānuśocanti paṇḍitāḥ ॥11 ॥

Śrī Kṛṣṇa said —

You grieve over those for whom no one is to grieve; whereas the words you speak are of a knowledge-able person. Neither for those who are gone nor for the not-gone, do the wise grieve.

O Arjuna, you speak in the words of a man of knowledge. Yet this knowledge does not help you to free yourself from grief. You are forgetting that you grieve for those who are not to be grieved for, not that there are some you should grieve for, and for others you should not. No one is to be grieved for — neither for those who have left the scene of life nor for those who are yet to do so. Such a griefless state is normal to *paṇḍitas,* wise ones. A wise one is called *paṇḍita,* for he possesses *paṇḍā* (wisdom).

What you need immediately is to become free of this sorrow. The knowledge you possess does not help you to do this. There is a knowledge that wipes out all grief; you require only to raise your knowledge to that level. The knowledge you have now is not wrong, it is only conditioned, and its appropriateness is also conditional; it is not that integral knowledge from which nothing concerning life is excluded. Relative in nature, the value of this knowledge is also relative and limited. It requires a transformation to make it unconditional, all-inclusive, unlimited in value, and absolute in nature. Then you will find that your sorrows have vanished, that you have become firm in understanding, that you are standing on a firm ground.

All that I am going to tell you in detail hereafter could thus be considered a sort of elaboration on what is condensed in this beginning verse.

न त्वेवाहं जातु नासं न त्वं नेमे जनाधिपाः।
न चैव न भविष्यामः सर्वे वयमतः परम् ॥१२॥

na tvevāhaṁ jātu nāsaṁ na tvaṁ neme janādhipāḥ ।
na caiva na bhaviṣyāmaḥ sarve vayam ataḥ param ॥12॥

I had never been non-existent, nor you, nor these kings; neither shall all of us become non-existent hereafter.

O Arjuna, your worry is that you would have to kill your own *gurus*; this is because you perceive as real their apparent forms. Now I will reveal to you a secret: it is one Substance alone that underlies the appearance of all these kings, of us all. This alone really exists, it has always existed; it has never come into being; it will never cease to be;

it is indestructible. I am that Reality, you are that Reality, all these great warriors are that Reality in essence.

Considering me, yourself, and all these kings as existing separately, as seperate realities, leads you to grieve. These apparent entities are only evanescent forms assumed by the one Reality; all such forms will disappear; the Reality remains unchanged. For example, a gold ornament is gold in essence; the gold-substance can never be made non-existent, but its form can be altered and given any new shape. I, you, these kings, all are such ornaments, one distinct from another, yet the essential substance in all of us always remains one and indestructible.

Unaware of the indestructible substance that you are, you saw yourself as a mere ornament and saw all those assembled here also likewise, and that is why they all seem mortal. When you look at yourself and everyone as the gold that assumes different forms, then you will see that all are indestructible, all are immortal.

Arjuna, it will become clear to you as we proceed that this one indestructible Substance is nothing but "I," not the individual but the Absolute "I" in all of us. That Reality was never originated, and it will never cease to exist. It appears here in many forms — in my form, your form, the forms of all these great warriors. Being that Reality in essence, we too have always existed and will always exist. The final goal of this wisdom teaching is to make the immortality of this one Substance ours, by realizing our oneness with It.

देहिनो ऽस्मिन्यथा देहे कौमारं यौवनं जरा ।
तथा देहान्तरप्राप्तिर्धीरस्तत्र न मुह्यति ॥१३॥

dehino 'smin yathā dehe kaumāraṁ yauvanaṁ jarā ।
tathā dehā 'ntara-prāptir dhīras tatra na muhyati ॥13॥

As the embodied passes through childhood, youth and old age in this body, so is its assuming another body; the wise are not bewildered thereby.

O Arjuna, the ornament-form, in the ornament-gold analogy, is body (*deha*), and the gold is that which is embodied (*dehin*). The Sanskrit word *deha,* signifying body, literally means "that which grows constantly." *Dehin* is the substance that assumes the form of the constantly emerging, growing and decaying body. You will see later (XIII.5-6), when I detail the constituents of *deha* or *śarīra,* that what is called "soul" (*cetanā*) is also included, for souls also emerge and disappear. One gold ornament can be melted down and reshaped into another any number of times. Each time it assumes a new body (*deha*) though the gold-substance remains indestructible. We also directly experience this: you and I were all infants once, passing through childhood, adolescence and youth, we have now assumed manhood. Eventually we will pass to old age and then vanish from this world. The "I" in all of us, through all these transformations, remains unchanging. Who or what is this unchanging "I"? Once that has been discovered, all the problems are solved.

The words *dehāntara-prāpti* (attaining a different body), which I have used here do not denote a soul leaving one body and entering another in the womb of an expectant woman, as is often construed. It means only attaining a different *deha,* like one ornament getting reshaped into a new form. What is to be looked at is not how body and soul are related, but how the Reality in each of us is indestructible. The *deha-dehin* relationship, such as between ornament and gold, is not to be confused with the hypothetical body-soul relationship. It should now be clear to you that *dehin* does not mean soul.

As we have become accustomed to treating the apparent as real, when an apparent form ceases to be in what we call death, we are overcome by fear. The state of mind in which the unreal appearance and the reality are mixed up, causing bewilderment is called *moha.* The one who is certain as to what is real or unreal is called *dhīra,* meaning "firm in mind," but strictly speaking, connoting "one who imparts knowledge to others," which is possible only to those who know.

In order to link what I have just told you with what I am going to say, I may point out in advance that *dehin* (the embodied) stands for *sat* and *deha* for *bhāva. Sat,* being what really exists underlying all appearances, is immutable, and *bhāva*, the changeful forms that *sat* assumes, always changeful.

मात्रास्पर्शास्तु कौन्तेय शीतोष्णसुखदुःखदाः।
आगमापायिनोऽनित्यास्तांस्तितिक्षस्व भारत ॥१४॥

mātrā-sparśās tu kaunteya śītoṣṇa-sukha-duḥkhadāḥ ।
āgamāpāyino 'nityās tāṁs titikṣasva bhārata ॥14॥

Momentary sense contacts, and the pains and pleasures such as heat and cold they cause, are all transient and of the habit of coming and going; do endure them, O Arjuna.

Considering oneself *dehin*, it becomes clear that we are all one indestructible Reality in essence. When looked at from the *deha* point of view, change alone is visible; growth and decay are normal; bodily states cyclically alternate; heat and cold, pleasures and pains, all alternate likewise. The emergence of new entities — birth — and merger of old entities — death — also appear natural in the state of *deha*-hood.

यं हि न व्यथयन्त्येते पुरुषं पुरुषर्षभ।
समदुःखसुखं धीरं सोऽमृतत्वाय कल्पते ॥१५॥

yaṁ hi na vyathayanty ete puruṣaṁ puruṣarṣabha ।
sama-duḥkha-sukhaṁ dhīraṁ so 'mṛtatvāya kalpate ॥15॥

One who is not disturbed by these (contacts), even-minded in pleasures and pains, and firm in mind, O Best of Men, he is destined for immortality.

O Arjuna, you, supposedly being one among the best of men, should not see appearances as real and give yourself cause to grieve. You, on the other hand, should perceive the one changeless Reality underlying all these changeful appearances, and see your inseparable oneness with this Reality. Then alone will you have the equanimity to treat both pleasure and pain as equal. The word *sama*, here meaning equality, connotes more than simple equality; it is an equality deriving from the universality of what underlies all existence.

After perceiving ourselves from the point of view of *sat* and that of *bhāva*, we are now required to use the *yogic* vision in which *sat* and *bhāva* are intuitively perceived as inseparable. It is this that makes life meaningful.

नासतो विद्यते भावो नाभावो विद्यते सतः ।
उभयोरपि दृष्टो ऽन्तस्त्वनयोस्तत्त्वदर्शिभिः ॥१६ ॥
nāsato vidyate bhāvo nābhāvo vidyate sataḥ I
ubhayor api dṛṣṭo 'ntas-tv anayos tattva darśibhiḥ II16 II

The unreal cannot manifest itself; the Real never ceases to manifest itself; the inherent truth of these two has thus been perceived by the seers of ultimate Reality.

O Arjuna, to return to the gold and ornament analogy, an ornament cannot be made of a non-existent gold, gold has to exist. Likewise, it is impossible for the existent gold, to remain without some form or other. Just as these two co-exist inseparably, so too is the relationship between the apparent world and the one underlying Reality. Individuals may be considered as being the ornament-forms, and Reality as being gold that is behind all the ornament-forms.

One crucial point is to be kept in mind: that though gold and ornaments may be always *conceived* separately, they cannot *exist* separately. They are inseparably one and non-dual. It is in the same way that we are inseparable from, and exist in a state of non-duality with the one Reality. The world has no existence apart from the one Reality, and this Reality cannot exist other than in the form of the world. This state of being inseparable is the secret signified by the Sanskrit words in this verse, *anayoḥ ubhayoḥ api antaḥ*, rendered here as "the inherent truth of these two."

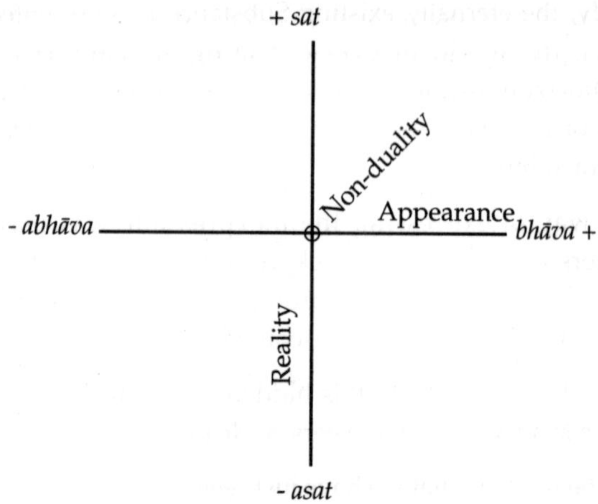

Arjuna, what I am teaching you is *brahma-vidyā,* known also as *yoga-śāstra* or the science of *yoga*. We have just looked at how the inseparable oneness of *sat* and *bhāva* forms the crux of what makes this teaching a *yoga-śāstra*. The word *yoga* meaning "the state of being united," is derived from the verb root *yuj,* signifying "to join," "to unite." Inseparably united are *sat* and *bhāva, dehin* and *deha,* like gold and ornament. Though what really exists is one alone, seen from two different angles, it appears as though there are two. Like gold and ornament, though they are inseparable, when looked at as substance it is gold, and as apparent form it is ornament. Gold and ornament are already one and need no uniting. Though their separateness is merely a mental image, without referring to such a separateness, it is not possible to express in words their state of oneness. No single word exists that can signify the state in which gold and ornament are inseparable. Inherent even in the words "gold-ornament" is the indestructible gold aspect and the destructible ornament aspect. Similarly ineffable is that state of non-duality in which the world and the Real exist. What is possible then in the realm of verbal expression is to say that without the one the other cannot exist. Two statements are made here from the points of view of the *sat* and *bhāva.* The unreal (*asat*) cannot manifest; the Real (*sat*) never ceases to manifest. Without *sat* there can be no *bhāva,* and without *bhāva, sat* cannot exist.

Graphically, the eternally existing Substance is represented by a vertical axis, the world of ever-changing appearances by a transversing horizontal line. Non-duality is represented by the meeting piont of the two, which is neither vertical nor horizontal, neither plus nor minus.

This rare way of expressing the inexpressible was used by wisdom teachers of all religious background from ancient times. Arjuna, I will also put it in use all through this wisdom discourse. And it is this facet that makes this discourse of mine a *yoga-śāstra*.

It is those who are awake to this hidden aspect of my teaching, who are to be considered the real seers of Reality (*tattva-darśin*).

Let us, in the light of what we have just seen, look at our life in its entirety. First, we look at ourselves as *sat:*

अविनाशि तु तद्विद्धि येन सर्वमिदं ततम्।
विनाशमव्ययस्यास्य न कश्चित्कर्तुमर्हति ॥१७ ॥

avināśi tu tad viddhi yena sarvam idaṁ tatam ।
vināśam avyayasyāsya na kaścit kartum arhati ॥17 ॥

Know That by which all this is pervaded to be indestructible. Undecaying as it is, no one can bring about its destruction.

The visible shape or form is destroyed; the essential substance is indestructible. When we realize our oneness with this essence, we realize our own indestructible nature.

अन्तवन्त इमे देहा नित्यस्योक्ताः शरीरिणः।
अनाशिनोऽप्रमेयस्य तस्माद्युध्यस्व भारत ॥१८ ॥

antavanta ime dehā nityasyoktāḥ śarīriṇaḥ ।
anāśino 'prameyasya tasmād yudhyasva bhārata ॥18 ॥

That these bodies, assumed by the eternal, indestructible, inscrutable embodied, have their end, is well known. You therefore go on with the battle, O Arjuna.

O Arjuna, *dehin*, the Reality that assumes all appearances (*dehas*) could as well be called *śarīrin*, meaning that which has *śarīra*. Signifying body, *śarīra* means "that which perishes." This Reality is inscrutable (*aprameya*) as it cannot be grasped through any means of knowledge, such as perception, inference and so on.

We are under the impression that we see the gold substance in ornaments; in fact the perceptible gold appears in varying ornament forms while the immutable gold, as such, has no immutable form of its own. Gold as a substance is formless. Anything formless is invisible, so too is the gold-substance. What we see then is not the gold-substance but some transient, visible form assumed by it. The same is true of the world. All the fleeting elements that constitute the apparent shapes of individual beings are part of the body; including physical elements, the I sense (*ahaṁkāra*), the mind, the indistinct (*avyakta*), sense organs, organs of action, their respective objects, desire, hatred, pleasure, pain, the coalescence of all these, the animating principle (*cetanā*), fortitude and all. Everything perceptible and conceivable in our being is thus part of mere appearance and is destructible. The indestructible Substance (*śarīrin*) always remains inconceivable.

Therefore, dear Arjuna, know that what is going to be destroyed in this battle are such apparent forms never the Real — whom you call the enemies. That Reality continues to exist, though it is unknown to us what form it will assume in future. Your not fighting will not stop the perishing of those bodies.

It is inevitable that bodies will perish, neither your participation in this battle nor even your withdrawal from it can prevent that.

य एनं वेत्ति हन्तारं यश्चैनं मन्यते हतम्।
उभौ तौ न विजानीतो नायं हन्ति न हन्यते ॥१९॥

ya enaṁ vetti hantāraṁ yaś cainaṁ manyate hatam ।
ubhau tau na vijānīto nāyaṁ hanti na hanyate ॥19॥

He who thinks of This (embodied) as the killer, and he who takes It as the killed — both fail in knowing the truth. It does not kill, nor is It killed.

What caused you to become despondent was the thought that you would have to kill those who are dear to you. You thought of yourself as the killer, and of them as being killed. Arjuna, remember that neither you, I, or any of these people, are anything but fleeting apparent forms of the one Reality. Each one of us is that Reality in essence. As that Reality, you are no killer, nor can those others be killed, for that Reality neither kills nor can be killed. I shall now tell you what this Reality is. Hear me with a keen mind, for this is one of the basics to be constantly kept in mind all through this teaching and all through your life.

न जायते म्रियते वा कदाचिन्नायं भूत्वा भविता वा न भूयः।
अजो नित्यः शाश्वतोऽयं पुराणो न हन्यते हन्यमाने शरीरे ॥२०॥

na jāyate mriyate vā kadācin nāyaṁ bhūtvā bhavitā vā na bhūyaḥ ।
ajo nityaḥ śāśvato 'yaṁ purāṇo na hanyate hanyamāne śarīre ॥20॥

That (Reality) is never born, nor does It ever die; once having been, It does not cease to be either. Unborn, eternal, perpetual, ancient, It is not destroyed at the destruction of the body.

वेदाविनाशिनं नित्यं य एनमजमव्ययम्।
कथं स पुरुषः पार्थ कं घातयति हन्ति कम्॥२१॥

vedāvināśinaṁ nityaṁ ya enam ajam avyayam ।
kathaṁ sa puruṣaḥ pārtha kaṁ ghātayati hanti kam ॥21॥

One who knows that Reality as indestructible, everlasting, unborn, undecaying — whom and how does he kill, and whom does he make kill?

It must be clear to you now that the one Substance, *sat*, underlying and pervading everything, is indestructible. Whosoever knows the *sat* realizes, "I am that eternal *sat*." There would be an accompanying realization that the Reality in oneself, the real Self, is neither killed, nor itself kills. Ordinarily understood, death is the destruction of the body, an event like the melting down of an ornament. The disappearance of one apparent form leads to the appearance of a new one, as *sat* cannot exist without assuming some transient form. This phenomenon of merger and emergence of *bhāvas* goes on incessantly while the one *sat* continues to exist in and through all the altering forms. Such is life.

It is *śāśvata* in the sense that It has neither increased nor decreased. It is *purāṇa* as It has existed timelessly. I shall make this point clearer:

वासांसि जीर्णानि यथा विहाय नवानि गृह्णाति नरो ऽपराणि ।
तथा शरीराणि विहाय जीर्णान्यन्यानि संयाति नवानि देही ॥२२॥

vāsāṁsi jīrṇāni yathā vihāya navāni gṛhṇāti naro 'parāṇi ।
tathā śarīrāṇi vihāya jīrṇāny-anyāni saṁyāti navāni dehī ॥22॥

As a person casts off worn-out garments and changes into other new ones, so does the embodied (Reality) cast off worn-out bodies and assumes new ones.

Arjuna, one does not count how many times one has thrown away worn-out clothes and acquired new ones. No matter how often one does this, one continues to be the same. Life, in one respect, is also of a like nature.

Old and worn-out bodies are discarded by the embodied Reality, which assumes new forms just as ornaments which become old-fashioned are melted down and recast into new shapes. A person casting off old clothes and putting on new ones does not become different; melting one ornament to recast it into another form does not make the gold substance different. In this manner, when old bodies are discarded and new ones taken on, it does not make the embodied different or non-existent. *Śarīra* (body) here is to be understood in its broadest sense, which does not exclude what we call soul (*cetanā*), as already made clear. That bodies constantly change and the embodied Reality remains changeless, is the fundamental rule governing life.

What I have said in the present verse might be construed as supporting the theory of reincarnation, however to conceive of the embodied (*dehin*) as undergoing rebirth would imply admitting both birth and death, which, as you know, we have already seen to be unreal earlier in Verse 20. The concept of reincarnation also requires admitting souls as many and real, a concept in no way acceptable to Vedānta. Popular belief in reincarnation of souls exists as a fallout of the stories of the *Purāṇa*s and *Itihāsa*s.

Now look at the verse carefully. *Dehin* (the embodied) is referred to in it in singular form, meaning, one *dehin* alone exists. *Śarīrāṇi* (bodies), literally the perishable, at the same time, is in the plural form, signifying that the perishable appearances are many. What I really mean is this: one all-underlying Reality, remaining immutable, assumes ceaselessly changing numerous appearances. Therefore is it that in the analogy also, the man who changes clothes is referred to in singular form and the clothes he changes in plural.

Acquiring and putting on new clothes does not make a person many. Above all, the topic we are concerned with in the particular context is not what will happen to an individual soul after death, but, even from Verse 11, it is how the overall flow of nature works, with the one eternal Reality and the innumerable apparent forms it assumes remaining inseparable. The same theme will continue from the next verse onwards also. Interpolating the idea of reincarnation of individual souls into its middle would be inappropriate and quite unbecoming of a *śāstra* text. Of course, there will be contexts in this discourse where the question of reincarnation will arise.

I should now like to dwell more on the indestructibility of the one *dehin* that continues to exist, despite the incessant altering of its visible forms.

नैनं छिन्दन्ति शस्त्राणि नैनं दहति पावकः ।
न चैनं क्लेदयन्त्यापो न शोषयति मारुतः ॥२३॥

nainaṁ chindanti śastrāṇi nainaṁ dahati pāvakaḥ ।
na cainaṁ kledayanty āpo na śoṣayati mārutaḥ ॥23 ॥

Weapons do not cut It asunder, nor does fire burn It down; Water does not drench It, nor wind dries It up.

It is only the visible forms that are vulnerable to being cut down, or burnt up, becoming damp, or getting dry. How is it possible that the invisible and inscrutable *sat* can be subjected to any of these conditions?

अच्छेद्यो ऽयमदाह्यो ऽयमक्लेद्यो ऽशोष्य एव च ।
नित्यः सर्वगतः स्थाणुरचलो ऽयं सनातनः ॥२४ ॥

acchedyo 'yam adāhyo 'yam akledyo 'śoṣya eva ca ।
nityaḥ sarvagataḥ sthāṇur acalo 'yaṁ sanātanaḥ ॥24 ॥

It cannot be cut, It cannot be burnt, It cannot be wetted, nor can It be dried. The eternal, the all-pervading, the stable, the immovable, It is ever the same.

अव्यक्तो ऽयमचिन्त्यो ऽयमविकार्यो ऽयमुच्यते ।
तस्मादेवं विदित्वैनं नानुशोचितुमर्हसि ॥२५ ॥

avyakto 'yam acintyo 'yam avikāryo 'yam ucyate ।
tasmād evaṁ viditvainaṁ nānuśocitum arhasi ॥25 ॥

Unmanifest is It; unthinkable is It; immutable is It; so It is told of. Having known It to be so, no need is there for you to grieve.

Arjuna, all that appears to be distinct, one different from another, is *vyakta,* a manifest form, and each such entity is called a *vyakti,* an individual. We have already seen that all such individual forms are part of *bhāva* and not *sat*. That *sat* may therefore appropriately be called *avyakta,* the indistinct unmanifest. The constant changes that we see in nature are called *vikāra*; that which is subject to no *vikāra* is *avikārya*; the *sat* is thus *avikārya* as well. Changes occur only to *bhāvas*, never to the *sat*. Regardless of all the apparent changes, *sat* always remains immutable.

Once this fundamental truth is known, you will never consider yourself as an individual being, as *bhāva*, but only as the immutable *sat* become manifest. You will also see all these great kings not as individuals, but as the very same *sat* which can neither be killed, nor itself kills.

Looked at from the *sat* point of view, you will thus realize that nothing that happens unavoidably in life is to be grieved for. Your present grief is no exception.

अथ चैनं नित्यजातं नित्यं वा मन्यसे मृतम्।
तथापि त्वं महाबाहो नैनं शोचितुमर्हसि ॥२६॥

atha cainaṁ nitya-jātaṁ nityaṁ vā manyase mṛtam ।
tathāpi tvaṁ mahābāho nainaṁ śocitum arhasi ॥26॥

If you think of It as ever being born and ever dying, even then, O Mighty Armed (Arjuna), you do not have to grieve.

Arjuna, you have just seen that there is no need to grieve when life is seen as *sat*. Let us now see life as *bhāva;* then too you don't have to grieve. For, to be constantly changing is intrinsic with *bhāva*. One *bhāva* is always replaced by another. The vanishing of an old form is what we call death, and the emergence of a new one, birth. The hatching of an egg signals the emergence of a chick, one disappears and gives place to the appearance of another; the death of one becomes the birth of another. Both birth and death, even if considered as real, pertain to *bhāva*. Both are seen happening as part of the eternal flux of *bhāva* or becoming. Here again, you have no cause to grieve.

जातस्य हि ध्रुवो मृत्युर्ध्रुवं जन्म मृतस्य च।
तस्मादपरिहार्येऽर्थे न त्वं शोचितुमर्हसि ॥२७॥

> *jātasya hi dhruvo mṛtyur dhruvaṁ janma mṛtasya ca* |
> *tasmād aparihārye 'rthe na tvaṁ śocitum arhasi* ||27 ||
>
> Those born, for sure, will die, the dead, for sure, has to be born again; therefore over the inevitable you should not grieve.

The ornament has no existence of its own; it is merely a form assumed by gold. The ornament form has birth; it necessarily has to die. All forms in all the worlds appear as a result of the disappearance of some other form. It is inevitable that the disappearance of one form results in the appearance of a new one. This is natural in the realm of *bhāva*s; and it is not right to grieve over such an unavoidable sequence.

Arjuna, once again my words, "Those born, for sure, will die, and the dead, for sure, will be born again" might be misinterpreted as my acceptance of the notion of reincarnation. The present context looks at life from the side of *bhāva* as against that of *sat,* and thus it seems that we were all born, and are destined to die. However, since it is clear that the *sat* in all of us is without birth and death, there is no cause to be carried away by inappropriate grief. And I want you to remember this as a vital part of my teaching to be kept in mind at all times.

Do you still think of yourself as a born being? If so, you are still seeing yourself as *bhāva,* and not as *sat,* which is what I intend for you. All *bhāva* has beginning and end. The taking of such appearances to be real, unmindful of the unborn *sat* within, is known as *avidyā,* to be translated as 'ignorance,' or more correctly as 'nescience.' Understanding the unborn *sat* as real and all appearances as unreal is called *vidyā* (proper knowledge). In order to discriminate between the two, I will deal with the *avidyā* aspect and its effects as well. You must however keep in mind that this is meant merely to give clarity to the backdrop against which the real teaching is to be set. Such references are not to be mixed up with the doctrine that I teach.

The message I intend to convey here is only this: You do not have to grieve even if you look at life from the *bhāva*'s angle, for birth and death are inevitable in that realm.

अव्यक्तादीनि भूतानि व्यक्तमध्यानि भारत।
अव्यक्तनिधनान्येव तत्र का परिदेवना ॥२८॥

avyaktādīni bhūtāni vyakta-madhyāni bhārata ।
avyakta-nidhanāny eva tatra kā paridevanā ॥28॥

Indistinct were all beings in the beginning, distinct in the middle they are all; indistinct they become at dissolution, O Bhārata, what is therein to bemoan?

Arjuna, let us look at ourselves as individual beings, each a distinct *bhāva*. Each one of us is an entity that has come into being, a *bhūta*, meaning that which has attained a *bhāva*. Where was our beiginning? An egg, for example, when hatched, emerges as a chick. It contains not merely the physical content that was already in the egg. The bodily warmth of the mother-hen, the contact with the surrounding atmosphere, many other factors along with a mysterious creative aspect — all play a vital role. The mother-hen needs food to produce warmth for the egg, in addition to all the biological processes that take place within its being. No one knows in what form the substance in an egg was existing before. In short, its existence was indistinct before its hatching. So is our beginning. Each one of us supposedly has a distinct form. What were the factors that brought together in forming the being of each of us? It is quite indistinct. Similarly, no one knows what each being will disintegrate into or how they continue and are reformulated into new beings. The "before" and the "after" of our life, thus, are indistinct. The vague "before" extends back into the beginning, if any, of the world, and the "after" reaches out into the world's end. Only that which is in between these two indistinct immensities seems distinct — what we call our worldly existence. Compared to that part which remains indistinct, what we experience as distinct is an insignificant dot. That insignificant dot is our life, the problems of which torment us. Instead of seeing our life as a separate entity, try to view it as a minute part of the beginningless and endless flux of cosmic life. What you feel then will not be the problems that torment you, but the great wonder that life is.

आश्चर्यवत्पश्यति कश्चिदेनमाश्चर्यवद्वदति तथैव चान्यः ।
आश्चर्यवच्चैनमन्यः शृणोति श्रुत्वाप्येनं वेद न चैव कश्चित् ॥२९॥

āścaryavat paśyati kaścid enam āścaryavad vadati tathaiva cānyaḥ ।
āścaryavac cainam anyaḥ śṛṇoti śrutvāpy enaṁ veda na caiva kaścit ॥29॥

Some see It as a mystery! Others speak of It as a mystery! Still others hear of It as a mystery! Even having seen, spoken of or heard of, no one does understand It at all!

Arjuna, now don't you know life as a beginningless and endless flux of becoming where the one immutable *sat* assumes ceaselessly the forms of every fleeting apparent form? What that *sat* is and how it assumes all such apparent forms, no one knows. Those who know It perceive It as a great mystery. There are certain others who try to express in words, what It is. Unable to say anything definite without contradictions, they too end up saying, "It is a great mystery" or are meaningfully silent. The case of those who hear such wisdom is not very different.

Those who know the Real are to be called *jñānins*. It is as a *jñānin* that I have been speaking so far, but here what I say is, "It is a mystery." Anything mysterious cannot be known; no definite concept can be formulated of it. Then how can I know what it is? Or how can other *jñānins* know this Reality? The truth is that a *jñānin* is not to be understood as one who knows clearly and distinctly what Reality is, but rather as one who is aware that this Reality cannot be conceived of, who knows it is ineffable.

Indian thinkers, unlike their Western counterparts, rarely insist on the final conclusion of their philosophical speculations being logically tenable. A willingness to admit that Reality is a mystery, which defies all attempts at reasoning out or to be expressed, is fundamental to Vedānta.

Now to summarize how *dehin* and *deha*, *sat* and *bhāva*, are related, and what the benefit of knowing them as so related is:

देही नित्यमवध्यो ऽयं देहे सर्वस्य भारत ।
तस्मात्सर्वाणि भूतानि न त्वं शोचितुमर्हसि ॥३० ॥

dehī nityam avadhyo 'yaṁ dehe sarvasya bhārata ।
tasmāt sarvāṇi bhūtāni na tvaṁ śocitum arhasi ॥30 ॥

The embodied in all these bodies, O Bhārata, is eternal and incapable of being killed; you should, therefore, not grieve for any of all that has come into being.

Arjuna, this is how bodies (*dehas*) and the embodied Reality (*dehin*) are related: *dehas* constantly change; they appear and disappear; the *dehin* in all *dehas* remains immutable; it cannot be killed. In battling, you will destroy only the bodies, not the embodied Reality. Why should you grieve for the destruction of unreal bodies?

स्वधर्ममपि चावेक्ष्य न विकम्पितुमर्हसि ।
धर्म्याद्धि युद्धाच्छ्रेयो ऽन्यत्क्षत्रियस्य न विद्यते ॥३१ ॥

svadharmam api cāvekṣya na vikampitum arhasi ।
dharmyād dhi yuddhācchreyo 'nyat kṣatriyasya na vidyate ॥31 ॥

In view of *svadharma* also, you don't have to be wavering; for nothing better is there for a kṣatriya than to be in a war that accords with *dharma*.

Arjuna, we tried to clarify the nature of life, looking at it variously from the side of *sat* and of *bhāva*. Let us now look at it from the view of *svadharma*. *Svadharma* means one's own *dharma*. It does not simply mean adhering to one's ancestral profession. Persons are born with certain inherent personal traits, and the ideal life is that does full justice to these traits. It is only when each of these qualites is fully expressed that a person feels the satisfaction of having lived as he should. To seek and become aware of one's own personal traits and then to find an appropriate way of living and occupation, is one's *svadharma.* An idea of paramount importance in the *Gītā, svadharma* needs to be dealt with in detail later.

As far as you are concerned, your personal traits are those of a kṣatriya. The urge to provide protection to enable people to live a righteous life, and the willingness and capability to fight for this without retreating, could be considered the distinguishing qualities of a kṣatriya. You being one, this war is an opportunity for you to fully express your self-entity, the entity of a warrior. It is a war necessitated by the desire for *dharma* to prevail. As a kṣatriya, there can be nothing more meritorious for you than waging a righteous war.

Looking upon both sides of the battlefield, what you saw were reasons to dissuade you. You were confounded, making you oblivious to the reasons that should rightly persuade you into taking part in it. It is those factors that, I point out to you now, as a sort of counterbalance to your confusion and the negativity it caused, along with taking you to the notion of *svadharma.*

यदृच्छया चोपपन्नं स्वर्गद्वारमपावृतम्।
सुखिनः क्षत्रियाः पार्थ लभन्ते युद्धमीदृशम्॥३२॥

yadṛcchayā copapannaṁ svarga-dvāram apāvṛtam ।
sukhinaḥ kṣatriyāḥ pārtha labhante yuddham īdṛśam ॥32॥

Come-unsought-for is this war, as an open door to heaven; kṣatriyas who get such a war-chance, O Pārtha, do feel happy.

Arjuna, the wisdom I teach you is not aimed at attaining heaven; its goal is attaining *mukti* or *mokṣa,* the final liberation, a liberation from both heaven and hell, by realizing your inseparable oneness with the Absolute Reality; you might then doubt why I have told you, "the doors of heaven are open before you." These words, though mine, do not convey my final teaching, I am simply countering your fear of having to "go to hell." That way of understanding life is more Vedic, where heaven and hell are meaningful; finding yourself in that realm, you were suddenly overwhelmed by the prospect of being in hell. The same scriptures which teach you that those who kill their own gurus and kith and kin are destined to go to hell, teach also that the kṣatriya who fights righteous wars attains heaven. It is brought to your notice simply to free you from the despondency you are in.

अथ चेत्त्वमिमं धर्म्यं सङ्ग्रामं न करिष्यसि।
ततः स्वधर्मं कीर्तिं च हित्वा पापमवाप्स्यसि॥३३॥

atha cet tvam imaṁ dharmyaṁ saṅgrāmaṁ na kariṣyasi ।
tataḥ svadharmaṁ kīrtiṁ ca hitvā pāpam avāpsyasi ॥33॥

Should you be not engaging in this battle that accords with *dharma*, then you would be incurring sin by ignoring your *svadharma* and good fame.

Arjuna, you are frightened of the sinfulness of fighting your own kith and kin and of the resultant hell. There is another side: to ignore one's *svadharma* means, being unjust to oneself which is as much a sin as ruining one's own reputation. Both are sins of omission. You perceived the sin in participation, I show you the sin in not doing so.

Though fame is a worldly value, much lower than that of adhering to *svadharma*, yet it is not to be ignored; ignoring it may also be considered sinful. Looking at life in terms of fame, you should not retreat from this battle. The value of fame, though a worldly one related to the present context, needs a little more elucidation, which I do in the next three verses.

अकीर्तिं चापि भूतानि कथयिष्यन्ति तेऽव्ययाम्।
सम्भावितस्य चाकीर्तिर्मरणादतिरिच्यते॥३४॥

भयाद्रणादुपरतं मंस्यन्ते त्वां महारथाः।
येषां च त्वं बहुमतो भूत्वा यास्यसि लाघवम्॥३५॥
अवाच्यवादांश्च बहून्वदिष्यन्ति तवाहिताः।
निन्दन्तस्तव सामर्थ्यं ततो दुःखतरं नु किम्॥३६॥

akīrtiṁ cāpi bhūtāni kathayiṣyanti te 'vyayām ।
sambhāvitasya cākīrtir maraṇād atiricyate ॥34॥

bhayād raṇād uparataṁ maṁsyante tvāṁ mahārathāḥ ।
yeṣāṁ ca tvaṁ bahumato bhūtvā yāsyasi lāghavam ॥35॥

avācya-vādāṁś ca bahūn vadiṣyanti tavāhitāḥ ।
nindantas tava sāmarthyaṁ tato duḥkhataraṁ nu kim ॥36॥

Besides, people will continue forever to tell stories disgracing you; to a man of honour, ill fame is worse than death.

These great chariot-generals will think, you fled from the battle out of fear; they, having held you once in high esteem, will belittle you.

Those who don't like you will speak words ill of you and will deride your dexterity. Is there anything more painful than this?

To sum up what I have said so far: Once you know the ultimate nature of life, perceivable either as *sat* or *bhāva*, you will never grieve. Considering your *svadharma* also you don't have to be wavering. Viewed from the realm of the worldly value of fame also, you should neither sorrow nor retreat. In every way, thus, what is proper to you is not to be lost in despondency, but to stand up all-alert and battle.

हतो वा प्राप्स्यसि स्वर्गं जित्वा वा भोक्ष्यसे महीम्।
तस्मादुत्तिष्ठ कौन्तेय युद्धाय कृतनिश्चयः॥३७॥

hato vā prāpsyasi svargaṁ jitvā vā bhokṣyase mahīm ।
tasmād uttiṣṭha kaunteya yuddhāya kṛta-niścayaḥ ॥37॥

> If killed, you will reach heaven; if victorious, you will enjoy this earth. Therefore, O Son of Kuntī, stand up resolved to fight.

In a battle, one side must win and the other side be defeated. If defeated and killed, you will reach heaven, and if victorious, you will become the ruler of this earth. The result is good either way, and so you need not have to sorrow.

In your estimation, both fighting and not fighting are bad, for, you think that if you win, you will be a sinner enjoying pleasures splattered with the blood of your own *gurus*; and if you retreat, you think you will have to lead the life of a beggar. Here, I am showing you how these same results may be seen as positive.

This teaching, though being given to you, is really meant for everyone. It is not that everyone should get armed and go for battle. Life's struggle is the battlefield here, and it is different for each one. You, as a warrior by inborn nature, have to resolve to fight. Everyone who makes use of this wisdom teaching is required to identify his personal traits, and resolve to battle through life remaining true to those traits. The happiness thus gained is nothing but the happiness of self-realization.

The attitude towards life you should have, could well be summarized thus in the wake of what we have discussed so far.

सुखदुःखे समे कृत्वा लाभालाभौ जयाजयौ ।
ततो युद्धाय युज्यस्व नैवं पापमवाप्स्यसि ॥३८॥

sukha-duḥkhe same kṛtvā lābhālābhau jayājayau ।
tato yuddhāya yujyasva naivaṁ pāpam avāpsyasi ॥38॥

> Treating both happiness and suffering evenly, both gain and loss evenly, both victory and defeat evenly, do unite yourself to the war; thus you will remain unaffected by sin.

Attaining the firmness of mind to treat both happiness and suffering evenly is one of the most important benefits gained by acquiring the wisdom I teach. You will then be capable of regarding all opposing experiences in life, such as gain and loss, victory and defeat, with the same firmness and equanimity. The word *samam* I use here to mean evenness, not mere equality between two or more things, signifies that equality which two or more things have in the capacity of their being parts of one universal whole. One in whom such an attitude becomes natural is to be called a *yogī*. The contrariness between sin and merit is similar to that between suffering and happiness. Once you are capable of treating happiness and suffering or sin and merit evenly, you transcend both. To be a *yogī* is the way I recommend — the only way available — to be absolutely free from sins.

To treat both victory and defeat evenly, and putting yourself into the war situation you are already in, is what is required of you at the moment. It is a sort of *yoga*. No one can live cut-off from total existence. Any attempt to consider yourself as existing independent of the whole leads to sufferings. Seeing yourself as part of the whole, as part of the cosmic system, is the essence of *yogī* in you. In short, you have to fight this battle with the mind of a *yogī*, instead of being in the deranged mental state of a *rogī* (an ill person).

In the rest of this chapter I'll be concentrating more on the attainment of this *yoga* state.

एषा तेऽभिहिता साङ्ख्ये बुद्धिर्योगे त्विमां शृणु ।
बुद्ध्या युक्तो यया पार्थ कर्मबन्धं प्रहास्यसि ॥३९॥

eṣā te 'bhihitā sāṁkhye buddhir yoge tvimāṁ śṛṇu ।
buddhyā yukto yayā pārtha karma-bandhaṁ prahāsyasi ॥39॥

What I have just laid bare is *sāṁkhya-buddhi*. Hear it now in terms of *yoga-buddhi*; being united to this *buddhi*, one shakes off all bindings of *karma*.

We now enter a new phase of our inquiry. What I had been expounding till now could be called *sāṁkhya-buddhi*. The meaning of *sāṁkhya* was clarified at the start of this chapter. *Buddhi* is not just intellect; it is the sum of the knowledge one acquires about any topic of one's interest. Here our interest is nothing less than life and our place in it. We tried to view life from different angles; the knowledge we gained thus is *sāṁkhya-buddhi*.

Yoga is the state in which two are inseparably united. Our understanding of life with such an outlook, or rather inlook, is *yoga-buddhi*. It is more an experience of being one with the whole than a specific understanding. Reasoning gives shape to *sāṁkhya-buddhi*, and intuitive experience formulates *yoga-buddhi*. To be free from the happiness-suffering duality is the benefit we gain through *sāṁkhya buddhi*; attaining the transcendental state is the benefit of *yoga-buddhi*, as will be underscored in Verse 51: *padaṁ gacchanty anāmayam* (they reach the state without suffering).

The attainment of the final goal known as *paramānanda* implies two aspects: being rid of sufferings and reaching the abode of happiness. The first is to avert the unwanted; the other to achieve that which is coveted. The two are like the sides of a coin, the real is that which has these two for apparent facets and which unites the two into its being. Uniting two opposite facets into a non-dual being is thus the secret of *yoga-buddhi*.

One who unites himself with this understanding of life will find himself free from all the bindings of *karma*. How this happens will become evident in the next chapter, *Karma-yoga*.

I shall tell you one of the peculiarities of this *buddhi*:

नेहाभिक्रमनाशो ऽस्ति प्रत्यवायो न विद्यते ।
स्वल्पमप्यस्य धर्मस्य त्रायते महतो भयात् ॥४० ॥

nehābhikrama-nāśo 'sti pratyavāyo na vidyate ।
svalpam apy asya dharmasya trāyate mahato bhayāt ॥40 ॥

In this (*yoga-buddhi*) no effort goes fruitless; neither will be felt any hindrance in getting the rightful fruit.

Even a little of this *dharma* redeems one from great fear.

Karmas (actions) done are usually motivated by the fruits they are expected to yield. There may be occasions when one does not gain the expected fruit in spite of all one's best efforts. The unfavourability of such nature is known as *abhikrama-nāśa.* Some unexpected slip between the cup and the lip may also occur at times. Such hindrances to the rightful enjoyment of the fruits of one's own *karma* is known as *pratyavāya*. Life and its value, in either of the cases, are evaluated confining oneself to the limited circle of one's own *karmas* and their fruits. Erase that circle and see life as extending to infinity. Then you will see an overall system, a *dharma,* sustaining life in its entirety, you and your *karmas* being merely a part of it.

Coming back to your personal problem: the fear and despondency you experienced was basically caused by your treating the actions (*karmas*) you happen to do as "your *karmas*," confining yourself in the closed circle of *karmas* and their fruits. Erase that little circle and see yourself as part of an infinite life system, and you will realize the insignificance of those *karmas* — though inevitable — freeing you of all these fears. This direct experience of your oneness with the whole is the core of yoga as understood here. Even a trace of it is sufficient to redeem you from all such fears.

व्यवसायात्मिका बुद्धिरेकेह कुरुनन्दन ।
बहुशाखा ह्यनन्ताश्च बुद्धयो ऽव्यवसायिनाम् ॥४१ ॥

vyavasāyātmikā buddhir ekeha kuru-nandana ।
bahu-śākhā hy anantāś ca buddhayo 'vyavasāyinām ॥41 ॥

Fully convincing and resolute knowledge, in this case, O Joy of Kurus, is unitary; many-branched and endlessly diverse is the knowledge of those who are unconvinced and irresolute.

The contentment of having known what is to be ultimately known about Reality, about life, about ourselves, is what one finally gains by pursuing this *yoga-buddhi*. Such knowledge is one alone, of its own kind with no other knowledge to compare with. Seeing everything in all the worlds as one self-manifesting Reality is the essential content of this knowledge. In that vision alone can the act of knowing find firm ground, where it attains finality. Then alone one feels, nothing remains to be known.

The other knowledge is that of knowing all apparent entities as real on their own; such entities being countless, knowledge of them is also endless. Knowing these, one will never have the contentment of having come to the end of knowledge, nor will such knowledge be conclusive, convincing or resolute, for how can there be conclusive knowledge concerning things spread out endlessly and many-branched?

The latter is the way people like you are familiar with. It may also develop into many sciences in the future. Whatever be the number of such sciences, however penetrating their enquiries be, they will never arrive at a conclusive knowledge. One of the aims of the present wisdom teaching is to steer seekers like you away from that way of thinking, and to lead you on to the unitive way of knowing. Knowing the one Reality marks the end of all knowledge, which the word "Vedānta" means — *veda* meaning "knowledge" and *anta* "the finality."

Arjuna, what I am teaching you is none other than the essence of Vedānta. It is Vedānta also in the sense that it is the wisdom teaching that forms the concluding part (*anta*) of the Vedas. Though Vedānta thus has the Vedas for its background, the two are widely at variance in content. Vedanta teaches the wisdom of one Reality; its goal being freedom from all bondage, while the Vedas, in contrast, are ritualistic in import and with a view that the worlds are many in number and beings are many, reality is also likewise seen as many, and the goal of Vedas is to reach heaven and enjoy its pleasures. The Vedas and their rituals together is the best example in the Indian spiritual tradition, of inconclusive and irresolute knowledge. Let us now look at its nature more closely with a view to contrasting it with the unitive way of Vedānta.

यामिमां पुष्पितां वाचं प्रवदन्त्यविपश्चितः।
वेदवादरताः पार्थ नान्यदस्तीति वादिनः ॥४२॥
कामात्मानः स्वर्गपरा जन्मकर्मफलप्रदाम्।
क्रियाविशेषबहुलां भोगैश्वर्यगतिं प्रति ॥४३॥
भोगैश्वर्यप्रसक्तानां तयापहृतचेतसाम्।
व्यवसायात्मिका बुद्धिः समाधौ न विधीयते ॥४४॥

yām imāṁ puṣpitāṁ vācaṁ pravadanty avipaścitaḥ ।
vedavāda-ratāḥ pārtha nānyad astīti vādinaḥ ॥42॥
kāmātmānaḥ svarga-parā janma-karma-phala-pradām ।
kriyā-viśeṣa-bahulāṁ bhogaiśvarya-gatiṁ prati ॥43॥
bhogaiśvarya-prasaktānāṁ tayāpahṛta-cetasām ।
vyavasāyātmikā buddhiḥ samādhau na vidhīyate ॥44॥

The undiscerning, delighting in the letter of the Vedas, and professing, O Pārtha, that nothing else aspirable is there, discourse about it in such flowery words;

Saturated with desires, with heaven for their goal, (those words of theirs) proclaim repeating birth and *karma* as final reward, and prescribe various specific rites with a view to ensuring worldly enjoyments.

To them, desirous of mastering worldly enjoyments as they are, with minds allured by such words, the convincing and resolute knowledge will not avail for attaining *samādhi*.

Arjuna, the promises of the Vedas are alluring to the ignorant. The longing for more pleasure leads the ignorant to hope to reach heaven one way or another. However great may be heaven's enjoyments, the longing for these makes man more and more bound to the means of attainment — the *karma*s — rather than being a liberating force. Such a pleasurable heaven as the Vedas teach, is reached as an outcome of the *karma*s one performs while in this world. How can those who are after such pleasures attain and stand by one resolute and convincing knowledge?

Arjuna, to be peaceful and happy in life is desired by all. It is to be attained only when one finds one's proper abode and remains unwaveringly one with it, like an ornament that finds its abode in gold and remaining one with it. The word *samādhi* has two parts: *sam* standing for *samyak* meaning "proper," and *ādhi*, "abode." *Samādhi* thus is the state in which mind finds its proper abode and remains well stabilized there. That this *samādhi*-experience and the *yoga-buddhi* we are concerned with presently, are inseparable will gradually become clear as we proceed.

I shall now tell you what should therefore be your attitude as a seeker, towards the Vedas as well as towards all that which makes you see reality as many.

त्रैगुण्यविषया वेदा निस्त्रैगुण्यो भवार्जुन ।
निर्द्वन्द्वो नित्यसत्त्वस्थो निर्योगक्षेम आत्मवान् ॥४५ ॥

traiguṇya-viṣayā vedā nistraiguṇyo bhavārjuna ।
nirdvandvo nitya-sattvastho niryogakṣema ātmavān ॥45 ॥

The (realm of) three *guṇa*s is the Vedas' concern; go beyond the three *guṇa*s, O Arjuna; go beyond all the dualities; find your being in the one eternal Existence; don't find identity with possessions; be possessed of the Self.

Arjuna, it must be quite clear to you by now that the Vedas view reality as many. The notion of many is relevant only in the realm of *bhāva*, never in that of *sat*, as was made explicit in the section on *sāṁkhya-buddhi*. The process by which one *sat* or *dehin* assumes many *bhāva*s or *deha*s is called *prakṛti*. It has inherent in it three *guṇa*s or modes of activeness: *sattva*, *rajas* and *tamas*. The incessant mixing together of these *guṇa*s in constantly varying proportions, causes all apparent changes and variety, resulting also in the appearance and disappearance of forms. These aspects are explored at greater length in Chapter XIV.

To return to your problem: though unconsciously, you are still under the pull of Vedic moorings, which is the reason you think in terms of "killer," the "killed," the act of killing, this world, heaven, hell and suchlike, as many realities. All these that you count as real are all fleeting appearances, mere *bhāvas,* always changing owing to the activeness of *prakṛti.* You, in other words, are under the spell of the three *guṇas*. Go beyond, and you will find yourself going past the Vedas' teaching as well as dualities such as sin and merit, success and failure. Seek in yourself the one Substance (*sat*) that not only underlies all but also unfolds as all these dualities. That Substance is none other than *ātmā* (the Self) and one who is well founded in It, possesses It. Then you will feel the meaninglessness of the worldly possessions with which you have been identifying yourself. You become an *ātmavān,* one who possesses the Self and is possessed by the Self. In other words, you become a *yogī.* The word *niryoga-kṣema* is interpretable in two ways: as "one who does not care for worldly possessions"; and as "one who considers one's own *yoga* state as true prosperity."

यावानर्थ उदपाने सर्वतः सम्प्लुतोदके ।
तावान्सर्वेषु वेदेषु ब्राह्मणस्य विजानतः ॥४६ ॥

yāvān artha udapāne sarvataḥ samplutodake ।
tāvān sarveṣu vedeṣu brāhmaṇasya vijānataḥ ॥46 ॥

All the Vedas, to an enlightened brāhmaṇa, are of no more use than is a small pool in a place flooded all over.

Arjuna, imagine a village where water is held in pools, wells, ponds and suchlike, from where people fetch water for their daily needs. Imagine a flood of good potable water inundating all of these. People will no longer need to go to the pools or wells or ponds for water, as good water is freely available everywhere. Though the pools and wells are still there, their usefulness has gone underneath the value of the flooding water.

Similar is the difference between the values held high by the Vedas and Vedānta. The former, based on the notion of many realities, are like small pools of limited value that become inundated by the flood of the all-inclusive value of Vedānta, which wisdom I am restating here. So too, *yoga-buddhi* engulfs ordinary knowledge into its perception of all as one. The many are not simply denied existence, rather they are subsumed under the one all-inclusive Existence, rendering the former of no significance.

Any close study of history reveals a peculiar fact: it is not by totally nullifying an already existing cultural phase that a new upheaval happens. The limited significance of the previous culture is subsumed into the new and wider significance of the latter. The Vedāntic way of correcting the Vedic way is also the same, known in history as "dialectical revaluation."

कर्मण्येवाधिकारस्ते मा फलेषु कदाचन ।
मा कर्मफलहेतुर्भूर्मा ते सङ्गो ऽस्त्वकर्मणि ॥४७॥

karmaṇy evādhikāras te mā phaleṣu kadācana ।
mā karma-phala-hetur bhūr mā te saṅgo 'stv akarmaṇi ॥47॥

Doing actions as such alone is appropriate for you; never being concerned with their benefits. Do not (therefore) be benefit-motivated in actions, be not attached to inaction either.

Arjuna, you have just seen how the Vedas along with their rituals (*karma*s), in the wake of Vedāntic wisdom, are like small pools and wells subsumed under a flood. In the broadest sense, all the activities that unceasingly take place in *prakṛti* owing to its three *guṇa*s, are *karma*s. *Prakṛti* and all the *karma*s together are subsumed under the flood of the *sat* that is beyond the *guṇa*s. We are yet to go into the details of the place of *karma* in the overall system of life in Chapter III.

By your having discovered yourself as *sat* and remaining as That, *prakṛti* (translated vaguely as "nature") is not rendered inactive. As part of that *prakṛti*, you also will continue to be active. All those activities are nothing but *prakṛti* finding self-expression.

Running away from such activities is not possible. Becoming engaged in these should never be for attaining any predetermined benefit, rather, they are to be done for the sheer joy of doing them. Each such action leading to some result also forms part of the unfoldment of *prakṛti*.

People in the usual course of life, do *karma*s motivated by desire for benefits, immediate or future, and disappointment follows when they do not get the expected result. On the other hand, if you were to make the motive of your action the joy of doing them, the benefit is achieved even as you are doing actions. It is comparable to children playing for the joy of playing. Similar should be all your actions, fighting in this battle included. The favourable or unfavourable events that occur from such *karma*s are also to be treated as part of *prakṛti*, not as the end-result of your *karma*. Thus you will find yourself neither attached to actions nor attached to inaction.

What I have just stated summarily, when elucidated, becomes *karma-yoga*, also sometimes called *niṣkāma-karma* (*karma*s done not motivated by desires). Doing some *karma* and relinquishing its outcome does not make *niṣkāma-karma*.

योगस्थः कुरु कर्माणि सङ्गं त्यक्त्वा धनञ्जय ।
सिद्ध्यसिद्ध्योः समो भूत्वा समत्वं योग उच्यते ॥४८॥

yogasthaḥ kuru karmāṇi saṅgaṁ tyaktvā dhanañjaya ।
siddhy-asiddhyoḥ samo bhūtvā samatvaṁ yoga ucyate ॥48॥

By being in *yoga,* O Dhanañjaya, perform actions with attachments abandoned, and with evenness towards getting and not-getting; for evenness of mind is said of as *yoga.*

Arjuna, the world on its own is an eternal and universal flow of *karma*s. Constant change is normal with the world. Every change involves an event; every event is a *karma,* one leading to another. You and I, individuals, came into being as a result of such *karma*s. We too do *karma*s as part of the universal flow of *karma*s. Once visualized thus, no one will feel: "I am doing a *karma,*" but rather that, "I am partaking in the universal flux of *karmas*, in universal life." My *karma* and the world's *karma* are thus merged as one *karma*, which is a state of *yoga*. Place yourself in that state and do whatever *karma* that crops up as part of the flow. There you will never feel attached to those actions. One's attachment towards anything is called *saṅga*. To give up all attachments is considered a spiritual discipline; but, nevertheless, its fulfilment becomes fruitful only when complemented by the other half: being in the *yoga* state. Practising non-attachment helps one reach the *yoga* state; conversely, being in the *yoga* state makes one unattached. Being in *yoga* and having a sense of detachement are thus mutually complementary in the seeker's life.

The feeling, "I am the doer of this *karma*" is followed by the thought, "Its fruits should also be mine." Done in a *yoga* state with full detachment, all *karmas* become of even value, regardless of whether the results are favourable or unfavourable. This evenness of mind (*samatvam*) could thus be considered a sign of the *yoga* state.

दूरेण ह्यवरं कर्म बुद्धियोगाद्धनञ्जय ।
बुद्धौ शरणमन्विच्छ कृपणाः फलहेतवः ॥४९॥

dūreṇa hy avaraṁ karma buddhi-yogād dhanañjaya ।
buddhau śaraṇam anviccha kṛpaṇāḥ phala-hetavaḥ ॥49॥

Far inferior to *buddhi-yoga* indeed is *karma*, O Arjuna; resort, (therefore), to *buddhi-yoga* for final refuge; despicable indeed are the benefit-motivated.

Arjuna, as you know, *karma* becomes sublimated into *karma-yoga*, when the individual does a *karma* after finding his being to be one with totality or *prakṛti*. To understand the role of one's *karma* in the overall scheme of existence is what matters then, not whether one is actually engaged in actions or not. Understanding (*buddhi*), in other words, is what transmutes *karma* into *karma-yoga*. The state in which one always relies on understanding, in which one is united with understanding, could be called *buddhi-yoga*. If this understanding is lacking, all actions will arise from the notion, "I am the doer of this *karma*, and its fruits are also mine!" The guilty conscience of having committed sin, or the pride of having done something meritorious, always follows such *karmas*. One may even be constantly anticipating the prospect of enjoying or suffering the results of those *karmas*. Far inferior are thus the *karmas* of the ignorant than the desireless *karmas* of those who resort to understanding. All benefit-motivated actions, even those aimed at attaining heaven, render us more bonded whereas what we need is liberation. Take refuge, therefore, in understanding; only then will you be rid of the feeling of being bound to do *karma*. Despicable (*kṛpaṇa*) are those who undertake benefit-motivated *karmas*. The state of being a *kṛpaṇa* is *kārpaṇya*. It is this state you were earlier in, as indicated by your words *kārpaṇya doṣa* in Verse 7. Lack of discrimination, greed, misery — these are some other signs of *kārpaṇya*. Without your knowing, such blemishes have crept into your being. There is only one remedy: rely on understanding, resort to *buddhi-yoga,* and what you attain will be *yoga-buddhi*.

बुद्धियुक्तो जहातीह उभे सुकृतदुष्कृते ।
तस्माद्योगाय युज्यस्व योगः कर्मसु कौशलम् ॥५० ॥

buddhi-yukto jahātīha ubhe sukṛta-duṣkṛte ।
tasmād yogāya yujyasva yogaḥ karmasu kauśalam ॥50 ॥

One in unison with understanding casts off here both good and evil deeds. Therefore find your union with *yoga*; *yoga* is propitiousness in action.

The *yogī*, you know, is the one who lives in union with understanding — the understanding that one exists in union with the totality. As mere *kṛtis* (actions) of *prakṛti*, the *karmas* one does are neither sinful nor meritorious. Only *yogīs* are thus absolutely free from sins; the freedom of others is merely relative and shortlived.

You are engaged now in a search for release from the sense of sin. Seek that understanding which will make a *yogī* of you, make yourself united to that wisdom context, to be freed from all sin for ever. The actions a *yogī* does may seem right or wrong, sinful or meritorious, to a non-yogic observer, but for the *yogī* they are simply actions of the *prakṛti* of which he is a part. The *yogī* experiences self-contentment and peace, knowing himself to be one with *prakṛti*. The original word *kauśalam*, rendered here as "propitiousness," strictly means the state in which one feels fulfilled. "*Yoga* is propitiousness in action" is yet another of my definitions of *yoga*; and another, that "evenness of mind is *yoga*," was given in Verse 48 above.

Self-fulfilment, as with other experiences, is to be experienced in the living moment, not in some unknown hypothetical future. Each moment of one's life should be a moment of self-fulfilment. None experiences the future except as a hope at the present. There are many who make the living present torturous, in the hope of making the future happy. That happy future may remain just a dream, and it may so happen that they die without having lived the happy life they hoped to live. To avoid this tragedy, what you have to do is to transform everything that you happen to do at every moment of the present into an occasion of self-fulfilment, which is itself the propitiousness indicated here.

कर्मजं बुद्धियुक्ता हि फलं त्यक्त्वा मनीषिणः ।
जन्मबन्धविनिर्मुक्ताः पदं गच्छन्त्यनामयम् ॥५१ ॥

karmajaṁ buddhi-yuktā hi phalaṁ tyaktvā maniṣiṇaḥ ।
janma-bandha-vinirmuktāḥ padaṁ gacchanty anāmayam ॥51 ॥

The wise, united as they are to proper understanding, having renounced action-born-fruits, and thus liberated from birth-born-bondages, attain the state of sufferinglessness.

Arjuna, the Sanskrit word for liberation is *mukti* or *mokṣa*. Its opposite is *bandha*, meaning bondage or boundedness. The liberation we need is from the bondage, the boundedness we feel towards our own actions which, according to Vedism, results in repeated births and deaths. Only a *yogī*, through his resorting to *buddhi-yoga*, becomes free of *karmas*. He never feels, "This is my *karma*." He really is to be called the wise (*manīṣin*). The transcedental state he finds himself in is without suffering, beyond pleasure and pain, beyond sin and merit, beyond birth and death — the final goal anyone can aspire to in life.

Your grief was also the result of the boundedness you felt towards your *karmas*. The remedy is to become a wise one (*manīṣin*) and thus attain liberation.

यदा ते मोहकलिलं बुद्धिर्व्यतितरिष्यति ।
तदा गन्तासि निर्वेदं श्रोतव्यस्य श्रुतस्य च ॥५२॥

yadā te moha-kalilaṁ buddhir vyatitariṣyati ।
tadā gantāsi nirvedaṁ śrotavyasya śrutasya ca ॥52॥

When your understanding crosses the dross of indecisiveness, then will you attain detachment towards what is yet to be heard and what is already heard.

Arjuna, unless and until you attain fully convincing and resolute knowledge, unless you resort to *buddhi-yoga* and thus attain *yoga-buddhi*, you will continue to view reality as many. Seeing many, you will find it difficult to decide which is real and which is unreal, which is good and which is bad, or which is graceful and which is disgraceful. Such indecisiveness is called *moha*. Crossing over it, you find the one Reality where knowledge becomes convincing and resolute. You will then be not interested in that which was of interest till then, that is, in Vedism, which considers reality as many not only in respect of what you are yet to learn, but also what you have already learnt. The words *śrotavya* (what is yet to be heard) and *śruta* (what is already heard) are both derived from the root word *śruti*, meaning "hearing" which in the Vedic context stands for "learning" those scriptures. The word *nirveda*, a synonym of *vairāgya*, meaning indifference and a sense of detachment towards those of little value, suggests also the denial of the Vedas (*nir+veda*).

श्रुतिविप्रतिपन्ना ते यदा स्थास्यति निश्चला।
समाधावचला बुद्धिस्तदा योगमवाप्स्यसि ॥५३॥

śruti-vipratipannā te yadā sthāsyati niścalā I
samādhāv acalā buddhis tadā yogam avāpsyasi II53 II

When your understanding, presently bewildered by Vedic teachings, stands unshaken, steadfast in *samādhi*, then will you attain *yoga*.

अर्जुन उवाच —

स्थितप्रज्ञस्य का भाषा समाधिस्थस्य केशव।
स्थितधीः किं प्रभाषेत किमासीत व्रजेत किम्॥५४॥

arjuna uvāca —

sthita-prajñasya kā bhāṣā samādhisthasya keśava I
sthita-dhīḥ kiṁ prabhāṣeta kim āsīta vrajeta kim II54 II

Arjuna said —

What are the signs of a man of well founded knowledge? Who is in a state of *samādhi*, O Keśava? How does the man of steadied intellect express himself? How does he live? How does he move about?

O Kṛṣṇa, your teaching, I realize, is meant to help me attain the state of *samādhi* where the mind is unshaken, the one who has attained such a state being a *sthita-prajña.*

What actually takes place within the mind of anyone, being purely a personal experience, though incomprehensible to another, still becomes reflected in the person as external visible signs. What are some such external signs that distinguish a *sthita-prajña*?

श्री भगवानुवाच —

प्रजहाति यदा कामान्सर्वान्पार्थ मनोगतान्।
आत्मन्येवात्मना तुष्टः स्थितप्रज्ञस्तदोच्यते॥५५॥

śrī bhagavān uvāca —

prajahāti yadā kāmān sarvān pārtha mano-gatān ।
ātmany-evātmanā tuṣṭaḥ sthita-prajñas tadocyate ॥55 ॥

Śrī Kṛṣṇa said —

A man who drives away all desires that crop up in mind, remaining satisfied in himself by himself, is said to be a *sthita-prajña.*

Arjuna, *sthita-prajña* is an apt name for the one of well-founded knowledge. Such a one does not derive joy either from pleasurable objects, or from the company of others. Fulfilment of desires for such is in no way near the contentment obtained from self-fulfilment. A *sthita-prajña* is fully satisfied in himself; on finding the Real that makes his being, he thenceforth lives considering himself a small ripple in the boundless ocean of that Reality. My words *ātmani eva ātmanā tuṣṭaḥ* might possibly be misconstrued to indicate that the *sthita-prajña* becomes satisfied with an entity called *ātman* within himself. The simplest meaning of the word *ātman* is "I" or oneself, and the *sthita-prajña* may be understood to live fully satisfied in being himself rather than emulating someone else.

दुःखेष्वनुद्विग्नमनाः सुखेषु विगतस्पृहः ।
वीतरागभयक्रोधः स्थितधीर्मुनिरुच्यते ॥५६ ॥

duḥkheṣv anudvigna-manāḥ sukheṣu vigata-spṛhaḥ ।
vīta-rāga-bhaya-krodhaḥ sthita-dhīr munir ucyate ॥56 ॥

He whose mind remains unwavering in the midst of sorrows, and not longing in the midst of pleasures, free from attachment, free from fear, and free from anger — is said to be a silent recluse (*muni*) of well-founded knowledge.

Arjuna, a *sthita-prajña* does not like to speak out what he knows nor will be boasting of his self-fulfilment. He, on the other hand, would prefer to remain a silent recluse, a *muni*, in the stability of his certitude.

यः सर्वत्रानभिस्नेहस्तत्तत्प्राप्य शुभाशुभम्।
नाभिनन्दति न द्वेष्टि तस्य प्रज्ञा प्रतिष्ठिता ॥५७॥

yaḥ sarvatrānabhisnehas tat-tat prāpya śubhāśubham ।
nābhinandati na dveṣṭi tasya prajñā pratiṣṭhitā ॥57॥

He who has no undue fondness towards anything, who neither exults the good nor detests the bad when facing each — his knowledge is well-founded.

Arjuna, the fear of committing a dreadful sin was worrying you, but once *buddhi-yoga* has been attained, you will consider both good and bad, sinful and meritorious deeds, as equally part of *prakṛti*'s *kṛti* (action). You will then have no particular desire for meritorious deeds, nor will you detest what are called "sinful" actions. Instead, you will treat all that occurs with a neutral mind, while reacting to each as the situation demands.

यदा संहरते चायं कूर्मोऽङ्गानीव सर्वशः।
इन्द्रियाणीन्द्रियार्थेभ्यस्तस्य प्रज्ञा प्रतिष्ठिता ॥५८॥

yadā saṁharate cāyaṁ kūrmo 'ṅgānīva sarvaśaḥ ।
indriyāṇīndriyārthebhyas tasya prajñā pratiṣṭhitā ॥58॥

Again, a man who withdraws his senses from their objects, as a tortoise draws its limbs in from all sides — his knowledge is well-founded.

Arjuna, the habit of withdrawing the senses form the objects that they habitually pursue, is another sign of a *sthita-prajña*. Self-fulfilment, rather than sense-gratification, keeps such a one happy. The *sthita-prajña,* in the midst of pleasures, withdraws the mind and sense-organs, rather than surrender to the urge for enjoyment. He seeks protection within the indestructible shell of the Self. Withdrawing the mind from sense-interests is known as *śama,* and withdrawing the sense-organs from their objects is called *dama.*

Longing for sense-pleasures is one of the most potent distractions that deter seekers from their life-goal. Unless a firm stand is taken in this matter, backed by a mind willful enough to stand by this decision, none of the seeker's efforts will become fruitful. It is, therefore, essential to be aware of some of the subtler aspects that this self-restraint implies.

विषया विनिवर्तन्ते निराहारस्य देहिनः ।
रसवर्जं रसोऽप्यस्य परं दृष्ट्वा निवर्तते ॥५९॥

viṣayā vinivartante nirāhārasya dehinaḥ ।
rasa-varjaṁ raso 'py asya paraṁ dṛṣṭvā nivartate ॥59॥

Sense objects turn away from the embodied when starved into restraint, the relish for them still persisting; the relish too ceases on perceiving the Transendental.

Arjuna, by now it must have become evident to you that a sense of detachment towards pleasure is an essential prerequisite for gaining the wisdom I teach here. With this awareness, there are many who practise self-restraint as part of their spiritual discipline. The senses and the mind are naturally inclined to seeking out interesting things to feast on. Merely to deny their natural food is in effect equal to starving the senses and the mind. Mere forced suppression of mind and senses does not put an end to their longing for pleasures. Such longing also ceases to be when the mind comes face to face with that happiness beyond which nothing remains to relish. Once the mind relishes the bliss of the Absolute, it withdraws from momentary pleasures in a natural process. Once the mind has this treasure to rejoice in, it will cease to be affected by other passing pleasures.

यततो ह्यपि कौन्तेय पुरुषस्य विपश्चितः ।
इन्द्रियाणि प्रमाथीनि हरन्ति प्रसभं मनः ॥६०॥

yatato hy api kaunteya puruṣasya vipaścitaḥ ।
indriyāṇi pramāthīni haranti prasabhaṁ manaḥ ॥60॥

> Even a discerning man of self-restraint (at times) gets excited by senses. O son of Kuntī, forcefully they drag his mind along.

Merely being a discerning person or one keen on attaining self-knowledge, does not make one capable of self-restraint. The temptation of sense pleasures are strong and require an uncompromising willfulness to keep them at bay. The genuine seeker must cultivate the kind of self-restraint, with its two facets mentioned in the last verse.

तानि सर्वाणि संयम्य युक्त आसीत मत्परः ।
वशे हि यस्येन्द्रियाणि तस्य प्रज्ञा प्रतिष्ठिता ॥६१ ॥

tāni sarvāṇi saṁyamya yukta āsīta mat-paraḥ ।
vaśe hi yasyendriyāṇi tasya prajñā pratiṣṭhitā ॥61 ॥

> Restraining all of them (the senses), let him remain in *yoga*, with Me alone as goal; his knowledge is well-founded whose senses are in his own control.

Arjuna, I explained how self-restraint becomes effective and fruitful only when the mind is directed to the highest of all values. That highest value which is to be the goal is nothing but "I," the Absolute Reality, the *sat* that underlies everything, *Brahman*. This disposition of the mind to consider Me, *Brahman*, as the one goal that ensures self-fulfilment, is what I mean by *mat-paraḥ* (with Me alone as goal).

I shall now proceed to tell you what will happen to those who are not self-restrained.

ध्यायतो विषयान्पुंसः सङ्गस्तेषूपजायते ।
सङ्गात्सञ्जायते कामः कामात्क्रोधो ऽभिजायते ॥६२ ॥
क्रोधाद्भवति सम्मोहः सम्मोहात्स्मृतिविभ्रमः ।
स्मृतिभ्रंशाद् बुद्धिनाशो बुद्धिनाशात्प्रणश्यति ॥६३ ॥

dhyāyato viṣayān puṁsaḥ saṅgas teṣūpajāyate ।
saṅgāt sañjāyate kāmaḥ kāmāt krodho 'bhijāyate ॥62 ॥

krodhād bhavati sammohaḥ sammohāt smṛti-vibhramaḥ ।
smṛti-bhraṁśād buddhi-nāśo buddhi-nāśāt praṇaśyati ॥63 ॥

Man, brooding on objects of pleasure, develops attachment towards them; from attachment arises desire; from desire springs anger.

Anger makes him deluded; from delusion arises lapse of memory; because of memory-lapse is lost proper understanding; lack of understanding results in perishing.

Arjuna, here is a picture of the vicious circle that is triggered off when one becomes infatuated with sense pleasures. In contrast, those who avoid this trap through proper self-restraint, live in a serene state.

रागद्वेषवियुक्तैस्तु विषयानिन्द्रियैश्चरन् ।
आत्मवश्यैर्विधेयात्मा प्रसादमधिगच्छति ॥६४ ॥

rāga-dveṣa-viyuktais tu viṣayān indriyaiś caran ।
ātma-vaśyair vidheyātmā prasādam adhigacchati ॥64 ॥

By contrast, he who keeps himself free from attachment as well as aversion even when his senses, under his own control, are engaged in their objects, attains supreme serenity because he is possessed by the Self.

Arjuna, by all this, you are not to understand that the sense-organs of those who are of full self-restraint remain inactive. The senses are active as they should be, but the individual does not become yoked to them or controlled by them, rather remaining in control, the senses also function under control. Such a person is to be called a *vidheyātmā*, one under one's own control. Though such a person may be moving amongst objects, remaining uninterested in them, he does not forget his ultimate goal, nor do his efforts deviate form the path of its attainment. The senses in such cases, instead of hindering the attainment of this final goal, may function as helpful aids. All experiences, whether originating from sense-contact or not, are perceived by such a one as simply many sparks of the one great fire of pure Consciousness.

प्रसादे सर्वदुःखानां हानिरस्योपजायते ।
प्रसन्नचेतसो ह्याशु बुद्धिः पर्यवतिष्ठते ॥६५॥

prasāde sarva-duḥkhānāṁ hānir asyopajāyate ।
prasanna-cetaso hy āśu buddhiḥ paryavatiṣṭhate ॥65॥

Serenity having been attained, one feels the extinction of all sorrows; understanding also indeed soon becomes well-founded with the serene-minded.

Arjuna, one who is not serene and happy, is not a *sthita-prajña.* The state of being *sthita-prajña* and serenity of mind are co-existent. A person in whom these two find unity is to be called a *yogī* or *yukta*; or else he is an *ayukta.* To contrast an *ayukta* with a *yukta:*

नास्ति बुद्धिरयुक्तस्य न चायुक्तस्य भावना ।
न चाभावयतः शान्तिरशान्तस्य कुतः सुखम् ॥६६॥

nāsti buddhir ayuktasya na cāyuktasya bhāvanā ।
na cābhāvayataḥ śāntir aśāntasya kutaḥ sukham ॥66॥

He who is not thus united lacks in proper understanding; nor is there the vision of the origin (*bhāvanā*) in the not-united; the person lacking in vision of origin has no peace; for the peaceless, how could there be happiness?

Arjuna, we are now trying to describe the visible signs of a *sthita-prajña*, the one who is of well-founded knowledge. This kind of well-founded knowledge marks the life of a *yogī* or *yukta,* one who is united with the One. Whatever the changeful facets of life the *yogī* encounters, he sees in all of these only one Reality. The *yogī* 's interest is held not by the evanescent outer sparks called *bhāvas,* but by the one Substance, *sat.* It is this form of perception — of seeing all the *bhāva*s as one with the *sat,* what I call *bhāvanā* (the vision of the origin). He, who perceives in such a manner, is the *yukta* or *yogī.* To him, the sense, sense-contacts, sense-pleasures — these are all nothing but a part of those *bhāvas.*

इन्द्रियाणां हि चरतां यन्मनो ऽनुविधीयते ।
तदस्य हरति प्रज्ञां वायुर्नावमिवाम्भसि ॥६७ ॥

indriyāṇāṁ hi caratāṁ yan mano 'nuvidhīyate ।
tad asya harati prajñāṁ vāyur nāvam ivāmbhasi ॥67 ॥

With mind wandering behind the wandering senses, one's discerning faculty is carried away by it, as a ship in waters is by wind.

Arjuna, our senses, their objects, their contact with these, the resultant pleasures and pains — these are all of a fleeting nature, all part of *bhāvas.* Pleasure-seekers are always on the lookout for enjoyment from fleeting objects. When one object passes having given pleasure, another appears. This is followed by yet another and so on ceaselessly. Rarely is one aware of where this lust for enjoyment leads one's life. Like a boat drawn hither and thither by uncertain winds, one's life just follows the course of momentary temptations. Perhaps by the end of one's life's term one looks back to see what was gained. What seemed to have been gains may appear to be no gain at all. Then the feeling that time has run out will create a sense of frustration and futility. Disenchantment fills one's being. To avoid this disillusionment in life requires that one stay tuned to the ultimate goal all the time, transforming one's sense of experience into means, helpful to attaining this goal. The *sthita-prajña*'s life is marked by this peculiarity.

तस्माद्यस्य महाबाहो निगृहीतानि सर्वशः ।
इन्द्रियाणीन्द्रियार्थेभ्यस्तस्य प्रज्ञा प्रतिष्ठिता ॥६८ ॥

tasmād yasya mahābāho nigṛhītāni sarvaśaḥ ।
indriyāṇīndriyārthebhyas-tasya prajñā pratiṣṭhitā ॥68 ॥

Therefore, O Mighty Armed, he whose senses are fully held back from their objects that surround him — his knowledge is well-founded.

Arjuna, one of the distinguishing features of a *sthita-prajña* is that the senses are not let loose to follow their objects. Instead they are held back under control (*nigṛhīta*) and his interest is always in the one Reality. Even one with highly developed sharp mind that can delve deep into basic principles, need not be a *sthita-prajña.* One who is endowed with the discrimination to use such capabilities to attain the final goal, and with a mind firm enough to keep the senses and mind in control — such a one is a *sthita-prajña.* Thus a *muni,* who is a *sthita-prajña,* is easily distinguishable:

या निशा सर्वभूतानां तस्यां जागर्ति संयमी ।
यस्यां जाग्रति भूतानि सा निशा पश्यतो मुनेः ॥६९ ॥

yā niśā sarva-bhūtānāṁ tasyāṁ jāgarti saṁyamī ।
yasyāṁ jāgrati bhūtāni sā niśā paśyato muneḥ ॥69 ॥

What is night for all beings, therein the self-controlled is awake; wherein all beings are awake, that is night for the silent recluse (*muni*).

Arjuna, here I do not mean that the self-controlled remain awake at night and sleep during the day. All beings live dictated by animal instincts; among humans, only those with discriminative powers and capable of self-control can live otherwise. There is that world in which others concentrate their interests with a wakeful mind — the world of pleasures. There, the mind of self-controlled persons will not be awake, but they remain in this world as though asleep. There is another world of which others are oblivious — the world of

Supreme Self-contentment. It is in this world that the *yogī* remains always awake.

आपूर्यमाणमचलप्रतिष्ठंसमुद्रमापः प्रविशन्ति यद्वत्।
तद्वत्कामा यं प्रविशन्ति सर्वे स शान्तिमाप्नोति न कामकामी ॥७०॥

āpūryamāṇam acala-pratiṣṭhaṁ samudram āpaḥ praviśanti yadvat ।
tadvat kāmā yaṁ praviśanti sarve sa śāntim āpnoti na kāma-kāmī ॥70॥

All waters enter the ever-full, unmoving, well-founded ocean; likewise, he in whom all desirables enter, attains peace; not he who relishes desirables.

Arjuna, look at the ocean; it is always full, its fullness neither increases nor decreases. All rivers flow into it and yet its fullness remains unaffected. Likewise is a *sthita-prajña* remaining in a state of perfect peace, fully content with a satisfaction that does not depend on anything. Nevertheless, he too has needs for survival, like food, clothing, shelter and so on. Being a *yogī* living one with the whole, his needs are also met as part of the functional system of that whole, not as the fulfilment of his desires. It happens because it cannot be otherwise. Whether such needs are met or not, his peacefulness remains unaffected. Look now at how such a peaceful man moves in this world.

विहाय कामान्यः सर्वान्पुमांश्चरति निःस्पृहः।
निर्ममो निरहङ्कारः स शान्तिमधिगच्छति ॥७१॥

vihāya kāmān yaḥ sarvān pumāṁś carati nispṛhaḥ ।
nirmamo nirahaṁkāraḥ sa śāntim adhigacchati ॥71॥

The man who leaves behind all desires, and moves about desireless, free from the sense of "I" and "mine" — he attains to Peace.

Arjuna, the most outstanding outer sign of a *sthita-prajña* is the state of Peace that he is in at all times. No misfortune can move him out of that state, just as no joy can.

As the life of all individual entities is nothing more than manifestations of the one *sat*, the *sthita-prajña* sees himself only as one such manifestation. When this transparency of awareness has been attained, it results in the cessation of "I" as a reality existing on its own. One's sense of being "I" is called *ahaṁkāra* or *ahaṁta*. Along with this "I"-sense comes the mine-sense called *mama-kāra* or *mamata*. As long as one thinks of oneself as existing distinct from others, the feeling that one's life depends on such "others" will also arise. This sense of dependence leads to the urge to possess or hold on to "others" that one likes, and to hate the "others" that one dislikes. That is how desire (*kāma*) buds within us. *Ahaṁkāra* lacking, *mamakāra* would not sprout up. Devoid of both, one attains to real Peace, thus becoming a *sthita-prajña.*

The all-abiding Reality is known in Vedānta as *Brahman. Sthita-prajña* thus is one who finds himself in *Brahman,* which state could be called *brāhmī-sthiti.* What kind of state it is, I shall tell you:

एषा ब्राह्मी स्थितिः पार्थ नैनां प्राप्य विमुह्यति ।
स्थित्वा स्यामन्तकाले ऽपि ब्रह्मनिर्वाणमृच्छति ॥७२ ॥

eṣā brāhmī sthitiḥ pārtha naināṁ prāpya vimuhyati ।
sthitvā syām antakāle 'pi brahma-nirvāṇam ṛcchati ॥72 ॥

This is the state of being in *Brahman* (*brāhmī-sthiti*), O Pārtha; it attained, one no more suffers delusion. Having become well-founded in It, be at the last moments of life, one attains final absorption in *Brahman* (*Brahma-nirvāṇa*).

Arjuna, the beingness (*sthiti*) of *Brahman* is *brāhmī-sthiti.* One who feels oneness with *Brahman* has already attained that state of beingness. Once this transparency of vision is attained, no more will one be deluded as to what is real and what is not.

The attaining of this vision of certitude may come as a sudden all-engulfing effulgent experience at any moment in the life of a mature seeker. This moment is when, he begins to see himself in *Brahman,* as *Brahman.* An experience in which "I" the individual burns in the great bon-fire of *Brahman,* it could also be called *brahma-nirvāṇa, nirvāṇa* meaning "to become extinguished."

Though what I teach here in the *Bhagavad-Gītā* is *brahma-vidyā,* the word *Brahman* is used in the text for the first time here. The word, derived from the verb root *bṛh,* meaning "to grow," literally means "that which is in a constant process of growth." It signifies the one Substance that underlies all appearances in all the worlds, whose extensiveness is beyond all notions of extensiveness. The words *dehin* and *śarīrin* used at the beginning of this chapter connotes the same. Finding one's beingness in *Brahman,* as *Brahman,* is what is signified by *brāhmī-sthiti.*

To recapitulate what we now discussed in this chapter:

One *sat* alone exists. It is birthless and deathless. It cannot exist as pure *sat* without manifesting as the world and its beings. All such manifest forms incessantly appear and disappear in this one Substance. As the Substance that underlies whatever grows, it is called *dehin;* as the Substance that underlies all apparent and decaying forms, it is called *śarīrin;* as the all-inclusive, ever-growing Reality, it is *Brahman;* as the Substance that makes one's own being, it is *ātman.* The appearance of new forms assumed by It is called "birth" and the disappearance of old forms is "death." You, I and all those who are gathered here are all such apparent forms. The Substance in us is not destroyed by the destruction of its present form, the body. No one is thus really killed; no one kills either. This is the essence of what we understand of our life according to *sāṁkhya-buddhi.*

We have seen from the viewpoint of *sāṁkhya-buddhi* that our existence as living entities is one with *Brahman;* and living as one with *Brahman* is the *yoga-buddhi.* One alone, and not the many, is perceived as Real. Reality is living and active, and as part of It, we too are alive and active. When that activeness finds expression, it is called *karma.* Whosoever perceives the *karmas* taking place in himself as not different from *Brahman,* is to be called a *yogī*. When *karmas* are done with this awareness of Reality, one is not bound to those *karmas*. What binds one to *karmas* is not the actual doing, but considering oneself as the doer.

The knower of Reality, even when engaged in *karmas,* remains free. It is thus knowledge or lack of it, not the doing or not doing of *karmas,* that makes one free or bound. One who knows Reality, lives as one with *Brahman,* with no "I"-sense or "my"-sense, while being alive and active.

All the basic truths to be understood concerning life, have in a sense, been laid out in this second chapter, though many details yet remain to be discussed. The chapter ends with marking out the characteristic signs of a *sthita-prajña,* whose state was also named *brāhmī-sthiti.* Knowing such signs for the sake of understanding them, is not of any value in life. One has to become a *sthita-prajña* oneself, and this requires ascension of many more steps. Transmuting the basic principles understood into actual living experience requires purification of our being. This ascent towards purification is discussed next.

Thus ends Chapter Two entitled Sāṁkhya-Yoga of the Bhagavad-Gītā, the essense of the Upaniṣads, that embodies the yoga-śāstra of brahma-vidyā in the form of a dialogue between Śrī Kṛṣṇa and Arjuna.

III

Karma-Yoga
— The Yoga of Action —

अर्जुन उवाच —

ज्यायसी चेत्कर्मणस्ते मता बुद्धिर्जनार्दन ।
तत्किं कर्मणि घोरे मां नियोजयसि केशव ॥1॥
व्यामिश्रेणैव वाक्येन बुद्धिं मोहयसीव मे ।
तदेकं वद निश्चित्य येन श्रेयो ऽहमाप्नुयाम् ॥2॥

arjuna uvāca —

jyāyasī cet karmaṇas te matā buddhir janārdana ।
tat kiṁ karmaṇi ghore māṁ niyojayasi keśava ॥1॥

vyāmiśreṇaiva vākyena buddhiṁ mohayasīva me ।
tad ekaṁ vada niścitya yena śreyo 'ham āpnuyām ॥2॥

Arjuna said —

If knowing, in your opinion, O Janārdana, is superior to performing deeds, then why do you, O Keśava, direct me to this terrible action?

With apparently mixed-up words, it seems, you are confounding my ability to comprehend. So, decisively tell me that one by which I can attain the best.

Kṛṣṇa, I was attentively listening to you, and it seems the picture is becoming clear to me now. I understand that doing actions is unavoidable, but what counts is not whether one does something or not, but how one thinks of such actions. What makes life satisfying, in other words, is one's understanding rather than what one actually does. At the same time, you are directing me to engage in this fighting, while being fully united to *yoga*, with a sense of full detachment. I do not know how to fight with detachment. Bringing the two together seems to be out of my grasp, perhaps because of my immature understanding of life. I find these words of yours confounding. What I need at this moment is not an open-ended direction, but rather a decisive teaching that can ensure my attaining the best in life.

श्रीभगवानुवाच —

लोके ऽस्मिन्द्विविधा निष्ठा पुरा प्रोक्ता मयानघ ।
ज्ञानयोगेन साङ्ख्यानां कर्मयोगेन योगिनाम् ॥3 ॥

śrī bhagavān uvāca —

loke 'smin dvividhā niṣṭhā purā proktā mayānagha ।
jñāna-yogena sāṁkhyānāṁ karma-yogena yogināṁ ॥3 ॥

Śrī Kṛṣṇa said —

Two paths are there in this world, O sinless one, as set forth by Me of old: The *yoga* of wisdom (*jñāna-yoga*) for men of knowledge and the *yoga* of action (*karma-yoga*) for men of action.

Arjuna, I see nothing wrong in your finding my words confounding. The ideas of the last chapter, especially those concerning desireless action (*niṣkāma-karma*), were so compressed. To make it easier, let us begin from the basics, particularly regarding *karma* (actions).

The paths that enable man to attain the best in life are two. My words "as set forth by Me," here as well as everywhere else in this discourse, only mean, "as is natural with the spontaneous unfoldment of life." It in no way means that it is so as decided by Śrī Kṛṣṇa the individual. I represent the Absolute, *Brahman*, the indestructible Reality that unfolds as everything. These two paths are known as *jñāna-yoga* and *karma-yoga*. There are those who give much importance in life to knowledge; the natural way for them to attain the best in life is through *jñāna-yoga*. Others find themselves happy in being active and so the best way for them is through *karma-yoga*.

The best of life (*śreyas*) that you seek is to be attained on freeing yourself of all the fetters that bind you. The obverse side of this freedom is nothing other than the experience of unconditioned happiness (*paramānanda*), the state of supreme self-contentment, farthest from the pleasures one gains from worldly objects. Such worldly pleasures and fulfilment of needs are known as *preyas,* as against *śreyas.*

What I am teaching you is the science of *yoga* (*yoga-śāstra*). As to the number of kinds of *yogas*, there are various opinions. Some think *karma-yoga, jñāna-yoga, bhakti-yoga* and *rāja-yoga* are the four *yogas* I teach in this *Gītā. Mantra-yoga* (the *yoga* of sacred formulas), *laya-yoga* (the *yoga* of merger), *kriyā-yoga* (the *yoga* of active devotion), *haṭha-yoga* (the *yoga* of forced physical postures), *kuṇḍalilnī-yoga* (the *yoga* of arousing the *kuṇḍalinī* snake) are some of the other *yogas* propagated by the concerned cults. The original source book of *yoga* is Patañjali's *Yoga-Sūtras,* which makes no mention of any such divisions. So far as the re-presentation of *brahma-vidyā* as a *yoga-śāstra* is concerned, only two types of *yoga* are relevant: *karma-yoga* and *jñāna-yoga.* How this is so will become clear as we proceed. The present chapter deals with *karma-yoga* and the next one with *jñāna-yoga* and the fifth chapter will clarify how the two are not different in essence.

न कर्मणामनारम्भान्नैष्कर्म्यं पुरुषो ऽश्नुते ।
न च सन्न्यसनादेव सिद्धिं समधिगच्छति ॥4 ॥

na karmaṇām anārambhān naiṣkarmyaṁ puruṣo 'śnute ।
na ca sannyasanād eva siddhiṁ sam adhigacchati ॥4 ॥

Not by abstaining from initiating activities does man enjoy the attainment of freedom from actions; nor by mere renouncing actions does one achieve final attainment.

Arjuna, as we saw at the end of the last chapter, the state of being in *Brahman* (*brāhmī-sthiti*) is the ultimate goal one can reach in life, and the means of attaining that state is by acquiring wisdom. What kind of wisdom this is, we will see in the next chapter. One in that state feels no obligation to initiate any action. This state in which one is free from obligations to initiate action is known as the *siddhi* (attainment) of *naiṣkarmya* (having transcended actions). However, if one with this attainment in mind deliberately abstains from all actions, such self-enforced inactivity will not result in *naiṣkarmya siddhi*.

Renouncing everything, on the other hand, becomes natural to those who follow the path of wisdom. In short, whether the path one choses is *karma-yoga* or *jñāna-yoga,* its practice should not be mechanistic. What this practice is to be, will become clear as we proceed.

We have to be mindful of an important aspect that differentiates the *karma* understood here from the *karma* of the Vedic context. Two spiritual paths, of *karma* and *jñāna*, both of Vedic background, have become well rooted in Indian culture. The former enjoins performing rituals, called *karmas,* with the first *Saṁhitā* part of the Vedas as its basis, while the latter teaches how to make life meaningful and free of fetters by realizing what is Real in us, with the Upaniṣads for basis. But the *karma* of the *Gītā* is any action that man or any being happens to do as part of the eternal flux of nature. Nature in itself is understood as an eternal stream of *karmas*. To realize how such *karmas* work in us as part of the whole, is the *karma-yoga* as a spiritual practice recommended in this chapter, as a result of which we find ourselves existing in *Brahman* as one with It. Now let us see how crucial is the role of such *karmas*:

न हि कश्चित्क्षणमपि जातु तिष्ठत्यकर्मकृत् ।
कार्यते ह्यवशः कर्म सर्वः प्रकृतिजैर्गुणैः ॥5 ॥

na hi kaścit kṣaṇam api jātu tiṣṭhaty akarma-kṛt ।
kāryate hy avaśaḥ karma sarvaḥ prakṛtijair guṇaiḥ ॥5 ॥

> No one indeed remains actionless even for an instant; for helplessly is everyone driven to activities by the *guṇa*s born of nature.

Arjuna, you complain that I am directing you into performing ghastly actions such as that of conducting this battle. The actions that one may happen to engage in may be frightful or otherwise; yet it is impossible to remain inactive, not only for humans but for all beings. The truth may be that the *karma* which happens, for the time being, as part of nature, may seem ghoulish to you.

All of us are born, live and die as part of the eternal *karma*-stream of nature of which we are all a part. The Sanskrit word for nature, *prakṛti,* has within it the word *kṛti; prakṛti* cannot be *prakṛti* without *kṛti. Prakṛti,* being constantly creative, brings forth from itself its own *guṇa*s (modalities) — *sattva, rajas* and *tamas*. If at all *prakṛti* can be defined, it would be somewhat like this:

> It is well known as *prakṛti* in that it is spontaneously active, marvellously bringing about distinct *guṇa*s from itself.
>
> — Narayana Guru, *Darśanamālā,* IV.10

As a part of this *prakṛti,* humans are also active and are engaged in *karmas.* In this aspect, we are rather helpless and it is for this reason that it was stated in the previous verse that neither abstaining from initiating activities nor giving up actions altogether would enable you to attain the final goal. However, since *karma* is an integral part of *prakṛti,* it cannot be so easily renounced and the predicament of those who headstrong give up all activities is this:

कर्मेन्द्रियाणि संयम्य य आस्ते मनसा स्मरन्।
इन्द्रियार्थान्विमूढात्मा मिथ्याचारः स उच्यते ॥6॥

karmendriyāṇi saṁyamya ya āste manasā smaran ।
indriyārthān vimūḍhātmā mithyācāraḥ sa ucyate ॥6॥

> He who physically restrains his organs of action, while mentally dwelling on sense objects, self-deluded — he is to be called a hypocrite.

Arjuna, as we know, the organs of action are five: speech, hands, feet, excretory organ and genitals. A person might possibly force oneself to restrain the activities of any of these organs, but still relish mentally the fruits of activities, mostly sense pleasure. Such, though apparently actionless and passionless, are attached to pleasures and are to be considered hypocrites, all this being the ill-results of forcibly restraining natural activities, brought about by a wrong notion of self-restraint.

I shall tell you how it is possible to avoid this plight, how to keep yourself free, while being in the world of action.

यस्त्विन्द्रियाणि मनसा नियम्यारभते ऽर्जुन ।
कर्मेन्द्रियैः कर्मयोगमसक्तः स विशिष्यते ॥7 ॥

yas tv indriyāṇi manasā niyamyārabhate 'rjuna ।
karmendriyaiḥ karma-yogam asaktaḥ sa viśiṣyate ॥7 ॥

But, he who, controlling senses by the mind, commences *karma-yoga* engaging organs of action with no attachment — he excels, O Arjuna.

Arjuna, it is natural for fire to flame upwards while water naturally flows downwards and winds blow at will in any direction. Similar is the capability of our ear to hear, eyes to see, feet to walk, hands to grasp and work. All activities are part of nature, it is when the mind becomes obsessed with the results of these activities as giving pleasures that one becomes attached to activities. Then one begins to think, "This *karma* is mine, its fruits also are mine." It is this mind that has to be brought under contol, rather than allow ourselves to be controlled by the temptations of the mind. Such a person of restraint will remain a neutral witness to the natural activities taking place within, viewing these activities as part of nature's incessant flow. In this state, engaging in *karma*s is felt to be an occasion to feel your oneness with the whole. It is thus that *karma* is transformed into *karma-yoga, yoga* being that state where the individual feels identified with the whole.

The *karma-yogin* does not feel himself to be the doer of actions; instead of abstaining from actions the *karma-yogin* undertakes natural activities without a sense of agency, rather with a sense of detachment. In your case, Arjuna, the present one is a situation where you cannot avoid performing those actions which are natural to you. The natural course of events brought you to this, though the actions you are required to perform, might well seem horrific. What I say is that you must proceed in the manner of a *karma-yogin*, with no concern or attachment to the possible outcome.

I shall now tell you what should be our general attitude towards the activities natural to each of us:

नियतं कुरु कर्म त्वं कर्म ज्यायो ह्यकर्मणः ।
शरीरयात्रापि च ते न प्रसिद्ध्येदकर्मणः ॥8 ॥

niyataṁ kuru karma tvaṁ karma jyāyo hy akarmaṇaḥ ।
śarīra-yātrāpi ca te na prasiddhyed akarmaṇaḥ ॥8 ॥

Do the *karma*s that are inevitable, for doing *karma*s is much better than remaining inactive. Even bodily existence would be rendered impossible by your remaining actionless.

Arjuna, as we proceed, we will see how complex is the nature of *karma.* Presently what we are concerned with is how one can free oneself from the bondage of natural *karma*s, by tranforming them into *karma-yoga*.

Kṛti being part of *prakṛti*, it is but natural that we continuously and in a rather helpless manner, are engaged in *karma*s. The most viable way to free ourselves of the bondage of *karma*, cannot therefore be to abstain from *karma*s. To engage in doing natural *karma*s with a sense of detachment as far as their fruits are concerned, is the more appropriate way of *karma-yoga*. In the incarnate world, existence is not possible without *karma*s.

How is one who desires to become a *karma-yogī* to view the *karma*s he undertakes?

यज्ञार्थात्कर्मणो ऽन्यत्र लोको ऽयं कर्मबन्धनः ।
तदर्थं कर्म कौन्तेय मुक्तसङ्गः समाचर ॥९॥

yajñārthāt karmaṇo 'nyatra loko 'yaṁ karma-bandhanaḥ ।
tad arthaṁ karma kaunteya mukta-saṅgaḥ samācara ॥9॥

People become bound by actions, unless they are performed as *yajña*. Therefore, O Arjuna do actions free from attachments, in the sense of *yajñas*.

Arjuna, a *karma-yogin* treats as *yajña* all actions undertaken by him, he treats all actions as part of nature's unfoldment. The real significance of *yajña* will become clear in the verses to follow. How attaining wisdom could be treated as a sort of *yajña* will be made explicit in the next chapter. *Yajña*, thus, is a subtle element implicit in *yoga*, whether of *karma* or *jñāna*.

As we know, all actions emerge in *prakṛti* because of its three *guṇas*, and human emergence and actions are part of this. Every action we eagage in is part of *prakṛti*'s *kṛti* or action. Unaware of this fact, we often foolishly think, "This is my *karma*, its fruits are mine." When one becomes aware of the truth that it is all part of *pṛakrti*, one feels like offering back to *prakṛti* what one considered as one's own. Once that happens, every moment of one's life and all one's *karma* are experienced as a sort of oblation at the sacrificial fire of *prakṛti*. Such is the symbolic significance of the *yajña* under reference here.

To treat one's *karmas* as forming a *yajña*, requires a clear understanding of all that we have discussed so far. Those who have not acquired such an awareness, will remain ignorant. Their actions continuously create bondage, for to each action they attach a sense of ownership, thinking "This is my *karma*" and have expectations from the fruits of these actions.

Now, you must understand that *yajña* is not just a principle that is related to Vedic *karmas* and their results, rather it is the principle underlying all of life.

सहयज्ञाः प्रजाः सृष्ट्वा पुरोवाच प्रजापतिः।
अनेन प्रसविष्यध्वमेष वो ऽस्त्विष्टकामधुक् ॥10॥

saha-yajñāḥ prajāḥ sṛṣṭvā purovāca prajāpatiḥ ।
anena prasaviṣyadhvam eṣa vo 'stv iṣṭa-kāmadhuk ॥10॥

Having created mankind along with *yajña* in ancient times, the Lord of Creations told mankind: by this *yajña* shall you prosper; this shall be your milch cow of all desires.

Arjuna, I desire you to understand that whenever I say "Prajāpati did this or that" or "I ordained such and such a thing," it means that whatever is said to be done is part of the overall scheme of nature. Here I say, Prajāpati emanated beings along with *yajña*. *Prajā*, meaning "that which is born," could be any being born anywhere in all the worlds. *Yajña* is that principle which enables one to see oneself as a part of the entirety of life. How this scheme of life works, I shall describe to you soon. It is possible to experience life as prosperous only when *yajña* is its guiding principle. From a worldly point of consideration, what assures happiness in life is the availability of enjoyable objects. Put in worldy terms, Vedic *yajña* is the cow that yields the milk of fulfilment of all desires. Indian mythology calls this cow *Kāmadhenu* or *Kāmadhuk* (the milch cow of all desires).

Who are thus linked together by Prajāpati using the principle of *yajña*, and in what manner, I shall now tell you:

देवान्भावयतानेन ते देवा भावयन्तु वः।
परस्परं भावयन्तः श्रेयः परमवाप्स्यथ ॥11॥

devān bhāvayatānena te devā bhāvayantu vaḥ ।
parasparaṁ bhāvayantaḥ śreyaḥ param avāpsyatha ॥11॥

By making use of this (*yajña*) you shall satisfy gods; they will in return satisfy you. Satisfying one another, you shall attain the supreme good.

Each being that is born is a *prajā*, but of all *prajā*s humans are the only ones who are aware of being so, who are in search of the meaning of birth and death. Through experience humans learn that it is impossible to live life as one wills, and it is then that they begin to premise the existence of a controlling Reality, Power or Principle to life. Though the nature of that Reality remains unknown, humans imagine it to be conscious, or even consciousness in essence, because of the fact that life is a well regulated functional system. Since consciousness is an experience of brightness, rather than of darkness, humans invented the word *deva* meaning "the shining one," to signify such a controlling or directing power.

Like humans, the gods (*deva*s) are also the creation of Prajāpati. Creations, in our view, are thus spread over two different worlds — the known human world and the unknown world of the *deva*s, both together forming one life system. The existence and happiness of each entity ensures the existence and happiness of all others. This web of mutually affirming coexistence is what scientists of a future, with emphasis on the external world, may declare as "deep eco-system." Symbolically this is all that is suggested by the notion that human beings satisfy the gods and vice versa. Such instances of mutual satisfaction are found everywhere. When mango trees bloom as spring arrives, along with it come thousands of bees to enjoy the nectar of mango blossom. The pollination that takes place with the help of the bees, ensures the happiness of the tree. This kind of interdependent actualization of the happiness of trees, animals and humans is provided for by the elements earth, water, air, heat and the like natural phenomena. Should these be conscious (modern science asserts that there is nothing in nature that is not conscious) they too must feel a gratitude in ensuring the happiness of all that depend on them, thus making their own existence meaningful. Everything in the world is connected with happiness (*ānanda*). In other words, the existence and life of every individual transient entity, is an oblation offered into the sacrificial fire, the effort for actualizing *ānanda.* Having become part of this *yajña*, the individual realizes the meaningfulness of being born. The satisfaction that one feels as a part of the *yajña* is said to be the eating of the *yajña-śiṣṭa* or *yajña*'s remainder.

Portraying this process in ritualistic terminology is to say that humans, by performing *yajñas*, please the gods and make them benevolent. The gods, in turn through the *yajña* of becoming benevolent, make humans pleased.

Life, lived with this awareness, takes on a new character, a new dimension derived from having attained the best. The life that lacks this understanding, on the contrary, not only deters this attainment but also binds one to one's actions. Thus it was earlier stated, "People become bound by actions unless they are performed as *yajña*."

Knowing this *yajña*-principle and treating one's own life and its natural activities as an offering or oblation, requires a discerning mind, which many lack. They think, "I do this *karma* because I am capable of it. I am its doer; no one else can claim its benefits." How such people should be treated, I shall tell you:

इष्टान्भोगान्हि वो देवा दास्यन्ते यज्ञभाविताः।
तैर्दत्तानप्रदायैभ्यो यो भुङ्क्ते स्तेन एव सः ॥१२॥

iṣṭān bhogān hi vo devā dāsyante yajña-bhāvitāḥ ।
tair dattān apradāyaibhyo yo bhuṅkte stena eva saḥ ॥12॥

Satisfied by the *yajña*, gods certainly bestow the enjoyments you desire. But he who enjoys what they give, with nothing offered in return, is merely a thief.

The gods, as conceived by the Vedas, on being satisfied with the *yajñas* offered to them by men, fulfil all their wishes, and the men in turn become satisfied, offer more oblations. This Vedic concept, understood in the context of *karmas*, undergoes a transformation here. Each individual performs activities natural to him/her as part of the overall scheme of life, and it is a sort of *yajña*. As part of the same scheme of life, each gets what is needed for sustenance and satisfaction, as if with an unseen helping hand. Whether or not one actually treats one's activities as *yajñas* and the enjoyment of favours as *yajña-śiṣṭa*, it makes no difference in the overall state of existence. When an individual thinks that the favours he enjoys are the result of his own actions, and that he is not bound to share it, such a man is to be treated as a thief. A thief takes by force that which is not really his. The present one takes to be his that which is really owned by *prakṛti* and is, further, even unwilling to share it with anyone else. This difference between those who treat life as a *yajña*, and those who do not, is reflected in their gains in life.

> यज्ञशिष्टाशिनः सन्तो मुच्यन्ते सर्वकिल्बिषैः ।
> भुञ्जते ते त्वघं पापा ये पचन्त्यात्मकारणात् ॥१३॥
>
> *yajña-śiṣṭāśinaḥ santo mucyante sarva-kilbiṣaiḥ* ।
> *bhuñjate te tv aghaṁ pāpā ye pacanty ātma-kāraṇāt* ॥13॥
>
> The virtuous, who eat the remains of *yajña*, are absolved of all blemishes; but those who prepare food for themselves alone, truly are devouring sin.

Arjuna, the significance of *yajña* has already been seen. Those who treat their life and its activities as an offering at the altar of the ever active *prakṛti*, and treat both the pleasures and pains of life as the eating of the remains of that sacrifice, are to be considered the virtuous (*santaḥ*). Activities performed with the awareness that no action is of one's own and that all actions are nature's activities, are neither righteous nor unrighteous. One feels guilty on committing a sin only where the distinction between right and wrong is relevant. The actions of *prakṛti* is neither righteous nor unrighteous. Treating all life experiences as the partaking of the remains of the said *yajña*, thus makes one free from this sense of sin. The case of others is far different from this. They think of every action as their own, and worry that their actions may be unrighteous. Even enjoyment may be marked by the worry, "Am I not enjoying the fruit of my sinful act?" In short, every experience is tainted with a sense of sin; in effect, what is eaten is thus sin alone.

We have just seen how individual life is experienced when the *yajña* principle does or does not guide it. The picture will not be complete unless its cosmic counterpart is also seen alongside it. Whether conceived as related to individual or cosmos, life in itself is neither individual nor cosmic, but rather neutral and non-dual, to be perceived with an intuitive yogic eye. These two opposing facets are pointed out simply to enable the seeker to use his yogic insight with these two facets as an aid, in the manner in which a magnet is discerned perceiving its two opposite poles. Now let us examine the cosmic aspect of the *yajña*-principle:

अन्नाद्भवन्ति भूतानि पर्जन्यादन्नसम्भवः ।
यज्ञाद्भवति पर्जन्यो यज्ञः कर्मसमुद्भवः ॥१४॥
कर्म ब्रह्मोद्भवं विद्धि ब्रह्माक्षरसमुद्भवम् ।
तस्मात्सर्वगतं ब्रह्म नित्यं यज्ञे प्रतिष्ठितम् ॥१५॥

annād bhavanti bhūtāni parjanyād anna-sambhavaḥ ।
yajñād bhavati parjanyo yajñaḥ karma-samudbhavaḥ ॥14॥

karma brahmodbhavaṁ viddhi brahmā 'kṣara-samudbhavam ।
tasmāt sarvagataṁ brahma nityaṁ yajñe pratiṣṭhitam ॥15॥

From food beings come into being; from rain is food produced; from *yajña* comes forth rain; and *yajña* has its origin in *karma*.

Know that *karma* is born of Brahmā (the Creator); and Brahmā did originate from the Imperishable. The all-pervading *Brahman* is, therefore, ever founded on *yajña*.

This is a portrayal of how life in all the worlds is strung together with the *yajña* principle. That all living beings emerge because of food and are basically sustained by food which requires no explanation. But saying that rain comes forth from *yajña* is a bit of a riddle. That *yajña* emerges from *karma, karma* from Brahmā the Creator, and the Creator from the Imperishable Reality, are all statements concerned with the unknowable realms of life. Beings, food, rain, *yajña, karma,* Brahmā the Creator, and the Imperishable are sequentially linked here as each factor being caused by the next. The first three are known to us, while the last three are unknown and unknowable. *Yajña* comes between these, connecting the known and unknown factors controlling life. This is a revised version of the concept of *yajña* that links together the life of humans and that of the gods.

Life is the stage upon which is enacted this intermingling of knowable and unknowable aspects of existence; within this enactment *yajña* may be looked upon as the catalyst. This explains why I say, "The all-pervading *Brahman* is ever founded on *yajña*." The usage "the all-pervading *Brahman*" (*sarvagataṁ brahma*) is to be understood in its strict literal sense. *Brahman* means that which is far-extended in dimension (*bṛhat*). What we call the totality of all the worlds is nothing other than the one Reality, become manifest and far-extended. To directly perceive what that expansiveness is, you have to wait till we reach Chapter XI. For the time being, the one Reality becomes manifest as all the worlds may be taken as connoted by the phrase "the all-pervading *Brahman*" (*sarvagataṁ brahma*).

Rain coming forth from *yajña* can then be understood to mean that no life is possible without water; rain therefore symbolizes everything that sustains life, and it comes forth in turn as part of the overall scheme of life in which are interlinked, all the above said factors.

Ritualistically, *karma* is not the source of *yajña;* on the other hand, *yajña* itself is *karma*. What the *Gītā* understands by *karma* we have already seen. Every activity, every pulsation, that takes place in nature, is a *karma*. It will later (VIII.3) be defined thus:

> The creative urge, that causes the coming forth of that which has come into being, is to be termed as *karma*.

And the Imperishable, it will be stated there, is wherein this creative urge is inherent. The same Imperishable is being referred to here. Brahmā, the mythological Creator, is none other than this creative urge, activated. Therefore, it is said, all *karma*s have their origin in Brahmā. It is through *karma*s that all the knowable and unknowable aspects of existence are interlinked in life, the connecting factor being *yajña*. If no *karma* existed, no *yajña* would be necessary and so it can be said, "*yajña* has its origin in *karma*." Rain is a part of the life system where all factors are in unison, and thus its emergence is from *yajña*.

Arjuna, the sequence from the Imperishable to rain, seemingly causally related, need not be taken to be literal. It suggests only that life is an endless wheel that rolls on with *yajña* for its hub. Let us see the place of individuals in the wheel of life:

एवं प्रवर्तितं चक्रं नानुवर्तयतीह यः ।
अघायुरिन्द्रियारामो मोघं पार्थ स जीवति ॥१६ ॥

evaṁ pravartitaṁ cakraṁ nānuvartayatīha yaḥ ।
aghāyur indriyārāmo moghaṁ pārtha sa jīvati ॥16 ॥

Arjuna, he who lives not complying with that revolving wheel, is sinful in life; rejoicing in senses, he lives in vain.

Arjuna, the line of phenomena, beginning from the Imperishable and ending with living beings, may seem to be a linear process, but it is not really so. The Imperishable, urged on by the *karma* principle inherent in itself, appears as all beings, and this happens in a cyclic process, where it is difficult to pinpoint how and where the knowable and unknowable factors are linked. The wheel of life rolls on without either a beginning or an end. No being exists in any of the worlds, whether of the gods, humans, demons or other beings, that does not form a part of this wheel. What man can do is simply to live as part of it, it is not possible to stand apart and be an onlooker; even the seeming observations we make of the wheel are part of the movement of the very same wheel. It is possible to find peace and contentment in life only when we experience ourselves as part of that wheel. Such a life requires the capability to perceive the nature of this wheel. Those lacking this perception will only see their activities as their own *karma*s. Expecting personal gains from *karma*s is instigated by the longing for sense pleasures. Without a proper understanding of the life-wheel, man is destined to live life in vain.

How one, who sees himself and lives as part of that wheel, feels, I shall now tell you:

यस्त्वात्मरतिरेव स्यादात्मतृप्तश्च मानवः ।
आत्मन्येव च सन्तुष्टस्तस्य कार्यं न विद्यते ॥१७॥

yas tvātma-ratir eva syād ātma-tṛptaś ca mānavaḥ ।
ātmany eva ca saṁtuṣṭas tasya kāryaṁ na vidyate ॥17॥

But the man who delights in himself, who is content in himself, who rejoices only in the Self — for him there is no action that he is obliged to do.

Arjuna, we have just seen that wheel, the rolling of which is what we call life. This wheel is Reality. He who lives knowing himself to be part of this wheel will see what is real in him and all the worlds as nothing but that which is Real in the wheel. What role does *rati,* which means "pleasure," have here? He who is aware of the wheel of life knows that objects of pleasure also are part of this same wheel. Therefore, he knows what he enjoys is not the pleasure derived form objects, but the pleasure of rejoicing in himself. Whosoever constantly experiences the feeling of rejoicing in himself is called *ātmārāma.*

Such a man sees all that is good or desirable as a part of nature's wheel, and thus as part of himself. He thus feels the satisfaction of having gained all that can be gained, and he is constantly in the state of having satisfied all desires. The *tṛpti* of a *karma-yogī* is *ātma-tṛpti,* the satisfaction of being satisfied in oneself.

As nothing worries him, he is always pleasant (*prasanna*). Knowing his activities to be a part of nature's wheel, he does not feel bound to or refrain from doing particular things. He simply does what occurs moment after moment as part of nature's flow. He remains always active, but without the obligation of having to do anything. Why is he not obliged to do any *karma*? I shall tell you:

नैव तस्य कृतेनार्थो नाकृतेनेह कश्चन ।
न चास्य सर्वभूतेषु कश्चिदर्थव्यपाश्रयः ॥१८॥

naiva tasya kṛtenārtho nākṛteneha kaścana ।
na cāsya sarva-bhūteṣu kaścid artha-vyapāśrayaḥ ॥18॥

He does not have anything to gain in this world from doing something; nor anything from not doing. Neither is there for him any gain by depending on any being whatsoever.

Arjuna, ignorant of the reality of nature (*prakṛti*), and about one's own life, one does actions motivated by the desire for particular benefits. A *karma-yogī*, on the other hand, engages in actions as his participation in the rolling on of the *prakṛti*-wheel. The results of these actions, whether favourable or unfavourable, are also seen as part of the *kṛti* (action) of *prakṛti*. For this reason, the *karma-yogī* does not expect a particular personal benefit. If at all such a person depends on anything, it is on *prakṛti* alone. Every entity is seen by the *yogī* as equal to himself, as having come into being like himself, depending like himself, on *prakṛti*.

Now I will point out to you, in the context of all that I have just said, what is befitting to your character, which is also the best for you:

तस्मादसक्तः सततं कार्यं कर्म समाचर।
असक्तो ह्याचरन्कर्म परमाप्नोति पूरुषः ॥१९॥

tasmād asaktaḥ satataṁ kāryaṁ karma samācara ।
asakto hyācaran karma param āpnoti pūruṣaḥ ॥19॥

Therefore, remaining unattached, always perform actions that are to be done by necessity. Engaged in actions unattached, one truly attains the Supreme.

Arjuna, my words *"param āpnoti"* (attains the Supreme), looked at from the overall theme of the *Gītā*, would mean attaining final Release (*mukti or mokṣa*) or merging in the Absolute. At the same time, in each chapter it is necessary to understand this in a more specific way that fits in with the nature of the particular chapter. In the present chapter, *Karma-Yoga*, for example, attaining to the Supreme signifies seeing one's own *kṛti*s (actions) and *prakṛti*'s *kṛti*s as one *kṛti*. In the next chapter it will mean seeing one's own existence and the total existence as one Existence. Though there is a change in the angle of significance in different chapters, the essential import is the same.

Actions performed without attachment enables one to see one's *krti* and the *kṛti* of *prakṛti* as a single *kṛti*. There are not many who perform such unattached actions. Of these few, King Janaka always stands out as an ideal *karma-yogī*.

कर्मणैव हि संसिद्धिमास्थिता जनकादयः ।
लोकसङ्ग्रहमेवापि सम्पश्यन्कर्तुमर्हसि ॥२० ॥

karmaṇaiva hi saṁsiddhim āsthitā janakādayaḥ ।
loka-saṁgraham evāpi saṁpaśyan kartum arhasi ॥20 ॥

Through action, indeed, Janaka and others accomplished final attainment. Concern for the integrity of the world also requires you to do actions.

Arjuna, many are there who were able to attain the Supreme goal of life while being engaged in normal activities. They did not give up those activities that were natural to their personal character. King Janaka was one such. While being an ideal ruler, his founding on wisdom was so firm that he could even put to public test the integrity of vision of seers like Yājñavalkya. He has always been treated as an ideal *karma-yogī*.

Concern for the integrity of the world order demands that you be active. All the worlds and all beings together constitutes an integral whole. Our coming into being and disappearing at death, are all part of nature's wheel rolling on. No man should go against it, and none should disregard it. Each has his role to play in the rolling of the wheel. Though it is not possible to know the nature of the entire wheel, it is desirable that man should try and find out what his role is. This individual role of each human being in nature, is known as his/her *svadharma*. Discovering it and living accordingly, makes one's life happy. The upkeep of the total system will be in danger unless each individual fulfils the function expected of him. Therefore, no one is free to be inactive, and you are no exception to this.

Another reason also is assignable for people like you not to be inactive:

यद्यदाचरति श्रेष्ठस्तत्तदेवेतरो जनः।
स यत्प्रमाणं कुरुते लोकस्तदनुवर्तते ॥२१॥

yad yad ācarati śreṣṭhas tat tad evetaro janaḥ ।
sa yat pramāṇaṁ kurute lokas tad anuvartate ॥

Whatsoever a great man does, the very same is done by others also. Whatever standard he sets, the people follow it.

Arjuna, one step down from being part of the wheel of nature, you can see yourself as part of society. Here too, you cannot back off from *karmas*. Whatever great people like you do, is considered an ideal by common people and they try to follow suit. Such is the nature of man's social mind. You remaining inactive and others following you will certainly jeopardize the social order and in turn the world order. You may consider me as an ideal in this matter:

न मे पार्थास्ति कर्तव्यं त्रिषु लोकेषु किञ्चन।
नानवाप्तमवाप्तव्यं वर्त एव च कर्मणि ॥२२॥

na me pārthāsti kartavyaṁ triṣu lokeṣu kiñcana ।
nānavāptam avāptavyaṁ varta eva ca karmaṇi ॥22॥

In the three worlds there is no action I ought to do, O Pārtha, nor is there anything for me worth attaining unattained. Still I am engaged in actions.

Arjuna, as an individual I am Śrī Kṛṣṇa, and symbolizing the Absolute, I am *Bhagavān*. I may thus be treated both as an individual and the Absolute Reality. As an individual I am a *Brahman*-knower, and all *Brahman*-knowers incessantly experience their being as one with *Brahman*. Such people do not feel anything to be lacking in life, nor that anything needs to be gained to make life happier. As

Bhagavān, I have control over everything. There is nothing for me to gain. For ordinary people, making efforts or doing actions is always prompted by the benefit motive. As one with nothing to gain, I am not bound to do anything either. Yet I don't remain idle; I am always active. My coming here as your charioteer is also part of such activities. Do you know what will happen to the world if people like you and me take to idleness? I shall tell you:

यदि ह्यहं न वर्तेयं जातु कर्मण्यतन्द्रितः ।
मम वर्त्मानुवर्तन्ते मनुष्याः पार्थ सर्वशः ॥२३ ॥

yadi hy ahaṁ na varteyaṁ jātu karmaṇy atandritaḥ ।
mama vartmānuvartante manuṣyāḥ pārtha sarvaśaḥ ॥23 ॥

If I remain inactive even for a moment, people in every walk of life, O Arjuna, will take to my way.

Arjuna, people look at me as a *jñanin*, even as *Bhagavān*, and thus I am an ideal. Seeing me inactive, they could take to idleness; seeing me active they too would become active. Whatever I do, good or bad, becomes a model for them. I therefore have the responsibility of being a role model though I myself have nothing to gain personally by doing any *karma*. Look at what will happen to the world as a whole if I remain idle:

उत्सीदेयुरिमे लोका न कुर्यां कर्म चेदहम् ।
सङ्करस्य च कर्ता स्यामुपहन्यामिमाः प्रजाः ॥२४ ॥

utsīdeyur ime lokā na kuryāṁ karma ced aham ।
saṅkarasya ca kartā syām upahanyām imāḥ prajāḥ ॥24 ॥

The life system would perish should I not be engaged in *karma*s, and thus I would become one who causes confusion, destroying in effect the systematic existence of living beings.

Arjuna, as you know, my own *prakṛti* rolls on as a wheel of *karmas*. The entire life system is ordered in such a way that each being has a place in this wheel, a role to play. The withdrawal of any one from this would, in effect, bring in chaos into the world order. In my role as the ideal human being, if I remain idle, others too would follow suit, thus disrupting the rolling on of this wheel. This would bring total confusion into the world order and of values (*saṁkara*) followed by the eventual wasting away of life system as a whole.

Arjuna, you fear the total destruction of all the men of your clan in this battle. You fear also the eventual inevitability of the women of your clan having to mix with men of other castes, resulting in the evil known as *varṇa-saṁkara*, and thus in the ruin of the prevailing caste system. But your withdrawal from this battle will bring about another sort of confused state (*saṁkara*), not of the blood of different castes, but of the entire life system itself. The confuion of castes is only of relative significance, for it is limited to a system in the social order, born of ignorance. The other confusion is of an absolutist dimension, its ill-effects are universal.

Like me, you too have to live as an ideal for people, with regard to *karmas*. However, though externally, your *karmas* and the *karmas* of the ignorant may seem similar, they are marked by a difference in the attitude with which the *karmas* are done. I shall make it clearer:

सक्ताः कर्मण्यविद्वांसो यथा कुर्वन्ति भारत।
कुर्याद्विद्वांस्तथासक्तश्चिकीर्षुर्लोकसङ्ग्रहम् ॥२५॥

saktāḥ karmaṇy avidvāṁso yathā kurvanti bhārata ।
kuryād vidvāṁs tathāsaktaś cikīrṣur lokasaṅgraham ॥25॥

As the unwise act out of their attachment to actions, O Arjuna, so should the wise act, but with no attachment, with the upkeep of the world order in view.

Arjuna, the wise and the unwise both are seen to be engaged in activities. The only difference is in the attitude with which they do these *karmas*. The wise do not feel, "This is my *karma*," neither are they urged into doing anything by the desire to enjoy the fruits of the *karmas*. For the wise one, it is only the upkeep of the world order that urges him to be active. Those who are not wise on the other hand, do everything with a feeling, "This is my *karma;* its fruits, whether sweet or bitter, also will be mine." Thus, attachment keeps the foolish active. Among such beings, how the wise are to remain as ideals, I shall tell you:

न बुद्धिभेदं जनयेदज्ञानां कर्मसङ्गिनाम्।
जोषयेत्सर्वकर्माणि विद्वान्युक्तः समाचरन्॥२६॥

na buddhi-bhedaṁ janayed ajñānāṁ karma-saṅginām ।
joṣayet sarva-karmāṇi vidvān yuktaḥ samācaran ॥26॥

The wise should not cause disruption in the minds of the ignorant attached to actions. A *yogī* should encourage them in doing actions, by he remaining active himself.

Arjuna, it is not many who become engaged with the kind of discussion we are having. Rarely do people become seekers, and still rarer is it for them to get real insight into what I am disclosing to you now. Others live ignorant of the meaning of life. As a part of the *prakṛti*-wheel, they continue to engage in *karmas*. And overlooking the fact that they too are part of *prakṛti*, they become attached to their *karmas* and are constantly worried about the outcome. You and I are unlike them, for we, knowing the meaning of life, do not look upon any *karma* as our own. If this knowledge were to make us take up a course of inaction, the ignorant, then taking our example, will also take to that path. It is not right that we should be the cause of a disruption of order. The ideal is to engage in actions like the ignorant, but unlike them, to do so with detachment.

In the light of all I have said so far, I should like to look at the question, "Whose really is *karma?*"

प्रकृतेः क्रियमाणानि गुणैः कर्माणि सर्वशः ।
अहङ्कारविमूढात्मा कर्ताहमिति मन्यते ॥२७॥

prakṛteḥ kriyamāṇāni guṇaiḥ karmāṇi sarvaśaḥ ।
ahaṅkāra-vimūḍhātmā kartāham iti manyate ॥27॥

Actions in every way take place because of the *guṇa*s of *prakṛti*. Deluded by the I-sense, one holds, "I am the doer."

Arjuna, now we know how the *prakṛti*-wheel rolls on. *Sattva* (pure), *rajas* (active), *tamas* (inert), the three *guṇa*s inherent in *prakṛti*, keep it restless or active, because of the inequalities among them. It is thus that *karma*s are really being done impelled by *prakṛti*. It is also *prakṛti* in action that assumes human form as each of us. Caught up with the "I" and "mine," in all aspects of life, we often overlook the good of the entire world, and the happiness of all beings. Life is evaluated with the measure of personal interests. Such deluded attitude is to be understood as indiscriminate (*vimūḍhātmā*).

How *karma* is perceived by those who know *prakṛti* and its activeness, I shall now tell you:

तत्त्ववित्तु महाबाहो गुणकर्मविभागयोः ।
गुणा गुणेषु वर्तन्त इति मत्वा न सज्जते ॥२८॥

tattva-vit tu mahā-bāho guṇa-karma-vibhāgayoḥ ।
guṇā guṇeṣu vartanta iti matvā na sajjate ॥28॥

But he who knows the basic truth about the distinction between *guṇa*s and *karma*s, O Mighty-armed, remains unattached, knowing that (*karma*s are) just *guṇa*s acting upon *guṇa*s.

One who knows what is basically, undeniably Real (*tattva*) is to be called a *tattvavit*, rendered here as "a knower of basic truth." Relating to the present stage of our reflections, *tattvavit* is one who sees his life and all its *karma*s as forming part of the rolling of *prakṛti*'s giant wheel. As this wheel rolls on, individual entities emerge one after another with different blends of *guṇa*s becoming predominant at any particular moment. The *karma*s engaged in at a particular moment are defined by the particular blend of *guṇa*s at that moment. None of us is exempt from this. This wheel of life — of individual and cosmos — rolls on and at every moment individual *guṇa*s realize their oneness with the *guṇa*s of *prakṛti*. A *tattvavit* lives always seeing this principle (*tattva*) in all his *karma*s. At every moment he is aware of himself and his *karma*s and their fruits as part of *prakṛti*, and is totally detached at all times. Such ones are called *karma-yogī*s.

Now I shall tell you what happens to others and how they are to be treated by knowers of truth:

प्रकृतेर्गुणसम्मूढाः सज्जन्ते गुणकर्मसु ।
तानकृत्स्नविदो मन्दान्कृत्स्नविन्न विचालयेत् ॥२९ ॥

prakṛter guṇa-sammūḍhāḥ sajjante guṇa-karmasu ।
tān akṛtsna-vido mandān kṛtsna-vin na vicālayet ॥29 ॥

Those who are confused regarding *prakṛti* and its *guṇa*s, become attached to the actions of the *guṇa*s. Such dullards, whose knowledge is but little, should not be disturbed by those of perfected knowledge.

Arjuna, those living unaware of *prakṛti*, its *guṇa*s and their creativity, are to be considered dullards. Such lives cannot be compared even with animal life. Animals are born, they remain active and die as part of the wheel of *prakṛti*. They do not have any conceptions of the fact that the *karma*s they engage in are "their" *karma*s, and are not bound by their *karma*s. Dull-headed humans are not so, they are not only unaware of the wheel of *prakṛti* as are animals, but in addition, they hold fast to a sense of agency in actions, making their predicament worse.

Teaching them the reality concerning *karma*s is practically impossible for the reason that they generally are unwilling to listen to any wisdom teaching. The best thing to do then is to leave them alone. It will help at least to have the world order undisturbed. The upkeep of the world order is the duty of the enlightened also, the reason why I asked you earlier to be engaged in activities to keep the world order up (*loka-saṁgrahaṁ*). Towards such actions, your attitude has to be this:

मयि सर्वाणि कर्माणि संन्यस्याध्यात्मचेतसा।
निराशीर्निर्ममो भूत्वा युध्यस्व विगतज्वरः ॥३०॥

mayi sarvāṇi karmāṇi saṁnyasyādhyātma-cetasā |
nirāśīr nirmamo bhūtvā yudhyasva vigata-jvaraḥ ||30 ||

Renouncing all actions in Me, mindful of the Self that you are, freed from longings and mine-sense, you fight with no feverishness.

Arjuna, we saw that the central notion around which thought developed in this chapter was that of the *prakṛti*-wheel rolling on. The previous chapter dealt with the one Substance that underlies all manifestations, where it was also noticed that this Substance is nothing but *Brahman*. We understood this to be a living, conscious Reality or rather that this Reality is life itself, Consciousness itself, which does not remain inert or inactive. It is this activeness, this creativity, that is called *prakṛti* in the present chapter.

I alone am that one Substance. *Prakṛti* too is active in Me, or rather I am *prakṛti*. When we say that all actions take place in *prakṛti*, it thus means all actions take place in Me. To offer all actions back to *prakṛti* means renouncing them in Me. A Sanskrit word for "giving up" is *nyāsa* and so we call the one who practises this giving up a *saṁnyāsin*. Thus, what the knower of truth (*tattvavit*) does, is renounce all actions in Me.

Such a *tattvavit* is said to be *adhyātma-cetas* or one who tries to understand the meaning of one's own life and of the entire world, taking as basis that which is ultimately real in oneself. This basis termed *dehin* (the embodied) and the *Brahman* of the previous chapter are nothing but Me.

Arjuna, be a *tattvavit*, and perform actions with the vision of a *tattvavit*. In your life, the *karma* that is unavoidable, as a part of *prakṛti*'s self-unfoldment, is the *karma* of a warrior, of fighting this war, and is the *karma* that squares with your own personal nature. What is required of you now is to fight, but without the feverishness of attachment. You spoke of experiencing a burning feeling when your mind dwelt on the battle to come. This was caused by your identifying yourself with your kith and kin, of your clan, and your tradition. If you remain always identified with the one Reality, the one *prakṛti*, then, and then alone, will you be a *tattvavit*. Only for those who do not know the Reality of life does life become a fevered rush.

I shall now proceed to tell you how one is to live with the universal truth that was just revealed.

ये मे मतमिदं नित्यमनुतिष्ठन्ति मानवाः ।
श्रद्धावन्तो ऽनसूयन्तो मुच्यन्ते ते ऽपि कर्मभिः ॥३१॥

ye me matam idaṁ nityam anutiṣṭhanti mānavāḥ ।
śraddhāvanto 'nasūyanto mucyante te 'pi karmabhiḥ ॥31॥

Those who, full of faith and devoid of envy, always follow this teaching of mine, they too become liberated from *karma*s.

What I have just spoken of is not merely my opinion, rather it is my well-considered, conclusive teaching (*matam*). You have already seen that this teaching is not understood by all. Earnest seekers attain it only with the help of a proper guide, a *guru*; exceptions to this are very rare indeed. The most important prerequisite for the seeker to attain the secret of this teaching is to have absolute faith in the *guru* and the teaching, which faith, in Vedānta, is known as *śraddhā*.

Arjuna, what I mean by these words may not straightaway be clear to you. You will have to subject what you have heard to intense cogitation in your own way, using the ways of reasoning familiar to you, past experiences, universally accepted norms and valid means of knowledge (*pramāṇa*s), and finally the *yoga-buddhi* we have spoken of earlier. The clarity thus gained regarding Reality has then to be meditated on as the essential content of your own beingness. Only then can that Reality become a living experience. The initial stage of hearing or learning the instruction with full faith is *śravaṇa,* the intense cogitation that follows is *manana,* and the final stage of meditation and realization is *nididhyāsana.* Initially if faith be lacking, no cogitation or final realization would be possible. Such is the crucial role of *śraddhā* (faith) in attaining wisdom, aided by a *guru.*

Initially, because of *śraddhā,* you will accept what I say as true, though you have not properly understood it. Later, after realization, when Reality has been rendered transparent, you will become fully aware of the value of that initial faith. The truth that was taken for granted at first, now becomes revealed as being so, and it no more remains a matter of faith. In that sense, *śraddhā* is quite unlike the belief in religious dogmas. The latter will always remain a matter of belief, whereas the former leads to final realization, after which, of course it no more remains a matter of faith. *Śraddhā* is thus merely the first stepping stone in attaining wisdom; it could be towards one's own personal *guru* or towards the *guru*s of the past who have left behind a record of wisdom teaching. These records, whether basic textbooks or scriptures, are in general known as *śāstra*s.

Śraddhā is thus a main element in the bipolarity of the *guru*-disciple relationship. If that is lacking, the disciple may feel mistrust in the *guru*'s teaching. Teaching that is not trusted cannot form the basis for further cogitaion and meditation. In such cases, the seeker may even experience envy of the master. It has therefore become a well recognized rule of *guru*s, that their teaching is imparted only to trusting seekers, the ultimate benefit being final release from all bondage, all *karma*s.

What happens to those seekers who have no faith in Me and masters like me, I shall tell you now:

ये त्वेतदभ्यसूयन्तो नानुतिष्ठन्ति मे मतम्।
सर्वज्ञानविमूढांस्तान्विद्धि नष्टानचेतसः ॥३२॥

ye tv etad abhyasūyanto nānutiṣṭhanti me matam ।
sarva-jñāna vimūḍhāṁs tān viddhi naṣṭān acetasaḥ ॥32॥

> But those who cavil and do not follow this teaching of Mine — know them as deluded as to the knowledge of the whole, as mindless, and fated to be lost.

See how helpless we are as a part of the rolling on of *prakṛti*:

सदृशं चेष्टते स्वस्याः प्रकृतेर्ज्ञानवानपि ।
प्रकृतिं यान्ति भूतानि निग्रहः किं करिष्यति ॥३३॥

sadṛśaṁ ceṣṭate svasyāḥ prakṛter jñānavān api ।
prakṛtiṁ yānti bhūtāni nigrahaḥ kiṁ kariṣyati ॥33॥

> Even a man of wisdom behaves in accordance with the *prakṛti* within him. Creatures always follow *prakṛti*. Of what avail then is restraint?

Arjuna, both *jñānins* and *ajñānins* are born, live and die as part of the rolling wheel of *prakṛti*. The same is true of all beings. To try to curb these actions that emerge inevitably in the course of overall changes in nature is futile. One's best would be to use that very same *karma* (action) as a means to directly experience one's own inseparable oneness with the total *prakṛti*. Then what steers our life will no longer be the longing for doing actions (*karmas*). How do such longings arise?

इन्द्रियस्येन्द्रियस्यार्थे रागद्वेषौ व्यवस्थितौ ।
तयोर्न वशमागच्छेत्तौ ह्यस्य परिपन्थिनौ ॥३४॥

indriyasyendriyasyārthe rāga-dveṣau vyavasthitau ।
tayor na vaśam āgacchet tau hy asya paripanthinau ॥34॥

> Attachment and aversion for sense objects abide in senses by their nature. You are not meant to come under their spell. These two indeed are enemies besetting your path.

Arjuna, to be in contact with the concerned object is natural with every sense organ. When felt pleasant, the sense gets attached to the object, and when unpleasant feels aversion. This attachment and aversion happen in the realm of sense organs. Your mind is meant to remain as witness; but what happens is you yourself get attached to or feel an aversion towards the object. This is caused by your wrongly taking upon yourself the agency of all actions, including the functions of sense organs. Your existence is really as a part of the *prakṛti*-wheel, and your sense organs and their functions form part of your existence. If you perceive yourself thus, "you" cease to feel attachment or aversion towards objects. Those who desire to make their life peaceful and free of fetters have, therefore, to treat these two — attachment and aversion towards sense objects — as enemies that block their proper life-path.

Going one step up from seeing the Kauravas as enemies, you have now come to seeing your own feelings of attachment and aversion as enemies. War-tactics have also necessarily to be changed in accordance with the nature of the enemies. Further sublimation of the nature of the enemy will be encountered in the next chapter.

What I told you so far about *karma* could be summarized thus:

श्रेयान्स्वधर्मो विगुणः परधर्मात्स्वनुष्ठितात्।
स्वधर्मे निधनं श्रेयः परधर्मो भयावहः ॥३५॥

śreyān svadharmo viguṇaḥ para-dharmāt svanuṣṭhitāt ।
svadharme nidhanaṁ śreyaḥ para-dharmo bhayāvahaḥ ॥

Better is it to be engaged in activities that conform to one's own inner nature even when ill-done, than to be engaged in activities not proper to oneself, though well-done. Even if resulting in death, to be engaged in activities proper to oneself is much better; applying oneself to activities improper to oneself is frightful.

Arjuna, the concept of *svadharma* was hinted at in Verse 31 of the last chapter and I explained what it meant then. Following that, we have examined *karma-yoga*, where alone, applying oneself to *svadharma* is possible. Let us now make the picture of *svadharma* (activities proper to one's own inner nature) clearer, with the *karma-yoga* concept added.

Our life, as you know, is a part of the rolling wheel of nature (*prakṛti*). We are minuscule outgrowths that emerge from and re-merge into this wheel, lasting a short while at some point in that boundless wheel. Yet, each one has a place and a role to play in the rolling. What is this place and this role, we have to find out on our own. It will vary in accordance with one's inner nature and disposition, and we must seek it out so as to enable us to live accordingly. The way of life as well as the vocation we choose should give full expression to our role in this context, and the proper goal of any well-conceived educative process should be to make this possible. When one is thus engaged in activities attuned to inner propensities, at the same time seeing oneself to be one with *prakṛti*, then one could be considered to be in one's own *svadharma*. Those who choose a way of life or vocation not fitting in with their inner nature are said to be doing *paradharma* (activities not proper to oneself).

You asked me at the beginning to define what would be best for you, in this critical life-situation. Finding your own *svadharma* and holding fast to it at all costs is best for you. Even if such an adherence to *svadharma* causes you inconvenience or even death, it would still be best for you, for in doing your *svadharma*, you will experience the joy of expressing yourself, the joy of making evident to yourself what possibilities are latent within you. Such activities will then never be just a means of livelihood. Each moment will be one of self-contentment and blissfulness. The case of those who are engaged in activities not conforming with their inner nature will be far different: boredom arises from having to do something not liked, and there will also be the fear that what was done may have been wrong. The person's strongest emotion will be the desire to get the job done somehow and leave. *Paradharma* (activities not proper to oneself) thus renders every moment of life insipid and fearsome, while engaging in *svadharma* fills life with self-contentment and there is also the experience of the individual's oneness with the rolling wheel of *prakṛti.*

By character you are an outright kṣatriya, a man of valour whose best is revealed while in battle. The rolling wheel of *prakṛti* has provided you a chance to express yourself fully and to see for yourself who and what you are; in other words, a chance to realize yourself is there through the action of battling that has emerged unasked for. This is the reason for my asking you earlier *tasmād yuddhyasva bhārata* (therefore go on battling, O Arjuna) (II.18).

अर्जुन उवाच —

अथ केन प्रयुक्तो ऽयं पापं चरति पूरुषः।
अनिच्छन्नपि वार्ष्णेय बलादिव नियोजितः ॥३६॥

arjuna uvāca —

atha kena prayukto 'yaṁ pāpaṁ carati pūruṣaḥ ।
anicchann api vārṣṇeya balād iva niyojitaḥ ॥36॥

Arjuna said —

Impelled by what, O Kṛṣṇa, is man given to commit sins even unwillingly, as though driven by force?

Kṛṣṇa, you now know in what way everything that we do forms part of the activeness of *prakṛti.* When seen as *prakṛti*'s, no *karma* is good or bad. Our feelings are not so; we consider certain actions to be "good" and certain others to be "bad." We usually intend to avoid doing wrong but often we still do; sometimes we feel that our own will is overpowered by some force that pushes us from behind, compelling us to do the very things we did not intend. What is that force?

Cannot some use as an excuse the notion that, "All actions are *prakṛti*'s" to commit crimes such as murder, on the claim, "It was done by *prakṛti,* not by me"?

श्रीभगवानुवाच —

काम एष क्रोध एष रजोगुणसमुद्भवः ।
महाशनो महापाप्मा विद्ध्येनमिह वैरिणम् ॥३७॥

śrī bhagavān uvāca —

kāma eṣa krodha eṣa rajo-guṇa-samudbhavaḥ ।
mahāśano mahā-pāpmā viddhy enam iha vairiṇam ॥37॥

Śrī Kṛṣṇa said —

It is desire, it is anger, born of *rajo-guṇa* (the active, affective modality of nature), the all-consuming and the most evil, that causes it. Know it to be your real enemy here.

Arjuna, in Verse 34, both attachment and aversion (*rāga* and *dveṣa*) were mentioned as enemies hiding within us. The same may be designated "desire" (*kāma*) and "anger" (*krodha*) and are part of our inner nature, created by *rajo-guṇa*, one of the modalities of *prakṛti.*

The rolling on of the wheel of *prakṛti* becomes possible by the three *guṇas* (modalities) — *sattva, rajas* and *tamas* — inherent in it. As part of *prakṛti*, these three *guṇas* are in us also, at times working against us, especially in relation to our life's goal. Yet it is these *guṇas* that have endowed us with the discriminatory powers to discern what is right and wrong, the value-sense to discern good and bad, the sense of responsibility to abide by what is good, the wilfulness to stand by the truth. It is our responsibility to make use of these qualities properly as a part of the rolling on of *prakṛti's* wheel of activities — a responsibility towards not any other being or group, but to *prakṛti* as a whole. One who knows this, will never do anything that goes against the normal flow of events in nature. Such is the case of those who know Reality, not of those who are bent on exploiting a basic philosophical truth for one's own evil ends. The knowledge of Reality is to be lived, not to be argued about, much less to be exploited. Only those who are interested in the logic behind Reality, not in the Reality as such, will doubt the worth of this knowledge. Instead of arguing, become enlightened; then you will find that you have no mind to do anything wrong.

The active and effective modality called *rajo-guṇa* is what instills the emotions of desire and anger. For a detailed analysis of this psychological factor we have to wait till Chapter XIV. You may take note of one thing for the time being: this *rajo-guṇa* is fire-like; it is never satisfied, no matter how much fuel is consumed; the more the fuel the stronger the desire becomes. Finally, desire and anger together will consume our own life's purport and to that extent, they are considered our enemies, though a part of us, and must be conquered. Since the enemy is within, no one else can help us conquer it, we ourselves have to seek it out and vanquish it.

In the usual course of life no one notices this enemy within. Why it is so, I shall now tell you:

धूमेनाव्रियते वह्निर्यथादर्शो मलेन च ।
यथोल्बेनावृतो गर्भस्तथा तेनेदमावृतम् ॥३८ ॥

dhūmenāvriyate vahnir yathā'darśo malena ca ।
yatholbenāvṛto garbhas tathā tenedam āvṛtam ॥38 ॥

As is fire enveloped by smoke, as is mirror by dust, as is embryo by amnion, so is This (Wisdom) veiled by that (desire and anger).

आवृतं ज्ञानमेतेन ज्ञानिनो नित्यवैरिणा ।
कामरूपेण कौन्तेय दुष्पूरेणानलेन च ॥३९ ॥

āvṛtaṁ jñānam etena jñānino nitya-vairiṇā ।
kāma-rūpeṇa kaunteya duṣpūreṇānalena ca ॥

Wisdom is veiled by this insatiable fire of desire, the eternal enemy of the wise, O son of Kuntī.

Arjuna, to be a *karma-yogin,* one must be fully aware of the rolling of the *prakṛti*-wheel as well as one's own place and role in it. But *rajo-guṇa* and the desire and anger it gives rise to, are always present in us, hiding this awareness from ourselves. It is necessary to constantly remain awake to this awareness, and to fight its veiling power. The veiling power of *rajo-guṇa,* in short, is an eternal enemy. The peculiarity of this enemy — desire — is that it is never satisfied, as is fire never satisfied. Those who have taken the decision to transform their own lives into a constant flow of *karma-yoga*, must therefore be willing to combat this desire-enemy within.

Just as every battle has its appropriate tactics, so too does this one. A primary war tactic is to create all kinds of obstructions in the path of approaching enemy-troops. Desire also has within each of us its own safe camps, which necessarily has to be prevented from reaching. I shall show you where that safe camp is:

इन्द्रियाणि मनो बुद्धिरस्याधिष्ठानमुच्यते ।
एतैर्विमोहयत्येष ज्ञानमावृत्य देहिनम् ॥४० ॥

indriyāṇi mano buddhir asyādhiṣṭhānam ucyate ।
etair vimohayaty eṣa jñānam āvṛtya dehinam ॥40 ॥

The senses, mind and understanding are said to be its seat. Veiling wisdom with these, it deludes the embodied.

Arjuna, desire does all its maneuvering using our sense organs, the organs of action, as well as our mind and understanding as safe harbours. It may even be said that desire uses these as a veil to hide itself. For this reason, we usually do not see the desire that drives us from behind when our sense organs, mind and understanding become interested in enjoyable objects. Further, it makes us think of wrong as right, bad as good, unfavourable as favourable, resulting finally in the capsizing of our life's boat. Thus deluded, we remain always ignorant of the Real in us. What we should do to avert such tragic ends, I shall tell you now:

तस्मात्त्वमिन्द्रियाण्यादौ नियम्य भरतर्षभ ।
पाप्मानं प्रजहि ह्येनं ज्ञानविज्ञाननाशनम् ॥४१ ॥

tasmāt tvam indriyāṇy ādau niyamya bharatarṣabha ।
pāpmānaṁ prajahi hy enaṁ jñāna-vijñāna-nāśanam ॥41 ॥

> To begin with, therefore, master your senses, O best of the Bharatas (Arjuna), and slay this sinful one, the annihilator of *jñāna* and *vijñāna.*

Arjuna, desire, as you know, makes use of our senses and other faculties as a veil to hide itself. The best way to put an end to this is to master the senses. *Niyama,* the original word, a technical term of the *yoga* system, is rendered here as "mastering." The eight-tiered *yoga* system has for its second tier the five disciplines called *niyama: śauca* (cleanliness), *santoṣa* (contentment), *svādhyāya* (self-learning), *tapas* (austerity), *īśvara praṇidhāna* (thinking always of God). The *niyama* I mean here is even more than these five disciplines.

Our lives should not be left uncontrolled like a boat caught in rough seas, to be carried away by the currents of senses, mind and various forms of understanding. It should instead be brought to the peaceful sea of *karma-yoga,* and the very senses and other faculties could very well be made instrumental in that attainment. As you know, it is the nature of senses to get into contact with and be interested in respective objects, all this taking place as a part of *prakṛti* rolling on. This awareness keeps one aloof, as a witness to all that takes place in oneself as part of *prakṛti.* The senses, active in their own way, will not then allure you and tempt you. They cannot persuade you to do the wrong that you do not intend.

Once the enemy's camp, the abode of desire, having been brought under your full control, their powers of offence are weakened. This is the only way of conquering desire and anger. Unless thus conquered, they will annihilate our *jñāna* and *vijñāna.* What *jñāna* is we will see in the next chapter and what *vijñāna* is in Chapter VII.

Battle tactics are devised taking into account who the enemy is, how mighty they are, how they are organized, under whose control they are and other similar factors. Before encountering the present enemies — desire and anger — these factors are all to be taken into account.

इन्द्रियाणि पराण्याहुरिन्द्रियेभ्यः परं मनः ।
मनसस्तु परा बुद्धिर्यो बुद्धेः परतस्तु सः ॥४२॥

indriyāṇi parāṇy āhur indriyebhyaḥ paraṁ manaḥ ।
manasas tu parā buddhir yo buddheḥ paratas tu saḥ ॥42॥

Higher (than desirable objects), it is said, are the senses; still higher is the mind; greater than mind are our understanding; what is beyond understanding is That indeed.

Arjuna, all around us are a variety of tempting desirable objects. We are tempted when the senses, which are part of our being, come into contact with them. Being subjective, and therefore subtler than objective, the sense organs are in that sense higher than objects.

The function of the sense organs is controlled by mind (*manas*) which is a more subjective and subtler aspect of being. The function of *manas* is to create images (*saṁkalpa*s) capable of driving the sense organs towards their objects.

In us, *buddhi* is the faculty that controls even the mind. *Buddhi* is the faculty of clearly understanding anything that is to be known. Our clear and definite understanding creates new images and layers of imagination in our mind. Our understanding about anything is nothing but pure, unconditioned Consciousness appearing as conditioned by the object known. Put differently, it is in one Consciousness that all ideas and understandings get formulated. Such is the way in which the factors that control our desires are related. Keeping all these in mind, I shall now tell you how to work out tactics against your enemy:

एवं बुद्धेः परं बुद्ध्वा संस्तभ्यात्मानमात्मना ।
जहि शत्रुं महाबाहो कामरूपं दुरासदम् ॥४३॥

evaṁ buddheḥ paraṁ buddhvā saṁstabhyātmānam ātmanā ।
jahi śatruṁ mahā-bāho kāma-rūpaṁ durāsadam ॥43॥

> Knowing yourself as *ātman* beyond understanding, and restraining yourself, do kill, O Mighty Armed, the difficult-to-subdue-enemy of desire-form.

Arjuna, as the sense organs are higher than enjoyable objects, restraining the senses will help to conquer the temptations of objects. The mind being superior to the sense organs, bringing the mind under restraint will help to keep one's senses under control. One's understanding being above the mind's fancies, stabilizing the understanding helps to control the mind's vagaries. What can we keep our understanding anchored to? Every form of understanding, every kind of knowledge, is formulated in consciousness, as a conditioned mode of the unconditioned, immutable Consciousness-Substance, *ātman* (the Self). That which was earlier called *dehin* (the embodied) and *Brahman* (the Absolute) in the last chapter is nothing else. Once we see that all knowledge, all understanding, exists in and as one with *ātman*, then we will find for ourselves that everything from sense objects to understanding, desires included, have been conquered.

This should be the crux of spiritual practice, to be practised not simply at particular scheduled time; it is to be observed all through the flux of life's *karma*s.

To summarize what we learnt from the present chapter:

The one embodied Reality or Substance (*dehin*), known as *Brahman*, that fills the being of everything is indestructible. This Substance is creative on its own. When active, that creativity is called *prakṛti*, loosely translated as "nature." *Kṛti* or activity is ever present in *prakṛti*. This *kṛti* of *prakṛti* is called *karma*. It is as part of this *karma* that we are born, live and die. This *kṛti* exists and is active even in the minutest aspect of nature, and so we too remain active in life. Doing away with *karma* is impossible. Unaware that all *karma*s are *prakṛti*'s, we may think, "I am the doer of actions; their fruits are also mine." Those who are aware of the reality concerning *prakṛti* and its *karma*, engage in activities knowing that no individual, but *prakṛti*, is the real doer of *karma*s. *Karma*s are thus transformed into a sort of *yajña* (sacrificial offering). Since the individual is neither the doer (*kartā*) nor the enjoyer (*bhoktā*) of *karmas*, no sin or merit accrues to him. One who perceives *prakṛti*'s *kṛti* and individual's *kṛti* as one, is to be called a *karma-yogī*. For such a person, *karma* is the best means of directly experiencing inseparable oneness with the whole. Even while engaged in activities, *ātma-darśana* (perceiving the Self-Reality) goes on endlessly.

Each one of us has to do something different as a part of the creativity of the overall *prakṛti*, depending on the inner nature or characteristics of the individual concerned. Activity proper to one's own inner nature is called *svadharma*. Being engaged in *svadharma* transforms life into a constant flow of contentment, free of all external compulsions, and also transforms *karma* into *karma-yoga*.

The emotions of desire and anger are present in us, distracting us from this noble path of *svadharma* and *karma-yoga*. These emotions emerge from the *rajo-guṇa* of *prakṛti*, and are the mighty enemies a would be *karma-yogī* has to encounter. What transforms *karma* into *karma-yoga* is our knowledge of *prakṛti*, and thus the decisive role in *karma-yoga* is that of knowledge. Knowledge of Reality pure and simple is called *jñāna*. We can remain *yogī*s in the realm of that knowledge where we become *jñāna-yogī*s. One becoming a *yogin* as a *jñānin* is the theme of the next chapter.

Thus ends Chapter Three entitled Karma-Yoga of the Bhagavad-Gītā, the essence of the Upaniṣads, that embodies the yoga-śāstra of brahma-vidyā in the form of a dialogue between Śrī Kṛṣṇa and Arjuna.

IV

Jñāna -Yoga
— The Yoga of Wisdom —

श्री भगवानुवाच —

इमं विवस्वते योगं प्रोक्तवानहमव्ययम् ।
विवस्वान्मनवे प्राह मनुरिक्ष्वाकवे ऽब्रवीत् ॥१॥

śrī bhagavān uvāca —

imaṁ vivasvate yogaṁ proktavān aham avyayam ।
vivasvān manave prāha manur ikṣvākave 'bravīt ॥1॥

Śrī Kṛṣṇa said —

This unexpending *yoga* I first declared to Vivasvān. He taught it to Manu, who in turn imparted it to Ikṣvāku.

एवं परम्पराप्राप्तमिमं राजर्षयो विदुः ।
स कालेनेह महता योगो नष्टः परंतप ॥२॥

evaṁ paramparā-prāptam imaṁ rājarṣayo viduḥ ।
sa kāleneha mahatā yogo naṣṭaḥ paraṁtapa ॥2॥

Thus handed down in line, this *yoga* was known to sagely kings. With the long lapse of time, O Scorcher of Enemies, it came to be lost to the world.

Arjuna, we have just seen how one, living in the world of *karmas*, can become a *yogī*. You must have noticed the very subtle element in it, that sublimates *karma* into *karma-yoga*. It is this very element that also transforms *jñāna* into *jñāna-yoga*. Neither this element of *yoga*, nor its application in *karma* and *jñāna*, are new. It was known to *gurus* of the past from time immorial without beginning. Knowledge of this *yoga* through generations has been handed down in succession from *gurus* to disciples. Many such lines of *gurus* have existed; of them, one alone is mentioned here.

It must be pointed out that it was sagely kings who knew this secret of *yoga* in olden days. These kings, being sages, were kings capable of applying wisdom in statescraft. The best example is Janaka. Upaniṣads like the *Bṛhadāraṇyaka* testifies that this *yoga* secret was known to kings — who were kṣatriyas — rather than to brāhmins who supposedly are meant to occupy the topmost rung in the caste-based social order of India. Pointing though to one of the main aspects of Indian History, lingering on it at length will be out of place here.

This *yoga* secret, handed down in line, at times gets clouded, sometimes even becoming lost to sight. Sometimes, when a disciple does not have the clear intuitive wisdom of the *guru*, the line of succession may even get snapped. The present is such an occasion and against such a back drop is to be seen and appreciated what I teach you now.

स एवायं मया तेऽद्य योगः प्रोक्तः पुरातनः ।
भक्तोऽसि मे सखा चेति रहस्यं ह्येतदुत्तमम् ॥३॥

sa evāyaṁ mayā te 'dya yogaḥ proktaḥ purātanaḥ ।
bhakto 'si me sakhā ceti rahasyaṁ hy etad uttamam ॥3॥

The very same age-old *yoga* is again being declared to you now by me, for you are devoted to me, you are a close friend of mine. It indeed is the highest secret.

Arjuna, this *Gītā*-teaching has a purpose of its own: reclaiming the *yoga*-secret that was lost in the course of being handed down through generations, so that posterity may be benefitted. For this reason I say, "I am declaring to you the very same age-old *yoga*-secret."

Arjuna, Reality is ineffable and remains a mystery, no matter how detailed an elucidation is made to explain it. It is revealed to the listener only after his subjecting what he hears to intensive meditation making use of the *yoga-buddhi* we have already studied in Chapter II. Ineffable intuitive perception becomes an accomplished fact only when the listener with full faith accepts what I say — what any *guru* says — and follows it up with *manana* and *nididhyāsana*. Only that listener who is filled with devotion and love for me, can attain an experience of the ineffable Reality. The role of faith, called *śraddhā*, we have already discussed (see commentary under Verse III.31). Devoutness (*bhakti*) is a disposition in which one constantly pursues (*anusaṁdhāna*) something; this act of pursuing is known as *bhajanā*. What is pursued here is nothing but the one Reality, *ātman*. I am fully convinced that you, Arjuna, are one who pursues *ātman*. In that sense, you are a *bhakta* (devotee) of Mine. You are also a dear friend, one who has developed perfect bipolarity with Me. All this being so, I now willingly reveal to you My inner being, Myself, which you have to perceive and experience as your own being and self. It is this disposition that leads one to such a perceptual awareness which is *bhakti*.

अर्जुन उवाच —

अपरं भवतो जन्म परं जन्म विवस्वतः ।
कथमेतद्विजानीयां त्वमादौ प्रोक्तवानिति ॥४ ॥

arjuna uvāca —

aparaṁ bhavato janma paraṁ janma vivasvataḥ ।
katham etad vijānīyāṁ tvam ādau proktavān iti ॥4 ॥

Arjuna said —

Recent was your birth and that of Vivasvān much earlier. How then am I to understand that you declared this *yoga* to Vivasvān first?

Kṛṣṇa, you are telling me that you imparted this *yoga*-secret to Vivasvān first. But Vivasvān, a Purāṇic character, was born, if at all, long long ago, while you are my own contemporary. How come then that you taught the *yoga* to Vivasvān first? It sounds like a puzzle. Kindly make it clear to me.

श्री भगवानुवाच —

बहूनि मे व्यतीतानि जन्मानि तव चार्जुन।
तान्यहं वेद सर्वाणि न त्वं वेत्थ परंतप ॥५॥

śrī bhagavān uvāca —

bahūni me vyatītāni janmāni tava cārjuna ।
tāny ahaṁ veda sarvāṇi na tvaṁ vettha paraṁtapa ॥5॥

Śrī Kṛṣṇa said —

O Arjuna, many are the births I have passed through, and so have you too. I am aware of them, but you are not so, O Scorcher of Enemies.

Arjuna, every step I make forward in this *Gītā*-teaching is to be understood and appreciated in the light of all that I have said before. Unless you do so intentionally, you are most likely to be misled. The "I" mentioned here just now does not denote the individual called Śrī Kṛṣṇa. I told you in Chapter II, you may remember, that "I" had never been non-existent, you had never been non-existent, all these chariot-masters had never been non-existent. What I meant as ever existing is the one Substance that has assumed our apparent forms for a short while, not as individuals as such. That one embodied Substance in all of us is none other than *Brahman*. Imperishable, it assumes the perishable, constantly changing forms of all. Such apparent forms are called *śarīra*s or *deha*s. The one Substance assuming a new form is what we call birth, and its disappearance death. You and I are all such constantly changeful forms assumed by the one Substance, and to that extent we both are equal. But you and I are unequal at a higher level — in that I am fully aware of life being so, and you are not, in that I am a *jñānin* who knows the meaning of life, and you are still a seeker yet to know. This difference between us, a part of the transient appearance, is to be considered as that between a *jñānin* and an *ajñānin*. Whether *jñānin* or *ajñānin*, the Reality that underlies both is one alone. Life flows on without stop, and the birth and death, the emerging of new forms and the re-merging of these forms, constantly take place in that Reality. One gold substance, unchanging, could be altered in any form we choose, so too the one Substance appears as many forms of beings. What underlies and appears as an *ajñānin* is also the one *Brahman*, but, being ignorant, he remains completely unaware of being so. For this reason, he considers birth as marking the beginning of life, and death the end.

This basic understanding which I helped you arrive at the very beginning, should be kept in mind when you try to understand my words, "I revealed the *yoga*-secret before" and "I reveal it now to you." The real "I" in me, and in you, is birthless and deathless.

अजो ऽपि सन्नव्ययात्मा भूतानामीश्वरो ऽपि सन्।
प्रकृतिं स्वामधिष्ठाय सम्भवाम्यात्ममायया ॥६॥

ajo 'pi sann avyayātmā bhūtānām īśvaro 'pi san ।
prakṛtiṁ svām adhiṣṭhāya sambhavāmy ātma-māyayā ॥6॥

The unborn and undiminishing *ātman* though I am, the supreme controller of all that has come into being though I am, residing in my own *prakṛti*, I emerge as beings, owing to my own *māyā*.

Arjuna, that I am the one unborn, indestructible, undiminishing *ātman*, is clear to you. Similar am I to the imperishable gold-substance in all the perishable ornament forms. I am the one indwelling Substance, the one inner controller (*īśvara*), of everything that has come into being.

How *prakṛti* is inherent in Me and how *karma*s take place in it, was explicated to you in Chapter III. It is the activating of the *kṛti* in *prakṛti* that results in the ever-changing world with all its vagaries. Truth concerns life in its entirety. The same is true in the restricted context of handing down the *yoga*-secret in succession. The *guru*-principle that works in the *guru*s of olden days and of the present days is one and the same; it is birthless and deathless. However, this abstract principle cannot stand face to face with you and help solve your problems, or teach you. All this has to be done by a flesh-and-blood-mortal *guru*. Yet he has to be the embodiment of the immortal *guru*-principle. The *guru* in me is thus not a person, not a mortal being, it has always been living. It, in the form of another living *guru*, taught Vivasvān in olden days, and the same in the form of a living Kṛṣṇa is teaching you at this moment. It is the immortal principle of *guru*-hood, called *gurutva*, that is denoted by my use of "I" here.

How this one immortal *gurutva* manifests itself as all the mortal *gurus*, prophets, masters and mystics of all ages, might seem a mystery. The *prakṛti* inherent in *Brahman*, we know, causes the emergence of all the worlds. So too, the one *gurutva* emerges as numerous *gurus* when and where needed as a part of the very same *prakṛti*'s *kṛti*. The one Reality — Myself — itself is an enigma. That enigmatic element in the emergence of the many from the one, the many not existing apart from the one, is what is known as *māyā*.

Though how the one *gurutva* manifests as numerous specific *gurus* is inexplicable, their emergence is clearly shown to us by history, and this appearance of *gurus* always happens to be turning points in history. When do such occur, I shall point out to you:

यदा यदा हि धर्मस्य ग्लानिर्भवति भारत।
अभ्युत्थानमधर्मस्य तदात्मानं सृजाम्यहम्॥७॥

yadā yadā hi dharmasya glānir bhavati bhārata ।
abhyutthānam adharmasya tadātmānaṁ sṛjāmy aham ॥7॥

Whenever laxity with regard to *dharma* comes about, *adharma* asserting itself, O Bhārata, then I Myself come forth.

In the previous chapter we spoke of how the overall system of human life remains intact only when guided by the wise whose lives are ideals. Those who are at the zenith of wisdom are to be called *yogins*. The *yoga*-secret of such *yogins* may become lost in the process of being handed down through generations. At times when such decadence happens, the role models readily available would naturally be those who claim to be *yogins*, rather than real *yogins*. The ideals of such charlatans can never be genuine, but will be revered as by the general populace, resulting in decline of *dharma. Dharma*, in fact, is much more than honouring and abiding by moral values in life. The word *dharma*, as pointed out earlier, denotes the overall system that sustains life and the cosmic order. A person's life becomes fully in tune with *dharma* when he respects the overall existence of life and its system in his personal life. Ignoring that system and leading a life controlled by one's own personal likes and dislikes is *adharma*, the opposite of *dharma*. The most important cause, significant in the present context, for such decline of *dharma* and the prevailing of *adharma*, is the contingency of having to live a life guided by the unwise who play the role of the wise, and lead the unwary into more darkness. It becomes imperative in such critical junctures of history to reclaim lost wisdom and the *yoga*-secret contained therein for posterity. To become fully aware of such a need is a natural part of My creativity. If asked how I take cognizance of these historical exigencies, the only possible answer would be, *ātma-māyayā* (owing to My own *māyā*). I, the immortal *guru*, in such junctures, cause Myself to emerge as new living, flesh-and-blood *gurus*. Each such *guru* will have a specific mission to fulfil, depending on the peculiarity of the particular historical exigency. Detailing it is impossible. I shall therefore point out simply what kind of mission it could be, viewed in general.

परित्राणाय साधूनां विनाशाय च दुष्कृताम् ।
धर्मसंस्थापनार्थाय सम्भवामि युगे युगे ॥८ ॥

paritrāṇāya sādhūnāṁ vināśāya ca duṣkṛtām ।
dharma-saṁsthāpanārthāya sambhavāmi yuge yuge ॥8 ॥

For the protection of the sustainer of *dharma* (*sādhus*), for the destruction of evil-doers, and for firmly re-establishing *dharma*, I do emerge age after age.

Arjuna, *sādhu* means one who helps sustain *dharma*. Those who hinder the sustenance of *dharma* and live inconsiderate to *dharma*, are to be considered evil-doers (*duṣkṛtas*). *Gurus* are born at that juncture of time when such evil-doers flourish, as though in answer to some inner call of history. Such *gurus* take upon themselves as life's mission, the restoration of the lost purity of wisdom.

Arjuna, to consider me as an incarnation of Viṣṇu according to the legends of the *Bhāgavata Purāṇa* gives rise to chances of misinterpreting what I have spoken of in this verse. The stories of Viṣṇu's incarnations meant for the protection of the good and the destruction of evil-doers are many. Those conditioned by such stories might take the present *Gītā* verse as referring to the incidents of such stories. But in the *Bhagavad-Gītā*, a science in its own right, I may remind you, I am to be understood as a representative of the one eternal *guru*-hood, and true to the present context of the *Gītā*, I am now born to restore the *yoga*-secret of wisdom.

A scientifically conceived philosophical treatise (*śāstra*), the *Gītā* follows its own system of thought and deals with many related topics in order to make fully transparent, an integral vision of life. It is only natural that nothing incongruous to the topic under discussion will be brought into the middle of any particular context of such a scientifically conceived text. The present discussion is centred around the restoration of lost wisdom, and this continues into the next verse as well. To bring in the topic of Viṣṇu's incarnation is out of tone here and does not become the seriousness of the *Gītā* as a *śāstra*. Even if taken as part of the present chapter in general, such an interpretation is out of place, as this chapter deals with *jñāna-yoga* (*yoga*-secret of wisdom); it does not give room for reflections on the incarnations of Viṣṇu.

I am not referring in this verse to any *avatāra*, the popular name that incarnations of Viṣṇu are known by, literally meaning, "coming down from above." Rather the word I use here is *sambhavāmi*, meaning, "I emerge again and again" or "I come forth," a process of welling up, that has to take place from something already existing, quite unlike the *avatāra* concept. Such details are also to be taken into account when you try to understand what I say, not only here, but all through the *Gītā*.

The creative urge, known as *karma*, inherent in Me, is the force that urges such phenomena to occur. You should know how great that creative force is:

जन्म कर्म च मे दिव्यमेवं यो वेत्ति तत्त्वतः ।
त्यक्त्वा देहं पुनर्जन्म नैति मामेति सोऽर्जुन ॥९॥

janma karma ca me divyam evaṁ yo vetti tattvataḥ ।
tyaktvā dehaṁ punar-janma naiti mām eti so 'rjuna ॥9॥

My taking birth thus and the *karma* that actuates it are divine. By knowing it in its true nature, one attains Me, leaving behind the body and attaining to no birth any more.

Arjuna, as you know, I am birthless and deathless Reality. The phenomena of birth, death and the resultant life-span of individuated entities, appearing constantly, are all made possible by the creative urge in Me, called *karma*.

Arjuna, likewise am I, the one immortal *guru*. It is Myself who appears phenomenally as the many mortal *gurus* bound by birth and death. This too is urged by the *karma* hidden in Me.

Arjuna, we have seen (in Verse II.16) how reality (*sat*) and appearance (*bhāva*) are inseparably one. Though this is beyond logical thinking, we do experience this oneness in life, and it is intuitively perceived by those endowed with *yoga-buddhi* or dialectical vision. This awareness is referred to here as, "by knowing it in its true nature" (*tattvato jñātvā*). In this unitive vision, the one Reality, all mortal forms emerging therein and the creative urge that causes the emergence of such forms, are all seen as forming part of one functional whole. Whosoever attains such a level of perception, knows himself to be the immortal Reality, and ceases to feel that he is an individual, born at a particular time and destined to die at a time in the future. In effect, such a person may be said to have left behind identity with the body. He has realized that he is that immortal Reality. Attaining identity with that Reality means attaining Me, for I am that Reality.

Once immortality is attained, the phenomena of birth and death, which pertain to appearance, are of no consequence. It is one's identity with the body that makes one feel that birth and death mark the beginning and end of life. Identity with Me reveals life to be without beginning and end.

Arjuna, trying to unravel the essence of *karma*, we have reached the essence of *jñāna* (wisdom), which is the state where the seeker perceives his existence as inseparably one with the existence of the whole, perceives that what exists in him as that which exists in the whole.

The benefit gained from this wisdom is release from birth and death, the freedom known as *mukti* or *mokṣa*, which also is suggested in this verse.

वीतरागभयक्रोधा मन्मया मामुपाश्रिताः ।
बहवो ज्ञानतपसा पूता मद्भावमागताः ॥१० ॥

vīta-rāga-bhaya-krodhā manmayā mām upāśritāḥ ।
bahavo jñāna-tapasā pūtā mad bhāvam āgatāḥ ॥10 ॥

Rid of attachment, fear and anger, being Myself in essence, taking refuge in Me alone, and purified by the austerity of wisdom, many have come to the state of being Myself.

Arjuna, the one who seeks Reality becomes Reality; the one who seeks Me becomes Myself. Such experience marks the finality of *jñāna* (wisdom).

How this wisdom might at times be hindered by the *rajo-guṇa* in oneself and the resultant emotions such as attachment, aversion, desire, anger, egoism and competitive attitude, we have seen earlier at the close of Chapter III. The one who, armed with a strong will, braves this challenging path of wisdom, will naturally have to undergo *tapas*, the word meaning, a self-imposed process of self-heating, which is usually translated as "austerity." *Tapas* brings about a sort of self-purification such as when gold is heated and beaten out. This purification is here called *sattva-śuddhi*, indicating that the seeker is purged of all accretions, finally becoming what he really is in essence. And he, as every other seeker, is really Me. Now this "Me" that I refer to could be the "Me" in the seeker, or the "Me" in Me, the *guru*. These two "Me"-s are really one "Me" alone. The seeker, realizing himself to be this one "Me," becomes absorbed in Me, and feels identified with Me. He thus comes to a state of being Myself.

However, different is the way in which each attains "Me," and I shall now speak of this:

ये यथा मां प्रपद्यन्ते तांस्तथैव भजाम्यहम् ।
मम वर्त्मानुवर्तन्ते मनुष्याः पार्थ सर्वशः ॥११ ॥

ye yathā māṁ prapadyante tāṁs tathaiva bhajāmy aham ।
mama vartmānuvartante manuṣyāḥ pārtha sarvaśaḥ ॥11 ॥

As I am approached, so am I availed, for, people from every side are in pursuit of Me, O Pārtha.

Arjuna, the only animal endowed with thinking faculty, man, knows, and also knows that he knows. This faculty compels him, regardless of whether he be intelligent or not, to think of Reality and seek Reality, that is to say, to seek Me. Yet the real "Me" is attained only by those who were referred to in the last verse. Others, though in search of Me, remain satisfied with some partial or wrong knowledge about Me. Their notion would be that the partial or wrong knowledge they have acquired is the true knowledge. One's true knowledge of Reality, in other words, depends on one's aptitude, interests, the way of approach that one prefers and similar factors.

(For example, it is taken for granted by modern science and its orthodox proponents that all natural phenomena are caused by matter — a preconceived notion unproved and unprovable by any scientific method. The method of enquiry of such science — that of subjecting physical objects to laboratrory experiments — also is fully in line with this notion. And the conclusions they arrive at are also concerning what is physical, never concerning such factors as mind and life, what is beyond physical. Their conclusions are not wrong, but their rightness has validity only at the material level. Those in search of Reality that is neither material nor mental, with an unprejudiced mind, are also there, and naturally their method of enquiry will be much different. What they attain, if at all, will also be different — the Reality pure and simple, neither material nor mental.)

Similar is it with the religions of the world. Each one tries in one or another way to know the meaning of ultimate Reality and to attune human life with it. The original seer, *guru* or prophet of each religion is seen to have been born at a critical time, and evident in his expressions will be a hue of the cultural background to which he belongs. At the same time, this does not indicate that his teaching is bounded by any cultural barrier. While their basic teachings, what they perceived within themselves, what they tried to express, remain the same Reality — the Real Me — one's way of giving expression to it might be by relying more on reasoning while another might give stress to belief. Such differences in their inclinations might leave their tinges in the way the one Reality — "I" — finds expression in their words.

Endless are such ways of approaching Me, and endless are the ways in which I am expressed in words and conceived as ideas. Intuitively perceiving the unconditioned and uncoloured Me as such becomes possible through two such ways alone: the *karma-yoga* detailed in the last chapter, and the *jñāna-yoga* now being elucidated. It was when trying to understand certain aspects of *karma-yoga*, you know, that we found ourselves landed in *jñāna-yoga*.

The *karma* in the Vedic context, means ritualism. Even such *karma* could well be transformed as ways, though inapt, of seeking "Me."

काङ्क्षन्तः कर्मणां सिद्धिं यजन्त इह देवताः।
क्षिप्रं हि मानुषे लोके सिद्धिर्भवति कर्मजा ॥१२॥

kāṅkṣantaḥ karmaṇāṁ siddhiṁ yajanta iha devatāḥ ।
kṣipraṁ hi mānuṣe loke siddhir bhavati karmajā ॥12॥

> Intent on gaining fruits of action people in this world do offer oblations to deities. In the human world, the action-born attainments are seemingly proximate.

Karma (action), in its broadest sense, takes place always everywhere in the world. Its complexity is such that, discerning which results in which is practically impossible. Man, in a planned effort to make life happier, undertakes delibrate actions aimed towards specific results. The Vedas have laid down many such *karma*s and as a consequence, such Vedic *karma*s also are, in a way aimed at ensuring maximum happiness in life, that is to say, to attain "Me." Seeing *karma*s and their results as closely linked, is but natural in such contexts. Even in the case of ordinary activities of life it is common that certain events are seen as the outcome of certain things done earlier. Human *karma*s and fruits of *karma*s thus appear to human mind as closely linked and proximate, despite the reality that all *karma*s ultimately are Mine.

One basic factor differentiates the constant flow of *karma*s that fill the world from the *karma*s of human being: the former is planned, if at all, by the will of *Brahman*, whereas the latter is planned by human will. Determining the nature of the flow of the former is humanly impossible; therefore an element of indeterminism accompanies it. In the case of human *karma*s, on the other hand, which result will be gained by which is conceived in advance and each *karma* is therefore performed expecting a particular result. Yet, the decision taken by each individual in respect of *karma* varies, so too does the nature of *karma* each does. I shall tell you why it is so:

चातुर्वर्ण्यं मया सृष्टं गुणकर्मविभागशः ।
तस्य कर्तारमपि मां विद्ध्यकर्तारमव्ययम् ॥१३॥

cāturvarṇyaṁ mayā sṛṣṭaṁ guṇa-karma-vibhāgaśaḥ ।
tasya kartāram api māṁ viddhy akartāram avyayam ॥13॥

> The four-fold colouration of human character was created by Myself, according as the *guṇa*s in each,

> according to the *karmas* (vocations) that go with it. Though I am their originator, know Me to be the unexpended non-doer of *karmas*.

Arjuna, that each strives to attain Me in his own way, in order to make life happier, I have made clear to you. The reason for this difference is that each individual is different in character and personal traits. Living beings are endless in variety. Of the countless living species, human being is one; and any one individual in that species is unlike another. Even the thumb-impressions of no two of the millions and millions of human beings, as you know, are never alike. Similar to this bodily uniqueness is the uniqueness of character. So also, the *karma* one prefers to do, the vocation one chooses, varies accordingly. This variety is caused by *prakṛti* with the three *guṇas* (nature-modalities), present always in varying proportions in different individual entities.

Nevertheless, as ancient Indian psychologists have shown, human character, based on certain common features, could be classified into four groups, and hence each such group is called a *varṇa* (literally, colouration, here of character). These psychological types are brāhmaṇa, kṣatriya, vaiśya and śūdra.

These four types of humans, these four groups of human nature, are part of *prakṛti;* and whatever is part of *prakṛti* is nothing but Myself assuming an apparent form. To that extent, I am the originator of this classification, the sense in which I said, "The four-fold colouration of human character was created by Me."

I am the Absolute Reality, the Substance that is always creative. Becoming apparent, this creativity is *prakṛti*, and in *prakṛti*, events are but natural — apparent forms will be constantly changing. As the underlying Substance for all such changes, I may be considered the doer of all the actions in *prakṛti* or of all the changes. Yet, I am not the doer of anything. A *karma* has to have a doer (*kartā*). Though the doer of all *karmas* in *prakṛti,* I have no sense of agency of actions, and so am no doer of *karmas*. For the same reason, I am not the author of the said classification.

Arjuna, you have to be cautious of these words of mine. There is every chance of mistaking Me for the creator of the caste system of the Indian social order. Even the value of the teachings of the *Gītā* might be belittled on that count. That the four colour-groups I distinguish here are in no way of a hierarchical nature and that they are all equal in status, will become clear as we deal with it in detail in Chapter XVIII, Verse 45. What I teach you here is not sociology, but *brahma-vidyā*. Each of us, while being part of the whole, naturally has our own personal traits and personalities, and thus the vocation befitting one's inner nature will vary from another's. Knowing what one's inner nature is and choosing a pattern of life that fits in with that nature is essential to live a content and peaceful life.

If those with vested interests choose to misuse my words and exploit fellow human beings, it is their own ignorance and greed that prompts them to do so. Even such people are in search of happiness and to that extent, in search of Me, but the means they choose, being guided by ignorance, are wrong.

There are also those people who, with no such shortcomings, do actually know, not only what is real in them, but also have a clear understanding of what their personal traits are. Such people are able to engage in activities proper to them, which keep them always content. It is they who really attain Me. I shall tell you now how they do so:

न मां कर्माणि लिम्पन्ति न मे कर्मफले स्पृहा ।
इति मां यो ऽभिजानाति कर्मभिर्न स बध्यते ॥१४॥

na māṁ karmāṇi limpanti na me karma-phale spṛhā ।
iti māṁ yo 'bhijānāti karmabhir na sa badhyate ॥14॥

No *karma* adheres to Me; nor do I desire any fruit of *karma*. He who knows Me thus is not bound by *karmas*.

Arjuna, "being Myself in essence" (*man-maya*) and "coming to a state of being Myself" (*mad-bhāva*) were seen in Verse 10 as marking the highest attainment — a state in which one directly experiences oneself as being one with the Absolute. I am the Absolute, and you are the seeker supposedly in this highest state of attainment. In that state of absolute Oneness, the "I" in you and the "I" in Me are not at all two. It is this non-dual "I" that I refer to here as "Me" when I say, "No *karma* adheres to Me, nor do I desire any fruit of *karma*." This non-dual "I" is what is denoted by the word *ātmā* or *ātman* (the Self) in Vedānta. Ceaselessly creative on its own, It is always active; *karma*s always take place in It. Yet It does not think or feel that It is the doer of those *karma*s. Having no sense of agency of actions means in effect that It is *karma*-less even when being incessantly active. No *karma* binds one who is devoid of the sense of agency of action. One who has this experience of Self-existence is to be counted as a liberated one (*mukta*). He is a *jñānin* free of bondage caused by *karma*. The *karma*s he happens to do are really non-action (*akarma*) in effect. The *jñānin*, in short, is not one who remains idle doing no *karma* at all, but rather one who has been able to transform these *karma*s that *prakṛti* makes him do into non-*karma* or *akarma*, knowing that all *karma*s are really *prakṛti*'s. Therefore,

---

एवं ज्ञात्वा कृतं कर्म पूर्वैरपि मुमुक्षुभिः।
कुरु कर्मैव तस्मात्त्वं पूर्वैः पूर्वतरं कृतम्॥१५॥

evaṁ jñātvā kṛtaṁ karma pūrvair api mumukṣubhiḥ ।
kuru karmaiva tasmāt tvaṁ pūrvaiḥ pūrvataraṁ kṛtam ॥15॥

Knowing thus, our predecessors seeking liberation, had been performing *karma*s; you too, therefore, have to do *karma*s as were done by our ancient predecessors.

Arjuna, as long as one is embodied, remaining inactive is impossible. The *karma*s so done take on qualifications of "sinful" or "meritorious" only when one considers oneself as the doer of those *karma*s. You too, Arjuna, are ensnared by a sense of sinfulness. Give up the idea that you, the individual, are the one who does *karma*s; realize that all *karma*s are nothing but a part of the actualization of the creative urge in the real "I" both in me and you. Then you will find yourself freed from all sins. Sin, thus, is not caused by *karmas*, but by attributing the doing of these *karmas* to individuals. Seeing *karmas* as pertaining to *ātman* or "Me" makes one a *jñānin*. Become a *jñānin* thus, and do all actions that chance requires you to do, without a sense of attachment towards them as well as the results they bring. Seekers like you, in the past, have done the same.

Our speculation about *karma* is here touching a new depth of subtlety. If you think the "I" in you, the individual, is the doer of *karmas*, then you become bound to the *karmas*, which is the bondage known as *karma-bandha*. If, on the other hand, you do *karmas* with the awareness that all *karmas* take place in the one "I," in the *ātman*, in the one Substance in both you and me, then you become liberated of all *karmas* and the sins that accompany them. Look at the subtlety of *karmas*:

किं कर्म किमकर्मेति कवयो ऽप्यत्र मोहिताः ।
तत्ते कर्म प्रवक्ष्यामि यज्ज्ञात्वा मोक्ष्यसे ऽशुभात् ॥१६ ॥

kiṁ karma kim akarmeti kavayo 'py atra mohitāḥ ।
tat te karma pravakṣyāmi yaj jñātvā mokṣyase 'śubhāt ॥16 ॥

What is *karma*, and what is non-*karma* — even the wise seemingly are confused in this regard. I shall therefore tell you of that *karma*, which, on knowing, liberates you from all evils.

Arjuna, you have to be all ears to what I am going to say now to understand clearly what *karma* and non-*karma* are. Our final goal is not this knowledge, but to liberate ourselves from *karma*-caused bondage.

कर्मणो ह्यपि बोद्धव्यं बोद्धव्यं च विकर्मणः ।
अकर्मणश्च बोद्धव्यं गहना कर्मणो गतिः ॥१७ ॥

karmaṇo hy api boddhavyaṁ boddhavyaṁ ca vikarmaṇaḥ ।
akarmaṇaś ca boddhavyaṁ gahanā karmaṇo gatiḥ ॥17 ॥

> One should know what *karma* is. What wrong *karma* is also should be known. Non-*karma* too is to be known. Elusive indeed is the course of *karmas*.

Arjuna, it must be clear to you from what we have discussed so far that *karma* can be perceived in different ways: as happening in the overall *prakṛti*, as done by each individual, or as the unfoldment of the creative urge of the one Reality. Therefore, each time we refer to *karma*, we should be clear in our mind which of these contexts we are relating it to. Otherwise, there is every likelihood of being caught in a tangle without free ends.

Arjuna, I am going to expound till the very end of this chapter, how *karma* dims and finally vanishes in the all engulfing brightness of *jñāna* (wisdom). It would therefore be advantageous to be clear beforehand as to what *karma* (action), *vikarma* (wrong action) and *akarma* (non-action) are.

Seen from the individual's viewpoint, everything done by him with the sense "I am the doer of this acton" is an individual's *karma*. It is relevant when one considers oneself as existing independently.

Seen from the viewpoint of overall existence, all that happen as part of the rolling on of the wheel of *prakṛti* are *karmas*. These take place in the one all-underlying Substance, the *ātman*.

When an individual deliberately retreats from the action that becomes necessary as a part of the natural course of events in *prakṛti*, it is to be treated as *akarma* (non-action).

You are well aware that all *karmas* take place in the one *ātman* as the actualization of the creative urge inherent in it finding expression as the rolling of the wheel of *prakṛti*. *Ātman* does not have the feeling, "I am the doer of all these *karmas*." *Ātman*, thus, being no doer, the *karma* that takes place in it, in principle, becomes *akarma* (non-action) in a slightly different sense.

Many are those who engage in activities motivated by desires for momentary pleasures. They do not think of the overall flux of activities of nature, nor of the overall system of life that unfolds as a result. They are unmindful even of their own personal traits and what makes them happy. The activities they are engaged in, mostly urged on by the weakness of the moment, are to be counted as *vikarmas* (wrong actions). What distinguishes *vikarma* from *akarma* is that the doer later mostly regrets it.

Karma thus is rooted in many directions, some of which are uplifting and others letting down, which is the reason for my stating, "elusive indeed is the course of *karmas*."

Though, elusive, one who knows the basics of *karma*, is not affected by it. How he looks at the *karmas* he does himself, I shall tell you:

कर्मण्यकर्म यः पश्येदकर्मणि च कर्म यः ।
स बुद्धिमान्मनुष्येषु स युक्तः कृत्स्नकर्मकृत् ॥१८ ॥

karmaṇy akarma yaḥ paśyed akarmaṇi ca karma yaḥ ।
sa buddhimān manuṣyeṣu sa yuktaḥ kṛtsna-karma-kṛt ॥18 ॥

He who sees non-action in action, and action in non-action, he, among men, is wise; he is a *yogī*, he is the doer of all actions.

Arjuna, practise seeing yourself, your life, everything you happen to do in life, as part of the rolling on of the wheel of *prakṛti*. Then you will feel that it is not you but *prakṛti* or *ātman* that is the sole doer of all actions. But, *prakṛti* or *ātman*, on its part has no sense of being the doer of actions. *Karmas*, then, are neither yours, nor *prakṛti*'s, nor *ātman*'s, they are simply non-actions (*akarmas*).

Arjuna, you are in the middle of a field of actions now, but you connot remain so continuously. Not only you but none. Descent follows ascent; night follows day; so too being active has to be followed by being inactive, taking rest. Only thus can the rolling of the *prakṛti*-wheel work; every point in a wheel goes up and comes down the other way round; so too is life. One's state of being inactive is also thus part of the eternal activity of the wheel of *prakṛti*. What looks like inactivity too, in other words, is, in principle, part of the eternal flux of *karma*.

One who thus sees *akarma* in *karma* and *karma* in *akarma* is to be counted as really wise. He sees his own existence, active or not, always as one with the existence of the whole, similar to a wave seeing itself as not different from the ocean. He sees one and many, reality and appearance, *sat* and *bhāva*, as inseparable, just as gold and ornament are inseparable. This inseparable unity of seemingly opposite pairs, is what is known as *yoga*. One who knows this is a *yogī*.

Such a *yogī*, as you know, sees himself as the Self-Reality in essence. This Reality, never remaining inactive, is creative on its own. Experiencing that creative Reality as his own essential content, the *yogī* will even perceive all the activities in all the worlds as taking place in his own being. Thus, while being a non-doer of any *karma*, he feels himself the doer of all *karma*s. What his attitude towards all those *karma*s will be, I shall tell you:

यस्य सर्वे समारम्भाः कामसङ्कल्पवर्जिताः ।
ज्ञानाग्निदग्धकर्माणं तमाहुः पण्डितं बुधाः ॥१९॥

yasya sarve samārambhāḥ kāma-saṅkalpa-varjitāḥ ।
jñānāgni-dagdha-karmāṇaṁ tam āhuḥ paṇḍitaṁ budhāḥ ॥19॥

He whose initiatives for action are not motivated by desires or pre-conceived idea of results, whose *karma*s are all burned down in the fire of wisdom — him the wise call a *paṇḍita*.

Arjuna, those who are aware of the wheel of *prakṛti* will have to do many things as part of its rolling, but none of these actions will be motivated by the yearning for desire-fulfilment. He will not have pre-conceived ideas of any particular result from any particular *karma*. To know life as a part of *prakṛti*'s wheel rolling on, means to become a *jñānin*. How a *jñānin* perceives himself, as you may recall, was stated in Verse 10 above. Done without a sense of agency (*kartṛtva*), all his *karma*s in effect become non-*karma*s. Seen from the point of view of *jñāna*, all his *karma*s are burnt down in the fire of wisdom.

Arjuna, a *jñānin,* thus, is the one who is capable of seeing his own actions as non-actions. Not guided by any desire, he never deliberately gets involved in activities. He simply does actions that become necessary as part of the natural course of life events, seeing them as non-actions. His contentment in doing these actions does not depend on the benefit they yield nor on their success or failure. His contentment is in the very doing of it, as made clearer in the next verse.

त्यक्त्वा कर्मफलासङ्गं नित्यतृप्तो निराश्रयः।
कर्मण्यभिप्रवृत्तोऽपि नैव किञ्चित्करोति सः॥२०॥

tyaktvā karma-phalāsaṅgaṁ nitya-tṛpto nirāśrayaḥ ।
karmaṇy abhipravṛtto 'pi naiva kiñcit karoti saḥ ॥20॥

Giving up attachments towards fruits of action, ever content, never seeking shelter, he, though engaged in *karmas*, does no *karma* at all (in principle).

Arjuna, it is our attachment towards the fruits of our actions that makes our life restless and full of misery. One who does not feel oneself to be the doer of actions will not be attached to their results either. He will ever experience contentment — the contentment of flowing with the flux of *prakṛti* by doing actions that emerge as part of the flow. He, in other words, experiences the oneness of the flow of the whole and the flow of his life, through his performance of *karmas*. Content in being himself, in being what is real in him, he does not take shelter anywhere but in himself. The *karmas* done by him also form a part of the eternal flow of *karmas*. Thus, while engaged in actions, he remains absolutely free from their bondage. It is not possible to deliberately avoid natural activities. Therefore,

---

निराशीर्यतचित्तात्मा त्यक्तसर्वपरिग्रहः।
शारीरं केवलं कर्म कुर्वन्नाप्नोति किल्बिषम्॥२१॥

nirāśīr yata-cittātmā tyakta-sarva-parigrahaḥ ।
śārīraṁ kevalaṁ karma kurvan nāpnoti kilbiṣam ॥21 ॥

Desireless, mind fully in his control, owning nothing, he does *karmas* simply as pertaining to the perishable aspect; so he amasses no sin.

Arjuna, whoever knows that everything belongs to *prakṛti,* owns nothing. The whole world, the form in which the one Reality appears, is a huge body or *śarīra,* literally, "that which perishes," with one's own body being part of it. And this world of appearance is a boundless flux of *karmas*, with our *karmas* being a part of it. Living with this awareness and doing all *karmas* that become necessary as part of the flow of life, with no attachment towards them, one remains always free of all sins. The guilty conscience of having committed sin has place only when one thinks, "I am the doer of this *karma*." In short, fully aware of Reality, one remains free from sins. The normal course of behaviour of such a *yogī* will be thus:

यदृच्छालाभसंतुष्टो द्वन्द्वातीतो विमत्सरः ।
समः सिद्धावसिद्धौ च कृत्वापि न निबध्यते ॥२२॥

yadṛcchā-lābha-saṁtuṣṭo dvandvātīto vimatsaraḥ ।
samaḥ siddhāv asiddhau ca kṛtvā 'pi na nibadhyate ॥22 ॥

Fully content with what chance brings about, going beyond all pairs of opposites, non-competitive, equipoised in gain and no-gain, he, though remaining active, is not bound.

Arjuna, a *yogī*'s contentment does not come from the fulfilment of his desires, for he has no desires. And yet, like everyone else, he too has needs of sustenance. The difference is that he does not concentrate on them, but remains satisfied with whatever is brought about by the rolling of *prakṛti*'s wheel. And *prakṛti* does not fail to fulfil his needs either. Pairs of opposites like good and evil, pleasure and pain, merit and sin, do not in any way affect his contentment.

Knowing that all such dualities are natural in the flux of *prakṛti*-events, he remains undaunted, always finding oneness with the total. Since *karma*s done as part of *prakṛti* do not make one bound to them; while *karma*s go on, the *yogī* remains above them. What is more, the *karma*s themselves become naught as far as the *yogī* is concerned. To clarify further:

गतसङ्गस्य मुक्तस्य ज्ञानावस्थितचेतसः ।
यज्ञायाचरतः कर्म समग्रं प्रविलीयते ॥२३॥

gata-saṅgasya muktasya jñānāvasthita-cetasaḥ I
yajñāyācarataḥ karma samagraṁ pravilīyate II23 II

Of the one whose attachments are gone, fully liberated, mind always remaining firm in wisdom, the entire *karma* performed as *yajña* becomes dissolved.

Arjuna, how a *yogī*'s *karma* becomes a *yajña,* we have seen in the last chapter. The same *yogī,* as the one who perceives what is ultimately Real in his own being, sees himself as a part of the one Reality which I am, in essence, even when engaged in *karma*s. Such *karma*s, in principle, are no *karma* for they have no existence apart from Me, they become dissolved in Me, doer and all. *Karma-yoga,* thus, in its pure form, attains the sublimity of *jñāna-yoga.*

As with *karma, jñāna* could also be seen as a *yajña*. What is offered as oblation in the *yajña* of *karma-yoga* is one's *karma*s. In *jñāna-yajña,* on the other hand, what is sacrificed is oneself. Put otherwise, it is not "mine" but "I" that is offered. A sacrificer thus offering himself in Me, the Absolute or *Brahman,* what remains after would be Me alone. A *jñānin* thus sees himself as Myself in essence (*man-maya*), as *Brahman* in essence (*brahma-maya*). Life as a whole, thus, turns out to be an offering of oblation into the Absolute. A *yogī* or *jñānin* perceives the *yajña* of life thus:

ब्रह्मार्पणं ब्रह्म हविर्ब्रह्माग्नौ ब्रह्मणा हुतम्।
ब्रह्मैव तेन गन्तव्यं ब्रह्मकर्मसमाधिना ॥२४ ॥

brahmārpaṇaṁ brahma havir brahmāgnau brahmaṇā hutam ।
brahmaiva tena gantavyaṁ brahma-karma-samādhinā ॥24 ॥

The act of offering oblation, for him, is *Brahman*; the object offered is *Brahman*. Offering is made by *Brahman* in the fire of *Brahman*. The goal he attains on finding his proper abode (*samādhi*) in the *karma* of *Brahman*, also is *Brahman*.

The picture I portrayed in this verse is of a *jñāna-yogī* who sees not only his *karma*s but also his entire life as a *yajña*. The essential content of his existence, the goal he aims at, and the means of attaining it, are all nothing but the one Reality — *Brahman* or Me — variously manifested.

Numerous are the means that many resort to in order to attain Me. None among such means is either superior or inferior to one another. As means of attaining Me, these are also to be counted as *yajña*s. I shall now point out to you some such prevailing systems of spiritual discipline, that are countable as *yajña*s.

दैवमेवापरे यज्ञं योगिनः पर्युपासते ।
ब्रह्माग्नावपरे यज्ञं यज्ञेनैवोपजुह्वति ॥२५ ॥

daivam evāpare yajñaṁ yoginaḥ paryupāsate ।
brahmāgnau apare yajñaṁ yajñenaivopajuhvati ॥25 ॥

Certain *yogī*s adoringly resort to fire-sacrifice intended for gods. Some others sacrifice the very *yajña* into the fire of *Brahman*.

Arjuna, certain seekers, interested as they are in conducting Vedic rituals, perform *yajña*s intended for propitiating the gods in heaven. Since their goal is attaining happiness in life, which is the same as attaining Me, their rituals, the actual *yajña*s, could well be considered as *yajña*s of a wisdom significance.

There are certain others, whose understanding is deeper, and they, rather than perform a fire sacrifice, burn down the very need for such sacrifices in the fire of wisdom. They, in other words, feel no need for the actual ritual. This *yajña* comes closer to the one we prefer here.

श्रोत्रादीनीन्द्रियाण्यन्ये संयमाग्निषु जुह्वति ।
शब्दादीन्विषयानन्य इन्द्रियाग्निषु जुह्वति ॥२६ ॥

śrotrādīnīndriyāṇy anye saṁyamāgniṣu juhvati ।
śabdādīn viṣayān anya indriyāgniṣu juhvati ॥26 ॥

Some offer as oblation the senses like hearing into the fire of self-restraint; still others offer sense objects like sound into the fire of senses.

Self-restraint is a common feature of most spiritual disciplines. Knowledge of the meaning and aim of life is not enough; one has to adhere to it with full self-restraint. The most forceful temptation distracting one from one's chosen path is that of sense pleasures, and this is why restraining senses has been accepted by all spiritual disciplines as an essential pre-requisite. This does not mean that other temptations are not to be taken seriously. The reference here to restraining senses stands for all of these.

This practising of self-restraint has also an element of *yajña* or sacrifice: the fire into which oblations are poured is nothing but self-restraint, and the oblations, the senses.

There are also those who practise self-restraint at a deeper level. They do not curtail the natural activities of the sense organs; instead, the senses are allowed to have contact with their objects, but every resulting experience of contacts is perceived as a new facet of his or her own Self-Reality — *ātman*, pure, unconditioned Consciousness — becoming manifest. On seeing something beautiful, for example, instead of becoming enchanted by it, one of such a practice perceives his own consciousness-content finding self-expression as that particular experience, and enjoying its mystery as a witness. When thought of as a *yajña*, the fire into which the offerings are poured is the sense organs, while the things offered are the sense objects. The brightness that results is nothing but *jñāna* or wisdom.

सर्वाणीन्द्रियकर्माणि प्राणकर्माणि चापरे।
आत्मसंयमयोगाग्नौ जुह्वति ज्ञानदीपिते ॥२७॥

sarvāṇīndriya-karmāṇi prāṇa-karmāṇi cāpare ।
ātma-saṁyama-yogāgnau juhvati jñāna-dīpite ॥27 ॥

All the functions of senses as well as of *prāṇa*s are offered by some into the wisdom-kindled fire of *yoga* consisting of self-restraint.

Arjuna, some seekers attain *jñāna* with the backing of *yoga*. They restrain all their vital functions, not as any mechanical interruption in the natural course of life, but as a natural consequence of enlightenment. This could also be considered a sort of *yajña*, and its sacrificial fire would be the wisdom-kindled self-restraint, and the things offered would consist of all the vital functions such as those of the sense organs, organs of action, the five *prāṇa*s, and so on.

द्रव्ययज्ञास्तपोयज्ञा योगयज्ञास्तथापरे।
स्वाध्यायज्ञानयज्ञाश्च यतयः संशितव्रताः ॥२८॥

dravya-yajñas tapo-yajñā yoga-yajñas tathapare ।
svādhyāya-jñāna-yajñaś ca yatayaḥ saṁśita-vratāḥ ॥28 ॥

Some offer materials as oblations; some treat austerity as a sacrifice; some practise *yogic* disciplines as a sacrifice. Attaining wisdom through self-learning is yet another *yajña* practised by some. All these accomplishers of self-restraint (*yati*s) are commendable in their well-intentioned firmness.

अपाने जुह्वति प्राणं प्राणे ऽपानं तथापरे।
प्राणापानगती रुद्ध्वा प्राणायामपरायणाः ॥२९॥

apāne juhvati prāṇaṁ prāṇe 'pānaṁ tathāpare ।
prāṇāpāna-gatī ruddhvā prāṇāyāma-parāyaṇāḥ ॥29 ॥

Some, interested as they are in breath-control (*prāṇāyāma*), offer *prāṇa* into *apāna* and *apāna* into *prāṇa*, by restraining their breathing process.

Arjuna, with some the means of attaining Me is practising *prāṇāyāma*. They control their incoming and outgoing breaths as prescribed in the source books of certain *yoga* schools. This practice could also be treated as *yajña* performed for attaining Me, where the inward and outward breaths become mutual oblation and sacrificial fire.

अपरे नियताहाराः प्राणान्प्राणेषु जुह्वति ।
सर्वे ऽप्येते यज्ञविदो यज्ञक्षपितकल्मषाः ॥३० ॥

apare niyatāhārāḥ prāṇān prāṇeṣu juhvati ।
sarve 'py ete yajña-vido yajña-kṣapita-kalmaṣāḥ ॥30 ॥

Some others, controlling their food habit, make an offering of vitalities in the fire of vitalities. All such are knowers of *yajña*, and by means of *yajña*, they annihilate sin.

Arjuna, some observe certain religious vows as a means to attain Me. Fasting or controlled diet are usually part of such schemes. Such food habits help purify the physical body. Uncontrolled food habits render one's vital functions too uncontrolled; controlled food habits, on the other hand, keeps one's vitalities controlled. Treated as a *yajña*, this sort of spiritual discipline has vitalities for both the sacrificial fire and oblation.

Arjuna, how some of the various spiritual disciplines could be perceived as *yajña*, I have just shown you. It does not mean that I recommend all of them as means to be adopted by you or the learners of the *Gītā*. I was just re-evaluating some of the prevailing practices. The practice I really recommend will be stated in Verse 33.

What is of importance is this: the practice one follows is not what matters. What makes any practice laudable is one's understanding of the *yajña* principle inherent therein. If practised with this awareness, its adherent, no matter which system he follows, is to be considered a knower of *yajña*. Total emancipation from sin is the chief goal of the *yajña* we are concerned with now. That emancipation too becomes an accomplished fact for the adherent of such *yajña*s.

Irrespective of the system one follows, seeing it as a *yajña* brings different systems to this one common goal:

यज्ञशिष्टामृतभुजो यान्ति ब्रह्म सनातनम्।
नायं लोको ऽस्त्ययज्ञस्य कुतो ऽन्यः कुरुसत्तम ॥३१॥

yajña-śiṣṭāmṛta-bhujo yānti brahma sanātanam ।
nāyaṁ loko 'sty ayajñasya kuto 'nyaḥ kuru-sattama ॥31॥

The partakers of the immortal remainders of *yajña* attain *Brahman* the Eternal. To those who make efforts not as *yajña*, even this world remains unattainable, much less the other, O Best of the Kurus (Arjuna).

Arjuna, partaking of the sacred remnants of *yajña* forms a part of such rituals. Such remnants are known as *yajña-śiṣṭa*. The wisdom sacrifice (*jñāna-yajña*) we are concerned with here too has its own *yajña-śiṣṭa*: the peace and blissful contentment experienced on offering back to the total *prakṛti* whatever was till then considered as belonging to oneself. Thenceforth, not only that he himself enjoys, but also his own being will be perceived as the sacred remnants of sacrifice. It is the experience of a transient being while living, attaining the Eternal *Brahman*.

Unless perceived and practised as a *yajña*, any spiritual discipline may be limited to a mechanical process. Neither peace nor contentment follows it, which means life in this world itself is not felt to be peaceful or meaningful, let alone experiencing transcendental blissfulness.

The urge for undergoing such spiritual disciplines as *yajña* arises always from one *karma* principle, which I shall clarify:

एवं बहुविधा यज्ञा वितता ब्रह्मणो मुखे ।
कर्मजान्विद्धि तान्सर्वानेवं ज्ञात्वा विमोक्ष्यसे ॥३२॥

evaṁ bahuvidhā yajñā vitatā brahmaṇo mukhe ।
karmajān viddhi tān sarvān evaṁ jñātvā vimokṣyase ॥32॥

Many and varied are such *yajñas* spread out as the manifest facets of *Brahman*. Know all these as having originated from one *karma* principle. Knowing thus, you become emancipated.

Arjuna, all *yajñas* have their origin in *Brahman*. *Yajña*, as we know, is a *karma* enjoined by the Vedas; many and varied are the *yajñas* thus prescribed. The word *Brahman* stands also for the Vedas.

But the *yajña* we are concerned with is of another sort: the *jñāna-yajña* meant for attaining *Brahman*, the Absolute. This *yajña*, as the means of attaining *Brahman*, is inherent in the very same *Brahman*. To clarify it: the effort to attain *Brahman* is made by seekers like you, such seekers being nothing but momentary apparent manifest forms of that *Brahman*. The seeker, on his part, perceives the effort he makes as a *yajña*, an offering in which the object sacrificed is himself; he offers himself back to *Brahman*. It could thus be said that *yajña* is something that forms part of the functional aspect of *Brahman*.

In every *yajña*, whether Vedic or of wisdom import, is implied an offering. Every offering is a *karma*. The capability to do *karmas* is present in every being as part of the creative urge of the one all-underlying Substance finding expression. Neither creation nor the *yajñas* performed by creations would be possible in the absence of such an urge. It is this creative urge in the one Reality that is to be truly understood as *karma*. As part of this total being, individual beings also have in them the same *karma*. It is this *karma* that urges an individual being to perform *yajñas*.

Whoever undergoes spiritual discipline, treating it as a *yajña,* and considering his own life also as a *yajña,* does not think of it as his own. The *karma*s he does are not considered his, but as *Brahman*'s or *prakṛti*'s. Having no *karma* of his own, he is not bound by them either. That is how he becomes freed from the bondage caused by *karma*s, and thus from all sins.

After having told you that you can treat some of the prevailing spiritual disciplines as *yajña*s, I shall now tell you of that spiritual discipline which I prefer above all others:

श्रेयान्द्रव्यमयाद्यज्ञाज्ज्ञानयज्ञः परंतप ।
सर्वं कर्माखिलं पार्थ ज्ञाने परिसमाप्यते ॥३३॥

śreyān dravya-mayād yajñāj jñāna-yajñaḥ paraṁtapa ।
sarvaṁ karmā 'khilaṁ pārtha jñāne parisamāpyate ॥33॥

Higher than material sacrifice in value is the wisdom-sacrifice, O Killer of Foes. All *karma*s, in their entirety, terminate, O Arjuna, in wisdom (*jñāna*).

Arjuna, certain material objects are offered as oblation in all the Vedic *yajña*s or rituals. Other spiritual practices also have aspects that are rather "physical." The *yajña* I recommend, on the other hand, is that of wisdom (*jñāna-yajña*), where nothing material is offered into a physical fire. What is offered is simply the being of the seeker himself, and the fire into which the offering is made is *Brahman* — an offering that takes place purely in one's understanding. Seeing his own beingness in the one beingness of the ultimate Reality, the seeker experiences inalienable oneness with that Reality. He will then see all the *karma*s that take place in life, all the efforts made by him and all the spiritual disciplines he undergoes, as happening in the being of *Brahman*. He, himself being not the doer, in effect, has no *karma*s of his own. The experience of oneness with *Brahman* thus puts an end to all *karma*s — this being the way in which *karma* becomes *akarma* (non-action).

Arjuna, the essential content of this wisdom sacrifice is not open to many. To whom is it easily accessible I shall tell you:

तद्विद्धि प्रणिपातेन परिप्रश्नेन सेवया ।
उपदेक्ष्यन्ति ते ज्ञानं ज्ञानिनस्तत्त्वदर्शिनः ॥३४ ॥

tad viddhi praṇipātena paripraśnena sevayā ।
upadekṣyanti te jñānaṁ jñāninas tattva-darśinaḥ ॥34 ॥

Learn it by greeting the wise ones prostratingly, by asking searching questions, by doing personal services; they, the seers of "That" pure and simple, will duly enlighten you on wisdom.

Arjuna, rarely it happens that one may become enlightened on one's own, without help from another about the secret of that wisdom sacrifice, where one's life itself is its remainder. Such people are known as *ṛṣis*, literally "the seers." All others need the help of a guide, a *guru*. The wisdom a *guru* imparts to a disciple is not knowledge of the sort that is taught in schools and universities. The seeker's search is not for the knowledge of anything objective, but for self-Reality, the Substance that constitutes and appears as his own existence. What the *guru* is enlightened on, and directly experiences, is the Substance that constitutes his own existence — he is the knower of the self-Reality in *himself*. As a *guru*, what he, at *his* utmost, can do is somehow reveal to the seeker the Reality of *his* own existence. What the seeker-disciple has to imbibe and make *his* own is not the Reality in the *guru*'s being. He has to transform what the *guru* reveals into *his* own self-experience. The actualization of this transformation depends on the intimacy established between them: the intimacy known as *guru-śiṣya-pārasparya* (the bipolarity between *guru* and disciple). The seeker greeting the *guru* with prostration, doing personal services for him, asking pertinent questions, are all part of the external signs of an internal bipolarity. Formally asking a question may not actually take place, for a real *guru* will always be fully aware of the problem that smoulders in the mind of the seeker. The clarity and definiteness of a *guru*'s answer depends on the pertinence and exactness of the question that forms in the seeker. The final certitude the seeker arrives at is that the one Substance alone constitutes the being of the *guru* as well as himself. It is this oneness that reflects as the personal intimacy between them. This is what makes the personal bipolarity between *guru* and disciple an essential prerequisite in the context of imparting wisdom.

Arjuna, one Reality alone really exists. It assumes the forms of *guru* and disciple. It assumes the form of everything in all the worlds. As the Reality to be sought and realized, It is often referred to as *tat*, meaning "That." The state of *tat* being itself pure and simple, is known as *tattva*. One who realizes one's own being as that *tattva* in essence is called a *tattva-darśin*, the seer of "That," pure and simple.

Arjuna, you may be wondering what this wisdom is, what its ultimate benefit is. I shall tell you:

यज्ज्ञात्वा न पुनर्मोहमेवं यास्यसि पाण्डव।
येन भूतान्यशेषेण द्रक्ष्यस्यात्मन्यथो मयि ॥३५॥

yaj jñātvā na punar moham evaṁ yāsyasi pāṇḍava ।
yena bhūtāny aśeṣena drakṣyasy ātmany atho mayi ॥35 ॥

By knowing that, you will not get into confusion any more. You will then see everything that has come into being in yourself, and yourself in Me.

Arjuna, you were in a state of utter confusion when you first approached Me as a seeker. You were incapable of discriminating good from evil, the meritorious from the sinful, the true from the untrue. Such a confused state of mind is known as *moha*. It is a result of looking at your life from the narrow and closed perspective of the orthodox notion of the traditional virtue of your clan (*kula-dharma*), the erroneous concept of the caste system and its obligations (*jāti-dharma*), your duties and obligations to your masters and elders of the family. The wisdom I reveal, on the other hand, enables you to perceive life in total, the world in total, Reality in total. The all-inclusiveness of this open perspective subsumes all the narrower considerations, rendering them irrelevant, just as small pools become irrelevant in a flood of pure water. You thus become free from all confusions. That is the ultimate benefit of this wisdom.

Everything that has come into being in all the worlds is nothing but various apparent manifestations of one Self-Reality. Seeing all beings in oneself, and then oneself merging in the total being of *Brahman*, the Absolute — the *Bhagavān* of the *Gītā* — is the essential content of what is known as *jñāna*.

To clarify: An earthen pot, for example, realizes what is real in it — that it is clay in essence. This knowledge concerns not merely that particular pot but all earthen pots, for the earth-content in that pot is the earth-content in all pots. The realization attained by the pot will be this: I, in essence, am the clay that forms the substance of all the earthen pots in the world. Attaining this realization, the pot begins to see all earthen pots in itself. The present seeker has to see himself in the place of this pot and realize what substance he is in essence. It is the very same Substance that unfolds itself and appears as all the entities in all the worlds. He thus realizes: I am really the Substance in all beings. He, in other words, sees all beings in himself.

This one Substance in all entities is what is referred to as *ātman* (the Self) or *Brahman* (the Absolute) in Vedānta, which in the *Gītā* is represented by Me, the *Bhagavān*. Therefore, as a continuation of seeing all beings in himself, the realized individual sees himself in Me or *Brahman*. Such is the overall picture represented in the present verse.

Everything living and not living together constitute the perceptual world. Conducting enquiries into Reality, you will come to perceive that the entire visible world exists as your experience, that its existence is in your experience, in you, the perceiver. Try to find out how extensive your perceiving mind or consciousness is; you will then realize that all the worlds are in it, that it is infinite in extension. That which is of infinite extensiveness cannot be more than one in number either. This infinitely extensive one mind or consciousness is nothing but "Me" the *Bhagavān*, or *Brahman*. This "Me" is that which manifests as this endlessly extensive cosmic system. All the worlds, thus, you will first see in yourself, and then yourself in "Me". One of such a perception is to be called a *tattva-darśin*.

Arjuna, the word *ātmani* (in the *ātman*) of this verse is to be specially noted. Though translated here as "in yourself," it really means "in oneself," "in the self." Only on knowing the one underlying Substance in one's being, like clay in a pot, can one claim to know oneself. Therefore, more than meaning "I" or "Me," the word *ātman* signifies the one Substance that constitutes one's being.

Almost all nouns in the Sanskrit language, unlike in many other languages, are derived from verb roots, the word *ātmā* (*ātman*) being no exception. Strangely enough, the word *ātmā* has more than one derivation, thus naturally has more than one meaning.

One root from which it is derived is *ad*, meaning "to eat," "to enjoy." *Ātmā*, thus derived, means the eater, the enjoyer, of everything (*atti iti ātmā*).

Another root is *at* which means "to constantly move on" (*ata sātatya-gamane*). *Ātmā,* thus, means that substance which reaches everywhere and everything knowable and thinkable, assuming their forms.

A secondary root derived from *at* is *āt*, meaning "to pervade everything" (*ād vyāpane*). Derived from this root, *ātmā* means, that which pervades everything (*ātata*), the sense in which the *Praśna Upaniṣad* conceives *ātmā*. This pervading is not like that of fragrance in air, but is like clay in a pot or metal in a coin. *Ātmā* thus is the one Substance which assumes the form of everything, from the subtlest animating principle to the grossest physical bodies. An enquiry into the essential content of this Substance, *ātmā,* reveals that it is imperceptible and unthinkable, for everything perceptible and thinkable is an object, while what we seek is the Substance in all such objects.

A popular idea is that *ātmā* means soul or *jīva,* thinking of it as the principle that animates the physical body. I am aware of this but the *ātmā* I mean is entirely different. Every individual living entity has inherent in it numerous constituent factors, ranging from the subtlest soul principle to the tangible physical body. The one Substance that assumes the forms of all these is what I refer to as *ātmā*. All these apparent aspects, inclusive of the animating principle, together constitutes what I call *śarīra* as will be made explicit in Verses XIII.5, 6. The word *jīva,* translated usually as "soul," in the Sanskrit language, actually means, an entity that exists through breathing (*jīva prāṇa-dhāraṇe*). The word *jīvātmā,* one of the key words in Vedānta, if at all admissible, should therefore be accepted as denoting the substance that assumes the apparent form of the individual living entity, not the soul principle in a living being.

I have made clear that perceiving everything in the "I" in you, in the Self (*ātman*), constitutes wisdom. This "I," the Self, is nothing other than pure and unconditioned Consciousness. Everything other than this Consciousness that constitutes my being is "mine" only; so we say, "my body," "my hands," "my sense," "my mind," "my world" and so on. We won't hesitate even to say "my self" or "my *ātmā*," as though the *ātmā* can be "mine." Really the *ātmā* is not "mine," but is "myself." *Ātmā* or Self is that Consciousness which is conscious of all that are considered "mine." That Consciousness is the real Substance of my being, of your being, and of the being of all. In other words, all become one in that Consciousness. Such is the significance of my words *yena bhūtāny aśeṣeṇa drakṣyasi ātmani* (because of which you see everything that has come into being in yourself).

How one Consciousness alone is the Substance that underlies all appearances can be further clarified with the help of an example:

Take a piece of cloth. Take it apart into its yarns. The identity of the cloth disappears in the yarns. It was the yarns that till that moment appeared as the cloth. Further, part the yarn into its fibres, and then you will see that the yarn has disappeared in the heap of fibres. Separate the component elements in the fibres; then the fibres disappear in the reality of basic elements. Those elements, further divided, become atoms, and these split again, become pure energy which is non-matter as will be conceived by future scientists. According to ancient Indian conception, anything physical is made of the five basic elements — space, air, fire, water and earth. Their existence being purely conceptual, none of these elements on its own, is physical. All the actual physical entities are combinations of those basic elements. The basic substance that exists on its own, therefore, is conceptual, that is to say, its existence is in consciousness, as consciousness alone. Whether seen with the modern mind or with the scientific mind of the ancient Indian thinkers, what ultimately exists is consciousness pure and simple alone. Put otherwise, pure and unconditioned Consciousness become conditioned, assumed the form of energy particles, atoms, fibres, yarns, pieces of cloth, ultimately, of everything in the world, in all the worlds. You are that Consciousness in essence; I am that Consciousness in essence; all the worlds are that Consciousness in essence. All find unity in That. You being "That," everything attains unity in you. I being "That," you attain unity in Me. For this reason I said: *yena bhūtāni aśeṣeṇa drakṣyasi ātmani atho mayi.* You will then see everything that has come into being in yourself, and yourself in Me.

This Self-Reality, being Consciousness in essence, must have made some people unmindful of subtleties, take *ātmā* for a synonym for *jīva*, for a common notion is that consciousness is one of the distinguishing characteristics of *jīva*. Anyway, what I do mean by *ātmā* has been made sufficiently clear to you, and any study of the *Gītā* lacking a clear understanding of this, will be a futile effort. In short, the "I" in you and the "I" in Me are no two consciousnesses. They are one in essence. That one Consciousness is infinite in extension. That is the Self-Reality; That is *ātman*; That is *Brahman*; That is you; That is Me.

Beyond attaining this experiential unity, there is no higher knowledge. Being an enlightenment on the whole of existence, its realizer no more feels there is something yet remaining to be known. On this enlightenment vanish all confusions. Your approaching Me, you know, was in a state of utter confusion caused mainly by your sense of sinfulness in killing kith and kin. How you, of such a state of mind, will be benefitted by this highest wisdom, I shall show you:

अपि चेदसि पापेभ्यः सर्वेभ्यः पापकृत्तमः ।
सर्वं ज्ञानप्लवेनैव वृजिनं सन्तरिष्यसि ॥३६ ॥

api ced asi pāpebhyaḥ sarvebhyaḥ pāpa-kṛttamaḥ ।
sarvaṁ jñāna-plavenaiva vṛjinaṁ santariṣyasi ॥36 ॥

Even if you be the most sinful of all sinners, you will cross over all the sins by this wisdom-raft.

Arjuna, those who are enlightened on what I have just revealed to you, see one Consciousness (*cit*) alone, Me alone, as really existing. All the activities in all the worlds will then be seen as taking place in Me. Such *karma*s by themselves are neither good nor bad, neither meritorious nor sinful; they are just *karma*s. Those who are not enlightened on this Reality are to be counted as ignorant; their perception naturally will be very narrow and closed; their understanding of life will be but little. They see the *karma*s taking place in them as theirs. Classifying them as meritorious and sinful is based simply on whether their immediate results are favourable or unfavourable, as also on certain Vedic notions. Doing actions thus counted as sinful, one becomes frightened of the prospect of having to go to hell. The only unconditioned means of saving man from this trap-like situation is this wisdom. It is the only raft that takes you across the otherwise uncrossable river of sin.

You wrongly thought of yourself as the doer of the *karma* of this battling; it resulted in your guilty conscience of committing a horrible sin. What happens to such *karma*s on one getting enlightened? I shall tell you:

यथैधांसि समिद्धोऽग्निर्भस्मसात्कुरुतेऽर्जुन ।
ज्ञानाग्निः सर्वकर्माणि भस्मसात्कुरुते तथा ॥३७ ॥

yathaidhāṁsi samiddho 'gnir bhasmasāt kurute 'rjuna ।
jñānāgniḥ sarva-karmāṇi bhasmasāt kurute tathā ॥37 ॥

Just as flaming fire reduces fuel to ashes, so too, O Arjuna, this fire of wisdom reduces to ashes all *karmas*.

Arjuna, experienced wisdom has in it neither knower nor known, it does not have knowledge as such; no doer of *karma*, no enjoyer of *karmas* and indeed, no *karmas* as such. All these are burnt like fuel in its flaming fire. A *jñānin*, thus, has no *karma* and hence, how can there be then good *karmas* and evil *karmas*? How can there be past *karmas*, present *karmas* or future *karmas*? I know that the notion prevails among some Vedāntins that even *jñānins* are bound to *prārabdha-karmas*, the *karmas* which are already begun but whose fruits are not yet fully enjoyed.

It is true that a *jñānin* also is externally seen to be engaged in normal activities, but he does not see these as his *karmas*. It is the ignorant who, on seeing a *jñānin* engaged in activities, interpret these as the *jñānī*'s *prārabdha-karmas*. The *jñānin*'s enlightened state of existence is experienced only by him, and is quite incomprehensible to the ignorant.

न हि ज्ञानेन सदृशं पवित्रमिह विद्यते ।
तत्स्वयं योगसंसिद्धः कालेनात्मनि विन्दति ॥३८ ॥

na hi jñānena sadṛśaṁ pavitram iha vidyate ।
tat svayaṁ yoga-saṁsiddhaḥ kālenātmani vindati ॥38 ॥

Nothing so purificatory as wisdom is there in this world. One who has attained perfection in *yoga*, experiences it in himself in due course.

Who has this unworldly purificatory experience? Listen to me:

श्रद्धावांल्लभते ज्ञानं तत्परः संयतेन्द्रियः ।
ज्ञानं लब्ध्वा परां शान्तिमचिरेणाधिगच्छति ॥३९ ॥

śraddhāvān labhate jñānaṁ tat-paraḥ saṁyatendriyaḥ ।
jñānaṁ labdhvā parāṁ śāntim acireṇādhigacchati ॥39 ॥

Only one endowed with *śraddhā*, intent always on attaining what is denoted by *tat* (That), i.e., Me, with full mastery over the senses, obtains *jñāna*. Obtaining it, one immediately attains the state of Supreme Peace.

Arjuna, what *śraddhā* is and what its implications and importance are, we have already made sufficiently clear (Verse III.31). Being fully intent on realizing what is signified by the word *tat* (That), the one Supreme Reality, makes one a seeker. Mastery over the senses and giving up the desire for objects of pleasure are essential prerequisites. How these are mutually complementary and supporting, we have seen in detail earlier. One endowed with these qualities experiences the shining of the effulgent sun of the Self as his own beingness. All the fever of transactional life, all *karmas* and the bondage caused by them along with sin and merit, then slide off revealing his own natural, supremely peaceful, existence. Anyone who is not so, is to be called *ajñānin* — the ignorant. I shall tell you what becomes of him:

अज्ञश्चाश्रद्दधानश्च संशयात्मा विनश्यति ।
नायं लोकोऽस्ति न परो न सुखं संशयात्मनः ॥४० ॥

ajñaś cāśraddadhānaś ca saṁśayātmā vinaśyati ।
nāyaṁ loko 'sti na paro na sukhaṁ saṁśayātmanaḥ ॥40 ॥

The ignorant, the *śraddhā*-less and the doubts-embodied, end up in perishing. Neither the happiness of this world nor of the other is theirs.

Arjuna, it is with full conviction that you are no doubting person, but one full of *śraddhā*, that I am imparting this wisdom to you. No *guru* will teach one who lacks *śraddhā*. *Saṁśaya* (doubt) is the state of mind opposite to *śraddhā*.

Now let us have a review of what was covered in the present chapter:

योगसन्न्यस्तकर्माणं ज्ञानसञ्छिन्नसंशयम् ।
आत्मवन्तं न कर्माणि निबध्नन्ति धनञ्जय ॥४१ ॥

yoga-saṁnyasta-karmāṇaṁ jñāna-sañchinna-saṁśayam ।
ātmavantaṁ na karmāṇi nibadhnanti dhanañjaya ॥41॥

With all *karmas* renounced on attaining *yoga*, with all doubts sundered on attaining *jñāna*, one possessing *ātmā*, and possessed by *ātmā*, does not become bound by *karmas*, O Arjuna.

Arjuna, he who sees himself as existing as inseparable with total *prakṛti*, perceives his *karmas* as part of *prakṛti*'s changes. A *karma-yogī*, thus, is one who attains *yoga*, with his being engaged in natural activities as means. The last chapter discussed its details, and in it is hidden a *yoga* secret, a mystery element in the wisdom teaching of the *gurus* of the past from time without beginning. In the process of handing down this wisdom teaching through generations of *gurus* and disciples, at times its clarity is temporarily lost, and the present context is one such instance of unclear wisdom. Reclaiming it, reviving it, and cleansing it to make it available again to posterity through teaching it to you — that is what I am presently doing.

Guru-hood is a principle without beginning or end, and the *gurus* of the past were embodiments of this, and so too am I. The ceaseless existence of this *guru*-principle through generations of *gurus* is similar to that of the eternal Substance (*sat*) in and through the ever changing apparent forms (*bhāvas*). He who is aware of the *karma*-principle inherent in the one eternal Substance and the resultant phenomenon of the constant birth of new apparent forms, sees himself only as one of many such forms. Such a person will see Me, the Absolute, alone as that which is Real in him. He will see himself as Me in essence. Such a one is to be called a *jñāna-yogī*. Seeing his being in My being, he forgets all his *karmas*. Becoming enlightened that what is Real in oneself is Real in the whole, constitutes wisdom (*jñāna*). This transparent vision concerning all the worlds, life in these worlds, and one's own life, brings about the contentment that nothing more remains to be known, nothing more remains to be done. Such a one is to be qualified as *jñāna-saṁchinna-saṁśayaḥ* (he whose doubts are all sundered on attaining wisdom). Fully aware of the Self-Reality that himself is, he remains firmly in the Self; as the

Self; so he is an *ātmāvān* (possessor of the Self and possessed by the Self).

Only those who have *karmas* of their own, are bound by them. The one who is fully enlightened of his having no *karma* of his own, has no *karma*-caused bondage. He is also free from sin and merit. He sees everything in all the worlds as being in himself, and himself in Me or *Brahman*. He is a *jñāna-yogī*.

Just as *karma-yoga* was seen as a *yajña*, so too can be seen *jñāna-yoga*. What is offered in the *yajña* of *karma-yoga* is one's own *karmas*, and the fire into which offering is made is total *prakṛti*. In the *yajña* of *jñāna-yoga*, on the other hand, the oblation offered is oneself, and the fire, the Absolute or *Brahman*. This *jñāna-yoga* becomes a living experience only for a person who is *tat-paraḥ* (one who is intent on *Brahman* alone) and *samyatendriyaḥ* (one who has mastered his senses), endowed with *śraddhā* as well. One who lacks such qualities, the ignorant one, never attains this experience. A real seeker of *jñāna* has, therefore, to treat the *saṁśaya* (the absence of *śraddhā*) in himself as the gravest of all enemies.

तस्मादज्ञानसम्भूतं हृत्स्थं ज्ञानासिनात्मनः ।
छित्त्वैनं संशयं योगमातिष्ठोत्तिष्ठ भारत ॥४२॥

tasmād ajñāna-sambhūtaṁ hṛtsthaṁ jñānāsinātmanaḥ ।
chittvainaṁ saṁśayaṁ yogam ātiṣṭhottiṣṭha bhārata ॥42॥

Therefore, chopping down the ignorance-born doubt that clings to your heart, with the sword of wisdom of the Self, become a *yogī* and thus stand up, O Arjuna.

Arjuna, I am sure, you are fully aware of the role of *śraddhā* in attaining wisdom. *Saṁśayātmā* is the one who has no real faith (*śraddhā*) in what his own *guru* teaches, in what the *gurus* of the past have taught, as well as in the existence of an undeniable and indisputable Reality. He, therefore, finds no firm ground from which to begin systematic enquiry, for belief in such a ground has to come first. *Saṁśaya* or the doubting mind has to be chopped down mercilessly with the sword of discrimination, then only can one become a *jñānin* or a *yogī*. Only such people can wage the war of life with the fully emancipated mind of a *yogī*. You, I know, are already a *yogī*. Stand firm in that *yoga*-state, and rise up fully determined to face what is unavoidable.

As we pass through each chapter of the *Gītā*, we take one more step further towards the finality of wisdom. As a result of it, the nature of the enemy we are required to face also undergoes change. At first the enemies you were required to fight appeared to be the Kauravas; at the end of the third chapter the foes appeared to be the desire and anger in yourself, and now the enemy is revealed as your own doubting mind, the doubt caused by ignorance. Stand up firm in mind to fight that enemy.

Thus ends Chapter Four entitled Jñāna-yoga of the Bhagavad-Gītā, the essence of the Upaniṣads, that embodies the yoga-śāstra of brahma-vidyā in the form of a dialogue between Śrī Kṛṣṇa and Arjuna.

V

Karma-Saṁnyāsa-Yoga

— The Yoga of Renouncing Actions —

अर्जुन उवाच —

संन्यासं कर्मणां कृष्ण पुनर्योगं च शंससि।
यच्छ्रेय एतयोरेकं तन्मे ब्रूहि सुनिश्चितम् ॥१॥

arjuna uvāca —

saṁnyāsaṁ karmaṇāṁ kṛṣṇa punar yogaṁ ca śaṁsasi ।
yac chreya etayor ekaṁ tan me brūhi suniścitam ॥1॥

Arjuna said —

Kṛṣṇa, you praise renunciation of *karmas*, so also you do praise *yoga*. Please tell me clearly which one of these two is higher in value.

Kṛṣṇa, *karma-yoga* seemed commendable as Chapter III ended, but the next chapter ended glorifying *jñāna-yoga*. Which of the two is better and befits me, I find myself unable to decide. Kindly make it clear to me.

श्री भगवानुवाच —

संन्यासः कर्मयोगश्च निःश्रेयसकरावुभौ।
तयोस्तु कर्मसंन्यासात्कर्मयोगो विशिष्यते ॥२॥

śrī bhagavān uvāca —

saṁnyāsaḥ karma-yogaś ca niḥśreyasa-karāv ubhau ।
tayos tu karma-saṁnyāsāt karma-yogo viśiṣyate ॥2॥

Śrī Kṛṣṇa said —

Both renunciation of *karma* and *karma-yoga* are emancipation-making. Yet, of the two, *karma-yoga* is superior to mere renunciation of *karmas*.

Arjuna, whether one resorts to *karma-yoga* or *jñāna-yoga* as the means, the goal aimed at is final emancipation, known as *mukti* or *mokṣa*. It signifies one's liberation from all bondages. The Nyāya system likes to call it *niḥśreyas*, that which is of the highest value.

Karma-yoga, as a spiritual means, does not do away with *karmas* that form a part of nature's flow of life. *Jñāna-yoga*, on the other hand, moves beyond being conscious of *karmas*, even those that seem unavoidable. Practically, to do away with *karmas* or to be completely oblivious of them, is an impossibility for humans and so *karma-yoga* could be thought of as superior. Efforts to attain liberation is comparable to a mountaineering expedition. When more than one trekking path is available the climber will naturally prefer the easiest; so is the superiority of *karma-yoga* over *jñāna-yoga*.

Saṁnyāsa, though meaning proper renouncing, does in no way imply any wilful giving up of all activities. Who a real renouncer of *karmas* is, I shall tell you:

ज्ञेयः स नित्यसंन्यासी यो न द्वेष्टि न काङ्क्षति।
निर्द्वन्द्वो हि महाबाहो सुखं बन्धात्प्रमुच्यते ॥३॥

jñeyaḥ sa nitya-saṁnyāsī yo na dveṣṭi na kāṅkṣati ।
nirdvandvo hi mahā-bāho sukhaṁ bandhāt pramucyate ॥3॥

He is to be known as perpetual renouncer (*nitya-saṁnyāsin*) who neither detests nor covets anything. Free from pairs of opposites, he becomes easily released from all bondages, O Mighty Armed.

Arjuna, a *jñānin* detests nothing; he desires nothing; he hates nothing; he adores nothing. Only such, who are above all duality of opposites (*nirdvandva*) are real *saṁnyāsins* (renunciates). They remain always free from *karma*-caused bondage, whether they remain active or not.

My telling you in the last verse that *karma-yoga* is superior to renouncing *karmas* altogether, does in no way mean that an enlightened one remaining *karma*-less, is inferior. It is indicated by the word *nitya-saṁnyāsī* (perpetual renouncer) here. What marks a *nitya-saṁnyāsī* is not his renouncing *karmas* altogether, but his unattached attitude towards both doing and not doing *karmas*, an attitude that becomes spontaneous in *jñānins*. *Karmas* performed with such a sense of detachment are to be termed *karma-yoga*. To discriminate precisely between *karma-yoga* and *jñāna-yoga*, between remaining a *karma-yogīn* and renouncing *karmas*, is therefore an impossibility. The two, as life-experiences, are no two. I shall make it clearer:

साङ्ख्ययोगौ पृथग्बालाः प्रवदन्ति न पण्डिताः ।
एकमप्यास्थितः सम्यगुभयोर्विन्दते फलम् ॥४ ॥

sāṅkhya-yogau pṛthag bālāḥ pravadanti na paṇḍitāḥ ।
ekam apy asthitaḥ samyag ubhayor vindate phalam ॥4 ॥

The *sāṁkhya* and *yoga* as different, only the unwise, never the wise, speak of. Well-established in one, one gains the fruits of both.

यत्साङ्ख्यैः प्राप्यते स्थानं तद्योगैरपि गम्यते ।
एकं साङ्ख्यं च योगं च यः पश्यति स पश्यति ॥५ ॥

yat sāṁkhyaiḥ prāpyate sthānaṁ tad yogair api gamyate ।
ekaṁ sāṁkhyaṁ ca yogaṁ ca yaḥ paśyati sa paśyati ॥5 ॥

The state attained by *sāṁkhya*-adepts is reached by *yoga*-adepts as well. He who sees *sāṁkhya* and *yoga* as one, alone sees.

Arjuna, you should remember the *sāṁkhya-buddhi* I taught you in the first half of the second chapter, and it was the way of thinking dominant in Chapter IV. It led us to the *yoga* state where all doubts are sundered on attaining wisdom (*jñāna-saṁchinna-saṁśayaḥ*, IV. 41) — a state in which one perceives everything in oneself and then oneself in the Absolute. In the second half of Chapter II was taught another way of looking at life, called *yoga-buddhi*, leading us to the state of *karma-yoga* where all natural activities are performed without a sense of attachment, as shown in Chapter III. This explains why I term *jñāna-yoga* and *karma-yoga* here simply as *sāṁkhya* and *yoga*. Seeing the two as two is natural with those of undeveloped child-like thinking. For this reason, designating the unwise as children (*bālāḥ*) is common place in Vedāntic parlance.

The science of life I teach you here has a definite goal enabling one to live life meaningfully, whatever the means one resorts to. As living experience, the goals of *sāṁkhya-buddhi* and *yoga-buddhi* are the same, and to that extent the two can be counted as being not different. Those who are able to see in this way are *yogī*s; they alone are the seers of Truth.

Without realizing the secret of *jñāna-yoga* no one can become a real *karma-yogīn*; in the world of actualities, no *jñāna-yogīn* can live other than as a *karma-yogīn*.

संन्यासस्तु महाबाहो दुःखमाप्तुमयोगतः ।
योगयुक्तो मुनिर्ब्रह्म नचिरेणाधिगच्छति ॥६॥

saṁnyāsas tu mahā-bāho duḥkham āptum ayogataḥ ।
yoga-yukto munir brahma nacireṇādhigacchati ॥6॥

Saṁnyāsa is verily hard to attain without *yoga*; united with *yoga* (on the other hand), a sage attains *Brahman* soon.

Arjuna, seeing one's own existence as being one with total existence, as you know, constitutes the essence of *jñāna*. Living every moment with this awareness, the *jñānin* does not feel bound to do any *karma*, all *karma*s having been offered into the fire of wisdom. He, nevertheless, does not remain actionless; he will be doing everything that nature's flow of actions makes necessary, with the awareness that those actions are not his, but *prakṛti*'s, and this constitutes the essence of *karma-yoga*. In short, other than as *karma-yoga*, no one can practise *jñāna-yoga* in life. What we call *yogī* or *yoga-yukta* henceforth, for this reason, will neither mean *karma-yogī* nor *jñāna-yogī*, but that *yogin* in whom the two are inseparably one, whom I have termed *muni* (sage) in the present verse. He, at every moment of life, in everything he happens to do, will see only the one unchanging Reality — *Brahman* — variously manifesting. What the word *Brahman* signifies I have made sufficiently clear, you may remember, under Verse 72 of Chapter II. A wave, seeing itself as ocean in essence, feels itself identified with it. Similar is the *yoga-yukta* state of the sage — his living is a ceaseless flow of experiencing oneness with *Brahman*. It is in this sense I said that the sage attains *Brahman* soon. How such a sage lives and moves in this world I shall tell you:

योगयुक्तो विशुद्धात्मा विजितात्मा जितेन्द्रियः ।
सर्वभूतात्मभूतात्मा कुर्वन्नपि न लिप्यते ॥७॥

yoga-yukto viśuddhātmā vijitātmā jitendriyaḥ ।
sarva-bhūtātma-bhūtātmā kurvann api na lipyate ॥7॥

Unified through *yoga*, pure Self in essence, conquering oneself, conquering the senses, with the self having become the Self of all that has come into being, he, even while being active, remains unattached.

Arjuna, a wave realizes, "I am water." That is its self-realization; this is its state of being united through *yoga*, its state of being a *yogin*. It thus forgets its individuating wave-qualities and remains as nothing but water. This is its remaining pure self in essence. So too with individual *yogīs*. They reject personal likes and dislikes, for, in the absence of such rejection, the knowledge, "I am the one Reality in essence" remains mere theoretical understanding unrelated to life. With the I-sense and sense of possession gone, one becomes self-conquered. Immersed in the blissfulness of being the Absolute, he does not become interested in momentary sense-pleasures, thus becoming one who has conquered the senses.

A wave, realizing water to be its self-content, also realizes the same water to be the self-content of all waves. So too, a *yogī* perceives his own self-content pervading the being of everything. In all his activities too he perceives only the creative beingness of the one Self-Reality. He does not, then, feel that he is doing anything on his own, and is thus not bound to any *karmas*.

नैव किञ्चित्करोमीति युक्तो मन्येत तत्त्ववित्।
पश्यञ्शृण्वन्स्पृशञ्जिघ्रन्नश्नन्गच्छन्स्वपञ्श्वसन् ॥८॥
प्रलपन्विसृजन्गृह्णन्नुन्मिषन्निमिषन्नपि ।
इन्द्रियाणीन्द्रियार्थेषु वर्तन्त इति धारयन् ॥९॥

naiva kiñcit karomīti yukto manyeta tattva-vit ǀ
paśyañ śṛṇvan spṛśañ jighrann aśnan gacchan svapañ śvasan ǁ8 ǁ

pralapan visṛjan gṛhṇann unmiṣan nimiṣann api ǀ
indriyānīndriyārtheṣu vartanta iti dhārayan ǁ9 ǁ

The *yogī*, knowing the beingness of That, thinks, "I do not act at all," even as he sees, hears, touches, smells, eats, moves, sleeps, breaths, speaks, emits, grasps, opens and closes his eyes. He just maintains, "The senses are engaged with their objects."

Arjuna, *karmas* are going on everywhere in *prakṛti*: wind blows, fire blazes, water flows, the sun shines, the earth supports everything. No one stops to ask who the doer of all these *karmas* is, for everyone knows that they take place as part of *prakṛti*. It is as part of the very same *prakṛti* that we human beings too see, speak, hear, engage in activities using our hand, think and do other such things; however, instead of seeing all such actions as *prakṛti*'s, we choose to see ourselves as their doers. Here the *yogī* differs from others; he remains a witness to all the activities that take place in his own being fully aware that each sense, as part of nature, is engaged with its object. He, in other words, perceives all *karmas* as pertaining to *Brahman*, not to him the individual. To clarify further:

ब्रह्मण्याधाय कर्माणि सङ्गं त्यक्त्वा करोति यः।
लिप्यते न स पापेन पद्मपत्रमिवाम्भसा ॥१०॥

brahmaṇy ādhāya karmāṇi saṅgaṁ tyaktvā karoti yaḥ ।
lipyate na sa pāpena padma-patram ivāmbhasā ॥10॥

Placing all *karmas* in *Brahman*, with attachments given up, he who acts is untouched by sin, as is a lotus leaf by water.

All the actions that take place in the entire *prakṛti* as well as in oneself, are seen by a *yogī* as pertaining to *Brahman*. Even the chosen actions performed wilfully are looked upon as an offering to *Brahman*, for his own free will is nothing but part of *prakṛti*'s functioning. Not feeling himself to be doing anything, he remains free from any sense of sin or merit. What makes one bound to *karmas*, in fact, is not whether one performs them or not, but the attitude with which they are performed. Lotus leaves float on water, but water does not wet them. Likewise is a *yogī* remaining unattached to *karmas*. A sense of sin or merit is meaningful only when one thinks of oneself as the doer of actions.

To clarify further the attitude of such a *yogī*:

कायेन मनसा बुद्ध्या केवलैरिन्द्रियैरपि।
योगिनः कर्म कुर्वन्ति सङ्गं त्यक्त्वात्मशुद्धये ॥११॥

kāyena manasā buddhyā kevalair indriyair api ।
yoginaḥ karma kurvanti saṅgaṁ tyaktvātma-śuddhaye ॥11॥

Yogīs, by means of body, mind, intellect or even mere senses, do perform actions abandoning all attachments, aimed simply at self-purification.

Arjuna, whichever the kind of action he does, a *yogī* never thinks of it as his. He lives as part of *prakṛti*; he does actions also as part of *prakṛti* as every moment of its unforeseeable unfoldment demands. To back off from such exigencies causes guilt — another form of self-defilement. What a *yogī* achieves by performing *karmas* is avoiding all such defilements. The attitudes of a *yogī* or *yukta* and a non-*yogī* or *ayukta* towards *karma* are totally different. To clarify it further:

युक्तः कर्मफलं त्यक्त्वा शान्तिमाप्नोति नैष्ठिकीम्।
अयुक्तः कामकारेण फले सक्तो निबध्यते ॥१२॥

yuktaḥ karma-phalaṁ tyaktvā śāntim āpnoti naiṣṭhikīm ।
ayuktaḥ kāma-kāreṇa phale sakto nibadhyate ॥12॥

United with the Total, with fruits of action abandoned, one attains to well-founded Peace spontaneously. The non-united, desire-motivated and attached to fruits of actions as he is, on the other hand, remains bound.

Arjuna, a *yogī* continues to do those *karma*s that the exigencies of nature bring, never thinking of them as his. Experiencing uninterrupted Peace will also be normal and natural with him. The actions of non-*yogī*s, on the other hand, are always motivated by desire for particular results, which achieved makes them happy and failure to achieve brings unhappiness and disappoinment. So strongly attached are they to the fruits of what they do, that at times they curse themselves or even God.

One's becoming *karma*-bound or not, in short, depends not on doing or not doing, but on attachment or non-attachment towards the *karma*s and their results. How a real *yogī* renounces *karma*s I shall tell you now:

सर्वकर्माणि मनसा संन्यस्यास्ते सुखं वशी।
नवद्वारे पुरे देही नैव कुर्वन्न कारयन्॥१३॥

sarva-karmāṇi manasā saṁnyasyāste sukhaṁ vaśī ।
nava-dvāre pure dehī naiva kurvan na kārayan ॥13॥

Mentally renouncing all actions, the self-possessed remains happy with the awareness, "The embodied dwells in the nine-gated city, neither acting nor causing others to act."

Arjuna, renouncing *karmas*, as we have seen, is what marks a *jñānin*. His renunciation of *karmas* is not giving them up altogether, but mentally disowning them. Physically he will be seen doing *karmas* just as anyone else is, for to be active is normal with the physical body. Having nine orifices, the human body is often metaphorically concieved as a nine-gated city. Even as the activities normal to the city are taking place, its "dweller," the *yogī* or the Self, remains actionless, not making anyone else act either, as a constant witness of all actions.

Most live unaware of life being so, and so they always live bound to the *karmas* they do. They, doing each *karma*, think, "This *karma* is mine." This sense of being the doer of *karmas* is known as *kartṛtva*. What place this *kartṛtva* as well as the *karmas* has when looked at from My point of view, from the point of view of *Brahman*, I shall clarify now:

न कर्तृत्वं न कर्माणि लोकस्य सृजति प्रभुः ।
न कर्मफलसंयोगं स्वभावस्तु प्रवर्तते ॥१४ ॥

na kartṛtvaṁ na karmāṇi lokasya sṛjati prabhuḥ ।
na karma-phala-saṁyogaṁ svabhāvas tu pravartate ॥14 ॥

Neither *kartṛtva* nor *karmas* themselves is disposed by the Lord among beings of the world, nor is the doer's union with the fruits of action allocated. What works out here is simply the creative becoming of the Self.

Arjuna, I am the one Substance that appears as everything. This "I" is not simply the "I" in the person named Sri Kṛṣṇa; the "I" in you is also the same. That "I" is nothing but *ātmā*, the Self. It could also be called *prabhu* in the sense it emerges as everything (*prabhavati*). This emergence of everything is made possible by the invincible creative urge, called *karma* inherent in Me. I, actively finding Self-expression as everything, am known as *prakṛti* (Nature). Being part of My active self-unfoldment, every being thus emerged too remains active, yet is not the doer of any action. In this sense, I say here that I have not made anyone the doer of any *karma*. And more, no being is destined to do some pre-ordained *karma*s or to enjoy or suffer the fruits of such *karma*s.

Then what is all this that is going on in this world? It is My own *bhāva* or creative self-unfoldment (*sva-bhāva*) — *sva*, meaning "my own" or "one's own"— finding expression. Should there be a doer for all these actions, it should be the one Self-Reality or Myself. No individual is thus the doer of any action. Not only the physical activities, but the mental activities like deciding what to do and not to do, also are part of the *karma* of Mine.

A possible way of interpreting My teaching would be that everyone should do his duty as an offering to Me. It may look easily understandable to the common man as well. Such an interpretation implies that one is duty-bound. Being duty-bound is naturally followed by *kartṛtva* (the sense of agency of actions). But here I clearly say, no *kartṛtva* or *karma* has been imposed by Me on any being. Entirely different from duty-bound *karma*s — be they done as an offering to Me — are the *karma*s performed without attachment or sense of agency. These are not duty-bound, for they are done seeing all *karma*s as part of *prakṛti*'s boundless flow of action. My later words like *tat kuruṣva mad arpaṇam* (do it as an offering unto Me,IX.27) signify only that all *karma*s really belong to Me and that your mistaken notion of being their doer should be given up. Subtle though the difference in this interpretation is, not taking cognizance of it will result in losing sight of one of the main points of my teaching and its benefit.

Along with the sense of agency of actions go the sense of sin and merit. How are they counted by Me as well as by a *yogī*, and how they confound human life, I shall make clear now:

नादत्ते कस्यचित्पापं न चैव सुकृतं विभुः।
अज्ञानेनावृतं ज्ञानं तेन मुह्यन्ति जन्तवः॥१५॥

nādatte kasyacit pāpaṁ na caiva sukṛtaṁ vibhuḥ ।
ajñānenāvṛtaṁ jñānaṁ tena muhyanti jantavaḥ ॥15 ॥

The all-pervading One does not take cognizance of anyone's sinful or meritorious actions. Wisdom being veiled by non-wisdom, beings simply remain deluded.

Arjuna, the doubt whether what has been done is right or wrong arises only when one thinks of oneself as the doer. Finding it wrong, one is filled with remorse and fear of sin, and finding it to be right makes one satisfied with having done a meritorious deed. *Karma*s done with no sense of agency, on the contrary, are neither good nor evil, neither meritorious nor sinful; they simply are the workings of one's own inner creative urge.

One who perceives his own inseparable oneness with the beingness of the whole, one who perceives his own actions to be inseparably one with the actions of the whole, is a *yogī*. Others, are non-*yogī*s; they are unwise. They feel that they are the doers of actions; they feel that they are duty-bound. They are anxious about the outcome of what they have done; they are scared of sin; they long for merit; all of these having a single basis: non-wisdom (*ajñāna*). Due to *ajñāna* they remain confounded about their existence as well as *karma*s. How can one, ignorant of one's own reality, know the reality of the world? Not many ways are there to get rid of this non-wisdom. What the proper way is, I shall tell you:

ज्ञानेन तु तदज्ञानं येषां नाशितमात्मनः ।
तेषामादित्यवज्ज्ञानं प्रकाशयति तत्परम् ॥१६ ॥

jñānena tu tad ajñānaṁ yeṣāṁ nāśitam ātmanaḥ ।
teṣām ādityavaj jñānaṁ prakāśayati tat param ॥16 ॥

Verily, in whom non-wisdom is destroyed by the wisdom of the Self, in them wisdom, shining as the sun, reveals "That," the Transcendental.

Arjuna, what constitutes the essence of wisdom, as you may recall, was clarified in the last chapter. It is no knowledge that becomes clear step by step. Abrupt is its dawning, like a wave realizing itself to be ocean in essence, like an ornament realizing itself to be gold in essence — an inner transparence that dawns when searching for the Substance that oneself is constituted of. The absence of that wisdom is called *ajñāna* (non-wisdom), and the only way of removing this is by bringing in the light of wisdom, like dispelling darkness by bringing in a lamp.

The usage *tat param* ("That," the Transcendental) is to be specially noted. The Reality we are in search of is always referred to as *tat* (That) in Vedānta. To have that Reality alone as the one and only goal and the one and only guiding principle in life, is known as *tat-paratā*. And the search for "That" is to be made in the interior of one's own being, like an ornament searching for gold within itself. This search for Reality within oneself results in the realizing of the one Reality underlying everything. Suggestive of all these is the usage *tat param*.

What do such realized persons attain? I shall tell you:

तद्बुद्धयस्तदात्मानस्तन्निष्ठास्तत्परायणाः ।
गच्छन्त्यपुनरावृत्तिं ज्ञाननिर्धूतकल्मषाः ॥१७ ॥

tad-buddhayas tad-ātmānas tan-niṣṭhās tat-parāyaṇāḥ ।
gacchanty apunar-āvṛttiṁ jñāna-nirdhūta-kalmaṣāḥ ॥17 ॥

Thinking of "That" alone, finding oneself "That" alone in essence, established in "That," intent on "That," they, cleansed of all impurities by wisdom, attain to the state whence there is no return.

Arjuna, thoughts of sin, of being doomed to go to hell because of sin, or of having to be reborn to finish suffering the fruits of the sins committed in this life — all these have one basis: the belief that one is the doer (*kartā*) of one's actions. And this feeling is the outcome of non-wisdom (*ajñāna*). When this non-wisdom is dispelled with the brightness of wisdom, the sense of agency of action disappears, and one becomes freed of notions of both sin and merit, as well as of the thought that one needs to be reborn. A *jñānin* or *yogī* sees himself as unborn and deathless, without *karma* and *kartṛtva,* the one Reality in essence. As that Reality is indestructible, the question of its dying or being reborn does not arise at all.

The one and only Reality that a *yogī* sees in his being is seen by him as also underlying all beings. As every being is thus known to be one Substance in essence, one *ātmā* in essence, discrimination among human beings, based on caste, religion, gender or any form of social prejudice, appears senseless to him. To clarify it further:

विद्याविनयसंपन्ने ब्राह्मणे गवि हस्तिनि ।
शुनि चैव श्वपाके च पण्डिताः समदर्शिनः ॥१८ ॥

vidyā-vinaya-saṁpanne brāhmaṇe gavi hastini ।
śuni caiva śvapāke ca paṇḍitāḥ sama-darśinaḥ ॥18 ॥

In a brāhmin adorned with learning and humility, in a cow, in an elephant, in a dog and even in a dog-eater (out-caste), the enlightened perceives the same (Reality) alone.

Arjuna, what the word *paṇḍita*, rendered here as "the enlightened," signifies, has already been made clear to you. Here it stands for the *yogī* who perceives and experiences as undifferentiated both *karma-yoga* and *jñāna-yoga*. He sees the "same" (*samam*) in everything. The equality meant by the Sanskrit word *samam* is not simply the externally visible equality of things, but rather the internal equality owing to the sameness of substance, like the equality of gold in different ornaments. This perception of sameness is double-faced: to see one Substance alone in everything everywhere, and to see oneself as not different from that one Substance. To clarify this latter facet of sameness further:

इहैव तैर्जितः सर्गो येषां साम्ये स्थितं मनः।
निर्दोषं हि समं ब्रह्म तस्माद्ब्रह्मणि ते स्थिताः ॥१९॥

ihaiva tair jitaḥ sargo yeṣām sāmye sthitaṁ manaḥ ।
nirdoṣaṁ hi samaṁ brahma tasmād brahmaṇi te sthitāḥ ॥19॥

Even here, in this life, the creation-mystery of birth and death, is conquered by those with minds well stabilized in sameness. Blemishless indeed is the sameness of *Brahman*. And, therefore, they find themselves well stabilized in *Brahman*.

Arjuna, a seer of sameness perceives everything as one in essence, treats everything as equal. This Reality that exists equally in all, as all, is *Brahman*. The seer's own existence is also perceived as being in the same *Brahman*. The inseparable sameness of *Brahman* and himself is thus what the seer experiences and enjoys at every moment of life, no matter what its vagaries may be. This world, all worlds, the mysterious phenomenon of life in all the worlds, all are seen by the seer as one Reality — *Brahman* — unfolding itself, and he and his life appear simply as a minute, transitory part of that vast and boundless scheme of unfoldment. *Brahman*'s existence, birthless and deathless in itself, is what the seer sees in his own existence, thus seeing himself also as birthless and deathless. Equally without beginning and end is the phenomenal becoming that manifests in *Brahman*, each detail of it being transitory. What we call the world, the ever changing cyclic phenomenon of life (*saṁsāra*), all its pleasures and pains, are but part of that manifestation. Seeing oneself as inseparable from that Reality, is what makes one a *yogin*, a *jnanin*, a realized person, a liberated person, a seer of sameness.

Such seers of sameness live in this world seeing themselves as one with *Brahman*. In the life of such would be evident certain peculiarities perceptible to the discerning, some of which I shall point out to you now:

न प्रहृष्येत्प्रियं प्राप्य नोद्विजेत्प्राप्य चाप्रियम्।
स्थिरबुद्धिरसम्मूढो ब्रह्मविद्ब्रह्मणि स्थितः ॥२०॥

> *na prahṛṣyet priyaṁ prāpya nodvijet prāpya cāpriyam* |
> *sthira-buddhir asammūḍho brahma-vid brahmaṇi sthitaḥ* ||20 ||
>
> He does not rejoice on obtaining what is dear, and does not grieve on obtaining what is unpleasant either. With his understanding well stabilized and delusion-free, that *Brahman*-knower finds himself existing in and as *Brahman*.
>
> बाह्यस्पर्शेष्वसक्तात्मा विन्दत्यात्मनि यत्सुखम् ।
> स ब्रह्मयोगयुक्तात्मा सुखमक्षयमश्नुते ॥२१ ॥
>
> *bāhya-sparśeṣv asaktātmā vindaty ātmani yat sukham* |
> *sa brahma-yoga-yuktātmā sukham akṣayam aśnute* ||21 ||
>
> He will be unattached to the external sense contacts. That joy he finds thus in himself, in essence, is the undiminishing bliss enjoyed as the one united with *Brahman* through *yoga*.

Arjuna, the seer of sameness sees the same alone and no "other." Enjoyable objects spread out around pertain to "the other," the seer of sameness always remains unattached to and uninterested in them. The joy he feels always is that of himself being the Self. The eye seeing, the ear hearing, and all like sense perceptions are visualized by the seer as the one Self unfolding itself as the enjoyer, the enjoyed and the act of enjoying. The joy he experiences thus is not of his enjoying any object, but of the Self perceiving its own specific functional modes. Life and all the events in it are seen by him only as the never ceasing Self-contentment realized.

One who lives life seeing *Brahman* in himself and seeing everything as being the same as he himself, is a *yoga-yuktātmā* (one united with *Brahman* through *yoga*). This state of the *yoga-yuktātmā* is no other than that which is known as *ātma-sākṣātkāra* (Self-realization) and *brahma-sākṣātkāra* (*Brahman*-realization). Its ultimate value is in the experiencing of undiminishing bliss. This bliss and the never ceasing Self-contentment mentioned earlier are not two in essence. The non-difference of these two is not to be described; it may only be experienced. Viewed in one way, it is ceaseless Self-contentment; in another way, it is the undiminishing bliss of being one with *Brahman*. The two are like the two sides of a coin — neither side is reality, what is real is the coin that encompasses both sides. Similar is the experience of non-dual *ānanda* of the realized person, which has the above two forms of bliss for its two sides.

Wherein the seers of sameness find happiness has now become clear. Now I shall tell you wherein they do not find happiness:

ये हि संस्पर्शजा भोगा दुःखयोनय एव ते ।
आद्यन्तवन्तः कौन्तेय न तेषु रमते बुधः ॥२२॥

ye hi saṁsparśajā bhogā duḥkha-yonaya eva te ।
ādyantavantaḥ kaunteya na teṣu ramate budhaḥ ॥22॥

The contact-born pleasures, having beginning and end as they are, are verily the source of sorrows. They are not rejoiced in, O Arjuna, by the enlightened one.

शक्नोतीहैव यः सोढुं प्राक्शरीरविमोक्षणात् ।
कामक्रोधोद्भवं वेगं स युक्तः स सुखी नरः ॥२३॥

śaknotīhaiva yaḥ soḍhuṁ prāk śarīra-vimokṣaṇāt ।
kāma-krodhodbhavaṁ vegaṁ sa yuktaḥ sa sukhī naraḥ ॥23॥

He who is able, even here, before liberation from the body, to resist the agitation arising from desire and anger, is the *yogī*; he is the happy man.

Arjuna, we have alrealy seen that desire originates from the *prakṛti*'s *rajo-guṇa* (active modality of nature), as well as that anger always accompanies desire. Desire is felt for things external which are transient and a source of sorrow. In one who is a seer there is the will to resist desire, and only such seers become *yogī*s; only they experience Absolute Happiness.

The happiness a *yogī* experiences, is not derived from anything external. Where is it then derived from? I shall tell you:

योऽन्तःसुखोऽन्तरारामस्तथान्तर्ज्योतिरेव यः ।
स योगी ब्रह्मनिर्वाणं ब्रह्मभूतोऽधिगच्छति ॥२४॥

yo 'ntaḥ-sukho 'ntar-ārāmas tathāntar-jyotir eva yaḥ ।
sa yogī brahma-nirvāṇaṁ brahma-bhūto 'dhigacchati ॥24॥

He who finds happiness within, whose restful rejoicing is within, who is all effulgence within — he is a *yogī*. Having become *Brahman*, what he attains is self-effacement in *Brahman* (*brahma-nirvāṇa*).

Arjuna, the happiness a *yogī*, a seer of sameness, experiences within himself also derives from within. A busy man, after a restless day, may find some rest in a flower garden which he finds greatly pleasing. For a *yogī*, on the other hand, every moment is restful and filled with rejoice, all deriving from within. The one Reality that has assumed the form of the *yogī*, that also assumes the form of everything, is pure effulgence in essence — an effulgence that is aware of itself and thus self-effulgent. Since he knows that nothing exists other than that, the *yogī* feels that nothing external exists. What is thought of as external is nothing but various apparent facets of the same effulgence manifesting, of which one facet is the *yogī* himself. The *yogī* feels his existence thus simply to be a facet of *Brahman*'s existence. The flame of his existence as an individual thus dies out in *Brahman*. This experience of self-effacement could be called *brahma-nirvāṇa*. Who does actualize this experience in the life here and now, I shall clarify:

लभन्ते ब्रह्मनिर्वाणमृषयः क्षीणकल्मषाः ।
छिन्नद्वैधा यतात्मानः सर्वभूतहिते रताः ॥२५॥

labhante brahma-nirvāṇam ṛṣyaḥ kṣīṇa-kalmaṣāḥ ।
chinna-dvaidhā yatātmānaḥ sarva-bhūta-hite ratāḥ ॥25॥

Seers, with sins withered away, dualities eradicated, self-restrained, and delighting in the good of all beings, attain self-effacement in *Brahman*.

Arjuna, how a *yogī* always remains free from sins, above the duality of sin and merit, we have just seen. Finding himself to be one with *Brahman*, his doubts about Reality and meaning of life totally vanishes. Seeing nothing as external, the necessity of depending on something else does not arise at all. Thus, self-restraint and finding happiness in himself becomes natural for the *yogī*. Perceiving everything as various manifestations of one self-effulgent *Brahman*, the seer of sameness sees his interests and others' interests as identical; what he does for his benefit will therefore naturally turn out to be also for the benefit of all. As such, self-effacement in *Brahman* is spontaneous. A few more apparent signs of this effacement, I shall point out to you:

कामक्रोधवियुक्तानां यतीनां यतचेतसाम् ।
अभितो ब्रह्मनिर्वाणं वर्तते विदितात्मनाम् ॥२६॥

kāma-krodha-viyuktānāṁ yatīnāṁ yata-cetasām ।
abhito brahma-nirvāṇaṁ vartate viditātmanām ॥26॥

Self-effacement in *Brahman* is immediately around those of self-restraint, who know themselves full well, who are freed from desire and anger, who are of controlled mind.

Arjuna, self-effacement in *Brahman* is a state attained by those who have conquered desire and anger. The minds of those who have not vanquished their anger, do not remain in their own control, dragged hither and thither not by the infatuation of sense pleasures. Those who have gained victory over their own minds need wait no longer for the attainment of self-effacement, for to conquer desire and anger and to attain this goal are, as we have already seen, like the two sides of a single coin, one meaningless and impossible without the other. Such *yogīs* are to be considered the real Self-knowers, those who know what they are in essence. These are really the liberated and their spiritual discipline aimed at this attainment is made up of constantly seeing themselves as tiny sparks in the bon-fire of the self-effulgent *Brahman*. To go into more details of that discipline:

स्पर्शान्कृत्वा बहिर्बाह्यांश्चक्षुश्चैवान्तरे भ्रुवोः।
प्राणापानौ समौ कृत्वा नासाभ्यन्तरचारिणौ ॥२७॥
यतेन्द्रियमनोबुद्धिर्मुनिर्मोक्षपरायणः।
विगतेच्छाभयक्रोधो यः सदा मुक्त एव सः ॥२८॥

sparśān kṛtvā bahir bāhyāṁś cakṣuś caivāntare bhruvoḥ ।
prāṇāpānau samau kṛtvā nāsābhyantara-cāriṇau ॥27॥

yatendriya-mano-buddhir munir mokṣa-parāyaṇaḥ ।
vigatecchā-bhaya-krodho yaḥ sadā mukta eva saḥ ॥28॥

Putting aside external contacts, with gaze fixed well mid-way between the eyebrows, having the breaths going in and out through the nostrils well balanced, with senses, mind and intellect ever in control, the silent recluse ever intent on liberation, with wilful desires, fears and anger cast aside, does ever remain liberated.

Arjuna, there are some silent recluses (*munis*) who hold themselves back from sensual and intellectual temptations, keeping them in control, who conquer desire, anger, greed, and other passions, and having final liberation alone for the ultimate goal. All the above said qualities become naturally stabilized in them as though impelled by an inner clarity. These are the real seers of sameness. For them, to be one-pointedly interested in that which is of highest value in life, and to hold back from all that is of less value, is a constant spiritual practice. The two sides — spontaneous stabilization in the one and deliberate withdrawal from the many, along with a deliberate one-pointedness in the onward progression of life and a resultant spontaneous withdrawal from the distractions of life — thus become united in the inner being of a *yogī*. That inner being is nothing but

"Me," the Absolute or *Brahman*. The *yogī* then sees "Me" alone everywhere, as a result of which his being is filled with an unworldly peace.

भोक्तारं यज्ञतपसां सर्वलोकमहेश्वरम्।
सुहृदं सर्वभूतानां ज्ञात्वा मां शान्तिमृच्छति ॥२९॥

bhoktāraṁ yajña-tapasāṁ sarva-loka-maheśvaram ।
suhṛdaṁ sarva-bhūtānāṁ jñātvā māṁ śāntim ṛcchati ॥29॥

It is the peace one attains to on knowing "Me" as the enjoyer of all the sacrifices and austere self-disciplines, as the great ruler of all the worlds, as the friend of all beings.

Arjuna, let us now look back and see where we have reached:

Externally seen, we are all active, doing *karmas*. Every activity of ours is really a part of the total activity of *prakṛti*. Seeing the *karma* one does as really *prakṛti*'s and still remaining active totally unattached to the actions, makes a *karma-yogin* of one. Inwardly viewed, each has the experience of existing, an existence not differentiable from the existence of the whole, of *Brahman*. Intuitively experiencing oneness with *Brahman*, makes one a *jñāna-yogin*. In that these two *yogīs* realize their oneness with the whole, the two *yogas* are essentially one. A real *yogī*, therefore, is the one who experiences *karma-yoga* and *jñāna-yoga* as one *yoga*. Such a *yogī* perceives his own existence and all the activities in it, as a sort of offering of oblation into the sacrificial fire of *Brahman*. All *karmas* having been offered back to *Brahman*, he is no more the doer of actions (*kartā*). Having no *karma* of his own, such a *yogī* is not bound to the fruits of those actions. The *karmas* he happens to do thus are not on their own either good or evil, either sinful or meritorious. Living though in the world of *karmas*, he always remains untouched by them, like a lotus leaf that floats above the water without getting wet. No *karma* binds him despite *karmas* always going on; he perceives himself to be one with *Brahman*, as the one self-effulgent

Consciousness (*cit*) that witnesses all that is happening. His being undergoes self-effacement in *Brahman*.

What he does to make himself happy as a part of *prakṛti*'s activity, naturally makes every being in *prakṛti* happy. Being interested in the attainment of the one final goal, and not in any of the distractions of life, becomes spontaneous in him. He practises them as a spiritual discipline as well. What spontaneously develops in oneself and what one practises deliberately, thus come in unison making of him a perfect *yogin* who unceasingly experiences an unworldly Peace within, no matter what the vagaries of life's events are.

That the inner purity and clarity one attains as though impelled by an inner urge, could well be made more stable by making of it a deliberate spiritual practice, we have just seen. What we are going to deal with in the next chapter is the details of that pursuit.

Thus ends Chapter Five entitled Karma-Saṁnyāsa-Yoga of the Bhagavad-Gītā that embodies the yoga-śāstra of brahma-vidyā in the form of a dialogue between Śrī Kṛṣṇa and Arjuna.

VI

Dhyāna-Yoga

—The Yoga of Meditation—

Vyāsa:

The *Gītā* now enters its sixth chapter of teaching and the chapter is named *Dhyāna-Yoga. Dhyāna,* as you know, means meditation or contemplation. It is something rather to be practised with a wilful mind than to be described in detail.

There may be those who begin their spiritual pursuit with *dhyāna.* But what is to be meditated on or contemplated on should be clear before one begins to practise it, and that exactly is what we have so far been trying to make clear till the last chapter. At the close of Chapter V was indicated why we should practise it as well. What was taught in the first five chapters, in short, should be clearly kept in mind before one begins to practise meditation as the *Gītā* intends it, and that explains why *dhyāna* is taught as its sixth chapter. *Dhyāna,* in short, is not the first step any spiritual pursuit is to begin with. Any practice of meditation without an understanding of the basics of what is to be meditated on, will turn out to be a mechanical process; its result also naturally will be so.

The meditation taught in the *Gītā* in this chapter is to be practised not merely at any particular time at a chosen, secluded place. The seeker, on the other hand, has to transform his entire life as a progression of meditation. As part of it there is included the notion of sitting down at a quiet place comfortably and remaining absorbed in the Reality that one really is.

Without Arjuna asking any question, Kṛṣṇa here continues his teaching from where he stopped at the end of the last chapter. Any wisdom teaching, when it enters its higher and subtler realms, has necessarily to be so. Questions gradually vanish from the mind of the seeker and the *guru* freely enters new realms of revealing Truth enlightening the disciple.

श्री भगवानुवाच —

अनाश्रितः कर्मफलं कार्यं कर्म करोति यः ।
स संन्यासी च योगी च न निरग्निर्न चाक्रियः ॥१॥

śrī bhagavān uvāca —

anāśritaḥ karma-phalaṁ kāryaṁ karma karoti yaḥ ।
sa saṁnyāsī ca yogī ca na niragnir na cākriyaḥ ॥1॥

Śrī Kṛṣṇa said —

He who performs necessary actions, expecting of them no fruits, he is a *saṁnyāsin*, he is a *yogin*; not he who has left off fire-sacrifiecs; not he who has left off all actions.

Arjuna, what I am going to teach you in this chapter is not meant just to be understood properly, but is rather to be practised earnestly.

Our goal, looked at from wisdom's side, is to become a *jñāna-yogin*; looked at from actions' side, it is to become a *karma-yogin*; seen neutrally, the goal is to become a *yogin* who is also a *samadarśin* (seer of sameness). The self-effort one has necessarily to undergo to achieve this goal is what I am about to tell you in detail.

The first step of the meditation I teach you is none other than practising to see oneself as living as part of *prakṛti*, inseparably one with *prakṛti*, performing all actions that *prakṛti* inadvertently and unavoidably brings about, without thinking of oneself as their doer, and without expecting any personal gain out of them.

Spiritual aspirants may be there who think, giving up all Vedic rituals makes one a *saṁnyāsin*. Some may think one becomes a *saṁnyāsin* just by remaining doing nothing. Helping only to curb the natural urges in one's being as such practices are, they are never means of becoming a *saṁnyāsin* or *yogin*.

The urge for doing actions crops up from one's fancying of prospects. Giving up such fancying is the next step. To clarify it:

यं संन्यासमिति प्राहुर्योगं तं विद्धि पाण्डव।
न ह्यसंन्यस्तसङ्कल्पो योगी भवति कश्चन ॥२॥

yaṁ saṁnyāsam iti prāhur yogaṁ taṁ viddhi pāṇḍava ।
na hy asaṁnyasta-saṁkalpo yogī bhavati kaścana ॥2॥

That which is known as *saṁnyāsa*, know it to be *yoga* as well, O Pāṇḍava. Without giving up one's fancying of prospects, no one becomes a *yogin*.

Arjuna, from the essential oneness of *jñāna-yoga* and *karma-yoga*, seen in the last chapter, it must be clear to you how *saṁnyāsa* and *yoga* are also not different in essence. A *yogī* sees all the actions he does as *prakṛti*'s activity working in him. He is never urged to do anything by the idea, "This is my *karma*," "Its fruits are mine," "Such and such will be the resulting prospects." Such fancying in the minds of non-*yogī*s is what I call *saṁkalpa* here. By renouncing it alone one becomes a *yogī*. Without *saṁnyāsa* (renouncing), in other words, there is no *yoga*.

The meditation I teach here is not to be practised by seekers alone, but by *yogī*s who have attained their goal as well; but slightly different are the ways the two view their own practising. To clarify it further:

आरुरुक्षोर्मुनेर्योगं कर्म कारणमुच्यते।
योगारूढस्य तस्यैव शमः कारणमुच्यते ॥३॥

ārurukṣor muner yogaṁ karma kāraṇam ucyate ।
yogārūḍhasya tasyaiva śamaḥ kāraṇam ucyate ॥3॥

> For a silent recluse who is an aspirant, attainment of *yoga* is caused by *karma*s (without *saṁkalpa*). For the same recluse, on ascending *yoga*, withdrawal from activity is the motive force (for renouncing *saṁkalpa*).

Arjuna, the *yoga* I mean here is the one in which *karma-yoga* and *jñāna-yoga* find unity as we saw in the last chapter. Ascending to it is the goal of a seeker. His self-effort for such an ascent too is a sort of *karma*, and so he cannot simply do away with *karma*. He therefore performs, with complete sense of detachment, all the necessary actions that come about as *prakṛti* rolls on, thus sublimating all *karma*s as *karma-yoga*. *Karma*, for him, including his own spiritual effort, becomes thus a means of attaining *yoga*.

One who has already attained *yoga* is called *yogārūḍha*. He is a *jñānin* as well. Doing *karma*s, as was made sufficiently clear earlier, is of no concern for him. He is the one who has completely renounced all *karma*s, even as bodily activities are going on. Withdrawing himself from the world of actions — a withdrawal by renouncing all *saṁkalpa*s — is what a *yogī* has to continue to practise as a discipline. To clarify the nature of this renouncing of *saṁkalpa* further:

यदा हि नेन्द्रियार्थेषु न कर्मस्वनुषज्जते ।
सर्वसङ्कल्पसंन्यासी योगारूढस्तदोच्यते ॥४॥

yadā hi nendriyārtheṣu na karmasv anuṣajjate ।
sarva-saṁkalpa-saṁnyāsī yogārūḍhas tadocyate ॥4॥

> When one feels no attachment either to objects of senses or to actions, one who has renounced all fancying of prospects, he then is said to have ascended to *yoga*.

Arjuna, each of our five senses of knowledge offers a different sort of pleasure. Five organs of action — speech, hands, feet, excretory organ, genitals — are also there in us offering us momentary pleasures.

What happens to one who fancies such pleasures was shown to you in Verses 62 and 63 of Chapter II. Saving oneself from such a peril is possible only by restraining one's mind from the infatuation of such pleasures, and fixing it as the one goal of rejoicing eternally in the Self. Along with it has to happen the renouncing of all *saṁkalpas*. These have to become a constant practice in life.

No *yogī* can and is meant to withhold the natural functions of both the sense organs and organs of action, and any effort of that sort will be an unhealthy practice. The best attitude a *yogī* can have towards them is this: to remain an indifferent witness to all such functions. One remaining liberated from all actions and all *saṁkalpas* thuswise alone can actualize in life the state of ascending to *yoga*. I had pointed this out to you earlier in Verse II.28, as a basic principle to be understood. Now you have to practise it as a part of your *dhyāna*. What happens to oneself on constantly practising it, I shall tell you:

उद्धरेदात्मनात्मानं नात्मानमवसादयेत्।
आत्मैव ह्यात्मनो बन्धुरात्मैव रिपुरात्मनः ॥५॥

uddhared ātmanātmānaṁ nātmānam avasādayet ।
ātmaiva hy ātmano bandhur ātmaiva ripur ātmanaḥ ॥5॥

Let one uplift oneself by the self. Let one not let oneself down. Oneself, verily, is the friend of oneself; oneself is one's own enemy as well.

Arjuna, having made all that I have taught so far a constant practice, you will experience an upliftment that is effected by none other than yourself. On the other hand, if you do not practice it, you will unwittingly be letting yourself down. Not practising this discipline is caused by your own ignorance, and it is this same ignorance that keeps you unaware of being let down. One thus turns out to be the enemy of oneself. I shall now make explicit to you when it is that we become our own friends, and when our enemies.

बन्धुरात्मात्मनस्तस्य येनात्मैवात्मना जितः ।
अनात्मनस्तु शत्रुत्वे वर्तेतात्मैव शत्रुवत् ॥६ ॥

bandhur ātmātmanas tasya yenātmaivātmanā jitaḥ ।
anātmanas tu śatrutve vartetātmaiva śatruvat ॥6 ॥

Conquered by oneself, self remains friend of oneself. Not known and conquered by oneself, self remains enemy-like to oneself.

Arjuna, imagine that one knows what one really is in essence, as an ornament knowing itself to be gold. Then one's existence is not apart from the existence of the one Reality. The peace that this awareness brings about impels one to withdraw from momentary sense pleasures and pleasurable activities, and one makes such a self-withdrawal a constant practice in life. Such a one can be considered a *jitātmā* (one who has conquered oneself), and he will be a friend to himself. He in whom the opposite practices have become deep rooted will be an enemy to himself.

Such a *jitātmā* transforms his life as a pilgrimage through a golden mean in respect of all conflicting dualities. To make it clearer:

जितात्मनः प्रशान्तस्य परमात्मा समाहितः ।
शीतोष्णसुखदुःखेषु तथा मानापमानयोः ॥७ ॥

jitātmanaḥ praśāntasya paramātmā samāhitaḥ ।
śītoṣṇa-sukha-duḥkheṣu tathā mānāpamānayoḥ ॥7 ॥

One who, absorbed in Peace, has conquered himself, sees the Supreme Self alone abiding steadfast in all dualities such as heat and cold, pleasure and pain, honour and disgrace.

Arjuna, I have just told you who a *jitātmā* is. Remaining absorbed ceaselessly in peace, no matter what goes on all around, is one of his attainments. Though he exists among conflicting pairs of opposites such as heat-cold, pleasure-pain, success-failure, honour-dishonour, friend-foe, in all of these he will intuitively visualize the one Supreme

Self-Reality. Such a visualization is a constant practice, forming part of his *dhyāna*.

ज्ञानविज्ञानतृप्तात्मा कूटस्थो विजितेन्द्रियः ।
युक्त इत्युच्यते योगी समलोष्टाश्मकाञ्चनः ॥८ ॥

jñāna-vijñāna-tṛptātmā kūṭastho vijitendriyaḥ ।
yukta ity ucyate yogī sama-loṣṭāśma-kāñcanaḥ ॥8 ॥

A well stabilized *yogī*, remaining fully content with *jñāna* and *vijñāna*, with full control over senses, is said to be united (with Me). A lump of earth, a stone and gold look equal to him.

Arjuna, the differentiation of *jñāna* and *vijñāna* is to be discussed in detail in the next chapter. Lingering on it here therefore will be out of place. Suffice it to say for the present that knowing one Reality as constituting the essence of oneself and everything, is *jñāna*, and preceiving that Reality alone in each and every phenomenal appearance constitutes *vijñāna*. Understanding is important in *jñāna;* its application in life characterizes *vijñāna*. Unapplied theory, as we know, is of no value in life. To apply in actual life a theory or idea that is unsound, is equally senseless. Life is the field wherein philosophical understanding and its application have to find common ground. One who has attained this is a *jñāna-vijñāna-tṛptātmā* (one who remains fully content with *jñāna* and *vijñāna*).

The word *kūṭastha*, meaning "unwavering like a rock," in Vedānta signifies *Brahman*, referring to Its motionlessness. The same epithet is given to the *yogī* here, for he finds himself to be *Brahman* in essence. We have already seen how he restrains his senses and mind with his one-pointed interest always fixed in *Brahman*. All these characteristics are unceasingly evident in the life of a *yogī*.

A *yogī* sees a lump of earth, a stone and gold as one substance appearing in different forms, despite the vast difference in their market value, which is simply attributed to various commodities in the context of money and commerce. A *yogī* treats a clod and lump of gold on equal terms, for each, as he knows, has its own utility value, and one is not superior to the other.

A *yogī*'s behaviour pattern also is marked by certain thoughtful peculiarities which too form a part of his *dhyāna*.

सुहृन्मित्रार्युदासीनमध्यस्थद्वेष्यबन्धुषु ।
साधुष्वपि च पापेषु समबुद्धिर्विशिष्यते ॥९॥

suhṛn-mitrāry-udāsīna-madhyastha-dveṣya-bandhuṣu ।
sādhuṣv api ca pāpeṣu sama-buddhir viśiṣyate ॥9॥

He excels, who maintains sameness with regard to well-wishers, friends, foes, the indifferent, those in between, those who are hostile and those who are kinsmen, and also in respect of the virtuous and sinner.

Arjuna, the *yogī*, seeing the one Reality alone in everything, sees none as inferior or superior to another, regardless of how they may vary in appearance and character. For him, maintaining such a perception is part of his *dhyāna*.

Since this neutrality to all things is his natural disposition, it is to be seen that such people seek out secluded places and in the solitude there, become absorbed in the one Reality. How this is to be done properly, I shall tell you:

योगी युञ्जीत सततमात्मानं रहसि स्थितः ।
एकाकी यतचित्तात्मा निराशीरपरिग्रहः ॥१०॥

yogī yuñjīta satatam ātmānaṁ rahasi sthitaḥ ।
ekākī yata-cittātmā nirāśīr aparigrahaḥ ॥10॥

A *yogī*, remaining in seclusion, alone, with mind and body restrained, with no hopes, with no possessions, should constantly gather himself to the Self.

Arjuna, just by finding a place of seclusion such as a lonely cave and practising meditation, does not make one a *yogī*, nor does his practice become real *dhyāna*. Having a clear understanding of the Reality underlying life, restraining oneself and making one's day-to-day life and lifestyle fully in accordance with that understanding, should precede the beginning of any meditation. If one, as a natural continuation of all these, finds a secluded place and practises self-absorption in the one Supreme Self, casting off all the individuating conditioning factors, it will then be a fruitful *dhyāna*. Being in a secluded place will then help him constantly subdue his otherwise uncontrollable mind. Such a place will also help him practise desirelessness. Sitting in an uninhabited place will also be conducive to interiorizing one's interests. Where and how those who feel the need for such meditation should seat themselves and how to practise, I shall now give some suggestions on:

शुचौ देशे प्रतिष्ठाप्य स्थिरमासनमात्मनः ।
नात्युच्छ्रितं नातिनीचं चैलाजिनकुशोत्तरम् ॥११॥
तत्रैकाग्रं मनः कृत्वा यतचित्तेन्द्रियक्रियः ।
उपविश्यासने युञ्ज्याद्योगमात्मविशुद्धये ॥१२॥

śucau deśe pratiṣṭhāpya sthiram āsanam ātmanaḥ ।
nātyucchritaṁ nāti-nīcaṁ cailājina-kuśottaram ॥11॥

tatraikāgraṁ manaḥ kṛtvā yata-cittendriya-kriyaḥ ।
upaviśy āsane yuñjyād yogam ātma-viśuddhaye ॥12॥

At a clean place, having set his own firm seat, neither too high nor too low, made of *kuśa* grass, deer-skin and cloth one on top of the other,

And seated there, having made the mind aimed at the One with activities of senses and thought restrained, let him make himself firm in *yoga* for the sake of self-purification.

Arjuna, the mind remaining always interested in the one Reality is what I call *ekāgratā*, a word usually considered in Sanskrit equivalent to one-pointedness or concentration of mind. That one Reality is no one else than I, the Absolute. This very same "I" exists and functions as the "I" in everybody. The main obstacles to this *ekāgratā* are the activities of the senses and mental faculties, and therefore subduing these is a must. That this restraint does not mean mere withholding of their natural functions, has already been made sufficiently clear. The present practising of *dhyāna*, in short, has two facets: letting oneself merge with "Me" and restraining the faculties that cause distractions. One's own being, undifferentiated as body and mind, should, in short, find itself inseparably one with the One, in the present practising of *dhyāna*. To go into its details:

समं कायशिरोग्रीवं धारयन्नचलं स्थिरः।
संप्रेक्ष्य नासिकाग्रं स्वं दिशश्चानवलोकयन् ॥१३॥
प्रशान्तात्मा विगतभीर्ब्रह्मचारिव्रते स्थितः।
मनः संयम्य मच्चित्तो युक्त आसीत मत्परः ॥१४॥

samaṁ kāya-śiro-grīvaṁ dhārayann acalaṁ sthiraḥ I
saṁprekṣya nāsikāgraṁ svaṁ diśaś cānavalokayan II13 II

praśāntātmā vigatabhīr brahmacāri-vrate sthitaḥ I
manaḥ saṁyamya maccitto yukta āsīta matparaḥ II14 II

With body, head and neck erect and immovably steady, directing his gaze at the nose-tip and not looking in any direction;

With his being deep in serenity and fears gone, settled in the vow of a *brahmacārin*, with mind settled and thought given over to Me, let him sit unitedly aspiring to Me alone.

By practising such a meditation, what attainment one gains, I shall tell you:

युञ्जन्नेवं सदात्मानं योगी नियतमानसः।
शान्तिं निर्वाणपरमां मत्संस्थामधिगच्छति ॥१५॥

yuñjann evaṁ sadātmānaṁ yogī niyata-mānasaḥ ।
śāntiṁ nirvāṇa-paramāṁ mat-saṁsthām adhigacchati ॥15॥

Himself thus ever uniting with Me, the *yogī* of subdued mind, attains to the Supreme Peace of self-effacement and of abiding in Me.

Arjuna, one's meditation can be considered to have become fruitful, if a contentment that nothing remains yet to be known, that no more goal remains to be reached, fills one's being. This is comparable to the state of a wave that experiences oneness with the ocean.

Many are the possible hindrances — all of them hiding in oneself — to such an attainment. I shall now point out to you some of these:

नात्यश्नतस्तु योगो ऽस्ति न चैकान्तमनश्नतः।
न चातिस्वप्नशीलस्य जाग्रतो नैव चार्जुन ॥१६॥

nātyaśnatas tu yogo 'sti na caikāntam anaśnataḥ ।
na cāti-svapna-śīlasya jāgrato naiva cārjuna ॥16॥

This *yoga*, to be sure, is not for the one who eats too much, nor for one who does not eat at all. Neither is it, O Arjuna, for him who is given to sleep, nor yet for him who always keeps awake.

Arjuna, it should be clear to you, what kind of eating habit and sleeping habit one who yearns to become a *yogī* should practise. To be explicit:

युक्ताहारविहारस्य युक्तचेष्टस्य कर्मसु।
युक्तस्वप्नावबोधस्य योगो भवति दुःखहा ॥१७॥

yuktāhāra-vihārasya yukta-ceṣṭasya karmasu ।
yukta-svapnāvabodhasya yogo bhavati duḥkhahā ॥17॥

He who is moderate in eating and moderate in recreation, who engages in activities moderately, who is moderate in sleep and waking — he attains the sorrow-eradicating-*yoga*.

Arjuna, eating, recreation, sleeping, waking and all such are bodily needs. Apart from being moderate in respect of these, the *yogī*-to-be has also to be conscious of the impediments that crop up from his own mind. Not being able to control the mind, and having intense desire to possess things pleasurable are two such. Only a wilful mind can get over such obstacles, and, therefore, doing so also forms part of meditation. I shall clarify the imperativeness of such a discipline:

यदा विनियतं चित्तमात्मन्येवावतिष्ठते ।
निःस्पृहः सर्वकामेभ्यो युक्त इत्युच्यते तदा ॥१८॥

yadā viniyataṁ cittam ātmany evāvatiṣṭhate ।
niḥspṛhaḥ sarva-kāmebhyo yukta ity ucyate tadā ॥18॥

When his well-settled mind, desireless in respect of all desirables, finds itself well-stabilized in his own being (in the Self), then he is said to be a *yogī*.

Arjuna, the urges that distract a *yogī* from his chosen path could be bodily as well as mental. An uncompromising wilful mind alone helps him get over these — something that has to be accomplished on his own. What one feels on accomplishing it, I shall tell you:

यथा दीपो निवातस्थो नेङ्गते सोपमा स्मृता ।
योगिनो यतचित्तस्य युञ्जतो योगमात्मनः ॥१९॥

yathā dīpo nivātastho neṅgate sopamā smṛtā ।
yogino yata-cittasya yuñjato yogam ātmanaḥ ॥19॥

A lamp at a windless place flickers not. Comparable to it is the *yogī* of restrained mind, who unites himself with *yoga*.

Arjuna, a transparent vision of Reality, mind's steadiness, unrelenting meditation, the resulting experience of fruitfulness — all these become united in a real *yogī*. Such a *yogī* looks like this:

यत्रोपरमते चित्तं निरुद्धं योगसेवया।
यत्र चैवात्मनात्मानं पश्यन्नात्मनि तुष्यति ॥२०॥
सुखमात्यन्तिकं यत्तद्बुद्धिग्राह्यमतीन्द्रियम्।
वेत्ति यत्र न चैवायं स्थितश्चलति तत्त्वतः ॥२१॥
यं लब्ध्वा चापरं लाभं मन्यते नाधिकं ततः।
यस्मिन् स्थितो न दुःखेन गुरुणापि विचाल्यते ॥२२॥
तं विद्याद्दुःखसंयोगवियोगं योगसंज्ञितम्।
स निश्चयेन योक्तव्यो योगो ऽनिर्विण्णचेतसा ॥२३॥

yatroparamate cittaṁ niruddhaṁ yoga-sevayā ।
yatra caivātmanātmānaṁ paśyann ātmani tuṣyati ॥20॥

sukham ātyantikaṁ yat tad buddhi-grāhyam atīndriyam ।
vetti yatra na caivāyaṁ sthitaś calati tattvataḥ ॥21॥

yaṁ labdhvā cāparaṁ lābhaṁ manyate nādhikaṁ tataḥ ।
yasmin sthito na duḥkhena guruṇāpi vicālyate ॥22॥

taṁ vidyād duḥkha-saṁyoga-viyogaṁ yoga-saṁjñitam ।
sa niścayena yoktavyo yogo 'nirviṇṇa-cetasā ॥23॥

Wherein the well-restrained mind finds rest by the practising of *yoga*, and wherein one feels the contentment of the self perceiving the Self (of oneself perceiving oneself);

Wherein one understands what the ultimate happiness is, imperceptible to senses yet perceptible to awareness; established wherein one swerves not from the one Reality;

Obtaining which one thinks of no other greater gain, and established wherein one is not moved even by intense suffering;

> Such dissociatedness from the context of associating oneself with sufferings, is to be known by the name *yoga*. This *yoga* is to be adhered to with determination, free from despondence.

Arjuna, the *Bhagavad-Gītā* is a *yoga-śāstra* (a science of *yoga*). With *yoga* at its core, thought is developed systematically here. *Yoga* was first seen in Chapter II as a basic philosophical principle. The same was then perceived in Chapter III as *karma-yoga* and in Chapter IV as *jñāna-yoga*. How *karma-yoga* and *jñāna-yoga* get merged in one *yoga* was clarified in Chapter V. All these are rather conceptual in import. Transforming that *yoga* into a direct experience through meditation is what the present chapter accomplishes. *Yoga* thus attains a new dimension, deriving a new definition, not in terms of concepts, but rather as a value experience.

Well stabilized in this *yoga*, the *yogī* feels a constant serenity within. Understanding that the real happiness is to be found within, he rejects seeking happiness without. Becoming aware that his own being is nothing but *ānanda* in essence, he remains rejoicing in his own being. Finding joy in himself is a happiness that is unconditional, happiness that depends on nothing, and is to be considered the ultimate happiness (*sukham ātyantikam*). It is beyond the bounds of sense perception, beyond the bounds of mental perception, and its realization comes only as an illumination of inner transparence (*buddhi-grāhyam*). As a mental faculty, *buddhi* is our reasoning power, but here the word is used in its broadest sense, of "being aware."

The *yogī* of this experience will neither desire nor be likely to swerve from the conceptual *yoga* already seen. He remains content that nothing more remains to be known or attained. Even the most "miserable" situations in life will not make the *yogī* swerve from his stability for he remains aware that pain and pleasure together are part of nature. The contentment the *yogī* feels is untouched by what others see as misery; it is beyond the duality of pleasure and pain. The constant experience of this contentment is *yoga*.

Arjuna, this much should now be clear to you: that the conceptual awareness of *yoga* to be transformed into experiential transparence and Absolute contentment, needs the backing of a clear mind along with uncompromising will power. Restraining one's own mind, in other words, has a crucial role in *yogic* meditation. How to practise it, I shall tell you now:

सङ्कल्पप्रभवान्कामांस्त्यक्त्वा सर्वानशेषतः ।
मनसैवेन्द्रियग्रामं विनियम्य समन्ततः ॥२४ ॥
शनैः शनैरुपरमेद्बुद्ध्या धृतिगृहीतया ।
आत्मसंस्थं मनः कृत्वा न किञ्चिदपि चिन्तयेत् ॥२५ ॥
यतो यतो निश्चरति मनश्चञ्चलमस्थिरम् ।
ततस्ततो नियम्यैतदात्मन्येव वशं नयेत् ॥२६ ॥

saṁkalpa-prabhavān kāmāṁs tyaktvā sarvān aśeṣataḥ ।
manasaivendriya-grāmaṁ viniyamya samantataḥ ॥24 ॥

śanaiḥ-śanair uparamed buddhyā dhṛti-gṛhītayā ।
ātma-saṁsthaṁ manaḥ kṛtvā na kiñcid api cintayet ॥25 ॥

yato-yato niścarati manaś cañcalam asthiram ।
tatas-tato niyamyaitad ātmany eva vaśaṁ nayet ॥26 ॥

Abandoning without reserve all desires arising from wilful motives, curbing in the aggregate of sense-functionings on every side,

Slowly and steadily let him withdraw his mind, holding it up with understanding and wilfulness, and thus let him establish his mind reflexively in the Self, not letting it think of anything.

As and when the fickle and unsteady mind strays out, then and there it is to be kept a tight rein on, bringing it back under the sway of one's own Self-content.

Arjuna, what I said just now is not meant to be practised at any specific moment. The mind by nature is fickle; to motivate us is part of its function, every motivation creating in us desire. Every seeker needs to be constantly alert to the arising of such motives and desires. This awareness, backed by wilfulness, should be used in withdrawing the wandering mind and directing it towards oneness with one's own Self-content. Such motives and desires may arise at any moment, and so one's vigilance has to be constant.

The desire to go to a secluded place to meditate, as we know, arises only in the seeker willing to transform his entire life into a process of meditation. What should mainly happen internally in such a meditation, as pointed out in these verses, has two facets: one, the seeker distancing himself from the temptation of pleasurable objects, and two, keeping himself always attuned to the Absolute, the one Self-Reality or Me. These two, one ineffective and meaningless without the other, are mutually complementary and compensatory.

Now I shall tell you what one who practises meditation thus, experiences within himself:

प्रशान्तमनसं ह्येनं योगिनं सुखमुत्तमम् ।
उपैति शान्तरजसं ब्रह्मभूतमकल्मषम् ॥२७ ॥

praśānta-manasaṁ hy enaṁ yoginaṁ sukham uttamam ।
upaiti śānta-rajasaṁ brahma-bhūtam akalmaṣam ॥27 ॥

This *yogī*, his mind deep in peace, his *rajo-guṇa* (the spur to activities) pacified, himself becoming *Brahman*, free from blemishes, attains to unsurpassed happiness.

Arjuna, a peacefulness fills the being of the *yogī* who sees life as a continuous flow of meditation, and whose meditative practices are also seen as part of this whole. This is an internal condition, not discernible to others. Once the *rajo-guṇa* (the active modality of nature that spurs one to activities) is pacified, and desire, anger and other life-obstructing emotions are subdued, and the *yogī* perceives himself to be undifferentiated from *Brahman*, he is filled with the supreme contentment of knowing, "I am that supreme Self-Reality." Attaining *Brahman*-realization is somewhat like this:

युञ्जन्नेवं सदात्मानं योगी विगतकल्मषः ।
सुखेन ब्रह्मसंस्पर्शमत्यन्तं सुखमश्नुते ॥२८॥

yuñjann evaṁ sadātmānaṁ yogī vigata-kalmaṣaḥ ।
sukhena brahma-saṁsparśam atyantaṁ sukham aśnute ॥28॥

Ever thus uniting himself with *yoga*, rid of all sins, the *yogī* enjoys with ease the ultimate Happiness of having constant contact with *Brahman*.

Arjuna, what the nature of meditation is, and the experience of peace it results in, have been made clear to you. The *yogī* of that experience sees himself as a small ripple that emerged fleetingly in the infinite ocean of *Brahman*. He sees not only himself but also every entity in all the worlds in the same light. In his vision, all that exists is seen as ripples in the *Brahman*-ocean. *Brahman* alone is everywhere. The senses and whatever they come into contact with, the knowing mind and whatever arises as objects of knowledge, all ideas, concepts and imaginations formulated in the mind — all these are seen as nothing but ripples in the one infinite *Brahman*. Constantly having such an experiential vision is like having tactile contact with *Brahman*, and is to be considered the ultimate benefit of applying oneself to the *Bhagavad-Gītā*. How such a *yogī* perceives himself and all beings as inseparably one, I shall tell you:

सर्वभूतस्थमात्मानं सर्वभूतानि चात्मनि ।
ईक्षते योगयुक्तात्मा सर्वत्र समदर्शनः ॥२९॥

sarva-bhūtastham ātmānaṁ sarva-bhūtāni cātmani ।
īkṣate yoga-yuktātmā sarvatra sama-darśanaḥ ॥29॥

One of unified Self-being, the seer of sameness, perceives himself abiding in all beings and all beings abiding in himself.

Arjuna, what I said in this verse is simply another version of Verse 6 of the *Īśa Upaniṣad*. An ornament, realizing "I am gold," forgoing its identity with the ornament shape, is identifying itself with the one substance in all the ornaments in all the worlds. This new self-identity, in effect, means, "All ornaments abide in me, the gold-substance." Similar is the vision of the *yogī* who sees *Brahman* alone as real in himself and in everything. His identity being with *Brahman*, rather than with individual form, he sees himself abiding in everything that has come into being.

How does he visualize Me, the one Supreme Self-Reality and the world together as inseparably one, like gold and ornament, in his meditation, I shall depict to you:

यो मां पश्यति सर्वत्र सर्वं च मयि पश्यति ।
तस्याहं न प्रणश्यामि स च मे न प्रणश्यति ॥३० ॥

yo māṁ paśyati sarvatra sarvaṁ ca mayi paśyati ।
tasyāhaṁ na praṇaśyāmi sa ca me na praṇaśyati ॥30 ॥

He who sees Me everywhere, and sees everything in Me, for him I never cease to be, nor he ceases to be for Me either.

Arjuna, you know Me to be eternal and the one ultimate Reality. Yet I cannot actually exist without assuming some transient form. Every entity in all the worlds is a transient form assumed by Me. All those forms are changing while I remain changeless. How the eternal Reality (*sat*) and transient appearances (*bhāva*) remain inseparably one and non-dual, was made clear as early as Verse 16 of Chapter II, and the present verse is to be meditated on in that light. A *yoga* secret is implicit in this inseparability. Those who have realized it through the meditation we have just described, see Me alone in all the worlds. In Me they see all the worlds and all appearances. It is like seeing all ornaments in one gold, and one gold in all ornaments.

I, in their vision, am the one and only Reality; they see themselves too are this same Reality.

I am, as you know, immortal, and attaining immortality is the final goal of all beings. This goal is attained by seeing Me, the one immortal Reality, in themselves. Seeing oneself as immortal and seeing Me as immortal are but like two sides of the same coin.

Where does such a realized *yogī* find himself, the vagaries of his apparent form and events in life notwithstanding, I shall tell you:

सर्वभूतस्थितं यो मां भजत्येकत्वमास्थितः ।
सर्वथा वर्तमानो ऽपि स योगी मयि वर्तते ॥३१॥

sarvabhūtasthitaṁ yo māṁ bhajaty ekatvam āsthitaḥ ।
sarvathā vartamāno 'pi sa yogī mayi vartate ॥31॥

The *yogī* who, established in unity, meditatively perceives Me as abiding in all beings, even as passing through every mode of existences, he lives in Me.

Arjuna, you know that I am the one Substance abiding in everything, assuming the form of everything while remaining intrinsically unchanged. When an individual seeker constantly perceives My unchanging existence in his own being, that is *bhajanā* (meditative perception), which in essence is not different from *dhyāna,* the central theme of the present chapter. Though vagaries may still appear in the life of such a *yogī,* in his perception, these take place in Me rather than in his personal being. Such a *yogī* not only exists in Me, but he is also always conscious of existing in Me, as Me.

You should also be aware of how a *yogī* differs from a non-*yogī*. In fact, the non-*yogī*'s existence too is in Me, but he is quite unaware of this, and he thinks of himself as existing on his own. Then naturally, both birth and death are taken for granted as marking the beginning and end of life, and therefore the non-*yogī* remains always in fear of death. The *yogī,* on the other hand, sees Me alone in himself, and knowing Me to be both birthless and deathless, does not fear death. To make it clearer:

आत्मौपम्येन सर्वत्र समं पश्यति यो ऽर्जुन।
सुखं वा यदि वा दुःखं स योगी परमो मतः ॥३२॥

ātmaupamyena sarvatra samaṁ paśyati yo 'rjuna ।
sukhaṁ vā yadi vā duḥkhaṁ sa yogī paramo mataḥ ॥32॥

He who sees everything everywhere, whether pleasurable or painful, with a vision of evenness on a par with the Self, he is considered a perfect *yogī*.

Arjuna, the apparent forms I assume are both unpredictable and unimaginably varied, some pleasurable and some painful. A *yogī* considers all of these to be part of the Self's unfoldment, as the different ways in which the one *ānanda*-content of the Self becomes manifest. He neither rejects the painful, nor accepts the pleasurable, both considered to be simply natural parts of life.

This awareness is not to be treated as just a philosophical principle to be understood. Each one needs to make a self-examination and see how far from such a state oneself is.

अर्जुन उवाच —

योऽयं योगस्त्वया प्रोक्तः साम्येन मधुसूदन।
एतस्याहं न पश्यामि चञ्चलत्वात्स्थितिं स्थिराम् ॥३३॥

arjuna uvāca —

yo 'yaṁ yogas tvayā proktaḥ sāmyena madhusūdana ।
etasyāhaṁ na paśyāmi cañcalatvāt sthitiṁ sthirām ॥33॥

Arjuna said —

You have just expounded *yoga* as sameness in essence. O Madhusūdana, I do not see it steadily enduring owing to the wavering state of mind.

चञ्चलं हि मनः कृष्ण प्रमाथि बलवद्दृढम्।
तस्याहं निग्रहं मन्ये वायोरिव सुदुष्करम् ॥३४॥

cañcalaṁ hi manaḥ kṛṣṇa pramāthi balavaddṛḍham ।
tasyāhaṁ nigrahaṁ manye vāyor iva suduṣkaram ॥34॥

Wavering indeed is the mind, O Kṛṣṇa; it, for sure, forcibly keeps us turbulent. Holding it in control, I think, is very difficult, as is wind.

Kṛṣṇa, this is how I understand the *yoga* you have so far been kindly teaching me: *Brahman*, the Self-Reality, is one and the same in everything and It is the Substance that forms the essential content of everything. Realizing oneself as that Reality in essence, and always remaining steady in that sameness is *yoga*. Two-pronged is the way of attaining to it: one, restraining one's own mind from the temptations of sense pleasures, and two, keeping the mind always aimed at You, the most high, eternal Value. Both require a firmness of mind, but mind, as is well known, is by nature fickle. It changes every moment. We may hold something as of high value in life and try to attain it, but the wavering mind distracts us as if forcibly, from our own chosen path and goal, often making us remorseful later. Controlling this mind is as difficult as leashing the blowing wind. I am unable to find a means to fix myself firmly in the *yoga* state.

श्री भगवानुवाच —

असंशयं महाबाहो मनो दुर्निग्रहं चलम्।
अभ्यासेन तु कौन्तेय वैराग्येण च गृह्यते ॥३५॥

śrī bhagavān uvāca —

asaṁśayaṁ mahābāho mano durnigrahaṁ calam ।
abhyāsena tu kaunteya vairāgyeṇa ca gṛhyate ॥35॥

Śrī Kṛṣṇa said —

O Mighty Armed, difficult to control and restless doubtlessly is the mind; yet by repeated practice and sense of non-attachment, it can be held back.

Arjuna, it is a mere truism that mind is fickle and difficult to control, yet it is not totally uncontrollable. You are a mighty warrior. Your bodily might may not help in controlling your mind; what helps is *abhyāsa* (repeated practice) and *vairāgya* (constantly cultivating a sense of non-attachment) together. *Abhyāsa* means repeatedly reminding oneself of one's main interest, and directing the mind towards it again and again. The mind, owing to its fickleness, may stray away again and again; at every such instance one must become aware of it, restrain it, and direct it towards the goal. Repeatedly practising this makes the mind less vulnerable to temptations. In order to strengthen this new tendency being learnt by the mind, is to be practised *vairāgya*. With the constant and deliberate practising of this double-headed self-discipline, one's mind becomes controlled, and only then can one effectively practise *dhyāna* and become a *yogī*. To make it more explicit:

असंयतात्मना योगो दुष्प्राप इति मे मतिः ।
वश्यात्मना तु यतता शक्यो ऽवाप्तुमुपायतः ॥३६ ॥

asaṁyatātmanā yogo duṣprāpa iti me matiḥ ।
vaśyātmanā tu yatatā śakyo 'vāptum upāyataḥ ॥36 ॥

One with no self-restraint finds it hard to attain *yoga*; that is My conviction; but to the endeavouring one who is in his own control it is attainable through properly applied means.

Arjuna, self-restraint, in short, is the most important prerequisite for an effective *dhyāna*. *Dhyāna* practised by an unrestrained person never results in becoming a *yogī*, whether or not the *dhyāna* practised is as I have taught here.

Vyāsa:

Janmejaya, the *Bhagavad-Gītā*, as you know, is a dialogue between Śrī Kṛṣṇa and Arjuna. But rare are the occasions in which Kṛṣṇa answers Arjuna's questions direct to the point; the present one being such. This answer points out that there is no other alternative to self-restraint in the matter of attaining *yoga*, and that a real seeker has to be uncompromising in this respect.

अर्जुन उवाच —

अयतिः श्रद्धयोपेतो योगाच्चलितमानसः ।
अप्राप्य योगसंसिद्धिं कां गतिं कृष्ण गच्छति ॥३७ ॥
कच्चिन्नोभयविभ्रष्टश्छिन्नाभ्रमिव नश्यति ।
अप्रतिष्ठो महाबाहो विमूढो ब्रह्मणः पथि ॥३८ ॥
एतन्मे संशयं कृष्ण छेत्तुमर्हस्यशेषतः ।
त्वदन्यः संशयस्यास्य छेत्ता न ह्युपपद्यते ॥३९ ॥

arjuna uvāca —

ayatiḥ śraddhayopeto yogāc calita-mānasaḥ ।
aprāpya yoga-saṁsiddhiṁ kāṁ gatiṁ kr̥ṣṇa gacchati ॥37 ॥

kaccinnobhaya-vibhraṣṭaś chinnābhram iva naśyati ।
apratiṣṭho mahā-bāho vimūḍho brahmaṇaḥ pathi ॥38 ॥

etan me saṁśayaṁ kr̥ṣṇa chettum arhasy aśeṣataḥ ।
tvad-anyaḥ saṁśayasyāsya chettā na hy upapadyate ॥39 ॥

Arjuna said —

Kr̥ṣṇa, one of unsubdued mind, endowed with faith though, wandering away from the path of *yoga*, being unable to reach the final *yogic* attainment — what then is his destiny?

Fallen from both, deluded in the path of *Brahman*, with no footing, does he get destroyed like a rent cloud, O Mighty Armed?

You, O Kr̥ṣṇa, have to dispel this doubt of mine, for truly there is none save you who is competent to dispel it.

Kr̥ṣṇa, I am fully convinced that self-restraint is an essential prerequisite for the practising of *dhyāna* and thus becoming a *yogī*. One such effective self-restraint is known as *yati;* the others being called *ayatis*. There are many who are fully aware that they aim at *mukti*, the final freedom, and know also how to live in ways conducive to that attainment, but often fail to attain their goal merely for want of self-restraint. Deeply intent on *mukti* as they are, they give up all worldly interests, but they do not reach the final goal. It is as though they have lost both. What is the destiny of such? Is it similar to that of a cloud that scatters at the blowing of strong winds? Do all their good intentions and efforts go in vain? Please clear this doubt of mine.

श्री भगवानुवाच —

पार्थ नैवेह नामुत्र विनाशस्तस्य विद्यते ।
न हि कल्याणकृत्कश्चिद्दुर्गतिं तात गच्छति ॥४०॥

śrī bhagavān uvāca —

pārtha naiveha nāmutra vināśas tasya vidyate ।
na hi kalyāṇa-kṛt kaścid durgatiṁ tāta gacchati ॥40॥

Śrī Kṛṣṇa said —

O Pārtha, neither in the world here nor hereafter, is there destruction for him, for the destiny of one of propitious efforts, My son, will never be woeful.

Arjuna, your present question concerns not a *yogī*, but one who by chance has wandered away from the path of *yoga*. My teaching in general is aimed towards man becoming a *yogī* while living actively. A *yogī* sees himself as fully identified with Me, the birthless and deathless Reality; thus he himself also becomes birthless and deathless. A non-*yogī*, one who strays away from the path of *yoga*, never sees himself so; he, on the other hand, sees himself as an individual being existing on his own, as a being who was born once and will die once. Though everyone, both *jñānin* and *ajñānin*, both *yogī*s and non-*yogī*s, emerge from and exist in Me as My own modes of appearance, a *jñānin* or *yogī* only knows that reality. An *ajñānin*, ignorant of it, is worried about many things. One who strays away from the path of *yoga* is still such an *ajñānin*, though knowing what he aims at in life. He is, so to say, fallen from *yoga*, fallen from *jñāna*. He, thus, cannot have a *yogī*'s clear vision of life. Since your question concerns such aspects, my answer also will be along those lines rather than in line with My final conclusive teaching. What I am about to tell you now is, therefore, not meant to be considered part of the final teaching of the *Gītā*.

The one referred to above as having failed in attaining this final goal, though ignorant, is still intent on the most high value and so he should not be dissuaded in his efforts. His efforts, therefore, are being evaluated here in such a way as to encourage him further while not going against the general stand I have taken in the *Gītā* regarding *karma*. I take good advantage for this purpose of the already prevailing popular notion of *karma* and rebirth, knowing full well that it has relevance only for the ignorant, never for a *jñānin* or a *yogī*, and thus not forming part of the core teaching of the *Gītā*.

All *karmas* really have their origin in *prakṛti*, yet no *karma* goes fruitless. Each *karma*, each event in nature, is followed by an effect as its fruit, the propitious efforts made by the non-*yogīs* are no exception. Their effects have necessarily to exist somewhere in *prakṛti*. Being a non-*yogī*, he does not consider his efforts, his *karmas*, as pertaining to *prakṛti*, but takes them as his own and so thinks of their fruits also as his. Though ignorant, such good intentioned are not to be discouraged. The non-*yogī* does not understand that all *karmas* and their fruits belong to *prakṛti;* had he understood this, he too would be a *yogī*. The appropriate teaching which he can comprehend would be that he and his good deeds will neither be destroyed nor be fruitless. In his view, there is a world of sufferings reached by evil-doers, and a world of happiness reached by those of meritorious deeds. His efforts being propitious, he can easily be given the hope that he will reach the world of merits. Therefore I say,

---

प्राप्य पुण्यकृतां लोकानुषित्वा शाश्वतीः समाः ।
शुचीनां श्रीमतां गेहे योगभ्रष्टो ऽभिजायते ॥४१ ॥

prāpya puṇya-kṛtāṁ lokān uṣitvā śaśvatīḥ samāḥ ।
śucīnāṁ śrīmatāṁ gehe yoga-bhraṣṭo 'bhijāyate ॥41 ॥

Having attained the worlds of the meritorious, and having lived there for countless years, he who fell

> from the path of yoga (*yoga bhraṣṭa*) is reborn in the house of the pure and well-to-do.

Arjuna, My conclusive teaching in the *Gītā* is that all the worlds are but various manifest forms of the one Self-Reality. What exists everywhere as everything is one *ātmā* alone. That *ātmā*, all abiding, neither goes anywhere nor returns. The *yogī* is he who finds himself to be one with that omnipresent Reality, he too becoming omnipresent. But what we are concerned with at the moment is not the case of such *yogīs*, but of those who have fallen from *yoga* due to their lack of self-restraint. Such, being naturally ignorant of the one all-abiding Reality or *ātmā*, think of reaching heaven by doing meritorious deeds in this life. They hold that, reaching heaven after death, they can live there enjoying pleasures for a long time, and afterwards when the effect of the acquired merit runs out, they will come back to be reborn in this world. It is to persuade those fallen from *yoga* to continue their efforts that I say that faithfully doing meritorious acts, you will reach heaven after death, will live there for countless years, then return to this world to be reborn in the family of some pure and well-to-do people.

The notions that each individual has a different self, and that the selves departed go to the other world and come back are all against the basic stand of the *Gītā*.

Further persuading those who fell from yoga, I say:

अथवा योगिनामेव कुले भवति धीमताम्।
एतद्धि दुर्लभतरं लोके जन्म यदीदृशम्॥४२॥

athavā yoginām eva kule bhavati dhīmatām ।
etaddhi durlabhataraṁ loke janma yad īdṛśam ॥42॥

> Or else he may even be born in a family of some wise *yogīs*. Such a birth is rare indeed in this world.

Arjuna, being born in the families of the pure and well-to-do or in the families of wise *yogīs*, is not so common in this world. What matters is not which family the rebirth occurs in, but whether the rebirth enables the continuance of efforts made in the previous life.

These words in no way acknowledge the concept of rebirth as forming a part of My core-teaching. It admits only that such a notion prevails among the ignorant, which is helpful in persuading them to strive for a better life. My real teaching is that *ātmā* has neither birth nor death. How can a birthless *ātmā* have rebirth?

How the one thus reborn, according to his own belief, furthers his efforts to become a *yogī*, I shall tell you:

तत्र तं बुद्धिसंयोगं लभते पौर्वदेहिकम्।
यतते च ततो भूयः संसिद्धौ कुरुनन्दन ॥४३॥

tatra taṁ buddhi-saṁyogaṁ labhate paurva-dehikam I
yatate ca tato bhūyaḥ saṁsiddhau kuru-nandana II43 II

There he regains the awareness related to the previous body, and then strives futher for attainment, O Joy of the Kurus.

पूर्वाभ्यासेन तेनैव ह्रियते ह्यवशो ऽपि सः।
जिज्ञासुरपि योगस्य शब्दब्रह्मातिवर्तते ॥४४॥

pūrvābhyāsena tenaiva hriyate hy avaśo 'pi saḥ I
jijñāsur api yogasya śabda-brahmātivartate II44 II

By virtue of the former practice itself, he is irresistibly borne on, for even by becoming the seeker of *yoga* one transcends the *Brahman* understandable from scriptural words.

Those who have fallen once from *yoga* and still strive in successive births, will certainly attain their final goal as the next verse will state. That goal is none other than to directly experience oneness with Me or *Brahman*. This experience is not merely a principle to be understood; it is that ineffable state of being in which the experiencer-experienced duality totally vanishes — referred to in Vedāntic parlance as *aparokṣa anubhūti*. One may gain a clear understanding of *Brahman* through learning scriptures and basic textbooks on Vedānta. Such a conceptual *Brahman* is what is termed here as *śabda-brahman, śabda* meaning "the word," particularly of the scriptures. The *Brahman* realized by a *yogī* transcends this conceptual *Brahman*.

On who yearns to be a *yogī*, be it in one life or many lives, certainly crosses over the realm of conceptual *Brahman* and attains experiential realization, thus:

प्रयत्नाद्यतमानस्तु योगी संशुद्धकिल्बिषः।
अनेकजन्मसंसिद्धस्ततो याति परां गतिम् ॥४५॥

prayatnād yatamānas tu yogī saṁśuddha-kilbiṣaḥ ।
aneka-janma-saṁsiddhas tato yāti parāṁ gatim ॥45॥

But the *yogī* who strives with perseverence, purified of all sins and perfected through many births, thereupon reaches the transcendental goal.

Arjuna, the attainment a *yoga-bhraṣṭa* gains through the efforts of successive lives and that gained by practising *dhyāna* are not two in essence. The only difference is that the former seeker thinks of it as gained by sustained effort in many successive lives, while the latter knows the same as an experience in this very birth that comes about through transcending the realm where birth and death are meaningful and by attaining oneness with Me.

My answer to your question concerning the *yoga-bhraṣṭa* ends here. Now I shall tell you how great is the state of a *yogī*.

तपस्विभ्यो ऽधिको योगी ज्ञानिभ्यो ऽपि मतो ऽधिकः।
कर्मिभ्यश्चाधिको योगी तस्माद्योगी भवार्जुन ॥४६॥

tapasvibhyo 'dhiko yogī jñānibhyo 'pi mato 'dhikaḥ ।
karmibhyaś cādhiko yogī tasmād yogī bhavārjuna ॥46॥

Greater than ascetics is a *yogī*; greater than the wise is a *yogī*; greater than men of action is a *yogī*; O Arjuna, you therefore become a *yogī*.

Arjuna, the search for Reality is, in a way, a sort of self-heating, known in India as *tapas*. Those who practise it are called *tapasvins* (ascetics). Every such effort regardless of the religious or cultural background to which it belongs, involves a self-imposed austere discipline and is aimed at a final goal. This *tapas* implies another *tapas* undergone by Me or *Brahman*, in order to bring about the world from Myself. The Upaniṣads compare this latter *tapas* to eggs being brooded on for hatching, with the world emerging as a result. Man who is the present seeker is one of the beings thus emerged. He, in his turn, is now in search of the Reality that brooded on Itself, resulting in his own emergence. Finally he realizes, "I am that Reality." Similar to My brooding on Myself and creating man, is man's brooding on himself and finding "Me" as the causal Reality in him. The *tapas* understood here thus is a double-faced one, the ascetic's *tapas* being one of its faces.

The *tapas* a seeker undergoes is simply a means with a specific end in view. A *yogī*, on the other hand, has already reached that goal, and in that sense he is much greater than an ascetic.

Wisdom (*jñāna*) was seen in Chapter IV as a means to become a *yogī*. The *jñānin* (wise one) who knows Me, is greater than the *ajñānin* (ignorant) but inferior to a *yogī* who has realized oneness with Me and lives as Myself.

We saw that *karma-yoga* is a means to attain *yoga*. One, who performs actions unattached to their fruits and with no sense of agency, is far greater than the ordinary doer of actions attached to the fruits of action. A *yogī* is one who does not see *karma-yoga* and *jñāna-yoga* as being different, he is one who finds himself always in Me. From now on the *yogī* or *yukta* I refer to is such a one. He definitely is greater than those who are interested in actions (*karmins*), and even *karma-yogīs*. Your aim therefore should neither be to become a *tapasvin* nor to become a *jñānin* or *karmin*, but to become a *yogī*. Who such a superior *yogī* is, I shall make clear to you:

योगिनामपि सर्वेषां मद्गतेनान्तरात्मना ।
श्रद्धावान्भजते यो मां स मे युक्ततमो मतः ॥४७ ॥

yoginām api sarveṣāṁ mad-gatenāntarātmanā I
śraddhāvān bhajate yo māṁ sa me yuktatamo mataḥ II47 II

And of all *yogīs*, I hold him most fully united, who, full of faith, with his inner being abiding in Me, meditatively perceives Me alone in his being.

Arjuna, in Chapter IV we dealt with those who try to attain Me following various disciplines. All of them in a way could well be considered *yogīs*. Who a *karma-yogī* is and who a *jñāna-yogī* is were also examined adhering more strictly to the backing of the *Gītā*. Yet the best of all *yogīs* is the one who sees his inner being in Me and Me in his being, in the same way as a wave sees its non-difference with the ocean or an ornament sees its non-difference from gold. His meditative perception will always be, "I am *Brhaman*" (*aham brahma asmi*), which is one of the great dicta (*mahā-vākyas*) of Vedānta. Such a realized *yogī* is the one I call *yogārūḍha*.

Arjuna, let us now summarize what we saw in the present chapter:

Seeing the oneness of *karma-yoga* and *jñāna-yoga* marked the conclusion of the last chapter. To attain such a *yoga* state and find ourselves firmly existing in it is our goal. The only way for attaining this is, transforming life into a process of meditation, which is what this chapter focuses on.

No one else can render any help in this matter; one has to make efforts on one's own and uplift oneself. One should deliberately practise treating dualities such as heat and cold, pleasure and pain, honour and dishonour, with equanimity. One should also practise conquering oneself through self-restraint. Going beyond discriminations such as friends and foes, good and bad, should constantly be practised. The firmness of seeing not the external appearances but the indwelling lone Substance as Real, and uniting oneself always with that Substance should be attained through repeated practice. Viewing this inner aloneness may make one desire solitude to sit and concentrate on what is within. One will then find happiness in being desireless and in possessing nothing, which also has to be stabilized through practice.

The place one chooses to sit and meditate should neither be too high nor too low. One must sit there erect with the spine, neck and head held vertically, with the mind one-pointedly directed towards Me, and fully withdrawn from pleasurable external temptations. Then one feels as if one is burning down in My being (*brahma-nirvāṇa*), a state of mind comparable to that of the flame of a lamp burning in a windless place. Fully detached from sufferings of any kind, this state provides us with yet another definition of *yoga*.

All the experiences just described are to take place within one's own mind which in itself is flickering by nature. The ideas and imaginations arising in the mind arouses new desires, which the meditator should be fully conscious of, for it is this awareness of being tempted that enables him to restrain himself then and there and re-orient the mind towards the goal. This has to be a constant practice (*abhyāsa*) which helps the mind to become calm and capable of keeping at bay the temptations of *rajo-guṇa*.

He who is in such a state sees only himself everywhere, and everything in himself. With his inner being always abiding in Me, he sees Me alone in his being. He is the best of all *yogī*s; he is the *yogārūḍha*.

Thus ends Chapter Six entitled Dhyāna-Yoga of the Bhagavad-Gītā the essence of the Upaniṣads, that embodies the yoga-śāstra of brahma-vidyā in the form of a dialogue between Śrī Kṛṣṇa and Arjuna.

VII

Jñāna-Vijñāna-Yoga

— The Yoga of Wisdom and Experiential Wisdom —

Śrī Kṛṣṇa:

Arjuna, as you know, I am the one Reality that abides in everything. The one who realizes Me to be so, finds himself in Me. Such a one is the *yogārūḍha*; he is the one fully content with *jñāna* and *vijñāna*. The present chapter seeks to clarify what this contentment is like.

I am not an inert Reality, as you know full well. I do not remain inactive, always appearing in My own manifested forms. Though immutable as a substance in its abstract sense, My manifestations are all changeful, each having its own unique peculiarities. To use the gold-ornament analogy, gold as substance is immutable; its manifestations, the ornaments, are changeable, each having its own peculiarity and specific use. So is everything in all the worlds; each entity in it is unique and has its own value. Every such peculiarity is nothing but an aspect of My own manifestations, and in it should be seen My own being. Seeing Me as the one all-underlying Reality constitutes *jñāna*; seeing Me alone in every peculiarity of all apparent forms is *vijñāna*, *vi* stands for *viśeṣa* (specificity). One who is content with both sees Me alone in unity and in multiplicity. Now let us proceed:

श्री भगवानुवाच —

मय्यासक्तमनाः पार्थ योगं युञ्जन्मदाश्रयः ।
असंशयं समग्रं मां यथा ज्ञास्यसि तच्छृणु ॥१॥

śrī bhagavān uvāca —

mayy āsakta-manāḥ pārtha yogaṁ yuñjan mad-āśrayaḥ I
asaṁśayaṁ samagraṁ māṁ yathā jñāsyasi tac chṛṇu II1 II

Śrī Kṛṣṇa said —

With mind clinging to Me fervently, experiencing *yoga* and depending on Me alone, how you will know Me comprehensively, having no doubt, do hear now.

Arjuna, the *yogārūḍha* referred to in the last chapter knows Me, as a wave knows the ocean. This being no knowledge of something else, it is necessarily comprehensive, having no chance for doubt. Comprehensive knowledge leaves nothing unknown beyond its bounds. Its doubtlessness is in being non-mediate, intuitive perception (*aparokṣa anubhūti*). What are included in this comprehensive vision and how unique it is, I shall tell you:

ज्ञानं ते ऽहं सविज्ञानमिदं वक्ष्याम्यशेषतः ।
यज्ज्ञात्वा नेह भूयो ऽन्यज्ज्ञातव्यमवशिष्यते ॥२॥

jñānam te 'haṁ savijñānam idaṁ vakṣyāmy aśeṣataḥ I
yaj jñātvā neha bhūyo 'nyaj-jñātavyaṁ avaśiṣyate II2 II

I shall elucidate to you the nature of *jñāna* along with *vijñāna* leaving out nothing, which known, nothing will remain yet to be known.

Arjuna, by comprehensive knowledge I mean *jñāna* along with *vijñāna*. There is, in fact, nothing to be known other than the one Reality and Its manifestations; the Reality is one and manifestations many. Both the one and the many are thus included in this comprehensive knowledge. The ultimate benefit of adopting the *Gītā* and its teaching as a life-guide is that this knowledge brings the contentment of realizing that nothing more remains to be known in life. This knowledge is no common place one. See how rare it is:

मनुष्याणां सहस्रेषु कश्चिद्यतति सिद्धये ।
यततामपि सिद्धानां कश्चिन्मां वेत्ति तत्त्वतः ॥३॥

manuṣyāṇāṁ sahasreṣu kaścid yatati siddhaye ।
yatatām api siddhānāṁ kaścin māṁ vetti tattvataḥ ॥3 ॥

Among thousands of men, one perchance strives for the perfection of attainment. Even among those who strive thus and attain the goal, one perchance knows Me right to the core.

Arjuna, I, the one and non-dual Reality, as has been indicated, have two apparent facets: one immutable and the other mutable; the one attributeless and the other full of attributes; the one unconditioned and the other conditioned. The non-dual Me, appears as having these two facets owing to the creativity inherent in Me. This creativity finding expression is called *prakṛti*, as we saw in Chapter III. Changefulness and changelessness, therefore, are to be considered the two aspects of My own *prakṛti* that brings forth from Me all multitudinous appearances. How this *prakṛti* finds expression in Me, I shall tell you:

भूमिरापो ऽनलो वायुः खं मनो बुद्धिरेव च ।
अहंकार इतीयं मे भिन्ना प्रकृतिरष्टधा ॥४॥
अपरेयमितस्त्वन्यां प्रकृतिं विद्धि मे पराम् ।
जीवभूतां महाबाहो ययेदं धार्यते जगत् ॥५॥

bhūmir āpo 'nalo vāyuḥ khaṁ mano buddhir eva ca ।
ahaṁkāra itīyaṁ me bhinnā prakṛtir aṣṭadhā ॥4 ॥

apareyam itas tv anyāṁ prakṛtiṁ viddhi me parām ।
jīva-bhūtāṁ mahā-bāho yayedaṁ dhāryate jagat ॥5 ॥

Earth, water, fire, air, space, mind, intellect, I-sense — these are the eightfold divisions of My *prakṛti.*

Know this to be My immanent (*aparā*) *prakṛti.* Different is My transcendental (*parā*) *prakṛti,* O

Mighty Armed, that, becoming life-element, sustains the entire changeful world.

Arjuna, the first five sub-divisions of my *aparā-prakṛti* constitute the five physical elements and the other three mental functions. What we call the world, as you know, is an aggregate of physical and mental aspects of experience, all of which together form the apparent aspect of My existence, and hence is called the *aparā-prakṛti*.

The world, for sure, is more than an aggregate of such elements, it is a living world — a life principle sustains each entity separately as well as the entire existence as a cosmic system. That aspect is My *parā* (transcendental) *prakṛti*.

My having these two *prakṛtis* does not in any way mean that My being is divided into two or many. I remain one always. These two *prakṛtis* are mentioned here only as an aid to seeing Me as one, and at the same time as having countlessly multiple apparent forms. Just because something is conceived of in two different ways, the entity conceived does not become divided into two. Likewise, My non-duality remains unaffected in spite of conceiving two *prakṛtis* in Me. How I, urged by My own *prakṛti*, assume the form of the ever changing world, I shall tell you:

एतद्योनीनि भूतानि सर्वाणीत्युपधारय ।
अहं कृत्स्नस्य जगतः प्रभवः प्रलयस्तथा ॥६ ॥
मत्तः परतरं नान्यत्किञ्चिदस्ति धनञ्जय ।
मयि सर्वमिदं प्रोतं सूत्रे मणिगणा इव ॥७ ॥

etad-yonīni bhūtāni sarvāṇīty upadhāraya ।
ahaṁ kṛtsnasya jagataḥ prabhavaḥ pralayas tathā ॥6 ॥

mattaḥ parataraṁ nānyat kiñcid asti dhanañjaya ।
mayi sarvam idaṁ protaṁ sūtre maṇi-gaṇā iva ॥7 ॥

Know that all beings have this (*prakṛti*) for their common source. I am the origin and dissolution of this entire changeful world.

Nothing whatsoever superior to Me is there, O Dhanañjaya. In Me is strung all this, as are rows of pearls on a string.

Arjuna, two are the questions all philosophical enquiry tries to answer: Who am I? Whence is this world? The only possible and plausible answer is: I, the Absolute, having the above-said two inherent *prakṛtis*, am the only source of all that has come into being. The two-faced *prakṛti* is what makes Me emanate everything from My own being. Such beings, like waves from the ocean, do not exist different from Me. Waves are many and the ocean only one, but the two are undifferentiably one. Likewise, beings are many and I am one; but the two are inseparably one. No Reality higher than this all-underlying Me exists. Though My being is as the one Reality that appears as all, it remains invisible, for what is visible everywhere are only the apparent forms. My existence in beings is comparable to that of the invisible string in a necklace of pearls. Without it the pearls cannot form a necklace; without Me the beings cannot exist either as themselves or as the world.

All beings have their own unique distinguishing qualities. They are as they are because I abide in all of them. Those keen in perception, therefore, will intuitively see Me even in the specifying qualities and aspects of each and every entity that forms part of the world, which perception is what we call *vijñāna* here. To show you a few instances:

रसोऽहमप्सु कौन्तेय प्रभास्मि शशिसूर्ययोः ।
प्रणवः सर्ववेदेषु शब्दः खे पौरुषं नृषु ॥८॥

raso 'ham apsu kaunteya prabhāsmi śaśi-sūryayoḥ ।
praṇavaḥ sarva-vedeṣu śabdaḥ khe pauruṣaṁ nṛṣu ॥8॥

The quality of taste in water is Myself, O son of Kuntī; the quality of brightness in sun and moon is Myself; the sound *Auṁ* (*praṇava*) in all the Vedas is Myself; the sound-quality in space is Myself; the human quality in men is Myself.

Arjuna, the physical world, as conceived by the *ṛṣis* of India, is constituted of five basic elements: space, air, fire, water and earth. Each of these, having its own specifying quality, also has the qualities of the preceding elements. Thus water, while also having the sound-quality of space, touch-quality of air, form-quality of fire, is itself qualified specifically by taste. Tasting water, you should therefore, perceive My being. It thus becomes a part of *vijñāna.*

The sun and the moon similarly, with brightness for their specifying quality, shine in the sky forming part of the cosmic system, simply because of Me. You, seeing and enjoying their brightness, therefore, should perceive My existence in them.

The one Reality all the scriptures try to reveal through words is Myself, and the one-syllabled word that signifies Me is *AUṀ*. It is, therefore, the one word that makes all the words of all the scriptures meaningful. Pronouncing or hearing the sound *AUṀ*, too, you should perceive Me, which perception transforms your *jñāna* into *vijñāna.*

That which functions as space (*khaṁ* or *ākāśa*), having sound for its specifying quality, is Myself become manifest, and so in all the sounds you hear you should perceive Me. Similar is the human quality in Men.

पुण्यो गन्धः पृथिव्यां च तेजश्चास्मि विभावसौ ।
जीवनं सर्वभूतेषु तपश्चास्मि तपस्विषु ॥९॥

puṇyo gandhaḥ pṛthivyāṁ ca tejaś cāsmi vibhāvasau ।
jīvanaṁ sarva bhūteṣu tapaś cāsmi tapasviṣu ॥9॥

The pure fragrance of earth and the luminosity of fire are Myself. So is the aliveness in all living beings, and the *tapas* in ascetics (*tapasvins*) as well.

Arjuna, earth is the grossest of all physical elements, and its specifying particular quality is fragrance while it also has the qualities of the other four elements. The one all-supporting element, earth and its specifying quality could be thought of as having a special divinity and purity of its own. In this peculiarity also you should see Me. Similar are the qualities of luminosity in fire, aliveness in living beings, *tapas* (austere self-discipline) in the ascetics, all of which are explicable. Even as I am all these specifying qualities I am also the causal Substance in all of these. Seeing both the aspects together:

बीजं मां सर्वभूतानां विद्धि पार्थ सनातनम्।
बुद्धिर्बुद्धिमतामस्मि तेजस्तेजस्विनामहम् ॥१०॥
बलं बलवतां चाहं कामरागविवर्जितम्।
धर्माविरुद्धो भूतेषु कामो ऽस्मि भरतर्षभ ॥११॥

bījaṁ māṁ sarva-bhūtānāṁ viddhi pārtha sanātanam |
buddhir buddhimatām asmi tejas tejasvinām aham ||10 ||

balaṁ balavatāṁ cāhaṁ kāma-rāga-vivarjitam |
dharmāviruddho bhūteṣu kāmo 'smi bharatarṣabha ||11 ||

Know Me, O Pārtha, as the eternal seed of all beings. I am the intellect in intellectuals, and brightness in the brilliant too.

I am strength in the strong, devoid of desire and attachment. Desire in living beings which are not contrary to the all sustaining system, also I am, O Best of the Bharatas.

Arjuna, every being is endowed by Me with a strength of its own that urges it on with its life-activities, which are meant to keep them in flow with the unpredictable creativity of nature. Man is no exception. He too should use it to enable himself to live as one with nature, rather than for personal gains at the expense of the cosmic order and the interests of other beings in it. The freedom of man to make use of his strength with discretion also gives him responsibility. The quality of strength in man thus utilized with a sense of responsibility, unmotivated by personal attachments, sentiments and desires, is to be considered Myself. Not that man has to be desireless altogether. Desire, as everyone knows, is the only force that ensures the continuance of life, for no propagation of life is possible in the absence of desire (*kāma*). My creating the world from Myself, too, you should remember, is urged by My own desire. That desire is present in every being that has emerged from Me. This desire sustains the total life and it is to be seen as marking My presence.

That all such particular entities having particular qualities originate from Me owing to the two-faceted *prakṛti* of Mine, I have made clear to you. This *prakṛti* too has its own qualities known as *guṇas* — *sattva, rajas* and *tamas* — that keep it restless and thus the cosmic system ever flowing. How these *guṇas* are related to Me I shall now clarify:

ये चैव सात्त्विका भावा राजसास्तामसाश्च ये ।
मत्त एवेति तान्विद्धि न त्वहं तेषु ते मयि ॥१२॥

ye caiva sāttvikā bhāvā rājasās tāmasāś ca ye ।
matta eveti tān viddhi na tvahaṁ teṣu te mayi ॥12॥

The manifestations that are pure and clear (*sāttvika*), active (*rājasa*), and inert and dark (*tāmasa*) in nature — know them as originating from Me. Still I am not to be seen in them, but they in Me.

The specifics of these three *guṇas* (nature-modalities) remain to be dealt with in detail in a later chapter. For the present, you have to remain satisfied by understanding that My *prakṛti* has inherent in it three modalities or *guṇas* named *sattva, rajas* and *tamas*, causing the appearance of all the changeful manifestations in the otherwise immutable Me. Mentioning it here in advance has a special relevance: It could be thought that I am to be seen in these three *guṇas* become manifest as well, similar to seeing Me in the taste of water or in the brightness of sun and moon. But this is not so as the next verse will make it clear. These *guṇas* cause the delusion of seeing the various beings and their peculiarities as Real in themselves, instead of seeing Me in them. For this reason I say, I am not to be seen in them, though their activities take place in My own *prakṛti*. See how these *guṇas* delude ordinary human beings:

त्रिभिर्गुणमयैर्भावैरेभिः सर्वमिदं जगत्।
मोहितं नाभिजानाति मामेभ्यः परमव्ययम्॥१३॥

tribhir guṇamayair bhāvair ebhiḥ sarvam idaṁ jagat ।
mohitaṁ nābhijānāti mām ebhyaḥ param avyayam ॥13॥

Deluded is this entire world by these three *guṇa*s become manifest, and so I, the transcendental and the unexpended, remain unknown.

Arjuna, *prakṛti* My creative urge become manifest — essentially composed of three *guṇa*s, and these in their ever changing proportion are the cause of the never ending flow of ever changing appearances in nature. This very *prakṛti* deludes its own creations by giving the impression that appearances are real, as well as by keeping them oblivious of Me, the undiminishing Reality in all of them. The world and its beings, in other words, are so created by Me in Myself that they remain unaware of the need of knowing Me as if the very creativity in Me puts a veil over Myself. There is an undefinability, a mystery, here.

दैवी ह्येषा गुणमयी मम माया दुरत्यया।
मामेव ये प्रपद्यन्ते मायामेतां तरन्ति ते॥१४॥

daivī hy eṣā guṇamayī mama māyā duratyayā ।
mām eva ye prapadyante māyām etāṁ taranti te ॥14॥

This mysterious *māyā* of Mine, three *guṇa*s in essence, is hard indeed to overcome. Nevertheless, this *māyā* is crossed over by those who attain Me.

Arjuna, *māyā* is my mysterious potency to create from Myself all specific entities, each with its own specific form, name and characteristics. *Māyā* also makes of the very same appearances a veil to overcover Me. "So is it," is the only explanation we can give for it. The peculiar characteristics of everything that emerges of this mysterious, undefinable factor occurs as if guided by chance though cohering to an overall structure. This element of chance or fate in

Sanskrit is known as *daivam; daivī,* its feminine form, is used to qualify the feminine word *māyā*.

I gave the name *māyā* to this mysterious potency in Me because it is something non-existent, the word *māyā* meaning "that which does not exist." What really exists is Myself alone, the world being only a phenomenon that appears in Me. Though there is no need of a third factor existing between Me and the world, there is a mystery that veils My being. That is *māyā*. It is a very hard obstacle to overcome, but he who sees Me, equally inexplicably, overcomes it. Indeed there exists no other means of accomplishing this.

To say that *māyā* obstructs knowing Me and that attaining Me alone is the way to overcome *māyā,* may look logically implausible. But logic is not the means to attaining Me. No logic or evidence is needed for an earthen pot to look at itself and realize its being clay in essence. Likewise, the seeker, without having recourse to any logical means looks inwards at himself to see Me, the essential content of all. That non-indirect intuitive perception (*aparokṣa anubhūti*) is far from any direct or indirect knowledge arrived at logically.

This possibility of having the intuitive perception of Reality in one's own being is taken away by the very same *māyā*. See what happens to those who are completely under the spell of *māyā*:

न मां दुष्कृतिनो मूढाः प्रपद्यन्ते नराधमाः ।
माययापहृतज्ञाना आसुरं भावमाश्रिताः ॥१५॥

na māṁ duṣkṛtino mūḍhāḥ prapadyante narādhamāḥ ।
māyayāpahṛta-jñānā āsuraṁ bhāvam āśritāḥ ॥15॥

The evil-doers, the foolish, the lowest among men — they do not attain Me, for, with wisdom taken away by *māyā*, they embrace demonic nature.

Arjuna, knowing that what causes the emanation of beings from Myself is *māyā*, purifies one's mind, making it of divine (*daivī*) characteristics. Others, under the spell of *māyā,* remain ignorant (*ajñānins*); infatuated by the pleasures that apparent forms offer, they remain pleasure-mongers. The more they become so, the more they are distanced from Me, thus becoming filled with demonic nature (*āsurī-bhāva*). How the *daivī* and *āsurī* natures in men are to be distinguished is reserved to be detailed in Chapter XVI. This much you may keep in mind for now: those aptitudes which help one attain wisdom and thus the release from all bondage, are *daivī* (divine), and those that make one fall into the mire of ignorance and thus into bondage, are *āsurī* (demonic). One who is under the spell of *māyā*, can only be of demonic character.

Those who see Me alone as Real, live free of all *karma* — causing bondage — for in their perception, all *karma*s take place in Me, and so are not theirs. Those who are engaged in activities with such a perception can be counted as *sukṛti*s (those who do good deeds) from the point of view of My teaching. Those who do *karma*s, thinking, "This is my *karma*; its fruits too are mine," live in constant fear of sin (*pāpa*) and of the hell that they think they are destined to go to. Such, in the present context, are to be considered evil-doers (*duṣkṛti*s). I am not the goal they reach, for they do not see Me as their goal at all.

Evil-doers also have their own concept of life's goals though wrongly conceived. They too pray to God for the fulfilment of their personal desires. Those who are not deluded, on the other hand, seek God as the Reality in themselves. The deluded and the undeluded seek God or Me, each in his own way, each having his own end in view. I shall, therefore, give an overall classification of those who seek Me based on the goal they aim at:

चतुर्विधा भजन्ते मां जनाः सुकृतिनोऽर्जुन ।
आर्तो जिज्ञासुरर्थार्थी ज्ञानी च भरतर्षभ ॥१६॥

caturvidhā bhajante māṁ janāḥ sukṛtino 'rjuna ।
ārto jijñāsur arthārthī jñānī ca bharatarṣabha ॥16॥

Arjuna, of four types are the virtuous who adore Me meditatively: the distressed, wisdom seekers, aspirants of wealth and the wise, O Best of the Bharatas.

Arjuna, of the four, those in distress seek Me with the prayer, "O God, please save me from all these miseries." Those in search of worldly well-being pray thus, "O God, please make me wealthier." Not knowing the real Me within themselves and aspiring to worldly ends and comforts, they are to be considered as of demonic character. Those of divine character seek Me in a different way. Their seeking has no end in view other than to realize Me as what they really are. The *jñānin* (the wise one) is the one who has already so realized Me.

Calling all of them *sukṛtis* (the virtuous or the doers of good deeds) deserves special attention. The distressed and the aspirants of wealth are ignorant. They willingly perform rituals strictly conforming with scriptural injunctions, and to that extent they are *sukṛtis* (doers of meritorious deeds) true to Vedism. Wisdom seekers and the wise are not so; the former yearn to realize Me within and the latter have already realized Me. The former perform deeds that emerge as part of the flow of nature, as an offering unto Me; the latter do them with the awareness that all *karmas* take place in Me. That is the sense in which their deeds are virtuous.

Of the four, *jñānin* is the one who has realized Me, and to tell you more about him:

तेषां ज्ञानी नित्ययुक्त एकभक्तिर्विशिष्यते ।
प्रियो हि ज्ञानिनो ऽत्यर्थमहं स च मम प्रियः ॥१७॥

teṣām jñānī nitya-yukta eka-bhaktir viśiṣyate ।
priyo hi jñānino 'tyartham ahaṁ sa ca mama priyaḥ ॥17॥

The wise (*jñānin*), of these, always one with Me and meditatively perceiving Me alone, surpasses others. I am extremely dear to him, and he likewise to Me.

Arjuna, of these four types of people who seek Me, it is the *jñānin* who surpasses others in that he experiences himself to be one with Me while the others are just My seekers. The *jñānin* sees only one Reality as existing, one Reality alone worthy of worship, and that is Myself. His adoration thus is one-pointed (*eka-bkaktiḥ*).

For all of us, we hold ourselves most dear. Seeing Me as the Reality in oneself, I Myself — considered as *ātmā, Brahman* or God — becomes the dearest; I too have the same attitude towards such seekers, which is the reason for their life appearing to be blessed. This reciprocity between Me and the *jñānin* is not merely a personal one, but is like that between waves and the ocean, or ornaments and gold. To make the nature of this reciprocity more explicit:

उदाराः सर्व एवैते ज्ञानी त्वात्मैव मे मतम्।
आस्थितः स हि युक्तात्मा मामेवानुत्तमां गतिम्॥१८॥

udārāḥ sarva evaite jñānī tv ātmaiva me matam ।
āsthitaḥ sa hi yuktātmā mām evānuttamāṁ gatim ॥18॥

Dignified, indeed, are all of them; but I hold the *jñānin* as Myself. He of unified self-being, steadfastly exists in Me, the unexcellable goal.

Arjuna, many are those who rely on their own capabilities to attain their goals. Much better are those who bank on Me, for they at least have the awareness that everything in life is not in their control. But the best of them, the *jñānin* is not an individual relying on Me, but is Myself. This stand is a finalized certitude of Mine. A *jñānin's* final goal is Myself; his ultimate being too is in Myself.

All are born *ajñānin*s. Only later a few turn out to be seekers and finally become *jñānin*s. Becoming a *jñānin*, an *ajñānin*'s perception of life alters altogether. How is it I shall tell you:

बहूनां जन्मनामन्ते ज्ञानवान्मां प्रपद्यते।
वासुदेवः सर्वमिति स महात्मा सुदुर्लभः॥१९॥

bahūnāṁ janmanām ante jñānavān māṁ prapadyate ।
vāsudevaḥ sarvam iti sa mahātmā sudurlabhaḥ ॥19॥

Marking the end of many births, one, becoming a *jñānin*, attains Me, realizing, "Everything is but Vāsudeva." Such great ones are rare indeed to find.

Arjuna, as you know, the distressed as well as aspirants of worldly well-being, are ignorant. What they consider real is not Me, but the apparent forms that emerge and re-merge in Me, which they look upon as the birth and death of themselves. Life, in their view, begins with birth, and ends with death. What happens after death is a fearful question that haunts their waking and sleeping hours. The notion that the self is to be reborn entering a new womb is an idea fixed in their minds, which is strengthened by references to such things in secondary scriptures or by misinterpreted references in the cardinal scriptures. The ignorant thus believe in having passed through many such incarnations. It is in such a person that arises by chance the intense desire to know the ultimate Reality. Through unrelenting enquiry and austere self-discipline and restraint, he finally realizes that the Self is birthless and deathless, and that he too is that Reality in essence. Only then it dawns on him that what till then he had thought of as birth, death and rebirth are all the arising, disappearing and re-emerging of little ripples in the one boundless ocean of Self. All ripples are one with the ocean; all beings exist as one with the Self. The seeker then realizes that the state in which he saw himself as having birth and death has come to an end, as he now knows everything to be the one immortal Vāsudeva.

As you know, one of my numerous names is Vāsudeva, for I am the son of Vasudeva, but it is not that sense which fits into the present context. Here I am Vāsudeva as the one Reality that abides (*vāsa*) the entire cosmos, owing to the latent tendency (*vāsanā*) inherent in Itself. Those who treat this name to mean only he who is the son of Vasudeva, are considering as real only this apparent form. Those who see Me as the all-underlying Vāsudeva, on the other hand, see me as the final goal; they alone see their own greatness. Such are to be called "the great" (*mahātmā*) and they indeed are very rare.

Those who think of the apparant forms as real, seek Me also as having such a form. How do they seek Me and realize Me, I shall tell you:

कामैस्तैस्तैर्हृतज्ञानाः प्रपद्यन्ते ऽन्यदेवताः ।
तं तं नियममास्थाय प्रकृत्या नियताः स्वया ॥२० ॥

kāmais tais tair hṛta-jñānāḥ prapadyante 'nya-devatāḥ ।
taṁ taṁ niyamam āsthāya prakṛtyā niyatāḥ svayā ॥20 ॥

Dictated by their own inner nature, they, with wisdom taken away by this or that desire, take to other divinities, resorting to precepts pertaining to them.

Arjuna, those who think of appearances as real find meaning and fulfilment in enjoying these, for all appearances are objects of sense pleasure. Infatuated with such pleasures, they do not see Me. They live ignorant, and unaware of being ignorant.

The pleasure-seekers too, from experience, learn that everything is not in their control, that enjoying life requires the support of something unknown which they call "God." They seek God or gods' favour for the fulfilment of their desires. I too am a god in their perception, a god full of attributes, all of which depend on the wishes they seek to fulfil. Many such are the forms I am conceived in, resulting in many divinities that are worshipped. The fulfilment of varied desires being different, the ways of worship for the wish-fulfilling divinity also become different, with each one being thought of as inviolable. Those who worship their chosen divinities in this way, do reach their goal. Whoever are the aspirants, whatever their aspirations, whichever the divinities they propitiate, whatever are the ways in which they worship, the one underlying Reality in all of them is Myself — a truth that they remain oblivious of. How do I dwell in them I shall make clearer:

यो यो यां यां तनुं भक्तः श्रद्धयार्चितुमिच्छति ।
तस्य तस्याचलां श्रद्धां तामेव विदधाम्यहम् ॥२१ ॥

yo yo yāṁ yāṁ tanuṁ bhaktaḥ śraddhayārcitum icchati ।
tasya-tasyācalāṁ śraddhāṁ tām eva vidadhāmy aham ॥21 ॥

Whoever the supplicant intending to worship with full faith whichever form of divinity, that unwavering faith in him is bestowed on by Myself.

Arjuna, a supplicant's unshaken faith in being able to achieve his goal through worshipping a particular deity in a specific way, I call *śraddhā* (faith) here. You know, I am the Reality that appears as the supplicant and thus his faith too is Myself. I am also the one who brings forth the result intended, as is stated in the next verse:

स तया श्रद्धया युक्तस्तस्याराधनमीहते ।
लभते च ततः कामान्मयैव विहितान्हि तान् ॥२२॥

sa tayā śraddhayā yuktas tasyārādhanam īhate ।
labhate ca tataḥ kāmān mayaiva vihitān hi tān ॥22॥

He, endowed with that faith, intends to worship that particular (deity). His desires thus get fulfilled too. Yet, I am the one who so decrees all these.

Arjuna, many are those who worship Me thus in the form of different deities having different forms, but few are those that worship Me as the attributeless Reality in all specific forms. The benefits the two thus achieved are also different:

अन्तवत्तु फलं तेषां तद्भवत्यल्पमेधसाम् ।
देवान्देवयजो यान्ति मद्भक्ता यान्ति मामपि ॥२३॥

antavat tu phalaṁ teṣāṁ tad bhavaty alpa-medhasām ।
devān deva-yajo yānti mad-bhaktā yānti mām api ॥23॥

Terminable indeed are the benefits gained by those of little understanding. Those who offer oblations to divinities reach the divinities; and those who meditatively adore Me reach Me.

Arjuna, all the specific forms have beginning and end; those who seek happiness in such forms consider themselves also as having beginning and end; the happiness they derive from worshipping specific divinities, thus has also necessarily to be ephemeral. I, the indwelling Substance in all, on the other hand, am eternal; and those who meditatively adore Me, reach Me and become eternal themselves. See how the deluded have their own specific concepts concerning Me:

अव्यक्तं व्यक्तिमापन्नं मन्यन्ते मामबुद्धयः।
परं भावमजानन्तो ममाव्ययमनुत्तमम्॥२४॥

avyaktaṁ vyaktim āpannaṁ manyante mām abuddhayaḥ ।
paraṁ bhāvam ajānanto mamāvyayam anuttamam ॥24॥

Those devoid of reason think of Me, the unmanifest, as having a specific form, unaware as they are of My unexpended, unsurpassed, Supreme beingness.

Arjuna, those who are not *yogī*s see themselves as distinct and definable entities, and they think of Me also in this way. These seekers, the objects they seek for pleasure, the divinities they rely on, are all thus terminable. They are incapable of knowing Me as the one eternal Reality. Only in knowing Me can seekers realize that there is no other reality that transcends Me or surpasses Me in greatness.

Why is it that the ignorant do not see Me? They could at least see what is real in themselves if not in all things, but they do not. Why it is so, I shall tell you:

नाहं प्रकाशः सर्वस्य योगमायासमावृतः।
मूढो ऽयं नाभिजानाति लोको मामजमव्ययम्॥२५॥

nāhaṁ prakāśaḥ sarvasya yoga-māyā samāvṛtaḥ ।
mūḍho 'yaṁ nābhijānāti loko mām ajam avyayam ॥25॥

Veiled as I am by My own *yoga-māyā*, I do not become revealed to all. Deluded, these people do not see the unborn, unexpended Me.

वेदाहं समतीतानि वर्तमानानि चार्जुन।
भविष्याणि च भूतानि मां तु वेद न कश्चन ॥२६॥

vedāhaṁ samatītāni vartamānāni cārjuna I
bhaviṣyāṇi ca bhūtāni māṁ tu veda na kaścana II26 II

I know the beings that are past, present and yet to come in future, O Arjuna, but no one knows Me.

इच्छाद्वेषसमुत्थेन द्वन्द्वमोहेन भारत।
सर्वभूतानि संमोहं सर्गे यान्ति परंतप ॥२७॥

icchā-dveṣa-samutthena dvandva-mohena bhārata I
sarva-bhūtāni saṁmohaṁ sarge yānti paraṁtapa II27 II

Beguiled by the dualities arising from attraction and repulsion, O Bhārata, all beings genetically go deluded, O Burner of Foes.

Arjuna, how our desires and the anger that follows when these are not fulfilled, lead us to our own ruin, we have discussed. Dualities such as pain and pleasure, sin and merit, good and evil, our like for pleasure, merit and good, and dislike of pain, sin and evil — all have one origin only: our desires, which in turn are caused by My own *māyā*. Though born veiled by this *māyā*, no one is aware of being so, for only someone not subject to it can see it to be so. Nevertheless, there are a few, graced by God, as it were, who become enlightened on the *māyā*-caused delusion, and realize Me as the indweller in them as well as everything else. I shall tell you who they are:

येषां त्वन्तगतं पापं जनानां पुण्यकर्मणाम्।
ते द्वन्द्वमोहनिर्मुक्ता भजन्ते मां दृढव्रताः ॥२८॥

yeṣām tv anta-gataṁ pāpaṁ janānāṁ puṇya-karmaṇām ।
te dvandva-moha-nirmuktā bhajante māṁ dṛḍha-vratāḥ ॥28 ॥

Those who habitually do pure deeds of terminated sins, freed from the duality-caused delusion, with firm reslove, meditatively perceive Me.

Arjuna, the pure deeds meant here are not the Vedic rituals nor are they the works of public benefit. They, on the other hand, are the day-to-day activities of those who are fully aware that all *karma*s that take place in all particular entities in all the worlds are nothing but My own creativity or *prakṛti* become manifest. Such beings do not act out of desire. They are *yogī*s, and remain beyond sin and merit, as we have already seen. Seeing Me alone in themselves and all else, they are not deluded by the dualities apparent in life. Sense pleasure is never their aim; what they aim at, is liberation.

जरामरणमोक्षाय मामाश्रित्य यतन्ति ये ।
ते ब्रह्म तद्विदुः कृत्स्नमध्यात्मं कर्म चाखिलम् ॥२९ ॥

jarā-maraṇa-mokṣāya mām āśritya yatanti ye ।
te brahma tad viduḥ kṛtsnam adhyātmaṁ karma cākhilam ॥29 ॥

Those who, turning to Me, strive for liberation from old age and death, are the knowers of *Brahman* designated as "That." They understand all as self-based; they are the knowers of everything concerning *karma*.

Arjuna, those who meditate on Me with firm resolve aim at liberation — from old age, death and other miseries of life. What are old age and death? Merely aspects of changefulness of the apparent forms I assume. They too are not different from Me. As I am to be seen in the taste of water, so am I to be perceived in old age and death as aspects of life. Seeing Me in these states makes one free from the fear of old age and death.

Brahman, as the goal to be attained, is often designated as "That" (*tat*) in the Upaniṣads. But in the perception of the enlightened such as those we speak of here, *Brahman* is no longer "That," for they themselves have become *Brahman*. They perceive *Brahman* as the self-reality in every individuated being (*adhyātma*), and they see *Brahman* alone in all *karmas*. Even the problems of day-to-day life are perceived by them as *Brahman* manifesting. I shall point out to you some aspects of such manifestations:

साधिभूताधिदैवं मां साधियज्ञं च ये विदुः ।
प्रयाणकालेऽपि च मां ते विदुर्युक्तचेतसः ॥३०॥

sādhibhūtādhidaivaṁ māṁ sādhiyajñaṁ ca ye viduḥ ।
prayāṇa-kāle 'pi ca māṁ te vidur yukta-cetasaḥ ॥30॥

By knowing Me as based in physical elements, as based in universal effulgent entities, and as based in sacrificial offerings, at least at the time of departure, those of well-united mind do really know Me.

Arjuna, all the individuated entities (*adhyātma*) and all *karmas*, we have seen to be My own manifestations. So too physical existence and universal existence, and their presiding deities and sacrificial offerings have Me for their Substance. Perceiving Me in every aspect or quality of existence, even if attained at the time of death, makes a person a *yogī* and he attains Me. How blessed then will be the life of the one who sees Me so all through life!

Let us now summarize what we learnt in the present chapter:

Attaining Me and seeing oneself as one with Me is the state reached as a result of meditation, seen at the end of the last chapter. Rare indeed are persons of that attainment.

Prakṛti is the creativity in Me finding expression leading to the emanation of beings. This *prakṛti* has two aspects: *aparā* (immanent) and *parā* (transcendental). As dictated by this *prakṛti* exist all the worlds, all the specific entities in these worlds, and all their specifying qualities. And therefore, your meditative perception should go to the extent of seeing Me in all the specificities of nature. Water, for example, is one of the basic physical elements and its specifying quality is taste. So when tasting water, you have to meditatively perceive Me in that taste. So with everything else.

All the apparent forms emerge from Me; and each of these has its own specifying characteristic because of Me. Yet such entities and their qualities, in the usual course, are looked upon as real, forgetting that I am the Real in all of these. It is my *māyā* that causes this.

Those under the spell of *māyā* look upon Me for succour. Those who seek Me could in a general way be classified into four types: the distressed, aspirants after wealth, wisdom-seekers and the wise. The seekers are those who fight for mastery over *māyā,* whereas the wise have already won it over, and so it is the latter who are the best of all who pursue Me.

Those who, subject to *māyā,* treat individual entities and their specifying characteristics as real on their own, treat Me also as having a specific form and characteristics that depend on the desires they seek to get fulfilled. Such forms are known as *devatā*s (deities). The ignorant worship these and they reach the goals they aim at, but only as being dispensed by Myself, by the Absolute. The wise, on the other hand, worship Me directly, and what they gain as a result is nothing short of Myself. Those who think of Me as having any distinct form are ignorant, for I am indistinct and indestructible. The *māyā* that makes people see Me as distinct is inborn in all beings. Only by winning over it and seeing Me in all individual entities can one transcend the sufferings of old age and death. I, then, become perceptible as *adhyātma, adhibhūta, adhidaivata* and *adhiyajña*. Seeing Me thus, one becomes fully content with *jñāna* and *vijñāna,* the ultimate goal of the meditation taught to you in the last chapter.

Thus ends Chapter Seven entitled Jñāna-Vijñāna-Yoga of the Bhagavad-Gītā, the essence of the Upaniṣads, that embodies the yoga-śāstra of brahma-vidyā in the form of a dialogue between Śrī Kṛṣṇa and Arjuna.

VIII

Akṣara-Brahma-Yoga

—The Yoga of Imperishable Brahman—

अर्जुन उवाच —

किं तद्ब्रह्म किमध्यात्मं किं कर्म पुरुषोत्तम ।
अधिभूतं च किं प्रोक्तमधिदैवं किमुच्यते ॥१॥

arjuna uvāca —

kiṁ tad brahma kim adhyātmaṁ kiṁ karma puruṣottama ।
adhibhūtaṁ ca kiṁ proktam adhidaivaṁ kim ucyate ॥1॥

Arjuna said —

What is that *Brahman*? What is *adhyātma*? O Puruṣottama, what is *karma*? What is spoken of as *adhibhūta*? And what is called *adhidaivam*?

अधियज्ञः कथं को ऽत्र देहे ऽस्मिन्मधुसूदन ।
प्रयाणकाले च कथं ज्ञेयो ऽसि नियतात्मभिः ॥२॥

adhiyajñaḥ kathaṁ ko 'tra dehe 'smin madhusūdana ।
prayāṇa-kāle ca kathaṁ jñeyo 'si niyatātmabhiḥ ॥2॥

Who is the *adhiyajña* that is in this body, and how, O Madhusūdana? And how are you to be known by the one of self-restraint at the time of departing?

श्री भगवानुवाच —

अक्षरं ब्रह्म परमं स्वभावो ऽध्यात्ममुच्यते ।
भूतभावोद्भवकरो विसर्गः कर्मसञ्ज्ञितः ॥३॥

śrī bhagavān uvāca —

akṣaraṁ brahma paramaṁ svabhāvo 'dhyātmam ucyate ।
bhūta-bhāvodbhava-karo visargaḥ karma-saṁjñitaḥ ॥3॥

Śrī Kr̥ṣṇa said —

The Indestructible, the Supreme, is *Brahman*. Its own manifestation as individual entities is what is known as *adhyātma*. The specific creative urge that causes the emerging of individual entities is designated as *karma*.

Arjuna, the contemplative inward gaze I spoke of in the last chapter was capable of perceiving Me alone in every specific entity appearing in nature. In other words, it is My own varied facets of appearance that people think of as separately existing entities. Some generalized aspects of My manifestations were looked at in the concluding verses of the last chapter, and now you desire that I speak about each of these in detail.

In this teaching, only on very rare occassions do I answer your questions right to the point, and the present is one such. You have asked Me eight different questions and I shall answer each of these one by one:

First, *Brahman*: That Substance which is Supreme or Transcendental and Indestructible is *Brahman*. By "Supreme" (*paramaṁ*) I mean "that beyond which nothing exists." *Kṣara* means "that which perishes," and *akṣara*, its opposite, means "the indestructible." What was qualified as the birthless and deathless *sat* in Chapter II is none other than this *Brahman*. The word itself literally means, "that which ceaselessly grows," deriving from the verb root *bṛh*, meaning "to grow." It is the one Substance that underlies all that is perceived and all that which is conceived. It is more extensive than the imagination can conceive of; all things — subjective and objective — are Its outgrowth and it never ceases to grow.

Secondly, the word *adhyātma:* The *Brahman* I speak of here, is nothing but Myself. It does not exist as an abstract reality with no concrete form, just as gold, to exist, necessarily assumes some form, whether of ornaments, coins, blocks or even of the ore itself. All these forms are changeful whereas the substance gold is changeless; so too are *Brahman* and Its apparent forms related. (This inseparability of *sat* and *bhāva* we have discussed in detail under Verse II.16.) Every individual entity along with its various specifying qualities, emerges from Me, and seeing Me, alone in each of these we call *vijñāna*. Each such entity, inseparable from Me, should be counted as My own normal and natural individuated aspect (*sva-bhāva*), *sva* meaning "My own," or "one's own" and *bhāva* "individualized aspect." Each such form of Mine is to be termed *adhyātma*. The word means, "that which has oneself or the self for basis, *adhi* standing for *adhiṣṭhāna*, meaning "basis" or "firm ground," and *ātmā* "the self or oneself." The name *adhyātma-śāstra* for all scriptures also is derived in this way. To know what the ultimate reality is, one need not go searching but only look inwardly at oneself and perceive how the one indestructible Reality assumed his own form as well as that of everything else. Since the search for Reality is thus made with oneself as the firm basis, the science of that search is known as *adhyātma-śāstra*. The wisdom thus attained is also at times called *adhyātma-jñāna*.

It is individual seekers, who are in search of Reality in the *adhyātma* way, and all individual entities in essence are Myself. Every individual, thus, is an *adhyātma* aspect of Myself or *Brahman*.

And now for *karma*: Just as transformations occur in gold as ornaments are formed from it, so too in the emerging of all the worlds from Me, some events take place resulting in their emergence. Every individual thus emerged is a *bhūta* (that which has already come into being). Such new *bhūta*s constantly emerge and old ones merge back. Events in nature always have some underlying, impelling urge that makes it happen inevitably — an external force or an internal urge. With *Brahman*, no "other" existing, this urge has necessarily to be from within and invincible. Individual entities thus emerging have their own specific attributes. The specific creative urge in Me or *Brahman* that makes all individual entities with specific characteristics emerge from Myself and appear as the ever changing world and the phenomenon of life in it, is to be understood as *karma*.

Indicating this urge in *Brahman*, the *Chāndogya Upaniṣad* (VI.ii.3) conceives of *Brahman* as desiring, *bahuḥ syām prajāyeya* (let Me take birth as many).

Remember this, Arjuna: *karma* (action), without doubt, takes place in Me, and the phenomenon of birth and death of beings is a result of *karma* finding expression. I am that Reality which is creative by Itself, and everything that emerges from Me and merges back into Me is also naturally creative. The *karmas* of human beings are to be understood simply as that creativity finding expression. So it is that such human *karmas* — physical, mental and verbal — are to be seen as Mine. Ignorant of this reality, human beings often think of the actions they do as "their" *karmas*. This is where you too erred. When fighting became unavoidable in your life as part of the unfoldment of events in nature, instead of seeing these events as taking place in "Me," you thought of them as "your" *karma*, causing fear of sin and punishment.

अधिभूतं क्षरो भावः पुरुषश्चाधिदैवतम् ।
अधियज्ञो ऽहमेवात्र देहे देहभृतां वर ॥४॥

adhibhūtaṁ kṣaro bhāvaḥ puruṣaścādhidaivatam ।
adhiyajño 'ham evātra dehe deha-bhṛtāṁ vara ॥4॥

Perishable manifestations constitute *adhibhūta*, and *puruṣa* is the *adhidaivata*. Myself underlying the body here is the *adhiyajña*, O Best of the Embodied.

Arjuna, I shall now tell you what *adhibhūta* is. *Bhūta,* as you know, is "that which has come into being"; when that *bhūta* aspect is the basis of something, it is *adhibhūta*. I shall make it clearer. The perishable forms in which I, the Imperishable Substance, appears in a constantly changing state, are called *adhibhūta*.

Now as to *adhidaivata*: *Daivata* means "that which is self-effulgent," and what is always so is pure consciousness, what would later be called mind in western psychology. When I shine as this mind in individuals, it could be considered my *adhidaivata* aspect.

This mind is always referred to as *puruṣa* (person, literally "the city-dweller") by our ancient *ṛṣis*, because the human body is conceived of as a city of nine gates. The cosmos as a whole is also treated likewise and the *puruṣa* dwelling in it is called *virāṭ-puruṣa*, usually translated as "the cosmic person." Whether conceived of as the individual mind or the cosmic mind, its essence is brightness and both are to be considered *adhidaivata* aspects of Mine.

Now about the what and how of *adhiyajña*: The *karma* in Me ceaselessly finds expression resulting in the constant emergence of new forms and re-mergence of old ones. Every such form is a *deha* (body) literally, "that which grows." Each *deha* forms part of the *adhibhūta*, and is perishable, yet as long as it lasts My *puruṣa* aspect is inherent in it arousing the I-sense. This I-sense too has its origin in Me, and so does not exist apart from Me. An individual who realizes this would be willing to offer oneself as an oblation into Me, the Absolute. An I-sense in such a state is to be understood as *adhiyajña*. How this I-sense is related to *yajña* needs further elucidation:

What creates an impression that I and you are different, or that my *karmas* are different from yours, is the "I"-sense in each of us. However, with the understanding that it is *Brahman* that appears as all these, one tends to see oneself as united with *Brahman*, and to offer to *Brahman* what was till then considered as one's "own." Such offerings were seen in Chapters III and IV as constituting the essence of all *yajñas*. And every *yajña* is performed by an individual having an I-sense.

अन्तकाले च मामेव स्मरन्मुक्त्वा कलेवरम् ।
यः प्रयाति स मद्भावं याति नास्त्यत्र संशयः ॥५॥

anta-kāle ca mām eva smaran muktvā kalevaram ।
yaḥ prayāti sa mad-bhāvaṁ yāti nāsty atra saṁśayaḥ ॥5॥

He who goes forth casting off body, thinking of Me alone, reaches the state of being Myself. No room for doubt is there as regards this.

Arjuna, your last question was, "How do those of self-restraint reach Me?" Those of self-restraint as a natural way of life are known as *yatis*. *Yatis* see only Me everywhere and in everything. For a *yati*, the present body is nothing but an evanescent apparent form assumed by the eternal Me. In their last moments it is Me alone that they think of. When their body vanishes the real Substance in it continues to be as it must. Since I am that Substance, when the *yatis* cast off their bodies they become Me only, just as ornaments melted can become only gold.

The present chapter intends to accomplish a discrimination between *akṣara* and *kṣara*, and to perceive all the *kṣara*-forms also as having their being in the *akṣara* or Me.

There are those who think of the perishable, apparent forms as real; they are known as *ajñānins* (the ignorant). There are also others who perceive the indestructible Substance as real and they think of body, the apparent, transient aspect of existence, merely as appearing to be. Those are known as *jñānins* (the wise). It is possible to answer your question from the point of view of either type, and this is the reason for the puzzle. I am not sure whether you, while asking the question, were aware of this.

To make it clearer: your question was, "How do *yatis* attain Me at the time of departing (*prayāṇa-kāle*)?" *Prayāṇa* ordinarily is taken to mean death, a phenomenon treated as real only by the ignorant who are naturally worried about the hereafter. They interpret my words in this verse, to mean that one of self-restraint who thinks of Me alone till the last moment of life, reaches Me after death. This is the idea or belief the ignorant have formulated in their mind concerning the afterlife of *yatis*.

True to its literal sense, the word *prayāṇa* means only "proper going forward" — a going forward from ignorance to wisdom, from one's identity with the perishable body to one's identity with the imperishable *Brahman*. Casting off the body in this context means becoming free of the notion "I am this body," and along with becoming free there shines the awareness, "I am *Brahman* indeed." One's casting off of the body is not at the time of death but rather at the time he frees himself of ignorance. His attaining immortality is not an afterlife experience, but an experience of being immortal while living here and now. With the realization, "I am the birthless and deathless *Brahman*" he goes forward from death to immortality. This going forward is his *prayāṇa-kāla* (the time of departing). Thus, even though it is one Reality alone that underlies the life of both *jñānin* and *ajñānin*, though it is one law of life that controls the life of both, the understandings the two have of it are different; likewise different are their notions of "casting off the body." Their concepts of "attaining Me" also therefore must be different. To clarify that difference:

यं यं वापि स्मरन्भावं त्यजत्यन्ते कलेवरम्।
तं तमेवैति कौन्तेय सदा तद्भावभावितः ॥६॥

yaṁ yaṁ vāpi smaran bhāvaṁ tyajaty ante kalevaram ।
taṁ tam evaiti kaunteya sadā tad-bhāva-bhāvitaḥ ॥6॥

Whatever phase of existence one thinks upon intently as one abandons body, always identified as he is with that phase, that phase alone one attains to, O Son of Kuntī.

Arjuna, you are now well aware that the "abandoning" of the body has different meanings for *jñānin*s and *ajñānin*s. In both cases is there without doubt an envisaging of a particular phase of existence at that particular moment. For a *jñānin*, his last moment is when he forgoes his identity with the body. What fills his being at that time is that he is one with *Brahman* or Me. He thinks of Me alone while living here as well as when dying, and so his existence is in Me, while living as well as after death.

An *ajñānin* is different; he sees death as being as real as transient appearances. *Ajñānin*s hold fast to the idea that one attains after death that which one's thoughts dwell upon at the time of death. With the earnest desire to attain God, an ignorant man might think of Me on his deathbed with an attitude of prayer. The God in his mind, needless to say, is not the *jñānin*'s *Brahman*. His idea of God may be of a Viṣṇu living in Vaikuṇṭha, a Śiva residing in Kailāsa, the lotus-born-Brahmā the Creator, the Mother Goddess (Devī) or some other favourite personal deity. Such one dies peacefully with the hope of reaching My abode. Some others think of the possibility of going to the world of manes (*pitṛloka*) and to be reborn again in this world.

In spite of all our attempts to understand with reason, a vagueness continues to shroud the matter we are now discussing. This vagueness disappears only when one becomes enlightened as to the ultimate nature and Reality of life, revealing how our life is related to *Brahman*. From *Brahman* alone does every being emerge, and back to *Brahman* itself do they merge. Regardless of whether a being is organic or inorganic, regardless of whether one is a *jñānin* or an *ajñānin*, all merge into the one *Brahman* alone. To consider that the afterlife of *jñānin*s is different from that of *ajñānin*s is to defy this basic reality. The *ajñānin* considers that the two have different afterlives, whereas the *jñānin* understands that both *jñānin*s and *ajñānin*s merge back in *Brahman*.

Arjuna, it has been made clear to you how each being, body abandoned, reaches either *Brahman* or the world he fancies, depending on how he thinks of the afterlife. You may now be wondering what your own fate will be after death. You have already left behind the underworld of ignorance and attained the higher realms of wisdom, and thus you, a *yogī*, have already given up your body. How you, being such, should attain Me, I shall make clear:

तस्मात्सर्वेषु कालेषु मामनुस्मर युध्य च।
मय्यर्पितमनोबुद्धिर्मामेवैष्यस्यसंशयः ॥७॥

tasmāt sarveṣu kāleṣu mām anusmara yudhya ca ।
mayy arpita-mano-buddhir mām evaiṣyasy asaṁśyaḥ ॥7॥

Therefore always remember Me and fight. Single-minded on Me in your imaginations and reasoning, you will, no doubt, come to Me alone.

Arjuna, having properly understood what I have been teaching you at length so far, you now see Me alone as the one essential content in your being. You may recall what I said in the last chapter: that what is real in the element water is Myself, so too what is real in taste, the distinguishing quality of water, is also Myself alone. Likewise, being a warrior through and through is the quality that makes you, and it too is not other than one of My manifestations. Therefore, it behoves you to continue fighting, and by that very act you will attain Me.

Though I am thus attainable to all, all the same I am not actually attained by all. How everyone can make Me accessible, I shall tell you:

अभ्यासयोगयुक्तेन चेतसा नान्यगामिना ।
परमं पुरुषं दिव्यं याति पार्थानुचिन्तयन् ॥८ ॥

abhyāsayoga-yuktena cetasā nānya-gāminā ।
paramaṁ puruṣaṁ divyaṁ yāti pārthānucintayan ॥8 ॥

With disposition repeatedly attuned to *yoga* and meditating on Him, undistracted by anything else, is reached the *Puruṣa*, the Supreme Effulgence.

Arjuna, the *Puruṣa*, Supreme Effulgence in essence, referred to here, is but Myself. I manifest as every being. But such beings — here we are more concerned with human beings — in general are unware that both they themselves as well as their actions are Myself.

Those who have closely followed my teaching so far, may remember intermittently the necessity of that awareness, but suddenly the mind will jump to something interesting and thus be distracted. The recollection that even that distracting something is Myself become manifest, may bring the mind back to Me once again. Bringing one's mind repeatedly back to Me, as said earlier, is called *abhyāsa* (repeated practising). *Abhyāsa* causes one to incessantly perceive oneself as inseparable from Me, and one who has reached this state is to be called *yoga-yukta* (one attuned to *yoga*). Seeing always, everywhere and in all, My own effulgent beingness, he constantly finds himself in Me. You too, fighting with your mind always attuned to Me, attain oneness with Me; so also it is for all others. Doing whatever is in natural accordance with their personal traits and the natural outcome of the overall flow of events, seeing

Me alone in themselves as well as in all actions, they are already in Me, and they also are *yoga-yuktas*.

Quite similar is the attainment of *yogīs* whose natural activity is remaining absorbed in meditation. How they attain the same Supreme Goal, I shall tell you:

कविं पुराणमनुशासितारमणोरणीयांसमनुस्मरेद्यः ।
सर्वस्य धातारमचिन्त्यरूपमादित्यवर्णं तमसः परस्तात् ॥९॥
प्रयाणकाले मनसाचलेन भक्त्या युक्तो योगबलेन चैव ।
भ्रुवोर्मध्ये प्राणमावेश्य सम्यक् स तं परं पुरुषमुपैति दिव्यम् ॥१०॥

kaviṁ purāṇam anuśāsitaram aṇor aṇīyāṁsam anusmared yaḥ ।
sarvasya dhātāram acintya-rūpam āditya-varṇaṁ tamasaḥ parastāt ॥9॥

prayāṇa-kāle manasācalena bhaktyā yukto yoga-balena caiva ।
bhruvor madhye prāṇam āveśya samyak sa taṁ paraṁ puruṣam upaiti divyam ॥10॥

The all-knower, the most ancient, the one who conducts everything, minuter than the minutest, the supporter of all, of unimaginable form, effulgent as the Sun, beyond all darkness — Him meditating on,

At the time of departing with mind unshaken on the strength of *yoga* and contemplation, with breathing process properly concentrated between the eyebrows, one reaches that Supreme Effulgent *Puruṣa*.

Arjuna, we have seen how, as a part of wishing to transform life into a ceaseless process of meditation, one feels at times like retreating into solitude and meditating. As the first step, we also studied what was the proper way to pursue — forgoing one's identity with the body which itself, as far as a *yogī* is concerned, is his time of departing. The mind has to be kept unwavering in this contemplation. How the otherwise fickle mind can be brought to firmness by showing it the highest goal and its value, was also clarified in the same chapter. Such a *yogī*, contemplating Me alone, experiences oneness with Me. Constant contemplation on something is called *bhakti*, derived from the root *bhaj*, meaning "to contemplate"; and we will have to examine it in detail later in Chapter XII. The inner firmness or strength one thus feels is called here *yoga-bala* (the strength of *yoga*). In the absence of such a strength, no meditation becomes stable and fruitful, the reason why the *Muṇḍaka Upaniṣad* puts it emphatically thus: "Unattainable is this *ātmā* to the weak minded" (*nāyam ātmā balahīnena labhyaḥ*, III.ii.3).

One should then regulate respiration and perceive its alternating process as taking place in between the eyebrows, resulting in feeling the in-breath as an upward movement and the out-breath as a downward one. This helps to fully direct the attention from external enjoyables to one's own interior being. That one's being is not confined to the outer skin of the body — identity with body already being foregone — and that one's real essential content is boundless pure Consciousness (*cit*) becomes a direct experience then. Visualizing oneself as that boundless *cit*, one should concentrate on the upward and downward movement of *prāṇa* in between the eyebrows; then one feels this pulsating movement also to be taking place in the boundless expanse of *cit*. This *cit* is the *Puruṣa*, and one directly experiences it to be neither individual nor cosmic. All that remains then is one blissful effulgence.

This *Puruṣa* is Consciousness pure and simple; not consciousness about anything but rather the mind that unfolds itself as consciousness about everything. In the sense that It is effulgence in essence, It is to be considered *divyam*, meaning "the effulgent." In it do all the worlds exist and in it all events take place. Being consciousness in essence, It is conscious of every event and thus It is to be considered *kavi*, the all-knower.

Each of us, as individuals who emerged in that *cit*, has a beginning, but the *cit* can have no such temporal beginning, and so It is known as the most ancient, *purāṇa*.

Since all events take place in *cit*, as dictated by It, It is the one who conducts everything ancient (*anuśāsitā*).

Our individual minds being mere momentary sparks of that *cit*, knowing Its greatness and way of functioning is beyond the comprehension of our minds.

Enquiring into how large It is takes us nowhere. Since it is not at all visible, It could be thought of as minuter than the minutest; the original word for the minutest is *aṇu*, which literally means, "that which is indivisibly small." At the same time, nothing existing outside it, It is also greater than the greatest. Then it goes without saying that *cit* is the one supporter of everything (*sarvasya dhātā*).

Those who look for Its form realize that *cit* is incomprehensibly formless. Any enquiry made by our mind is nothing but a tiny spark of the very same *cit*. How can a spark comprehend the form of its own source, the fire? Yet there are very rarely persons who intuitively visualize that *cit* or *Puruṣa*. They simply praise the wonder of the experience in such words as,

> Like millions of Suns rising all at once, It comes up submerging all the worlds in Its glory![1]

Such being the supreme *Puruṣa*, meditating on Him as one's own essential content is often compared to the event of one drop of pure water falling into an ocean of pure water.[2] In the form of that all-engulfing effulgence-experience of a *yogī*, is My being, and that is the *akṣara* (imperishable) understood in this chapter.

यदक्षरं वेदविदो वदन्ति विशन्ति यद्यतयो वीतरागाः ।
यदिच्छन्तो ब्रह्मचर्यं चरन्ति तत्ते पदं संग्रहेण प्रवक्ष्ये ॥११॥

yad akṣaram veda-vido vadanti viśanti yad yatayo vīta-rāgāḥ ।
yad icchanto brahmacaryaṁ caranti tat te padaṁ saṁgraheṇa pravakṣye ॥11॥

That which the Veda-knowers speak of as the Imperishable, that which the passion-free self-

1. See *Piṇḍanandi*, verse 1, of Narayana Guru.
2. See *Kaṭha Upaniṣad* II.i.15.

> controlled go into, that aiming at which *brahmacarya* is adhered to in life, that state I shall declare to you in brief.

Arjuna, all the Vedas, the scriptures of all religions, all source books of spirituality, all forms of self-restraint, have only one goal: to attain the Imperishable, to attain Me. This is suggested here by the fact that the present verse is a slightly altered version of a verse of the *Kaṭha Upaniṣad* (II.15). The Upaniṣadic verse says that the goal mentioned here could well be encapsulated in the monosyllable *AUṀ*. My intention here too is nothing else.

AUṀ, also called *praṇava*, is at times made an object of meditative adoration (*upāsanā*) by spiritual aspirants. They too seek Me alone; what they reach at the end too is Myself. How to practise that *upāsanā*, I shall tell you:

सर्वद्वाराणि संयम्य मनो हृदि निरुध्य च।
मूध्न्यर्धायात्मनः प्राणमास्थितो योगधारणाम्॥१२॥
ओमित्येकाक्षरं ब्रह्म व्याहरन्मामनुस्मरन्।
यः प्रयाति त्यजन्देहं स याति परमां गतिम्॥१३॥

sarva-dvārāṇi saṁyamya mano hṛdi nirudhya ca ।
mūrdhny ādhāyātmanaḥ prāṇam āsthito yoga-dhāraṇām ॥12॥

om ity ekākṣaraṁ brahma vyāharan mām anusmaran ।
yaḥ prayāti tyajan dehaṁ sa yāti paramāṁ gatim ॥13॥

> One who, with all gates (senses) in one's own control, with all imagining and fancying functions of mind held convergent in the heart, having found stability of adhering to *yoga* by concentrating *prāṇa*'s functions at the crown of the head, abandons body and goes forth uttering *AUṀ*, the Absolute-in-one-syllable, constantly thinking upon Me as well — he attains to the Supreme Goal.

Arjuna, wisdom was seen to predominate in the practice of meditation and attaining the goal of meditation described in Verses 9 and 10 above, whereas here *yoga* is seen to be predominant. Part of this *yoga*-practice is uttering the syllable *AUṀ* (pronounced *OṀ*) and at the same time thinking upon Me. Those who follow these two ways, and those who engage in activities natural to their personal traits with their minds always filled with Me, attain the one Imperishable Goal, attain Me. *AUṀ* is understood as the linguistic sign that denotes Me. How it is to be properly meditated upon as signifying Me as *cit* in its various functional states is made sufficiently clear in the *Māṇḍūkya Upaniṣad*.

Arjuna, I showed you three different meditative methods of attaining Me. Such ways need not necessarily be confined to three. How one meditates on Me really depends mainly on the personal traits of the seeker. A method that suits one may not be equally suitable for another. Hence any basic scripture can only give some general directions with regard to meditating on Me.

Whether the method thus selected is one of the three I have suggested here or any other, there will always be one common factor, lacking which the method itself will have to be discounted as bogus. I shall tell you what that common factor is:

अनन्यचेताः सततं यो मां स्मरति नित्यशः ।
तस्याहं सुलभः पार्थ नित्ययुक्तस्य योगिनः ॥१४ ॥

ananya-cetāḥ satataṁ yo māṁ smarati nityaśaḥ ।
tasyāhaṁ sulabhaḥ pārtha nitya-yuktasya yoginaḥ ॥14 ॥

He who remembers Me day in and day out with mind undistracted by anything else, to that ever attuned *yogī*, I am easy of attainment, O Pārtha.

Arjuna, to keep one's thoughts and interests from getting distracted is common to all forms of meditation, so too is remembering Me always and remaining fully attuned to Me. The result is that I become easily accessible. Experiencing inseparable oneness with the Imperishable and Immortal Me and thus realizing one's own

Imperishability and Immortality, is what is ultimately gained by making the teaching of the *Gītā* a way of life. Birth, death and all the miseries that go with life pertain entirely to the realm of perishable appearances (*kṣara-bhāva*). Transcending these as well as reaching and becoming identified with the imperishable Reality (*akṣara-sat*) comprise our goal. Having become one with the birthless and deathless Me, there is no more worry about death, the state after and rebirth, for all these are then revealed as unreal and meaningless. Thus is transcended the need to be reborn. To clarify further the nature of this ultimate gain:

मामुपेत्य पुनर्जन्म दुःखालयमशाश्वतम् ।
नाप्नुवन्ति महात्मानः संसिद्धिं परमां गताः ॥१५॥

mām upetya punar-janma duḥkhālayam aśāśvatam ।
nāpnuvanti mahātmānaḥ saṁsiddhiṁ paramāṁ gatāḥ ॥15॥

Me realized, the great ones, having attained the highest goal, do not come again to birth in this transitory abode of sufferings.

Arjuna, the crux of the teaching in this chapter comprises of learning to discriminate the perishables from the Imperishable, and then seeing the Imperishable Me alone in all perishable appearances. The perishables and the Imperishable are differentiated in the next verse:

आब्रह्मभुवनाल्लोकाः पुनरावर्तिनोऽर्जुन ।
मामुपेत्य तु कौन्तेय पुनर्जन्म न विद्यते ॥१६॥

ā-brahma-bhuvanāl lokāḥ punar-āvartino 'rjuna ।
mām upetya tu kaunteya punar janma na vidyate ॥16॥

All worlds from the realm of Brahmā down to the earth, O Arjuna, are subject to phenomenal coming and going, but on reaching Me, O Son of Kuntī, no more birth is there.

Arjuna, in the realm of perishables newer and newer forms appear and old ones disappear. This process is known as *punar āvartti* (continuous coming and going). Emergence of new forms is called birth and the merger of older ones death, both relevant only in the realm of perishables.

Everything perceptible, as we know, is perishable. Even conceivable worlds, the highest of which is thought of here as that of Brahmā the Creator, are also so.

The imperishable is one alone and that is Myself. One who sees Me alone as ultimately Real and as the one Substance in everything perishable, by that very act of seeing so, is already merged in Me, and he is already the Imperishable Me. Birth and death thus are of no relevance for him. The question of rebirth then does not come up at all. But those who treat all the perishables in all the worlds up to that of Brahmā as real, find their identity also with that realm that is subject to repeated coming and going. It is but natural that the one who finds identity with that realm too is subject to coming and going. How this coming and going, in an overall sense, happens, I shall tell you:

सहस्रयुगपर्यन्तमहर्यद्ब्रह्मणो विदुः ।
रात्रिं युगसहस्रान्तां ते ऽहोरात्रविदो जनाः ॥१७ ॥

sahasra-yuga-paryantam ahar yad brahmaṇo viduḥ ।
rātriṁ yuga-sahasrāntāṁ te 'ho-rātra-vido janāḥ ॥17 ॥

Brahmā's day is one thousand *yuga*s in duration, and night too is likewise. People who know thus are the real knowers of day and night.

Arjuna, events happening continuously with apparently alternating phases, we call *punar-āvartti*. The *punar-āvartti* we are most familiar with is the alternation of day and night here on the earth. An other-worldly day and night, pertaining to the world of Brahmā, the farthest extreme of conceivable perishables, could also be looked at. The day and night of the earth are twelve hours each, and that of the other extreme are imagined to be one thousand *yugas* each in duration. (The ancient *ṛṣis* of India thought of one cosmic cycle as constituted of four *yugas*: Kṛtayuga, Tretāyugu, Dvāparayuga and Kaliyuga. We are living in the Kaliyuga. The four *yugas* together is 43,20,000 years in duration.) Every conceivable stage within the range of these two extreme poles of the world of perishables, has its own day and night. Whichever the stage, the alternation of distinct and indistinct phases of existence is present in each, and these phases are symbolized here as day and night. Those who understand the realm of perishables thus as having two poles with alternating phases are to be counted as real knowers of the physical world. Look at what happens in such a physical world:

अव्यक्ताद्व्यक्तयः सर्वाः प्रभवन्त्यहरागमे ।
रात्र्यागमे प्रलीयन्ते तत्रैवाव्यक्तसंज्ञके ॥१८॥

avyaktād vyaktayaḥ sarvāḥ prabhavanty aharāgame |
rātry-āgame pralīyante tatraiva 'vyakta saṁjñake ||18 ||

From the indistinct emerge all that is distinct at the coming of day; at the coming of night they do merge in the very same, named the indistinct.

Arjuna, one entity, which becomes distinguishable from another, is said to be *vyakta* (distinct), and each such entity is a *vyakti* (individual). Every individuated phase of existence we know to be perishable. From where do all such entities emerge? Since we cannot be sure, we look upon that source-reality as something indistinct, *avyaktu* (the indistinct or the unmanifest). We can conveniently compare this emerging of distinct forms from one indistinct Reality as the arrival of day, for it is at day time that everything becomes distinctly visible. Every entity thus emerged is also dissolved once again into that very same indistinct state which we can think of as the coming of night.

This emerging — what we call creation, and merger — conceived as dissolution, unlike day and night, do not take place in temporal alternation. Neither creation nor dissolution is at a particular point of time; they occur simultaneously as the creative and destructive phases involved in every event in the cosmic system. The symbolic language of Indian Mythology represents this concept clothed in highy sublime poetical imagery: creation takes place as Brahmā awakes after a night's sleep lasting a thousand *yugas*, and dissolution happens at the end of his day of the same duration.

Transformations in the cosmic system are so structured that the disappearance of one phase of existence appears as another phase of existence, creation and dissolution thus being simultaneous. Hence the alternation of Brahmā's days and nights conceived here cannot be a temporal one, the two representing only the emerging and merger phases of existent beings.

How these constructive and destructive phases alternate, like days and nights, making for the ceaseless appearance of the world, I shall clarify:

भूतग्रामः स एवायं भूत्वा भूत्वा प्रलीयते ।
रात्र्यागमे ऽवशः पार्थ प्रभवत्यहरागमे ॥१९॥

bhūta-grāmaḥ sa evāyaṁ bhūtvā bhūtvā pralīyate ।
rātry-āgame 'vaśaḥ pārtha prabhavaty ahar-āgame ॥19॥

This very same multitude of beings, having emerged repeatedly, of necessity, does merge back at the onset of night, O Pārtha, and they come into being at the coming of day.

Arjuna, an indomitability is there in the emergence and merger of beings in the one Indestructible. This indefatigable urge is what we called *karma* earlier in Verse 3. How the Imperishable that houses this *karma*, is inalienably related to perishable beings, I shall point out to you now:

परस्तस्मात्तु भावो ऽन्यो ऽव्यक्तो ऽव्यक्तात्सनातनः ।
यः स सर्वेषु भूतेषु नश्यत्सु न विनश्यति ॥२०॥

paras tasmāt tu bhāvo 'nyo 'vyakto 'vyaktāt sanātanaḥ ।
yaḥ sa sarveṣu bhūteṣu naśyatsu na vinaśyati ॥20 ॥

Beyond this indistinct is there another eternal unmanifest; It remains undestroyed even as all beings are destroyed.

Arjuna, the alternation of day and night is temporal whereas the emergence and merger of beings are existential in import. The Indistinct denotes merger and the distinct emergence. Another unmanifest Reality (*avyakta*) that gives room for both emergence and merger has also to be there. This *avyakta* has to be of an order much higher than that of the indistinctness caused by night alone. Night is a time-related phenomenon whereas the indistinct-ness of the causal Reality transcends time concept, and therefore is *sanātana* (timeless). It must remain ceaselessly existing even as all entities perceptible emerge and merge, just as the gold substance remains undestroyed even when all ornament-forms come and go. This unmanifested is none other than the Imperishable Me. To clarify this aspect:

अव्यक्तो ऽक्षर इत्युक्तस्तमाहुः परमां गतिम् ।
यं प्राप्य न निवर्तन्ते तद्धाम परमं मम ॥२१ ॥

avyakto 'kṣara ity uktas tam āhuḥ paramāṁ gatim ।
yaṁ prāpya na nivartante tad dhāma paramaṁ mama ॥21 ॥

That unmanifested is called the Imperishable (*akṣara*). It is spoken of as the highest goal. Its attainers return not. It is My supreme abode.

Arjuna, this imperishable unmanifested is the one all-underlying Existence (*sat*), also signified by the words *ātmā* and *Brahman*. One who has realized that it is this one Existence that manifests as one's own being, perceives in all ups and downs of life, in all pleasures and pains of life, that one Existence alone becomes manifest. Even in what we consider as birth and death, he sees only the creativity of that Substance becoming actualized. There is for him no return from that Existence. Attaining this experience makes life meaningful, for that Existence alone is the meaning content of life. That Existence is My abode; nay, I am that Existence. Seeking Me out and searching for that Existence are not two. How one who has thus found Me, the Supreme *Puruṣa*, in his own being, will perceive the world around, I shall tell you:

पुरुषः स परः पार्थ भक्त्या लभ्यस्त्वनन्यया।
यस्यान्तःस्थानि भूतानि येन सर्वमिदं ततम्॥२२॥

puruṣaḥ sa paraḥ pārtha bhaktyā labhyas tv ananyayā ।
yasyāntaḥ sthāni bhūtāni yena sarvam idaṁ tatam ॥22 ॥

That (Imperishable unmanifested) is the Supreme *Puruṣa*, O Pārtha, attainable through contemplating as not different from oneself. Within Him all beings have their being. By Him everything here is pervaded.

Arjuna, the one Supreme *Puruṣa* unfolds Himself as all the worlds and as everything in these worlds, with each of us being a tiny speck of Him. Being so, in search of the *Puruṣa*, we need not look around, but only to look for the substance in our own being. Contemplating the *Puruṣa* thus as inalienable from oneself is proper *bhakti*, the only way to attain Him.

The *Puruṣa* thus having been attained, what one perceives all around as the world is but the same *Puruṣa* become manifest, or oneself become manifest. Other than reaching Him, other than realizing oneself as the *Puruṣa* in essence, there is no other goal to attain.

Arjuna, I have been differentiating between the *kṣara* and *akṣara* as seen by a *jñānin* who sees one *akṣara* (imperishable) *puruṣa* alone in all the perishable appearances. But all are not *jñānin*s; for the most part people remain ignorant (*ajñānin*s). They too have their own perception of life. Ignorant of the Imperishable which they are, they live treating all the apparent perishable forms as real. Birth is a reality for them, just as death and rebirth. The afterlife therefore, becomes problematic and a source of worry for them. For a *jñānin*, as you know, such things have no relevance. But in the perception of the ignorant, a *jñānin*'s hereafter appears to be different from his own, and the words of some *ṛṣis* too appear to support such a concept. Having heard that a *jñānin* becomes finally released, the ignorant interprets it to mean that the souls of *jñānins* go to a world from where they do not return, whereas the *ajñānins*' souls go to another world from where they return to be reborn. The *ajñānins*' concepts of *punar-āvṛtti* (repeated coming and going) and *anāvṛtti* (the state of no-return), though much different from that of a *jñānin*, must also be familiar to us. Therefore,

---

यत्र काले त्वनावृत्तिमावृत्तिं चैव योगिनः।
प्रयाता यान्ति तं कालं वक्ष्यामि भरतर्षभ ॥२३॥

yatra kāle tv anāvṛttim āvṛttiṁ caiva yogīnaḥ ।
prayātā yānti taṁ kālaṁ vakṣyāmi bharatarṣabha ॥23॥

I shall tell you now of that time wherein going forth *yogīs* return not, and that wherein going forth they return, O Best of the Bharatas.

Arjuna, our ordinary concept is that all events take place in time. The ignorant think birth and death, which are meaningful events in life, also as taking place in time. For this reason what I say about the hereafter is in terms of time — that the hereafter depends on the time of departing. This in no way means that *ajñānins*' and *jñānins*' departings take place at different times and that all that I state here, you must keep in mind, is as it appears in the perception of the ignorant, and is not my teaching proper. How the ignorant conceive of the *jñānins* departing of no return, I shall tell you:

अग्निज्योतिरहः शुक्लः षण्मासा उत्तरायणम्।
तत्र प्रयाता गच्छन्ति ब्रह्म ब्रह्मविदो जनाः ॥२४॥

agnir jyotir ahaḥ śuklaḥ ṣaṇmāsā uttarāyaṇam ।
tatra prayātā gacchanti brahma brahma-vido janāḥ ॥24 ॥

> The knowers of *Brahman,* passing through fire, light, day-time, the bright fortnight, the six months of the northern course of the sun, do reach *Brahman.*

Arjuna, the belief that the soul of a *jñānin,* on departing, reaches *Brahman,* passing along a bright path, has been prevalent among religious-minded Indians. Some references to it appear in scriptures like the Upaniṣads and Purāṇas and are taken to be the source of such beliefs. The fact that such references either do not form a part of the cardinal teaching of those scriptures or that such citations are mostly misinterpreted, often remains unnoticed, and the result is that such references continue to be quoted in support of this belief as though they are part of the basic tenets of Indian spirituality. The *Chāndogya Upaniṣad,* for instance, says thus in its Verses V.x.1-2:

> This is known to those who, living in forests, devote themselves to *tapas* with full faith. They go first to light; from light they go to day time; from day time to the brighter fortnight; from the brighter fortnight to the six months during which the sun moves towards the north. From those six months to year; from year to the sun; from the sun to the moon; from the moon to the lightning — do they go. From there a non-human person leads them on to *Brahman.* This is the path known as *deva-yāna.*

Fire, light, day-time, brighter fortnight, the six months of the northern course of the sun — all these denote the bright side. This path is popularly known as *arcir-mārga,* the brighter path (*arcis* meaning "brightness," and *mārga* "path"). But when seen related to the preceding stanzas, it will become quite evident that the above citation does not signify the states after death as it is believed to be. The Upaniṣadic passage is simply part of the description of the overall scheme of life, in which beings emerge and re-merge in the one Reality that is effulgence (*deva*) in essence. Still the common man, not very deep in his understanding of the Upaniṣadic teachings, treats the *deva-yāna* as another name for *arcir-mārga* as the afterdeath course of the souls of *jñānins*. A similar concept about the souls of *ajñānins* also is popular. It is thus:

धूमो रात्रिस्तथा कृष्णः षण्मासा दक्षिणायनम्।
तत्र चान्द्रमसं ज्योतिर्योगी प्राप्य निवर्तते ॥२५॥

dhūmo rātris tathā kṛṣṇaḥ ṣaṇmāsā dakṣiṇāyanam ।
tatra cāndramasaṁ jyotir yogī prāpya nivartate ॥25 ॥

The *yogī* who reaches lunar light, passing through smoke, night-time, the darker fortnight, the six months of the southern course of the sun, does return.

Arjuna, Verses 24 and 25 are the summarization of what the *Chāndogya Upaniṣad* supposedly says about the afterlife of *jñānins* and *ajñānins*. The Upaniṣadic passage concerning the latter reads as follows:

Now, those who, living in villages, adore *iṣṭa-karmas*, *pūrta-karmas* and *dāna-karmas*, thinking of these as meritorious, go first to smoke, from smoke to night, from night to the darker fortnight, from the darker fortnight to the six months during which the sun moves towards the south; from those six months they do not reach year.

From the six months they go to the *pitṛ-loka* (the world of manes), from the *pitṛ-loka* to space, and from space to the moon. It is Soma the King. It is food for the *devas* and they eat it.

Having remained in the moon till the time of fall, they return by the same way they ascended. They come back first to space, and from space they come back to air. Having become air, they become white clouds.

Having become white clouds, they become rain clouds; having become rain clouds, they fall as rain. Then they are born here as rice and barley, herbs and trees; sesame plants and beans. Getting out of this is hard indeed. Whoever happens to eat them and sow his seed in a womb, like him one becomes.

Among them, those of good conduct while in this world, quickly go into noble wombs: of brāhmaṇas, kṣatriyas or vaiśyas. But those of evil conduct while living here, quickly enter base wombs: of dogs, hogs or *caṇḍālas* (Verses V.X.3-7).

All the stages in this path being dark, beginning with smoke (*dhūma*), it is known as *dhūma-mārga*. The souls destined to return to the earth being called *pitṛs* (manes), the path is known also as *pitṛ-yāna* (the path of the manes).

The picture of these two paths might have been drawn up from the flames and smoke that arise from funeral pyre. Be that as it may, we have just described the essence of what is called *deva-yāna* and *pitṛ-yāna*, known also as *śukla-gati* and *kṛṣṇa-gati*, meaning white and black paths. How people evaluate these two paths, I shall tell you.

शुक्लकृष्णे गती ह्येते जगतः शाश्वते मते ।
एकया यात्यनावृत्तिमन्यया वर्तते पुनः ॥२६ ॥

śukla-kṛṣṇe gatī hy ete jagataḥ śāśvate mate ।
ekayā yāty anāvṛttim anyayā vartate punaḥ ॥26 ॥

These two paths, the white and the black, related to the world, are thought of as everlasting; by one, one attains to non-returning, while by going through the other one comes back.

Arjuna, I have told you in brief the nature of prevailing beliefs regarding the departed souls, non-return as well as their return through rebirth. You should not forget that these are ideas become fixed in the minds of the ignorant, for it overlooks the fact that the Reality in us is birthless and deathless, making us worried about death and afterlife.

Jñāna and *ajñāna,* death and afterlife, are relevant in the life of human beings alone. Other beings too are born and die but their afterlife does not find place here in the *Gītā*. Nevertheless, reference to it occurs in the *Chāndogya Upaniṣad*. Its Verse V.x.8 says, "Souls that do not go through either of the paths are also there: the brute creatures. Birth and death occur to them endlessly, and theirs is known as the third state (*tṛtīyam sthānam*)." Such beings are born and die simply as part of nature's creative unfoldment. Unmindful of birth and death and, therefore, not worried about death and afterlife, what is real for them is life alone. No detailed discussion on the two paths is made here for the reason that they are mere artefacts of human ignorance.[1]

Having imbibed the essence of wisdom and thus having realized your being immortal, the two paths are of no relevance to you. You are already a *jñānin*, you are already a *yogī*, engaged in activities seeing Me alone in every specific phase of actions. How *yogī*s such as yourself treat the said two paths, I shall tell you:

नैते सृती पार्थ जानन्योगी मुह्यति कश्चन ।
तस्मात्सर्वेषु कालेषु योगयुक्तो भवार्जुन ॥२७ ॥

naite sṛtī pārtha jānan yogī muhyati kaścana ।
tasmāt sarveṣu kāleṣu yogayukto bhavārjuna ॥27 ॥

Aware of what these two paths are, a *yogī* does not become deluded at all by these. Arjuna, you, therefore, always be firm in *yoga*.

Arjuna, it is the ignorant, the non-*yogī*s, who, facing the problem of the hereafter, become confused and deluded. A *yogī*, on the other hand, seeing himself as inseparably one with the birthless and deathless Me, knows himself to be birthless and deathless, and so, never thinks of what will happen after death. You too therefore are not to be worried about it; remain a *yogī* who sees himself beyond the realm of the two paths we have spoken of. Concluding this chapter, I shall tell you what that state beyond is:

---

1. For our interpretation of this topic see our commentary on the *Chāndogya Upaniṣad*.

वेदेषु यज्ञेषु तपःसु चैव दानेषु यत्पुण्यफलं प्रदिष्टम्।
अत्येति तत्सर्वमिदं विदित्वा योगी परं स्थानमुपैति चाद्यम्॥२८॥

vedeṣu yajñeṣu tapaḥsu caiva dāneṣu yat puṇya-phalaṁ pradiṣṭam ।
atyeti tat sarvam idaṁ viditvā yogī paraṁ sthānam upaiti cādyam ॥28॥

The meritorious rewards shown as of learning the Vedas, performing *yajñas*, undergoing austere self-discipline, offering religious gifts, are all transcended by the *yogī* who, knowing this, attains to the Supreme Primal State.

Arjuna, learning the Vedas, performing fire-sacrifices, offering religious gifts, and undergoing austere self-discipline, are all meritorious deeds prescribed by the Vedas. The rewards of the first three take one towards the black path of return, and that of the last towards the white path of no-return. What *yogīs* think of constantly is neither of death nor of after-death, but of the birthless and deathless Reality that he himself is. Experiencing himself to be that Reality is his attaining the Supreme Goal. Though aware of other notions held by non-*yogīs*, the *yogī* remains untouched by such notions.

Those who consider *kṣara* (the perishable appearances) as real are compelled to think of the hereafter; on the other hand, those who know the *akṣara* (imperishable) as the Reality, themselves become that *akṣara*, which is deathless, and which has no hereafter.

To recapitulate the present chapter:

The one Reality that assumes the appearance of everything phenomenal is *Brahman* or Myself, and this forms the core of what the entire *Gītā* intends to teach. Becoming enlightened to this Reality comprises *jñāna* (wisdom). Every apparent form being an aspect of My manifestation, I alone am to be seen in each and every such phenomenal entity, and all its specifying characteristics are Me alone; this understanding constitutes *vijñāna*. One enlightened on and contented with this two-faced perception of life is to be called *jñāna-vijñāna-tṛptātmā*.

The one all-underlying Substance, being imperishable, is termed *akṣara*, and all the perishable apparent forms are called *kṣara*. The *akṣara* is one and immutable, and the *kṣara* many and ever changing. The indescribable and mysterious creative urge in the one *akṣara* that causes the emergence of the many *kṣara*-forms from itself, within itself, is called *karma*. We individual beings, with all our peculiar personal traits, are here as an outcome of the actualization of this *karma*. Part of those personal traits is the warrior-quality in you. Therefore, while seeing Me as the *akṣara* Substance in you, you should see Me also in your act of fighting. Then you will be able to battle perceiving always your inseparable oneness with Me, the Supreme Goal attainable for you. Finding identity with Me virtually means your leaving the body.

The case of the one who finds one's identity with the *kṣara*-form or body is different; leaving body, for him, means death. Since such a leaving behind follows from being identified with the body, it follows that a new body will be attained. On the other hand, one who leaves body in principle by seeing one's identity with Me, attains Me.

You are a *karma-yogī;* all are not like you. Some give more importance to meditative self-enquiry. They, contemplating always on Me, concentrate their *prāṇa*'s functions between the eyebrows, and, on the strength of *yoga*, realize their oneness with Me. Some others choose the path of concentrating the *prāṇa* at the crown of the head. They, foregoing their body-identity, realize their oneness with *Brahman* along with uttering the syllable *AUṀ*. They too attain Me. Whichever the means adopted, one thing remains common: thinking upon nothing other than Me and remembering Me alone. Those of such attainments are free from birth and death, and consequently from rebirth. This is what is to be understood as the real *anāvṛtti* (the no-return).

The realm of changeful appearences, what we call *kṣara,* extends from the world around us to the imaginary world of Brahmā, and they are all subject to *punar-āvṛtti* (coming back again), for the emerging and merging back of distinct forms goes on without beginning and end. The ignorant who take such distinct forms as the real conceive their own ideas, based on their misconceptions of the hereafter. Such are the concepts of the white path and the black path. Such people believe that those who follow the former do not return to this world, and those who follow the other have to return to be reborn.

The *jñānin*, unlike the *ajñānin*, sees the leaving of the body differently: for the former it is his realizing that he is the one *akṣara*, and for the latter it is his leaving one *kṣara* body for another. A *jñānin* who is also a *yogī*, is never concerned with either path, for being a *jñānin* itself means attaining the Supreme Goal, for him. You too are free of the two paths for the same reason. The *yogī*'s state you are in now is much higher than all the rewards one can expect of all sorts of meritorious deeds as well.

Thus ends Chapter Eight entitled Akṣara-Brahma-Yoga of the Bhagavad-Gītā, the essence of the Upaniṣads, that embodies the yoga-śāstra of brahma-vidyā in the form of a dialogue between Śrī Kṛṣṇa and Arjuna.

IX

Rājavidyā-Rājaguhya-Yoga
—The Yoga of Kingly Wisdom, the Kingly Secret—

Śrī Kṛṣṇa:

Arjuna, by now, you are fully aware that it is in Me that all apparent forms appear and disappear. This perception having become well-founded through the meditations of Chapter VI, it is possible to see the imperishable Me alone, even in the minutest detail and quality of all apparent perishable forms. When this vision becomes an incessant experience, the highest state of wisdom has been attained, and this is the crowning secret of *brahma-vidyā*. Since this central chapter reveals the core aspects of this wisdom it has been given the name of *Rājavidyā-Rājaguhya-Yoga* (The Yoga of the Kingly Wisdom, the Kingly Secret).

श्री भगवानुवाच —

इदं तु ते गुह्यतमं प्रवक्ष्याम्यनसूयवे ।
ज्ञानं विज्ञानसहितं यज्ज्ञात्वा मोक्ष्यसे ऽशुभात् ॥१ ॥

śrī bhagavān uvāca —

idaṁ tu te guhyatamaṁ pravakṣyāmy anasūyave ।
jñānaṁ vijñāna-sahitaṁ yaj jñātvā mokṣyase 'śubhāt ॥1 ॥

Śrī Kṛṣṇa said —

To you who has no mistrust verily I shall declare the most profound secret of *jñāna* together with *vijñāna*. It known, you will be freed from all that is ominous.

Arjuna, as a wisdom dialogue enters its subtlest aspects, the disciple may be at a loss to frame precise questions, therefore the *guru* must take the initiative himself. This is the reason why I am entering the most profound part of My teaching without waiting for you to ask any question.

It must be clear to you, especially in the light of my teaching of Chapters VII and VIII, what I mean by *jñāna* together with *vijñāna*. Your desperate thoughts of being on the verge of committing a grave sin was instrumental in initiating this wisdom dialogue of ours. There is only one way out from all such situations, and that is to attain transparency of the wisdom I teach. Let us see how very subtle and profound it is to understand, but so easily put into practice.

राजविद्या राजगुह्यं पवित्रमिदमुत्तमम् ।
प्रत्यक्षावगमं धर्म्यं सुसुखं कर्तुमव्ययम् ॥२॥

rāja-vidyā rāja-guhyaṁ pavitram idam uttamam ।
pratyakṣāvagamaṁ dharmyaṁ susukhaṁ kartum avyayam ॥2॥

The crowning secret of a royal science is this, the best of all sanctifiers, yet perceptually realizable, all-supporting, and very easy to apply in life is it.

Arjuna, as you know, it is the one *cit* (Consciousness) alone, that underlies everything. At the same time, there exists also a limitless possibility of it becoming manifest as numerous forms and branches of knowledge. The crown of all such knowledge and sciences is the proper understanding of that *cit*. This knowledge is the Science of all sciences.

The basis of every science that we are familiar with, is the knowing mind trying to know something else. The knowing mind trying to know itself is a science of a different order, where the subject itself becomes the object, or to be more precise, where the subject-object duality vanishes. The science of knowing oneself or of the mind trying to know itself, thus, differs from other sciences both in the method of enquiry as well as the style of exposition. Those accustomed to the exact sciences may find the science of Self puzzling and incomprehensible at times. In respect of subtlety too, the science of Self excels all other sciences. Since this science has the capacity to release one from all ominous thoughts, its purificatory effect is limitless. No other science exists, which is higher than this, with respect to the sense of certitude and contentment it results in. Thus, it is to be considered the best of all knowledge (*uttamaṁ*).

Though esoteric and thus royal, this wisdom is in no way unattainable. On the contrary, of all knowledge, this may be understood as the simplest for it is as simple as a wave realizing its inseparable oneness with all waves like it, and with the ocean. Thus, it is to be qualified as being perceptually realizable (*pratyakṣa avagamaṁ*).

The word *dharmyaṁ*, rendered here as "all-supporting," means "that which accords within *dharma*" which in turn means "that which supports everything." This all-supporting Reality is nothing but *Brahman*. Whosoever has realized *Brahman* will live as *Brahman* become manifest, and such a life will be perfectly in accordance with *dharma*; such a life will be absolutely righteous. The word *dharma* also signifies righteousness in life. The Reality we are concerned with, in other words, is actualizable in our day-to-day affairs as an absolutely righteous life.

Living life in such a manner will not be a matter of effort for a realized person; it will simply be spontaneous, and thus very easy, (*susukhaṁ kartuṁ*). But with others, it will be a strenuous task. Unable to discern which is right and which is wrong, they become confused. The fear of doing wrong unintentionally torments them all through their lives, whereas nothing of the sort worries the wise one. The attainment of this wisdom requires *śraddhā* in the one Reality, in Me, and in what I teach. Those endowed with *śraddhā* realize Me and become one with Me. What happens to the others, I shall now tell you:

अश्रद्दधानाः पुरुषा धर्मस्यास्य परंतप ।
अप्राप्य मां निवर्तन्ते मृत्युसंसारवर्त्मनि ॥३॥

aśraddadhānāḥ puruṣā dharmasyāsya paraṁtapa ।
aprāpya māṁ nivartante mṛtyu-saṁsāra-vartmani ॥3 ॥

Men lacking *śraddhā* in this *dharma*, O Burner of Foes (Arjuna), not attaining Me, go back in the path of *saṁsāra* where (birth and) death are meaningful.

Arjuna, those who have no *śraddhā* in this wisdom, do not attain Me, for one's *śraddhā* decides the goal one attains. A goal one doesn't believe in, cannot be attained by one. I being the only birthless and deathless Reality, the only goal, those who have no *śraddhā* in Me, naturally live life in the realm of births and deaths and all the accompanying miseries, which is what we call *saṁsāra*. Life for such people is an ocean of sufferings; any escape becomes possible only when *śraddhā* is directed to Me and they attain wisdom. In the present chapter we are meditating on the hidden aspects of this very same wisdom. I shall now describe the core of that mystery.

मया ततमिदं सर्वं जगदव्यक्तमूर्तिना ।
मत्स्थानि सर्वभूतानि न चाहं तेष्ववस्थितः ॥४ ॥

mayā tatam idaṁ sarvaṁ jagad avyakta-mūrtinā I
mat-sthāni sarva-bhūtāni na cā 'haṁ teṣv avasthitaḥ II4 II

This changeful world is pervaded by Me; I am the one Reality that is described here as "indistinct" (*avyakta*). However, though all that has come into being exists in Me, my being is not to be found in them.

Arjuna, the word *jagat*, denoting the world, literally means "that which always changes." All worlds are subject to change. In all these worlds there exists the one Substance that underlies the being of all that changes. This Substance has necessarily to be unchanging, like the water in waves and gold in ornaments, and I Myself am that Substance.

This is the most secret aspect of wisdom — to perceive the one immutable "I" in all that is mutable. Everything is "I," everything is *Brahman* — attaining this certitude is the royal science (*rāja-vidyā*).

When, in this verse, I refer to Myself as *avyakta-mūrti,* it deserves special attention. *Avyakta* means something indistinct, whereas *mūrti* means that which has a concrete tangible form. The compound word *avyakta-mūrti* is, therefore, seemingly paradoxical. Though I am Really indistinct, all distinct forms are Myself become manifest, and I cannot remain abstract without assuming those forms. The seeming paradox thus vanishes when seen with a meditative inward gaze that sees beyond the bounds of words.

Everything that has come into being is called a *bhūta,* each of these having a beginning and an end, and their being is in Me alone just as waves exist in the occan.

A wave can easily and directly experience itself as the ocean, but trying to understand the ocean by looking for it in another wave, by thinking of it as an external object, will be in vain. In vain too are all our attempts to understand the ultimate Reality by analysing other entities like us. Such enquiries lead us to contradictory conclusions rather than to any certitude. It is in this sense that I say, "My being is not in them."

Those who worship idols, thinking of Me as existing in them, are not aware of the real essence of My existence which is not in any particular form but in all forms. Logical reasoning does not help to reach an understanding of the oneness of Myself, or the reason that I always remain one and indistinct, while appearing as the countless distinct entities of the manifest world. With all this in mind, you should attempt to understand the next two verses. We can consider the rest of this chapter as an elucidation of what I have said in this verse.

न च मत्स्थानि भूतानि पश्य मे योगमैश्वरम्।
भूतभृन्न च भूतस्थो ममात्मा भूतभावनः॥५॥

na ca mat-sthāni bhūtāni paśya me yogam aiśvaram ।
bhūta-bhṛn na ca bhūtastho mamā 'tmā bhūta-bhāvanaḥ ॥5॥

Yet beings have no existence in Me. This all-reigning *yoga*-state of Mine, you will have to perceive

> intuitively. Though reigning over all apparent forms causing their emergence, My self-being is not in them.

Arjuna, I being the one Reality in everything that has come into being, to say that those beings do not exist in Me may sound paradoxical. But our concern here is not the logical strictness of statements, but the transparency of the vision of Reality contained in them.

Just as a wave is simply a momentary formation on the surface of the ocean, without existence of its own, so too is the state of beings in Me. We cannot say that something which does not exist, can have being in something that exists. The total ocean does not exist in waves, and similar is My non-existence in the entire range of beings. All appearances, with no existence of their own, are unreal, what is Real is Myself alone.

Though waves are unreal, the ocean has in it the inherent potential to ceaselessly make both waves rise up as well as to control them. Likewise in Me too, there is the urge to make all apparent but unreal forms emerge and to reign over these. In that sense I am their *Īśvara*, meaning God, but literally "one who controls." *Aiśvara* means "that which is related to *Īśvara*." This mysterious element as well as its effects (the emerging of apparent forms and I) cannot be separated out; they are in a *yoga* state of inseparable oneness.

I, as you know, am *cit* (unconditioned Consciousness) in essence, and in that Consciousness are formulated numerous images, each appearing as a perceptible distinct entity. My being the one pervading Substance (*ātmā*) in all such images and entities, makes Me their *bhartā* (the indwelling controller). Eager to seek Me, people may scrutinize some such entities. What they face will be some or other inert aspect of Me, and never the living Me. Only that seeker who turns his attention inwards, to himself, will perceive Me as a living Reality.

How all the apparent entities find place in Me, I shall make clear to you with the help of an analogy:

यथाकाशस्थितो नित्यं वायुः सर्वत्रगो महान्।
तथा सर्वाणि भूतानि मत्स्थानीत्युपधारय ॥६॥

yathākāśa-sthito nityaṁ vāyuḥ sarvatrago mahān ।
tathā sarvāṇi bhūtāni mat sthānīty upadhāraya ॥6॥

Know that, as the air of great expanse that moves around everywhere has its being in space, so all that has emerged have their being in Me.

Arjuna, We know that air exists in space. Unlike that of water and the pitcher containing it, the relation between air and space is that of inseparable oneness — air cannot exist without space and space does not exist without air. Though, future astro-physics will assert the existence of empty space without air, its being so will be, in our calculations, not as actual experience. Even on our reaching that empty space, our existence is possible only in an artificially created atmosphere of air. Space in the realm of life is thus always filled with air. Likewise related are I and the beings that exist in Me.

Look at the way in which those beings emerge from and merge in Me:

सर्वभूतानि कौन्तेय प्रकृतिं यान्ति मामिकाम्।
कल्पक्षये पुनस्तानि कल्पादौ विसृजाम्यहम्॥७॥

sarva-bhūtāni kaunteya prakṛtiṁ yānti māmikāṁ ।
kalpa-kṣaye punas tāni kalpādau visṛjāmy ahaṁ ॥7॥

All beings, O Arjuna, go into the *prakṛti* of Mine at the end of a *kalpa*, and at the beginning of it, I cause their emanation again.

Arjuna, what a *kalpa* (world-cycle) is, we have seen in Verse 17 of the last chapter. In Verse 3 of the same chapter, we learnt also of the indomitable creative urge inherent in Me, which we termed *karma*. When that *karma* is active, I am called *prakṛti*, the word literally meaning "that which goes on working properly" (*prakarṣeṇa karoti iti*). I could well be thought of, also as existing inactive with all these potential *karma*s hidden within. Then all beings could be imagined to have gone back into Me. That, in principle, is the *kalpa-kṣaya* (the end of the world-cycle). I could equally well be thought of with all the *karma*s having found expression, resulting in the emergence of all beings. (Emerging of a new phase always involves the merger of the previous one). Then I am the one Substance that has assumed the form of all beings. Seeing Me thus, is the philosophical connotation of the mythological concept *kalpādi* (the beginning of a world-cycle). In fact, it is impossible for Me to exist without My *karma*s manifesting, and thus emerging as everything.

You should take special notice of the "I" understood here, as being neither simply Śrī Kṛṣṇa the Lord, nor Kṛṣṇa the *guru*, nor even *Brahman* the Absolute. As we have already seen, it is when the "I" in Me and the "I" in you become one "I" that *jñāna* reaches its highest. It is from that unitive "I" that everything emerges, and into which everything merges back. Such is My all reigning *yoga* state. The one *prakṛti* in Me is in you as well.

To clarify it further:

प्रकृतिं स्वामवष्टभ्य विसृजामि पुनः पुनः ।
भूतग्राममिमं कृत्स्नमवशं प्रकृतेर्वशात् ॥८ ॥

prakṛtiṁ svām avaṣṭabhya visṛjāmi punaḥ-punaḥ ।
bhūta-grāmam imaṁ kṛtsnam avaśaṁ prakṛter vaśāt ॥8 ॥

Resorting to My own *prakṛti* and helplessly subject to it, I bring forth again and again the entire multitude of beings.

Arjuna, subject to the *prakṛti* in Me are my activities; so too are your activities subject to the *prakṛti* in you. Even I myself cannot stop the flow of *prakṛti*'s creative unfoldment happening in Me, so too is it with you. As a result of this flow, everything in this cosmic system has come into being from Me. Do you know what My attitude is towards those *karma*s taking place in Me? I shall tell you:

न च मां तानि कर्माणि निबध्नन्ति धनञ्जय।
उदासीनवदासीनमसक्तं तेषु कर्मसु ॥९॥

na ca māṁ tāni karmāṇi nibadhnanti dhanañjaya ।
udāsīnavad āsīnam asaktaṁ teṣu karmasu ॥9॥

Remaining indifferent and unattached to them as I am, O Arjuna, those *karma*s do not bind Me either.

Arjuna, *prakṛti* is an essential part of Me, and it does its job. Not considering it as my *karma*, I remain a witness and thus no *karma* binds Me. The sense of sin, as you know, is born from one's being bound by *karma*s, with the conception of "This is my *karma;* its fruits are also mine." You see yourself in My place; then everything will be transparent. You will find your problem also solved or rather to have dissolved. Neither I nor you can curb the flow of events in nature; we can only be mere witnesses. How the cosmic system remains in a constant state of flux, I shall now tell you:

मयाध्यक्षेण प्रकृतिः सूयते सचराचरम्।
हेतुनानेन कौन्तेय जगद्विपरिवर्तते ॥१०॥

mayādhyakṣena prakṛtiḥ sūyate sacarācaram ।
hetunānena kaunteya jagad viparivartate ॥10॥

Presided over by Me, the *prakṛti* gives birth to everything, living and non-living. Because of it, O Arjuna, the world constantly evolves.

Arjuna, *prakṛti,* the creative urge in Me, makes everything arise from Myself, whereas I, as consciousness, remain always a witness to such events. You too are like this. Your earlier decision not to act when action was inevitable as part of the flow of nature, was in a sense, an attempt to curb the flow of nature, which none of us is capable of doing. You and I, as witnesses, are, strictly speaking, not to be counted as individual human beings, either as Kṛṣṇa or Arjuna. I shall tell you how wrong such a notion is:

अवजानन्ति मां मूढा मानुषीं तनुमाश्रितम् ।
परं भावमजानन्तो मम भूतमहेश्वरम् ॥११॥

avajānanti māṁ mūḍhā mānuṣīṁ tanum āśritam ।
paraṁ bhāvam ajānanto mama bhūta-maheśvaram ॥11॥

The foolish, ignorant as they are of My transcendental being as the Supreme Lord of beings, misunderstand Me as body-based.

Arjuna, I really am the Supreme Self; so are you and all else. But ignorance makes people unaware of being so, and foolishly they think of themselves as identified with human forms. They treat Me as Śrī Kṛṣṇa the individual and you as Arjuna the individual. You too were prey to this misconception when you thought of yourself as Arjuna the individual, gave rise to the idea that, since you were the doer of the *karma* required at the moment, you would accumulate sin. See yourself as the Supreme Self; then you will see the same Self in all else as well. You realize thus that the real being (*ātmā*) in you is the Supreme Lord of all beings (*bhūta-maheśvara*).

How people misconceive themselves and thus unwittingly make their own life meaningless and miserable, I shall tell you:

मोघाशा मोघकर्माणो मोघज्ञाना विचेतसः ।
राक्षसीमासुरीं चैव प्रकृतिं मोहिनीं श्रिताः ॥१२॥

moghāśā mogha-karmāṇo mogha-jñāna vicetasaḥ ।
rākṣasīm āsurīṁ caiva prakṛtiṁ mohinīṁ śritāḥ ॥12॥

Futile become their hopes; futile become their *karmas*; futile become their knowledge. Of perverted understanding, they submit themselves to the confounding natures of malignant titans and demons.

Arjuna, the fools we saw in the last verse see themselves as individuals, each with a set of his own hopes and aspirations. All of such hopes or aspirations cannot be fulfilled, and this causes the feeling that their life has been futile.

The *karmas* such people do are not treated as part of *prakṛti*'s unfoldment of creativity, but are meant for the fulfilment of personal ends. Such *karmas* do not always lead them to the expected goals, thus causing the feeling that their *karmas* have been futile.

The root cause of all this is a perverted understanding of oneself. Instead of searching for what is real in oneself and all others, the knowledge gained has been about appearances. Instead of living with the awareness of what is real in oneself, the foolish make use of their knowledge in exploiting others for the fulfilment of personal gains. In place of contentment, such lives become filled with frustration.

Those who are frustrated may at times act hard-heartedly, and when this becomes a habit, a certain malevolent and demonic character gradually strikes root. (The details of such human character will be discussed in Verses 7 to 20 of Chapter XVI.) Those who are enlightened and know what they really are, are to be called *mahātmā*s (the great). What will their life be like, I shall now tell you:

महात्मानस्तु मां पार्थ दैवीं प्रकृतिमाश्रिताः ।
भजन्त्यनन्यमनसो ज्ञात्वा भूतादिमव्ययम् ॥१३॥

mahātmānas tu māṁ pārtha daivīṁ prakṛtim aśritāḥ ।
bhajanty ananya-manaso jñātvā bhūtādim avyayaṁ ॥13॥

The *mahātmās*, on the other hand, O Pārtha, resorting to their *deva*-like nature and knowing Me, as the unexpended primal source of all beings, meditatively perceive and adore as not-another.

Arjuna, those who see themselves and Me as one Supreme Self, (*paramātmā*) are to be considered *mahātmā*s (the great), the word literally meaning "those who are the great *ātmā* worthy of worship," *mah* literally meaning "to worship." They in their day-to-day life resort always to the god-like aspect of their nature (*daivī-prakṛti*), turning a blind eye to demonic nature (*āsurī-prakṛti*) in themselves. That I, depending on My own *prakṛti,* assume the forms of all the worlds, was seen in Chapter VIII. This *prakṛti* of Mine has in it characteristics that we usually consider as good and bad, here termed *daivī prakṛti* (god-like nature-modality) and *āsurī-prakṛti* (demon-like nature-modality). Put in other words, the one Self-Reality, unfolding itself, assumes the appearance of both good and bad. My *prakṛti,* unlike in the view of some religionists, is not always to be taken as good. In fact, the goodness of the good is not discernible unless contrasted with the badness of the bad, and for this reason, what is bad is a part of the overall scheme of life. Yet those who are capable of discriminating good and bad always feel the imperativeness of overpowering badness and resorting to goodness. This discrimination, in its absolutist sense, requires seeing oneself not as an individual, but as the one Self-Reality — I — become manifest. Seeing Me not as something other, but as oneself, is the *ananya manas. Mahātmās* always remain perceiving Me thus as what is real in themselves, as what is real in everything, as the unexpended source of all. They meditate on Me, they adore Me, they worship Me; this state of mind is called *bhajanā*. Life for them will be a ceaseless flow of this *bhajanā*. Look at how such persons live in this world:

सततं कीर्तयन्तो मां यतन्तश्च दृढव्रताः।
नमस्यन्तश्च मां भक्त्या नित्ययुक्ता उपासते ॥१४॥

satataṁ kīrtayanto māṁ yatantaś ca dṛḍha-vratāḥ ।
namasyantaś ca māṁ bhaktyā nitya-yuktā upāsate ॥14॥

Constantly praising Me, avowedly striving, always devotedly saluting Me, and eternally united with Me as they are, they meditatively adore Me alone.

Arjuna, in themselves and everywhere they perceive Me alone. Their life process as a whole becomes part and parcel of praising Me. Whatever activities they are engaged in, they see Me alone creatively finding expression as those acts. Finding themselves fully identified with Me or *Brahman,* thus, becomes habitual to them even when engaged in their own natural activities.

Seeing Me alone everywhere, they cannot help taking note of My glory and so naturally salute Me, for they will see that there is nothing else worthy of salute. Perceiving Me alone even in themselves, they are always in a state of union with Me; this state is to be called *yoga*. Comparable is this state to an ornament finding its oneness with the gold-substance. Such, therefore, are to be called *nitya-yukta*s (eternally united with Me). They see nothing else to adore (*upāsanā*). Literally, the word *upāsanā* means to be seated close by and do service. What is nearest to anyone, we know, is nothing but the substance of one's own being, that is to say Myself, the Absolute. The Absolute thus is the most adorable.

The act of adoring Me with full awareness of My real glory is not necessarily expressed in the same way by everyone. What I give emphasis to here in this verse is the case of a *karma-yogī*, who finds himself in Me while being engaged in life's natural activities. How the *karma-yogin* and *jñāna-yogin* are to be differentiated was clarified in Chapter V. A *jñāna yogin*'s way of adoring Me is described in the next verse.

ज्ञानयज्ञेन चाप्यन्ये यजन्तो मामुपासते ।
एकत्वेन पृथक्त्वेन बहुधा विश्वतोमुखम् ॥१५॥

jñāna-yajñena cāpy anye yajanto mām upāsate ।
ekatvena pṛthaktvena bahudhā viśvato-mukham ॥15॥

Certain others are there who meditatively adore Me with wisdom sacrifice. They may adore Me, as having face everywhere, in different ways as one or many.

Arjuna, what the essence of *jñāna-yoga* is and how *jñāna* (wisdom) can be treated as a *yajña* (fire-sacrifice), were well clarified in Chapter IV. Those who perform such a *yajña* see themselves in Me, the Supreme Self. Understood as the all-underlying Substance, that Me is one, but understood as manifest as countless changeful entities forming the world, I am many. The difference between the two perceptions is only that of *sat* and *bhāva* "understandable" as separate, but never "actually" separable.

The entire cosmos and all life in it being My apparent manifestation, anything that forms a part of it could well be made instrumental in meditating on Me. Of such countless forms, I shall point out a few to you now:

अहं क्रतुरहं यज्ञः स्वधाहमहमौषधम् ।
मन्त्रो ऽहमहमेवाज्यमहमग्निरहं हुतम् ॥१६ ॥

ahaṁ kratur ahaṁ yajñaḥ svadhāham aham auṣadhaṁ ।
mantro 'aham aham evājyaṁ aham agnir ahaṁ hutaṁ ॥16 ॥

What is real in *kratu* is Myself; what appears as *yajña* too is Myself. *Svadhā* also really is Myself. The herbal products offered are Myself. I am the sacred formula uttered; I am the clarified butter offered; I am the sacrificial fire; the act of offering too is Myself.

Arjuna, manifesting as I am into endlessly various forms, My apparent faces are countless. However, certain functional situations of life can be separated and their constituent elements understood as being Me. One such situation, well known to Vedism, is that of *yajña* performed to please the *deva*s (gods). *Yajña*s are both with and without animal sacrifice, the former are known as *kratu*s and the latter simply *yajña*s. There are also other offerings made to appease departed souls (*pitṛ*s), known as *svadhā*s. Most of the materials offered in all such rituals are herbal products and all offerings are made along with the utterance of sacred Vedic *mantra*s. Offering *ghī* (clarified butter) is an essential part of all such rituals and all offerings are made into the sacred fire. The one real Substance in all such elements of any kind of sacrifice is to be understood as Myself.

पिताहमस्य जगतो माता धाता पितामहः ।
वेद्यं पवित्रमोङ्कार ऋक्साम यजुरेव च ॥१७ ॥

pitāham asya jagato mātā dhātā pitāmahaḥ ।
vedyaṁ pavitram oṁ-kāra ṛk sāma yajur eva ca ॥17 ॥

The father of this changeful world is Myself, its Mother, its sole support, its one Grandsire too. So are the sacred syllable *AUṀ* the knowable, and the *Ṛgveda, Sāmaveda* and *Yajurveda*.

Arjuna, this world, if thought of as a creation, should have a father and mother. I am both. Ever changing is the world, yet it constantly and consistently maintains a coherent order as though something unknown supports it; that unknown support (*dhātā*) is Myself. That *dhātā*, taken as Viṣṇu, the sustainer of the world, too is Myself. If everything should have a grandsire, a fore-father (*pitāmahaḥ*), suggesting Brahmā the creator, is also Myself.

Anything that is capable of being known is *vedya*, the most sacred of all such being *AUṀ*. That *AUṀ* is Myself, the Consciousness-Substance (*cit*) that unfolds itself and assumes the form of all knowledges, ideas and emotions. And Myself or *cit* is the Reality all the Vedas teach. The Vedas (Indian basic scriptures), being divided into the *Ṛgveda, Sāmaveda* and *Yajurveda* also constitute thus another instance of *cit* becoming unfolded as many. That one *cit* is Myself, so are all those Vedas Myself.

गतिर्भर्ता प्रभुः साक्षी निवासः शरणं सुहृत् ।
प्रभवः प्रलयः स्थानं निधानं बीजमव्ययम् ॥१८ ॥

gatīr bhartā pabhuḥ sākṣī nivāsaḥ śaranaṁ suhṛt ।
prabhavaḥ pralayaḥ sthānaṁ nidhānaṁ bījam avyayam ॥18 ॥

The goal, the protector, the ruler, the observer, the abode, the refuge, the friend of all, the ground of origin and dissolution, the repository of everything, the undiminishing seed of everything — all these are Myself.

Arjuna, different people have different concepts of the absolute Reality. The life problems faced by those people also vary; the nature of the trouble shooter each individual seeks out is also naturally different. It is the one Me, that people thus see variously.

Some live with an ultimate goal of life in view; that goal is Myself. Some think of God as the one protector or Ruler of everything. What they see so is none other than Myself. Certain others think of the ultimate Reality as the one immutable witness to everything mutable. That observer is Myself. For some, God is a friend of all. That friend too is Myself.

Man's eternal quest is to know the origin of the world and of himself. I am the one source into which everything returns, whatever the form and qualities attributed to it. The philosophical-minded conceive the absolute Reality as the imperishable and undiminishing repository of all that constitutes the world. There are others who think of the Reality as a primeval seed. All such varying concepts signify simply one Reality alone: Myself.

तपाम्यहमहं वर्षं निगृह्णाम्युत्सृजामि च ।
अमृतं चैव मृत्युश्च सदसच्चाहमर्जुन ॥१९॥

tapāmy aham ahaṁ varsaṁ nigr̥hṇāmy utsr̥jāmi ca ।
amr̥taṁ caiva mr̥tyuś ca sad asac cāham arjuna ॥19॥

Arjuna, the summer is Myself, the rain is Myself. The seasons are withheld by Me and sent forth by Me. The immortal is Myself, so is death. The Reality is Myself, so is the unreal.

Arjuna, in the context of weather conditions, both scorching summers as well as torrential rains may occur. Sometimes we feel that when warm weather is needed, someone holds it back, and when rain is needed there is one who restrains it. I am the only Reality that underlies all such phenomena of nature, whether unfavourable or favourable.

Some see only one immortal Reality in everything with the changeful appearances being merely Its evanescent manifestation. What they see as the Immortal is Myself. Death is not a problem for such people. But most live always in fear of death as though it is a terrifying fiend — these are the ignorant who treat individual beings that are born and die, as real on their own. What they see as death also is a functional facet of Mine.

Even the experiences of the Real and the unreal, O Arjuna, are Myself manifesting. Both existence and non-existence are experiences, and no experience can occur unless consciousness or mind functions as a common ground. That common ground — Consciousness — is Myself.

Arjuna, to perceive My facets everywhere in all things can become a habit only with those who can meditatively perceive and adore Me as "not-another" (*ananya-manas*). Attaining such an inner vision is where all Vedāntic search reaches its term. Those who are otherwise do not consider attaining Me to be the goal of life. They, instead, take recourse to Vedism and its rituals, and aim at accumulating religious merits in order to reach heaven to enjoy its pleasures. Though it is evident that this doctrine has an inherent deficiency, most do not care for it, being blinded by thoughts of the heavenly pleasures that supposedly await them. What this deficiency of Vedism is, I shall tell you:

त्रैविद्या मां सोमपाः पूतपापा यज्ञैरिष्ट्वा स्वर्गतिं प्रार्थयन्ते ।
ते पुण्यमासाद्य सुरेन्द्रलोकमश्नन्ति दिव्यान्दिवि देवभोगान् ॥२०॥
ते तं भुक्त्वा स्वर्गलोकं विशालं क्षीणे पुण्ये मर्त्यलोकं विशन्ति ।
एवं त्रयीधर्ममनुप्रपन्ना गतागतं कामकामा लभन्ते ॥२१॥

traividyā māṁ soma-pāḥ pūta-pāpā yajñair iṣṭvā svar-gatiṁ prārthayante ।
te puṇyam āsādya surendra-lokam aśnanti divyān divi deva-bhogān ॥20॥

te taṁ bhuktvā svarga-lokaṁ viśālaṁ kṣīṇe puṇye martya-lokaṁ viśanti ।

evaṁ trayī-dharmam anuprapannā gatāgataṁ kāma-kāmā labhante ॥21॥

Those who take recourse to the three Vedas, purified of sins by drinking *soma* juice, pray for attaining heaven by worshipping Me with fire sacrifices; reaching the world of the chief of gods, they enjoy the divine pleasures of heaven.

They, after having enjoyed the extensive world of heaven, and thus their acquired merits having become exhausted, re-enter the world of mortals. The pleasure-seekers, following the teachings of the Vedas as they are, thus attain the state of having to come and go (between heaven and earth).

Arjuna, an *ananya-manas* is the one who perceives the attainable Reality not as something else, but as comprising his own being (*ātmā*). This perception puts an end to the search for Reality and renders life peaceful. Only a few obtain this perception. Others think of life's goal as something far away, as far away as the heavens above, where it is all pleasure. The way to reach there, as the Vedas teach, is through pleasing the gods (*deva*s), its inhabitants, by performing *yajña*s, and the Vedas teach the performance of such. At one level, it may appear that the best way of life man can choose is that of Vedism. Imbibing the intoxicating *soma* juice — symbolic of man's quest for pleasure — is an essential part of these *yajña*s. Performing them purifies man of all sins and qualifies him to enter heaven.

Since I am really the one Reality in everything, what the Vedists think of as heaven is nothing other than Myself become manifest, and thus Myself in essence. And in that sense, though the way they conceive of Me is wrong, what such seekers aim to attain is Myself.

They, as taught by the Vedas, acquire merit and on their strength, after death, reach heaven and enjoy its pleasures. But no Veda assures that one can eternally remain in heaven. Enjoying the pleasures of heaven terminates when the merits acquired while in the human world are exhausted, and then one inevitably has to return to the human world. Continuing to acquire merits again, he can go again to heaven, of course to come back once again. This coming and going between heaven and earth is what Vedism holds as the highest goal of life.

Such journeying terminates only when realizing that what appears as the worlds here and hereafter is nothing but *Brahman* variously manifesting. Then the realization dawns that there is no "other" world existing other than the Reality in oneself. How such enlightened ones live, I shall tell you:

अनन्याश्चिन्तयन्तो मां ये जनाः पर्युपासते ।
तेषां नित्याभियुक्तानां योगक्षेमं वहाम्यहम् ॥२२॥

ananyāś cintayanto māṁ ye janāḥ paryupāsate ।
teṣāṁ nityābhiyuktānāṁ yoga-kṣemaṁ vahāmy aham ॥22॥

People who meditatively adore Me with the awareness that I am not different from themselves, are there. The *yogic* easement of life of those eternally united ones, I do take care of.

Arjuna, very rare are those who realize that the only adorable Reality, the only attainable Goal, is none other than the Substance that constitutes their own being, and that no other reality exists therefore to be sought out. That Substance being Myself, they constantly see Me alone everywhere; their mind is always filled with and guided by the thought of Myself; they meditatively adore Me alone. They are to be termed *nityābhiyukta*s (those eternally united with Me). Distracted by nothing else, such enlightened ones find themselves always in Me and Me in them. In their day-to-day affairs, in the pains and pleasures of life, such see nothing but My own Being manifesting. They see Me alone as the one to depend on, for I am the one Reality that appears as everything. It is their dependence on Me that results in the fulfilment of day-to-day necessities as part of My own self-unfoldment. Such people constantly feel at ease in life because of their awareness of being one with Me, which is to be termed *yoga kṣema* (the yogic easement of life).

The one Reality that manifests as everything is Myself, and thus, what we call the other worlds and other deities worthy of worship are all Myself. However, there are many pious people who worship gods and deities, treating them to be different and apart from themselves. How such adorations are to be treated, I shall tell you:

ये ऽप्यन्यदेवता भक्ता यजन्ते श्रद्धयान्विताः।
ते ऽपि मामेव कौन्तेय यजन्त्यविधिपूर्वकम् ॥२३॥

ye 'py anya-devatā-bhaktā yajante śraddhayānvitāḥ ।
te 'pi mām eva kaunteya yajanty avidhi-pūrvakam ॥23॥

Pious people devoted to other deities are also there, who worship them with full faith and attention. Me alone they too worship, though not in conformity with the basics.

Treating anything as worthy of worship is not wrong, for I am the one essential content in everything. The religious practices of worshipping deities or the gods of heaven, as though they exist different from the worshipper, are prevalent. What manifests as those deities and gods being Myself, such worshippers too can be treated as worshipping Me, though they remain unaware of the implications of their worship. Outgrowths of that ignorance are all such practices, and its dark shade tainting them is but natural. Any practice lacking understanding can go wrong in any aspect, and hence are to be considered *avidhipūrvakam* (not conforming to basics). How such practices deviate from the basics, I shall make clearer:

अहं हि सर्वयज्ञानां भोक्ता च प्रभुरेव च।
न तु मामभिजानन्ति तत्त्वेनातश्च्यवन्ति ते ॥२४॥

ahaṁ hi sarva-yajñānāṁ bhoktā ca prabhur eva ca ।
na tu mām abhijānanti tattvenātaś cyavanti te ॥24॥

I am the enjoyer of all sacrifices as also their Lord. Unaware of Me being so, they happen to deflect from the basics.

Arjuna, acquiring merits and thus enjoying the pleasures of heaven, we know, are the aims of Vedic rituals, whereas Vedāntic wisdom attains finality in perceiving Me alone in everything. What appears as merits, as the pleasures of heaven and even as the enjoyers of such pleasures, are all thus really Myself variously manifesting. Vedism and its gods, in other words, are lost to view in the all-inclusive wisdom of Vedānta, like small pools disappear in an all-inundating flood.

Yajamāna, whose enjoyment the *yajña* supposedly ensures, is one of My manifest forms. Opinion differs as to who ensures this enjoyment: whether it is the gods (*deva*s) or the mysterious principle called *apūrva*. In either case, the existence of whoever ensures enjoyment, too, is one of My assumed forms. Yet, this Me, that appears as all the elements involved in rituals, in the normal course does not come to the view of ritualists, for in their view, the rituals, their performers, their enjoyers, their Lord, all exist as different from one another. It is this wrong notion that deflects them from the right path towards Me. Thus, they do not attain Me even though really I am in them. How this happens I shall clarify:

यान्ति देवव्रता देवान् पितॄन्यान्ति पितृव्रताः ।
भूतानि यान्ति भूतेज्या यान्ति मद्याजिनोऽपि माम् ॥२५॥

yānti deva-vratā devān pitṝn yānti pitṛ-vratāḥ ।
bhūtāni yānti bhūtejyā yānti mad-yājino 'pi mām ॥25॥

Those who persistently propitiate the gods, attain the gods; those who persistently propitiate the manes attain the manes; those who sacrifice for material beings attain material benefits; and those who sacrifice themselves in Me, attain Me.

Arjuna, notions of life and its goal differ from person to person, and what is considered adorable also thus varies. Some think of reaching heaven after death as the ultimate goal of life, and as a means to that end, they propitiate the gods (*deva*s). Some others consider appeasing the souls of the departed as enabling them to lead a peaceful present life; they perform rituals like *śrāddha* and *svadhā*. Those who consider material gains as making life meaningful are also there; they make efforts accordingly and do gain what they look for. One's attainments, in short, depends on what one weighs up as the goal of life and the efforts made therefor.

I being the one Reality that appears as gods, manes and materials, why their worshippers' attainment also cannot be that of Me? Ignorant of Me, they, when attaining and enjoying the goals they long for, remain in the dark as to the reality that I am the result attained and its bestower too. They, instead, think the deity or god they adore bestows the results. In effect, what they feel thus is not that they attain Me, but the gods and their bounties. Had they realized Me in themselves, in all the gods and deities and in the benefits they bestow, they would very well have become fully aware of the meaning-lessness of rituals, and disavowed them, to find joy in the Self alone, in Me alone.

Me alone seen in everything, what one happens to do physically, verbally or mentally will form a *yajña* (sacrifice) unto Me. Seeing My presence alone in themselves and other entities is the way they attain Me. Virtually no action is there, no worshipping is there, no prayer is there, in that *yajña*, which may sound deficient in some respect mainly because of the conditioning our mind has become subject to, owing to the millenniums-long ritualistic culture. Should one feel so, it could be amended by performing some minimal and least troublesome ritual as I suggest here:

पत्रं पुष्पं फलं तोयं यो मे भक्त्या प्रयच्छति ।
तदहं भक्त्युपहृतमश्नामि प्रयतात्मनः ॥२६ ॥

patraṁ puṣpaṁ phalaṁ toyaṁ yo me bhaktyā prayacchati ।
tad ahaṁ bhakty-upahṛtam aśnāmi prayatātmanaḥ ॥26 ॥

One leaf, one flower, one fruit, a little water — these when offered to Me with full dedication, that devout offering of the pure-hearted, I accept with joy.

Arjuna, though such a minimal ritual is recommended, what is important is not the actual doing of it, but the attitude with which it is done. To clarify it:

यत्करोषि यदश्नासि यज्जुहोषि ददासि यत्।
यत्तपस्यसि कौन्तेय तत्कुरुष्व मदर्पणम्॥२७॥

yat karoṣi yad aśnāsi yaj juhoṣi dadāsi yat ।
yat tapasyasi kaunteya tat kuruṣva mad-arpaṇam ॥27॥

Arjuna, whatever you do, whatever you consume, whatever you offer as oblation, whatever austerity you subject yourself to, do it as an offering unto Me.

Arjuna, one Supreme Self-Reality alone exists here as you and me. Do live with this awareness, and then you will feel that whatever you happen to do in life is simply part of the unfoldment of the *prakṛti* of that Self-Reality. Your attitude towards those acts, then, will be that of offering all of them unto Me. All acts will then be of the Self, of *prakṛti,* not of Arjuna the individual. Do everything that is natural, knowing that they are the acts of the Self. You will then feel a sense of freedom that is known as *mukti* or *mokṣa.* How do you experience it, I shall tell you:

शुभाशुभफलैरेवं मोक्ष्यसे कर्मबन्धनैः।
संन्यासयोगयुक्तात्मा विमुक्तो मामुपैष्यसि॥२८॥

śubhāśubha-phalair evaṁ mokṣyase karma-bandhanaiḥ ।
saṁnyāsa-yoga yuktātmā vimukto mām upaiṣyasi ॥28॥

Both good and evil results of the *karma*-caused bondages you thus become free of. United with the Self through self-renunciation, you attain Me, becoming absolutely Free.

Arjuna, the act of fighting you were destined to do was wrongly thought of by you as your *karma,* instead of seeing it as the *karma* that takes place in My being, in My *prakṛti*. This wrong notion made you scared of the evil of having to kill your own *gurus* and kith and kin. All this arose from your not knowing Me as the one Reality that underlies you, your *karmas*, all the great warriors gathered here, the entire world. Had you seen Me so, you would have found in all your doings only the variety of specific ways in which My *prakṛti* finds self-expression. This is the only way you can get rid of bondages caused by *karmas*.

Whether a *karma* is meritorious or sinful is of concern for the doer of it. Though all *karmas* take place in Me, I have no sense of being the doer of any *karma*, and hence neither does their outcome, good or evil, worry Me. *Karma* being good or bad has some man-made value notions for criterion, all necessarily relative and conditional. I, the only absolute and unconditioned Reality, am concerned with *karma* as such alone, not with its goodness or evilness. Such *karmas* of mine, wrongly taken as his own and then subjected to evaluation, are felt to be good or bad by man. Done with the awareness that all *karmas* are mine, your doings will neither be good nor evil, thus making you free of both sin and merit. This is the only way open to man to set himself free of all sins. The basic requirement for this attainment is your renouncing (*nyāsa*) yourself unto Me. Such a proper (*samyak)* self-renunciation is to be called *saṁnyāsa*, wherein you directly experience your inseparable oneness with Me, as is a wave one with the ocean. One of such experience is called here *saṁnyāsa-yoga-yuktātmā* (one united with the Self through self-renunciation). I am not bound by anything; one who is one with Me too is so; he is liberated (*vimukta*) and no doubt he already has attained Me.

Though I am the one Reality underlying everything, everyone does not attain Me; only those who meditatively adore Me have that attainment. Why is it so? I shall tell you:

समो ऽहं सर्वभूतेषु न मे द्वेष्यो ऽस्ति न प्रियः।
ये भजन्ति तु मां भक्त्या मयि ते तेषु चाप्यहम्॥२९॥

samo 'haṁ sarvabhūteṣu na me dveṣyo 'sti na priyaḥ ।
ye bhajanti tu māṁ bhaktyā mayi te teṣu cāpy aham ॥29॥

Equally existing in every being am I; none is hated by Me, none is dear to Me either. Yet those who meditatively perceive Me with full devotion and dedication alone find themselves in Me and Me in themselves.

Arjuna, no further clarification is needed on My being the one Reality existing equally in every being. Comparable to water being the essential content of all the waves, is My uniform existence. But no wave can experience its identity with the ocean unless it is conscious of it being so. Likewise, those who are conscious of themselves being transitory apparent forms that emerge in one *Brahman,* in Myself, alone experientially live one with Me. Others, though really one with Me, do not have the experience of being so. To perceive Me thus constitutes the essence of *bhajanā* and those who do so incessantly are called *bhakta*s (those who are devout). Evaluating their doings as meritorious or sinful, seen from the prevailing worldly norms of ethics, will be incorrect. To clarify it further:

अपि चेत्सुदुराचारो भजते मामनन्यभाक् ।
साधुरेव स मन्तव्यः सम्यग्व्यवसितो हि सः ॥३०॥

api cet sudurācāro bhajate mām ananya-bhāk ।
sādhur eva sa mantavyaḥ samyag vyavasito hi saḥ ॥30॥

Be he a heinous evil doer, if he meditatively perceives Me as existing not different from himself, he must needs be counted as good, for his is the right resolve.

Arjuna, those who see themselves always one with Me, may at times, as part of the ongoing flow of *prakṛti*'s action, be doing things that could usually be counted as bad. Such *karma*s should not be treated as evil, for they were not done as their *karma*s nor was there any guilty conscience in them of having done something forbidden. What became unavoidable as part of *prakṛti*'s whirling actions was done, that is all; thus is their feeling. Even as they were doing so, their interest was neither in them nor in their goodness or badness, but in Me alone. Whatever thus destined to do in life, they, no doubt, attain Me. What kind of attainment is theirs, I shall make clearer:

क्षिप्रं भवति धर्मात्मा शश्वच्छान्तिं निगच्छति ।
कौन्तेय प्रतिजानीहि न मे भक्तः प्रणश्यति ॥३१॥

kṣipram bhavati dharmātmā śaśvac-chāntim nigacchati ।
kaunteya pratijānīhi na me bhaktaḥ praṇaśyati ॥31॥

Instantly, he becomes a *dharmātmā* and attains to lasting peace as well. O Arjuna, no one who meditatively perceives Me ever perishes.

Arjuna, one who does not desist from any *karma* unavoidable in life with the understanding that its real doer is the *prakṛti* of Myself, in effect finds his existence in Me, the Absolute. Actions are not discriminated by him as righteous and unrighteous, for he is *dharmātmā* himself — one who finds his being in the one all-sustaining world order. He, regardless of what he actually does, feels lasting joy and peacefulness in life — the peacefulness of being in Me, the Immortal, thus becoming immortal himself.

The right of attaining Me in this manner is not the monopoly of anyone, it is open to all, its doors are left open even to those who are considered sinners, provided they understand and perceive Me properly as detailed so far. To clarify it further:

मां हि पार्थ व्यपाश्रित्य येऽपि स्युः पापयोनयः ।
स्त्रियो वैश्यास्तथा शूद्रास्तेऽपि यान्ति परां गतिम् ॥३२॥

māṁ hi pārtha vyapāśritya ye 'pi syuḥ pāpa-yonayaḥ ।
striyo vaiśyās tathā śūdrās te 'pi yānti parāṁ gatīm ॥32॥

Arjuna, taking refuge in Me alone, even those of sinful origin attain the Supreme Goal; so do women, vaiśyas and śūdras as well.

Arjuna, it is an orthodox convention that women, vaiśyas (the merchant-farmer class) and śūdras (the servant class) do not have the right to learn the Vedas. With even less chance of learning the Vedas are those born illegitimately and thus supposedly are of sinful origin (*pāpa-yonayaḥ*). I would like you to understand this word as denoting those who are originated from sin as well as those who originate sin. I do not consider this an occasion for going into the legitimacy of this convention. The Vedāntic wisdom we are concerned with is of a much higher order than Vedic rituals, and much wider in scope than Vedism. Its final goal is not dependent on adhering to such conventions, which really are nothing but human prejudices. The goal of real wisdom is reached by seeing the Absolute in every detail of life and of the world, regardless of whether one is a woman, a vaiśya, a śūdra or an "outcaste," a *cāṇḍāla*. Once this wisdom is stabilized, attaining the ultimate goal becomes certain.

किं पुनर्ब्राह्मणाः पुण्या भक्ता राजर्षयस्तथा ।
अनित्यमसुखं लोकमिमं प्राप्य भजस्व माम् ॥३३॥

kiṁ punar brāhmaṇāḥ puṇyā bhaktā rājarṣayas tathā ।
anityam asukhaṁ lokam imaṁ prāpya bhajasva mām ॥33॥

How much more will it be so with brāhmins, with those who studiedly try to meditatively perceive Me, as also with royal seers! Having come into this world of impermanence and unhappiness, therefore, you do meditatively perceive Me.

Arjuna, you wrongly thought of your actions as "your" *karma*s, simply because you identified yourself with your apparent visible form, instead of seeing yourself as identified with Me. So long as you see yourself so, there can be no release from the bondage of actions (*karma-bandha*). The only way to release oneself from those bondages is to perceive Me alone as existing in your apparent form, and Me alone as the doer of all *karma*s. How this experience of ever-lasting release and peace, is to be effected in life, I shall tell you:

मन्मना भव मद्भक्तो मद्याजी मां नमस्कुरु ।
मामेवैष्यसि युक्त्वैवमात्मानं मत्परायणः ॥३४ ॥

manmanā bhava mad-bhakto mad-yājī māṁ namas-kuru ।
mām evaiṣyasi yuktvaivam ātmānaṁ mat-parāyaṇaḥ ॥34 ॥

Do become one of My mind; do become one who meditatively perceives Me alone; do become one who offers oneself unto Me; do bow down before Me alone. You thus, counting as you are attuned to Me alone, having united yourself as you are with Me alone, will attain Me alone.

Arjuna, it is in mind, as we know, that all ideas and notions are formulated. The notions of merit and sin too are mind-formed. Such notions may arise in your personal mind, but My mind knows neither sin nor merit. Let your mind become My mind, a natural consequence of you finding yourself in Me. You will then think with My mind and thus, be free of sin and merit. Then in your existence, in your thinking, in your doings, what you meditatively perceive (*bhaj*) will be Me alone.

We have already seen in Chapters III and IV, how all the *karma*s of life can be transformed into an offering (*yajña*) to Me. We also saw the wisdom too can be treated as such an offering. That these two sacrifices (*yajña*s), in essence, are one, became evident in Chapter V. Ultimately, what is sacrificed in these *yajña*s is nothing but you, the person. You and all others like you, are thus offered unto me the one Reality, the one to adore and to salute. There are those who consider worldly wealth as worthy of adoration, positions of power as worthy of adoration, status in society and other worldly gains as adorable. All such adoration helps to boost the ego. The ego fades out in Me only when I am adored in the light of all that I have said so far. Those who have attained that state, will without doubt find themselves in Me, in the state of a *yoga-yukta*.

Arjuna, this concluding verse of the 9th chapter marks the exact middle of the *Gītā*. The crux of My teaching is also contained here.

Underscoring this fact, an almost verbatim repetition of this verse occurs at the end of Chapter XVIII, when my teaching ends.

Let us now take an overview of what we covered in Chapter IX:

The perishable and imperishable aspects of existence were clarified in Chapter VIII. All the impermanant apparent forms have the same one imperishable underlying Reality — Myself. Everything, therefore, essentially is Myself, and I am indistinct. Everything distinct is really the one indistinct Me variously manifesting. This is the most secret aspect of all the knowledge contained here; this is royal wisdom (*rāja-vidyā*). From this indistinct Me may arise those of divine characteristics as well as those of demonic nature. Of these, the former alone will realize Me as being not different from themselves. They constantly see at work, even in their day-to-day activities, the *karma* principle inherent in the Supreme Self — Myself — never seeing themselves as doers. They are thus able to always remain free from *karma*-born bondage as well as from the bondage of "sin" and "merit." Seeing themselves as one with Me and seeing all *karmas* as My *karmas*, they are to be considered good in the absolutist sense, even if seen to be engaged in actions usually considered "evil." The right to such wisdom and the attainment of this wisdom is open to all, even to those who are viewed as of "sinful" origin. There is only one path to attain Me, and be freed from all sins. Become one whose mind has become My mind; become one who constantly perceives Me alone in meditation; become one who offers himself unto Me; salute Me alone.

Thus ends Chapter Nine entitled Rājavidyā-Rājaguhya-Yoga of the Bhagavad-Gītā, the essence of the Upaniṣads, that embodies the yoga-śāstra of brahma-vidyā in the form of a dialogue between Śrī Kṛṣṇa and Arjuna.

X

Vibhūti-Yoga

—The Yoga of Specific Manifestations—

Vyāsa:

Janmejaya, extremely subtle is the difference between what was taught in Chapter IX and what is going to be taught in the present chapter. The essence of the teaching of the former chapter is, "Everything is nothing but *Brahman.*" Kṛṣṇa in the present chapter will say, "*Brahman*'s manifestation is everything." The keen seeker should discern the difference between these two views. The step-by-step, upward search for the one ultimate Reality in what appears as many, brought us to the conclusion that Reality is *Brahman* (the Supreme Self, the Absolute). Kṛṣṇa, therefore, said, "Everything is Myself." The seeker, then identifying himself with *Brahman*, looks down upon the world of the many and sees the Absolute alone, manifesting as everything, and this latter view forms the essence of the *Vibhūti-Yoga, vibhūti* meaning, "specific forms of becoming." Chapter IX, in short, is an ascent from the many to the one, and Chapter X a descent from the one to the many.

These two form the two facets or dialectical counterparts, like the two sides of one coin, that enable the seeker on his own to attain the intuitive perception of the ineffable non-dual Reality. If this perception is not attained, the seeker misses the real message of the *Gītā*.

The overall structural scheme of the *Gītā* could be compared to that of a circular arch built up with eighteen differently shaped stones, nine on either side, and the 9th and the 10th meeting at the topmost portion, which is also the mid-point. This imperceptible mid-point represents the ineffable non-dual perception left inarticulate between the two middle chapters of the *Gītā*.

Let us now get into the text:

श्री भगवानुवाच —

भूय एव महाबाहो शृणु मे परमं वचः।
यत्ते ऽहं प्रीयमाणाय वक्ष्यामि हितकाम्यया ॥१॥

śrī bhagavān uvāca —

bhūya eva mahā-bāho śṛṇu me paramaṁ vacaḥ ।
yat te 'haṁ prīyamāṇāya vakṣyāmi hita-kāmyayā ॥1॥

Śrī Kṛṣṇa said —

Do hear again, O Mighty Armed, the crowning words of Mine. Desirous of your good, I impart this to you, for you are very dear to Me.

Arjuna, this is a wisdom-dialogue. Once its zenith is reached, the disciple may be found to become fully absorbed in it, with no questions to ask. On finding the disciple absorbed in this way, the *guru* might be found willing to elaborate further. The present situation is one such. For this reason, you are very dear to Me, making Me all the more intent on your welfare. See how rare is the wisdom I have just imparted to you:

न मे विदुः सुरगणाः प्रभवं न महर्षयः।
अहमादिर्हि देवानां महर्षीणां च सर्वशः ॥२॥

na me viduḥ sura-gaṇāḥ prabhavaṁ na maharṣayaḥ ।
aham ādir hi devānāṁ maharṣīṇāṁ ca sarvaśaḥ ॥2॥

My origin is not known even to gods and great seers, for I am the primeval cause of all the gods and great seers!

Arjuna, you know gods (*devas*) are the denizens of heaven; they do not know how great I am and what My origin is. This earth is inhabited by humans; of them, the great seers (*maharṣis*) are the best.

They too do not know My greatness. The simple reason is: all the worlds and their dwellers have Me alone for their source.

Any object of knowledge has to have an existence different from that of the subject or the one who seeks to know. The essential content of one's own being, the causal substance of one's origin, cannot become an object of knowledge for oneself, and this is the reason why I remain unknowable even to the gods of heaven. Though the word *devas* means "the bright ones" their brightness does not help them know that brightness which created them to be bright.

A *maharṣi* is a great *ṛṣi*, and *ṛṣi* is a seer of Truth. Yet even *ṛṣis* do not know the causal Substance that assumed their own forms. Those *maharṣis*, though *jñānins*, are not to be expected to know Me clearly and distinctly. A *jñānin* really is not one who clearly and precisely knows what the Reality is; on the other hand, he is the one who is fully aware of the fact that Reality never becomes an object of knowledge, that It is the greatest of all mysteries, and that his own existence and life in general are mysteries that form part of that great mystery. *Jñānins*, in other words, are those who know that the Reality is unknowable, as was made clear earlier in Verse II.29. Gods, *maharṣis*, their worlds are all Myself appearing in specific forms, called *vibhūtis*, *vi* standing for "specificity" and *bhūti* meaning "becoming or emerging." This aspect of life is the theme we concentrate on in this chapter.

The seeker and his search for Reality, you and your search for Me, are merely part of My *vibhūtis*, My assumed apparent forms. All such *vibhūtis* have beginnings and ends, whereas the Me in them is without beginning or end. How a seeker, who is simply a *vibhūti* of Mine, should therefore know Me, I shall tell you, along with telling you the benefits of such knowing.

यो मामजमनादिं च वेत्ति लोकमहेश्वरम् ।
असम्मूढः स मर्त्येषु सर्वपापैः प्रमुच्यते ॥३॥

yo mām ajam anādiṁ ca vetti loka-maheśvaram ।
asammūḍhaḥ sa martyeṣu sarva pāpaiḥ pramucyate ॥3॥

> As the unborn and the beginningless, he who knows Me, the one Supreme Controller of the world, he is the delusionless among human beings; he is the one released from all sins.

Arjuna, I am the one underlying Substance in all the *vibhūtis*, with the knower being merely one among these. Those who, instead of trying to know Me as an external object, realize Me directly as that which constitutes their own being, are the ones free from all delusions and all delusion-caused sins. Not merely their physical forms, but their internal emotions, mental activities and experiences as well, are all nothing but part of My *vibhūtis*. To clarify it:

बुद्धिर्ज्ञानमसम्मोहः क्षमा सत्यं दमः शमः ।
सुखं दुःखं भवो ऽभावो भयं चाभयमेव च ॥४ ॥
अहिंसा समता तुष्टिस्तपो दानं यशो ऽयशः ।
भवन्ति भावा भूतानां मत्त एव पृथग्विधाः ॥५ ॥

buddhir jñānam asammohaḥ kṣamā satyaṁ damaḥ śamaḥ,
sukhaṁ duḥkaṁ bhavo 'bhāvo bhayaṁ cābhayam eva ca ॥4 ॥

ahiṁsā samatā tuṣṭis tapo dānaṁ yaśo 'yaśaḥ ।
bhavanti bhāvā bhūtānāṁ matta eva pṛthag-vidhāḥ ॥5 ॥

> Reason, wisdom, non-deludedness, truthfulness, restraining the senses, restraining the mind, pleasure and pain, demonstrativeness and non-demonstrativeness, fear and fearlessness;

> Abstaining from killing or hurting others, equanimity, contentment, austerity, offering gifts, repute and no-repute — all these modes of mind in beings issue forth from Me alone.

Arjuna, not only the physical worlds and the beings in them, but all the mental states of these beings are also My own manifest forms. All the mental qualities from reasoning to restraining the mind are characteristic with the undeluded. All the pairs of opposites of experience such as pleasure and pain which are natural to all also, are sent forth from Me. Contentment, equanimity and the like are habits natural to those who are undeluded, who also maintain certain practices like austerity (*tapas*) and the offerings of gifts (*dāna*) to the needy. All such mental states too are My own *vibhūtis*. Even the imaginary mythological beings are so. I shall mention some of these characters as examples:

महर्षयः सप्त पूर्वे चत्वारो मनवस्तथा ।
मद्भावा मानसा जाता येषां लोक इमाः प्रजाः ॥६ ॥

maharṣayaḥ sapta pūrve catvāro manavas tathā ।
mad-bhāvā mānasā jātā yeṣāṁ loka imāḥ prajāḥ ॥6 ॥

The seven *ṛṣis* of olden times and the four Manus like-wise, all originated from Me as My mind materialized. And from them were born all the living beings.

Arjuna, the seven *ṛṣis* of mythological fame are Marici, Kratu, Vasiṣṭha, Aṅgīras, Pulastya, Atri and Pulaha. All the Purāṇas being My *vibhūtis*, their characters are also so.

Prajā means "beings that are born" and their originator is known as Prajāpati (the Lord of Beings). Each aeon is thought of as having a separate Prajāpati who is called Manu, and there are four such — Svayambhuva, Svārociṣa, Raivata, and Auttami. They too are My *vibhūtis*. Like water in ocean, I and My *vibhūtis* are inseparable. Each specific *vibhūti* experiencing its inseparable oneness with Me is *jñāna* (wisdom) proper, which is not knowledge concerning anything particular. Those immersed in the experience of totally being merged in Me are to be called *yogīs*. To clarify it,

---

एतां विभूतिं योगं च मम यो वेत्ति तत्त्वतः ।
सो ऽविकम्पेन योगेन युज्यते नात्र संशयः ॥७ ॥

etāṁ vibhūtiṁ yogaṁ ca mama yo vetti tattvataḥ I
so 'vikampena yogena yujyate nātra saṁśayaḥ II7 II

With this fundamental awareness of My *vibhūti* and *yoga* attained, one finds oneself unfalteringly united with that *yoga*; no doubt is there about it.

Arjuna, like that of ocean and waves is My inseparable oneness with My *vibhūtis*, each being one such. An individual being experiencing its oneness with Me, is the state known as *yoga*, and it marks the highest state of attaining Me, of knowing Me fundamentally (*tattvataḥ*) as well. Whatever its up and down movements, a wave will see itself forming part of the activeness of the ocean. Likewise will be the perception of a *yogī*. The pleasurable and painful, the meritorious and sinful, activities that form part of life's natural unfoldment will be seen by him as Myself manifesting, due to My own *māyā*. Internally unaffected by such ups and downs, he remains always a perfect *yogī*. How and where does he perceive Me, I shall make clearer:

अहं सर्वस्य प्रभवो मत्तः सर्वं प्रवर्तते ।
इति मत्वा भजन्ते मां बुधा भावसमन्विताः ॥८ ॥

ahaṁ sarvasya prabhavo mattaḥ sarvaṁ pravartate I
iti matvā bhajante māṁ budhā bhāva-samanvitāḥ II8 II

Knowing Me as the original source of all and that everything actively exists because of Me, the enlightened ones, who identify themselves as manifest forms (of Mine), meditatively perceive Me.

Arjuna, all the movements and actions of a wave are effected by the water-substance in it. I, likewise, am the one Reality that effects all the *karmas* in all beings. Aware of this, one sees oneself as existing and actively living as one with Me, the state called *bhāva-samanvitā* here. Those who remain content in the plenitude of this awareness are *budhās*, the enlightened ones.

The "I" mentioned here is not merely Kṛṣṇa the individual. You too, in union with Me, should be experiencing that everything originates from you and exists actively in you. The "I" in you and the "I" in Me are not two. Of what kind is the contentment of those who are thus well united, I shall tell you:

मच्चित्ता मद्गतप्राणा बोधयन्तः परस्परम् ।
कथयन्तश्च मां नित्यं तुष्यन्ति च रमन्ति च ॥९॥

mac-cittā mad-gata-prāṇā bodhayantaḥ parasparam ।
kathayantaś ca māṁ nityaṁ tuṣyanti ca ramanti ca ॥9॥

With minds become Mine, with vital functions having entered Mine, they remain ever contented and ever delighted by enlightening one another of Me, and mutually conversing about Me.

Arjuna, their mental functions are not seen by them as theirs, but as Mine; their vital functions too are seen to be likewise. They see Me alone everywhere, in everything. They find nothing else to converse about other than Me, no worldly matter finds place in their conversations. They remain *santuṣṭa*s, those who remain contented with the state which they are in at the moment. *Ram* (to be delighted) means "finding happiness from an external object." What the enlightened see as manifesting as external objects too is Myself or their own Self. They thus become *ātmārāma*s (those who find delight in the Self). This Self-delight could be considered either as acquired by them or as granted by Me, both meaning the same. The present verse conceives of it as acquired by them, whereas the same is seen in the next verse as granted by Me.

तेषां सततयुक्तानां भजतां प्रीतिपूर्वकम् ।
ददामि बुद्धियोगं तं येन मामुपयान्ति ते ॥१०॥

teṣāṁ satata-yuktānāṁ bhajatāṁ prīti-pūrvakam ।
dadāmi buddhi yogaṁ taṁ yena mām upayānti te ॥10॥

> On those who remain constantly united with Me and meditatively perceiving Me, do I bestow the conscious experience of being one with Me. Thus they attain Me as well.

Arjuna, the happiness *yogīs* have in life is that of being one with Me. This conscious experience is to be treated or can be treated as a blessing I bestow. It is equally appropriate to consider it as attained by finding Me in themselves. These two views are like two sides of a coin. The non-dual happiness of such people is to be intuitively perceived by treating these two views as its opposite sides. It is in such experiences that the darkness of ignorance vanishes totally and the radiance of wisdom shines, as the next verse shows:

तेषामेवानुकम्पार्थमहमज्ञानजं तमः।
नाशयाम्यात्मभावस्थो ज्ञानदीपेन भास्वता ॥११॥

teṣām evānukampārtham aham ajñānajaṁ tamaḥ ।
nāśayāmy ātmabhāvastho jñāna-dīpena bhāsvatā ॥11॥

> I, remaining as I am as their Self-content, becoming compassionate to them, destroy their ignorance-born darkness with the brilliant radiance of the lamp of wisdom.

Arjuna, I am the one Reality that underlies all, and thus the Self-content of all. Yet only very few realize Me to be so and thus, also as existing in themselves. Such are to be called *jñānins*. Though I am the Reality in all others as well, they do not realize this and thus remain ignorant. Veiled by the darkness of that ignorance, I remain imperceptible. As is quite evident, you are not one of these, and I can see the radiance of wisdom in you.

अर्जुन उवाच —

परं ब्रह्म परं धाम पवित्रं परमं भवान्।
पुरुषं शाश्वतं दिव्यमादिदेवमजं विभुम् ॥१२॥

आहुस्त्वामृषयः सर्वे देवर्षिर्नारदस्तथा ।
असितो देवलो व्यासः स्वयं चैव ब्रवीषि मे ॥१३॥

arjun uvāca —

paraṁ brahma paraṁ dhāma pavitraṁ paramaṁ bhavān ।
puruṣaṁ śāśvataṁ divyam ādi-devam ajaṁ vibhum ॥12॥

āhus tvām ṛṣayaḥ sarve devarṣir nāradas tathā ।
asito devalo vyāsaḥ svayaṁ caiva bravīṣi me ॥13॥

Arjuna said —

You are the transcendental *Brahman*; you are the transcendental abode; the supremely Pure too you are; the primeval god, the unborn one, you are !

Thus acclaimed are you by all the seers, by the *ṛṣi*s Nārada, Asita, Devala and by Vyāsa too. Now you are telling me the same yourself!

Kṛṣṇa, now I realize that you are the Reality that exists in my being and is engaged in my *svadharma* of waging battle. I also realize that I am not the doer (*kartā*) of this *karma* while you, unconditioned existence, pure effulgence in essence, have neither *karma* nor a sense of agency of action. This reality concerning the eternal you, has been the meaning content of the teaching of all the *ṛṣi*s of the past. And now your teaching the same confirms this. All the words of the *ṛṣi*s, all the scriptures, all the sciences, and your own words can thus be thought of as converging on You, the Absolute. Therefore,

---

सर्वमेतदृतं मन्ये यन्मां वदसि केशव ।
न हि ते भगवन्व्यक्तिं विदुर्देवा न दानवाः ॥१४॥

sarvam etad ṛtaṁ manye yan māṁ vadasi keśava ।
na hi te bhagavan vyaktiṁ vidur devā na dānavāḥ ॥14॥

O Keśava, every word of what you teach me now, I realize, is true. O Lord, neither the gods of heaven nor the demons of the underworld do know you clearly.

Who knows you, then?

> स्वयमेवात्मनात्मानं वेत्थ त्वं पुरुषोत्तम ।
> भूतभावन भूतेश देवदेव जगत्पते ॥१५॥
>
> *svayam evātmanātmānaṁ vettha tvaṁ puruṣottama* ।
> *bhūta-bhāvana bhūteśa deva-deva jagat pate* ॥15॥
>
> O Puruṣottama (the Highest *Puruṣa*), O the one who manifests as all the beings, O the Lord of all beings, O the Lord of all the worlds, you alone do know you, with yourself as means.

Kṛṣṇa, I do know myself now, not as "I" the person, but as You, the Reality. I see You alone in me; I see You alone in everything; I see You alone in all the happenings of this world. What I experience as my being and what takes place in me, I now realize, is but part of your knowing yourself. Everything is but your *vibhūti* (self-manifestation). Now I feel the urge to know how vast your *vibhūti*s are. Therefore,

---

> वक्तुमर्हस्यशेषेण दिव्या ह्यात्मविभूतयः ।
> याभिर्विभूतिभिर्लोकानिमांस्त्वं व्याप्य तिष्ठसि ॥१६॥
>
> *vaktum arhasy aśeṣeṇa divyā hy ātma-vibhūtayaḥ* ।
> *yābhir vibhūtibhir lokān imāṁs tvaṁ vyāpya tiṣṭhasi* ॥16॥
>
> Kindly tell me, omitting nothing, of your divine self-manifestations (*vibhūtis*). It is in and through such *vibhūtis* that you dwell in all these worlds.

And more,

> कथं विद्यामहं योगिंस्त्वां सदा परिचिन्तयन् ।
> केषु केषु च भावेषु चिन्त्योऽसि भगवन्मया ॥१७॥
>
> *kathaṁ vidyām ahaṁ yogiṁs tvāṁ sadā paricintayan* ।
> *keṣu keṣu ca bhāveṣu cintyo 'si bhagavan mayā* ॥17॥

O *yogin*, how am I, always thinking of you as I am, to know you really? Which are the manifest forms, O Lord, in which I can contemplate on you?

Kṛṣṇa, that you are the one who manifests as everything, I understand. Your existence is inseparably one with everything manifest, myself also one among them. I want to know now, in which of those manifest forms, I can easily perceive you meditatively. Though all are your own manifestations, it may be easier to meditate on you in certain specific forms. I would like to know which these are. And besides,

---

विस्तरेणात्मनो योगं विभूतिं च जनार्दन।
भूयः कथय तृप्तिर्हि शृण्वतो नास्ति मेऽमृतम्॥१८॥

vistareṇātmano yogaṁ vibhūtiṁ ca janārdana I
bhūyaḥ kathaya tṛptir hi śṛṇvato nāsti me 'mṛtam II18 II

O Janārdana, please tell me more about your inseparable self-unitiveness (*ātma-yoga*) and self-manifestation (*ātma-vibhūti*), for I never feel surfeited by hearing of the immortal.

श्री भगवानुवाच —
हन्त ते कथयिष्यामि दिव्या ह्यात्मविभूतयः।
प्राधान्यतः कुरुश्रेष्ठ नास्त्यन्तो विस्तरस्य मे॥१९॥

śrī bhagavān uvāca —
hanta te kathayiṣyāmi divyā hy ātma-vibhūtayaḥ I
prādhānyataḥ kuru śreṣṭha nāstyanto vistarasya me II19 II

Śrī Kṛṣṇa said —

Lo and behold! I shall tell you of my divine self-manifestations in the order of their importance. Their details, of course, are endless.

Arjuna, as you know, all the worlds and all the beings in them, are My own *vibhūtis*, My own being unfolded. Describing each of these in detail is humanly impossible, but since you want to hear about these *vibhūtis*, that make it easy for you to contemplate on Me, I shall point some out to you. Though I am the one all-underlying Substance, My presence is immediately felt in certain of My manifestations. I shall tell you now of some of these. The very fundamental aspect of My manifesting I shall tell you first:

अहमात्मा गुडाकेश सर्वभूताशयस्थितः ।
अहमादिश्च मध्यं च भूतानामन्त एव च ॥२०॥

aham ātmā guḍākeśa sarva-bhūtāśaya-sthitaḥ ।
aham ādiś ca madhyaṁ ca bhūtānām anta eva ca ॥20॥

Arjuna, I am the one all-pervading Substance. I am the meaning content in which all that have come into being abide. The beginning of beings I am, as also their middle and end.

Arjuna, it is clear to you that by *ātmā* I mean that Substance — invisible on its own — which pervades all the apparent forms that constitute the world. And this is the reason why I am referred to as *paramātmā*. *Ātmā* abides (*āśayasthitaḥ*) in all beings as the essential Reality. *Āśaya* means "one's proper seat" as well as "the meaning content." All the waves are "properly seated" in water, their "meaning content" is also water. Likewise is my being the *ātmā* in all beings.

From water emerge all waves; in water they have their being; and into water they dissolve. Likewise is the beginning, middle and end of all beings in Me. Meditating on Me in this way can be easier.

What I am going to tell you henceforth are only some details of this most fundamental of all My *vibhūtis*. They are simply some specifiable situations in which a discerning seeker feels the touch of *Brahman* in life.

आदित्यानामहं विष्णुर्ज्योतिषां रविरंशुमान्।
मरीचिर्मरुतामस्मि नक्षत्राणामहं शशी ॥२१॥

ādityānām ahaṁ viṣṇur jyotiṣāṁ ravir aṁśumān I
marīcir marutām asmi nakṣatrāṇām ahaṁ śasī II21 II

Among the Ādityas, I am Viṣṇu; among the luminaries, I am the radiant Sun; among the Maruts, I am Marīci; and among the stars, I am the Moon.

Arjuna, many are the types of beings imaginable as living and moving in the sky, and all of them are My *vibhūtis*. One set of such, being twelve in number are known as Ādityas, being the sons of Aditi. They are, Indra, Dhātā, Parjanya, Tvaṣṭā, Dṛṣṭā, Aryamā, Bhaga, Vivasvān, Viṣṇu, Aṁśumān, Varuṇa and Mitra. Of these, Viṣṇu is comparatively easier to meditate on as My manifest form, for the name itself means "the all-pervading."

Distinctly seeing all My manifestations is made possible by the Sun, and therefore the Sun, in the context of the luminaries could easily be meditated upon as My *vibhūti*. Maruts are Vedic gods who are friends of Indra, and their role in nature is making rain shower down from the skies. The suddenly appearing brightness of lightning is termed *marīci*. If all the luminaries visible at night together be treated as stars, then the importance of the Moon among them is well known. In the Moon as well as in Marīci, My *vibhūti* is easily perceptible.

वेदानां सामवेदो ऽस्मि देवानामस्मि वासवः।
इन्द्रियाणां मनश्चास्मि भूतानामस्मि चेतना ॥२२॥

vedānāṁ sāma-vedo 'smi devānām asmi vāsavaḥ I
indriyāṇāṁ manaś cāsmi bhūatānām asmi cetanā II22 II

Among the Vedas, I am the *Sāmaveda*; among the gods, I am Vāsava (Indra); among the senses, I am the mind; and of the living beings, I am the life-principle.

Arjuna, the four Vedas — *Ṛgveda, Yajurveda, Sāmaveda, Atharvaveda* — represent also the original source of all the sciences, all the branches of knowledge. Of them, the first is the most ancient and its essence musically re-rendered forms the *Sāmaveda*. Reciting part of it is essential in any Vedic fire-sacrifice and in that particular sense it is all-pervasive like Me.

Indra, also called Vāsava, is the chief of the *deva*s. Vasu means light-rays, and Vāsava symbolizes the light of all lights.

The five sense-organs, in order to engage in their own natural activities, need directives from the mind, and mind thus gains an absolutist dimension in that particular realm. Mind, at times, is also considered the sixth sense.

Everything that has come into being, from the most gross and inert minerals to the most subtle and dynamic life principle in beings, all called *bhūta*s, are My *vibhūti*s. Yet meditating on the life principle (*cetanā*) as My *vibhūti* helps one intuitively perceive the subtlety of My beingness.

रुद्राणां शंकरश्चास्मि वित्तेशो यक्षरक्षसाम्।
वसूनां पावकश्चास्मि मेरुः शिखरिणामहम्॥२३॥

rudrāṇāṁ śaṅkaraś cāsmi vitteśo yakṣa-rakṣasām ।
vasūnāṁ pāvakaś cāsmi meruḥ śikhariṇām aham ॥23॥

Among the Rudras, I am Śaṅkara; among the *yakṣa*s and *rākṣasa*s, I am Vitteśa; among the Vasus, I am Pāvaka; and among the mountains, I am Meru.

Arjuna, the Rudras are a group of divine beings who are various forms that Śiva assumes. The name literally means, "those who make others weep"; here it signifies those who cause suffering to the evil-minded. The Rudras, mythologically, are eleven in number: Aja, Ekapāda, Ahirbudhnya, Tvaṣṭā, Rudra, Hara, Śambhu, Tryambaka, Aparājita, Īśāna, Tribhuvana. To meditate on Śaṅkara (Śiva) himself, who has assumed all these apparent forms, as My *vibhūti*, is easier. The name Śaṅkara means "one who brings happiness"; and I also do the same. In other words, what makes life happy and peaceful is to be aware always of the one Absolute Reality.

Vitteśa (the Lord of wealth) or Kubera is the guardian deity of all wealth, yet not a god (*deva*); he is merely a *rākṣasa* (ogre). Too much wealth accumulated, we know, makes a monster of man. Even such a human character may assume an absolutist dimension, represented here by Vitteśa. Those, who are always after wealth may prefer to meditate on Me in the form of Kubera.

Vasus are another type of grouped deities (*gaṇa-devatā*), eight in number: Āpa, Dhruva, Soma, Adhvara, Anila, Pratyūṣa, Pāvaka and Prabhāsa. Because of its quality of purifying anything, fire is called Pāvaka, the verb root *pav* meaning "to purify." I too am the Reality in its purest. Therefore, meditating on Fire (Pāvaka) among the Vasus as Me is easier.

Indian mythology has a geographical concept of the world with the Mount Meru for its central pivot, around which it revolves. Of the nine continents, called *varṣa*s, Bhāratavarṣa (India) comes immediately around the axis. It is surrounded by Kiṁpuruṣa Varṣa, Hari Varṣa, Ilā Varṣa, Remyaka Varṣa, Hiraṇmaya Varṣa, Uttarakuru-Varṣa, Bhadrāśva Varṣa, Hetumalā Varṣa, each ten times the size of the previous one. These continents are separated by oceans each containing a different liquid. The Mount Meru at the centre, in height, touches the worlds of heavenly effulgence, the name also meaning the same. Meru, thus has an absolutism of its own. Those who are familiar with the life in mountain regions therefore can meditate on Meru as My *vibhūti*.

पुरोधसां च मुख्यं मा विद्धि पार्थ बृहस्पतिम् ।
सेनानीनामहं स्कन्दः सरसामस्मि सागरः ॥२४॥

purodhasāṁ ca mukhyaṁ māṁ viddhi pārtha bṛhaspatim ।
senānīnām ahaṁ skandaḥ sarasām asmi sāgaraḥ ॥24॥

Arjuna, among the priests, know Me as Bṛhaspati their chief; among the army generals, I am Skanda (Subrahmaṇya); and among the lakes, I am ocean.

Arjuna, gods (*devas*) of heaven, you know, exist depending on the oblations offered by human beings, represented by their priests, from here below. Those *devas* too have a priest of their own, who is also their *guru*: Bṛhaspati. He, thus, has an absolutism in the domain of priestcraft, and hence priests and those who are interested in priestcraft can easily meditate on Bṛhaspati as My *vibhūti*.

Subrahmaṇya was born, you know, of Śiva and Pārvatī in order to kill Tārakāsura, who had become a menace to all the worlds. He (Subrahmaṇya) fulfilled his mission even as a baby of seven days by giving lead to the grand army of the gods against Tāraka. In this unworldly leading of war there is implied a touch of *Brahman* wherein nothing is impossible, nothing is predictable. Those who are engaged in war activities, where also nothing is predictable, therefore can meditate on Subrahmaṇya, also called Skanda, in the sense that he encountered the enemies face to face, as My *vibhūti*.

Saras means "that which is always in a rocking state," and so all the lakes and pools are called so. Both in being in a rocky state and in being boundless, ocean is at its peak, and therefore those who are supported by lakes and pools can meditate on the ocean (*sāgara*) as My *vibhūti*. The word *sāgara* also means the abode of *amṛta* which means both "the immortal elixir" and "water." Really I am the immortal; those who attain Me also become immortal.

महर्षीणां भृगुरहं गिरामस्म्येकमक्षरम् ।
यज्ञानां जपयज्ञो ऽस्मि स्थावराणां हिमालयः ॥२५॥

maharṣīṇāṁ bhṛgur ahaṁ girām asmy ekam akṣaram ।
yajñānāṁ japa-yajño 'smi sthāvarāṇāṁ himālayaḥ ॥25॥

Among the great seers, I am Bhṛgu; and among words, I am the monosyllable (*AUṀ*). Among sacrifices, I am the sacrifice of meditative repetition of sacred words (*japa*); and among the immovables, I am the Himālayas.

Arjuna, a *ṛṣi* is a seer of Truth, and the great among such are called *maharṣis*, *maha* meaning "the great." *Tapas* (austerity) is their only wealth and strength. Bhṛgu, one of the greatest among them, was the very embodiment of *tapas*, his name meaning, "one who is well matured through *tapas*." Those who think of Me in terms of *tapas* can therefore easily meditate on Bhṛgu as My *vibhūti*.

How the monosyllable *AUṀ* (*oṁ*) represents Me is well known to anyone who has the least familiarity with the culture of India. It being My *vibhūti* requires no explanation.

We have seen *yajña* in its many aspects, particularly in Chapter III and IV, and the best one I recommended was *jñāna-yajña* (wisdom-sacrifice). *Japa* always forms part of any systematic search for wisdom. Meditative repetition of sacred words in practice, it literally means gaining clarity in thought and articulation simultaneously (*japa-vyaktāyām vāci mānase ca*). *Japa* as a spiritual practice gained universal acceptance cutting across all barriers of religion. This absolutist touch of it makes it considerable as My *vibhūti* by seekers.

Japa, at first, may not sound like forming any sacrifice as such, but given that everything that forms part of life is treatable as a *yajña*, *japa* is no exception.

Sthāvara means "that which cannot be moved from place to place," and the immovability of the Himālayas needs no explanation. Those who are interested in the immovables can meditate on the Himālayas as My *vibhūti*:

अश्वत्थः सर्ववृक्षाणां देवर्षीणां च नारदः ।
गन्धर्वाणां चित्ररथः सिद्धानां कपिलो मुनिः ॥२६ ॥

aśvatthaḥ sarva-vṛkṣāṇāṁ devarṣīṇāṁ ca nāradaḥ ।
gandharvāṇāṁ citrarathaḥ siddhānāṁ kapilo muniḥ ॥26 ॥

Among all the tree-varieties; I am *aśvattha* and among divine seers, I am Nārada. Among *gandharvas*, I am Citraratha; and among *siddhas*, I am the silent recluse Kapila.

Arjuna, a tree is called *vṛksa* in Sanskrit in the sense that it may be cut and felled at any moment, and therefore its life-span in practice is not what it should be. *Aśvattha* or *pīpal* tree is an exception in this respect; its life is very long which the very name means, and normally it is never felled for timber. This quality makes it meditatable as My *vibhūti*.

*Ṛṣi*s and *maharṣi*s are there in this world; so are they in heaven as well, Nārada one of the great among them. Unlike all the other *ṛṣi*s of heaven, he is interested in the affairs of the worlds below as well. Whenever any problem or doubt arises in the minds of the *ṛṣi*s of the other worlds, Nārada's presence will always be available to solve them. He, in other words, is a *ṛṣi* whose presence, like Mine, is felt in all the worlds. Hence My *vibhūti* can be seen in him.

*Gandharva*s are the musicians of heaven. The guardian deities of fine arts, they move about between the earth and heaven. Citraratha, a chief among them, is so named because he owns an extraordinary (*citra*) chariot (*ratha*). From the wondrousness of his chariot is to be assumed how skilled in fine arts he is. He, in short, represents perfection of skill in fine arts. Those who are interested in that field, therefore, find it easy to meditate on Citraratha as My embodiment.

Siddhi, literally "attainment," denotes certain unworldly psycho-physical attainments some spiritual practices result in, and those of such attainments are known as *siddha*s. Yet the best of all such attainments is that of wisdom. The *ṛṣi* Kapila, the proponent of the Sāṁkhya philosophy, was, so to say, the certainty of wisdom personified. His was the best systematized of all the schools of Indian philosophy, and its influence on the other systems was immense. Even his mother became his disciple. An absolutism thus is there in Kapila in respect of the certainty he attained in wisdom. Those who are interested in *siddhi*s therefore can meditate on Kapila as My *vibhūti*.

उच्चैःश्रवसमश्वानां विद्धि माममृतोद्भवम्।
ऐरावतं गजेन्द्राणां नराणां च नराधिपम्॥२७॥

uccaiḥśravasam aśvānāṁ viddhi mām amṛtodbhavam ǀ
airāvataṁ gajendrāṇāṁ narāṇāṁ ca narādhipam ǁ27ǁ

Among horses, understand Me as Uccaiḥśravas born of the immortal elixir; among lordly elephants, I am Airāvata; and among humans, I am the King.

Arjuna, *aśva*, the Sanskrit word for horse, means "that which takes you from one place to another very fast." The mythological horse Uccaiḥśravas of Indra was born of the milk-ocean when churned, and its name denotes its high fame. My nature, you know, too is likewise. I am here and everywhere at the same time, and need no time to reach anywhere: the state of being the fastest. It is being as fast as Me that makes Uccaiḥśravas famous among horses, giving him a touch of absolutism as well. And more, I am the immortal; he too is immortal. In virtue of all these, meditating on Uccaiḥśravas as My *vibhūti* is easy.

Elephant, the largest of all land-animals, is a unique one, and Airāvata, the elephant of Indra, also the product of the milk-ocean, is more so. The name means, "that which is born of ocean" (*irāvān*). Airāvata, thus, has an element of absolutism in its being, and hence meditatable as My *vibhūti* among elephants.

Man, among living beings, is the one who can control all others and thus he gained the name *nara*. Among such *nara*s, the one who leads them along the path of virtues, keeping them away from that of evils, becomes a king. His decisions, while being based on laws and basic principles of life, have to be taintless of personal motives and partiality. No one without a neutrality like Mine can, in short, become a good king, and hence good kings can be treated as an apparent *vibhūti* of Mine.

आयुधानामहं वज्रं धेनूनामस्मि कामधुक् ।
प्रजनश्चास्मि कन्दर्पः सर्पाणामस्मि वासुकिः ॥२८॥

āyudhānām ahaṁ vajraṁ dhenūnām asmi kāma-dhuk ।
prajanaś cāsmi kandarpaḥ sarpāṇām asmi vāsukiḥ ॥28॥

Of weaponry, I am Vajra (thunderbolt); among cows, I am Kāmadhenu; among progenitors, I am Kāma (Eros); among serpents, I am Vāsuki.

Arjuna, thunderbolt, called *vajra,* in the sense that it never returns without annihilating the enemy, is the main weapon of Indra. My creativity, My being the dissolver included, too, you know, is indomitable. Hence among weapons Vajra can be considered as an apparent *vibhūti* of Mine.

The place of Kāmadhenu, the mythological cow that yields all that is desired, is well known. Its origin was also from the same immortal milk-ocean and the *ṛṣi* Vasiṣṭha was its holder. All the desires of all beings of all the worlds really are created by Me and are satiated by Me. A similarity between Kāmadhenu and Me is thus evident and, therefore, that cow is easily meditatable as My *vibhūti.*

Life in this cosmic system is kept going, we know, by the process of procreation, where erotic feelings between males and females of a species and their sexual union have a crucial role. Kāmadeva (Eros of the East) is the imaginary presiding deity of all erotic feelings. If he remains inactive, life *in toto* comes to a standstill; that is to say, I the Reality goes inactive and inert. Yet it never happens — I never remain inactive — and Kāmadeva never ceases to function either. Therefore in the context of the continuance of life through procreation, I can be seen in Kāmadeva and thus meditated upon.

Snakes are called *sarpa*s in Sanskrit because of their serpentine movement. The onward process of My creative self-expression too is likewise; so serpentine and mysterious is My movement onward that nothing is predictable, though man makes many calculations. Vāsuki among serpents, is the one who carries within his head an invaluable gem (*vasu*) and thus deriving the name as well. My value too, as you know, is inestimable. Thus in regard to both unpredictability and invaluability, Vāsuki has much in common with Me, and hence is meditatable as My *vibhūti.*

अनन्तश्चास्मि नागानां वरुणो यादसामहम् ।
पितॄणामर्यमा चास्मि यमः संयमतामहम् ॥२९॥

anantaś cāsmi nāgānāṁ varuṇo yādasām aham ।
pitṝṇām aryamā cāsmi yamaḥ saṁyamatām aham ॥29॥

> Among the poisonless mountain-snakes, I am Ananta; among aquatic beings, I am Varuṇa; among the manes, I am Aryamā; and among the law-enforcers, I am Yama.

Arjuna, Nāgas are a kind of non-poisonous snakes seen in mountain areas, the name also meaning the same. Ananta, meaning "the endless," is one such snake well known in legends as forming the bed on which Viṣṇu reposes. I too am endless and harmless. Unapproachable without effort, I am like mountain dwellers as well. Those familiar with the world of non-poisonous snakes, therefore, can well mediatate upon Ananta as My *vibhūti*.

Varuṇa, as you know, is the presiding deity of oceans, and thus, he among aquatic beings, is somewhat like Me. *Pitṛ*s are the souls of the departed supposedly living in the world of manes, and Aryamā is their king. And both are meditatable as My *vibhūti*s.

Yama is the one who keeps in control all aspects of nature, so that they together form a coherent cosmic system. By allotting a specific role to each being and putting an end to the life of each being when its allotted life-span ends — the reason for conceiving Yama as the god of Death — Yama keeps nature from becoming stagnant and insipid. That Yama has thus a touch of the Absolute in his being is undeniable.

प्रह्लादश्चास्मि दैत्यानां कालः कलयतामहम् ।
मृगाणां च मृगेन्द्रो ऽहं वैनतेयश्च पक्षिणाम् ॥३०॥

prahlādaś cāsmi daityānāṁ kālaḥ kalayatām aham ।
mṛgāṇāṁ ca mṛgendro 'haṁ vainateyaś ca pakṣiṇām ॥30॥

> Among demons, I am Prahlāda; among those who are good in computation, I am Kāla (among those who diffuse and mix things up, I am Time); among animals, I am lion; and among birds, I am Vainateya (Garuḍa).

Arjuna, the demons (*asuras*) (also known as *daityas* because they are the progeny of Diti) are in general greedy and egoistic, the only exception being Prahlāda, who was an ardent devotee of Viṣṇu, that is to say, of Myself. Such devotees perceive Me, not as something existing outside them, but as the one substantial Reality having assumed their own form. Prahlāda knew himself as being Me in essence as indeed he is in truth.

Kāla (the god of time) makes precise calculations (*kālayati*) and fixes the length of time for which each being should live while keeping the basis of those calculations a mystery. With the word *kalanā*, which means "mixing up or diffusing" we are to bring to mind another function that is constantly occurring in the sphere of time — that of the crumbling of old forms and the shaping of new ones.

The superiority of lion among animals in the world is well known. Equally well known is the glory of the legendary bird Vainateya (Garuḍa), the vehicle of Viṣṇu.

पवनः पवतामस्मि रामः शस्त्रभृतामहम् ।
झषाणां मकरश्चास्मि स्रोतसामस्मि जाह्नवी ॥३१॥

pavanaḥ pavatām asmi rāmaḥ śastra-bhṛtām aham ।
jhaṣāṇāṁ makaraś cāsmi śrotasām asmi jāhnavī ॥31॥

Among purifying agents, I am air; among the armed, I am Rāma; among the fish, I am whale-shark; among rivers, I am Jāhnavī (Gaṅgā).

Arjuna, the quality of purifying by blowing everywhere gives air the name *pavana* (the purifier). Though the rule is, "no air no life" the blowing of air has no concern for the convenience of any; with perfect neutrality it blows towards all, at times even knocking everything in its path to the ground. Similarly, I the Absolute, with my unconditioned creativity which sustains life, too am like air; I have no concern for what may come in my path. Air can also thus be meditated on as My *vibhūti*.

Being armed with the famous Kodaṇḍa-bow and arrow is one of the distinguishing marks of Śrī Rāma in the *Rāmāyaṇa,* the arms signifying independence from all that is relative and conditioned. Hence, he can be taken as representing Me among those who are armed.

Fish are called *jhaṣa* in the sense they swallow anything smaller than them and the largest of them is the whale-shark (*makara*). It eats all fish species. I too am like that — all things being smaller than Me, I devour everything. I am the one all-engulfing Reality. Among the fish, therefore, the *makara* can be meditated on as My *vibhūti.*

The Gaṅgā, among rivers, has an absolutist touch of its own — it is always full whether it be summer or rainy season. And more, it is the central nerve of life in India. It is impossible to imagine life without the Gaṅgā. Without Me too life is impossible. Hence, I can be seen as represented by Gaṅgā among rivers.

सर्गाणामादिरन्तश्च मध्यं चैवाहमर्जुन ।
अध्यात्मविद्या विद्यानां वादः प्रवदतामहम् ॥३२॥

sargāṇāṁ ādir antaś ca madhyaṁ caivāham arjuna ।
adhyātma-vidyā vidyānāṁ vādaḥ pravadatām aham ॥32॥

Among the chapters of long works, O Arjuna, I am the first, the last and the middle. Among sciences, I am the science of the Self; and among those who are engaged in dialogue, I am the dialogue.

Arjuna, the word *sarga* means either "chapters of literary works" or "the creation of the world." In this verse too, we can use either interpretation. In the latter sense, the first two lines of this verse mean, "Of creation I am the beginning, the end and the middle," a point I have already covered in Verse 17. Besides, all that is considered in this verse pertain to the context of imparting knowledge.

All systematically written books, as you know, are usually divided into chapters or cantos. The cantos of longer poetical works in Sanskrit are called *sargas*, and of such, the first, the middle and the last are considered the most important. That the three together should contain the essential theme of the work is a convention, the other cantos being considered embellishments. As the one abstract and unconditioned Reality, I am like the essence of a literary work appreciated as indicated in its first, middle and last chapters. I, as manifesting in the form of everything in all the worlds and their specifying qualities, am comparable to the total body of a literary work.

I am sure I do not have to explain again at this juncture how the science of the Self, the very science I am engaged in teaching you, crowns all other sciences.

Among those engaged in dialogues such as the present one, what is essentially revealed through those words is nothing but Myself; the words of such dialogue may thus be considered My own manifestation. The last line of this verse can be interpretated in another way. Those who are engaged in arguments on matters of philosophical import are called *pravādins*, and among them, I am to be considered the argument (*vāda*). Such arguments were very common among the learned in ancient India. Mostly what was of interest to scholars was the logical strictness of argument rather than the veracity of what was being argued for or against. Yet, one thing was common to both contenders — the fact that they were arguing. Like the one neutral Reality underlying the other pairs of opposites, here too, I am the neutral element of argument (*vāda*) common to both parties engaged in dialogue.

अक्षराणामकारो ऽस्मि द्वन्द्वः सामासिकस्य च ।
अहमेवाक्षयः कालो धाताहं विश्वतोमुखः ॥३३॥

akṣarāṇām akāro 'smi dvandvaḥ sāmāsikasya ca ।
aham evākṣayaḥ kālo dhātā 'haṁ viśvato mukhaḥ ॥33॥

Among letters, I am "A"; among compound word-formations, I am *dvandva*; I am the imperishable Time; and I am the Creator with faces everywhere.

Arjuna, written languages are many and each of these has an alphabet of its own. But whatever may be the language, its first alphabet is always "A," representing the sound made spontaneously as we open our mouth. Considering this universality, the letter "A" can also be meditated on as My *vibhūti.*

Some languages, Sanskrit being one among them, have the special feature of combining words to form compound words. Sanskrit has developed a set of grammatical rules, called *samāsas*, for word-combining and one of these is *dvandva samāsa* in which both or all the compounded words are of equal importance, e.g., *rāmalakṣmaṇau*, meaning "Rāma and Lakṣmaṇa." I too am the Reality that equally underlies both the limbs of all dualities.

Anything may perish in time but time itself cannot. What we call time's headway is nothing but the sequentiality of actualization of My own creative self-expressions and, therefore, more than any of My *vibhūtis*, time is Myself.

I being the Reality that unfolds itself as this world, My face is everywhere. In Indian myths my creative urge finding actualization, is represented as Brahmā the Creator, also called Dhātā, with his four faces turned to the four directions symbolizing My having a face everywhere. Seeing Brahmā everywhere in the world and seeing Me everywhere thus in essence mean the same.

मृत्युः सर्वहरश्चाहमुद्भवश्च भविष्यताम् ।
कीर्तिः श्रीर्वाक्च नारीणां स्मृतिर्मेधा धृतिः क्षमा ॥३४॥

mṛtyuḥ sarva-haraś cāham udbhavaś ca bhaviṣyatām ।
kīrtiḥ śrīr vāk ca nārīṇāṁ smṛtir medhā dhṛtiḥ kṣamā ॥34॥

Death, the all-annihilator, is Myself; and the birth of all yet to emerge is also Myself. The values fame, grace, speech, memory, intelligence, firmness and forgiveness in women are also Myself.

Arjuna, to fear death and to be constantly thinking of death is a human habit. Your confusion on the battlefield was also a result of your dwelling on the horrifying eventuality that your dear ones would die because of you. Arjuna, you should realize that death is only one aspect of My endless *vibhūtis*. It must now be clear to you how I remain Myself while apparent forms constantly emerge from Me and merge back into Me. No new form can emerge without one already existing becoming destroyed first, as no chick is born without the destruction of the egg. The event of the egg becoming destroyed is what we call death, and that of the chick emerging, birth. A wave that emerges on the surface of the ocean must merge back; likewise is the inevitable merging back of all the apparent forms that emerge from Me. What we call death is that event of merging back. It too is not different from Me; it is a part of My "becoming." Aware of this reality, one will be able to meditate on death as one of My *vibhūtis*, instead of constantly fearing it. Life thus becomes fearless.

Death occurs only to something that has already come into being, and birth to beings yet to emerge, both forming part of My *vibhūti*.

Woman attains perfection in her fame, physical and mental gracefulness, appealing words, clarity of memory, quickness in intelligent response, firmness of mind and motherly patience. Such qualities in women can also be meditated on as My *vibhūti*.

बृहत्साम तथा साम्नां गायत्री छन्दसामहम् ।
मासानां मार्गशीर्षो ऽहमृतूनां कुसुमाकरः ॥३५॥

bṛhat-sāma tathā sāmnāṁ gāyatrī chandasām aham ।
māsānāṁ mārgaśīrṣo 'ham ṛtūnāṁ kusumākaraḥ ॥35॥

Among the *Sāman* songs, I am *bṛhat-sāma;* among Vedic texts or metres, I am Gāyatrī; among months, I am Mārgaśīrṣa (November-December); and among seasons, I am the flower-abounding spring.

Arjuna, what the peculiarities of the *Sāman* songs are I have already made clear to you. Of the numerous songs in the *Sāmaveda*, *bṛhat-sāma* is outstanding in its wisdom content, though forming part of the ritualistic section. In essence, it teaches that I am the one Absolute

Reality. The *Sāman*-singers, therefore, can meditate on the *bṛhat-sāma* as My *vibhūti*.

The texts of the Vedic hymns are known as *chandas*; the metres in which they are composed are also called *chandas*. The Gāyatrī in both the senses is particularly excellent. The *Gāyatrī mantra*, the most sacred of all Vedic hymns, prays thus: "May the Supreme Reality, effulgence in essence, enlighten my mind and through that enlightening may the Reality become more luminous." The more one meditates on the insights that are wrapped within these words the deeper it appears. The depth and extensiveness of My being, as you know, are unthinkable. Those, who are adepts in reciting Vedic hymns can, therefore, meditate on the Gāyatrī hymn as My *vibhūti*.

Gāyatrī is a Vedic metre as well. Containing 24 syllables in three lines, it is widely used in the Veda, particularly the *Ṛgveda*, and its usage remains limited to the Vedas. The hymn called the Gāyatrī is also composed in the same metre. Those who are interested in Vedic metres can meditate on Gāyatrī as My *vibhūti*.

Mārgaśīrṣa (November-December) is the most pleasant of all the twelve months of the year in India. It is common among human beings to consider the happiest moments of life as blessed by Me. The pleasantness of the month Mārgaśīrṣa can, therefore, be seen as having the touch of *Brahman* and thus meditated on.

The Reality that I am, is not inert; It is creative, and the blooming of that creativity becomes apparent in the spring season (*vasanta*), called here *kusumākara* meaning "the abode of flowers." The instinct in living beings for mating is also the strongest in this season. Among the seasons, spring may thus be seen as an apparent manifestation of Mine.

द्यूतं छलयतामस्मि तेजस्तेजस्विनामहम्।
जयो ऽस्मि व्यवसायो ऽस्मि सत्त्वं सत्त्ववतामहम्॥३६॥

dyūtaṁ chalayatām asmi tejas tejasvinām aham ।
jayo 'smi vyavasāyo 'smi sattvaṁ sattvavatām aham ॥36॥

Among those who cheat, I am gambling; among the brilliant, I am their brilliance; I am victory; I am certitude; among those who find themselves real, I am their beingness.

Arjuna, those of my *vibhūtis* that can be easily meditated on, which we have looked at in the previous verse, are all of positive values. Now this verse changes that. Gambling, a game that is considered to corrupt the human mind, and being deceitful, is never thought of positively. The pious devoted to Me might therefore doubt, "How can such a quality be treated as God's *vibhūti*?"

Considering that everything originates from Me, to conceive that My *vibhūtis* will always be good in quality is pointless. What we think of as good and evil, righteous and unrighteous, desire and desirelessness, all have Me alone for their source, and this is the reason why "evil" is not absent from life. The bent for gambling is just one such human urge. The unfoldment of events in nature is such that no one can predict for sure what will happen the next moment. An unpredictable element of chance always reigns supreme. The game of gambling too, depending totally on chance as it is, may be seen as having a touch of *Brahman*. Thus in gambling too you can very well meditatively perceive My *vibhūti*.

Though, My *vibhūtis* like decietfulness and gambling are evil, the best of all human qualities — brilliance — also is pointed out immediately as My own *vibhūti*, as if to cancel out the negativity of the former. The lustre of brightness seen in the wise can also be well meditated on as My *vibhūti*.

Victory being My *vibhūti* does not mean that failure is not so. Counting events as favourable and unfavourable is a human habit, and the criteria for such considerations are simply man's convenience and interest. Good and evil are also discriminated similarly. The forward movement of My creative self-unfoldment is not guided by such interests and goals. Whatever happens as a part of it simply forms one forward step in the successful advancing of My creativity. Had human beings also learnt to see all events in life as part of My victorious enduring, all problems that torment them would simply vanish.

Vyavasāya means "the certitude one attains when all doubts vanish" (*vyavasyati iti*). I am the one undoubtable Reality, and knowing Me dispells all doubts.

Sattva means beingness (*sato bhāvaḥ*). One who experiences one's own beingness is a *sattvavān*. "I am" is an experience each one of us undeniably has. The beingness so experienced by all is really *Brahman*'s. It was this one cardinal point that I stated summarily in the beginning and tried to elaborate afterwards. This beingness is not merely one of My *vibhūtis*, it is Myself. Those who experience themselves as existing, therefore, can perceive Me as their own beingness.

वृष्णीनां वासुदेवोऽस्मि पाण्डवानां धनञ्जयः ।
मुनीनामप्यहं व्यासः कवीनामुशना कविः ॥३७॥

vṛṣṇīnāṁ vāsudevos 'mi pāṇḍavānāṁ dhanañjayaḥ ।
munīnām apy ahaṁ vyāsaḥ kavīnam uśanā kaviḥ ॥37॥

Among those of the Vṛṣṇi clan, I am Vāsudeva; among the sons of Pāṇḍu, I am Arjuna; among silent recluses (*munis*), I am Vyāsa; and among seer-poets, I am Uśanas or Śukra.

Arjuna, that Śrī Kṛṣṇa, the individual, born in the Yādava or Vṛṣṇi clan, and now teaching you *brahma-vidyā*, is *Brahman* concretized needs no mention. You too are so. So are all, but they remain unaware of being so, and hence their being a *vibhūti* of Myself remains insignificant.

The present dialogue between you and Me, in fact, is an outcome of Vyāsa's intuitive vision of life; so is the epic *Mahābhārata* of which this dialogue is a part. The same vision represented in a more diluted and sweetened form clothed with legends, forms the Purāṇas, authored again by Vyāsa. More important, the Vedas, the most basic of all Indian scriptures and the most ancient of all world scriptures, were also collated and classified into four by Vyāsa. He, therefore, can very well be meditatively perceived as My *vibhūti* among silent sages (*munis*).

Though, Vālmikī is usually considered the most ancient of Indian poets, more ancient than him was Śukra, also called Uśanas. A *kavi* (poet) is more than a creative writer of poems; he is a *jñānin* who is also a poet. Hence, the poet Śukra, who was also the *guru* of the demons, may be meditated on as My *vibhūti*.

दण्डो दमयतामस्मि नीतिरस्मि जिगीषताम्।
मौनं चैवास्मि गुह्यानां ज्ञानं ज्ञानवतामहम्॥३८॥

daṇḍo damayatām asmi nītir asmi jigīṣatām ।
maunaṁ caivāsmi guhyānāṁ jñānaṁ jñānavatām aham ॥38॥

Of rulers, I am their sceptre; among those desirous of victory, I am justice; among mysteries, I am silence; and of *jñānins*, I am their *jñāna*.

Ancient Indians classified learning into three branches: *daṇḍa, ānvīkṣikī, vārtā.* These respectively are statecraft, philosophy and science of trades like agriculture and commerce. Those who rule a country need to be familiar with *daṇḍa* so that governance is neutral and just, as symbolized by the sceptre. The sceptre could, therefore, be meditated on as My *vibhūti* by those who are concerned with political affairs.

To be successful in life and to be victorious is a constant human aspiration. Yet attaining success at the expense of basic principles guiding life is not good. The success of human efforts in full consonance with such principles attains a new dimension called *nīti* (justice), literally "that which leads one forward." This *nīti* attains its zenith when human activities fully conform with My activities, with the spontaneous unfoldment of events in nature. This conformity attained, life is felt as an unceasing flow of success. In those who make efforts to attain such success in life, My *vibhūti* in the form of unfaltering and unconditioned *nīti* becomes evident.

The most mysterious of all knowledge is the *brahma-vidyā* that I am teaching you. What it really intends to teach is an ineffable experience of inner clarity. Masters, reaching this stage of teaching, turn silent, and the student too, likewise, remains immersed in the satisfaction of having all his doubts cleared, and of having attained what he was seeking. Hence, among all that is mysterious, the mystery of the silence of a *jñānin* can be meditated on as Myself.

It is by using words that I am teaching you now, but when the teaching reached its zenith, I pointed you to the silence that hides between the middle Chapters, IX and X. Unless this silent secret is intuitively perceived, what I really intend to teach in the *Gītā* as a whole will remain concealed, despite all other elaborations. Attaining this silent secret is what makes a *jñānin* of one. And thus *jñāna* in a *jñānin* is also Myself manifesting.

यच्चापि सर्वभूतानां बीजं तदहमर्जुन।
न तदस्ति विना यत्स्यान्मया भूतं चराचरम्॥३९॥

yac cāpi sarva-bhūtānāṁ bījaṁ tad aham arjuna ।
na tad asti vinā yat syān mayā bhūtaṁ carācaram ॥39॥

Above all, the original seed of all that has come into being is Myself. Whatever there is living or non-living, does not emerge in My absence.

Arjuna, till now I have been telling you of some of My *vibhūtis* wherein you can easily perceive Me meditatively. This in no way means that they are My only *vibhūtis*, for really everything in all the worlds is My own being manifesting variously. Though their variety is countless, the causal seed-substance in all of them is one alone, that is Myself. As no wave can emerge without water existing, so too no apparent entity in any world can exist without Me existing. In fact,

---

नान्तोऽस्ति मम दिव्यानां विभूतीनां परंतप।
एष तूद्देशतः प्रोक्तो विभूतेर्विस्तरो मया॥४०॥

nānto 'sti mama divyānāṁ vibhūtīnāṁ paraṁtapa |
eṣa tūddeśataḥ prokto vibhūter vistaro mayā ||40 ||

Having no end are My *vibhūtis*, O Arjuna. What I have detailed to you forms only some pointer examples of them.

Arjuna, endless are the ways in which I manifest Myself, everything living and non-living forming a part of My *vibhūti*. This immense potential for self-unfoldment is so divine (*divya*) that it is unimaginable to the human mind, for the very mind is nothing but a minute part of Myself manifesting. *Divya* literally means "that which can radiate light, that which reveals itself." I being effulgence in essence, everything that emerges from Me has necessarily to be effulgent and therefore *divya*.

My attempt was not to give a complete picture of My *vibhūtis*. I was just giving you some pointers (*uddeśa*) to help you or anyone to meditate on Me, as that was what you asked for.

यद्यद्विभूतिमत्सत्त्वं श्रीमदूर्जितमेव वा।
तत्तदेवावगच्छ त्वं मम तेजोंऽशसंभवम्॥४१॥

yad-yad vibhūtimat sattvaṁ śrīmad ūrjitam eva vā |
tat-tad evāvagaccha tvaṁ mama tejo ṁśa-saṁbhavam ||41 ||

Whatever there appears appealingly glorious, prosperingly beautiful and energetic, know all of them to be emanating from a mere spark of My splendour.

अथवा बहुनैतेन किं ज्ञातेन तवार्जुन।
विष्टभ्याहमिदं कृत्स्नमेकांशेन स्थितो जगत्॥४२॥

athavā bahunaitena kiṁ jñātena tavārjuna |
viṣṭabhyāham idaṁ kṛtsnam ekāṁśena sthito jagat ||42 ||

And after all, of what use for you is knowing Me in all details? (Keep this alone in your mind:) It is with

> a fragment of My being that I support the entire world as the pervading Substance of it.

Arjuna, though some *vibhūtis* of mine were just pointed out to you, knowing all of them in detail is of no use to any one in life, nor it is possible to know them all. The unimaginable greatness that I am, will be felt on your realizing that what appears as all the worlds together is merely a spark of the bon-fire that I am.

Arjuna, the teaching of this chapter is that whatever appears as all the worlds and life in these worlds is but My own being manifesting itself variously. Certain glorious and beautiful forms were also pointed out because you desired to hear from Me about those of My *vibhūtis* which could be meditated on easily. In fact, Śrī Kṛṣṇa, the individual, and Arjuna, the individual, are but different *vibhūtis* of that one Reality. It can be easily meditated on in many other forms also.

Thus ends Chapter Ten entitled Vibhūti-Yoga of the Bhagavad-Gītā, the essence of the Upaniṣads that embodies the yoga-śāstra of brahma-vidyā in the form of a dialogue between Śrī Kṛṣṇa and Arjuna.

XI

Viśvarūpa-Darśana-Yoga
—The Yoga of Cosmic Form Visualized—

अर्जुन उवाच —

मदनुग्रहाय परमं गुह्यमध्यात्मसंज्ञितम् ।
यत्त्वयोक्तं वचस्तेन मोहोऽयं विगतो मम ॥१॥

arjuna uvāca —

mad-anugrahāya paramaṁ guhyam adhyātma saṁjñitam ।
yat tvayoktaṁ vacas tena moho 'yaṁ vigato mama ॥1॥

Arjuna said —

Gone afar is my delusion as I heard your words on the Supreme mystery known to be self-based (*adhyātma*), you spoke out, out of your graceful favour for me.

Kṛṣṇa, this wisdom, most supreme and mysterious, you have taught me out of sheer love and compassion. I now understand in what sense it is supreme and mysterious. I know how it is *adhyātma* (self-based). I do realize what the ultimate Reality is; as well as the reason for treating this wisdom as *adhyātma* (the self-based). I now realize that I the individual and my *karma*s and you the individual and your *karma*s are all but conditioned appearances of the one unconditioned Reality, the Supreme Self. Before we began this dialogue I was confused as to what was *dharma* and what was *adharma* for me, merely because of the impression already fixed in my mind that all the *karma*s that take place through me are mine.

Now my attitude is totally transformed, knowing that I am not the doer of any *karma*. And besides,

---

भवाप्ययौ हि भूतानां श्रुतौ विस्तरशो मया।
त्वत्तः कमलपत्राक्ष माहात्म्यमपि चाव्ययम् ॥२॥

bhavāpyayau hi bhūtānāṁ śrutau vistaraśo mayā ।
tvattaḥ kamala-patrākṣa māhātmyam api cāvyayam ॥2 ॥

O Lotus-eyed, the genesis of beings as well as their dissolution in detail have been heard by Me from you; likewise your greatness that knows no decay too.

एवमेतद्यथात्थ त्वमात्मानं परमेश्वर।
द्रष्टुमिच्छामि ते रूपमैश्वरं पुरुषोत्तम ॥३॥

evam etad yathāttha tvam ātmānaṁ parameśvara ।
draṣṭum icchāmi te rūpam aiśvaraṁ puruṣottama ॥3 ॥

What you taught me of yourself, the Self, O Supreme Lord, I am fully convinced of. I do now wish to perceive directly that all-dominating Form of yours, O Puruṣottama.

Kṛṣṇa, I know you to be Parameśvara, the one Supreme Controller of everything. All that you have so far said of yourself concerning you, I now feel, I have understood. You yourself said that a real *tattvadarśin* is he who has directly perceived who and what you are. I too aspire to become such a *tattvadarśin* and therefore, I too wish to *see with my own eyes* the Form of yours that I have till now been trying to *understand* intellectually.

So far I have been attempting to *understand* you using the basics of common sense. This desire of mine to *perceive* your Form in all its conceptual details might perhaps be labelled a religious sentiment rather than a part of philosophical quest. I do not mind such a label, for our culture does not strictly separate religion and philosophy.

What I now pray for is that this longing of mine will, with your grace, be fulfilled. It is only on rare occasions that the aspirations of the seeker and the *guru*'s mind find unity, and a true imparting of wisdom becomes effective. For this reason,

मन्यसे यदि तच्छक्यं मया द्रष्टुमिति प्रभो ।
योगेश्वर ततो मे त्वं दर्शयात्मानमव्ययम् ॥४॥

manyase yadi tac chakyaṁ mayā draṣṭum iti prabho ।
yogeśvara tato me tvaṁ darśayātmānam avyayam ॥4॥

O Lord, O Master of *yoga*, if, in your opinion, I am worthy of seeing directly the decayless Form of yourself (the imperishable beingness of the Supreme Self) then please show it to me.

Kṛṣṇa, you are *yogeśvara,* the Lord or controller of all *yoga* states. If you think my aspiration and your grace can come together to a *yoga* state of union, then please make your being directly perceptible to me.

श्री भगवानुवाच —
पश्य मे पार्थ रूपाणि शतशोऽथ सहस्रशः ।
नानाविधानि दिव्यानि नानावर्णाकृतीनि च ॥५॥

śrī bhagavān uvāca —
paśya me pārtha rūpāṇi śataśo 'tha sahasraśaḥ ।
nānā-vidhāni divyāni nānā-varṇākṛtīni ca ॥5॥

Śrī Kṛṣṇa said —

O Pārtha, do behold My divine forms in their hundreds and thousands, multitudinous in variety, colour and form.

Arjuna, I do understand and appreciate your aspiration to perceive directly what I am and who I am, to perceive the one Absolute Reality in all Its multitudinous, apparent, changeful forms. That I am the one Reality of which everything is born and into which all are dissolved, you must be clearly aware of, particularly in the light of what was taught in the last chapter. Now you are about to *see* directly everything you previously *conceived* as ideas.

Countless are the manifest forms that emerge in their hundreds and thousands from Me, and merge back in Me, their variety of colour and form being indescribable and unpredictable. You may simply keep this in your mind: what you are going to see directly is a visual version of everything you have conceived of as My *vibhūtis*, in the last chapter. This Form you are going to see may be termed as *viśvarūpa*, in two senses: as all-inclusive, and as having the universe (*viśva*) for My form (*rūpa*). Some peculiarities of that form I shall tell you in advance:

पश्यादित्यान्वसून्रुद्रानश्विनौ मरुतस्तथा ।
बहून्यदृष्टपूर्वाणि पश्याश्चर्याणि भारत ॥६ ॥

paśyādityān vasūn rudrān aśvinau marutas tathā ।
bahūny adṛṣṭa-pūrvāṇi paśyāścaryāṇi bhārata ॥6 ॥

You will behold the Ādityas, the Vasus, the Rudras, the two Aśvins, and also the Maruts. Likewise will be seen many a not-seen-before-marvel, O Arjuna.

Arjuna, I told you in the last chapter that Viṣṇu among the Ādityas, Marīci among the Maruts, Śaṅkara among the Rudras, and some others were my *vibhūtis*. It is these very same Ādityas, Maruts and Rudras, in the flesh, that you are now going to see in Me. Nothing described verbally is as comprehensive as direct visual perception.

The cosmic system is peculiar: nothing therein is a carbon copy of another, even of the one that begot it. In this way each entity is a never-before-seen one. The marvel and mystery of this phenomenon is neither noticed nor appreciated simply because it is all too familiar for us. At any moment one may come across something inexplicable that has never been seen before. Many such wonders you are going to see in Me.

इहैकस्थं जगत्कृत्स्नं पश्याद्य सचराचरम् ।
मम देहे गुडाकेश यच्चान्यद्द्रष्टुमिच्छसि ॥७ ॥

ihaikastham jagat kṛtsnaṁ paśyādya sacarācaram ।
mama dehe guḍākeśa yac cānyad draṣṭum icchasi ॥7 ॥

Arjuna, the entire world with all its sentient and insentient beings, you will behold as located at one part of My body. What you will to see also you will see in it.

Arjuna, at the end of the last chapter it was mentioned that even a small part of My being can assume the form of the entire cosmos, and that also you will now directly see.

Another peculiarity of My Cosmic Form is that whatever you see will not simply be what I show you; what you wish to see will also be seen. This points to a hidden aspect of all our perceptual experiences: the nature of the perceived depends on the perceiving mind. Every perception is an experience and each experience occurs in the mind. The nature of perceptual experience at a particular moment depends not only on the object contacted by the senses but also on the state of the perceiving mind. The beauty of an excellent art work, for example, shown to one weary from a day-long monotonous job, is not properly appreciated. This is not because the art work lacks beauty, but because the mind was unwilling. Light entertainment, on the other hand, might at that moment be appealing to him. Each one's experience, even of the objective world being purely a subjective one, there is no way to contrast it with another's. What one sees is one's own world. It is with all this in mind I say, "What you will to see also you will see."

न तु मां शक्यसे द्रष्टुमनेनैव स्वचक्षुषा ।
दिव्यं ददामि ते चक्षुः पश्य मे योगमैश्वरम् ॥८ ॥

na tu māṁ śakyase draṣṭum anenaiva svacakṣuṣā ।
divyaṁ dadāmi te cakṣuḥ paśya me yogam aiśvaram ॥8 ॥

> Yet, you, with these eyes of yours, are not capable of perceiving Me; so I do give you a divine eye. With it you perceive the all-overseeing *yoga* of Mine.

Arjuna, the doubt you had about your own capability to directly see Me as I am, was not out of place. Transforming everything you have so far conceived into a perceptual experience requires not ordinary sight, but a special sight, an inner sight. This perception is an experience attained when the inner eye opens to see Me directly as though seen by the external eyes. At this present moment your mind is fully prepared to see that vision and therefore I give you unworldly sight to behold Me. The divine or unworldly (*divyam*) sight is nothing but the inexplicable capability one acquires at such rare moments in life. In this too there is a hidden *yoga*-secret — that of your mental preparedness and My graceful consent finding unity in an unworldly experience. In fact, the conceptual awareness you have had and the perception you are about to have are in essence not two. This *yoga*-secret is the mystery that underlies all the worlds, and controls all the worlds; thus it is *aiśvara,* rendered here as "the all-overseeing."

Vyāsa:

O Janmejaya, it was in the form of a dialogue between Kr̥ṣṇa and Arjuna that I conceived the *Bhagavad-Gītā.* Yet it begins and ends as a dialogue between Sañjaya and Dhr̥tarāṣṭra, a device that helps me weave the *Gītā* into the fabric of the epic *Mahābhārata.* The Sañjaya-Dhr̥tarāṣṭra dialogue, thus, naturally leans towards the epic story and the Kr̥ṣṇa-Arjuna dialogue towards the philosophy of life. The former which retreated as early as Chapter II, now re-emerges here in Chapter XI. Sañjaya is again brought to the forefront to describe to Dhr̥tarāṣṭra, the Cosmic Form of Kr̥ṣṇa that Arjuna is about to see.

In this description, three layers are to be separated out in order to appreciate it as relating fully to our own life and its problems.

1. Sañjaya describes the details of the Cosmic Form to Dhr̥tarāṣṭra — a description along the lines of the picture of Kr̥ṣṇa of the epic story and the *Bhāgavata Purāṇa.*

2. Arjuna's own appreciation of the Form. He sees in Kṛṣṇa's Form countless *vibhūtis* — all creative — arousing unstable feelings.

3. These appearances and feelings alter constantly till finally is seen the most terrible form of Kṛṣṇa, and a terrified Arjuna appeals to be shown a more gentle aspect. Kṛṣṇa himself makes an evaluation of the form, and only then Arjuna realizes that all those changeful appearances and the feelings they roused are nothing but a replica of individual experiences in life as a part of its total flow. The very beginning of the *Gītā,* as we know, was from such a situation.

सञ्जय उवाच —

एवमुक्त्वा ततो राजन्महायोगेश्वरो हरिः ।
दर्शयामास पार्थाय परमं रूपमैश्वरम् ॥९ ॥

sañjaya uvāca —

evam uktvā tato rājan mahā-yogeśvaro hariḥ ।
darśayāmāsa pārthāya paramaṁ rūpam aiśvaram ॥9 ॥

Sañjaya said —

O King, the Great Lord of Yoga, having spoken thus, showed to Arjuna his supreme lordly Form.

O King, "wondrous" is the only word with which the lordly Form of Kṛṣṇa could be described. See the details emerging in it!

अनेकवक्त्रनयनमनेकाद्भुतदर्शनम् ।
अनेकदिव्याभरणं दिव्यानेकोद्यतायुधम् ॥१० ॥

aneka-vaktra-nayanam anekādbhuta-darśanam ।
aneka-divyābharaṇaṁ divyānekodyatāyudham ॥10 ॥

Many are its faces and eyes; many are its wondrous features seen; many are the celestial ornaments it adorns itself with; many are the divine weapons it wields high.

O King Dhṛtarāṣṭra, Kṛṣṇa the individual, as we know, has only one face and two eyes, but Arjuna at this moment sees him as having countless faces and eyes. Kṛṣṇa has so far been teaching Arjuna in detail how the one and only Reality, represented here by Kṛṣṇa, the *guru*, unfolds itself and appears as everything in all the worlds. Every individual entity, then, is a particular face the Reality assumes for the moment, and it explains why Arjuna now sees Kṛṣṇa as having countless faces.

Seeing is the function of our eyes, but it has a limitation: it is capable of seeing clearly only one entity at a point of time. It, in other words, means our eyes are incapable of seeing the entire universe all at once, such a seeing requiring a special set of eyes — the ones Arjuna now has. It is such a special eye that every seeker should have to see Reality as such.

Nothing seen in the figure of Kṛṣṇa now is meant to be understood through the logical reasoning of mind. Anything not logically tenable is called a mystery (*adbhuta* or *āścarya*). Whatever is now seen in Kṛṣṇa is mysterious, for Reality in its ultimate sense and the appearing of the world are all a great mystery whether seen religiously, philosophically or scientifically.

Different stories in the Purāṇas and epics depict Kṛṣṇa as wearing various kinds of ornaments; all of them are now seen adorning his form. Viṣṇu whose incarnation Kṛṣṇa is, according to that story, had to engage in battles with *asuras* (demons) many times, each time using some special weapon; all those weapons are now seen held aloft by Kṛṣṇa now. Yet that form in general is extremely attractive.

दिव्यमाल्याम्बरधरं दिव्यगन्धानुलेपनम्।
सर्वाश्चर्यमयं देवमनन्तं विश्वतोमुखम् ॥११॥

divya mālyāmbara dharaṁ divya gandhānulepanam ।
sarvāścarya-mayaṁ devam anantaṁ viśvatomukham ॥11॥

Celestial garlands and vestures worn, and celestial cosmetics applied, that Form of the *deva* (the effulgent one) is but marvel embodied, endless and facing everywhere as it is.

O King Dhṛtarāṣṭra, all the good and beautiful things we have heard of as adorning the person of Kṛṣṇa or Viṣṇu are now seen all together in his Cosmic Form. Such visions are not to be described but to be experienced directly. That the Absolute is effulgence in essence (*deva*), Arjuna has been told many times; now he sees Kṛṣṇa to be so directly. That the Absolute is beginningless and endless is also taught repeatedly in the scriptures, and Kṛṣṇa taught it himself earlier; now the Lord is seen by Arjuna as beginninglessness and endlessness materialized. Another characteristic of *Brahman* is its having a face everywhere, hands everywhere, feet everywhere and so on. Kṛṣṇa gave emphasis to it himself when he said in the *Vibhūti-Yoga, dhātā'ham viśvato mukham* (X.33), meaning, "I am the Creator with faces everywhere." Now the same Kṛṣṇa is seen with the very same features.

Indescribable indeed is the glory of that vision. What I can tell you of it, is only this much:

दिवि सूर्यसहस्रस्य भवेद्युगपदुत्थिता ।
यदि भाः सदृशी सा स्याद्भासस्तस्य महात्मनः ॥१२॥

divi sūrya-sahasrasya bhaved yugapad utthitā ।
yadi bhāḥ sadṛśī sā syād bhāsas tasya mahātmanaḥ ॥12॥

Comparable to a thousand suns rising all at once in the vastness of the sky may be the blazing bright Form of the great Self.

O King, yet another marvel emerges visible within this blazingly effulgent form:

तत्रैकस्थं जगत्कृत्स्नं प्रविभक्तमनेकधा ।
अपश्यद्देवदेवस्य शरीरे पाण्डवस्तदा ॥१३॥

tatraika stham jagat kṛtsnaṁ pravibhaktam anekadhā ।
apaśyad deva devasya śarīre pāṇḍavas tadā ॥13 ॥

Located at a small part of this body of the God of gods is then seen by Arjuna, the entire changeful world variously divided well into all its specific entities.

O King Dhṛtarāṣṭra, Kṛṣṇa concluded the *Vibhūti-Yoga* (Chapter X) with these words: "It is with a fragment of my being that I support the entire world." Now, on the part of Arjuna, he sees the entire world with all its various and changeful entities, existing in a small part of the marvellous form of Kṛṣṇa. The effulgence of the body itself shines specifically as the entire world in a small insignificant part of the whole, while the other parts remain distant and misted over. Everything that Kṛṣṇa said about Himself and which was understood by Arjuna is now being directly perceived by him as forming a part of the cosmic body of Kṛṣṇa.

The rapturous response to this vision from Arjuna is thus:

ततः स विस्मयाविष्टो हृष्टरोमा धनञ्जयः ।
प्रणम्य शिरसा देवं कृताञ्जलिरभाषत ॥१४ ॥

tataḥ sa vismayāviṣṭo hṛṣṭa-romā dhanañjayaḥ ।
praṇamya śirasā devaṁ kṛtāñjalir abhāṣata ॥14 ॥

Wonderstruck as he became, Arjuna, his hairs standing on end, then bowed his head down before the effulgent Form and said, hands folded:

अर्जुन उवाच —
पश्यामि देवांस्तव देव देहे सर्वांस्तथा भूतविशेषसङ्घान् ।
ब्रह्माणमीशं कमलासनस्थमृषींश्च सर्वानुरगांश्च दिव्यान् ॥१५ ॥

arjuna uvāca —
paśyāmi devāṁs tava deva dehe sarvāṁs tathā bhūta-viśeṣa saṅghān ।

brahmāṇam īśaṁ kamalāsanastham ṛṣīṁś ca sarvān uragāṁś ca divyān ॥15 ॥

Arjuna said —

O the Effulgent One, I do see in your body all the gods of heaven and hosts of everything that has come into being. So do I see Brahmā the all powerful creator of beings, with lotus for his throne, all the *ṛṣis* and all the celestial serpents too.

O Kṛṣṇa, effulgence in essence is your bodily being. In it I do see all the worlds. I see heaven and its denizens in it. The earth and all its living and non-living beings are also seen in your body. Remaining one, you are assuming infinitely various forms. Now I *see* directly how there can be many in one and one in many. I recall now your explication of the way the one Reality and many appearances are inseparably non-dual in you. I am now having a direct experiential confirmation of this otherwise subtle philosophical point.

You being the beginning, the middle and the end of all beings is the most basic of all your *vibhūtis* (Verse X.20). That beginning is symbolized by Brahmā, the Creator. His celestial seat is within the lotus growing in the navel of Viṣṇu who, in his turn, represents the existence of beings (the middle).

The original cause of gods and *ṛṣis*, you remain unknown even to them as you yourself said earlier (X.2). They too are now seen in your being. Of your *vibhūtis*, you are Vāsuki among the serpents and Ananta among the poisonless mountain snakes (X.28, 29). Here I see those serpents and snakes also in your Cosmic Body. Besides,

---

अनेकबाहूदरवक्त्रनेत्रं पश्यामि त्वां सर्वतो ऽनन्तरूपम्।
नान्तं न मध्यं न पुनस्तवादिं पश्यामि विश्वेश्वर विश्वरूप ॥१६॥

aneka bāhūdara vaktra netraṁ paśyāmi tvāṁ sarvato 'nanta rūpam ।
nāntaṁ na madhyaṁ na punas tavādiṁ paśyāmi viśveśvara viśva-rūpa ॥16 ॥

The all-enveloping and endless Form of yours I do see as having countless arms, countless bellies, countless mouths, countless eyes, and of it I can see, O Lord of the Cosmos, O Cosmic Form, neither the end, nor the beginning, nor even the middle.

O Lord of All, I know that all beings are *vibhūtis* of yours, and such *vibhūtis* are countless, each having its own limbs, bellies, mouths and the like. All such distinctly seen limbs belong to your body, the cosmos. You are not only without beginning and end, but all that has beginning and end are your momentary *vibhūtis*. The famous *Puruṣa Sūkta* of the Vedas also depicts you in the same way.

किरीटिनं गदिनं चक्रिणं च तेजोराशिं सर्वतो दीप्तिमन्तम्।
पश्यामि त्वां दुर्निरीक्ष्यं समन्ताद्दीप्तानलार्कद्युतिमप्रमेयम् ॥१७॥

kirīṭinaṁ gadinaṁ cakriṇaṁ ca tejo-rāśiṁ sarvato dīptimantam
paśyāmi tvāṁ durnirīkṣyaṁ samantād dīptānalārka-dyutim aprameyam ॥17॥

Adorned with crown, weilding mace and discus, blazing brightly everywhere, is the Form of yours I see. That inconceivable, all-encompassing Form, like a blazing conflagration or the midday-summer-sun, is too difficult to look at.

O Lord, wearing a crown on your head and holding a mace and discus, two of your chief weapons, in your hands, is the form that I am familiar with. This very same form I do now see as all-encompassing. Pure brightness in essence, your being blazes everywhere, everything specific shines because of it as your own *vibhūtis*. Because of its overwhelming brightness, it is impossible to look at your form. Looking like all the fire of all the worlds blazing all at once, or a thousand suns shining in the midday sky of summer, it is impossible to imagine this Form of yours. In short, I do now perceive directly, comprehend fully, how you are *param* (the transcendental), how you are *akṣaram* (the imperishable), and how you are *aprameyam* (the inconceivable).

त्वमक्षरं परमं वेदितव्यं त्वमस्य विश्वस्य परं निधानम्।
त्वमव्ययः शाश्वतधर्मगोप्ता सनातनस्त्वं पुरुषो मतो मे ॥१८॥

tvam akṣaraṁ paramaṁ veditavyaṁ tvam asya viśvasya paraṁ nidhānam ।
tvam avyayaḥ śāśvata-dharma-goptā sanātanas tvaṁ puruṣo mato me ॥18॥

That transcendental and imperishable one meant to be finally known is yourself; the one supreme abode of the total cosmic system is yourself; the decayless you are; the immutable guardian of the eternal *dharma* you are; the most ancient *puruṣa* you are; and thus fully convinced I do become now.

O Lord, that one Reality alone is to be known by any seeker, and that this imperishable Supreme Reality is yourself was made clear earlier. It was also made explicit that you alone exist as supporting (*nidhānam*) the appearance of everything. You explained to me how you remained without diminishing, in and through all that grows and decays; that you are the most ancient *puruṣa* was also understood by me. All these I do see now as inherent in the Cosmic Body I behold before me. Though everything visible is ever changing and transient, a constant cosmic system, *dharma,* is always maintained and that is done by none other than you. You alone are the one *puruṣa,* you alone are the one Reality to be known; you alone are the one goal to be attained.

अनादिमध्यान्तमनन्तवीर्यमनन्तबाहुं शशिसूर्यनेत्रम्।
पश्यामि त्वां दीप्तहुताशवक्त्रं स्वतेजसा विश्वमिदं तपन्तम्॥१९॥

anādi-madhyāntam ananta-vīryam ananta-bāhuṁ śaśi-sūrya netraṁ ।

paśyāmi tvāṁ dīpta hutāśa-vaktraṁ sva-tejasā viśvam idaṁ tapantam ||19 ||

Beginningless, middleless and endless you are; of boundless vitality you are; of countless arms you are; having the sun and the moon for the two eyes you are. Such a being of yours is seen by me as having mouth emitting flames of fire, and scorching all this world with the fire of yours.

Kṛṣṇa, that *Brahman* is beginningless and endless, I have already become well aware of. The same beginninglessness and endlessness I am seeing now in your Form. The boundless creative vitality inherent in *Brahman,* I know, is what finds expression as all the worlds, and this process of creative self-expression of *Brahman* is what we call *prakṛti.* Now I am seeing all the worlds being shaped from your boundlessly vital Form. *Karma* is seen everywhere in it; arm being the main organ of *karma,* I see you as having countless arms.

This cosmos, imagined as having human form, has the sun and the moon for eyes, and exactly such is the form I see you now in.

Kṛṣṇa, look, your mood is changing as in life, and it assumes a terrible appearance. Your mouth now looks like a conflagration, and in its heat all the worlds become scorched. I am now thus witnessing directly how living beings bear sufferings in life.

द्यावापृथिव्योरिदमन्तरं हि व्याप्तं त्वयैकेन दिशश्च सर्वाः ।
दृष्ट्वाद्भुतं रूपमुग्रं तवेदं लोकत्रयं प्रव्यथितं महात्मन् ॥२० ॥

dyāvā-pṛthivyor idam antaraṁ hi vyāptaṁ tvay aikena diśaś ca sarvāḥ |
dṛṣṭvādbhutam rūpam ugraṁ tavedaṁ loka-trayaṁ pravyathitaṁ mahātman ||20 ||

By you, the one, alone is pervaded the entire extent between the earth and the sky, as also all the cardinal directions. This awe-inspiring wondrous Form of yours seen, O Great One, all the three worlds tremble with fear.

O Lord, I once again perceive how you are the all-pervading Reality. Your being fills the entire domain between the lowest and the highest regions of existence, as well as all around in all the directions of the compass. Mysterious is your Form and awful too. You are a mystery to those who try to understand you; you are fearsome to those who are unmindful of your boundless creative urge that finds expression as life and its events. Every living being, especially humans, intend to live life guided by personal interests and will, whereas the unfolding of all events in all the worlds is dictated by you alone. This conflict between your will and the will of each being creates dissatisfactions and disappointments in life. People feel the ground under their feet trembling when they find that their own life's progress is not guided by themselves, but by some unknown and unknowable will. Thus, though forming a part of your body, such people do not see themselves to be so and remain *ajñānins* (ignorant).

All such scenes of life I do witness now in your Cosmic Form.

अमी हि त्वां सुरसङ्घा विशन्ति केचिद्भीताः प्राञ्जलयो गृणन्ति ।
स्वस्तीत्युक्त्वा महर्षि सिद्धसङ्घाः स्तुवन्ति त्वां स्तुतिभिः पुष्कलाभिः ॥२१॥

amī hi tvāṁ sura-saṅghā viśanti kecid bhītāḥ prāñjalayo gṛṇanti ।
svastīty uktvā maharṣi siddha-saṅghāḥ stuvanti tvāṁ stutibhiḥ puṣkalābhiḥ ॥21॥

Lookẽ *suras* (gods of heaven), hosts of them, are entering your being; some of them, frightened, are with folded hands. Lots of *maharṣi*s (great seers) and *siddha*s (men of attainments), praying for the well-being of the world, sing your praise with beautifully composed meaningful hymns.

O Lord, there are certain people, who, as your own *vibhūti*s, realize that their own existence is only as your *vibhūti*s. Not seeing their own existence as real, they live always in identity with you. As though a perceptual version of this, I see now hosts of gods (inhabitants of heaven) entering your Cosmic Form.

Other types of your devotees are those who, though lacking in knowing you philosophically, are fully convinced that everything is in your control. They live in fear of you, always making supplications to you with folded hands. Many such I do see now in your Cosmic Form.

Maharṣis are great seers (*mahā*, great; *ṛṣi*, seer) and *siddhas* are men of wisdom-attainment; both know what is Real, both know you properly. As visualized by them, you are an experiential mystery. What such visionaries do is to simply sing your praises with the implicit or explicit prayer, "May all be well." Scriptures and devotional songs, poems and hymns, are an outcome of this. Such *maharṣis* and *siddhas* and all the invaluable works composed by them, are all now being seen in your Cosmic Form.

रुद्रादित्या वसवो ये च साध्या विश्वे ऽश्विनौ मरुतश्चोष्मपाश्च ।
गन्धर्वयक्षासुरसिद्धसङ्घा वीक्षन्ते त्वां विस्मिताश्चैव सर्वे ॥२२॥

rudrādityā-vasavo ye ca sādhyā viśve 'śvinau marutaś coṣmapāś ca ।
gandharva-yakṣāsura-siddha-saṅghā vīkṣante tvāṁ vismitāś caiva sarve ॥22॥

The Rudras, Ādityas, Vasus, Sādhyas, the Viśvedevas, the two Aśvins, Maruts, the manes, hosts of *gandharvas*, *yakṣas*, *asuras*, *siddhas* — all gaze at you amazed.

O Lord, describing your *vibhūtis*, you told me you were Śaṅkara among the Rudras, Viṣṇu among the Ādityas, Pāvaka among the Vasus and so on. All those Rudras, Ādityas, Vasus and others are now being seen in you, confirming what you described. Some other-worldly beings such as Sādhyas, Viśvedevas (the all-gods), the twin gods Aśvins, the manes (*pitṛs*), the Maruts, *gandharvas*, *yakṣas*, *asuras*, *siddhas* — all these are also seen in you. You have already mentioned some of them as forming your *vibhūtis*. Your *vibhūti* being endless, seeing more than what you had described is but natural. One thing I see as common in all of these is that they not only exist as a part of your being, but they are also fully aware of being so. While seeing their own existence, therefore, as a part of your ever-changing *vibhūtis*, they wondrously gaze at you.

There are also some others who, though a part of you, tremble with fear on seeing your unbelievable Form which at times turns terrible.

रूपं महत्ते बहुवक्त्रनेत्रं महाबाहो बहुबाहूरुपादम्।
बहूदरं बहुदंष्ट्राकरालं दृष्ट्वा लोकाः प्रव्यथितास्तथाहम् ॥२३॥

rūpaṁ mahat te bahu-vaktra-netraṁ mahā-bāho bahu bāhūru pādam ।
bahūdaraṁ bahu-daṁṣṭrā-karālaṁ dṛṣṭvā lokāḥ pravyathitās tathāham ॥23॥

O Mighty Armed (Kṛṣṇa), stupendous is your Form that has numerous faces, numerous mouths, numerous eyes, numerous hands, numerous thighs, numerous feet, numerous bellies, numerous teeth of fearsome appearance. Having seen it, beings of all the worlds are trembling in awe, so am I.

O Lord, every face is your face; every eye is your eye; every hand is your hand; every foot is your foot. The entities that thus become manifested in you are not always gentle. The everywhere-seen-mouth of yours is thus seen with fang-like teeth terribly protruding, making the entire Form of yours frightening. That the cosmic system as well as the life system in it, is not always gentle and smooth, must be the truth you are now revealing visually. Though normal with the world order, such facets of yours will no doubt make those who face them suffer. Indicating it must be the scene I see now, of all the beings in all the worlds trembling with fear on seeing this terrible aspect of yours. That all those beings have their being in you, while being thus frightened, is the most unbelievable mystery of it. I am also one among them.

Even that terrible Form seems to change its mood:

नभःस्पृशं दीप्तमनेकवर्णं व्यात्ताननं दीप्तविशालनेत्रम्।
दृष्ट्वा हि त्वां प्रव्यथितान्तरात्मा धृतिं न विन्दामि शमं च विष्णो॥२४॥

nabhaḥ-spṛśaṁ dīptam aneka varṇaṁ vyāttānanaṁ dīpta-viśāla-netram ।
dṛṣṭvā hi tvāṁ pravyathitāntarātmā dhṛtiṁ na vindāmi śamaṁ ca viṣṇo ॥24॥

Touching the sky, O the All-pervading One, you do loom luminous. Your being assumes many and varying hues. Wide open is your mouth, and burning fire-like are the large eyes of yours. Seeing you so, even the core of my being is trembling with fear. My mind does not find firmness, nor do I find any peace.

O Lord, being Viṣṇu, as the name signifies, you are the all-pervading Reality. Now I see you exactly so, touching heaven and earth. Ever actively creative, you are seen with your colour constantly changing. The mouth of yours seen everywhere, appears wide open and terrible, as though about to devour all the worlds. Likewise, terrible and fiery are your eyes. Having seen all these, My Lord, my inner being trembles, so does my mind, and my body feels as if losing the ground from under its feet. Behold! your Form becomes now ever more unbearable.

दंष्ट्राकरालानि च ते मुखानि दृष्ट्वैव कालानलसन्निभानि।
दिशो न जाने न लभे च शर्म प्रसीद देवेश जगन्निवास॥२५॥

daṁṣṭrā-karālāni ca te mukhāni dṛṣṭvaiva kālānala-sannibhāni ।
diśo na jāne na labhe ca śarma prasīda deveśa jagan-nivāsa ॥25॥

Having seen your mouths that blaze with inferno-like fires of cosmic destruction and your fiercely protruding fang-like teeth, I lose my sense of direction, O God of gods, O abode of the worlds, please be benign.

See, how fierce are the scenes I behold!

अमी च त्वां धृतराष्ट्रस्य पुत्राः सर्वे सहैवावनिपालसङ्घैः ।
भीष्मो द्रोणः सूतपुत्रस्तथासौ सहास्मदीयैरपि योधमुख्यैः ॥२६॥

वक्त्राणि ते त्वरमाणा विशन्ति दंष्ट्राकरालानि भयानकानि ।
केचिद्विलग्ना दशनान्तरेषु संदृश्यन्ते चूर्णितैरुत्तमाङ्गैः ॥२७॥

amī ca tvāṁ dhṛtarāṣṭrasya putrāḥ sarve sahaivāvani-pāla saṅghaiḥ ।
bhīṣmo droṇaḥ sūta-putras tathāsau sahāsmadīyair api yodha mukhyaiḥ ॥26॥

vaktṛāni te tvaramāṇā viśanti daṁṣṭrā-karālāni bhayānakāni ।
kecid vilagnā daśanāntareṣu saṁdṛśyante cūrṇitair uttamāṅgaiḥ ॥27॥

These sons of Dhṛtarāṣṭra, Bhīṣma, Droṇa, that Karṇa, along with the hosts of kings, the principal warriors with us as well — all are seen rushing headlong into your mouth with its terribly protruding teeth. Some are even seen getting stuck in the gaps between your teeth, heads crumbling.

O Lord, as this Cosmic Form of yours assumes a terrifying facet, this horrible battlefield and all these battling warriors also appear there. Not only are they part of your body but they, as if possessed by a frenzied urge, rush headlong into your horrible mouth and are destroyed. The heads of some are shattered between your teeth, and their fragments stick in the cavities of your teeth. By showing me this Cosmic Form of yours, you are visually teaching me that terrible things like war and destruction are only a natural part of the total scheme of life.

The urge for fighting, we know, is what brought these kings and warriors here standing face to face — facing death as well. Fighting simply means one is willing to be killed. I have now seen that this urge too is part of the total scheme of things, a minute part of your Cosmic Form. Look, how things are happening again!

यथा नदीनां बहवो ऽम्बुवेगाः समुद्रमेवाभिमुखा द्रवन्ति।
तथा तवामी नरलोकवीरा विशन्ति वक्त्राण्यभिविज्वलन्ति ॥२८॥

yathā nadīnāṁ bahavo 'mbu-vegāḥ samudram evābhimukhā dravanti ।
tathā tavāmī nara-loka-vīrā viśanti vaktrāṇy abhivijvalanti ॥28॥

As various rivers variedly flowing in various directions, do all course towards ocean, so do all these men of valour enter the flaming mouth of yours.

O Lord, the water of the oceans, evaporated, become rain clouds, and the rain from different terrains flows as rivulets, streams and rivers, into the very same ocean. So too are your *vibhūtis*: they are formulated in your being, they live as a part of your being, each living its own life, and finally merge in you. The warriors gathered here to fight each other are simply a facet of that cyclic process. Yet not many notice themselves as being so. What we do notice is the horror of perishing individuals. Not only these warriors but every being in all the worlds is also inevitably destined to reach your all-devouring mouth, the destructive aspect of the Absolute. Everyone, while living, is heading towards it. This particular aspect too, I do witness now in your Cosmic Form:

यथा प्रदीप्तं ज्वलनं पतङ्गा विशन्ति नाशाय समृद्धवेगाः।
तथैव नाशाय विशन्ति लोकास्तवापि वक्त्राणि समृद्धवेगाः ॥२९॥

yathā pradīptaṁ jvalanaṁ pataṅgā viśanti nāśāya samṛddha vegāḥ ।
tathaiva nāśāya viśanti lokās tavāpi vaktrāṇi samṛddha vegāḥ ॥29 ॥

As moths swarm swiftly into a flaming fire merely to perish, so do these people rush headlong into your mouths simply to be destroyed.

My Lord, moths are drawn by fire and they swarm towards a burning lamp or a flame. The very joy of flying into brightness results in their perishing. So also are human beings. Lured by pleasures, they jump into pleasure-giving situations, and find their doom therein. The present battle too is no exception. Greed for power is what lured both groups to become mutual enemies in this battle. The very same battle is going to be ruinous to both. Human life, taken generally, also is likewise. Every human being, at every moment, is engaged in calculated activities, thinking always of ensuring more pleasure. Such activities may either be constructive or destructive. Either way, man is unmindful always of his heading towards death, symbolically represented by the flaming fire of your all-devouring mouth. Now, I perceive this aspect more clearly in your Form:

लेलिह्यसे ग्रसमानः समन्ताल्लोकान्समग्रान्वदनैर्ज्वलद्भिः ।
तेजोभिरापूर्य जगत्समग्रं भासस्तवोग्राः प्रतपन्ति विष्णो ॥३० ॥

lelihyase grasamānaḥ samantāl lokān samagrān vadanair jvaladbhiḥ ।
tejobhir āpūrya jagat samagraṁ bhāsas tavogrāḥ pratapanti viṣṇo ॥30 ॥

You, mouths flaming, are lapping up all the worlds from every side and are devouring them. O Viṣṇu, your fierce brightness, filling the entire changeful world, scorches it.

O Lord, all beings, from every side, advance towards your flaming mouth, and you on your part, are devouring them, lapping them up one by one. Visible everywhere, thus is the brightness of your fiery mouth, its everywhere-radiating heat scorching all the worlds.

O Lord, how mysteriously changeful are the phenomena that appear and disappear in your being! First I saw all the gods, including Brahmā the Creator, in it; now I see you as all-devouring, signifying death and dissolution. Therefore,

---

आख्याहि मे को भवानुग्ररूपो नमोऽस्तु ते देववर प्रसीद।
विज्ञातुमिच्छामि भवन्तमाद्यं न हि प्रजानामि तव प्रवृत्तिम्॥३१॥

ākhyā hi me ko bhavān ugra-rūpo namo 'stu te deva-vara prasīda ।
vijñātum icchāmi bhavantam ādyaṁ na hi prajānāmi tava pravṛttim ॥31॥

O the One of Awe-inspiring Form, please tell me who you are. Salutations to you, O the Best of the Effulgent. Please be graceful and benign. I do desire to know you, the source of all, properly. In no way do I understand the activities of yours.

My Lord, I desired to perceive you in your Cosmic Form, and now what I behold is you as the all-devouring fire. I do not understand what you are showing Me! Are you visually teaching me how life is? The only urge this vision rouses in me is to salute you and to pray that you may once again appear to me as your benign self.

I do not understand the mysterious way you are activating yourself as the source of everything; may be it is not meant to be *understood* by anyone at all. Yet, I do have the insatiable urge to know you properly in all details as do other seekers.

श्री भगवानुवाच —
कालोऽस्मि लोकक्षयकृत्प्रवृद्धो लोकान् समाहर्तुमिह प्रवृत्तः।
ऋतेऽपि त्वां न भविष्यन्ति सर्वे येऽवस्थिताः प्रत्यनीकेषु योधाः॥३२॥

śri bhagavān uvāca —

kālo 'smi loka-kṣaya-kṛt pravṛddho lokān samāhartum iha pravṛttaḥ ।
ṛte 'pi tvāṁ na bhaviṣyanti sarve ye 'vasthitāḥ pratyanīkeṣu yodhāḥ ॥32 ॥

Śrī Kṛṣṇa said —

I am the always-advancing time that causes decaying of worlds. In order to destroy all these beings it is that I do ever remain active. None of these warriors arrayed in the hostile armies, shall remain alive even in case you do not fight.

Arjuna, you need not try to *understand* Me, nor to know how My activities are, for I am the unknowable original cause of everything knowable. I am the cause of the dissolution of everyting as well. Creation and dissolution, both are going on in Me simultaneously, one becoming dissolved results in the creation of another or many others. The emergence and merger of beings form part of My *karma* resulting in *vibhūtis*. This *karma* is such that no one, not even I, can predict exactly what will happen when and where. Therefore, instead of trying to *know* Me clearly and distinctly, you may rather *experience* your being in Me as a mystery. My nature and content, and the nature and content of life are not two.

The last thing you saw in My cosmic form was that everything was being consumed by my flaming mouth and among them were both those hostile to you as well as those who are with you. They are being destroyed, not because of you, but because of Me, the Absolute. Even if you people do not desire this war, still none is going to live for ever. Definitely all will attain death signified by my wide open flaming mouth. Therefore, do not feel the guilt that you are causing the death of these people.

तस्मात्त्वमुत्तिष्ठ यशो लभस्व जित्वा शत्रून् भुङ्क्ष्व राज्यं समृद्धम्।
मयैवैते निहताः पूर्वमेव निमित्तमात्रं भव सव्यसाचिन्॥३३॥

tasmāt tvām uttiṣṭha yaśo labhasva jitvā śatrūn bhunkṣva rājyaṁ samṛddham ।

mayaivaite nihatāḥ pūrvam eva nimitta-mātraṁ bhava savyasācin ||33 ||

Do, therefore, stand up and win renown, conquering your enemies, and do enjoy rulership of the prosperous kingdom. Already killed by Me are these enemies; you just become an incidental cause, O Master-Bowman.

Arjuna, death as you know, is inevitable and some cause for death has to emerge normally as a part of the flow of events in nature. The development of events in the present case happened to be such that these warriors are to die in this war. It could well be said, therefore, that it is My will that their death should be so. In other words, they have virtually already been killed by Me. Thus, you are only an incidental tool in making my will work, therefore don't think that you are the killer. The *karma* (activity) that is natural to you is fighting. Do it without a sense of being the doer, be fully aware that it is *prakṛti*'s creativity working through you. Stand up, be ready to fight with firm mind, you will become renowned as the one who successfully followed his *svadharma.* As a master-archer capable of shooting equally well with both hands, you are *savyasācin.* This special nature of yours, your conquering the enemies and your enjoying the rulership, all these should be understood as made possible, not by your skill, but by My will.

You experienced a sense of guilt that you were going to kill Bhīṣma, Droṇa and the like, who were really to be honoured. Do you know how their actual state is? I shall tell you:

द्रोणं च भीष्मं च जयद्रथं च कर्णं तथान्यानपि योधवीरान्।
मया हतांस्त्वं जहि मा व्यथिष्ठा युध्यस्व जेतासि रणे सपत्नान्॥३४॥

droṇaṁ ca bhīṣmaṁ ca jayadrathaṁ ca karṇaṁ tathānyān api yodha-vīrān |
mayā hatāṁs tvaṁ jahi mā vyathiṣṭhā yudhyasva jetāsi raṇe sapatnān ||34 ||

Droṇa, Bhīṣma, Jayadratha, Karṇa and other warriors like them are already doomed by Me; you just kill them. Have no compunction; do fight; you will conquer enemies.

Arjuna, *prakṛti*'s *karmas*, as they appear in My Cosmic Form right now, are such that Droṇa, Bhīṣma, Jayadratha, Karṇa and all other great warriors are to die of this war. We know that Bhīṣma can die only when he himself wills; but at the end of this war, he will be willing to die. If anyone is responsible for the death of these people, it is I, the Absolute. Creation and destruction are just two facets of the *karma* that goes on in Me. Becoming frightened at seeing the destructive phase of My *karma* is of no avail. It is as a part of the unfolding of My *karma* that the war occurred, and these warriors are to die as a part of the very same *karma*. That they have to die at your hands is merely incidental.

When a judge sentences a murderer to death and the executioner carries out the sentence, neither of them is responsible, but it is the overall social system and the state's law that are at work. Neither the judge nor the executioner can cut themselves off from it. Similar is the situation you and I are in now. I or *prakṛti* cannot go out of its way. You too cannot. What *prakṛti* enjoins you right now is to fight and conquer the enemies.

सञ्जय उवाच —

एतच्छ्रुत्वा वचनं केशवस्य कृताञ्जलिर्वेपमानः किरीटी।
नमस्कृत्वा भूय एवाह कृष्णं सगद्गदं भीतभीतः प्रणम्य ॥३५॥

sañjaya uvāca —

etac chrutvā vacanaṁ keśavasya kṛtāñjalir vepamānaḥ kirīṭī ।
namas-kṛtvā bhūya evāha kṛṣṇaṁ sagadgadaṁ bhīta-bhītaḥ praṇamya ॥35॥

Sañjaya said —

Having heard these words of Keśava (Kṛṣṇa) the Diadem-wearer (Arjuna), extremely frightened and with trembling body, bowed his head before Kṛṣṇa. With folded hands and faltering voice, he said to Kṛṣṇa, prostrating himself before him:

O King Dhṛtarāṣṭra, Arjuna, hearing these words of Kṛṣṇa, realized what his position really is: that he cannot exist and function simply as he wills, that his value notions and interests alone are not the factors that guide life. Extremely frightened is he now — a fear neither for his enemies, nor for the war in general. Kṛṣṇa has just revealed to him how life in its entirety is. Arjuna and his renowned skill in warfare are as nothing in this overall picture of life. This feeling of his own insignificance makes him tremble, for it has been a shock to his till-now-egoistic mind. The Upaniṣads speak of the fear that every natural phenomenon feels about *Brahman*. The *Taittirīya Upaniṣad,* for example, says, "Fearing It the wind blows; fearing It the sun rises; fearing It Agni and Indra perform their respective roles; fearing It hastens Death as the fifth." Similar is the fear Arjuna has now. This fear does not impel him to flee from the battlefield, but to do the bidding of *Brahman,* to dedicate himself to the cause of *Brahman,* to prostrate himself before Kṛṣṇa. So prostrating himself he says:

अर्जुन उवाच —

स्थाने हृषीकेश तव प्रकीर्त्या जगत्प्रहृष्यत्यनुरज्यते च।
रक्षांसि भीतानि दिशो द्रवन्ति सर्वे नमस्यन्ति च सिद्धसङ्घाः ॥३६॥

arjuna uvāca —

sthāne hṛṣīkeśa tava prakīrtyā jagat prahṛṣyaty anurajyate ca ।
rakṣāṁsi bhītāni diśo dravanti sarve namasyanti ca siddha-saṅghāḥ ॥36॥

Arjuna said —

O Hṛṣīkeśa (Kṛṣṇa), rightly do all find happiness and live in mutual accord just by singing your praise. *Rākṣasas*, frightened, are seen running away in all directions; *siddhas* (men of attainment), hosts of them, on the other hand, bow down before you in adoration.

Kṛṣṇa, I had a longing to know you properly and clearly; but now I realize you are unknowable and mysterious. I now desire to sing your praise rather than knowing you. Also I realize that life, particularly human life, will be peaceful only on seeing your being in the being of everything, in the being of oneself as well. Seeing myself thus enables me to see everything so. Now I see all such *vibhūti*s in mutual harmony, one's existence and happiness ensuring that of all others around. When this harmony and mutual trust are wanting, your *vibhūti*s will not form a cosmos, but will remain a chaos. The one Reality, the one Substance, that underlies all such *vibhūti*s is you; and seeing you as such and praising you as such makes life peaceful, no matter what happens moment after moment.

There are those who are incapable of perceiving life in this way, of course. They take to the idea that life's success consists in defeating their enemies. They may at times find themselves victorious, but will end up finally in total failure. The *rākṣasa*s represent them. Knowing you, the Reality, and paying due homage to you are quite unknown to them. They, therefore, always live scared of anything mightier than them; they live scared of Reality. Signifying this fact is this scene of frightened *rākṣasa*s running away in all directions seen in your cosmic form.

Much different is the case of those who live acknowledging you. Whatever they think desirable is felt by them as already attained, because you are everything and you are already attained. Such men of attainment are known as *siddha*s. Hosts of such I do see in your figure, saluting you.

कस्माच्च ते न नमेरन्महात्मन् गरीयसे ब्रह्मणो ऽप्यादिकर्त्रे ।
अनन्त देवेश जगन्निवास त्वमक्षरं सदसत्तत्परं यत् ॥३७॥

kasmāc ca te na nameran mahātman garīyase brahmaṇo 'py ādi kartre ।
ananta deveśa jagan nivāsa tvam akṣaraṁ sad asat tat paraṁ yat ॥37॥

O the Loftiest Self, for what reason they should not bow down to you, the original cause even of Brahmā, the Creator? O the Infinite One, O the Lord even of gods, O the Abode of All the Worlds, you are the Imperishable; you are the Real (*sat*), you are the unreal (*asat*), you are that which is beyond as well.

O Lord, you are the loftiest of all realities — the Absolute Self, the all-pervading Substance; thus the epithet *mahātman* (the Great Self) befits you well in all respects. Mythology thinks of Brahmā as the creator of the world; but you are the cause even of that creator. Likewise, you are the one into which everything is dissolved. Such being you, and knowing you so as those *siddhas* are, how can they remain without glorifying you? Beginningless and endless effulgence in essence, you control everything from within and thus you are *deveśa,* the *īśa* even of *devas; īśa* meaning controller, and *deva* the effulgent one or god. It is your Existence that becomes apparent as the existence of the world and of ours. You are thus *jagannivāsa,* the abode of all the worlds.

You are the one Reality (*sat*) that exists on its own, all the worlds being your apparent manifestations (*bhāva*), unreal by themselves. You, as *sat,* are imperishable (*akṣara*), and, as *bhāva,* are perishable (*kṣara*). How *sat* and *bhāva* are inseparably one in you we have already seen (II.16), thus you are beyond the *sat-bhāva* duality; beyond the *kṣara-akṣara* duality.

त्वमादिदेवः पुरुषः पुराणस्त्वमस्य विश्वस्य परं निधानम्।
वेत्तासि वेद्यं च परं च धाम त्वया ततं विश्वमनन्तरूप ॥३८॥

tvam ādi-devaḥ puruṣaḥ purāṇas tvam asya viśvasya paraṁ nidhānam ।
vettā'si vedyaṁ ca paraṁ ca dhāma tvayā tataṁ viśvam anantarūpa ॥38॥

You are the effulgent original cause of everything; you are the most ancient *puruṣa.* You are the supreme mainstay of this cosmos. You are the knower, and the known as well. You are the one supreme abode. O one of endless forms, by you as Substance is this entire world pervaded.

O Lord, you are the primeval causal effulgence; you are the one *puruṣa* (one who reposes in the city) of the world. Temporally you were existing even before the beginning of anything, and you are the one Substance that fills the being of everything that had a beginning. And thus you are the abode of the cosmos as well. The likes of me seeking you, the Reality, also are you yourself manifesting. Whatever is observed and studied anywhere in the universe forms only a tiny part of your mysterious being. The knower and the known being yourself, knowledge too is naturally yourself. In short, what is known as *tripuṭi* — the knower-known-knowledge-division — is but you manifest variously. All things everywhere in the cosmos being you, your manifest forms are endless, temporally as well as spatially. Those who know you thus, what else can they do than saluting you and praising you!

वायुर्यमो ऽग्निर्वरुणः शशाङ्कः प्रजापतिस्त्वं प्रपितामहश्च ।
नमो नमस्ते ऽस्तु सहस्रकृत्वः पुनश्च भूयो ऽपि नमो नमस्ते ॥३९॥

vāyur yamo 'gnir varuṇaḥ śaśāṅkaḥ prajāpatis tvaṁ prapitāmahaś ca,
namo namas te 'stu sahasra-kṛtvaḥ punaś ca bhūyo 'pi namo namas te ॥39॥

Vāyu (the god of air), Yama (the god of death), Agni (the god of fire), Varuṇa (the god of water), and the Moon, all are you. You are the Lord of beings (Prajāpati), the Grandsire of all as well. A thousand times salutations to you! Hail to you again and yet again!

O Lord, many are the deities people worship with fulfilment of their desires in view, and every deity thus worshipped is thought of as omnipotent. The form of such deities may vary according to the desires the supplicants seek to fulfil. Those who are interested in favourable wind conditions, worship the god of air (Vāyu), those interested in avoiding death, worship the god of death (Yama), those who pray for progeny, worship Prajāpati (the progenitor of all beings) and so on. Whichever deity is worshipped, as you had earlier pointed out to me, all worship goes to you; now I see in your cosmic form all deities such as Vāyu, Yama, Agni, Varuṇa, Prajāpati. Though thus seen in different forms, basically you remain unchanged. Such wonder fills my being and I want to salute you repeatedly in all humility and the more I salute you the more I feel like repeating the act.

नमः पुरस्तादथ पृष्ठतस्ते नमो ऽस्तु ते सर्वत एव सर्व ।
अनन्तवीर्यामितविक्रमस्त्वं सर्वं समाप्नोषि ततो ऽसि सर्वः ॥४० ॥

namaḥ purastād atha pṛṣṭhatas te namo 'stu te sarvata eva sarva ।
ananta-vīryāmita-vikramas tvaṁ sarvaṁ samāpnoṣi tato 'si sarvaḥ ॥40 ॥

O the All, I salute You from before; I salute You from behind; I salute You from everyside. Infinite in vigour and measureless in might, You reach everything; thus You are everything.

O Lord, first I saw you as touching heaven and earth, and also filling all the directions of the compass (Verse 20). Having realized now that you are the only adorable one, I do not know which side of you to face. Your boundless creative potential — now become literally apparent — is all becoming everywhere, all births anywhere, and also all death. I thus can see you in both the birth and death of everything. Nothing is seen anywhere without you. You being such, your real greatness has never become known to anyone, will never become known to anyone. Still,

---

सखेति मत्वा प्रसभं यदुक्तं हे कृष्ण हे यादव हे सखेति ।
अजानता महिमानं तवेदं मया प्रमादात्प्रणयेन वापि ॥४१ ॥

यच्चावहासार्थमसत्कृतो ऽसि विहारशय्यासनभोजनेषु ।
एको ऽथवाप्यच्युत तत्समक्षं तत्क्षामये त्वामहमप्रमेयम् ॥४२॥

sakheti matvā prasabhaṁ yad uktaṁ he kṛṣṇa he yādava he sakheti ।
ajānatā mahimānaṁ tavedaṁ mayā pramādāt praṇayena vāpi ॥41॥

yac cāvahāsārtham asat-kṛto 'si vihāra-śayyāsana-bhojaneṣu ।
eko 'thavāpy acyuta tat-samakṣaṁ tat kṣāmaye tvām aham aprameyam ॥42॥

O the undecaying one, I, ignorant of your grandeur, have thought of you as a friend. Owing to my fault, owing to my great love for you, owing to my inability to take the serious seriously, I have called you "O Kṛṣṇa," "O Yādava," "O friend" and the like, while playing, while resting, while sitting or while eating, when alone as well as when in the company of many. For all such jestings, for all such irreverence shown to you, I beseech you, the imponderable, to pardon me.

O Lord, I have all the while been treating you with the familiarity of a boyhood friend which you are. But your greatness as a *guru par excellence* was not noticed by me; and for this reason I have been treating you as a personal friend. Only now do I realize how wrong I was. Even when I accepted you as my *guru* and sought wisdom teaching, I was not fully aware of your real greatness as the one Transcendental Reality that manifests itself as all the worlds, as the phenomena of birth, life and death. You and the world have no separable existence. Please pardon my disrespect. Who you are and what you are I now realize:

पितासि लोकस्य चराचरस्य त्वमस्य पूज्यश्च गुरुर्गरीयान् ।
न त्वत्समो ऽस्त्यभ्यधिकः कुतो ऽन्यो लोकत्रये ऽप्यप्रतिमप्रभाव ॥४३॥

pitāsi lokasya carācarasya tvam asya pūjyasya gurur-garīyān ।
na tvat-samo 'sty abhyadhikaḥ kuto 'nyo loka-traye 'py apratima prabhāva ॥43 ॥

O the one of incomparable grandeur, you are the father of the world, of everything living and not-living too. Of the world, you are the one adorable great *guru*. None in all the three worlds is equal to you; how, then, can there be some one greater than you.

O Lord, you are the one Transcendental Reality with no equal. Comparing is possible only with two things of similar nature. With nothing else similar and nothing "else" existing, you are incomparable, and therefore you and your greatness are beyond comprehension. What can I then say about you other than that you are the only father of everything organic and inorganic? At the same time you are the *guru* who perceptibly revealed to me the otherwise incomprehensible Reality that you are. Who else is there then more adorable and greater than you? Is it possible to think of you, the father of everything in all the worlds, as equal to anything in those worlds? No. How then can there be anything greater than you?

तस्मात्प्रणम्य प्रणिधाय कायं प्रसादये त्वामहमीशमीड्यम् ।
पितेव पुत्रस्य सखेव सख्युः प्रियः प्रियायार्हसि देव सोढुम् ॥४४ ॥

tasmāt praṇamya praṇidhāya kāyaṁ prasādaye tvām aham īśam īḍyam ।
piteva putrasya sakheva sakhyuḥ priyaḥ priyāyārhasi deva soḍhum ॥44 ॥

Therefore, saluting you, I prostrate myself before you, the one adorable all-controller. Please be gracious unto me. O the effulgent one, please bear with me as a father with his son, as a friend with his friend, as a lover with his beloved.

अदृष्टपूर्वं हृषितो ऽस्मि दृष्ट्वा भयेन च प्रव्यथितं मनो मे।
तदेव मे दर्शय देव रूपं प्रसीद देवेश जगन्निवास ॥४५॥

adr̥ṣṭa-pūrvaṁ hr̥ṣito 'smi dr̥ṣṭvā bhayena ca pravyathitaṁ mano me ।
tad eva me darśaya deva rūpaṁ prasīda deveśa jagan-nivāsa ॥45॥

Overjoyed am I, seeing what I have never seen before. Still my mind shivers with fear. Therefore, please show me again that form of yours. Be gracious on me, O the controller of gods, the indweller of the world.

O Lord, you are *deveśa*; the god even of gods; the controller even of gods, the illuminator of all that shines. Incompetent was I so far to see such a form of yours, though living with you so long. Now that I have perceived it, I understand everything, now I perceive clearly what life is. I am fully contented with what I saw; a sense of fulfilment fills my entire being.

Now I realize, how events in life are not always agreeable as we expect them to be. A firmness to face calmly whatever occurs in life, with a sense of detachment, has now become natural with me. Though aware that life has its unpleasant and even terrible facets, no one wishes it to be so; what one always longs is to pass through the agreeable aspects of life alone. Even the learned shiver with fear when facing life's dreadful aspects, I too therefore pray, "Please show me your agreeable form."

किरीटिनं गदिनं चक्रहस्तमिच्छामि त्वां द्रष्टुमहं तथैव।
तेनैव रूपेण चतुर्भुजेन सहस्रबाहो भव विश्वमूर्ते ॥४६॥

kirīṭinaṁ gadinaṁ cakra-hastam icchāmi tvāṁ draṣṭum ahaṁ tathaiva ।
tenaiva rūpeṇa catur-bhujena sahasra-bāho bhava viśva mūrte ॥46॥

Crowned with diadem, mace and discus in hands, is the form of yours I wish to see again. O, the

> thousand-handed, O the one who has the cosmos for his visible form, please assume that four-handed form of yours.

O Lord, the first form of yours that was revealed to me as you showed me your Cosmic Form, was that of Viṣṇu with golden diadem on head, and mace and discus in hands, and the like. Seeing it again and quietening down my disturbed mind, I would like.

श्री भगवानुवाच —

> मया प्रसन्नेन तवार्जुनेदं रूपं परं दर्शितमात्मयोगात्।
> तेजोमयं विश्वमनन्तमाद्यं यन्मे त्वदन्येन न दृष्टपूर्वम्॥४७॥

śrī bhagavān uvāca —

> *māyā prasannena tavārjunedaṁ rūpaṁ paraṁ darśitam ātmayogāt* ।
> *tejomayaṁ viśvam anantam ādyaṁ yan me tvadanyena na dṛṣṭa-pūrvam* ॥47॥

Śrī Kṛṣṇa said —

> Arjuna, graceful as I was to you, you were able to perceive Me so, because of your inseparable oneness with Me, the Self (*ātmā-yoga*). This transcendental form of mine, effulgence in essence, endless cosmos in form, the original cause, has never been so perceived before by anyone else than you.

Arjuna, my Cosmic Form that you saw just now has never been perceived so directly by anyone before. You gained this extraordinary capability through My Grace. Equally right is to say that your *ātma-yoga*, your being one with Me, is what enabled you to perceive Me so. In a state of your selfhood being one with mine, your directly perceiving whatever form I can assume, is but natural. Really my assumed form is yours as well. Such a oneness of Self is what I meant by *ātma-yoga*.

न वेदयज्ञाध्ययनैर्न दानैर्न च क्रियाभिर्न तपोभिरुग्रैः ।
एवं रूपः शक्य अहं नृलोके द्रष्टुं त्वदन्येन कुरुप्रवीर ॥४८ ॥

na veda-yajñādhyayanair na dānair na ca kriyābhir na tapobhir ugraiḥ ।
evaṁ-rūpaḥ śakya ahaṁ nṛ-loke draṣṭuṁ tvad-anyena kurupravīra ॥48 ॥

Neither by learning the Vedas, nor by performing fire sacrifices, nor by offering gifts, nor by other ritualistic actions, nor by undergoing severe austerities, does anyone, you apart, in this human world, become capable of perceiving Me and this Form of Mine.

Arjuna, a real seeker's becoming fully enlightened about the mystery of *guru*-hood depends solely on the bipolar intimacy (*pārasparya*) with his *guru*. Likewise, a seeker fully realizing the mystery of *Brahman* depends solely on the extent of inseparable oneness established with *Brahman*. The plenitude of both is what you have just experienced. No religious practice like fire-sacrifice, offering gifts, learning the Vedas, is of any help in this respect. Blessed are you in having this vision.

मा ते व्यथा मा च विमूढभावो दृष्ट्वा रूपं घोरमीदृङ्ममेदम् ।
व्यपेतभीः प्रीतमनाः पुनस्त्वं तदेव मे रूपमिदं प्रपश्य ॥४९ ॥

mā te vyathā mā ca vimūḍha-bhāvo dṛṣṭvā rūpaṁ ghoram īdṛṅ mamedam ।
vyapeta-bhīḥ prīta-manāḥ punastvaṁ tad eva me rūpam idaṁ prapaśya ॥49 ॥

Do not be distressed, do not be confused on having seen this terrible form of mine. With all fear gone, with a mind rejoicing, do perceive again this form of mine.

Arjuna, that both gentle and terrible forms of appearance are normal with my manifestations, you have already seen quite well. When I alone am seen in all of them, then will all anguish and fears be vanquished. Now you can see the not-frightful form of mine.

सञ्जय उवाच —

इत्यर्जुनं वासुदेवस्तथोक्त्वा स्वकं रूपं दर्शयामास भूयः।
आश्वासयामास च भीतमेनं भूत्वा पुनः सौम्यवपुर्महात्मा ॥५०॥

sañjaya uvāca —

ity arjunaṁ vāsudevas tathoktvā svakaṁ rūpaṁ darśayāmāsa bhūyaḥ ।
āśvāsayāmāsa ca bhītam enaṁ bhūtvā punaḥ saumya-vapur mahātmā ॥50॥

Sañjaya said —

With this said to Arjuna, Vāsudeva revealed to him his normal form. Having assumed that gentle form, the *mahātmā* consoled again the fearful Arjuna.

अर्जुन उवाच —

दृष्ट्वेदं मानुषं रूपं तव सौम्यं जनार्दन।
इदानीमस्मि संवृत्तः सचेताः प्रकृतिं गतः ॥५१॥

arjuna uvāca —

dṛṣṭvedaṁ mānuṣaṁ rūpaṁ tava saumyaṁ janārdana ।
idanīm asmi saṁvṛttaḥ sacetāḥ prakṛtiṁ gataḥ ॥51॥

Arjuna said —

O Janārdana, this gentle human form of yours seen, I am now composed, and have gained back my normal state of mind.

O Lord, what I asked you to show me (Verse 46) is your diademed (divine) form holding mace and discus in hands; but what you showed me now is your gentle human form. Thus I see now once again the familiar form of my dearest Kṛṣṇa. The divine eye you gave me to perceive your Cosmic Form, I feel, is gone now. You, the one who has assumed this gentle human form, is he who manifests as all the worlds. Each individual like me, therefore, has to live with this awareness: that Reality that has assumed this apparent form of myself is the Reality that appears as everything.

श्री भगवानुवाच —

सुदुर्दर्शमिदं रूपं दृष्टवानसि यन्मम ।
देवा अप्यस्य रूपस्य नित्यं दर्शनकाङ्क्षिणः ॥५२॥

śrī bhagavān uvāca —

sudurdarśam idaṁ rūpaṁ dṛṣṭavān asi yan mama ।
devā apy asya rūpasya nityaṁ darśana-kāṅkṣiṇaḥ ॥52॥

Śrī Kṛṣṇa said —

Scarcely available to perceive is this Form of Mine you have just seen, which even gods (of heaven) do eternally long to see.

Arjuna, gods of heaven, like humans, are also my own manifest forms. Like humans, again, they too are seekers; they too long to perceive this Cosmic Form of Mine. Nevertheless this vision, is not availed by all who long for. Why? I shall tell you:

नाहं वेदैर्न तपसा न दानेन न चेज्यया ।
शक्य एवंविधो द्रष्टुं दृष्टवानसि मां यथा ॥५३॥

nāhaṁ vedair na tapasā na dānena na cejyayā ।
śakya evaṁ-vidho draṣṭuṁ dṛṣṭavān asi mām yathā ॥53॥

The Form of Mine you just saw now, is not perceptible either by proficiency in the Vedas, by undergoing austere penance, by offering free gifts, or by performing Vedic rituals.

Arjuna, perceiving me as you just saw, is a goal not attainable by following any of the popularly known religious or spiritual practices,

Vedic or otherwise. How then is it attained, I shall tell you:

भक्त्या त्वनन्यया शक्य अहमेवंविधोऽर्जुन ।
ज्ञातुं द्रष्टुं च तत्वेन प्रवेष्टुं च परंतप ॥५४॥

bhaktyā tv-ananyayā śakya aham evaṁ-vidho 'rjuna ।
jñātuṁ draṣṭuṁ ca tattvena praveṣṭuṁ ca paraṁtapa ॥54॥

Only through the *bhakti* in which one sees oneself not apart from Me, one becomes capable of knowing Me, true to basic principles, perceiving Me and entering Me in this manner.

Arjuna, only one way — that of *ananya-bhakti* — can lead to see Me as you did just now. *Ananya bhakti* means "perceiving contemplatively or intuitively the inseparable oneness with what one seeks." I, the one Reality always sought for, was seen by you in its Cosmic Form, of which the actual cosmos is merely a tiny part. Every individual seeker has to have this awareness: One's own existence is at some remote corner of this inconceivable Cosmic Form, as an inseparable part of it. Not only the individual's existence but even the devout effort to attain Me forms a part of the same Cosmic Form. In other words, what the seeker thinks of as his goal is itself the means he relies on to attain it. Therefore,

---

मत्कर्मकृन्मत्परमो मद्भक्तः सङ्गवर्जितः ।
निर्वैरः सर्वभूतेषु यः स मामेति पाण्डव ॥५५॥

mat-karma-kṛn mat-paramo mad-bhaktaḥ saṅga-varjitaḥ ।
nirvairaḥ sarva-bhūteṣu yaḥ sa mām eti pāṇḍava ॥55॥

He who carries out My *karmas*, who considers Me alone as the Supreme, who constantly contemplates on Me with all attachments gone, with no hatred towards any being, he attains Me, O Arjuna.

Arjuna, all *karmas*, as you know, are mine constantly taking place in my Cosmic Body. Each individual, while engaged in activities, should be aware that those *karmas* are not his or hers, but are part of his or her oneness with My active Cosmic Form. All, you included, then will see themselves as the performers of My (*Brahman's*) *karmas*. They will perceive nothing else higher than Me. Seeing Myself everywhere in every specific apparent form, is their *bhajanā* or contemplating or meditating on Me. Those who do *bhajanā* are called *bhaktas*. Such *bhaktas* are free from "I"-sense and "mine"-sense, and no being is seen as hateful by them for every being is a different apparent form of oneself, of the Supreme Self. They alone live seeing themselves in Me of Cosmic Form.

Thus ends Chapter Eleven entitled Viśvarūpa-Darśana-Yoga of the Bhagavad-Gītā, the essence of the Upaniṣads, that embodies the yoga-śāstra of brahma-vidyā, in the form of a dialogue between Śrī Kṛṣṇa and Arjuna.

XII

Bhakti-Yoga
— The Yoga of Meditative Adoration —

Vyāsa:

Janmejaya, the wisdom teaching of the *Gītā* reached its zenith in Chapters IX and X. That everything that appears to exist is nothing but *Brahman* in essence was revealed in Chapter IX, and the next chapter showed its reverse side: that one *Brahman* alone manifests itself as all the worlds of endless varied appearances. And then in Chapter XI, Arjuna, with the help of the divine sight given by Kṛṣṇa, perceived directly that it is so. How the entire world is merely a minute part of the Cosmic Form of *Brahman* was thus seen by Arjuna. The battlefield, the two armies arrayed against each other, all meeting with destruction, himself included, were all seen in the Cosmic Form. The chapter ended with the assertion that only those who perceive themselves as forming part of the Cosmic Form, who meditate on themselves in their inseparable oneness with the Cosmic Form, can know *Brahman* and enter *Brahman* in living terms.

Now what is required of Arjuna is seeing himself, while living, as a part of the Cosmic Form of *Brahman,* and that living should be as Arjuna with all his personal traits. The wisdom teaching of the *Gītā*, is meant for everyone. Therefore, what those, who have really taken in the crux of the teaching imparted so far, should do now is to see themselves, while living as themselves with their personal traits and peculiarities, as one with the Cosmic Form, as an inseparable manifestation of it.

Life in total could well be compared to a giant banyan tree, having a structural perfection of its own. Countless are the leaves, flowers and berries that bud forth and disappear, each having a place on some remote twig. Whatever its place, it does not cease to be a part of the tree. Likewise are we human beings. By being one with the entire life-tree, each has to play his role as a part of it, thus ensuring the eternal existence of the tree. It makes one's own personal life meaningful and worth living.

Every person becoming capable of perceiving himself as a part of the Cosmic Form while living as himself, is my ultimate goal in teaching. The guidelines on how to prepare oneself for attaining this goal is what I am going to give in the rest of the *Gītā*.

The wisdom taught in the *Gītā* in its first half could well be considered as consisting of perceiving oneself and the world together as the one Reality creatively unfolding itself. This creative self-unfoldment of Reality is what is known as *prakṛti* (nature). The second half, especially the chapters from twelve onwards, helps the seeker, whoever he may be, to explore for himself what his own inner nature is, while being one with the total nature, and thus enable him to live his life meaningfully. This search for one's inner nature requires a systematic self-examination. As an initial step, Chapter XII presents direction as to how one should meditatively adore *Brahman* in its Cosmic Form with oneself as inalienable from it. Such a meditative adoration is what is denoted by the word *bhakti* here.

अर्जुन उवाच —

एवं सततयुक्ता ये भक्तास्त्वां पर्युपासते ।
ये चाप्यक्षरमव्यक्तं तेषां के योगवित्तमाः ॥१॥

arjuna uvāca —

evaṁ satata-yuktā ye bhaktās tvāṁ paryupāsate ।
ye cāpy akṣaram avyaktaṁ teṣāṁ ke yoga-vittamāḥ ॥1॥

Arjuna said —

Those who meditatively adore you, seeing themselves thus eternally united with you, are there. And there are those who meditatively adore you as abstract and imperishable as well. Of these two, who are the best knowers of *yoga*?

Kṛṣṇa, I am in a dilemma now. For you have just told me that only those who experience inseparable oneness with you truly know you and enter you. But now having seen you in two aspects — one as having the Cosmic Form and the other your abstract, indistinct existence as pure *sat* as was represented in the entire first half of the *Gītā* — I am not sure which of these two I should meditatively adore.

I am not alone in my search for you, in search of "ultimate happiness." All seekers are really in search of you. Some of them meditate on you as the abstract, indistinct Substance (*sat*) that underlies all that is concrete and distinct. On the other hand, certain others meditate on you as having the Cosmic Form. Which of these two ways is better and easier?

श्री भगवानुवाच —

मय्यावेश्य मनो ये मां नित्ययुक्ता उपासते।
श्रद्धया परयोपेतास्ते मे युक्ततमा मताः ॥२॥

śrī bhagavān uvāca —

mayy āveśya mano ye māṁ nitya-yuktā upāsate,
śraddhayā parayopetās te me yukta-tamā matāḥ ॥2॥

Śrī Kṛṣṇa said —

That those who, with mind fully absorbed in Me, meditatively adore Me in an ever united state of existence, are the best of all *yogī*s, is my well-considered conclusion.

Arjuna, your perceiving My Cosmic Form was not a deviation form the normal course of my teaching, in fact in its light are to be seen all that I am going to teach you from here onwards. The word *yogī* will be used henceforth to refer to him who experiences himself as being one with My Cosmic Form. Though such *yogī*s may have the habit of thinking, formulating ideas and mental images about the world and about themselves, they are fully enlightened that all such actions take place nowhere else than in My Cosmic Form. Those who are enlightened thus are the best of all *yogī*s and their interest and faith (*śraddhā*) in Me will be absolute. Their meditative adoration of Me is to be counted as the best *upāsanā,* literally meaning "to be closeby and do service." To everyone, what is nearest is nothing but that substance they themselves are constituted of — as the water is nearest to the wave. Every action of a wave forms part of the ocean's being. So too those of this perception consider whatever they do as the *karma* that pertains to Me or *Brahman.* The performance of such *karmas*, in effect, becomes the best of all possible services to Me. Those who do such *upāsanā* are the best of all *yogīs*.

Not that those who meditatively adore Me as the abstract and indistinct Reality are in any way inferior. Because,

---

ये त्वक्षरमनिर्देश्यमव्यक्तं पर्युपासते ।
सर्वत्रगमचिन्त्यं च कूटस्थमचलं ध्रुवम् ॥३॥
संनियम्येन्द्रियग्रामं सर्वत्र समबुद्धयः ।
ते प्राप्नुवन्ति मामेव सर्वभूतहिते रताः ॥४॥

ye tv akṣaram anirdeśyaṁ avyaktam paryupāsate ।
sarvatragam acintyaṁ ca kūṭa stham acalaṁ dhruvam ॥3॥

saṁniyamyendriya-grāmaṁ sarvatra sama-buddhayaḥ ।
te prāpnuvanti mām eva sarva-bhūta-hite ratāḥ ॥4॥

Those who meditatively adore, with restrained and subdued senses, Reality as the abstract indestructible, the undefinable, the unmanifested, the all-pervading, the unthinkable, the rock-like support of all, the motionless, the eternal, and perceive sameness everywhere, they too attain Myself and live rejoicing in what is good for everyone.

Arjuna, whosoever intuitively experiences, with restrained mind and senses, the abstract Reality that constitutes his own being also attains Me alone. Therefore, such a means of attaining is not to be treated as inferior to that of adoring Me in the Cosmic Form. My statement in the last verse that those who find themselves as one with Me in the Cosmic Form are the best of all *yogīs*, took into account only the ease with which I could be adored meditatively. Therefore,

> क्लेशो ऽधिकतरस्तेषामव्यक्तासक्तचेतसाम् ।
> अव्यक्ता हि गतिर्दुःखं देहवद्भिरवाप्यते ॥५॥
>
> *kleśo 'dhikataras teṣām avyaktāsakta-cetasām* ।
> *avyaktā hi gatīr duḥkhaṁ dehavadbhir avāpyate* ॥5॥
>
> More difficult is it for those who attune themselves consciously to the abstract indistinct, for to follow the path of the indistinct is very hard indeed for those who are already embodied.

Arjuna, conducive to one and the same *yoga* state are both the ways of adoring Me: seeing Me with the Cosmic Form and as the abstract and indistinct Substance. The way chosen depends solely on the personal traits of each seeker. Being already conditioned with an apparent body as a part of the Cosmic Form as he is, the seeker will find it much easier to meditate and adore Me in My Cosmic Form. Those who are fully confident of trekking the harder path, of course, are free to do so. I am going to delineate in detail the easier path, but all of these are true of the other path as well.

Let us first look at it from the apparent activities natural with every individual.

> ये तु सर्वाणि कर्माणि मयि संन्यस्य मत्पराः ।
> अनन्येनैव योगेन मां ध्यायन्त उपासते ॥६॥
> तेषामहं समुद्धर्ता मृत्युसंसारसागरात् ।
> भवामि नचिरात्पार्थ मय्यावेशितचेतसाम् ॥७॥
>
> *ye tu sarvāṇī karmāṇi mayi saṁnyasya mat-parāḥ* ।
> *ananyenaiva yogena māṁ dhyāyanta upāsate* ॥6॥
>
> *teṣām ahaṁ samuddhartā mṛtyu-saṁsāra-sāgarāt* ।
> *bhavāmi nacirāt pārtha mayy āveśita-cetasām* ॥7॥
>
> Arjuna, those who are intent on Me existing in a state of *yoga* of inseparable oneness, meditatively

> adore Me after having renounced all his *karma*s in Me.
>
> For such, of mind already in Me, I become the one who lifts them up from the ocean of cyclic becoming and death.

Arjuna, that all actions really take place in My *prakṛti* and that no individual as such has *karma* of his own, had become sufficiently clear as early as Chapter III. Now the same *prakṛti* is to be perceived as forming part of My Cosmic Form that is ever creative, never inactive. Each minute element of it is constantly active and all such activities are *karma*s that take place in Me. Whatever specific activity an individual is engaged in, it really is My *karma.* What the individual who wrongly thinks he has his own *karmas,* should do is to renounce all such *karma*s in Me. This renunciation is equivalent to *yajña.* It is comparable to a leaf thinking that whatever it does is as a part of the tree's *karma,* not its own. No leaf exists and functions apart from the tree; likewise are all individual beings. They exist in Me and function in Me. Real *yoga* is the experience of this oneness. Those who know Me thus, those who meditate on Me thus, those who adore Me thus, realize that life is a totality, there is no life of individuals. Life, seen as belonging to individuals begins with birth, and ends with death; but seen as my creativity finding self-expression, life is without beginning and end, with the apparent phenomenon of birth and death ensuring as well as enriching the progression of life. Unaffected by the vagaries of the apparent forms emerging and merging back in the one Reality — in Me — life continues uninterrupted. This enlightenment and experiencing oneness with Me alone saves one from the ordeals of birth and death, from *saṁsāra.* Perceiving Me in oneself while living thus and adoring Me in this manner, is the real *bhakti,* and those who live so are the real *bhakta*s.

मय्येव मन आधत्स्व मयि बुद्धिं निवेशय।
निवसिष्यसि मय्येव अत ऊर्ध्वं न संशयः ॥८॥

mayy eva mana ādhatsva mayi buddhiṁ niveśaya |
nivasiṣyasi mayy eva ata ūrdhvaṁ na saṁśayaḥ ||8 ||

Embed your mind in Me; make your understanding properly go into Me. You will thereafter, no doubt, find yourself abiding in Me.

Arjuna, the above-mentioned *bhakti* leads to the realization of your stable existence in Me, with the awareness that even your mind, your thinking, your understanding, are all nothing but part of My Cosmic Form. You will then start seeing yourself well founded in Me, seeing Myself even in your apparent form as you are, you will give up your identity with that form unaware, and it virtually is your leaving the body. Finding such a stable identity with Me is no easy accomplishment.

अथ चित्तं समाधातुं न शक्नोषि मयि स्थिरम्।
अभ्यासयोगेन ततो मामिच्छाप्तुं धनञ्जय ॥९॥

atha cittaṁ samādhātuṁ na śaknoṣi mayi sthiram |
abhyāsa-yogena tato māṁ icchāptuṁ dhanañjaya ||9 ||

Arjuna, in case of your finding yourself incapable of stabilizing your mind thus in Me, you may, by repeated practising of *yoga*, seek to attain Me.

Arjuna, if you and others who follow My teachings find it difficult because of the fickleness of mind, to see their mind and their functions as being part of My Cosmic Form, you may then accomplish it by repeated practice of *yoga* (*abhyāsa-yoga*), as was taught earlier in Verse VI.26. Whenever one's mind, forgetful of what it is and where it is, is found wandering, one has to become aware of this happening and bring the mind back to Me, its source and basis. The mind may become fickle again and again; at every such instance it has to be restrained and brought back to Me. The continuous practice of keeping the mind aware of its inseparable oneness (*yoga*) with Me, is to be understood as *abhyāsa-yoga*, and it could well be invigorated by *vairāgya* (sense of detachment) as suggested as early as in Verse

VI.35. What was taught there rather as a theory, is to be actually practised here in relation to My Cosmic Body. This repeated bringing back of the mind to Me is also a form of *bhakti.* Of course, it requires on one's own part, the introspection of what happens to one's own mind, which is an aptitude not shared by many. I shall, therefore, point out to you yet another relatively easy way of attaining oneness with My Cosmic Form.

अभ्यासेऽप्यसमर्थोऽसि मत्कर्मपरमो भव।
मदर्थमपि कर्माणि कुर्वन्सिद्धिमवाप्स्यसि ॥१०॥

abhyāse 'py asamartho 'si mat-karma-paramo bhava ।
mad-artham api karmāṇi kurvan siddhim avāpsyasi ॥10॥

In case of you finding yourself incapable of even this repeated practice (of *yoga*), you can become one who performs actions considering them as Mine. By performing actions on My behalf also you can reach the attainment.

Arjuna, another way of attaining Me is, to remain engaged in one's natural activities, but to continually see them as forming a part of My Cosmic Form. You can do each *karma* as My *karma* finding specific expression. All such *karmas* then, virtually, are done on My behalf. This is an effective means for experiencing oneness with Me while actively living. Suppose one is incapable of practising even this. Then,

---

अथैतदप्यशक्तोऽसि कर्तुं मद्योगमाश्रितः।
सर्वकर्मफलत्यागं ततः कुरु यतात्मवान् ॥११॥

athaitad apy aśakto 'si kartuṁ mad-yogam āśritaḥ ।
sarva-karma-phala-tyāgaṁ tataḥ kuru yatātmavān ॥11॥

If incapable even of doing *karmas* in a state of union with Me, then, with full self-restraint, renounce all fruits of actions.

Arjuna, yet another easier alternative is to practise self-restraint, that is to say, to hold oneself back from motivated activities, subduing such urges as "I have to do this in order to get that. I must do this in order to enjoy certain results." This is to be supplemented by the attitude, "The fruits of these actions are not mine," concerning all *karmas* one happens to do as a part of the natural course of events in life. This practice also leads to Me.

श्रेयो हि ज्ञानमभ्यासाज्ज्ञानाद्ध्यानं विशिष्यते ।
ध्यानात्कर्मफलत्यागस्त्यागाच्छान्तिरनन्तरम् ॥१२ ॥

śreyo hi jñānam abhyāsāj jñānād dhyānaṁ viśiṣyate ।
dhyānāt karma-phala-tyāgas tyāgāc chāntir anantaram ॥12 ॥

Better indeed is *jñāna* than repeated practice (*abhyāsa*), and *dhyāna* is much better than *jñāna*. Renouncing fruits of action is better than *dhyāna*. As a result of renouncing is attained quietitude.

Arjuna, the superiority of one to the other mentioned here is not in any philosophical sense. Meditatively adoring Me in My Cosmic Form was considered superior to adoring Me in the abstract, you may remember, weighing the ease with which this adoration could be practised. Continuing the same line of thought, a comparison of the different ways of attaining Me in My Cosmic Form is also made here, considering how easy it is to practise in actual life.

What *abhyāsa* (repeated practice) signifies we have just seen. The implications of *jñāna* were laid bare in Chapter IV (particularly in Verse 35). *Jñāna* is an attainment related rather to theoretical understanding, and attaining oneness with Me through *jñāna* is also theoretical in essence. Such attainment is always hindered by the fickleness of the mind, and this hindrance can be overcome through *abhyāsa*; hence its superiority.

The details of *dhyāna* were given in Chapter VI; it is a persistent contemplative effort on the part of the seeker to realize his oneness with Me through treating *karma-yoga* and *jñāna-yoga* as one. More related to practical life, *dhyāna* is not mere theoretical certitude, and this peculiarity makes it superior to *jñāna*. Perceiving one's own inseparable unity with Me in practical life inevitably implies seeing Me in My Cosmic Form. The role of My Cosmic Form is thus more pronounced in *dhyāna* than in *jñāna,* and easier is the former to accomplish.

Still easier is the renouncing of the fruits of action mentioned in the last verse. Sin and merit, as you know, are meaningful only when you think of your actions as "your" *karma*s, and their fruits as "yours." Exactly the same is what happened to you. If one is stable in holding the position, "No *karma* is mine; no *karma*'s fruits are also mine," then the eagerness to perform favourable or meritorious actions will not be present. Detachment towards *karma*s becomes natural with such persons, even when constantly engaged in activities, and this brings about an abiding peacefulness in life. This experiencing of peace, in essence, is none other than practically finding oneness with My Cosmic Form.

I have pointed out to you many means of attaining oneness with Me. Each seeker is free to choose the way that is most appropriate to him or her. Whichever way is chosen, some common characteristics of the peace they experience will be evident in all. I shall tell you what they are:

अद्वेष्टा सर्वभूतानां मैत्रः करुण एव च।
निर्ममो निरहङ्कारः समदुःखसुखः क्षमी ॥१३॥
सन्तुष्टः सततं योगी यतात्मा दृढनिश्चयः।
मय्यर्पितमनोबुद्धिर्यो मद्भक्तः स मे प्रियः ॥१४॥

adveṣṭā sarva-bhūtānāṁ maitraḥ karuṇa eva ca ।
nirmamo nirahaṁkāraḥ sama-duḥkha-sukhaḥ kṣamī ॥13॥

santuṣṭaḥ satataṁ yogī yatātmā dṛḍha-niścayaḥ ।
mayy arpita-mano-buddhir yo mad-bhaktaḥ sa me priyaḥ ॥14॥

Hatredless, friendly and merciful towards every being, devoid of "I"-sense and "mine"-sense, equipoised in pleasure and pain owing to the perception of sameness, well composed, always content with himself in being one with Me, of self-restraint and firm conviction, mind and its thinking given over to Me, is the *bhakta* dear to Me.

Arjuna, nothing is despicable to one who sees everything as forming part of My Cosmic Form. Moreover to feel friendliness and mercy towards all beings will then be natural. What I teach here is not merely a lesson on human values — to be friendly, merciful and loving. On the contrary, all such moral values naturally become part of one who imbibes what I teach. The one who lives life with all such qualities expressed spontaneously, is the *bhakta* I mean here.

"I"-sense (*ahaṁkāra*) and "mine-sense" (*mama-kāra*) are two psychological factors that make one an "individual." These naturally fade out in those who find themselves as inseparably one with My Cosmic Form. For such people, pleasurable and painful events of life too are inseparable parts of My Cosmic Form, and thus as of the same value. Indifference filled with contentment will be the attitude of such people towards all events in life, and the abiding guideline for life will be the inseparable oneness (*ananya-yoga*) with Me. Self-restraint holds them back from engaging in activities motivated by desires, but it also guides them in doing activities natural to their course of life. Seeing not only their mind and its functions but even themselves in Me, such persons are to be called *yogīs*; they are the real *bhaktas*; they are the ones dear to Me.

Some apparent signs also could be easily discerned in My *bhaktas*.

यस्मान्नोद्विजते लोको लोकान्नोद्विजते च यः।
हर्षामर्षभयोद्वेगैर्मुक्तो यः स च मे प्रियः ॥१५॥

yasmān nodvijate loko lokān nodvijate ca yaḥ ।
harṣāmarṣa-bhayodvegair mukto yaḥ sa ca me priyaḥ ॥15॥

He who causes no fear and agitation to people, and to whom people cause no fear and agitation, who remains freed from euphoria, indignation, fear and anxiety, he is the *bhaktā* dear to Me.

Arjuna, becoming agitated and afraid because of others is common in life. Doing things that make others agitated and afraid is also usual. But one who sees oneself as a part of My Cosmic Form perceives others also so, though different in intrinsic nature. The responses and reactions coming from others will then be seen by him as happening in My Cosmic Form in accordance with the propensities of each part. This perception keeps him unagitated even by unfavourable and irritating reactions from others. So too the reactions that come from him will never be felt by others as affronting. He is neither found to be overjoyed, nor is he disturbed by indignation, fear or anxiety. Those, in whose life are seen such peculiarities are my *bhakta*s. And more,

---

अनपेक्षः शुचिर्दक्ष उदासीनो गतव्यथः।
सर्वारम्भपरित्यागी यो मद्भक्तः स मे प्रियः ॥१६॥

anapekṣaḥ śucir dakṣa udāsīno gata-vyathaḥ ।
sarvārambha-parityāgī yo mad-bhaktaḥ sa me priyaḥ ॥16॥

He who banks on nothing, who is pure, resourceful, well composed, and not worried, whose habit of taking initiative in motivated actions is renounced, is a *bhakta* dear to Me.

Arjuna, seeing themselves as inseparably one with Me, My *bhakta*s neither rely on anything, nor is there anything "else" for them to rely on. Put in religious terminology, his sole refuge is God, and philosophically understood, he sees nothing else other than the Self to rely on, and his life remains an open book always. Whatever he happens to do as a part of the natural course of events in life, is done with dexterity and heedfulness. No action done by him is treated as his own, and hence insisting on pre-planned motivated actions will be foreign to him. Besides,

---

यो न हृष्यति न द्वेष्टि न शोचति न काङ्क्षति।
शुभाशुभपरित्यागी भक्तिमान्यः स मे प्रियः ॥१७॥

yo na hṛṣyati na dveṣṭi na śocati na kāṅkṣati ।
śubhāśubha-parityāgī bhaktimān yaḥ sa me priyaḥ ॥17 ॥

He who remains unattracted while being detestless, griefless and cravingless, concernless for merit and demerit, endowed with *bhakti* as he is, is dear to Me.

Arjuna, seeing himself as one with My Cosmic Form, My *bhakta* neither craves for anything nor is he overjoyed at getting something desirable. Nothing to him is detestable either. Seeing everything in himself, he never grieves on account of anything. No doer of any *karma,* he remains concernless for the meritoriousness or otherwise of the *karma*s he happens to do. You know, the fear of having to do the supposedly sinful *karma* of killing your own kith and kin, *guru* and friends, was what was tormenting you. Now you do realize, such fears have no place as you and your *karma*s are inseparable from My Cosmic Form.

Some other peculiarities could also be noticed in the life of My *bhakta*s.

समः शत्रौ च मित्रे च तथा मानापमानयोः ।
शीतोष्णसुखदुःखेषु समः सङ्गविवर्जितः ॥१८ ॥
तुल्यनिन्दास्तुतिर्मौनी संतुष्टो येन केनचित् ।
अनिकेतः स्थिरमतिर्भक्तिमान्मे प्रियो नरः ॥१९ ॥

samaḥ śatrau ca mitre ca tathā mānāpamānayoḥ ।
śītoṣṇa-sukha-duḥkheṣu samaḥ saṅga-vivarjitaḥ ॥18 ॥

tulya-nindā-stutir maunī saṁtuṣṭo yena kenacit ।
aniketaḥ sthira-matir bhaktimān me priyo naraḥ ॥19 ॥

Same towards friends and foes, same towards honour and dishonour, same towards heat and cold, same towards pain and pleasure, devoid of all attachments, equal towards praise and reproach, silent, fully content with whatever happens, homeless, steady-minded, the man endowed with *bhakti* is dear to Me.

ये तु धर्म्यामृतमिदं यथोक्तं पर्युपासते ।
श्रद्दधाना मत्परमा भक्तास्ते ऽतीव मे प्रियाः ॥२० ॥

ye tu dharmyāmṛtam idaṁ yathoktaṁ paryupāsate ।
śraddadhānā mat-paramā bhaktās te 'tīva me priyāḥ ॥20 ॥

Those who meditatively adore as delineated here, the easily attained immortal [Cosmic Form] of Mine, with full faith, considering Me alone as the ultimate goal to be reached, such *bhakta*s are verily the dearest to Me.

Arjuna, it is really difficult to conceive Me — *Brahman,* as the all-underlying abstract Reality, but to perceive Me as having the cosmos for My body with the perceiver forming a part of it, is much more easy. In this sense my immortal form is *dharmya* (easily actualizable). As I am immortal, those who are inseparable from Me are also immortal. Those who meditatively adore Me thus, as the immortal adoring the immortal, are dearest to Me.

Arjuna, I shall summarize now what I taught you in the present chapter.

Theoretically conceiving Me as the one abstract all-underlying Reality and actualizing oneness with that Reality in life, though the most sublime of goals, is very difficult. On the other hand, realizing the same goal by seeing Me as having this cosmos for My body is much easier. Doing the groundwork for such a perception was My intention in showing you My Cosmic Form in the last chapter. How this inseparable oneness can be actualized in life and what peculiarities will be visible in the life of those of this attainment, were all detailed. Contemplation on this oneness is what is known as *bhajana,* and those who have accomplished it are to be called *bhakta*s. Such people are dearest to Me.

Thus ends Chapter Twelve entitled Bhakti-Yoga of the Bhagavad-Gītā, the essence of the Upaniṣads, that embodies the yoga-śāstra of brahma-vidyā in the form of a dialogue between Śrī Kṛṣṇa and Arjuna.

XIII

Kṣetra-Kṣetrajña -Vibhāga -Yoga

— The Yoga of Discriminating the Field and the Knower of the Field —

Śrī Kṛṣṇa:

ARJUNA, your living as yourself, as a part of Cosmic Form, i.e., the total nature, requires that you know your inner nature. As the first step to that end I shall now show you how to discriminate between the changeful form-aspect of your being and the changeless knowledge-aspect, the former I call *kṣetra* (field) and the latter *kṣetrajña* (the knower of the field).

श्री भगवानुवाच —

इदं शरीरं कौन्तेय क्षेत्रमित्यभिधीयते ।
एतद्यो वेत्ति तं प्राहुः क्षेत्रज्ञ इति तद्विदः ॥१ ॥

śrī bhagavān uvāca —

idaṁ śarīraṁ kaunteya kṣetram ity abhidhīyate ।
etad yo vetti taṁ prāhuḥ kṣetrajña iti tad vidaḥ ॥1 ॥

Śrī Kṛṣṇa said —

This perishable body, O Arjuna, is what is known as *kṣetra*. That which knows it is termed *kṣetrajña*. So say those who are well versed in this subject.

Arjuna, you have earlier seen the Cosmic Form of the Self, of Myself. As inseparably one with it is your own existence as an individual, as is mine as well. You also saw various and varying facets in My Cosmic Form — these are meant to be perceived in the being of each individual also. The ever changing body aspect of My Cosmic Form is to be differentiated in your understanding from the knowledge that knows it and controls it, while intuitively perceiving their inseparability. Such a conceptual differentiation and actual inseparability are also true with each individual. This differentiation could be considered equivalent to the mind-matter duality. Such a differentiation of the apparent aspects which are in actuality inseparable, is what I mean by *kṣetra-kṣetrajña-vibhāga* (distinction between the field and the knower of the field) in this chapter.

The body, in a general way, could be considered comprising the *kṣetra.* The Sanskrit term I use here to denote body is *śarīra,* meaning that which perishes. *Kṣetra* is a word of many meanings. In one context, it means "farmland." *Kṣetra* is the farm in which all our experiences grow. Another meaning of the word is "that which decays or undergoes change." Sometimes *kṣetra* is used in the sense of that which saves us from all harms. Here I use the word taking into account all these meanings as I shall clarify in Verses 5 and 6.

Kṣetrajña means "one who knows the *kṣetra.*" Though defined thus, *kṣetrajña* really is indefinable for the reason that everything definable comes under *kṣetra.* These definables and the indefinables remain inseparably non-dual in My Cosmic Form, in what still remains a mystery. Suggestive of this mysteriousness are my words, "So say those who are well versed in this subject."

क्षेत्रज्ञं चापि मां विद्धि सर्वक्षेत्रेषु भारत।
क्षेत्रक्षेत्रज्ञयोर्ज्ञानं यत्तज्ज्ञानं मतं मम ॥२॥

kṣetrajñaṁ cāpi māṁ viddhi sarva-kṣetreṣu bhārata ।
kṣetra-kṣetrajñayor jñānaṁ yat taj jñānaṁ mataṁ mama ॥2॥

Do understand also, O Bhārata, that I am the *kṣetrajña* in all the *kṣetras*. That knowing *kṣetra* and *kṣetrajña* together constitutes the essence of wisdom (*jñāna*) is my well-considered conclusion.

Arjuna, though *kṣetra* and *kṣetrajña* are imaginable as distinct, and it is easier to conceive of them so, the two have never existed and will never exist as separate. Pure consciousness in essence, I could well be the thought of as *kṣetrajña;* but *kṣetrajña* cannot exist without *kṣetra.* Neither can *kṣetra* exist without *kṣetrajña.* Though *understood* separately, the *kṣetra* and *kṣetrajña* are to be *experienced* non-dually as a part of My Cosmic Form. Therefore,

---

तत्क्षेत्रं यच्च यादृक्च यद्विकारि यतश्च यत्।
स च यो यत्प्रभावश्च तत्समासेन मे शृणु ॥३॥

tat kṣetraṁ yac ca yādṛk ca yad vikāri yataś ca yat ।
sa ca yo yat prabhāvaś ca tat samāsena me śṛṇu ॥3॥

What that *kṣetra* is, of what nature is it, of what kind of modes of appearance it is, how do all such arise, who the *kṣetrajña* is, of what grandeur he is — learn from me all these in brief.

Arjuna, the details of *kṣetra* and *kṣetrajña,* and their being inseparable are to be known as forming part of My Cosmic Form. Yet what I teach you now concerning this is no new finding of mine, or of any particular *guru.* Of what source it is, I shall tell you:

ऋषिभिर्बहुधा गीतं छन्दोभिर्विविधैः पृथक्।
ब्रह्मसूत्रपदैश्चैव हेतुमद्भिर्विनिश्चितैः ॥४॥

ṛṣibhir bahudhā gītaṁ chandobhir vividhaiḥ pṛthak ।
brahma-sūtra-padaiś caiva hetumadbhir viniścitaiḥ ॥4॥

Sung in praise of it in various ways in the various Vedic hymns, is this certitude that had logically well been ascertained in the aphorisms of the *Brahma-Sūtras.*

Arjuna, the wisdom secret I teach you now, was well known to the *ṛṣis* of the past, and its brightness makes lustrous many Vedic hymns and all the Upaniṣads. Bādarāyaṇa substantiated it with reasoning in his *Brahma-Sūtras.* This one certitude alone was thus arrived at by visionary-*ṛṣis* as well as logically-minded thinkers like Bādarāyaṇa.

First, I shall tell you what I mean by *śarīra* (body) or *kṣetra:*

महाभूतान्यहङ्कारो बुद्धिरव्यक्तमेव च ।
इन्द्रियाणि दशैकं च पञ्च चेन्द्रियगोचराः ॥५॥
इच्छा द्वेषः सुखं दुःखं सङ्घातश्चेतना धृतिः ।
एतत्क्षेत्रं समासेन सविकारमुदाहृतम् ॥६॥

mahābhūtāny ahaṁkāro buddhir avyaktam eva ca ।
indriyāṇi daśaikaṁ ca pañca cendriya gocarāḥ ॥5॥

icchā dveṣaḥ sukhaṁ duḥkhaṁ saṁghātaś cetanā dhṛtiḥ ।
etat kṣetraṁ samāsena savikāram udāhṛtam ॥6॥

The five primary elements, I-sense, intelligence, the indistinct, and likewise the ten sense-organs with mind as the eleventh along with the five objects of sense perception, longing, aversion, happiness, suffering, the state of all these being combined together, life-principle, firmness of mind — all these together, changeful as they are all, summarily constitute *kṣetra*.

Arjuna, changefulness is a peculiarity of the body (*śarīra*). To be precise, whatever is changeful is to be considered as a part of the body, whether seen individually or cosmically whether physical or mental. Some such main factors that form a part of our changeful aspect of existence are enumerated here.

Space, air, fire, water and earth are the most basic and subtle physical elements, their various and varying compounds forming the physical world. These elements do not *exist* in a separate, pure and simple state anywhere, though they are *understandable* as separate. The earth we stand on, for example, is not pure earth; in it are parts of the other four elements also and so too with the other elements. The systematic way in which these five assume their gross, perceptible forms, is known as *pañcīkaraṇa* (quintuplication).

The psychological "I"-sense is always involved in every experience that each of us has in life — like "I know," "I do." This "I"-sense, which always indicates oneself as the knower, doer or enjoyer, is called *ahaṁkāra.* Along with the "I"-sense comes the sense of "mine" called *mamakāra,* relating oneself with the "something" that is done, known or enjoyed.

Buddhi, rendered here as "intelligence" is a word having different connotations in different schools of Indian thought. In a general non-philosophical context, it stands for the psychological functions of grasping, understanding and recalling.

Vyakta means that which is distinct and distinguishable from all else; that which is indistinct is called *avyakta.* Everything distinct must have a substance underlying it, which will always be indistinct; for it has no definite form of its own. For instance, water poured into a tumbler assumes the distinct tumbler-form, poured into a broad pan assumes its distinct form, directed to a square field it assumes the distinct field-form, the substance water still remaining indistinct. No appearance of distinct forms is possible in the absence of an indistinct causal substance. The one substance that underlies the entire range of distinct forms in all the worlds is indistinct and therefore, is named *avyakta.* That this *avyakta* has invariably to be immutable, may be the first impression we get; but not. Everything indistinct, pure and simple being formless and therefore imperceptible, does exist only as concepts which, of course, have undeniable existence. All concepts in their turn, depend on the maturity of the conceiving mind, and to that extent are subject to change, hence we treat it as changeful and thus as a part of the body.

Ears, skin, eyes, tongue and nose are the five sense organs, and mind at times is counted as the sixth. Speech, hands, feet, excretory organ and genitals, treated usually as the five organs of action (*karmendriyas*), are also sometimes counted as forming part of the set of sense organs, which all together, thus are eleven in number. Ears hear sound, skin feels tactiles, eyes see forms, tongue tastes flavours, and nose smells odours; these five thus forming sense objects, each related to the five basic physical elements as their respective qualities.

Icchā (longing) is the mental action of aiming towards gaining pleasurable objects, and *dveṣa* (aversion) the mental effort to be rid of painful objects. The firmness of mind at conflicting situations in life is called *dhṛti,* remaining content in oneself.

All such constituent elements and aspects are present in each individual as a part of the Cosmic Form, and are present universally in the Cosmic Form as well. Though distinguished thus for the sake of convenience, in actuality they do not exist as distinct. This event, though imaginary, of the two appearing as distinct, makes the individual cease to be an individual and makes the universe cease to be universe. This point can be further clarified with the help of an example: A motor car is made up of thousands of parts, none of them being the car. Each part can play its role, only when it has been fitted in its appropriate place, in the correct way, and when all parts are thus fitted, there emerges the entity that is the car. Similar is the state of each constituent element and aspect mentioned here, which remains at its proper place playing its role as a part of the whole — the individual or the cosmos; this state is called *saṁghāta.* Given that both individuals and the universe are in a constant state of change, their constituent parts and their state of being together too are likewise.

A car is truly a car when it is on the road; the cosmos, likewise, is a cosmos, when it lives, that is to say, when it systematically functions as a whole. A car needs energy to make it run; the cosmos, on the other hand, lives on its own. This vitality that keeps both the cosmos and individuals alive is called *cetanā.* The cosmos being changeful, this *cetanā,* has also necessarily to be likewise. Of presumed existence, *cetanā* the subtlest of the constituent factors, is known as "soul" in theology.

Everything perceivable and conceivable, thus, from gross physical elements to the subtlest soul, together constitute *kṣetra.* The immutable consciousness that witnesses all this is called *kṣetrajña* (the knower of the field). This *kṣetrajña,* despite my agreeing earlier to clarify both, is both inconceivable and inexplicable. However, the two dialectical poles — knowledge (*jñāna*) and the knowable (*jñeya*) — which belong to *kṣetrajña*'s functional existence, are conceivable and hence also clarifiable. The real *kṣetrajña* could well be intuitively visualized in one's meditation, with these two counterparts as aids. I shall, therefore, first tell you what *jñāna* is.

The theoretical aspects of *jñāna* was covered earlier in Chapter IV, particularly in Verse 35, and it is the applied aspect, as seen to be alive in the Cosmic Form, that I explain to you as *jñāna* now. The external signs of a *jñānin* which I delineate upon here, will never be visible unless one is well stabilized in theoretical *jñāna*. No *jñānin* exists without the external signs either.

अमानित्वमदम्भित्वमहिंसा क्षान्तिरार्जवम् ।
आचार्योपासनं शौचं स्थैर्यमात्मविनिग्रहः ॥७ ॥
इन्द्रियार्थेषु वैराग्यमनहङ्कार एव च ।
जन्ममृत्युजराव्याधिदुःखदोषानुदर्शनम् ॥८ ॥
असक्तिरनभिष्वङ्गः पुत्रदारगृहादिषु ।
नित्यं च समचित्तत्वमिष्टानिष्टोपपत्तिषु ॥९ ॥
मयि चानन्ययोगेन भक्तिरव्यभिचारिणी ।
विविक्तदेशसेवित्वमरतिर्जनसंसदि ॥१० ॥
अध्यात्मज्ञाननित्यत्वं तत्त्वज्ञानार्थदर्शनम् ।
एतज्ज्ञानमिति प्रोक्तमज्ञानं यदतो ऽन्यथा ॥११ ॥

amānitvam adambhitvam ahiṁsā kṣāntir ārjavam ।
ācāryopāsanaṁ śaucaṁ sthairyam ātma vinigrahaḥ ॥7 ॥

indriyārtheṣu vairāgyam anahaṁkāra eva ca ।
janma-mṛtyu-jarā-vyādhi-duḥka-doṣānudarśanam ॥8 ॥

asaktir anabhiṣvaṅgaḥ putra-dāra-gṛhādiṣu ।
nityaṁ ca sama-cittatvam iṣṭāniṣṭopapattiṣu ॥9 ॥

mayi cānanya-yogena bhaktir avyabhicāriṇī ।
vivikta-deśa-sevitvam aratir jana-saṁsadi ॥10 ॥

adhyātma-jñāna-nityatvaṁ tattva-jñānārtha-darśanam ।
etat jñānam iti proktam ajñānaṁ yad ato 'nyathā ॥11 ॥

> Humility, modesty, non-hurting, forgiveness, straight-forwardness, attending on one's master, cleanliness, steadfastness, self-restraint;
>
> Feeling unattached to pleasurable sense objects, egolessness, insight into the painfulness and viciousness of birth, death, old age and disease;
>
> Dispassionateness towards, and absence of self-identification with, children, wife, house and the like, constantly maintained equanimity towards both favourable and unfavorable situations,
>
> Not swerving from the contemplative devotion of finding oneself inseparably one with Me (the Self), a liking to be at lonely places, a distaste for being in crowd;
>
> Constancy of perceiving the ultimate Reality in oneself, and the transparent intuitive perception of the most basic wisdom of the Reality-as-such — these do mark wisdom (*jñāna*); being contrary marks ignorance (*ajñāna*).

Arjuna, what I point out here as *jñāna* are certain distinguishing features seen in the life of *jñānins*. Many live proud of their personal capabilities, but *jñānins*, who perceive themselves as a part of the cosmos, count themselves as insignificant in contrast to the whole, and humility (*amānitva*), therefore, naturally marks their life.

The immodest give no value to the opinion of others. This trait is known as *dambha,* and one of such character is called *dambhin,* the state of being so is known as *dambhitva,* and its opposite is *adambhitva* (modesty). A *jñānin* always remains modest. If humility (*amānitva*) is related to one's knowledge, modesty (*adambhitva*) is concerned more with actions.

Ahiṁsā is one's habit of not intending to hurt any being, physically, mentally or verbally. Pointing out non-hurting as a high human value and at the same time asking you to fight might seem inconsistent. Becoming caught up in a predicament, where engaging in battle is unavoidable has not come about because you wanted to hurt anyone, rather it is an occasion of nature's events confluencing in a way that fighting becomes inevitable for you. At the same time, this course of action is appropriate to your personal traits as well, the reason for my asking you to fight. A *jñānin,* as you might recall, does all *karmas* — fighting not excluded — not as "his" *karmas*, but as a part of nature's insuperable flow of actions, and thus, as non-action (*akarma*). What I try to bring to your notice now is the behavioural peculiarities found in all *jñānins*. Even such a *jñānin,* though fully abiding by the principle of *ahiṁsā,* non-hurting, might at times, again as part of the flow of actions of nature, be constrained to hurt others. Such contingencies do not make false his general attitude of *ahiṁsā,* the deciding factor being the individual's intention.

Kṣānti is the presence of mind for forbearance and forgiveness towards adversaries. Not retaliating even when hurt by others is a natural part of this attitude.

Straightforwardness (*ārjava*) is marked by the habit of one's thoughts, words and deeds always tallying as if falling in a straight line, with one being a continuation of the other.

In India, *ācāryopāsanam* or *guru-śuṣruṣā* (doing personal services to one's *guru*), has always been valued as an essential part of spiritual life. This act is considered so noble that actual learning from the *guru* is held to be secondary, to be engaged in at the free time available after serving the *guru*. Such a high position being given to *ācāryopāsanam* indicates how in the acquiring of wisdom, mutual intimacy or bipolarity, the *pārasparya,* between *guru* and disciple is crucial.

A sense of cleanliness that spreads through life is suggested by *śauca,* and five types have been identified for easier understanding and practice: *manaḥ-śuddhi* (cleanliness of mind), *vāk-śuddhi* (cleanliness of words), *śarīra-śuddhi* (cleanliness of body), *indriya-śuddhi* (cleanliness of sense organs), and *parisara-śuddhi* (cleanliness of surroundings). This does not, however, mean that merely knowing and practising these makes of one a *jñānin.* On the other hand, what it does imply is that all such forms of cleanliness are natural to *jñānins*. Of course, one who aspires to wisdom can and should make them a part of systematized seeking.

Steadfastness of mind regarding the vagaries of life-events, as normal to the natural course of events in *prakṛti,* is denoted by *sthairya* (steadfastness).

Not permitting oneself to be tempted by momentary pleasures and thus be carried away, and holding oneself to one's master-interest in life, mark what is known as *ātma-vinigrahaḥ* (self-restraint). If that is lacking, life becomes aimless like a boat lost in an open sea of uncertain winds.

A person becomes vulnerable to momentary temptations when the senses become captivated by pleasurable objects. The habit known as *vairāgya* means becoming aware of this trap and keeping one's own mind detached from such pleasures.

Ahaṁkāra was clarified in Verse 5 above; keeping oneself free from *ahaṁkāra* or "I"-sense is *anahaṁkāra* (egolessness). "I"-sense, along with the sense of mine, is the most formidable impediment in one's search for the Self.

Treating life as an ocean of sufferings is more or less universal, the causes for such sufferings being birth, death, diseases, old age and the like. Only *jñānins* know that all such causes pertain to the realm of appearance, and that the sufferings they cause also have value only as appearance and do not affect Reality. His interest being in the Self alone, his identity being with the Self alone, his sufferings become relegated to nothingness. *Ātmā,* which one really is, has no birth, no death, no old age, no disease; and a *jñānin* lives always aware of this.

Liberation is a value cherished by all, and yet paradoxically, individuals keep themselves in bondage, and that cherished value is never realized. Hardly is there such a person who makes himself free from attachments such as "my wife," "my children," "my husband," "my wealth" and such like. Valued attachments towards which one always hastens, are called *eṣaṇās,* meaning "running or hastening towards something," and are generally classified into three: attachment towards one's children (*putraiṣaṇā*), attachment towards one's wife (*dāraiṣaṇā*) and attachment towards one's wealth (*vitteṣaṇā*). As long as these longings remain forceful, liberation will remain a mirage. The seekers of liberation, therefore, from the very beginning, practise developing a habit of distancing themselves mentally from all sources of bondage. With a *jñānin* this is a natural habit. This does not mean that one has to be irresponsible to one's natural family and its affairs. It is possible, however, to remain with the family and take care of everything, while also keeping oneself unattached. To attain this requires finding one's identity not with the family and its welfare, but with the one Reality, the Self, that is to say, with Me.

A *jñānin* sees identity with Me, the Supreme Self; he feels an inseparable oneness with Me, as wave with ocean or ornament with gold. Experiencing this oneness is what I refer here as *ananya-yoga.* The *jñānin*'s constant contemplation of Me, that lies behind this experience of inseparable oneness is *bhakti.* Such a *bhakti* is natural and constant with a *jñānin.*

Always absorbed in Me, a *jñānin* or *yogin* does not like to be amongst crowds or indulge in the company of others. What he yearns for is to be alone, always away from such situations. If at all he mingles with others, it would be guided by the perception of seeing Me alone in everything.

A *jñānin* perceives his own being as an evanescent manifestation of the one imperishable *ātmā;* he perceives the all-abiding *ātmā,* as the substance that constitutes his own being, and such a perception was earlier referred to as *adhyātma jñāna* (Verse 3 of Chapter VIII) Spontaneous, unchanging and enduring with a *jñānin,* this perception is characterized here as *adhyātma-jñāna-nityatva* (freely rendered as "the constancy of perceiving the ultimate Reality in oneself").

A transparent vision of Reality — perceiving all the manifest beings in oneself, and then, oneself in Me (as was conceived earlier in Verse IV.35) — is what guides all such behaviour patterns, and that vision is what I refer to here as *tattva-jñānārtha-darśanam* (rendered as "the transparent intuitive perception of the most basic wisdom of the Reality-as-such").

Jñāna, in short, is more than just an intellectual conviction of what is Real; this conviction has to fill one's own being and become the sole force that leads his life. And how such a conviction gets reflected in one's actual life is what these verses exemplify, though they do not cover the entirety of such external signs. The variety of life-events being endless, *jñāna* finding expression in life also is endless in variety. The absence of all such signs in life marks ignorance or *ajñāna.* The life of an ignorant person is not based on an awareness of Reality, nor is it systemized. Even one who strictly adheres to all moral codes of life is to be considered ignorant as long as he remains unaware of the Reality — *ātmā* — that underlies the being of everything; he does not feel life to be *ātmā* unfolding itself.

Arjuna, I have been trying to clarify how wisdom finds expression in the life of a *jñānin,* a person who knows. What is it, that he really knows? That everything is *Brahman* alone, and therefore if at all he has an object of knowledge (*jñeya*), it is *Brahman.* Thus what I speak of as "the knowable" (*jñeya*) is nothing but *Brahman.* Experientially, *Brahman* is no object of knowledge, for it is merely an inner experience of transparence. Yet to the extent that it is a concept, it is also a "knowable." Also, since it has become manifest as the Cosmic Form, *Brahman* is knowable.

ज्ञेयं यत्तत्प्रवक्ष्यामि यज्ज्ञात्वामृतमश्नुते ।
अनादिमत्परं ब्रह्म न सत्तन्नासदुच्यते ॥१२॥

jñeyaṁ yat tat pravakṣyāmi yaj jñātvā 'mṛtam aśnute ।
anādimat paraṁ brahma na sat tan nā 'sad ucyate ॥12॥

I shall now tell you what "the knowable" (*jñeya*) is; knowing it leads one to attain the state of enjoying immortality: It is *Brahman,* the transcendental, the beginningless; it is held to be neither existent nor non-existent.

Arjuna, the knowable, as far as a *jñānin* is concerned, is not anything that becomes an object of knowledge, but is the inconceivable Absolute or *Brahman,* particularly in its Cosmic Form. Though *Brahman* is beginningless and endless, birthless and deathless, every detail of its Cosmic Form has beginning and end. New individual forms, like you and me, constantly emerge in It unhindered. Being such, we have to live every moment with the awareness of our inseparable oneness with the Cosmic Form, and thus the immortality of the Cosmic Form becomes ours as well. What is immortal, birthless and deathless, is *Brahman;* It is *ātmā;* you are That; I am That. Neither you nor I have our own existence. *Brahman* alone is the Reality that exists on its own, assuming the appearance of everything. In other words, It is neither existent nor non-existent.

Brahman as such has never been seen by anyone nor has It existed other than in Its Cosmic Form — another sense in which It is non-existent. Yet without *Brahman* existing no other existence is possible; thus It is not non-existence either.

The knowable, for a *jñānin,* therefore, is what he intuitively perceives as the inseparable oneness of the formless, imperishable Reality and the perishable appearance of the Cosmic Form. How it appears as having form, I shall tell you:

सर्वतःपाणिपादं तत्सर्वतो क्षिशिरोमुखम् ।
सर्वतः श्रुतिमल्लोके सर्वमावृत्य तिष्ठति ॥१३॥

sarvataḥ pāṇi-pādaṁ tat sarvato kṣi-śiro-mukham ।
sarvataḥ śrutimal loke sarvam āvṛtya tiṣṭhati ॥13॥

With hands and feet everywhere, with eyes, heads and faces everywhere, with ears everywhere, is Its all-embracing existence.

Arjuna, contemplating on Me as having the Cosmic Form (as described in Chapter XI) makes clear how *Brahman* has hands, feet, eyes, faces, heads, ears and the like. Every specific aspect of that Form is perceptible, whereas the Substance that takes on this appearance remains imperceptible. Why It is imperceptible, I shall tell you:

सर्वेन्द्रियगुणाभासं सर्वेन्द्रियविवर्जितम् ।
असक्तं सर्वभृच्चैव निर्गुणं गुणभोक्तृ च ॥१४ ॥

sarvendriya-guṇābhāsaṁ sarvendriya-vivarjitam ।
asaktaṁ sarva-bhṛc caiva nirguṇaṁ guṇa-bhoktṛ ca ॥14 ॥

Itself having no sense organs, It shines as all the sense organs and their faculties. All-supporting, It remains attached to none. Qualityless, It is the enjoyer of all qualities.

Arjuna, perceiving is a function that takes place with the help of the sense organs, each with the quality of being able to make contact with the corresponding object. Since it is *Brahman* that assumes the form of these sense organs and their qualities, as a part of the Cosmic Form, how can It become an object of perception for the very same sense organs? Not only is *Brahman* thus beyond the bounds of sense perception, It has no sense organ either.

One alone being the Reality that underlies the entire Cosmic Form, It (the Reality) has no special preference for or attachment to any particular aspect of that Form. Remaining unattached to anything particular is thus normal with *Brahman* as well as with the one who finds identity with *Brahman*. Though unattached to everything, Its existence is not different from anything. On the other hand, being inseparably one with all apparent forms, is the existence of *Brahman*. Water ensures the appearance of waves; so too *Brahman* is the Reality that provides for the emanation and existence of the entire Cosmic Form. It, thus, is the all-supporter (*sarva-bhṛt*).

All qualities pertain to the Cosmic Form, whereas the Reality that assumes that Form is devoid of qualities, and yet It is fully conscious of all the qualities that merge in Itself.

Where does that one Reality exist, I shall clarify to you now:

बहिरन्तश्च भूतानामचरं चरमेव च।
सूक्ष्मत्वात्तदविज्ञेयं दूरस्थं चान्तिके च तत्॥१५॥

bahir antaś ca bhūtānām acaraṁ caram eva ca ।
sūkṣmatvāt tad avijñeyaṁ dūrasthaṁ cāntike ca tat ॥15॥

Its existence is both within and without every being. Its existence is as both the living and non-living entities. Because of subtlety, It is no object of knowledge. Its existence is both close at hand and far away.

Arjuna, the one Reality exists everywhere, as everything. Its existence is perceived as the existence of everything that has come into being, It is the essential Substance in everything, and It exists outside all things as well. If you make the subject-object division, then what appears as both is that one Reality.

That both living and non-living beings have their being only in My Cosmic Form, you have already noticed. The "knowable" is that which assumes these varied forms.

This Reality is neither object of sense perception nor an object of thinking, and as gold-substance in ornaments, having no form of its own, It is invisible. Hence the epithet *avijñeya* (not an object of knowledge).

There are many — perhaps most — philosophers who seek Reality conceiving of it as an object of knowledge and do not attain It, but end up feeling that it is too far away to reach. There are a few who become aware that the Reality they seek is within themselves and that they need only to seek out the Substance that makes their being, to know that Reality. Oneself being that Substance in essence, It turns out to be the closest of all realities.

Paradoxically, what I am telling you now may seem contradictary when logically viewed, but at the same time, without logical thinking no knowledge or knowable discrimination is possible. *Brahman* is not an object of knowledge, and conceptualizing It as an object inevitably brings in such contradictions, as you will see presently.

Where It exists having been shown, now I shall tell you how does It exist.

अविभक्तं च भूतेषु विभक्तमिव च स्थितम्।
भूतभर्तृ च तज्ज्ञेयं ग्रसिष्णु प्रभविष्णु च ॥१६॥

avibhaktaṁ ca bhūteṣu vibhaktam iva ca sthitam ।
bhūtabhartṛ ca taj jñeyaṁ grasiṣṇu prabhaviṣṇu ca ॥16॥

Undivided though, that "knowable" exists as if divided among beings. It exists supporting all beings, emanating all beings from Itself, and absorbing all beings into Itself.

Arjuna, that which is in a divided state is called *vibhakta*, and its opposite is *avibhakta*. Entities look different from one another in a *vibhakta* state, as are ornaments. Yet the gold-substance in all ornaments is one and undivided. Likewise, individual entities that constitute the Cosmic Form are *vibhakta*, but the Reality underlying them remains *avibhakta*. Though undivided, gold-substance cannot exist other than in divided forms; *Brahman* too, though one and undivided, does not exist other than in the divided forms that constitute the cosmos. Each ornament is supported by the gold-substance; likewise, every entity in the Cosmic Form is supported by the one Reality, by Me. From one gold-substance emerge all ornaments, and they merge back into the very same gold. So too, all beings emanate from the one Reality and merge back into Itself. Such is the way the Real exists. And now I shall tell you what It is in essence:

ज्योतिषामपि तज्ज्योतिस्तमसः परमुच्यते।
ज्ञानं ज्ञेयं ज्ञानगम्यं हृदि सर्वस्य विष्ठितम् ॥१७॥

jyotiṣām api taj jyotis tamasaḥ param ucyate ।
jñānaṁ jñeyaṁ jñāna-gamyaṁ hṛdi sarvasya viṣṭhitam ॥17॥

> That "knowable" is the effulgence in all that shines, and, it is said, is beyond darkness. It is knowledge; It is the knowable; It is what one attains through knowing. Its existence is in the innermost recess of everything.

Arjuna, distinguishing one thing from another in this cosmos is made possible by sun-light or some other light. In its absence, all disappear into darkness. Perceiving distinct entities in the presence of light involves the formulation of corresponding mental images. A consciousness functioning behind all this, making distinct entities visible to the senses in the presence of light, creating respective mental images, and always relating them with the individual's likes and dislikes, has naturally to be presumed as existing. And the essence of consciousness, as we directly experience, is effulgence rather than darkness, and thus that causal consciousness is the effulgence in all that shines.

Ordinary brightness has darkness for its other side, just as day is always followed by night. But there exists the effulgence of consciousness that arranges for the cosmic system of day and night, that systemizes life with waking and sleeping states related to brightness and darkness. That effulgence has no other side that is dark, the sense in which it is beyond darkness.

Arjuna, apparently now I am showing you how to discriminate the knowledge and knowable aspects of *Brahman*. Yet, closely examined, such a distinction will be found groundless, for the two are nothing but two apparent facets of what Really exists. Moreover, the final goal one aims at through knowing the Real, too is none other than *Brahman* that I portray here as "the knowable." *Brahman*, thus, is wherein knowledge, the knowable and the ultimate goal of knowing become inseparable in the knower.

The word *jñeya* (the knowable, that which is to be known) might mislead one to the impression that the "knowable" exists somewhere apart from the knower. The *jñeya* or "knowable" really is the Substance that makes the being of the knower, and is to be known or rather realized dialectically in a *yoga* state. The *kṣetra* (the Field) and *kṣetrajña* (the Knower of the Field) meant in this chapter, therefore, are to be discriminated as well as seen unitively. What the ultimate benefit of having such a transparent vision of *kṣetra* and *kṣetrajña* is, I shall tell you:

इति क्षेत्रं तथा ज्ञानं ज्ञेयं चोक्तं समासतः।
मद्भक्त एतद्विज्ञाय मद्भावायोपपद्यते ॥१८॥

iti kṣetraṁ tathā jñānaṁ jñeyaṁ coktaṁ samāsataḥ ।
mad bhakta etad vijñāya mad bhāvāyopapadyate ॥18॥

The Field (*kṣetra*), the knowledge (*jñāna*) and the knowable (*jñeya*) have thus been expounded to you summarily. Knowing it, My devotee is worthy of becoming Myself.

Arjuna, discriminating the Field (*kṣetra*) and the Knower of the Field (*kṣetrajña*), as you know, is the main theme of this chapter. First I detailed to you what the *kṣetra* comprises. Naturally what I should tell you about next is the details of *kṣetrajña,* which I did not do, except pointing out that *kṣetrajña* is the consciousness that remains aware of all that constitutes *kṣetra* and all that happens in *kṣetra. Kṣetrajña* really being indescribable is the reason for my giving a detailed description of *jñāna* and *jñeya* instead, enabling you to perceive the *kṣetrajña* intuitively on your own.

All the apparent signs of wisdom seen in the life of *jñānins,* enumerated in Verses 7 to 11, are conditioned manifestations of one Reality. All that I related as characterizing *Brahman* as "the knowable" (Verses 12 to 17), are yet some other conditioned aspects of the very same Reality. The one Reality, Consciousness in essence, that manifests itself differently as these two sets of conditioned appearances, by Itself is unconditioned. That unconditioned Consciousness is what I mean to be intuitively perceived by you as *kṣetrajña.* Any definition of It, if at all possible, would be somewhat like this:

What appears to be are conditioned aspects. The unconditioned never becomes apparent. That which

> is conditioned is unreal. The unconditioned is the *sat* (Existence) that alone is.*

Arjuna, anything apparently perceivable or conceivable is a conditioned aspect of what really exists. "The knowledge" (*jñāna*) and "the knowable" (*jñeya*) I told you about just now are such. The unconditioned Consciousness that unfolds itself in such conditioned forms, not only provides for them but is also fully aware of all of them and all that takes place in them. To know and to be aware of knowing, as you know, are both functions of consciousness (*cit*). The unconditioned Consciousness that finds expression as, and knows, all such conditioned knowledges, is what I mean by *kṣetrajña*, and the only way that leads you on to it, is *yoga-buddhi.*

Descriminating the *kṣetra* and *kṣetrajña* aspects of one's own existence that really is inseparably one with the Cosmic Form, is what makes one deserving to attain Me, to be one with Me, to live as Myself. He lives his own life that really is inalienable from My Cosmic Form. He is to be considered a real *bhakta* or devotee, as was clarified earlier in Chapter XII.

Vyāsa:

O, Janmejaya, the discrimination-cum-unitiveness of *kṣetra* and *kṣetrajña* that I attempted to clarify in this chapter so far, followed a line of thought of my own *yoga-buddhi* or dialectics. The same duo, following the more generally known method of the Sāṁkhya system, could be well considered equivalent to *prakṛti* (Nature) and *puruṣa* (Person). I shall, therefore, clarify the same point using the Sāṁkhyan terminologies as well, making it easier to grasp while breaking the ground for the further steps of self-examination to follow in the rest of the chapters, particularly in the next two.

---

* *yad bhāṣyate tad adhyastam anadhyastam na bhāṣyate* ।
yad adhyastam tad asad apy anadhyastam sad eva tat ॥

— Narayana Guru, *Darśanamālā,* (V.10)

प्रकृतिं पुरुषं चैव विद्ध्यनादी उभावपि।
विकारांश्च गुणांश्चैव विद्धि प्रकृतिसम्भवान्॥१९॥

prakṛtiṁ puruṣaṁ caiva viddhy anādi ubhāvapi I
vikārāṁś ca guṇāṁś caiva viddhi prakṛti-saṁbhavān II19 II

Prakṛti and *puruṣa,* know both as beginningless. All that is changeful and their differentiating qualities, know as emanating from the *prakṛti.*

Arjuna, causal realities are two — *prakṛti* and *puruṣa* — according to the Sāṁkhya system of thought. The world and everything in it are changeful, and what constantly evolves as all these is known as *prakṛti* (Nature), and it is beginningless. There exists also a consciousness, also beginningless, different in each individual living being, that knows this *prakṛti* and its evolutions, and is known as *puruṣa,* literally, the "person." Though I borrow these two terms, I use them in a slightly different sense so as to fit in with the Vedāntic line of thought I follow. I shall clarify it.

Both *kṣetra* and *kṣetrajña,* as you know, were perceived as inseparably one with My Cosmic Form; likewise are *prakṛti* and *puruṣa.* My Cosmic Form being beginningless and endless, the *prakṛti* and *puruṣa,* that are integral with It, are also so. These two, as held by the Sāṁkhya school, exist eternally with different functions, whereas in the present context of the *Gītā,* they are treated as two beginningless and endless facets of the Cosmic Form. Really what exists beginningless and endless is Myself alone.

Changefulness is what we saw as the distinguishing mark of *kṣetra; prakṛti* also is so. *Prakṛti* is changeful, the Sāṁkhya system claims, because of the three *guṇa*s (modalities or qualities) inherent in it, a stand acceptable to Vedanta also, as it explains easily how all entities that emerge in this world are different quality-wise. These basic inherent qualities of *prakṛti* are *sattva* (pure and clear), *rajas* (active) and *tamas* (dark, inert), to be elaborated on later in the next chapter. Inherent in *prakṛti,* these *guṇa*s have no other source. I shall clarify now how *puruṣa* and *prakṛti,* even as having their different functions, are one with My Cosmic Form.

कार्यकारणकर्तृत्वे हेतुः प्रकृतिरुच्यते ।
पुरुषः सुखदुःखानां भोक्तृत्वे हेतुरुच्यते ॥२० ॥

kārya-kāraṇa-kartṛtve hetuḥ prakṛtir ucyate ।
puruṣaḥ sukha-duḥkhānāṁ bhoktṛtve hetur ucyate ॥20 ॥

Prakṛti is called so because it activates the emergence of cause and effect. And *puṛusa* is that factor which causes the experiencing of pleasure and pain.

Arjuna, you have already seen how mysterious, how extensive, how active, how constructive and destructive, how diverse in appearance My Cosmic Form is; no one can predict or describe the variety of apparent entities that emerge and re-merge in it. Even as you pinpoint the active emergence of a particular entity, you notice that its apparent form is constantly changing, one phase of existence giving room for another the nature of the earlier one mostly deciding the nature of the later one. This is evident in every specific aspect of the existence of the cosmos, and altogether this forms its eternal flux. This series of phases of appearance of specific entities, is what we conceive in our thought-process as the cause-effect relationship or as causality. One effect naturally becomes the cause of some new effect, thus setting off an endless chain of causes and effects. The activating principle behind this chain is called *prakṛti* here.

Even as all these chains of action continue, creating an endless series of causes and effects, the fact that such events are taking place is becoming known to each conscious being. Apart from the knowing, there also takes place an evaluation of each event in relation to one's own pleasures and pains. Some events in life are thus felt to be pleasurable, others painful and some as neutral. That causal principle in My Cosmic Form, which is in this experiencing of pleasures and pains, I call *puruṣa* here.

Puruṣa and *prakṛti,* both have their being in My Cosmic Form alone; oblivious of this fact, we mostly think of the two as related to each other on their own. Look then at how we see their mutual relation:

पुरुषः प्रकृतिस्थो हि भुङ्क्ते प्रकृतिजान्गुणान्।
कारणं गुणसङ्गो ऽस्य सदसद्योनिजन्मसु ॥२१॥

puruṣaḥ prakṛtistho hi bhuṅkte prakṛtijān guṇān ।
kāraṇaṁ guṇasaṅgo 'sya sad asad yoni janmasu ॥21॥

Puruṣa, seated in *prakṛti,* enjoys the various attributes born of the latter. The attachment *puruṣa* has with these attributes is the cause of his continued incarnation in good and evil wombs.

Arjuna, admittedly it has become a fixed idea in our mind that our bodies are machine-like and that some energizing principle works in it. No one suspects its correctness; no one cares to explore for the grounds for these assumptions. Presenting it in a scientific-looking way, the Sāṁkhya system claims, "*Puruṣa* has his seat in *prakṛti.*" How the phenomenon of life and death is explained from that point of view is what we consider in the present verse.

Prakṛti has inherent in it the three *guṇas* — *sattva, rajas* and *tamas* — and each individual entity is necessarily endowed with these. Constantly changing in proportion, they cause incessant changefulness in the state of existence of nature both individually and cosmically, resulting in various corresponding experiences. This changeful *prakṛti* and the conscious *puruṣa* existing inseparable is what we consider to be an individual being. Individuals have different ways of living and differing experiences owing to the peculiar way the three *guṇa*s exist, act and react in each being. It could be well said in that sense that an individual being's birth is the result of a particular manner in which *puruṣa* becomes attached to *prakṛti*'s three *guṇa*s. Countless and endlessly various are such beings, for such is the diverseness of the intermingling of the three *guṇa*s. Counting such beings as of noble birth or ignoble birth is based simply on certain human value notions. Innately, none is noble, none is ignoble. Though changeless, the *puruṣa* is not functionless in *prakṛti.* Let us look at what his activities are:

उपद्रष्टानुमन्ता च भर्ता भोक्ता महेश्वरः ।
परमात्मेति चाप्युक्तो देहे ऽस्मिन्पुरुषः परः ॥२२ ॥

upadraṣṭā 'numantā ca bhartā bhoktā maheśvaraḥ ।
paramātmeti cāpy ukto dehe 'smin puruṣaḥ paraḥ ॥22 ॥

This *puruṣa* is the close perceiver of everything; is the permitter of everything; is the governor of everything; is the enjoyer of everything; is the supreme controller of everything. Abiding in this body though, this *puruṣa* is also styled the Supreme Self (*paramātmā*), the Transcendental.

Arjuna, the what and how of *prakṛti* we have already seen. *Prakṛti* always evolves, and the role of *puruṣa* is to be within whatever *prakṛti* evolves as, and to know all such evolutions; and that is why *puruṣa* is said to be the closest perceiver of everything (*upadraṣṭā*).

Though the evolution of *prakṛti* is inconceivably diverse and unpredictable, an overall structural integrity and coherence is always maintained, and all details of evolution take place only within the framework of that scheme. No human child, as we know, is ever born of a she-elephant, and no elephant-calf is born of a woman. Each phase, even of an insignificant event of evolution, needs the permission of a knowledge that knows the overall scheme of *prakṛti*. This permission-giver is none other than *puruṣa;* he thus is the *anumantā*. The governor of every event, he is the *bhartā;* the enjoyer of pleasures and pains arising from such events, he is the *bhoktā;* the all-abiding controller, he is the Maheśvara, also meaning the adorable God.

The Sāṁkhya system holds that there is one *puruṣa* in each body, but the *puruṣa* I re-introduce here as seen in Vedānta, is the one who abides within the one Cosmic Body, and in that sense, is called *paramātmā*, the Supreme Self. One of the many literal meanings of the word *ātmā* is "the one who enjoys." The *paramātmā* could then mean "the Cosmic Enjoyer in the Cosmic Body." Every individual is an integral part of the Cosmic Body, the enjoyer in each individual too is, therefore, a minute element of the Supreme *Puruṣa*. Along with discriminating these *puruṣa* and *prakṛti* aspects of one's own existence, we have to perceive also how these two are inseparable in the Cosmic Form. What a person of such a *yogic* perception attains in life is shown in the next verse:

य एवं वेत्ति पुरुषं प्रकृतिं च गुणैः सह।
सर्वथा वर्तमानो ऽपि न स भूयो ऽभिजायते ॥२३॥

ya evaṁ vetti puruṣaṁ prakṛtiṁ ca guṇaiḥ saha ।
sarvathā vartamāno 'pi na sa bhūyo 'bhijāyate ॥23॥

He who knows thus the *puruṣa* and *prakṛti* along with its *guṇas*, even as actively engaged in life in all respects, no more does he have repeated birth.

Arjuna, I am the Immortal Reality, and My existence is in the form of this cosmos. He who finds himself as one with My Cosmic Form naturally feels himself as immortal, for he and I are then no two. One of such a perception lives as a part of My Cosmic Form that always is in a changeful state owing to the ever evolving *prakṛti*, with *puruṣa* knowing all such change. He sees that it is one life alone that thrive ceaselessly without birth and death, and thus he sees himself as beyond birth and death. Living Immortality, in other words, is what he always experiences.

This experience is what one can expect to attain ultimately according to the teaching of the *Gītā*, and I am trying to clarify the way to attain this. However, this is not the only way that can be followed; there are many spiritual practices that lead to the same goal, each following a path natural to the particular system. What the individual seeker must do is to stick strictly to the path he chooses. Mixing different practices from different systems, simply because they seem attractive, is bound to be harmful. Such a mixing, instead of making a *yogī* of one, may make one indisposed (*rogī*). I shall point out to you some such practices presently existing:

ध्यानेनात्मनि पश्यन्ति केचिदात्मानमात्मना।
अन्ये सांख्येन योगेन कर्मयोगेन चापरे ॥२४॥

dhyānenātmani paśyanti kecid ātmānam ātmanā ।
anye sāṁkhyena yogena karma-yogena cāpare ॥24 ॥

Some, in their meditation, perceive the Self in the Self on their own. Some others do the same by following the Sāṁkhya way, the Yoga way or even the *karma-yoga*.

अन्ये त्वेवमजानन्तः श्रुत्वान्येभ्य उपासते ।
ते ऽपि चातितरन्त्येव मृत्युं श्रुतिपरायणाः ॥२५॥

anye tvevam ajānantaḥ śrutvā'nyebhya upāsate ।
te 'pi cātitaranty eva mṛtyuṁ śruti-parāyaṇāḥ ॥25 ॥

Certain others, ignorant of these basics, practise meditative adoration as taught by others. They too, adhering to what they learn, go beyond death.

Arjuna, the spiritual paths I point out here as different from what I teach could equally be considered as forming different steps of the one I teach here in the *Gītā* with a very broad and commonsense outlook. The word *śruti-parāyaṇāḥ,* strictly speaking, in the Vedic context, means "those who are well versed in the Vedas." The literal sense of the word *śruti* being "that which is heard," those who follow the paths heard of from others may also be called *śruti-parāyaṇāḥ*.

Whatever the path of practice followed, the ultimate goal is one only for each individual: to live engaged in activities in accordance with personal traits, knowing oneself to be inseparable from My birthless and deathless Cosmic Form, and thus to realize My Immortality as his or her own.

When looked at separately, each, being in My Cosmic Form, undergoes constant change, each change involving the disappearance of an old state of existence and the appearance of a new one. Related to this overall picture is the discrimination between *kṣetra* and *kṣetrajña* as well as between *prakṛti* and *puruṣa*. To clarify it further:

यावत्सञ्जायते किञ्चित्सत्त्वं स्थावरजङ्गमम् ।
क्षेत्रक्षेत्रज्ञसंयोगात्तद्विद्धि भरतर्षभ ॥२६ ॥

yāvat saṁjāyate kiñcit sattvaṁ sthāvara-jaṅgamam ।
kṣetra-kṣetrajña-saṁyogāt tad viddhi bharatarṣabha ॥26 ॥

Whatever being, living or non-living, that emerges, is to be understood as from the inseparable oneness of *kṣetra* and *kṣetrajña*.

Arjuna, the ultimate Reality is indistinct, formless and changeless; when become distinct, each of its apparent forms is changeful. The non-dual oneness of the distinct and indistinct, the changeful and the changeless, though difficult to understand logically, is an actuality. To render this actual inseparability into a perceptible form was also my intention in showing you My Cosmic Form. All that is living or non-living in all the worlds is nothing but minute parts of the changeful apparent form that I, the cosmic *puruṣa*, assume, and *kṣetra* and *kṣetrajña* are inseparably one in each of these. In order to make this inseparability easier to grasp, I brought in the Sāṁkhyan concept of the *prakṛti-puruṣa* duality. All events, all phenomena, in nature are thus to be seen as resulting from the constantly fluctuating states of the inseparability of *puruṣa* and *prakṛti*, personal traits of individuals not excepted. The *puruṣa* and *prakṛti*, their inseparability, all the multifarious forms and events that appear and disappear, are all within My Cosmic Form. Seeing oneself thus in Me alone ensures attaining immortality while actually living. In short, immortality is attained by those who perceive Me as pervading equally in everything everywhere in the cosmos. To clarify further:

समं सर्वेषु भूतेषु तिष्ठन्तं परमेश्वरम् ।
विनश्यत्स्वविनश्यन्तं यः पश्यति स पश्यति ॥२७ ॥

samaṁ sarveṣu bhūteṣu tiṣṭhantaṁ parameśvaram ।
vinaśyatsv avinaśyantaṁ yaḥ paśyati sa paśyati ॥27 ॥

He alone, who perceives the Supreme Lord as

existing equally in all that has come into being, as not perishing, even as all these perish, is the seer.

Arjuna, a real seer lives experiencing himself as immortal, always seeing the Real in himself and everywhere in Its Cosmic Form. Even as the Real always exists changeless, all the apparent entities that merge in It constantly undergo changes. All beings in all the worlds are nothing but such forms emerging and merging back into the Cosmic Form. I alone am the one Substance in all of these forms, I alone am the one controller of all changes, and I alone maintain the integrity of the Cosmic Form and the changefulness of all Its constituents. Thus I could well be called *parameśvara* (the Supreme Lord or Supreme Controller). One who discriminates between this imperishable aspect of Mine and the perishable nature of appearances, and lives the truth of this inseparability in himself, is the seer.

What a seer of this non-duality attains, I shall tell you:

समं पश्यन्हि सर्वत्र समवस्थितमीश्वरम् ।
न हिनस्त्यात्मनात्मानं ततो याति परां गतिम् ॥२८॥

samaṁ paśyan hi sarvatra sam avasthitam īśvaram ।
na hinasty ātmanātmānaṁ tato yāti parāṁ gatīm ॥28॥

Perceiving the one Lord alone underlying equally everywhere as he is, he killing anyone and he being killed by anyone are of no relevance for him. Besides, for the very reason, he attains the Supreme Goal as well.

Arjuna, you must now be fully aware that I am the one imperishable Substance or Lord that underlies all that perishes. Equally true is it to say that destructibility and indestructibility find in Me a unity without contradiction. The one who understands that I alone exist everywhere sees none else in himself either. As I am beyond birth and death, so too is the one who sees Me in himself. In the vision of such a one, to hurt or kill another or to be hurt or killed by another, does not make sense. When this dialogue began, your most fearsome doubt was, why you were destined to commit the sin of killing your own *gurus* and kith and kin. The problem of others in life may be different, but whatever their nature, they become insignificant the moment I alone am seen to be everywhere. The problem you faced may be well treated as representing all the problems of all human beings everywhere in practical life.

Becoming rid of all problems of life is not the only benefit of this wisdom; the clearing away of darkness is accompanied by the emergence of brightness. So too, being rid of crucial problems brings the feeling of contentment, which could be well named liberation, *mokṣa, sāyujya* or *kaivalya*. Doing away with problems and attaining liberation may thus be considered the two sides of what one ultimately gains as a result of following the teaching of the *Gītā*. Stated in a way more in line with the present phase of teaching, experiencing inseparable oneness with My Cosmic Form is felt, both as becoming free of all problems and as attaining liberation. Such a liberated one does not remain inactive in life; he too, as a part of the Cosmic Form, continues to live actively in accordance with the intrinsic nature of his being. How does he treat such actions?

प्रकृत्यैव च कर्माणि क्रियमाणानि सर्वशः ।
यः पश्यति तथात्मानमकर्तारं स पश्यति ॥२९॥

prakṛtyaiva ca karmāṇi kriyamāṇāni sarvaśaḥ ।
yaḥ paśyati tathātmānam akartāraṁ sa paśyati ॥29॥

Because of *prakṛti* alone do all kinds of *karmas* take place. One who lives seeing oneself thus as no doer of any *karma*, is the real seer.

Arjuna, you worried about your *karma* in fighting this great battle and about the sins that you would be committing as a result of killing your *gurus* and relatives. It must now have become sufficiently clear to you that all *karmas* take place in My Cosmic Form and are originated by Its *prakṛti* aspect, your own *karma* of fighting being no exception. All such *karmas* form part of the perishable aspect of My

Cosmic Form. The Imperishable "I," the *puruṣa,* that witnesses all *karmas*, is not the doer. Whosoever perceives himself to be one with such Me, also sees himself as imperishable and also as not the doer of any *karma.* No event that occurs in the Cosmic Form is a *karma* of any particular individual; they are simply evolutes of *prakṛti.* One of this perception lives unmoved by the vagaries of nature, seeing Me alone actively existing in and as all of these. This inflexible contentment experienced in actual life is none other than the attaining of *Brahman.* To elucidate further:

यदा भूतपृथग्भावमेकस्थमनुपश्यति ।
तत एव च विस्तारं ब्रह्म सम्पद्यते तदा ॥३० ॥

yadā bhūta-pṛthag bhāvam ekastham anupaśyati ।
tata eva ca vistāraṁ brahma sampadyate tadā ॥30 ॥

Constantly perceiving that the diversified apparent beings exist in one Reality, and that It opens out as all of these, marks one attaining *Brahman.*

Arjuna, as inseparable from My Cosmic Form, you saw the countless entities that constitute the cosmos, each having its own peculiar characteristics. He who constantly perceives himself and all beings as inseparable from the one Reality, which unfolds itself as all these beings, may be considered to have attained *Brahman.* For such a one, his own existence and My existence are not two.

This experiential attainment of oneness, in essence, is none other than the attainment of *Brahman.*

How does one of this perception treat all the *karmas*, is stated in the next verse.

अनादित्वान्निर्गुणत्वात्परमात्मायमव्ययः ।
शरीरस्थोऽपि कौन्तेय न करोति न लिप्यते ॥३१ ॥

anāditvān nirguṇatvāt paramātmāyam avyayaḥ ।
śarīrastho 'pi kaunteya na karoti na lipyate ॥31 ॥

Being beginningless and attributeless, this Supreme Self is imperishable. Though seated in perishable bodies, It does no *karma*, nor is It tainted by *karmas*.

Arjuna, how I am the beginningless must have become clear to you by now. All *guṇas* pertain to *prakṛti,* and the *ātmā,* the Self, Myself, that underlies *prakṛti,* is without *guṇas*. For one who is sure "I am that *ātmā,*" he no more perceives himself as an individual being experienceing himself. He thus is not *ātmā* but is *paramātmā,* the Supreme Self. "I am indestructible" is not an idea or ideal, but a living experience for him. Having a body (as defined in Verses 5 and 6 above) does not impinge upon his indestructibility, for he knows the body to be but a fleeting apparent form and merges into the Cosmic Form. Thus, one who sees himself as the Supreme Self lives freed from all *karmas*. *Ātmā*'s existence is not differentiable from that of body either; on the contrary, *ātmā* is the Substance that makes the being of the body as well, both individually and cosmically, yet *ātmā* remains free of all bodily confines. *Ātmā,* seen thus, exists in the body, but is free from bodily limitations. To clarify this liberatedness of *ātmā* further:

यथा सर्वगतं सौक्ष्म्यादाकाशं नोपलिप्यते ।
सर्वत्रावस्थितो देहे तथात्मा नोपलिप्यते ॥३२॥

yathā sarva-gataṁ saukṣmyād ākāśaṁ nopalipyate ।
sarvatrāvasthito dehe tathātmā nopalipyate ॥32॥

Space fills everywhere, and thanks to its subtlety, it remains untarnished. Likewise untarnished is the *ātmā* that makes the being of the entire cosmic body.

Arjuna, space is called *ākāśa* because it gives room for everything physical to exist, whereas its own physical existence is simply conceivable, never perceivable, for the reason that it is so subtle. Yet undeniable is its existence everywhere from the interior of a minute atom to the interior/exterior of the endlessly expanding universe or rather universes. Notwithstanding its existence everywhere, it is not attached to anything that exists in it; the sense of "O! this is mine" also does not occur to it. Similar is My existence everywhere in the Cosmic Form, never attached to anything that forms It. Nor do the vagaries of events that take place in the cosmos disturb My existence. The same is true of one who knows himself as inseparably one with Me.

I shall make now clear how I am unattached to and undisturbed by everything that happens in the cosmos, though all of it happens as an aspect of Myself becoming manifest.

यथा प्रकाशयत्येकः कृत्स्नं लोकमिमं रविः ।
क्षेत्रं क्षेत्री तथा कृत्स्नं प्रकाशयति भारत ॥३३॥

yathā prakāśayaty ekaḥ kṛtsnaṁ lokam imaṁ raviḥ ।
kṣetraṁ kṣetrī tathā kṛtsnaṁ prakāśayati bhārata ॥33॥

Arjuna, the Sun, remaining one, illuminates the entire world. Similarly illuminated by *kṣetrī* is the entire *kṣetra*.

Arjuna, the one sun illuminating the entire world is a phenomenon familiar to you. Similar to it is the role of *kṣetrī* or *kṣetrajña* in My Cosmic Form or *kṣetra.* Being consciousness or *puruṣa, kṣetrī* remains fully aware of all the transformations that take place in the *kṣetra* or *prakṛti.* In our own case, we know, all that takes place apparently in our body is witnessed by our mind. The same is true with the cosmos.

Though *kṣetrī* is thought of here as illuminating *kṣetra,* the two are not at all to be treated as existing separate, as the sun and the world it illuminates are thought to be. The two, on the other hand, always remain inseparable. In order to understand what I say now, you need the intuitive eye that can perceive these two distinctly, while they remain inseparable, as are mind and matter. Only the one endowed with such an eye can be considered a real seer, philosopher, a real *satya-darśin.* He alone attains the ultimate goal. Shedding more light on this aspect of *yoga* in the next verse, we shall conclude the present chapter.

क्षेत्रक्षेत्रज्ञयोरेवमन्तरं ज्ञानचक्षुषा ।
भूतप्रकृतिमोक्षं च ये विदुर्यान्ति ते परम् ॥३४ ॥

kṣetra-kṣetrajñayor evam antaraṁ jñāna-cakṣuṣā ।
bhūta-prakṛti-mokṣaṁ ca ye vidur yānti te param ॥34 ॥

Those who perceive thus with the intuitive wisdom-eye the distinction between *kṣetra* and *kṣetrajña,* along with one's Freedom from the *prakṛti*-related becoming, attain the Supreme Goal.

Arjuna, the *kṣetra* and *kṣetrajña* aspects of My Cosmic Existence as well as of individuated beings, have sufficiently been made clear, and comparing the two to the *prakṛti* and *puruṣa* concepts of the Sāṁkhya system has shed more light on this. Perceiving such a differentiation does not require the wisdom-eye, a logical mind alone will suffice. But the emphasis given here to the need of wisdom-eye is of utmost importance. I exist in the Cosmic Form — the distinctly perceivable *kṣetra* and *kṣetrajña* (*prakṛti* and *puruṣa*) aspects of My being, the being of individual entities, the *kṣetra-kṣetrajña* differentiation in such individual beings, all these together remain one whole as the Cosmic Form. The whole exists immutable whereas each entity that forms a part of it undergoes constant change. It results in the emergence of new apparent forms and merging back of the old ones. All these are to be intuitively and holistically perceived as one Living Reality, the perceiver being inseparable from It. Such a vision is what the wisdom-eye (*jñāna-cakṣus*) we speak of here ensures, and this eye is not different from the one I gave you earlier to see My Cosmic Form directly. It is with this eye that the *kṣetra* and *kṣetrajña* are to be distinguished as pertaining to a unitive whole. In other words, it is not just the mind-matter differentiation that we usually make.

In My Cosmic Form can be seen intuitively everything in all the worlds, and also *prakṛti* and its *guṇa*s that make every being in It undergo constant change. Even as such changes take place, one has to perceive what is Real in oneself, the *ātmā,* or what is Real in the entire Cosmic Form, the *paramātmā,* as remaining unaffected and as manifesting as *kṣetra* and *kṣtrajña,* as well as *prakṛti* and *puruṣa.* This existence of oneself unattached to anything changeful is the ultimate Freedom or *mokṣa* one can actualize in life.

Now to summarize what we learnt in this chapter:

Each individual finding his inseparable oneness with My Cosmic Form was seen to be the essense of *bhakti* in the last chapter. This oneness in no way abnegates one's own inherent personal traits and qualities. *Kṣetra* and *kṣetrejña* were introduced in this chapter as the two factors fundamentally distinguishable in one's personal beingness as a part of the Cosmic Form. *Kṣetra,* which can be treated as body (*śarīra*), also includes within its range what we normally treat as psychological factors and even the animating principle (*cetanā*) because it also appears and disappears and thus is a part of the changeful. The consciousness that always remains aware of all the constantly changing factors is the *kṣetrajña* and this is undefinable. And because it cannot be defined, I defined both *jñāna* (knowledge) and *jñeya* (the knowable). The keen student, with his intuitive and dialectical eye, should plunge into the inner vision of *kṣetrajña* with the two given definitions and the definition of *jñāna* given earlier in Verse IV.35, for his firm diving board.

The *kṣetra-kṣetrajña* distinction is peculiar to the way of approach I rely on in the *Gītā*. For the sake of easier understanding and further scrutiny in the coming chapters, the two could be equated to the *prakṛti-puruṣa* duality known to the Sāṁkhya system of Indian philosophy.

The unitiveness of *kṣetra* and *kṣetrajña* is present in everything creative in My Cosmic Beingness, and is to be perceived thus. Though understandable thus as distinct, existentially the two are inseparable and this unitiveness is what keeps My Cosmic Form living. What ensures this organic beingness of the cosmos is the *prakṛti* aspect of My Form, and the essential content of this *prakṛti* is its three *guṇas*. Therefore, the next chapter goes into the details of *prakṛti* and its *guṇas* as forming a part of My Cosmic Form.

Thus ends Chapter Thirteen entitled Kṣetra-Kṣetrajña Vibhāga-Yoga of the Bhagavad-Gītā, the essence of the Upaniṣads, that embodies the yoga-śāstra of brahma-vidyā in the form of a dialogue between Śrī Kṛṣṇa and Arjuna.

XIV

Guṇa-Traya-Vibhāga-Yoga
— The Yoga of Discriminating Three Nature-Modalities —

श्री भगवानुवाच —

परं भूयः प्रवक्ष्यामि ज्ञानानां ज्ञानमुत्तमम्।
यज्ज्ञात्वा मुनयः सर्वे परां सिद्धिमितो गताः ॥१॥

śri bhagavān uvāca —

paraṁ bhūyaḥ pravakṣyāmi jñānānāṁ jñānam uttamam ।
yaj jñātvā munayaḥ sarve parāṁ siddhim ito gatāḥ ॥1॥

Śri Kṛṣṇa said —

I shall teach you more of the best of all wisdom. Having it gained, many a silent recluse, crossing over the present state of existence, had reached the Supreme Attainment.

Arjuna, a further aspect of the wisdom I teach is now going to be clarified to you. It could more be considered a continuation of the signs of lived wisdom that I pointed out to you in the last chapter, than as a further elaboration on the philosophical core of wisdom taught you earlier in Chapter IV, particularly in Verse 35. I go down one step further to the details of the *prakṛti* aspect of My Cosmic Form. That the benefit of getting clarity on this aspect of wisdom is attaining "sameness with Me in functional existence" (*mama sādharmyam*) will be made clear in the next verse. What it means shall also be discussed in detail then. This much I shall tell you in advance: your experiencing inseparable oneness with Me even when engaged in activities natural to your inborn traits, is the core of this attainment. Many seekers like you had existed before, and they too had attained Me, not simply by muttering sacred chants or meditating in seclusion, but through engaging themselves in life-activities natural to them. They saw that it is My Cosmic Body alone that exists creatively in, and as, all those activities and as themselves. How they treated the phenomena of birth and death, the most crucial problems of life, as forming a part of *prakṛti*'s evolutionary phases as envisaged by them, I shall tell you:

इदं ज्ञानमुपाश्रित्य मम साधर्म्यमागताः ।
सर्गे ऽपि नोपजायन्ते प्रलये न व्यथन्ति च ॥२॥

idaṁ jñānam upāśritya mama sādharmyam āgatāḥ ।
sarge 'pi nopajāyante pralaye na vyathanti ca ॥2 ॥

With this wisdom relied on, and sameness with Me in functional existence attained, they do see no birth in the emergence of something; neither do they grieve at the dissolution of something apparent.

Arjuna, I intend to teach you now a transparent vision of the details of *prakṛti* as inherent in your own being, enabling you to attain *sādharmya* with Me (meaning, having the same *dharma* as Mine). I am the one and only Reality that has existence, and what appears as this cosmos is My *dharma* — as the all-supporting Reality, I assume the form of the supported, of which you are a part. Countless are the qualities of My Cosmic Form, and as a part of It you too have them, the warrior-quality being predominant among these. Whosoever lives in accord with his inner nature may be considered doing his *svadharma.* My *svadharma,* as the one and only Reality, is unfolding Myself as everything, your *svadharma,* is to live your life in perfect harmony with your personal traits of being a warrior, while seeing yourself as inseparably one with Me of Cosmic Form. Your *svadharma* and My *svadharma* thus come together to become non-dual, and attaining that state means you gain *sādharmya* with Me (sameness with Me in functional existence).

In essence, the *prakṛti* of the last chapter, is nothing but the creative way in which My *dharma* finds expression. The *kṛti* of *prakṛti* is what is known as *karma* or action. It takes place all through My Cosmic Form eternally, and its result is the apparent changefulness in nature (*prakṛti*). One state of existence of something changing into another is an event, and every event involves *karma* or *kṛti*. Every such event results in the emergence of a new phase of existence, in what we call the birth of something new (*sarga*). Really nothing new is born there, though the event is ordinarily counted as the joyous one, such as in the case of a new-born child. But this event is never considered by those who have attained *sādharmya* with Me as the birth of any new being, and therefore indifference is their attitude to such an event.

As the reverse side of the emergence of a new phase of existence occurs the disappearance of an old one, called *pralaya*, meaning "proper dissolution" (*pra+laya*), and this event in the usual course is treated as death. Nothing really dies; only an evanescent phase of appearance gives place to a new one, again as a part of My *dharma*. For this reason, the one who has attained My *sādharmya* does not ever grieve at such an event. *Jñānins* treat birth and death simply as a part of My *dharma* finding expression.

Each individual having a particular personal trait is also a part of My Cosmic Beingness, and a result of *prakṛti*'s creative unfoldment. If the emanation of such individual entities in My Cosmic Form is treated as a sort of giving birth, then how does their impregnation happen? It is to be understood thus:

मम योनिर्महद्ब्रह्म तस्मिन्गर्भं दधाम्यहम् ।
संभवः सर्वभूतानां ततो भवति भारत ॥३॥

mama yonir mahad brahma tasmin garbhaṁ dadhāmy ahaṁ ।
sambhavaḥ sarva-bhūtānāṁ tato bhavati bhārata ॥3 ॥

The womb — *Brahman* having assumed the form of *mahat* — is My own. I deposit the sperm therein Myself, and thus happens the coming into being of all living beings.

सर्वयोनिषु कौन्तेय मूर्तयः सम्भवन्ति याः ।
तासां ब्रह्म महद्योनिरहं बीजप्रदः पिता ॥४॥

sarva-yoniṣu kaunteya mūrtayaḥ saṁbhavanti yāḥ ।
tāsāṁ brahma mahad yonir ahaṁ bīja-pradaḥ pitā ॥4॥

Whatever the species of visible individual beings that emerge, O Arjuna, all of them have *Brahman* having-assumed-the-form-of-*mahat* for their mother, and I for the sperm-bestowing father.

Arjuna, countless beings are formulated in My Cosmic Form constantly, and also become dissolved likewise. In the context of deliberating on how individuals emerge with personal traits, the emphasis is here given to the former aspect. The emanation of every being is a sort of child-birth, a process that needs a mother and a father. Both roles, in the present case, are played by Me or *Brahman*. The changeful aspect of My Form was called *kṣetra*, and in order to make it easier to explore the details, this was equated to *prakṛti*, a Sāṁkhyan concept. *Prakṛti*, according to that school, formless on its own, evolves into all forms, and each such evolved form is called a *vikṛti*. It is such evolved forms that have specific attributes, and their aggregate is what we call "the world." This evolution takes place in various stages, and its first stage, the stage of inactive *prakṛti* becoming active, is called *mahat-tattva*. And then appear I-sense (*ahaṁkāra*), mental faculties (*antaḥkaraṇa*s) and the like, ending up with the five gross physical elements — space, air, fire, water, earth. *Mahat* thus being the point from where the actual evolution begins according to the Sāṁkhyans, and as we borrow their terminology for the sake of convenience, *Brahman*, in the capacity of being the original source of all emanations, is termed here *mahat*, though not strictly in a Sāṁkhyan sense. Hence My refering to it as *brahma-mahat*, instead of just *mahat*.

The role of the fertilizing father is also played by Me in a philosophical sense. This fertilization is not the biological one that operates purely within *prakṛti* alone. The present fertilization is the one that effects birth of every being with an impregnated element of consciousness or *puruṣa.**

This togetherness of *prakṛti* and *puruṣa,* evident everywhere in My Cosmic Form, is what effects the appearance of apparent individual living forms. *Prakṛti*'s three *guṇa*s are always apparent in all such forms, making one individual different form another. Now I shall tell you how these three *guṇa*s affect the existence of such individual forms.

सत्त्वं रजस्तम इति गुणाः प्रकृतिसम्भवाः।
निबध्नन्ति महाबाहो देहे देहिनमव्ययम्॥५॥

sattvaṁ rajas tama iti guṇāḥ prakṛti-saṁbhavāḥ ।
nibadhnanti mahā-bāho dehe dehinaṁ avyayam ॥5॥

Sattva, rajas and *tamas* are the three *guṇa*s born of *prakṛti,* and all of them alike, O Arjuna, bind the immortal living Reality to the (mortal) body.

Arjuna, *prakṛti* (Nature), that which is causal to everything changeful, according to the Sāṁkhya school, has three *guṇa*s or modalities inherent in it, and these, from within, urge *prakṛti* to evolve. Here we adopt these terms in a sense adapted to the basic stand of Vedānta for the sake of ease, in explaining how the inner nature of one man is different from another. *Guṇa*s literally mean qualities, but as a philosophical term, it signifies all the potentials that urge the self-unfolding Reality (*prakṛti*) to evolve into an endless variety of appearances, mental as well as physical. These *guṇa*s are three — *sattva, rajas, tamas* — and, becoming blended in various ways, they effect all the varieties of apparent nature. The three *guṇa*s have one thing in common: all three render the one all-underlying unconditioned Reality as conditioned and bound to the ever-changing apparent forms. The one Reality is termed here *dehin,* rendered as "the immortal living Reality," and the apparent forms,

---

* The words *nadam tiraṇṭu* (growing with consciousness blended) in the passage "Semen mixed with blood (ovum) and growing with consciousness blended, it was that I lay within (the womb)." of Narayana Guru in his *Piṇḍa-nandī* (Pre-natal Gratitude), sound very similar to the fertilization understood here.

deha. The implications of these two terms were made sufficiently clear as early as in Chapter II. *Dehi,* like gold in ornaments, is the Substance that underlies all that appear to be (*deha*s). All the appearances are *deha*s assumed by the *dehin,* as are all ornament forms assumed by the one ever existing gold-substance. *Deha,* meaning body, was called *śarīra* in the last chapter where it was equated to *kṣetra.* Root-wise, the word *deha* means "that which grows"; and *śarīra,* "that which perishes," both signifying the same. The *deha* of the present context is to be understood in the broad sense of *śarīra* defined in Verses 5 and 6 of the last chapter.

Pertaining to the apparent aspect of existence, the three *guṇa*s, while causing all mutations in nature, keep the unchanging Reality always out of sight. This veiling effect of the *guṇa*s makes each and every individual identify himself with his external form and individuating qualities. The effects of the three *guṇa*s make him think, "I am so and so," "I am of such and such peculiarities." All the characteristics that differentiate one person from another, in other words, are effectuated by the three *guṇa*s, and thus pertain to *prakṛti* or body, rather than to the essential content of *dehin.* The latter always remains unseen. Perceiving it is possible only in its form conditioned by and bound to *deha* or *śarīra.* Individuals, oblivious of being *dehin* and identifying themselves with *deha,* is but natural. *Deha* or *śarīra* being perishable, its perishing is thus wrongly taken as one's own perishing even when the *dehin,* the Reality that underlies oneself, remains imperishable.

The conditioning and bondage effected by each of the three *guṇa*s is different. I shall now show you how they differ:

तत्र सत्त्वं निर्मलत्वात्प्रकाशकमनामयम् ।
सुखसङ्गेन बध्नाति ज्ञानसङ्गेन चानघ ॥६॥

tatra sattvaṁ nirmalatvāt prakāśakam anāmayam ।
sukha-saṅgena badhnāti jñāna-saṅgena cānagha ॥6॥

Of these, *sattva,* being blemishless, is luminous and marked by the absence of unhappiness. It makes one bound to the desire for happiness and to the desire for wisdom, O sinless one (Arjuna).

Arjuna, now we go to the details of the three *guṇa*s. Even then you should not lose sight of the fact that the *guṇa*s and *prakṛti* have their being only as a part of My Cosmic Form. Each individual existing as an individual, each having his own personal characteristics, each remaining bound to *deha* in a different way, are all but a part of the Cosmic Form of Mine.

Purity and blemishlessness, related to mind, body or even inert matter, are the distinguishing marks of *sattva-guṇa.* Its predominance in humans makes life less afflicted, and makes them face calmly all events others may consider miserable, with the awareness that these are but natural in the over-all flow of life. Since all these qualities are commendable, one may think of being endowed with *sattva-guṇa* is the best, but this is a delusion. In those of *sattva-guṇa* will be strong the desire for happiness as well as the longing for acquiring more and more knowledge. Desire, even if for something noble, always is accompanied by attachment resulting in bondage. Those of *sattva-guṇa* are thus not free of bondage.

Now let us see how the *rajo-guṇa* binds us:

रजो रागात्मकं विद्धि तृष्णासङ्गसमुद्भवम् ।
तन्निबध्नाति कौन्तेय कर्मसङ्गेन देहिनम् ॥७॥

rajo rāgātmakaṁ viddhi tṛṣṇā-saṅga-samudbhavam ।
lun nibudhnāti kaunteya karma-sangena dehinam ॥7॥

Rajas (*rajo-guṇa*), emotion in essence, is to be understood as producing attachment and thirst in us. It, O Arjuna, binds the immortal living Reality to longing for action (*karma-saṅga*).

Arjuna, everywhere in My Cosmic Form, as you know, *karma*s take place constantly, and because of this, phases of nature ceaselessly change. All those activities are the effects of *rajo-guṇa* inherent in *prakṛti.* The emanation of individual entities in nature is also an outcome of this ceaseless *karma,* and those entities too, as a part of *prakṛti*'s unfoldment, have inherent in them, the same *rajo-guṇa.* Those individuals, who have this *guṇa* predominant in them, feel the urge to be intentionally active and their actions are always motivated by some expected good result. The attachment that mind develops towards such desirous results is called *rāga,* rendered here as "emotion" and thus *rajo-guṇa* and *rāga* always go together. The thirst for enjoying more good results of actions, and therefore to be engaged in more beneficial actions, never ceases in those in whom *rajo-guṇa* is dominant. They will not be willing to give up the already attained good results of actions. This state of mind is known as *saṅga,* translated here as "attachment." The increase of *rajo-guṇa* strengthens *rāga* and *tṛṣṇā* (thirst for pleasure), and conversely, the increase of *rāga* and *tṛṣṇā* strengthens *rajo-guṇa.* Therefore, those who feel the presence of too much of *rajo-guṇa* in themselves can well practise restraining *rāga* and *tṛṣṇā* as a self-imposed discipline. The *rajo-guṇa*, being such, in general results in attachment towards actions (*karma-saṅga*) whose apparent sign is the sense, "This is my *karma;* its fruit is also mine." It is from this *karma-saṅga* that arise the notions of sin and merit. We may, even being unwilling to do wrong, still feel the strong urge to do those very things, and this is caused by desire (*kāma*) and aversion (*krodha*) arising again out of the *rajo-guṇa* in us (as stated earlier in Verse III.37). Therefore, those who are bent on freeing themselves from all sins, have to treat the *rajo-guṇa* in them as a formidable enemy.

Now, let us see how the *tamo-guṇa* in us makes us bound:

तमस्त्वज्ञानजं विद्धि मोहनं सर्वदेहिनाम्।
प्रमादालस्यनिद्राभिस्तन्निबध्नाति भारत ॥८॥

tamas tv ajñānajaṁ viddhi mohanaṁ sarva-dehinām ।
pramādālasya-nidrābhis tan nibadhnāti bhārata ॥8॥

Tamas (*tamo-guṇa*), do understand, is begotten of ignorance (*ajñāna*) and begets ignorance. It causes delusion in everyone embodied. And it binds one to heedlessness in actions, indolence and sleepiness.

Arjuna, *tamas* literally means darkness, the absence of light. Ignorance too, likewise, is the absence of wisdom. *Tamas,* in other words, is seen wherever there is ignorance. The brightest phenomenon that emerges in My Cosmic Form, as a specific evolute of *prakṛti,* is the animating principle, often referred to as soul, in living beings. The *sattva guṇa* inherent in My *prakṛti* is its source. The *tamo-guṇa* in the very same *prakṛti* causes the emanation of all that is inert, like minerals. Inertia is what marks the presence of *tamo-guṇa.* This inertia may infect even the otherwise bright animating principle in beings, and those who are infected thus are incapable of perceiving Reality clearly, and thus remain ignorant. They perceive the embodied as many, as each *deha* having a separate *dehin,* instead of perceiving the immortal Reality living in all as one. Such *dehin*s, unable to discriminate the Real from the unreal, are in a deluded state. Once released from this delusion, individuals realize the oneness of Reality, and then the notion that *dehin*s are many also vanishes. Those who are subject to this ignorant notion of multiplicity of *dehin*s, would naturally be heedless in their actions (*pramāda*) along with being idle (*ālasya*) and sleepy (*nidrā*). *Pramāda* is the state of being unable to behave as situations demand. It means also misunderstanding a context and behaving accordingly. Not doing what is to be done, and doing what is not to be done also come under *pramāda.* A natural liking to be idle is *ālasya,* and appearing to be sleepy always or a tendency to sleep more than normal, is what *nidrā* signifies here. When these qualities are predominant in a person, it may be taken as a sign of his being tāmasic in nature. That they remain completely unaware of the fact that *tamas* is predominant in them, is what is peculiar with such persons, and for this reason correcting them is practically impossible.

Individuals with one *guṇa* dominating, say *sattva-guṇa,* could at times be seen under the spell of other *guṇa*s. For example, *tamas* is in complete control when one sleeps, whereas when one thinks and formulates new ideas, *sattva-guṇa* has the upper hand. In short, disentangling the ramifications of the three *guṇa*s in personal life as well as in the life of the cosmos is quite impossible.

Now let us summarize how the three *guṇa*s keep us in bondage:

सत्त्वं सुखे सञ्जयति रजः कर्मणि भारत ।
ज्ञानमावृत्य तु तमः प्रमादे सञ्जयत्युत ॥९॥

sattvaṁ sukhe sañjayati rajaḥ karmaṇi bhārata ।
jñānam āvṛtya tu tamaḥ pramāde sañjayaty uta ॥9॥

Sattva enslaves one to happiness, *rajas* to actions, O Bhārata, and *tamas* on the other hand, by shrouding wisdom, confines one to heedlessness in actions.

Arjuna, though the three *guṇa*s are equally bondage-causing, no *guṇa* exists anywhere, in anyone, in its pure state. How is it I shall clarify:

रजस्तमश्चाभिभूय सत्त्वं भवति भारत ।
रजः सत्त्वं तमश्चैव तमः सत्त्वं रजस्तथा ॥१०॥

rajas tamaś cābhibhūya sattvaṁ bhavati bhārata ।
rajaḥ sattvaṁ tamaś caiva tamaḥ sattvaṁ rajas tathā ॥10॥

O Bhārata, *sattva* at times becomes dominant over *rajas* and *tamas*. *Rajas*, likewise, at times becomes dominant over *sattva* and *tamas*. *Tamas* similarly at times dominates *sattva* and *rajas*.

Arjuna, the three *guṇa*s, in their infinitely varying blends, are operative everywhere in My Cosmic Form, their ratio undergoing constant change even in Its minutest parts. The *sattva-guṇa* in its cosmic aspect was symbolically seen as concretized in the form of Viṣṇu. Likewise, the concretized symbol of *rajo-guṇa* was called Brahmā and that of *tamo-guṇa*, Śiva. Though the embodiment of *sattva-guṇa*, Viṣṇu could be seen engaged in activities like fighting which is more befitting one with *rajo-guṇa*. Many are such stories about Brahmā and Śiva as well. The way the three *guṇa*s are operative is complex.

Each of the individual entities that emerge and merge back in My Cosmic Form also has inherent in it the three *guṇa*s in a constantly changing state. Though the blend of the three *guṇa*s is present in every individual, *sattva-guṇa* may gain a leading role in some, and they by convention are distinguished as *sāttvikas*. Similarly, those with *rajo-guṇa* leading are called *rājasic* and those with *tamo-guṇa* leading, *tāmasic.*

Now I shall point out to you what are the apparent distinguishing marks seen in those with the three *guṇas* dominant:

सर्वद्वारेषु देहेऽस्मिन्प्रकाश उपजायते।
ज्ञानं यदा तदा विद्याद्विवृद्धं सत्त्वमित्युत ॥११॥

sarva-dvāreṣu dehe 'smin prakāśa upajāyate ।
jñānaṁ yadā tadā vidyād vivṛddhaṁ sattvam ity uta ॥11॥

Consciousness manifesting luminously through all the sense-organs, do understand as marking the dominance of *sattva-guṇa.*

Arjuna, *sattva-guṇa,* as we know, is luminous in nature, its luminosity being nothing but that of the consciousness (*cit*) that exists as the Substance (*sat*) filling the being of everything. Yet its finding expression as knowledge and thought, as a part of the unfoldment of *prakṛti,* is seen only in living beings, especially in human beings. This manifestation of consciousness occurs with the sense-organs and mind as instruments. The clarity of sense perception and mental perception of an individual could well be considered the criterion for the predominance of *sattva-guṇa* in a human.

लोभः प्रवृत्तिरारम्भः कर्मणामशमः स्पृहा।
रजस्येतानि जायन्ते विवृद्धे भरतर्षभ ॥१२॥

lobhaḥ pravṛttir ārambhaḥ karmaṇām aśamaḥ spṛhā ।
rajasy etāni jāyante vivṛddhe bharatarṣabha ॥12॥

Avarice, activeness, undertaking new activities, restlessness, desire for enjoyment — these are born of the dominant *rajo-guṇa,* O best of the Bharatas (Arjuna).

Lobha (avarice) is the mental state of not feeling contented with one's gains in life, no matter how lofty they are. *Pravṛtti* (activeness) in this context means the state in which one yearns for and feels satisfied in all the faculties — sense-organs, organs of action, mental faculties — remaining active. *Āraṁbha* means taking initiative for a new venture with a specific end in view.

अप्रकाशो ऽप्रवृत्तिश्च प्रमादो मोह एव च ।
तमस्येतानि जायन्ते विवृद्धे कुरुनन्दन ॥१३ ॥

aprakāśo 'pravṛttiś ca pramādo moha eva ca ।
tamasy etāni jāyante vivṛddhe kuru-nandana ॥13 ॥

Consciousness remaining not luminous, having no bent to take any initiative, heedless in action, delusion — these are born of the dominant *tamas,* O Arjuna.

Arjuna, the three *guṇa*s, thus, becoming dominant and weak alternate everywhere in My Cosmic Form, and as a result there is the emergence and merger of all individuated entities.

No one worries about the particular blend of *guṇa*s that resulted in our emergence, but all of us worry about how the blend of *guṇa*s at the time of death decide the hereafter. In some, *sattva* may be dominant at the time of death, in others *rajas* or *tamas.* Whichever the dominant *guṇa,* doubtlessly it makes the *dehin* bound to *deha.* And because of this bondage, one thinks of one's merging back with My Cosmic Form, not as merger but as death. I shall tell you how those who find themselves caught in the whirl of *prakṛti* subject to the three *guṇa*s, think of their own state hereafter:

यदा सत्त्वे प्रवृद्धे तु प्रलयं याति देहभृत् ।
तदोत्तमविदां लोकानमलान्प्रतिपद्यते ॥१४ ॥

yadā sattve pravṛddhe tu pralayaṁ yāti deha-bhṛt ।
tadottama-vidāṁ lokān amalān pratipadyate ॥14 ॥

If *sattva* prevails at the time of dissolution, then the embodied attains the worlds of the knowers of the Highest.

Arjuna, those under the spell of the three *guṇas* are *ajñānins* (ignorant) bound to the *deha,* and consider birth and death as real, and nurture varied ideas regarding the hereafter. What I relate here is one such idea: that those in whom at the time of death, *sattva-guṇa* is dominant reach the pure world of the knowers of the Highest. That death, the hereafter, the world of the knowers of the Highest are all phenomenal appearances having no existence of their own, needs no reiteration. What really exists is Myself alone in My Cosmic Form.

Yet, as pertaining to the changeful apparent aspect of My Cosmic Form, all these are meaningful. The urge for *karma,* as you know, is always active in My Cosmic Form, and it is ceaseless. One *karma* is followed by another, and so on. It is this that results in the surging up of the three *guṇa*s in various blends with the overall effect of the emerging of new forms of appearance and the merging back of old ones, which we call death. What happens in death is merely the merging of individuated forms back into My being. Though it is unpredictable whether this merger happens when one *guṇa* or another is dominant, the urge of *karma* that resulted in the dominance of a particular *guṇa* cannot cease abruptly. It has to continue in the next stage of unfoldment, and this depends on how it is in the present stage. If the merger takes place when *sattva* is predominant, its repurcussions have to be felt in the forms that emerge immediately after. For example, a large wave that breaks forcefully on the sandy sea shore withdraws with almost equal force and this may be seen as the expression of the *karma* inherent in a particular wave. But the forceful receding also has an impact on the breaker that follows. In other words, the *karma* of the first wave decides the nature of the *karma* of the next one, and this goes on endlessly. The same is the case with the emerging and merging back of apparent individuated forms in My Cosmic Form. The merging of a particular entity with a particular dominant *guṇa,* decides the *guṇa* of the next one to emerge.

The defining characteristic of *sattva-guṇa,* as we know, is brightness, the brightness of consciousness or knowledge. If the dissolution of an individual happens when *sattva-guṇa* is dominant, its ramification, the manifestation of love for wisdom, will necessarily be seen in the next form the same Substance assumes. This is the sense in which the statement, "the embodied attains the worlds of the knowers of the Highest" is to be understood. "Worlds" (*lokas*) need not necessarily be taken in the mythological sense, like the earth, heaven and hell. Whatever is perceptible is *loka,* as the word literally means.

रजसि प्रलयं गत्वा कर्मसङ्गिषु जायते ।
तथा प्रलीनस्तमसि मूढयोनिषु जायते ॥१५॥

rajasi pralayaṁ gatvā karma-saṅgiṣu jāyate ।
tathā pralīnas tamasi mūḍha-yoniṣu jāyate ॥15॥

Having merged when *rajo-guṇa* is dominant, one is born among those who are attached to actions. Likewise, having become merged when *tamas* is dominant, one is born among idiots.

Arjuna, the principle seen in the last verse related to those who die when *sattva-guṇa* is dominant, is also true with the other two cases.

After examining the case of those who die when each of the three *guṇa*s has the upper hand, let us now look at the impact of the three *guṇa*s on those who live:

कर्मणः सुकृतस्याहुः सात्त्विकं निर्मलं फलम् ।
रजसस्तु फलं दुःखमज्ञानं तमसः फलम् ॥१६॥

karmaṇaḥ sukṛtasyāhuḥ sāttvikaṁ nirmalaṁ phalam ।
rajasas tu phalaṁ duḥkham ajñānaṁ tamasaḥ phalam ॥16॥

Sāttvika and pure are the fruits, it is said, of actions well done (*sukṛta*). The yield of *rajas* is sufferings, and that of *tamas,* ignorance.

Arjuna, activeness was earlier seen as the distinguishing mark of *rajo-guṇa*. This in no way means that the other two *guṇa*s are inactive; only that it is *rajo-guṇa* that incites one to take initiatives with the notion, "I am the doer of this action; and its fruit also is mine." Spontaneous actions, on the other hand, always take place everywhere in nature, including in those with *sattva-guṇa* predominant. All such actions are to be treated as *sukṛta*s (actions well done) though the word *sukṛta,* in the Vedic context, is taken to mean "meritorious actions." Philosophically, all actions that take place on their own (*svayam-kṛta*) as a part of the onward flow of *prakṛti,* is *sukṛta.*

Sattva is bright and it sheds its light on activities bringing about a proper channelization, with the result that these actions become *sukṛta* in the true sense. *Sukṛta*s alone are performed by one in whom *sattva-guṇa* prevails. On the other hand, by doing good by adhereing to ethical conventions, following scriptural instructions or following the directions of knowledgeable persons, it is possible to improve the *sattva-guṇa* already persent.

Those in whom *rajo-guṇa* dominates prefer always to be engaged in activities, and each such action is motivated by some desired benefit. This goal need not necessarily be always attained, for ultimately the way actions develop and the results they yield, depends less on the individual's intent and more on the flow of *prakṛti*'s unfoldment. This latter being unpredictable, engaging in benefit-motivated actions often leads to disappointment and grief. Thus, in general, *rajo-guṇa* usually causes suffering.

The consequence of the predominance of *tamas* is the ignorance that most of us are subject to. Inertia and darkness, as we know, are the defining qualities of *tamas.* This darkness puts a veil, so to say, on what is Real in oneself making It imperceptible. And with the help of *rajas, tamas* projects a variety of apparent forms over what is Real. This causes one to accept those forms as real. This basically is the cause of all fears in life. A man trapped in darkness may become terrified by forms that he imagines to be a ghost, without realizing that the ghost is a mental projection made by his own mind. Similarly, all fears are caused by one's own ignorance, the effect of *tamas.*

We have examined how the three *guṇas* affect the realm of activities. How the same *guṇas* act on the realm of knowing has also to be examined.

सत्त्वात्सञ्जायते ज्ञानं रजसो लोभ एव च।
प्रमादमोहौ तमसो भवतो ऽज्ञानमेव च ॥१७॥

sattvāt sañjāyate jñānaṁ rajaso lobha eva ca ।
pramāda-mohau tamaso bhavato 'jñānam eva ca ॥17॥

From *sattva* arises wisdom, and from *rajas*, greed. Both heedlessness and delusion, as also ignorance, arise from *tamas*.

How those who are dominated by the three *guṇas*, can be differentiated value-wise also, I shall tell you:

ऊर्ध्वं गच्छन्ति सत्त्वस्था मध्ये तिष्ठन्ति राजसाः।
जघन्यगुणवृत्तिस्था अधो गच्छन्ति तामसाः ॥१८॥

ūrdhvaṁ gacchanti sattvasthā madhye tiṣṭhanti rājasāḥ ।
jaghanya-guṇa-vṛttisthā adho gacchanti tāmasāḥ ॥18॥

Those who are established in *sattva* go upwards, and those of *rajas* remain in the mid-region. Steeped in the lowest of all qualities and functions, those of *tamas* go downwards.

Arjuna, one's value notion is decided by what one considers highly aspirable in life. Such notions can be brought serially into a vertical order. Then the value notion of those of *sattva-guṇa* is to be located at the highest point, and those of *tamo-guṇa* at the lowest. What is considered the best attainable in life by those of *rajo-guṇa* can be seen somewhere in the mid-region. Though seen at the highest point of the vertical series, those of *sattva-guṇa* are not yet fully liberated, because they are still attached to desire for happiness and for acquiring more knowledge. It is only that they, from among those subject to the whirling action of *prakṛti,* are the best. A *sāttvika* is no *yogī* yet. Now I shall tell you how a *yogī* perceives himself as related to the three *guṇa*s of *prakṛti:*

नान्यं गुणेभ्यः कर्तारं यदा द्रष्टानुपश्यति।
गुणेभ्यश्च परं वेत्ति मद्भावं सो ऽधिगच्छति ॥१९॥

nānyaṁ guṇebhyaḥ kartāraṁ yadā draṣṭānupaśyati ।
guṇebhyaś ca paraṁ vetti mad-bhāvaṁ so 'dhigacchati ॥19॥

As the seer perceives the (apparent) doer of actions as no other than the *guṇa*s, and himself (the real doer) as transcending the *guṇa*s, he attains the state of being Myself.

Arjuna, that *karma*s have two dimensions we have already noticed: one, seen as a part of *prakṛti,* and two, one *ātmā* or Myself, unfolding Itself creatively. The former are subject to the three *guṇa*s of *prakṛti* where the *dehin,* because of its identity with *deha,* remains oblivious of what it really is. And as a result one thinks, "I, the individual, am the doer of such and such actions." This is true with each of the individuated beings, especially human beings, forming part of My Cosmic Form. Nevertheless, one Reality — *ātmā* — underlies both individual beings and the Cosmic Form. Though it is Its creative urge that appears as *prakṛti;* It has no sense of being the doer of any action — It has no *kartṛtva.* It transcends all the three *guṇa*s of *prakṛti.* Yet no Cosmic Form exists apart form It; no *prakṛti* exists apart from It; no individual being exists apart from It.

Even when engaged in normal activities unavoidable in life, one has to be aware: These *karma*s are the handiwork of the three *guṇa*s; my feeling that I am their doer is because of my identity with *deha;* what is Real in me is beyond the ken of the three *guṇa*s. It is the universal facet of that Reality, identifying Itself with *deha,* that appears as the cosmos; and it is the particular facet of the very same Reality, become conditioned by *deha,* that appears as individual beings. The cosmos has no existence apart from that one Reality, nor do I have existence apart from that one Reality. One who has attained this certainty, even when engaged in normal activities, experiences oneness with Me, the Self or *ātmā*. This identity, in effect, is to attain Me. Such are they who are fully liberated while living. I shall clarify how is it:

गुणानेतानतीत्य त्रीन्देही देहसमुद्भवान्।
जन्ममृत्युजरादुःखैर्विमुक्तो ऽमृतमश्नुते ॥२०॥

guṇān etān atītya trīn dehī deha sam udbhavān ।
janma-mṛtyu-jarā-duḥkhair vimukto 'mṛtam aśnute ॥20॥

Transcending these three *guṇa*s that give rise to *deha*, the *dehin*, having become liberated from the sufferings of birth, death and old age, relishes the happiness of being immortal.

Arjuna, as it has become sufficiently clear to you now, My Cosmic Form has *prakṛti* inherent in it, and it is by virtue of its *guṇa*s that countless individuated beings, endlessly various in terms of quality, emerge in that Form. Such individuated appearances are what we call *deha* or body, literally that which grows. Innumerable are such *deha*s that emerge and merge in My Cosmic Form. Yet the Substance in all of them is one alone, and It is birthless and deathless.

Instead of realizing or becoming aware of their identity with the Substance or Me, humans usually identify with the *guṇa*-created *deha*s, and as a result, each thinks, "My being is constituted of this individual apparent form or *deha*." The *deha* is to be understood in the sense of *śarīra* or *kṣetra* detailed in Verses 5 and 6 of the last chapter. This *deha*-identity results in treating the emerging of *deha* as the birth of oneself, and its merger as the death of oneself. A *deha*, preparatory to its merger, naturally declines and decays, which state is counted as old age, always painful. All these are instrumental to suffering in one way or another, and for this reason even life as a whole happens to be treated as an ocean of sufferings. But there are people, though rare, who see the one birthless and deathless *ātmā* or Me as the Substance that underlies their being, the being of other individuals, and the being of the cosmos as a whole. They constantly experience oneness with Me. Since I am immortal, those who see themselves in Me also experience immortality.

At first sight, this final attainment may seem to have two apparent aspects: the negative side of getting rid of sufferings, and the positive side of attaining immortality. *Deha* is the root cause of all suffering, and getting rid of that identity itself, in effect, is the attainment of immortality, and therefore, the two aspects are really not two at all, but rather the dialectical counterparts of the unitive situation of life's fulfilment.

अर्जुन उवाच —

कैर्लिङ्गैस्त्रीन्गुणानेतानतीतो भवति प्रभो ।
किमाचारः कथं चैतांस्त्रीन्गुणानतिवर्तते ॥२१॥

Arjuna uvāca —

kair liṅgais trīn guṇān etān atīto bhavati prabho ।
kim ācāraḥ kathaṁ caitāṁs trīn guṇān ativartate ॥21॥

Arjuna said —

O Lord, what are the distinguishing marks of the one who has transcended the three *guṇas*? How does he conduct himself? And how can one transcend these three *guṇas*?

श्री भगवानुवाच —

प्रकाशं च प्रवृत्तिं च मोहमेव च पाण्डव ।
न द्वेष्टि सम्प्रवृत्तानि न निवृत्तानि काङ्क्षति ॥२२॥

śrī bhagavān uvāca —

prakāśaṁ ca pravṛttiṁ ca moham eva ca pāṇḍava ।
na dveṣṭi saṁpravṛttāni na nivṛttāni kāṅkṣati ॥22॥

Śrī Kṛṣṇa said —

O Arjuna, neither the brightness (of *sattva-guṇa*), nor the activeness (of *rajo-guṇa*), nor the delusion (of *tamo-guṇa*), when actively present, is despised by him. Nor does he long for these in their absence.

Arjuna, you are now well aware of the differentiating features of the three *guṇa*s. All the three make *dehin* bound to *deha,* only the nature of bondage varies in accordance with their predominance. For this reason, a person aspiring to transcend the three *guṇa*s might despise the dominance of any of them, or even wish to be rid of all the three, but such a move is wrong. *Guṇa*s, as you know, are always present in *prakṛti,* forming part of the apparent aspect of My Cosmic Form. Intending to do away with them virtually means desiring to get rid of My Cosmic Form — an impossibility. Within that Form, the activeness of each *guṇa* in each person is different, and even in a particular person their activeness may vary in different contexts. One or more of them can sometimes become too active and at other times too inactive. Only one who neither despises their active presence nor longs for them in their absence in oneself, is fully competent to transcend them. He perceives My Cosmic Form alone actively existing in their presence as well as absence. How does he treat the active presence of the *guṇa*s?

उदासीनवदासीनो गुणैर्यो न विचाल्यते ।
गुणा वर्तन्त इत्येव यो ऽवतिष्ठति नेङ्गते ॥२३ ॥

udāsīnavad āsīno guṇair yo na vicālyate ।
guṇā vartanta ity eva yo 'vatiṣṭhati neṅgate ॥23 ॥

He who transcends the three *guṇa*s remains unperturbed by them, as though indifferent. Thinking that the *guṇa*s are active in their own way, he keeps himself apart, unmoved.

Arjuna, *udāsīna* (the indifferent) is one who remains in a neutral state with no likes and dislikes, treating both pleasure and pain equally. Changeful events happening constantly, because of the presence of the three *guṇa*s, is normal with life; some may be felt to be pleasurable, others as painful. Undisturbed by the fickleness of *guṇa*s, the *udāsīna,* on perceiving their erratic nature, thinks, "How unpredictable and mysterious is the way the three *guṇa*s work in me!" Realizing that such fickleness is but natural with the cosmic system (My Cosmic Form) and is an essential part of it, he remains always identified with the one Reality that underlies the Cosmic Form.

Let us now see how this neutrality of the *udāsīna* finds expression in life:

समदुःखसुखः स्वस्थः समलोष्टाश्मकाञ्चनः ।
तुल्यप्रियाप्रियो धीरस्तुल्यनिन्दात्मसंस्तुतिः ॥२४ ॥
मानापमानयोस्तुल्यस्तुल्यो मित्रारिपक्षयोः ।
सर्वारम्भपरित्यागी गुणातीतः स उच्यते ॥२५ ॥

sama-duḥkha-sukhaḥ svasthaḥ sama-loṣṭāśma kāñcanaḥ ।
tulya-prīyāpriyo dhīras tulya-nindātma-saṁstutiḥ ॥24 ॥

mānāpamānayos tulyas tulyo mitrāri-pakṣayoḥ ।
sarvārambha-parityāgī guṇātītaḥ sa ucyate ॥25 ॥

One who values pain and pleasure as equals, who finds himself well stabilized in what is real in himself, who considers a lump of clay, a piece of stone and a piece of gold alike, who is equal towards the loving and the hateful, who is firm in his understanding and behaviour, who regards equally both being blamed and praised,

Who treats both honour and disgrace equally, who views friends and foes alike, who gives up all sorts of initiatives for actions — he is to be termed a *guṇātīta* (one who has transcended the three *guṇas*).

Arjuna, the *guṇātīta*'s state described here and the *brāhmī-sthiti* depicted earlier at the end of Chapter II are one. Emphasis there was on the theoretical understanding, and here the state is put in experiential terms of the individual's inseparable oneness with My Cosmic Form.

The awareness that all pairs of opposites mentioned here are normal with *prakṛti* as it assumes the form of the Cosmic Body, brings about an attitude of indifference towards their opposing nature. One with this awareness locates one's existence, not in the ever changing pleasurable or painful situations that arise in *prakṛti* or My Cosmic Body, but in the one all-underlying Reality, in Me. That is to say, he finds stability in the Self, in himself; he becomes a *svastha*, the Sanskrit term which means also "healthy state of existence." This state would be normal with a *guṇātīta*.

He sees a lump of clay, a gem-stone or a piece of gold as of equal value, not in terms of their market value, but taking into account their place in life-situations.

Similar is the *guṇātīta*'s attitude towards the loveable and the hateful. Those, who are subject to the three *guṇa*s feel dejected when someone betrays them, and elated on gaining praise. But a *guṇātīta* finds stability in what is Real in himself, not in the praise or rebuke of others. In friends and foes he sees only the Self manifesting itself variously.

He perceives the eternal flow of *karma*s taking place everywhere, even in himself. There is no need of any initiative in nature for a particular event to take place. This awareness keeps the *guṇātīta* away from taking initiative for any action with a particular motive; he simply does what the situation warrants as a part of the flow of nature.

Those, in whom such a behaviour pattern is found well stabilized naturally, can certainly be counted as *guṇātīta*s.

I shall now tell you what will be their inner disposition even when engaged in the spontaneous activities of the three *guṇa*s:

मां च यो ऽव्यभिचारेण भक्तियोगेन सेवते ।
स गुणान्समतीत्यैतान्ब्रह्मभूयाय कल्पते ॥२६ ॥

māṁ ca yo 'vyabhicāreṇa bhakti-yogena sevate ।
sa guṇān samatītyaitān brahma-bhūyāya kalpate ॥26 ॥

And he serves Me alone with the *yoga* of *bhakti*, with no swerving from My true path. He, transcending the *guṇa*s properly, becomes fit to become *Brahman*.

Arjuna, it should now be clear to you that only those who consider attaining the one Supreme Reality or Me as the ultimate goal of life, naturally transcend the three *guṇa*s. Attaining Me, in this context, means, perceiving oneself as an inseparable part of My Cosmic Form. This inseparability is what we saw as *bhakti* in Chapter XII and experiencing that oneness actually is to be called *bhakti-yoga.* Those of this experience perceive *Brahman* alone manifesting itself even in the form of *guṇa*s and their activeness, and this is how they become competent to attain *Brahman.*

The way of life following the path of *Brahman,* by seeing *Brahman* alone as existing and manifesting as everything, is known as *brahma-carya.* Any kind of swerving from that path is *vyabhicāra,* which also is the word for prostitution. No *vyabhicāra* is probable in the life of those who live as *bhakti-yogī*s.

The usage "to attain *Brahman*" might create the wrong impression that *Brahman* is something "other" to be attained, but it is not so. What is Real in me, is neither something I can attain, nor something I can theorize about. Such an ignorant notion may result in thinking of the *bhakti* and *bhakti-yoga* I speak of here, simply as following certain devotional disciplines and their promised results. Hence, I conclude this chapter by making it clear who or what "I" really am, or what the Real *ātman* or Self is. Apart from the Self there exists no *Brahman,* no Cosmic Form, no *prakṛti,* no *guṇa*s, none of their activities and the resultant painful and pleasurable experiences.

ब्रह्मणो हि प्रतिष्ठाहममृतस्याव्ययस्य च ।
शाश्वतस्य च धर्मस्य सुखस्यैकान्तिकस्य च ॥२७॥

brahmaṇo hi pratiṣṭhā 'ham amṛtasyāvyayasya ca ।
śāśvatasya ca dharmasya sukhasyaikāntikasya ca ॥27॥

For "I" (*ātmā,* the Self) is the stable abode of the immortal and unexpended *Brahman,* as also of the eternal *dharma* and of the ultimate Happiness of attaining the one goal.

Arjuna, *Brahman* is always said to be immortal (*amṛta*) and unexpended (*avyaya*) and many such attributes related to *Brahman* were referred to earlier. These references may have created the ideas that *Brahman* is such and such, but really none can say anything about *Brahman.* It is ineffable. Whatever is said about It creates only a conditioned knowledge of It, whereas *Brahman* is the one unconditioned Reality, the one unconditioned Consciousness (*cit*) in which are formulated countless conditioned ideas, images, emotions and the like. *Brahman* is the one unconditioned abode in which all the conditioned appearances have their being. That abode is the real *ātmā* or "I".

We have already examined what *dharma* signifies. It is to be understood here as related to My Cosmic Form. In that Form nothing is chaotic; it has an overall functional system of its own, which is inconceivable to the human mind, and *prakṛti* and its three *guṇa*s are part of it. That functional order is what *dharma,* literally "that which supports," stands for here. That *dharma* is eternal, and its eternal abode, Myself.

I am the eternal abode of ultimate Happiness as well, termed here *sukham aikāntikam,* meaning "the happiness one attains by living a life aimed at one goal only." This one goal is Myself. It is the "I" in you, in me, in everyone, and this "I" is the Self or *ātmā,* the one immortal Reality. It is with all this in mind that I told you at the very beginning of this instruction, "You have never been non-existent, I have never been non-existent, all these great warriors have never been non-existent, and none will become non-existent either" (II.12). Seeing oneself as this *ātmā* or "I" in essence, and living thus is the Supreme Happiness that can be actualized in life. All this is implied in my words, "abode of the ultimate Happiness of attaining the one goal" (*sukhasya ekāntikasya*).

Arjuna, let us now have an overall review of the present chapter:

Without Me no Cosmic Form (cosmos) can exist, and without assuming the form of the cosmos I can never exist either. You have seen as early as in Verse II.16 that the unreal (*asat*) can not assume appearance (*bhāva*) and that without appearing as the world (*bhāva*), Reality cannot exist either.

The activity of *sat* (Reality) assuming the apparent form of the world is what we call *prakṛti,* three *guṇa*s in essence. This *prakṛti* existing in My Cosmic Form provides for the emergence of each and every individual entity. This emergence, if considered as a process of child-birth, should have a father and a mother, and I am both. The three *guṇa*s of *prakṛti* have their own specifiable ramifications, all resulting in one's bondage in one way or another. Such apparent effects of the three *guṇa*s in individual beings will have their repurcussions in the Cosmic Body even after the merger of the concerned individuals, influencing the nature of the individual forms yet to emerge. This process continues endlessly.

What an individual, intending to become liberated, should do is to become aware of the particular way the three *guṇa*s of *prakṛti* are active in himself, and live accordingly, while realizing that he himself is the Reality or *ātmā* that underlies all the *guṇa*s and is beyond them. The kind of distinguishing marks present in such *guṇātīta*s, was also detailed. Whatever the events occurring in life, the *yogī* finds identity with the one Reality that underlies all events, and constantly experiences the blissfulness of self-absorption in *Brahman.*

Arjuna, two basic categories, *kṣetra* and *kṣetrajña,* also called *prakṛti* and *puruṣa,* were seen in Chapter XIII as constituting the Cosmic Form. The present chapter went into the details of the *prakṛti* aspect and examined how the presence of the three *guṇa*s of *prakṛti* can be discerned in one's own being as well as in the being of the cosmos, and how one can transcend the three *guṇa*s and liberate oneself. What is to be examined next is the *puruṣa* aspect, which we shall do in the next chapter, *Puruṣottama-Yoga.*

Thus ends Chapter Fourteen entitled Guṇatraya-Vibhāga-Yoga of the Bhagavad-Gītā, the essence of the Upaniṣads, that embodies the yoga-śāstra of brahma-vidyā in the form of a dialogue between Śrī Kṛṣṇa and Arjuna.

XV

Puruṣottama-Yoga

— The Yoga of the Supreme Person —

Vyāsa:

Janmejaya, each one of us is an inseparable part of the cosmos, of the Cosmic Form of Kṛṣṇa. At the same time, every individual is endowed with certain qualities and traits different from others. A person finds happiness in life only when engaged in activities befitting his personal qualities and traits, while also seeing himself as one with the whole.

The first step towards the actualization of this goal is finding oneness with the whole — oneness with the Cosmic Form of Kṛṣṇa. One who constantly keeps to this perception is the *bhakta* portrayed in Chapter XII.

The next step consists of making a self-examination in order to discern one's own personal traits in all its details, again as forming a part of the Cosmic Form. As a beginning of this process was seen in Chapter XIII, how to differentiate the two basic categories, *kṣetra* and *kṣetrajña,* that constitute the Cosmic Form, and individual beings. The two, in view of making it easier to detail, were then equated to the Sāṁkhyan concepts of *prakṛti* and *puruṣa.* An analysis of *prakṛti,* in terms of its three *guṇa*s, was then done in Chapter XIV. Every specific apparent form that emerges in the Cosmic Form is an effect of the activeness of these *guṇa*s, and is called a *vikṛti.* All the *vikṛtis,* no matter how various they are, have the one Reality underlying them, and It transcends the three *guṇa*s. Therefore, one, even while being a *vikṛti* has to remain fully aware of being one with the Reality or *ātmā,* the *guṇātīta,* and thus of himself as being *guṇātīta.* This is where Chapter XIV ended.

The *puruṣa* aspect in us is what we have to examine next. The *prakṛti* we analysed, as we know, is not merely the one understood by Sāṁkhyans, but is the one acceptable to the overall stand of Vedānta, as the creative self-unfoldment of *ātmā*. The *puruṣa* we speak of here, likewise, is also more than what the Sāṁkhyans conceive it to be.

The *puruṣa*, as held by the Sāṁkhya system, is the consciousness that witnesses all the evolutions of *prakṛti*, each individual being having a separate *puruṣa*. Considering the *puruṣa* as numerous, as you know, strictly speaking, does not fall in line with Vedāntic perception. Hence, it is used here simply to mean the consciousness aspect of existence.

Knowing is the function of consciousness, and it finds expression mainly in two ways. One is that of knowing each and every entity as distinct, one different from another. This is what was earlier (II.41) referred to as *avyavasāyātmikā buddhi*. The other is that of perceiving all specific forms of knowledge as one consciousness manifesting itself variously, and thus seeing that all knowledge is really one Consciousness (*cit*) in essence. It is this unitive perception that was earlier referred to as *vyavasāyātmikā buddhi*.*

Knowing reality as many also has two phases. First, the constantly changing flow of experiences everyone has. Purely personal, it is neither felt nor appreciated by another. Then there is the form in which the inner experiences find expression, its most popular medium being language. Such expressions make others guess what the inner experience of its originator was, though such guesses need not always be correct. Such expressed forms of knowledge constitute what we count as *śāstras* (sciences) and Vedas, both words meaning "that which helps one comprehend." All the various forms in which human knowledge has found expression could, in this sense, be treated as Vedas, the Sanskrit word for scriptures. Vedas, in the broadest sense, therefore, can be well treated as representing all kinds of expressed form of human knowledge.

---

* Narayana Guru, in modern times, called the former the *anya* (the other) aspect of the function of consciousness and the latter the *sama* (the same) aspect (see *Ātmopadeśa Śatakam*, Verses 36 to 42).

All such forms must necessarily have a consciousness underlying them, and it has to be unmanifest. All the experiences every individual has are nothing but the one unmanifest become manifest ceaselessly in various ways. This perception is what one can aim at in life, and it alone enables one to see himself in, and to live as, one with the Cosmic Form. Such is the clarity the present chapter leads one to. The chapter, therefore, begins with the portrayal of a giant fig tree symbolizing the endlessly branching human quest for knowledge.

श्री भगवानुवाच —

ऊर्ध्वमूलमधःशाखमश्वत्थं प्राहुरव्ययम्।
छन्दांसि यस्य पर्णानि यस्तं वेद स वेदवित्॥१॥

śrī bhagavān uvāca —

ūrdhva-mūlam adhaḥ śākham aśvatthaṁ prāhur avyayam ।
chandāṁsi yasya parṇāni yas taṁ veda sa veda vit ॥1॥

Śrī Kṛṣṇa said —

A holy fig tree with roots above and branches below is said to be there. It is unexpended. The Vedic hymns constitute its leaves. One who knows it, is really the *vedavit*.

Arjuna, all of us experience something continuously except when sleeping. Unconsciously enjoying the happiness of sleeping soundly is experienced even in deep sleep. No moment thus is there in our life when we do not experience anything. Where are all these experiences rooted? No one knows. The more we ponder on it, the more it becomes revealed that the root-cause cannot but be something effulgent in essense, something that transcends everything. This transendental causal effulgence can be thought of, if at all conceivable, only as above everything. The root-cause of all specific knowledges thus is conceived as hidden somewhere above everything.

The vast world of knowledges is here represented as a holy fig tree. Trees, we know, have their roots growing downwards and branches growing upwards; but contrary is the way the present tree strikes roots and grows, for its roots, as we have already seen, are above in the realm of the unknown, and its growth downwards creates a constantly widening world of knowledge, ideas and ideals. Scriptures, sciences, art, literature and the like are its main branches, each in its turn branching out endlessly. Its growth continues even now, creating new branches of knowledge and science never thought of before. Each such newly emerging branch of knowledge could be well symbolically termed a Veda, for the word Veda means, "scripture, knowledge and science." One who comprehends so the overall context of knowing alone can be termed a *vedavit*, which, in the religious context, means "one who is well-versed in scriptures," and in the broadest philosophical context, "one who knows what knowledge or science is."

Now let us go into the details of the tree.

अधश्चोर्ध्वं प्रसृतास्तस्य शाखा गुणप्रवृद्धा विषयप्रवालाः ।
अधश्च मूलान्यनुसंततानि कर्मानुबन्धीनि मनुष्यलोके ॥२॥

adhaś cordhvaṁ prasṛtās tasya śākhā guṇa-pravṛddhā viṣaya-pravālāḥ ।
adhaś ca mūlāny anusaṁtatāni karmānubandhīni manuṣya-loke ॥2॥

Downward-and-upward-growing are its branches, all nourished by *guṇas*. Its new buds are objects of knowledge. Its roots grow ramified downward as well, and *karma*s ensue them in the human world.

Arjuna, that the branches of the giant fig tree of the world of knowledge grow downwards, we have just seen; yet they grow upward as well. The realm of countless external objects of worldly interest alone is not what constitutes the field of human enquiry; the subtler realm of the nature and origin of knowledge also forms part of man's field of interest. All scriptures and philosophical studies, in a sense, are outcomes of this latter type of enquiry. All psychological enquiries could also be counted as coming around the periphery of the upward growing branches. Branching out of the growth of knowledge, thus, happens not only downwards to worldly interests, but upwards as well to the realms of higher thinking. To be more precise, some of the downward growing branches turn upwards in search of their own origin.

One assuming the form of many, wherever it be, means *prakṛti* is active. The one unconditioned Consciousness (*cit*) assuming the form of various fields of human interests also is activated by *prakṛti*, its presence being felt in the form of variegated ways in which the three *guṇa*s thrive. This thriving of the *guṇa*s conditions the pure and unconditioned Consciousness (*cit*) resulting in the emerging of new fields of knowledge and human interests, and that is how the world of sciences expands. In this sense it is conceived here, budding of new fields of interest in one universal Consciousness-Substance or *cid-vastu* has always behind it the nourishment provided by the three *guṇa*s (*guṇa-pravṛddhāḥ*).

The root-cause of knowledge, as we know, always remains concealed in the realm of the unknowable. Yet the very same cause is often made an object of enquiry by man, and then it is as if it has assumed objectivity. And many may be the branches that grow out of any such specified field of enquiry. The upward roots of the unknowable could thus be thought of as growing downwards to the realm of the knowables as well. To be short, the world of knowledge is an enormously vast one that extends between two extremely opposite realms of knowability and unknowability.

No conceivable limit is there for the variety of ways in which knowledge can find expression. Yet one thing is common to all of them, particularly related to experiences of humans, our main concern here: every new knowledge gained is followed by an urge to do something, to perform an action or *karma*, physical, verbal or mental. Performing any *karma* causes a new sort of bondage or *karma-bandha*, and freedom from all of them is our ultimate goal. The best way to attain this goal is intuitively perceiving that one pure Consciousness (*cit*) alone is it that manifests itself as all kinds of mental functions, experiences and knowledges. This perception brings about in us a sense of detachment towards the variety of experiences, whether pleasurable or painful. I shall clarify how this can easily be actualized:

न रूपमस्येह तथोपलभ्यते नान्तो न चादिर्न च संप्रतिष्ठा।
अश्वत्थमेनं सुविरूढमूलमसङ्गशस्त्रेण दृढेन छित्त्वा ॥३॥
ततः पदं तत्परिमार्गितव्यं यस्मिन्गता न निवर्तन्ति भूयः।
तमेव चाद्यं पुरुषं प्रपद्ये यतः प्रवृत्तिः प्रसृता पुराणी ॥४॥

na rūpam asyeha tathopalabhyate nānto na cādir na ca saṁ pratiṣṭhā ।
aśvattham enaṁ suvirūḍha-mūlam asaṅga-śastreṇa dṛḍhena chittvā ॥3॥
tataḥ padaṁ tat parimārgitavyaṁ yasmin gatā na nivartanti bhūyaḥ ।
tam eva cādyaṁ puruṣaṁ prapadye yataḥ pravṛttiḥ prasṛtā purāṇī ॥4॥

This fig tree's structural formation is not easy to grasp while being here. Where it ends, where it began and where and how it exists too are not knowable. This firmly rooted tree has to be cut down with the strong and sharp axe of non-attachment.

One can thus proceed to the Final Destination, entering wherein no return is there. It is from there that activities have ever been streaming forth. The search for It should be as, "I take refuge in that primordial *puruṣa* alone."

Arjuna, we are all conscious beings, and are conscious of being so. Yet we do not know what that consciousness is, where its origin is, what its nature and content is, where it ends, where and how does it exist. New ideas and new fields of interest bud in it ceaselessly, both in the up-growing roots and down-growing branches. We remaining aware of such new buddings also continues. All such specific experiences doubtlessly are provided for by an underlying Consciousness-Substance (*cid-vastu*) we are not at all aware of. But once this *cid-vastu* becomes revealed, it also becomes uncovered that the countless mental events and states that we experience are all nothing but tiny sparks that emerge from the ever burning bonfire of *cid-vastu.* Put in strict Vedāntic terms, all experiences are nothing but one unconditioned Consciousness-Substance (*cid-vastu*) become conditioned and appearing variously. Infinite is that *cid-vastu,* but all its conditioned manifestations are finite.

Realizing the one unconditioned Consciousness alone as *sat* and seeing It alone in all that appears to be, is the *vyavasāyātmikā buddhi,* and remaining involved and interested in all that appears to be and the multiplicity of experiences is the *avyavasāyātmikā buddhi.* As we know, that a different *puruṣa* exists in each and every individual entity is an idea repugnant to *vyavasāyātmikā buddhi.* No one becomes a *yogī* unless such a *buddhi* becomes well stabilized as was made sufficiently clear as early as in Chapter II (Verse 44). Keeping ourselves within the frame of reference of the present chapter, it could be said that we have to go beyond the realm of the multiplicity of *puruṣa*s to the realm of perceiving one primeval *puruṣa* alone as causal to the phenomenal appearance of multiplicity of *puruṣa*s. One path alone is there that leads us to this final goal, and it is double-sided. One side is that of cutting down the fig tree or cultivating a sense of non-attachment with a firm mind. How strong and how sharp should be the axe to use was indicated by Verses 62 to 64 of Chapter II. The other side of the path is taking refuge in that one *Puruṣa.* The yogic discipline that leads to the attainment of the final goal, in other words, has two mutually complementary and compensatory sides: one, giving up interest in the many by cultivating a firm sense of non-attachment, and the other, fixing one's interest fully on the One.

Attaining the one Supreme *Puruṣa* results in an experiential conviction that is also two-sided. One, that there is no returning from it; that means nothing else will be acceptable as real, for all that is experienced is seen only as multiple manifestaions of one Reality, pure Consciousness in essence, and there is no other to return to.

The other side of this conviction is that it is from this one *puruṣa* that all activities (*pravṛttis*) or *karmas* emanate ceaselessly. No activity, mental or physical, exists other than as the self-manifestation of the one *Puruṣa* or *cid-vastu.*

The ultimate goal, seen from the point of view of *prakṛti* that we examined in the last chapter, was becoming a *guṇātīta.* Here, on the other hand, from the side of *puruṣa,* the highest attainable goal is seen as consisting of going beyond the multiplicity of *puruṣas* and attaining the one transcendental *Puruṣa.* These two, though stated differently, are not two in essence. It is one goal being represented in two different ways, like the two sides of a single coin. What is intended is the realization of the one non-dual goal with these two statements as aids, by following the *yoga-buddhi* we have already dealt with in detail. I shall now tell you who are competent to attain this goal:

निर्मानमोहा जितसङ्गदोषा अध्यात्मनित्या विनिवृत्तकामाः ।
द्वन्द्वैर्विमुक्ताः सुखदुःखसञ्ज्ञैर्गच्छन्त्यमूढाः पदमव्ययं तत् ॥५॥

nirmāna-mohā jita-saṅga-doṣā adhyātma-nityā vinivṛtta-kāmāḥ ।
dvandvair vimuktāḥ sukha-duḥkha-saṁjñair gacchanty amūḍhāḥ padam avyayaṁ tat ॥5॥

Those who are devoid of self-esteem and delusion, who have won over the blemish of attachments, who are well-stabilized in being the Self by knowing oneself, who withdraw themselves from desirables, who have freed themselves from the duality of pleasure and pain, who are not benighted, they alone attain that decayless state.

Arjuna, as you know, we are presently examining the two mutually complementary and compensatory aspects of finding one's identity with My Cosmic Form. In the vision of one who has attained this goal, he and the Cosmic Reality are not two. He sees this oneness as making life meaningful, and so self-esteem does not find place in his life, and there is no delusion about what is Real. His mind will not become attached to particular things causing the mistaken identity with it. His understanding of himself will always be by identifying with what is Real in him. Such a well-founded understanding of oneself was earlier distinguished as *adhyātma* in Verse VIII.3. Such individuals naturally keep themselves neutral towards dualities such as pleasure and pain, heat and cold, merit and sin and so on. All these personal traits, in the case of those who see themselves as inseparably one with the Cosmic Form of Mine, are spontaneous. Cultivating such traits can also be practised as a spiritual discipline aiming at attaining the said goal.

What *puruṣa* signifies, as we know, is consciousness. The primeval *Puruṣa* therefore has to be the Consciousness causal to all knowledges and mental states. And consciousness obviously is effulgence in essence. The causal Consciousness is thus the effulgence that illuminates all effulgent experiences. To clarify it:

न तद्भासयते सूर्यो न शशाङ्को न पावकः ।
यद्गत्वा न निवर्तन्ते तद्धाम परमं मम ॥६॥

na tad bhāsayate sūryo na śaśāṅko na pāvakaḥ ।
yad gatvā na nivartante tad dhāma paramaṁ mama ॥6॥

That (primeval *Puruṣa*) is not illuminated by the sun, nor by the moon, nor by fire. Those who reach there do not return; that is My Supreme Abode.

Arjuna, the primary function of the sun, as you know, is to illumine all things making them visible at day time. Likewise, the moon at night does the same though in a mellowed manner. In a limited way, fire also does the same. But there has to be a Consciousness, a planning mind, that systematizes the cosmic order in such a way that the sun, the moon, fire and all else, by performing functions natural of them, maintain the cosmic order. And that Consciousness is never illumined by any luminary of the cosmic order. Yet one thing is definite: he who finds himself inseparably one with that Mind or *Puruṣa* does not return to the world of self-esteem, delusion, attachments and desires. And that is My abode; yours as well. Realizing your inseparable oneness with the Cosmic Form, you see yourself as having that *Puruṣa* alone for your supreme abode. So it is with everyone.

Let us now look at the world from the point of view of this supreme perception:

ममैवांशो जीवलोके जीवभूतः सनातनः ।
मनःषष्ठानीन्द्रियाणि प्रकृतिस्थानि कर्षति ॥७॥

mamaivāṁśo jīva-loke jīva-bhūtaḥ sanātanaḥ ।
manaḥ-ṣaṣṭhānīndriyāṇi prakṛti-sthāni karṣati ॥7॥

My own tiny but eternal portions, in the world of living beings, assume the form of individual living entities. Each in its turn attracts to itself sense organs with mind as the sixth, from their abode *prakṛti*.

Arjuna, you and I are all tiny constituent parts of the one Cosmic Form. In terms of consciousness, the one primeval *Puruṣa* functions in the likes of us as our many consciousnesses, designated by the word "mind" in future Western psychology. This is effected by the *pravṛtti* or *karma* that unceasingly emanates from the very same *Puruṣa,* as was stated earlier in Verse 4. All *karma*s pertain to *prakṛti,* and its *vikṛti* in the present context comprises all individuated units of consciousness. Each such individuated aspect of consciousness needs outlets to find expression as experiences. These outlets are also provided by *prakṛti* as its *vikṛti*s in the form of sense organs. *Manas,* the altering states of mind, also is at times considered forming a sixth sense organ. *Prakṛti,* on the one side, thus, makes the one consciousness appear as many, and on the other, sets the stage for them to play their respective roles. Even as every individual undergoes constant change physically, the individuated consciousness drawing sense organs to itself and finding expression as sense experiences goes on ceaseless. How is it, I shall make clearer:

शरीरं यदवाप्नोति यच्चाप्युत्क्रामतीश्वरः ।
गृहीत्वैतानि संयाति वायुर्गन्धानिवाशयात् ॥८॥
श्रोत्रं चक्षुः स्पर्शनं च रसनं घ्राणमेव च ।
अधिष्ठाय मनश्चायं विषयानुपसेवते ॥९॥

śarīraṁ yad avāpnoti yac cāpy utkrāmatīśvaraḥ ।
gṛhītvaitāni saṁyāti vāyur gandhān ivāśayāt ॥8॥

śrotraṁ cakṣuḥ sparśanaṁ ca rasanaṁ ghrāṇam eva ca ।
adhiṣṭhāya manaś cāyaṁ viṣayān upasevate ॥9॥

The perishable forms (*śarīra*) that the all controlling one (*Īśvara*) adopts while remaining above them, carry these sense organs with them, as air does with fragrance from its source.

And thus (an individual) enjoys sense objects resorting to the ear, the eye, touch, taste and smell, and also the mind, as instruments.

Arjuna, the primeval *Puruṣa,* as you know, is the one effulgence that illuminates all that is luminous. This *Puruṣa* could be well called *Īśvara,* the Sanskrit word for God, in the sense that He controls everything. *Īśvara* or God, in other words, is no other than the one Cosmic Consciousness. Conditioned by numerous *śarīra*s, it appears as numerous individual minds. That *śarīra* is to be understood not merely as constituted of our physical body, but in a broader sense inclusive of the animating principle in every being, as we have noticed in Verse 5 and 6 of Chapter XIII. Assuming such perishable forms or *śarīra*s ceaselessly is but natural with *Īśvara.* Even when doing so, He remains always above all of these as pure and unconditioned, as gold remains pure gold even when appearing as ornaments.

As this incessant process of assuming new *śarīra*s goes on, the instruments — sense organs — needed for their functional existence are also provided for by *prakṛti.* Thus is ensured the continuance of life. Put otherwise, *Puruṣa,* on the one side, becomes conditioned, assuming the form of individual minds. And on the other, *prakṛti,* persuaded by its three *guṇas*, evolves as senses and sense objects, setting the stage for the individual minds to flourish. In fact, it is this stage set by *prakṛti* that conditions the primeval *Puruṣa* causing the appearance of many *puruṣas*. This mutuality of *prakṛti* and *puruṣa* results in the upsurging of sense-experiences in individual beings, the five sense organs and mind, all evolutes of *prakṛti*, serving as instruments.

Arjuna, indescribable is the way the one immutable Consciousness assumes the forms of many minds and their variety of experiences. Yet it becomes crystal clear to the wisdom-eye of those who are free from the blemishes of *māyā*. To clarify it further:

उत्क्रामन्तं स्थितं वापि भुञ्जानं वा गुणान्वितम् ।
विमूढा नानुपश्यन्ति पश्यन्ति ज्ञानचक्षुषः ॥१० ॥

utkrāmantaṁ sthitaṁ vāpi bhuñjānaṁ vā guṇānvitam ।
vimūḍhā nānupaśyanti paśyanti jñāna-cakṣuṣaḥ ॥10 ॥

Even if understood as above the realm of *guṇas*, or as existing with *guṇas* inherent in, or even as, conditioned by *guṇas*, experiencing pleasures and pains, the deluded do not perceive the real Me. Those of wisdom-eye alone perceive Me.

Arjuna, how one perceives Me is not important; what is important is seeing Me alone as Real. There are some who think of Me as the one Reality that transcends all individuated minds and all the *vikṛtis* of *prakṛti*, and as the all underlying, immutable, self-effulgent Substance. Some others prefer to think of Me as Reality become conditioned by *prakṛti*, its *vikṛtis* and individual minds. There are also those who consider Me to be the enjoyer of everything. All enjoyments take place under the spell of the three *guṇas*, and pleasures and pains alternating is normal there. They see one *Īśvara* or Me alone manifesting Himself in the form of all such experiences.

The word *utkrāmantam* (that which is above the realm of the three *guṇas*) of this verse is to be understood as equal to the *avyakta* referred to in the *Bhakti-Yoga* (Chapter XII), and *sthitam* (existing with *guṇa*s inherent in) as referring to Me as existing with Cosmic Form, individuated minds gaining the status of enjoyers (*bhuñjānam*), forming part of it.

Many are the ways in which "I" can be perceived holistically; none is either absolutely right or wrong. Whichever the way of approach adopted, attaining a transparent vision of Me requires the eye of wisdom (*jñāna-cakṣus*), an eye to be understood in the light of the *jñāna* defined earlier in Verse IV.35. I will never be seen by those whose minds are boggled by the ignorance-caused delusion. Those endowed with the wisdom-eye are really to be called *yogī*s. How do they perceive Me, I shall clarify:

यतन्तो योगिनश्चैनं पश्यन्त्यात्मन्यवस्थितम्।
यतन्तोऽप्यकृतात्मानो नैनं पश्यन्त्यचेतसः ॥११॥

yatanto yoginaś cainaṁ paśyanty ātmany avasthitam ।
yatanto 'py akr̥tātmāno nainaṁ paśyanty acetasāḥ ॥11॥

And the *yogī*s who strive (to attain wisdom) perceive Me as the Substance that makes their own being. The unwise who do not perceive themselves as the handiwork of *ātmā* (*akr̥tātmā*), never visualize Me thus, even if they strive their best.

Arjuna, it should now be amply clear to you that *yogī*s who strive for wisdom, perceive Me or the one primeval *Puruṣa*, not as existing different from them, for they see Me alone as the Substance that makes their own being, like an ornament seeing gold as what is real in itself and all other ornaments. Many do strive to attain wisdom and to realize Me, but all do not attain this goal. The final attainment is only for those who interiorize their search and seek the Reality as the Substance in their own being. The Reality, in the perception of others, is some object of knowledge existing different from them; their search is exteriorized and they will not catch hold of the Reality even if they pursue it in all the worlds, for the simple reason that they are *akr̥tātmā*s — those who are incapable of perceiving themselves (*ātmā*) as the handiwork (*kṛta*) of the very Reality they are in search of. All their enquiry, however deep and strenuous, helps them only to come to certain well formulated concepts and theories concerning Me, not to realizing Me. The realized *yogīs*, on the other hand, intimately perceive Me as the effulgent *Puruṣa* that makes their own being. How they perceive that effulgence, I shall now describe:

यदादित्यगतं तेजो जगद्भासयतेऽखिलम् ।
यच्चन्द्रमसि यच्चाग्नौ तत्तेजो विद्धि मामकम् ॥१२॥
गामाविश्य च भूतानि धारयाम्यहमोजसा ।
पुष्णामि चौषधीः सर्वाः सोमो भूत्वा रसात्मकः ॥१३॥

yad āditya-gataṁ tejo jagad bhāsayate 'khilam ।
yac candramasi yac cāgnau tat tejo viddhi māmakam ॥12॥

gām āviśya ca bhūtāni dhārayāmy aham ojasā ।
puṣṇāmi cauṣadhīḥ sarvāḥ somo bhūtvā rasātmakaḥ ॥13॥

The brightness inhering in the sun that illumines the entire world, the brightness that inheres in the moon as well as in fire, do understand all as Mine.

Having entered the earth, I, with My own vital urges, sustain all that is born of it. Becoming *soma,* whose essential content is sap, I nourish vegetation.

Arjuna, as part of My Cosmic Form alone, the sun, the moon, fire, all have being. I, as *Puruṣa,* am the Consciousness that systematizes the entire cosmos. No cosmos and no life can exist in the absence of this planner-Consciousness. It could be well said in this sense that it is My brilliance that keeps all luminaries brilliant. The earth having the ability to emanate from itself and support all living beings, including vegetation, also forms part of My Cosmic Form. A *yogī* perceives Me to be thus. As I do keep up the cosmic order, so do I remain underneath the ordering of individual living organisms, as well. To clarify it further:

अहं वैश्वानरो भूत्वा प्राणिनां देहमाश्रितः।
प्राणापानसमायुक्तः पचाम्यन्नं चतुर्विधम् ॥१४॥

ahaṁ vaiśvānaro bhūtvā prāṇināṁ deham āśritaḥ ।
prāṇāpāna-samāyuktaḥ pacāmy annaṁ catur vidham ॥14॥

I, resorting to the bodies of living beings, become the digestive fire, and, functioning along with *prāṇa* and *apāna*, digest the four kinds of food.

Arjuna, what manifestly functions as the digestive system of a living being is Myself. Not that other organic functions are not Myself. In fact, the digestive system referred to stands for all such functions — the extremely complex network of nervous system, blood circulatory system, respiratory system, various muscular functions, different kinds of glands and their secretions, variously shaped bones that ensure a definite shape to the body, the reproductive system of begetting children through the mating of males and females and thus ensuring the eternal continuance of life, all these included. Every individual along with his or her functions, in other words, forms a part of the Cosmic Form.

सर्वस्य चाहं हृदि सन्निविष्टो मत्तः स्मृतिर्ज्ञानमपोहनं च।
वेदैश्च सर्वैरहमेव वेद्यो वेदान्तकृद्वेदविदेव चाहम् ॥१५॥

sarvasya cāhaṁ hṛdi sanniviṣṭo mattaḥ smṛtir jñānam apohanaṁ ca ।
vedaiś ca sarvair aham eva vedyo vedānta-kṛd veda-vid eva cāham ॥15॥

And I am what abides at the heart of all. From Me arise memory, wisdom, forgetfulness as well as the habit of clearing doubts. I am the one to be ultimately known from all scriptures. I am the one who brings about the end of knowing, the knower of knowledge too is Myself.

Arjuna, the vast domain in which *puruṣa* or conciousness functions, as you know, is what we are pondering on in the present chapter. It ranges from ordinary sense perception to extraordinary apperception or knowledge knowing itself. This *puruṣa* aspect or consciousness, in a conditioned form, is present in every being, though it finds expression differently. What one perceives within oneself is never understood, perceived or appreciated by another. One can only presume what is in the mind of another, mostly with one's own perceiving mind for norm. Whatever be the variety of such perceptual possibilities and probabilities, one thing is common to all: that each is a form in which one *Puruṣa* manifests Himself. The I-sense in each is nothing but Consciousness giving off sparks diversely. In short, it is Consciousness functioning in each individual, that stores up memories. What we consider as the storehouse of knowledge is no other than that of memories. All sciences emerge as systematization of memories. All the books ever written are also the memories of many authors finding expression in various ways.

To know, to store up in memory what is known, to doubt, to clear doubts, are some of the functions of consciousness. (The word *apoha* in this verse means both "to forget" and "to clear doubts").

Arjuna, to make it short, all the scriptures that have emerged so far in human history are all meant for knowing one Reality alone, and that Reality is Myself, the unconditioned Consciousness.

Knowing Me so marks the end of the search for Reality, for no reality other than Me does exist, and thus I am the maker of Vedānta, the end of knowledge.

As you know, I am the one and only *puruṣa,* consciousness in essence. To know *puruṣa,* therefore, means to know consciousness or knowledge. He who knows Me, thus, knows knowledge; that means he is a *veda-vit, veda* meaning "knowledge" and *vit,* "one who knows." That he who knows Me becomes Myself has been made evident before, and existing as Myself is the state of a real *yogī.*

Arjuna, we have so far been trying in this chapter to visualize the Cosmic Form and its constituent parts — individual beings — from the point of view of *puruṣa.* And as a part of this visualization was seen the nature of individuated *puruṣa*s or the personal consciousness or the mind each one of us has. Let me now summarize the basic philosophical principle implied in it.

द्वाविमौ पुरुषौ लोके क्षरश्चाक्षर एव च।
क्षरः सर्वाणि भूतानि कूटस्थो ऽक्षर उच्यते ॥१६॥

dvāv imau puruṣau loke kṣaraś cākṣara eva ca ।
kṣaraḥ sarvāṇi bhūtāni kūṭastho 'kṣara ucyate ॥16॥

Two are the *puruṣa*s conceivable in this world — the *kṣara* and the *akṣara* (the perishable and the imperishable). The *kṣara puruṣa* comprises all that has come into being, and the *akṣara puruṣa*, it is said, is the *kūṭastha* (that which exists firm rock-like).

Arjuna, the *puruṣa* seen as related to My Cosmic Form, has two facets — the universal and the particular, the cosmic mind and the individual mind. The latter is the mind that exists in and controls the being of individuals. Just as the individuals are perishable, so too are the *puruṣa*s in them perishable, and hence the epithet *kṣara puruṣa.* The universal *puruṣa* remains one and immutable, unaffected by the multiple forms he assumes. This imperishable (*akṣara*) aspect of *puruṣa,* being immutable, is often termed *kūṭastha,* meaning "firm like rock."

How *sat* and *bhāva* are to be discriminated while perceiving the two non-dually, was made clear earlier in Verse II.16. Very similar is the present context also; *sat* is replaced by the one *akṣara puruṣa* and *bhāva* by the many *kṣara-puruṣa*s. As inseparably one *sat* and *bhāva* are, so are the *akṣara puruṣa* and the *kṣara-puruṣa*s as well, one meaningless without the other. The ultimately Real *Puruṣa,* in other words, is who or what the many *kṣara-puruṣa*s and the one *akṣara-puruṣa* inhere in. What that non-dual *Puruṣa* is, I shall make clearer:

उत्तमः पुरुषस्त्वन्यः परमात्मेत्युदाहृतः।
यो लोकत्रयमाविश्य बिभर्त्यव्यय ईश्वरः ॥१७॥

uttamaḥ puruṣas tv anyaḥ paramātmety udāhṛtaḥ ।
yo loka-trayam āviśya bibharty avyaya īśvaraḥ ॥17 ॥

The *uttama-puruṣa* (Paramount Person) is yet another, generally known as *paramātmā* (the Supreme Self). He indeed is the *Īśvara* (God), who by pervading the three worlds, reigns over them.

Arjuna, the final goal, seen from *prakṛti*'s point of view (as in the last chapter) is becoming a *guṇātīta.* Equivalent to this, as seen from the side of *puruṣa,* is realizing one's identity with the *uttama-puruṣa* that transcends the duality of *kṣara puruṣa* and *akṣara puruṣa.* The *uttama puruṣa*'s non-duality is like the inseparable oneness of gold and ornament-forms. Likewise, realizing the *uttama-puruṣa* reveals that *kṣara puruṣa* cannot exist without the *akṣara puruṣa,* and the *akṣara puruṣa* cannot exist other than in the temporal assumed forms of the multiple *kṣara-puruṣas*. There is no wisdom higher than realizing this inseparable oneness. It is this *uttama puruṣa* that manifests itself as the two, as the worlds here and the hereafter. This one *Puruṣa,* being the one controller of all such worlds, could be well called *Īśvara,* literally "the controller." To clarify further:

यस्मात्क्षरमतीतो ऽहमक्षरादपि चोत्तमः ।
अतो ऽस्मि लोके वेदे च प्रथितः पुरुषोत्तमः ॥१८ ॥

yasmāt kṣaram atīto 'ham akṣarād api cottamaḥ ।
ato 'smi loke vede ca prathitaḥ puruṣottamaḥ ॥18 ॥

For the reason that I am the Highest that transcends both the *kṣara* and the *akṣara,* I am well known both in the realm of worldly knowledge and in the realm of scriptural wisdom, as *puruṣottama* (the Paramount Person).

Arjuna, the main realms of human enquiry are two: one concering the perceptible worldly reality and the other, related to the unknown, taught only by scriptures. Both are simply two branchings of the one search for reality, non-dual Consciousness or *uttama puruṣa* become differently manifest. What underlies the two and what the two try to glorify, is one alone: the *uttama-puruṣa,* hence My popular name *puruṣottama.*

यो मामेवमसम्मूढो जानाति पुरुषोत्तमम् ।
स सर्वविद्भजति मां सर्वभावेन भारत ॥१९॥

yo mām evam asammūḍho jānāti puruṣottamam ।
sa sarvavid bhajati māṁ sarva bhāvena bhārata ॥19॥

O Arjuna, the undeluded one who knows Me the *puruṣottama* thus, is the all-knower. He meditatively perceives Me, seeing Me alone in all the cosmic manifestations.

Arjuna, all that is apparently visible in the cosmos is nothing but Myself assuming various forms. Knowing Me properly, therefore, means knowing everything. How can I be perceived properly? In My Cosmic Form, as having assumed the form of the cosmos, like perceiving gold in all the apparent ornament-forms.

इति गुह्यतमं शास्त्रमिदमुक्तं मयानघ ।
एतद्बुद्ध्वा बुद्धिमान्स्यात्कृतकृत्यश्च भारत ॥२०॥

iti guhyatamaṁ śāstram idaṁ uktaṁ mayānagha ।
etad buddhvā buddhimān syāt kṛta-kṛtyaś ca bhārata ॥20॥

I have thus taught you the most secret of all the sacred teachings, O Sinless One. This secret known, anyone of discerning mind experiences the fulfilment of having finished with all that one is bound to do.

Arjuna, we have been trying from Chapter XII onwards to examine the details of each one of us perceiving ourselves as inseparably one with the Cosmic Form. The *prakṛti* aspect in each individual is not separable from the cosmic *prakṛti* with its three *guṇas*. Yet the one Reality that underlies all *prakṛti* is *guṇātīta,* and knowing ourselves as *guṇātīta* is our final goal.

The *puruṣa* or consciousness aspect of the existence of each being, likewise, is inseparable from the one cosmic consciousness or *viśva puruṣa.* If these two aspects are termed *kṣara puruṣa*s and *akṣara puruṣa,* then the non-dual *Puruṣa* is *puruṣottama.* The *guṇātīta* perceived at the end of the last chapter and the *puruṣottama* of this chapter are one when this non-duality becomes clear in one's inner perception. The secret of all secrets becomes revealed then on its own and then alone one feels the fulfilment of having found what one sought in life, and of having finished with all that one is bound to do in life. The attainment of this fulfilment thus is through *jñāna* and through *karma* both. The Sanskrit word for fulfilment is *kṛtakṛtya, kṛta* meaning "what is already done," and *kṛtya,* "what is yet to be done"; *kṛta-kṛtya* thus means, "one who has already done whatever one is bound to do." He who sees himself as forming part of the Cosmic Form never considers himself as having any *karma* of his own, nor as bound by any *karma.* He always remains constant in feeling the fulfilment, of perceiving all *karma*s as taking place in My Cosmic Form; what he performs then forms an integral part of It.

Thus ends Chapter Fifteen entitled Puruṣottama-Yoga of the Bhagavad-Gītā, the essence of the Upaniṣads, that embodies the yoga-śāstra of brahma-vidyā in the form of a dialogue between Śrī Kṛṣṇa and Arjuna.

XVI

Daivāsura-Sampad-Vibhāga-Yoga
—The Yoga of Discriminating Divine and Demonic Traits—

Vyāsa:

Janmejaya, everyone of us has his or her own personal traits even as part of the cosmic system. With a view to help us finding how we should live our own life as a part of the whole, we, in the last two chapters, tried to examine ourselves looking at from the point of view of *prakṛti* and *puruṣa,* and it enables us now to make a general classification of human character, as we are going to do in the present chapter.

One's character is so different from another's that comparing the two is practically impossible. It is like the face or fingerprint of one is never like another's. Nevertheless, certain commonalities are noticeable among many, and based on them we can classify human character into two: *daivī-sampat* (divine traits) and *āsurī-sampat* (demonic traits). Those of divine traits alone are naturally bent on attaining the final goal we have just visualized. Others, on realizing that demonic traits dominate them, can strive to correct themselves deliberately undergoing certain practices, mainly consisting of giving up desires and anger, the two main obstacles. Scriptures as well as directions given by Masters are there to guide us properly in this matter. This much is what we elaborate on in this chapter.

श्री भगवानुवाच —

अभयं सत्त्वसंशुद्धिर्ज्ञानयोगव्यवस्थितिः ।
दानं दमश्च यज्ञश्च स्वाध्यायस्तप आर्जवम् ॥१॥
अहिंसा सत्यमक्रोधस्त्यागः शान्तिरपैशुनम् ।
दया भूतेष्वलोलुप्त्वं मार्दवं ह्रीरचापलम् ॥२॥
तेजः क्षमा धृतिः शौचमद्रोहो नातिमानिता ।
भवन्ति संपदं दैवीमभिजातस्य भारत ॥३॥

śrī bhagavān uvāca —

abhayaṁ sattva-saṁśuddhir jñāna-yoga-vyavasthitiḥ ।
dānaṁ damaś ca yajñaś ca svādhyāyas tapa ārjavam ॥1॥

ahiṁsā satyam akrodhas tyāgaḥ śāntir apaiśunam ।
dayā bhūteṣv aloluptvaṁ mārdavaṁ hrīr acāpalam ॥2॥

tejaḥ kṣamā dhṛtiḥ śaucam adroho nātimānitā ।
bhavanti sampadaṁ daivīm abhijātasya bhārata ॥3॥

Śrī Kṛṣṇa said —

Fearlessness, a transparent vision of the Real and the ensuing purity of mind, being well stabilized specifically in *jñāna-yoga,* offering free gifts to the deserving, self-restraint, performing *yajña*s properly, studying scriptures on one's own, straightforwardness;

Non-hurting, honesty, being free from anger, willingness to renounce, calmness, aversion to slander, compassion to living beings, being uninterested in sense-pleasures, gentleness, modesty, absence of fickleness;

Alertness natural to brightness, forgiveness, fortitude, cleanliness, absence of malice, absence of self-esteem — all these are signs seen in those born with divine traits.

Arjuna, the word *sattva-saṁśuddhi* ordinarily means purity of mind. In the philosophical context or rather metaphysical context, *sattva* is the state in which one finds oneself to be what is Real (*sat*). This awareness is always accompanied by a sense of the purity of one's own being, mind-purity included. *Sattva-saṁśuddhi* signifies this sense of inner transparency.

Jñāna-yoga-vyavasthitiḥ (being well-stabilized in *jñāna-yoga*) is the state in which one directly experiences as *vijñāna* the secret of *jñāna-yoga* taught earlier in Verse IV.35.

Dama (self-restraint) is one's ability to keep one's mind and sense organs in one's own control so as to be conducive to the attainment of the final goal of life.

Yajña, as related to both *karma* and *jñāna,* was examined earlier in Chapters III and IV. Those who have absorbed its spirit see their own life as a sort of *yajña.*

Learning scriptures on one's own to ensure constant pondering on the basic problems of life is called *svādhyāya.* Doubts may arise in the course of such ponderings; then one has to approach someone well versed on the subject or one's own *guru* and get the doubts cleared. This latter process is known as *pravacana,* and it always goes with *svādhyāya.*

Tapas is the self-heating-up, one undergoes as a part of the search for Reality.

One has *ārjava* (straightforwardness) when one's thinking, spoken words and deeds agree with one another. Now let us look at the demonic traits:

दम्भो दर्पो ऽभिमानश्च क्रोधः पारुष्यमेव च ।
अज्ञानं चाभिजातस्य पार्थ सम्पदमासुरीम् ॥४॥

dambho darpo 'bhimānaś ca krodhaḥ pāruṣyam eva ca ।
ajñānaṁ cābhijātasya pārtha sampadam āsurīm ॥4॥

Pretentiousness, arrogance, sense of self-importance, anger, harshness, and likewise ignorance — these,

O Arjuna, are marks of those who are born with demonic traits.

The habit of pretending oneself to be important is known as *dambha* (pretentiousness). *Darpa* (arrogance) is the pride one feels owing to having much wealth or much education.

I shall now tell you how the divine and demonic traits affect human life:

दैवी सम्पद्विमोक्षाय निबन्धायासुरी मता।
मा शुचः सम्पदं दैवीमभिजातोऽसि पाण्डव॥५॥

daivī sampad vimokṣāya nibandhāyāsurī matā ।
mā śucaḥ sampadaṁ daivīm abhijāto 'si pāṇḍava ॥5॥

The divine traits are deemed to lead one to Liberation, and the demonic traits, on the other hand, tend to keep one down in bondage. Arjuna, you don't have to be worried about it, for you are surely born fit for divine traits.

Arjuna, everyone's intention is to be happy somehow. All efforts to be happy lead those of demonic traits, in one way or another, ultimately to unhappiness and bondage. Only the effort of those endowed with divine traits ensure happiness and Liberation.

You may be in doubt as to which of these two you belong. Don't worry. You are by birth quite fit for divine traits. In other words, you have all the qualities of a seeker, fit for attaining wisdom and thus final Liberation.

द्वौ भूतसर्गौ लोकेऽस्मिन्दैव आसुर एव च।
दैवो विस्तरशः प्रोक्त आसुरं पार्थ मे शृणु॥६॥

dvau bhūta sargau loke 'smin daiva āsura eva ca ।
daivo vistaraśaḥ prokta āsuraṁ pārtha me śṛṇu ॥6॥

> Two are the types to which all the creations in the world belong: the divine and the demonic. The details of the former have already been gone into. Hear from me now the details of the latter.

Arjuna, though the natural bent of living beings, especially of humans, can thus be classified, only those of divine traits become aware of being so, or only they can be taught about it. They distinguish the two traits and make themselves liberated while living. Those of demonic nature, on the other hand, remain completely ignorant of being so. Their natural bent, for this reason, have to be examined in detail in order to help them have a chance to become aware of their inner nature and to correct themselves if possible, and that is what we do in verses up to 20.

प्रवृत्तिं च निवृत्तिं च जना न विदुरासुराः ।
न शौचं नापि चाचारो न सत्यं तेषु विद्यते ॥७ ॥

pravṛttiṁ ca nivṛttiṁ ca janā na vidur āsurāḥ ।
na śaucaṁ nāpi cācāro na satyaṁ teṣu vidyate ॥7 ॥

> People of demonic traits do not discriminate the way of positive action and the way of negative withdrawal. No cleanliness, no proprieties, no truthfulness is found in them either.

Arjuna, most live by considering what they do as their own actions or *karmas*. They feel responsible for doing certain things and feel guilty if they fail to do these. If they do these things wrongly, they feel sinful. In short, they find the meaning of life in what they do, and this way of looking at life is known as *pravṛtti-mārga* (the way of positive actions).

There are some who are fully aware that no *karma* is theirs, and that all actions take place ceaselessly in *prakṛti*. Theirs is not the way of planning activities in life motivated by certain benefits. Instead, they withdraw from motivated activities and hence the name *nivṛtti-*

mārga (*nivṛtti* meaning "withdrawal") for their attitude. To be more conventional, *nivṛtti-mārga* is the way of those who withdraw from the Vedic rituals and their obligations and turn towards wisdom. Ritualists, in other words, follow *pravṛtti-mārga* and wisdom seekers *nivṛtti-mārga.* Nevertheless, to discriminate between the two occurs only to those of divine nature, the reason for those of demonic nature doing things indiscriminately. Cleanliness, both mental and bodily, is absent in the latter. Having no knowledge of truth, they cannot be expected to be truthful, and therefore not having propriety is natural for them.

असत्यमप्रतिष्ठं ते जगदाहुरनीश्वरम् ।
अपरस्परसम्भूतं किमन्यत्कामहैतुकम् ॥८ ॥

asatyam apratiṣṭhaṁ te jagad āhur anīśvaram ।
aparaspara-sambhūtaṁ kim anyat kāma-haitukam ॥8 ॥

The world exists, they claim, without a Reality; no Substance underlies it; its existence is not ensured by reciprocity. What else is there existing other than caused by lust?

Arjuna, those of demonic nature do not view life by admitting an all-underlying Substance as Real. They are simply incapable of conceiving that that substance, as *Īśvara*, the all-controlling principle, governs everything from within. They do not think also that this cosmos is so well systematized that everything that forms part of it exists supporting each other. What they perceive as the one force that pushes life on is desires. Their fulfilment is thought of as making life meaningful. Even the continuance of life system, they say, is made possible by one such desire — the carnal desire. They ask, why should we be worried about a Reality beyond or behind, when we are all happy here with the apparent things?

एतां दृष्टिमवष्टभ्य नष्टात्मानो ऽल्पबुद्धयः ।
प्रभवन्त्युग्रकर्माणः क्षयाय जगतो ऽहिताः ॥९ ॥

etāṁ dṛṣṭim avaṣṭabhya naṣṭātmāno 'lpa buddhayaḥ ।
prabhavanty ugra-karmāṇaḥ kṣayāya jagato 'hitāḥ ॥9 ॥

Willfully holding to this perception, they, having lost themselves because of their little understanding of themselves, happen to become doers of fierce deeds unmindful of the general interest and causing decline of the world.

काममाश्रित्य दुष्पूरं दम्भमानमदान्विताः ।
मोहाद्गृहीत्वा ऽसद्ग्राहान्प्रवर्तन्ते ऽशुचिव्रताः ॥१० ॥

kāmam āśritya duṣpūraṁ daṁbha-māna-madānvitāḥ ।
mohād gṛhītvā 'sad-grāhān pravartante 'śuci-vratāḥ ॥10 ॥

Surrendering themselves to insatiable desires, possessed with pretentiousness, arrogance and insanity, given to resolves unclean, they remain active in pursuit of false values, deluded by taking the unreal for the real.

चिन्तामपरिमेयां च प्रलयान्तामुपाश्रिताः ।
कामोपभोगपरमा एतावदिति निश्चिताः ॥११ ॥
आशापाशशतैर्बद्धाः कामक्रोधपरायणाः ।
ईहन्ते कामभोगार्थमन्यायेनार्थसञ्चयान् ॥१२ ॥

cintām aparimeyāṁ ca pralayāntām upāśritāḥ ।
kāmopabhoga-paramā etāvad iti niścitāḥ ॥11 ॥

āśā-pāśa-śatair baddhāḥ kāma-krodha-parāyaṇāḥ ।
īhante kāma-bhogārtham anyāyenārtha-sañcayān ॥12 ॥

Obsessed with numerous cares all through life and with the fixed idea that life ends with death, looking at sense pleasures as the highest attainable goal, cocksure that this much is the meaning of life;

They live tied up by hundreds of cords made up of their own desires, given over to lust and anger. They strive to accumulate wealth by unjust means for the fulfilment of their sensual desires.

इदमद्य मया लब्धमिमं प्राप्स्ये मनोरथम्।
इदमस्तीदमपि मे भविष्यति पुनर्धनम्॥१३॥
असौ मया हतः शत्रुर्हनिष्ये चापरानपि।
ईश्वरो ऽहमहं भोगी सिद्धो ऽहं बलवान्सुखी॥१४॥
आढ्यो ऽभिजनवानस्मि को ऽन्यो ऽस्ति सदृशो मया।
यक्ष्ये दास्यामि मोदिष्य इत्यज्ञानविमोहिताः॥१५॥

idam adya mayā labdham imaṁ prāpsye manoratham ।
idam astīdam api me bhaviṣyati punar dhanam ॥13॥

asau mayā hataḥ śatrur haniṣye cāparān api ।
iśvaro 'ham ahaṁ bhogī siddho 'haṁ balavān sukhī ॥14॥

āḍhyo 'bhijanavān asmi ko 'nyo 'sti sadṛśo mayā ।
yakṣye dāsyāmi modiṣya ity ajñāna-vimohitāḥ ॥15॥

This much I could gain today. The other wish I'll fulfil shortly. This much wealth do I possess now, and much more will be mine before long.

That enemy has been slain by me; the others will also be done away with by me. I do enjoy everything. I satisfy my ambitions. I am powerful. I am happy.

I am rich and high-born. Who is there equal to me? I will perform fire-sacrifices; I will give gifts, I will enjoy life. Deluded by ignorance are they.

अनेकचित्तविभ्रान्ता मोहजालसमावृताः।
प्रसक्ताः कामभोगेषु पतन्ति नरके ऽशुचौ॥१६॥

aneka-citta-vibhrāntā moha-jāla-samāvṛtāḥ ।
prasaktāḥ kāma-bhogeṣu patanti narake 'śucau ॥16॥

Involved in many things at a time, they make themselves confused and mad. They get entangled in the meshes of delusion. Addicted to lustful gratifications, they fall into hellish foulness.

Arjuna, what I mean is not that those of demonic nature will go to hell after death, but that they make a hell of their life here in this world itself.

आत्मसम्भाविताः स्तब्धा धनमानमदान्विताः ।
यजन्ते नामयज्ञैस्ते दम्भेनाविधिपूर्वकम् ॥१७॥

ātma-sambhāvitāḥ stabdhā dhana-māna-madānvitāḥ ।
yajante nāmayajñais te dambhenāvidhi-pūrvakam ॥17॥

Vainglorious, stubborn, intoxicated with the pride of wealth, they perform sacrifices, unmindful of scriptural instructions.

Arjuna, if you think those of demonic nature will not be interested in religion and spiritual matters, you are wrong. They too show interest in such matters, often spending much money. But what incites them to do so is desire for fame, for making themselves known as religious people. Their names becoming well known is what they think great.

अहंकारं बलं दर्पं कामं क्रोधं च संश्रिताः ।
मामात्मपरदेहेषु प्रद्विषन्तो ऽभ्यसूयकाः ॥१८॥

ahaṁkāraṁ balaṁ darpaṁ kāmaṁ krodhaṁ ca saṁśritāḥ ।
māṁ ātma-para-deheṣu pradviṣanto 'bhyasūyakāḥ ॥18॥

Dominated by egoism, use of force, arrogance, lust and anger, these envious ones violate even Me (the Supreme Self) dwelling in their form and of others.

तानहं द्विषतः क्रूरान्संसारेषु नराधमान् ।
क्षिपाम्यजस्रमशुभानासुरीष्वेव योनिषु ॥१९॥

tān ahaṁ dviṣataḥ krūrān saṁsāreṣu narādhamān ।
kṣipāmy ajasram aśubhān āsurīṣveva yoniṣu ॥19 ॥

These vilest of men, haters of the world and cruel as they are, are always hurled by Me unceasingly into demonic wombs in the cycle of worldly existence (*saṁsāra*).

आसुरीं योनिमापन्ना मूढा जन्मनि जन्मनि ।
मामप्राप्यैव कौन्तेय ततो यान्त्यधमां गतिम् ॥२० ॥

āsurīṁ yonim āpannā mūḍhā janmani janmani ।
mām aprāpyaiva kaunteya tato yānty adhamāṁ gatim ॥20 ॥

Arjuna, Me unattained and attaining demonic wombs birth after birth, those deluded ones sink into the lowest of depths.

Arjuna, at the end of this description of those of demonic nature, it sounds as if I include as a part of the core of My teaching, the idea that reincarnation is real. Those of demonic nature, no doubt, are ignorant. They are ignorant because they remain unaware of the one birthless and deathless Reality that assumes the form of everything, and because they consider the phenomenal appearance of birth and death as real. Thinking of themselves as mortals, they believe they are bound to be reborn after death. What is real for an individual is what one conceives a thing to be. They thus happen to live in a world of unceasing birth and death, thought of as real because of their ignorance.

Though ignorant they also originate from Me, and thus it could be well said I hurl them into *saṁsāra* (repeated births and deaths). Whatever happens as part of nature's flow of events is to be treated as caused by Me. All human beings, emanating as they are from Me, are naturally endowed with a free will that essentially is Mine, but they treat it as theirs and misuse it, unmindful of Me. They thus continue in the demonic world.

Knowing the implications of the two words *daivī* and *āsurī*, rendered here as "divine" and "demonic" will surely shed more light on the context. *Daivī*, derived from the root "*div*," meaning "to shine," signifies that which is essentially bright, suggesting "that which is in line with wisdom." *Āsurī* means "that which is related to *asura*," the mythological term for the enemies of *suras*, another word to mean *devas* (gods), or the effulgent ones. *Sura* literally means, "one who gives in plenty" (*suṣṭum rāti iti surah*). One feels the satisfaction of having got everything one needs, not when all the desires — they are endless — are fulfilled, but on attaining wisdom one feels that nothing more is to be gained in life. *Asura*, the opposite of *sura*, thus means "he who never feels satisfied with desire-fulfilment." All the mythological stories related to *asuras* show how insatiable are their desires. All such wishes, except that of deathlessness of theirs are willingly granted by Brahmā the Creator, as boons, but those very boons eventually become traps that lead to their own destruction. Men with such traits are to be considered as of *āsurī saṁpat* (demonic traits). Those of this nature, as we have already noticed make a hell of their life. This state too is not without escape. I shall now tell you how one can escape it:

त्रिविधं नरकस्येदं द्वारं नाशनमात्मनः ।
काम: क्रोधस्तथा लोभस्तस्मादेतत्त्रयं त्यजेत् ॥२१ ॥

tri-vidhaṁ narakasyedaṁ dvāraṁ nāśanam ātmanaḥ ।
kāmaḥ krodhas-tathā lobhas tasmād etat trayaṁ tyajet ॥21 ॥

Lust, anger, greed — these three are the infernal gates to one's own total destruction. Therefore these three are to be given up deliberately.

Arjuna, how desire, anger and greed lead us gradually to our own peril, we have seen in detail earlier in Verses 62 and 63 of Chapter II. These emotions lead us to express the demonic traits we have just discussed. Pride (*mada*), delusion (*moha*), and competitiveness (*mātsarya*) added, they become six, and are often referred to as *ari-ṣaḍ-varga* (six enemies) or *ṣaḍ-ūrmis* (six breakers that obstruct the normal course of life). Stifling these traits the moment any of them surfaces is the only way to escape from the grip of demonic traits. And this is not just a principle to be understood but rather a practice to be followed whenever these traits hold sway over us. This is possible only if one becomes conscious of becoming so. It is then possible to contain the trait then and there. It helps one to distance oneself from demonic traits and draw closer to divine ones. To triumph over such emotions occasionally is of no avail, it has to be a constant practice all through life, for these emotions can spring up again and again. One thus liberates oneself from their vice-like grip, and what one thus attains is stated in the next verse.

एतैर्विमुक्तः कौन्तेय तमोद्वारैस्त्रिभिर्नरः ।
आचरत्यात्मनः श्रेयस्ततो याति परां गतिम् ॥२२॥

etair vimuktaḥ kaunteya tamo-dvārais tribhir naraḥ ।
ācaraty ātmanaḥ śreyas tato yāti parāṁ gatim ॥22॥

The man who frees himself from these three gates to darkness, O Arjuna, endeavours for his own blessedness, and thus he attains the Supreme Goal.

Arjuna, lust, anger and greed, are the doors leading to the darkness of ignorance, which in its turn strengthens our demonic traits. One who manages to close those doors behind ignorance and win over the three passions, naturally reaches the goal of *śreyas*, the blessedness of wisdom, as against *preyas* or worldly gains. They attain eventually the Supreme Goal of experiencing themselves inseparably one with My Cosmic Form. How do people unintentionally become dominated by these passions? I shall tell you:

यः शास्त्रविधिमुत्सृज्य वर्तते कामकारतः ।
न स सिद्धिमवाप्नोति न सुखं न परां गतिम् ॥२३॥

yaḥ śāstra-vidhim utsṛjya vartate kāmakārataḥ ।
na sa siddhim avāpnoti na sukhaṁ na parāṁ gatim ॥23॥

He who, ignoring the guiding principles of scriptures, acts under the promptings of lust, does not reach the final attainment. Neither is he happy in life nor does he attain the Supreme goal of Liberation.

Arjuna, many are those who are incapable of discerning the real from the unreal, and making decisions about the do's and don'ts of life. The only source of guidance available to them are scriptures, of which those like the Upaniṣads and the present dialogue known as *śrutis*, enable them to decide on their own what is righteous and what is unrighteous. Other scriptures known as *dharma-śāstras* or *smṛtis* give instructions as to what acts are permissible or obligatory and what are taboo, based on certain general notions of righteousness. Those who follow the latter do not have to think much, for they simply have to abide by the prescribed codes. Neither of these two sets of scriptures is respected by those of demonic nature, resulting in their making a hell of their own lives. Hence this much I wish to assert:

तस्माच्छास्त्रं प्रमाणं ते कार्याकार्यव्यवस्थितौ ।
ज्ञात्वा शास्त्रविधानोक्तं कर्म कर्तुमिहार्हसि ॥२४॥

tasmāc chāstraṁ pramāṇaṁ te kāryākārya-vyavasthitau |
jñātvā śāstra-vidhānoktaṁ karma kartum ihārhasi ||24||

For this reason, scriptures are to be your authority in deciding what should be and should not be done. With the knowledge of what the scriptures enjoin should be your acts.

Thus ends Chapter Sixteen entitled Daivāsura-Sampad-Vibhāga-Yoga of the Bhagavad-Gītā, the essence of the Upaniṣads, that embodies the yoga-śāstra of brahma-vidyā in the form of a dialogue between Śrī Kṛṣṇa and Arjuna.

XVII

Śraddhā-Traya-Vibhāga-Yoga
—The Yoga of Discriminating Three Kinds of Reverence for Higher Values—

Vyāsa:

Janmejaya, each of us has to be fully aware, what peculiar personal traits are one's, as part of the entire cosmic system. As a guide to making self-examination with this end in view, Chapter XIV clarified how the three *guṇa*s of *prakṛti* influence human nature, along with showing how the very same *guṇa*s can be transcended. Then was examined in Chapter XV the *puruṣa* or knowing aspect of our being, showing how with roots above and branches downward, it forms the world of knowing the many as real, and also how, when well disciplined, it can function as our realization of the one Reality. The human character formulated as a result of the unpredictable combination of the three *guṇa*s of *prakṛti* and the equally unpredictable variety of knowing functions, could in a general way be classified into two – divine (*daivī*) and demonic (*āsurī*) as was laid bare in Chapter XVI. Each one of us lives every moment of our life influenced by all such intricate factors, and as a result each one's field of interest, pattern of behaviour and way of reacting are naturally different from those of others. One can make a guess about one's own inner nature by observing one's field of interest in life. And what Chapter XVII does is help accomplish this task by examining some of the basic fields of interest and habitual behaviours of humans. This otherwise exhaustive task is carried out here by treating three fields of interest counted as of high value by Vedism. They are *yajña* (sacrifice), *dāna* (offering free gifts) and *tapas* (austere discipline of self-heating), considered as symbolically representing the entire range of human interests. The three, though universally accepted by Vedism, are practised differently by each.

All living beings depend on food for existence, and food habits also vary from person to person. This aspect is also examined in this chapter.

The ultimate goal of all spiritual endeavour is realizing oneself as *Brahman*, and this *Brahman* is signified in Vedānta by three monosyllabled words: *AUṀ*, *tat* and *sat*. Oneself being *Brahman* in essence is true as related to these three terms in personal life as well; light is shed also on this aspect.

अर्जुन उवाच —

ये शास्त्रविधिमुत्सृज्य यजन्ते श्रद्धयान्विताः ।
तेषां निष्ठा तु का कृष्ण सत्त्वमाहो रजस्तमः ॥१ ॥

arjuna uvāca —

ye śāstra-vidhim utsṛjya yajante śraddhayānvitāḥ ।
teṣāṁ niṣṭhā tu kā kṛṣṇa sattvam āho rajas tamaḥ ॥1 ॥

Arjuna said —

O Kṛṣṇa, there are those who, unmindful though of scriptural injunctions, perform *yajña* with full faith. Of what sort is their faith? Is it *sattva, rajas* or *tamas*?.

Adhering to scriptural injunctions, as you hold, is the best means for effecting a shift from demonic traits to divine traits. It is, of course, to be accompanied by doing away with desire and anger, the two ever-open doors to hell. Many, though earnest in averting evil ways and reverting to commendable ones, do not always get the opportunity to become familiar with scriptures. Still they try their best, in their own way, without support from any scripture, to follow the path of goodness. It may so happen that those efforts do not agree with what the scriptures enjoin. How are such to be considered? This is my doubt. The *yajña* I refer to represents all deliberate acts with good intention.

श्री भगवानुवाच —

त्रिविधा भवति श्रद्धा देहिनां सा स्वभावजा।
सात्त्विकी राजसी चैव तामसी चेति तां शृणु ॥२॥

śrī bhagavān uvāca —

tri-vidhā bhavati śraddhā dehināṁ sā svabhāvajā ।
sāttvikī rājasī caiva tāmasī ceti tāṁ śṛṇu ॥2॥

Śrī Kṛṣṇa said —

Of three kinds is the reverence for higher values (*śraddhā*) innate in the embodied: *sāttvika* (pure and clear), *rājasa* (active and passionate), and *tāmasa* (inert and sluggish).

Arjuna, each person is born with a unique character on which depends the interest towards higher values. Going into its details is made unavoidable by your asking the present question. The character analysis I presently employ follows the trail of what I taught you in Chapters XIII, XIV and XV.

Man's reverence for higher values could be well classified as *sāttvika, rājasa* or *tāmasa* in accordance with the three *guṇa*s natural with each. Such variety of traits of human beings is not man-made, but rather a part of nature or *prakṛti*. I shall now tell you how the value notion of each varies.

सत्त्वानुरूपा सर्वस्य श्रद्धा भवति भारत।
श्रद्धामयो ऽयं पुरुषो यो यच्छ्रद्धः स एव सः ॥३॥

sattvānurūpā sarvasya śraddhā bhavati bhārata ।
śraddhāmayo 'yaṁ puruṣo yo yac-chraddhaḥ sa eva saḥ ॥3॥

One's reverence for higher values happens to be in accordance with the essential nature of one's being. What makes man, in fact, is his reverence for higher values (*śraddhā*). The high value one reverences constitutes the essential content of one's personality.

Arjuna, the intrinsic nature of each person's being decides what kind of higher values he or she becomes interested in. [The word *sattva* I use in this verse does not denote *sattva guṇa,* one of the three *guṇa*s, but rather means "the intrinsic nature of one's own beingness" (*sat-tva*).] To be more precise, the three *guṇa*s (examined in Chapter XIV), the endlessly branching knowledge (considered in Chapter XV) and the divine and demonic human traits (we saw in Chapter XVI) together, in different combinations, decides a person's intrinsic nature and also his/her sense of higher values.

To be involved in something that one thinks as being of high value is a peculiarity of the human mind. Without such a field of interest, life becomes meaningless, leading one possibly into a cureless psycho-pathological condition known in India as *aratī,* meaning "lack of zest for life," a condition that may even cause death. Those who lead a healthy life, therefore, always have a field of interest to be engrossed in, that makes life worth living. Implying all this are the words, "The high value one reverences constitutes the essential content of one's personality."

Look at, for example, how *yajña* or Vedic ritual, influenced by the three *guṇa*s, becomes diversified:

यजन्ते सात्त्विका देवान्यक्षरक्षांसि राजसाः ।
प्रेतान्भूतगणांश्चान्ये यजन्ते तामसा जनाः ॥४ ॥

yajante sāttvikā devān yakṣa-rakṣāṁsi rājasāḥ ।
pretān bhūta-gaṇāṁś cānye yajante tāmasā janāḥ ॥4 ॥

The *sāttvika*s perform *yajña*s propitiating gods (of heaven); the *rājasa*s do it to propitiate *yakṣa*s and *rākṣasa*s; and the *tāmasa*s do so to appease the souls of the departed and the elementals.

Arjuna, *deva*s are the inhabitants of Vedic heaven; *yakṣa*s are a class of demi-gods in guard of riches, gardens and treasures; and *rākṣasa*s are a sort of fiendish spirits.

Tapas forms a part of spiritual discipline, and is considered to be undergone by those of divine traits in view of attaining wisdom. But it is not so. Everyone, in one way or another, undergoes *tapas*. I shall tell you how it is practised by those of demonic traits:

अशास्त्रविहितं घोरं तप्यन्ते ये तपो जनाः ।
दम्भाहङ्कारसंयुक्ताः कामरागबलान्विताः ॥५॥
कर्शयन्तः शरीरस्थं भूतग्राममचेतसः ।
मां चैवान्तःशरीरस्थं तान्विद्ध्यासुरनिश्चयान् ॥६॥

aśāstra-vihitaṁ ghoraṁ tapyante ye tapo janāḥ ।
dambhāhaṅkāra-saṁyuktāḥ kāma-rāga-balānvitāḥ ॥5॥

karśayantaḥ śarīrasthaṁ bhūta-grāmam acetasaḥ ।
māṁ caivāntaḥ-śarīrasthaṁ tān viddhy āsura niścayān ॥6॥

Men are there who subject themselves to *tapas* in a terrible way unmindful of scriptural injunctions, given to arrogance, egoism, lust, passion and power, and who torture their own physical organs as well as Me that underlies them. Know them as of demonic resolves.

Arjuna, food, as you know, is the most basic of all needs for the sustenance of all living beings. Food habits too differ from individual to individual. Likewise also differ the *yajña* (fire sacrifice), *dāna* (offering free gifts) and *tapas*, each practises. I shall now clarify how do they differ.

आहारस्त्वपि सर्वस्य त्रिविधो भवति प्रियः ।
यज्ञस्तपस्तथा दानं तेषां भेदमिमं शृणु ॥७॥

āhāras tvapi sarvasya trividho bhavati priyaḥ ।
yajñas-tapas-tathā dānaṁ teṣāṁ bhedaṁ imam śṛṇu ॥7॥

Even the food liked by everyone is of three kinds. So too are the *yajña, tapas* and *dāna* observed by each. Now hear from Me how do they differ.

First I shall tell you of food habits:

आयुःसत्त्वबलारोग्यसुखप्रीतिविवर्धनाः।
रस्याः स्निग्धाः स्थिरा हृद्या आहाराः सात्त्विकप्रियाः ॥८॥

āyuḥ-sattva-balārogya sukha-prīti-vivardhanāḥ ।
rasyāḥ snigdhāḥ sthirā hṛdyā āhārāḥ sāttvika-priyāḥ ॥8॥

Foods that promote longevity, vitality, energy, health, joy and cheerfulness, that are delicious, rich and flavoursome, substantial and agreeable, are liked by *sāttvikas*.

Arjuna, recommending any particular food habit is not what I do here. How one's natural preference for food differs from another's alone is my concern. Yet the pure food habit of *sāttvikas* could be well practised by others as a supporting factor in acquiring divine traits and giving up desire and anger as enjoined in scriptures. But practising this food habit alone does not make a *sāttvika* of oneself, or one of divine traits.

कट्वम्ललवणात्युष्णतीक्ष्णरूक्षविदाहिनः।
आहारा राजसस्येष्टा दुःखशोकामयप्रदाः ॥९॥

kaṭv-amla-lavaṇātyuṣṇa tīkṣṇa-rūkṣa-vidāhinaḥ ।
āhārā rājasasyeṣṭā duḥkha-śokāmaya pradāḥ ॥9॥

Foods that are pungent, too sour, too salty, choleric, too peppery, hardened, burning and thirst-producing, causing uneasinnes, depression and disease, are liked by *rājasas*.

यातयामं गतरसं पूति पर्युषितं च यत्।
उच्छिष्टमपि चामेध्यं भोजनं तामसप्रियम् ॥१०॥

yāta-yāmaṁ gata-rasaṁ pūti paryuṣitaṁ ca yat ।
ucchiṣṭam api cāmedhyaṁ bhojanaṁ tāmasa-priyam ॥10॥

Cooked hours before, putrid and stale, leavings of others and unclean, is the food liked by *tāmasas*.

Now I shall clarify to you how those with any of the three *guṇas* predominant, by nature, perform sacrifices.

अफलाकाङ्क्षिभिर्यज्ञो विधिदृष्टो य इज्यते ।
यष्टव्यमेवेति मनः समाधाय स सात्त्विकः ॥११ ॥

aphalākāṅkṣibhir yajño vidhi-dṛṣṭo ya ijyate ।
yaṣṭavyam eveti manaḥ samādhāya sa sāttvikaḥ ॥11 ॥

The *yajña* performed in accordance with scriptural injunctions, unmotivated by particular gains, but with firm understanding of its necessity, is *sāttvika*.

अभिसंधाय तु फलं दम्भार्थमपि चैव यत् ।
इज्यते भरतश्रेष्ठ तं यज्ञं विद्धि राजसम् ॥१२ ॥

abhisaṁdhāya tu phalaṁ dambhārtham api caiva yat ।
ijyate bharata-śreṣṭha taṁ yajñaṁ viddhi rājasam ॥12 ॥

The *yajña* performed expecting some particular gain or for egoistic show, O Best of Bharatas, is to be understood as *rājasa*.

विधिहीनमसृष्टान्नं मन्त्रहीनमदक्षिणम् ।
श्रद्धाविरहितं यज्ञं तामसं परिचक्षते ॥१३ ॥

vidhihīnam asṛṣṭānnaṁ mantra-hīnam adakṣiṇam ।
śraddhā-virahitaṁ yajñaṁ tāmasaṁ paricakṣate ॥13 ॥

The *yajña* performed unmindful of scriptural injunctions, with no food prepared, without sacred chants, without offering *dakṣiṇa*, and devoid of faith, is said to be *tāmasa*.

Arjuna, *dakṣiṇā* is the token free gift offered to priests by the performer of sacrifices, or to a *guru* by a disciple.

Now I shall tell you how *tapas* — itself of three kinds: bodily, verbal and mental — differs from person to person in accordance with the *guṇa* predominant in each.

देवद्विजगुरुप्राज्ञपूजनं शौचमार्जवम्।
ब्रह्मचर्यमहिंसा च शारीरं तप उच्यते ॥१४॥

deva-dvija-guru-prājña-pūjanaṁ śaucam ārjavam ।
brahmacaryam ahiṁsā ca śārīraṁ tapa ucyate ॥14॥

Worship offered to gods, to the twice-born (*dvijas*), to *gurus*, to the wise in general, cleanliness, straightforwardness, *brahmacarya,* non-hurting, are said to constitute bodily *tapas.*

अनुद्वेगकरं वाक्यं सत्यं प्रियहितं च यत्।
स्वाध्यायाभ्यसनं चैव वाङ्मयं तप उच्यते ॥१५॥

anudvega-karaṁ vākyaṁ satyaṁ priya-hitaṁ ca yat ।
svādhyāyabhyasanaṁ caiva vāṅmayaṁ tapa ucyate ॥15॥

Saying inoffensive, truthful, pleasant and beneficial words, and constant contemplative self-study of wisdom-scriptures, are considered the *tapas* of speech.

मनःप्रसादः सौम्यत्वं मौनमात्मविनिग्रहः।
भावसंशुद्धिरित्येतत्तपो मानसमुच्यते ॥१६॥

manaḥ-prasādaḥ saumyatvaṁ maunam ātma-vinigrahaḥ ।
bhāva-saṁśuddhir ity-etat tapo mānasam ucyate ॥16॥

Cheerfulness, gentleness, noiselessness, self-restraint, transparency of perception — these are said to constitute mental *tapas.*

श्रद्धया परया तप्तं तपस्तत्त्रिविधं नरैः।
अफलाकाङ्क्षिभिर्युक्तैः सात्त्विकं परिचक्षते ॥१७॥

śraddhayā parayā taptaṁ tapas tat trividhaṁ naraiḥ ।
aphalākāṅkṣibhir-yuktaiḥ sāttvikaṁ paricakṣate ॥17॥

This three-fold *tapas,* when practised by not-benefit-motivated men, with utmost care and faith, is called *sāttvika.*

सत्कारमानपूजार्थं तपो दम्भेन चैव यत्।
क्रियते तदिह प्रोक्तं राजसं चलमध्रुवम्॥१८॥

satkāra-māna-pūjārthaṁ tapo dambhena caiva yat ।
kriyate tad iha proktaṁ rājasaṁ calam adhruvam ॥18॥

The *tapas* performed with the objective of gaining respect, honour and reverence from others and motivated by self-esteem, is named *rājasa;* it is unstable and of fleeting benefit.

मूढग्राहेणात्मनो यत्पीडया क्रियते तपः।
परस्योत्सादनार्थं वा तत्तामसमुदाहृतम्॥१९॥

mūḍha-grāheṇātmano yat pīḍayā kriyate tapaḥ ।
parasyotsādanārthaṁ vā tat tāmasam udāhṛtam ॥19॥

The *tapas* that involves self-torture, undergone out of foolish obstinacy, or to harm others, is named *tāmasa.*

Now see how *dāna* (offering gifts) is also of three kinds:

दातव्यमिति यद्दानं दीयतेऽनुपकारिणे।
देशे काले च पात्रे च तद्दानं सात्त्विकं स्मृतम्॥२०॥

dātavyam iti yad dānaṁ dīyate 'nupakāriṇe ।
deśe kāle ca pātre ca tad dānaṁ sāttvikaṁ smṛtam ॥20॥

The offering of gifts made with the clear understanding that such are to be offered, to a fit person who does nothing in return, at a fit time at a fit place, is counted as *sāttvika:*

यत्तु प्रत्युपकारार्थं फलमुद्दिश्य वा पुनः ।
दीयते च परिक्लिष्टं तद्दानं राजसं स्मृतम् ॥२१॥

yat tu pratyupakārārthaṁ phalam uddiśya vā punaḥ ।
dīyate ca parikliṣṭam tad dānaṁ rājasaṁ smr̥tam ॥21॥

The gift offered expecting some return benefit or motivated by its fruits, and offered with vexation, is considered *rājasa*.

अदेशकाले यद्दानमपात्रेभ्यश्च दीयते ।
असत्कृतमवज्ञातं तत्तामसमुदाहृतम् ॥२२॥

adeśa-kāle yad dānam apātrebhyaś ca dīyate ।
asatkr̥tam avajñātaṁ tat tāmasam udāhr̥tam ॥22॥

The gift given to an unworthy person improperly and with disrespect, at a wrong place, at a wrong time, is said to be *tāmasa*.

Arjuna, we have so far been examining how the three *guṇa*s have their impact on *yajña, dāna* and *tapas,* the three Vedic disciplines, that stand here for the variety of high human values. Similarly, various is the impact of the *guṇa*s on those of divine traits and demonic traits. Those who perceive knowledge unitively and those who perceive it as endlessly branched and spread out in the higher and lower worlds, too have their own food habits and ways of performing *yajña, dāna* and *tapas,* all depending on how the *guṇa*s blend in them. And more, such differences will be apparent in all the activities, happening naturally or done deliberately, that form part of the Cosmic Form of Mine. Such activities are neither good nor bad in themselves, they are just a part of the cosmic system into which *Brahman* (Myself) unfolds itself. What is important, therefore, is not differentiating *sattva, rajas* and *tamas* as good or bad, but perceiving them as inseparable from, and inevitable in, *Brahman*'s self-unfoldment.

Three words — *AUM, tat, sat* — denotes *Brahman.* These are to be seen here in relation to *yajña, dāna* and *tapas* also, whether *sāttvika, rājasa* or *tāmasa*. Seen thus, the three disciplines gain a new dimension as inseparable from *Brahman,* as inseparable from the Cosmic Form. Seeing thus, therefore, is what we do in the rest of the chapter.

ॐ तत्सदिति निर्देशो ब्रह्मणस्त्रिविधः स्मृतः ।
ब्राह्मणास्तेन वेदाश्च यज्ञाश्च विहिताः पुरा ॥२३॥

oṁ tat sad iti nirdeśo brahmaṇas-trividhaḥ smṛtaḥ ।
brāhmaṇās tena vedāś ca yajñāś ca vihitāḥ purā ॥23॥

AUṀ, tat, sat — these three words are considered indicative of *Brahman*. Based on these, of old, were the *Brāhmaṇa*s, Vedas and *yajña*s put in order.

तस्मादोमित्युदाहृत्य यज्ञदानतपःक्रियाः ।
प्रवर्तन्ते विधानोक्ताः सततं ब्रह्मवादिनाम् ॥२४॥

tasmād om ity udāhṛtya yajña-dāna-tapaḥ-kriyāḥ ।
pravartante vidhānoktāḥ satataṁ brahma-vādinām ॥24॥

The exponents of *Brahman,* therefore, perform *yajña, dāna* and *tapas* as ordained, always along with uttering the word *AUṀ*.

Arjuna, that anything intentionally done with a pure heart should begin with the uttering of the monosyllabled sacred word *AUṀ* (pronounced *OṀ*) is a very ancient custom. Its philosophical basis, though not always understood by adherents, pertains to the context we are dealing with now.

How *karma-yogī*s perceive their doing *karma*s as *yajña*s was discussed in Chapter III. Done with the awareness, "These *karma*s are not mine, but of *prakṛti,*" such *karma*s become instrumental in realizing one's identity with total *prakṛti* or with *Brahman. Yajña,* thus, in principle, is the offering back to *prakṛti* what was wrongly thought of as one's *karma*s. Over and above the individual's actions, he himself is inseparably one with the Total Reality, and attaining this realization was seen in Chapter IV to be the essence of *jñāna-*

yoga. What is offered as oblation, then, is not one's *karmas*, but oneself. Living itself is then felt to be a never-ending *yajña*. *Brahma-vādin*'s perception, therefore, is that *yajña* is a principle that governs a properly lived life, and is the contextual frame of *karma-yoga* as well as *jñāna-yoga*. For the reason that all such offerings are made unto *Brahman*, both *karma-yogins* and *jñāna-yogins* perform whatever they do in life by uttering *AUṀ*, the word denoting *Brahman*. Indicative of all this is the customary practice of starting all ritualistic actions with the uttering of the sound *AUṀ*.

The Vedic ritual *dāna* (offering free gifts) underscores the idea, "Nothing is mine; everything belongs to God or *Brahman*". The riches that happen to come under one's control, therefore, are shared with the deserving. *Brahma-vādins* (exponents of *Brahman*) alone offer gifts with the awareness of this principle, and they, as a sign of this awareness, utter the word *AUṀ* while offering gifts.

Tapas, as we know, is the process of self-heating-up one undergoes in view of realizing *Brahman*, the Reality that is the Substance of one's own being. Those who undergo *tapas* as a spiritual practice with this awareness, utter *AUṀ* as they enter every new step of their practice.

It is the *yajña*, *dāna* and *tapas*, performed with such an understanding that is to be considered ordained in scriptures (*vidhānokta*), wisdom-wise. In the ritualistic context, on the other hand, rites become *vidhānokta* when performed following strictly in all details the instructions given in scriptural texts. It is also *vidhānokta* (ordained in scriptures) that all rituals must begin with uttering *AUṀ* as a sacred formula.

Brahma-vādin, literally, is one who speaks (*vad*) of *Brahman*. Speaking of anything implies clear understanding about it. One who knows *Brahman* and speaks of *Brahman* is, thus, a *Brahmavādin*.

Now let us examine the same, *yajña*, *dāna*, and *tapas* as related to the *Brahman*-denoting word *tat* (That).

तदित्यनभिसंधाय फलं यज्ञतपःक्रियाः ।
दानक्रियाश्च विविधाः क्रियन्ते मोक्षकाङ्क्षिभिः ॥२५॥

tad ity anabhisandhāya phalaṁ yajña-tapaḥ-kriyāḥ ।
dāna-kriyāś ca vividhāḥ kriyante mokṣa-kāṅkṣibhiḥ ॥25॥

With the conviction that all this is *tat* ("That" or *Brahman*) in essence, it is that liberation-seekers perform *yajñas*, undergo *tapas* and offer gifts, in various ways, with no desire for fruits.

Arjuna, to have motivating desires behind *karmas*, whether *sāttvika, rājasa* or *tāmasa,* ties us down to their fruits. Fruit-motivated *karmas* do not ensure liberation, but rather lead us to bondage. Since no life is possible without *karmas* or activities, we saw that the only way to liberate ourselves is to perform all *karmas* as *yajñas* (as was shown in Verse III.19). By perceiving *tat* alone or *Brahman* alone in all *karmas*, bodily, mental or verbal, we keep ourselves fully liberated even when remaining fully active.

Now let us relate *yajña, dāna* and *tapas* to *sat,* the other *Brahman*-denoting word.

सद्भावे साधुभावे च सदित्येतत्प्रयुज्यते ।
प्रशस्ते कर्मणि तथा सच्छब्दः पार्थ युज्यते ॥२६॥
यज्ञे तपसि दाने च स्थितिः सदिति चोच्यते ।
कर्म चैव तदर्थीयं सदित्येवाभिधीयते ॥२७॥

sad-bhāve sādhu-bhāve ca sad ity etat prayujyate ।
praśaste karmaṇi tathā sac-chabdaḥ pārtha yujyate ॥26॥

yajñe tapasi dāne ca sthitiḥ sad iti cocyate ।
karma caiva tad-arthīyaṁ sad ity evābhidhīyate ॥27॥

O Arjuna, the term *sat* is used related to *Brahman* in the sense, "It is what ultimately exists," and also in the sense, "It is what is ultimately Good." In relation to laudable actions too the word is fittingly in use.

> Steadfastness in *yajña, dāna* and *tapas* also is referred to as *sat*. So also actions done with the perception that *tat* (*Brahman*) is their meaning content, are also termed *sat*.

Arjuna, it is that one Reality alone — *Brahman,* referred to as *sat* — which unfolds itself as everything in all the worlds and as all the worlds. The connotation of the word *sat,* therefore, is so extensive that it excludes nothing that appears to be, including life-activities, from its scope. Such are the implications of the word *sad-bhāva.* The term *sat* used earlier in Verse II.16 is to be recalled here.

Whatever is good, whatever emerges and exists as a part of the spontaneous unfoldment of nature, can be termed *sādhu,* meaning good. Therefore, all that happens everywhere as natural is to be considered *sādhu* and thus good; and what one does with such a perception is also good in the absolutist sense. Life also will generally be good if understood to be nothing but *Brahman* manifesting itself. What one does in life then will also be good. It is such life-activities that are to be considered laudable (*praśasta*). *Sat-karma* is a term often used in referring to such *karma*s. *Karma*s done adhering to man-made laws and social regulations need not necessarily be *sat-karma*s in this sense. A *karma* always becomes *sat-karma* when done with the perception that it is part of *Brahman*'s self-manifestation, even though these *karma*s may be unmindful of social conventions.

*Karma*s done as *yajña*s lead to liberation (*mukti*), and *dāna* and *tapas* are to be seen as forming a part of *yajña* in principle. Therefore, as *karma*s performed as *yajña, dāna* and *tapas* are *sat-karma*s (*karma*s done properly and well, or meritorious *karma*s, those approved of by scriptures).

Brahman or *sat,* as the causal Substance, underlies all that appears to be. It thus assumes the form of effects and their *karma*s as well. Humans and their doings form a part of it. Therefore, what the word *sat* signifies excludes nothing in the Cosmic Form of Mine.

Arjuna, all human doings and conduct, *yajña, dāna* and *tapas* representing them, seen as inseparable from *Brahman,* seen as forming part of the Cosmic Form, are to be counted as *sat-karmas* enjoying the approval of the scriptures. They can be well practised even without learning scriptures. Learning such texts, particularly those of ritualistic import, and behaving strictly in accordance with their instructions, are *sat-karmas* in the ritualistic context; but such *karmas* follow scriptural injunctions in a mechanical way only. Wisdom's way is different, making life well ordered in a way of its own, and the behaviour pattern that finds expression thus follows scriptural injunctions in an absolutist way. The latter way is far superior, for one's faith and interest always find unity in it. In the other way, relativistic as it is, one feels imposed upon and the scriptures are followed with no abiding faith or interest.

How the *yajña, dāna* and *tapas* performed with no abiding faith and interest are to be counted, is stated in the concluding verse of the chapter:

अश्रद्धया हुतं दत्तं तपस्तप्तं कृतं च यत्।
असदित्युच्यते पार्थ न च तत्प्रेत्य नो इह ॥२८॥

aśraddhayā hutaṁ dattaṁ tapas taptaṁ kṛtaṁ ca yat ।
asad ity ucyate pārtha na ca tat pretya no iha ॥28॥

The oblation offered, the gift given, the *tapas* performed, and whatever is done, when done with no abiding faith and interest, are said to be *asat* (unreal, not Good), O Arjuna. Such doings are of no value here or the hereafter.

Arjuna, a *jñānin* sees all *karmas* as inseparable from *Brahman*, as *Brahman* become manifest, as forming part of the living Cosmic Form, and for this reason, all his doings naturally are full of faith and abiding interest. With an *ajñānin* (ignorant), on the other hand, all doings are benefit-motivated, and what he looks for is pleasure here as well as in the hereafter. Unaware of the one all-underlying Reality, regarding unreal appearances as the real, the ignorant see the here and hereafter as having separate existences. All that is done backed by this wrong understanding is bound to be *asat* (unreal as well as not good). The ignorant never become liberated from the obligations to perform rituals. They always remain in bondage, always live fearing sin.

Thus ends Chapter Seventeen entitled Śraddhā-Traya-Vibhāga-Yoga of the Bhagavad-Gītā, the essence of the Upaniṣads, that embodies the yoga-śāstra of brahma-vidyā in the form of a dialogue between Śrī Kṛṣṇa and Arjuna.

XVIII

Saṁnyāsa-Yoga

—The Yoga of Renunciation—

Vyāsa:

Janmejaya, just as the battle was about to start, as you remember, Arjuna took the negative attitude of unwillingness to fight. The reasons given by him reflected the traditional values followed by his family and clan, non-compliance with which was considered sinful, resulting in having to live in hell hereafter. From such a narrow and closed perception of life, Kṛṣṇa led Arjuna step by step to perceive himself as one with the whole cosmic system, figuratively represented by the Cosmic Form of Kṛṣṇa. At the same time, Arjuna, the individual, his personal traits and the behaviour pattern natural to those traits were not disregarded. Arjuna finding his identity with the Cosmic Form virtually means he relinquishing himself unto that Form. How is such relinquishment (*tyāga*) to be practised? What is the difference between *tyāga* and *saṁnyāsa*? The last chapter begins with answering these questions of Arjuna, and the answer takes us back to the scene with which the *Gītā* began.

Kṛṣṇa first differentiates *tyāga* and *saṁnyāsa,* then shows how in living terms *tyāga* finds expression in different ways in each person, categorizable as *sāttvika, rājasa* or *tāmasa. Tyāgī*s (those who relinquish) are never worried about the fruits of their actions (*karma-phala*), such worries being natural only with *atyāgī*s (those who have not relinquished themselves into the Cosmic Form), or so to say, with *ajñānin*s. In their perception, such fruits may be favourable, unfavourable or indifferent. The ignorant do *karma*s thinking of themselves as the doers of actions. Such *karma*s have five determinant factors, but *ajñānins* are oblivious to this. They regard themselves as the lone deciding factor. All such pre-planned actions have some knowledge that prompts from behind. Such knowledge is also of three kinds; the *karmas* performed thus are also of three kinds. Likewise, categorizable into three, is the sense of agency of action (*kartṛtva*) in each such doer. All decision-making has reasoning (*buddhi*) behind it; this reasoning is also of three types. Only those endowed with a firm mind (*dhīra*) can reason out and take proper decisions. Such firmness of mind (*dhṛti*) is also likewise of three kinds.

Whether one is a *jñānin* or *ajñānin, tyāgī* or *atyāgī,* the ultimate goal is happiness; it is only in the matter of regarding what they do as their own *karmas* or as part of *prakṛti,* that *ajñānins* or *atyāgīs* differ from *jñānins* or *tyāgins*. This happiness (*sukha*) also is of three types. The variety of human nature is thus: to be happy in life, one has to become fully aware, in the light of what we have discussed from Chapter XII to XVII, of what one's own peculiar character is, as part of the Cosmic Form. Then we realize that all the endlessly varying human traits in general could be well brought under four psychological types: brāhmaṇa, kṣatriya, vaiśya, śūdra.

One has to decide on one's own, of what type he or she is. If brāhmaṇa, one should live accordingly engaged in activities that fit in with that type; if one is found to be a kṣatriya, as Arjuna is, one should live and act accordingly; so it is with other types also. Happiness or blissfulness is experienced by everyone when involved in activities that fully agree with their character that forms the essential content of their self-being. This happiness is of self-expression, self-fulfilment, the Happiness of Self-Realization actualizable in practical life. The field of activity that fully agrees with one's personal traits is known as *svadharma*. All other activities, as far as oneself is concerned, are *paradharmas*, and remaining engaged in *paradharmas* causes constant worry and fear.

Arjuna, by personal character, is an outright kṣatriya, and a kṣatriya fulfils self-realization by expressing his skill in warfare. The *Mahābhārata* war is an occasion where Arjuna the kṣatriya is provided with the opportunity to engage in his *svadharma* and thus to actualize and eventually realize his own self-content as a part of the Cosmic Form. It was exactly at this juncture that he decided to retract, an act totally inappropriate for the kṣatriya that Arjuna is. This was the only one error on the part of Arjuna though backed by an argument grounded on tradition. Kṛṣṇa's lengthy wisdom-discourse makes Arjuna fully aware of what and who he really is. Arjuna thus comes back to himself, realizes who he is, and what his part is in the whole, picks up the bow and arrow that he had dejectedly laid down earlier, and firmly stands to fight. Such is the picture of Arjuna we see as Kṛṣṇa's teaching ends with this chapter. Let us now go into the details of the chapter:

अर्जुन उवाच —

संन्यासस्य महाबाहो तत्त्वमिच्छामि वेदितुम् ।
त्यागस्य च हृषीकेश पृथक्केशिनिषूदन ॥१॥

arjuna uvāca —

saṁnyāsasya mahābāho tattvam icchāmi veditum ।
tyāgasya ca hṛṣīkeśa pṛthak keśi-niṣūdana ॥1॥

Arjuna said —

O Hṛṣikeśa, O the Killer of Kesi, O the Mighty-Armed, I like to know the essence of *saṁnyāsa* (renunciation) as distinct from *tyāga* (relinquishment).

O Kṛṣṇa, in the beginning, frightened as I was by the possibility of having to kill my own kith and kin and *gurus*, I desired to retract from the battlefield. My mindset then was to give up everything. Now, after listening to your wisdom teaching, I fully realize how I am an inalienable part of your living Cosmic Form. There too another sort of relinquishment — the relinquishment of whatever was thought of as mine — seems essential. Yet, how different is the sense of relinquishment I now feel, from what was felt earlier!

There are also those called *saṁnyāsins*, who live in this world and who have renounced everything. In them too is a sort of giving up. It thus seems to me that *tyāga* (relinquishment) can be of many levels. I would like to get all this cleared up; please tell me initially the essential difference between *tyāga* and *saṁnyāsa*.

श्री भगवानुवाच —

काम्यानां कर्मणां न्यासं संन्यासं कवयो विदुः ।
सर्वकर्मफलत्यागं प्राहुस्त्यागं विचक्षणाः ॥२॥

śrī bhagāvan uvāca —

kāmyānāṁ karmaṇāṁ nyāsaṁ saṁnyāsaṁ kavayo viduḥ ।
sarva-karma-phala-tyāgam prāhus tyāgaṁ vicakṣaṇāḥ ॥२॥

Śrī Kṛṣṇa said —

Renouncing desire-motivated actions is understood by the wise as *saṁnyāsa*. And those of insight declare that relinquishing fruits of action is *tyāga*.

Arjuna, it is well that you asked this question. It gives me an opportunity to elucidate on all *karma*-related matters so as to enable you and others to examine yourselves, and each to decide on your own what your personal traits are, and what your *svadharma* is.

First, I shall tell you the difference between *saṁnyāsa* and *tyāga*. *Karmas* willingly performed by individuals are of different kinds: *nitya-karmas* (acts of daily routine), *niyata-karmas* (inevitable actions), *naimittika-karmas* (incidentally done *karmas*), and *kāmya-karmas* (desire-motivated actions). Eating, performing daily ablutions and the like constitute *nitya-karmas*. Actions that one is well aware of being inevitable are *niyata-karmas*. *Naimittika-karmas* are those one does incidentally. *Karmas* performed with the motive of some particular gain are known as *kāmya-karmas*. Renouncing all the *kāmya-karmas* is the mark of *saṁnyāsa*, the word meaning proper (*samyak*) renouncing (*nyāsa*). *Tyāga*, on the other hand, is relinquishing or rather being unmindful of the resultant benefit of all kinds of actions. Both the words *tyāga* and *nyāsa* literally mean the same, but what a *saṁnyāsin* renounces is the desire-motivated *karmas*, and what a *tyāgī* renounces is the benefit that accrues from all kinds of *karmas*. This *tyāga* is to be understood in the light of the *karma-yoga* discussed earlier in Chapter III and *saṁnyāsa* in the light of the *jñāna-yoga* of Chapter IV. These are opinions prevalent amongst the wise, yet all of them are not of the same opinion in this regard.

त्याज्यं दोषवदित्येके कर्म प्राहुर्मनीषिणः।
यज्ञदानतपःकर्म न त्याज्यमिति चापरे ॥३॥

tyājyaṁ doṣavad ity eke karma prāhur manīṣiṇaḥ ।
yajña-dāna-tapaḥ karma na tyājyam iti cāpare ॥3॥

*Karma*s in general, some say, ought to be given up, for they are all evil. According to some others, *yajña, dāna* and *tapas* are *karma*s not to be given up.

Arjuna, those who consider *jñāna* as a value higher than anything else, think of *karma*s and the way of ritualism as much inferior and evil. On the other hand, those who prefer ritualism consider *yajña, dāna* and *tapas* as meritorious *karma*s and hence never to be given up. Now I shall clarify what My stand is in this regard.

निश्चयं शृणु मे तत्र त्यागे भरतसत्तम।
त्यागो हि पुरुषव्याघ्र त्रिविधः सम्प्रकीर्तितः ॥४॥
यज्ञदानतपःकर्म न त्याज्यं कार्यमेव तत्।
यज्ञो दानं तपश्चैव पावनानि मनीषिणाम् ॥५॥
एतान्यपि तु कर्माणि सङ्गं त्यक्त्वा फलानि च।
कर्तव्यानीति मे पार्थ निश्चितं मतमुत्तमम् ॥६॥

niścayaṁ śṛṇu me tatra tyāge bharata-sattama ।
tyāgo hi puruṣa-vyāghra trividhaḥ saṁprakīrtitaḥ ॥4॥

yajña-dāna-tapaḥ-karma na tyājyaṁ kāryam eva tat ।
yajño dānaṁ tapaś caiva pāvanāni manīṣiṇām ॥5॥

etāny api tu karmāṇi saṅgam tyaktvā phalāni ca ।
kartavyānīti me pārtha niścitaṁ matam uttamam ॥6॥

> O Best of the Bharatas, hear now My own well settled conclusion in respect of *tyāga: tyāga,* O the tiger among men, is well known as of three types.
>
> *Yajña, dāna* and *tapas* are *karmas* not to be given up; they are indeed to be performed, for these three *karmas* purify the wise.
>
> Yet such actions, O Arjuna, have to be done with attachments and desire for benefits given up. This is My settled and decisive conviction.

Arjuna, it should now be clear to you that My perception of *yajña, dāna* and *tapas* is much different from that of ritualists. These rites, as I see them, purify the individual who performs them. *Yajña,* according to My teaching, as you know, symbolizes offering unto the Total Cosmic Form whatever is thought of as belonging to individuals. This offering purifies the mind of the individual and absolves him of all sense of sin. However, only the wise can do this with such an understanding. What one possesses as personal property really belongs to the Cosmic Form; so also oneself as well. Sharing such properties with everyone is the principle behind *dāna.* Such a *dāna* keeps one always pure in mind. *Tapas* is the intense effort on one's part to realize the one all-underlying Reality as the substance of one's own being; this realization purifies the individual to the extent that even the sense of being an individual vanishes. *Yajña, dāna* and *tapas,* in this revised sense, I tell you, are commendable and are to be performed. Then alone the seeming contradiction between My inviolable oneness and the multiplicity of appearances in My Cosmic Form become resolved. In a ritualistic sense, these three rites are performed with a sense of attachment, that is to say, one does them with the sense of being their doer, motivated always by expected beneficial results. The very same rites, as I recommend, are done by the wise (*manīṣiṇaḥ*), and what prompts them to do so is the clarity of vision of their inseparable identity with Me. Therefore, while performing these apparent rites, they remain fully unattached to them, unmoved by expectancy of results. Such are the *karmas* I consider as the best, ideal and wise.

Tyāga, being such, can also be of three types: *sāttvika, rājasa* and *tāmasa.*

नियतस्य तु संन्यासः कर्मणो नोपपद्यते।
मोहात्तस्य परित्यागस्तामसः परिकीर्तितः॥७॥

niyatasya tu saṁnyāsaḥ karmaṇo nopapadyate ।
mohāt tasya parityāgas tāmasaḥ parikīrtitaḥ ॥7॥

Renouncing actions that are inevitable is not proper. Giving up such actions in a deluded state of mind is said to be *tāmasa-tyāga*.

Arjuna, each individual, as part of the Cosmic Form, has his own functional role, comparable to that of each leaf in a giant banyan tree. The tree's upkeep is ensured by each of its parts functioning properly. The refusal of any part to perform its functions could have an adverse effect on the existence of the tree as a whole. An individual, likewise, due to ignorance or delusion, might ignore his own natural role as part of the total functional cosmic system. Such renunciation of activities natural to oneself is to be termed *tāmasa.*

Now I shall tell you what kind of renunciation of *karma* is *rājasa* by nature:

दुःखमित्येव यत्कर्म कायक्लेशभयात्त्यजेत्।
स कृत्वा राजसं त्यागं नैव त्यागफलं लभेत्॥८॥

duḥkham ity eva yat karma kāya-kleśa-bhayāt tyajet ।
sa kṛtvā rājasaṁ tyāgaṁ naiva tyāga-phalaṁ labhet ॥8॥

To renounce *karma*s, thinking of them as difficult and fearing bodily pain, is *rājasa-tyāga*. The benefit of *tyāga* is not at all attained by such a *tyāga*.

Now let us see what kind of *tyāga* is *sāttvika:*

कार्यमित्येव यत्कर्म नियतं क्रियतेऽर्जुन।
सङ्गं त्यक्त्वा फलं चैव स त्यागः सात्त्विको मतः॥९॥

kāryam ity eva yat karma niyataṁ kriyate 'rjuna ।
saṅgam tyaktvā phalaṁ caiva sa tyāgaḥ sāttviko mataḥ ॥9॥

Arjuna, that relinquishment which consists of giving up attachments and thoughts of return benefits in respect of inevitable *karmas* performed with the feeling, "This indeed ought to be done," is *sāttvika*.

Arjuna, the *guṇas* — *sattva, rajas* and *tamas* — pertain to *prakṛti*. Transcending *prakṛti* and its three *guṇas* and thus becoming *guṇātīta*, was seen to be the highest goal at the end of Chapter XIV. A *guṇātīta* never perceives Me as having the Cosmic Form, but only as the abstract, Absolute Reality. It is only when My own beginningless and endless self-manifestation is perceived that My Cosmic Form becomes meaningful, with the three *guṇas* invariably having a place in it. Therefore, those who perceive themselves as forming part of My Cosmic Form, that is to say, as forming part of the cosmic system, have necessarily to admit the three *guṇas* in themselves. *Karmas* are present only where changes take place in the state of existence, and changes are always subject to the three *guṇas*. My Cosmic Form, the aggregate of those changeful forms, is also changeful. The *karmas* taking place in it as a result might be felt to be good or bad. What the attitude of an enlightened *tyāgī* will be towards such *karmas*, I shall tell you:

न द्वेष्ट्यकुशलं कर्म कुशले नानुषज्जते ।
त्यागी सत्त्वसमाविष्टो मेधावी छिन्नसंशयः ॥१०॥

na dveṣṭy akuśalaṁ karma kuśale nānuṣajjate ।
tyāgī sattva-samāviṣṭo medhāvī chinna-saṁśayaḥ ॥10॥

A wise *tyāgī* of sundered doubts, seeing himself filled with beingness as he is, never despises unpleasant *karmas*, nor does he become attached to pleasant ones.

Arjuna, practising the *sāttvika tyāga* defined in Verse 9 is natural only for those who feel themselves filled with what is Real in the Total (*sattva-samāviṣṭa*). They then see all *karmas* as originating from the Total Being or *paramātmā* or Cosmic Form, and as having their being in the very same Cosmic Form. Liking some *karmas* and disliking some other *karmas* then becomes impossible. For such persons even classifying *karmas* as good and bad, meritorious and evil, is meaningless, for all *karmas* are those of *paramātmā*. If individuals have no *karmas* of their own, why can't they remain inactive? That too is impossible. Why?

न हि देहभृता शक्यं त्यक्तुं कर्माण्यशेषतः ।
यस्तु कर्मफलत्यागी स त्यागीत्यभिधीयते ॥११ ॥

na hi deha-bhṛtā śakyaṁ tyaktuṁ karmāṇy aśeṣataḥ ।
yas tu karma-phala-tyāgī sa tyāgīty abdhidhīyate ॥11 ॥

No body-sustainer can give up actions altogether. A real *tyāgī*, therefore, is one who relinquishes fruits of action.

Arjuna, the cosmic system altogether could be well considered to be My — *paramātmā*'s — body, and it is ceaselessly creative. Countless are the individual apparent forms that emerge in it as a result of its creativity, they too are creative and each has a body as well. Every body undergoes changes in appearance to perish finally. Change in appearance always involves some kind of action. Therefore, as every individual has to sustain a body, it is impossible to remain actionless.

Can a person, on knowing what *paramātmā* is, and becoming fully convinced that no individual has any *karma*, remain totally inactive? No. The decision not to do anything would be impossible to put into practice by anyone, for bodily limbs like hands and feet will continue to be functional. Of course, they can be restrained forcefully to some extent, but the inner organs will continue to work, the digestive system will function compelling eating, which is again an external action. The senses too will continue to do their jobs, and the mental faculties are no exception. The spiritual discipline known as *ātma-saṁyamana* (self-restraint) does not in any way mean putting an end to all natural activities as has already been made clear.

In short, no being, remaining inseparably one with the Cosmic Form, can remain actionless. By acknowledging this inevitability alone should one put into practice the high ideal of *tyāga*. Then one realizes, a real *tyāgī* is not the one who relinquishes all activities, but rather the one who has given up the notion, "I am the doer of this *karma* and its fruits are also mine." What he relinquishes is not action (*karma*), but the fruits of action (*karma-phala*). Giving up the fruits of action neither means that one intends one's actions to go fruitless, nor that the fruits should not be enjoyed. On the other hand, while being engaged in activities, doing something or enjoying something natural to his personal traits, the *tyāgī* will not be concerned with results, as far as he is concerned; his actions are merely part of the creative unfoldment of the Cosmic Form. Those concerned with fruits of action are not *jñānins*; they are simply *ajñānins* (ignorant); they are not *tyāgīs* (relinquishers), they are *atyāgīs* (non-relinquishers). The fruits of action, in the perception of such *atyāgīs*, appear to be of different kinds. Therefore,

अनिष्टमिष्टं मिश्रं च त्रिविधं कर्मणः फलम्।
भवत्यत्यागिनां प्रेत्य न तु संन्यासिनां क्वचित्॥१२॥

aniṣṭam iṣṭaṁ miśraṁ ca trividhaṁ karmaṇaḥ phalam |
bhavaty atyāginām pretya na tu saṁnyāsināṁ kvacit ||12 ||

Desirable, undesirable and mixed — thus threefold is the result of actions, the non-relinquishers think, to be enjoyed hereafter; but none such is relevant with a real renouncer (*saṁnyāsin*).

Arjuna, it is clear that the belief that one will have to enjoy or suffer in the next life the fruits of actions of this life, is an idea become fixed in the minds of *atyāgīs* who are also *ajñānins*. Each *karma*, in their perception, has its own end result which depends solely on its doer. Granted that *karmas* and their fruits are real, the nature of the latter depends necessarily on more than one factor, as I shall show you now:

पञ्चैतानि महाबाहो कारणानि निबोध मे।
सांख्ये कृतान्ते प्रोक्तानि सिद्धये सर्वकर्मणाम् ॥१३॥
अधिष्ठानं तथा कर्ता करणं च पृथग्विधम्।
विविधाश्च पृथक्चेष्टा दैवं चैवात्र पञ्चमम् ॥१४॥
शरीरवाङ्मनोभिर्यत्कर्म प्रारभते नरः।
न्याय्यं वा विपरीतं वा पञ्चैते तस्य हेतवः ॥१५॥

pañcaitāni mahā-bāho kāraṇāni nibodha me ।
sāṁkhye kṛtānte proktāni siddhaye sarva-karmaṇām ॥13॥

adhiṣṭhānaṁ tathā kartā karaṇaṁ ca pṛthag-vidham ।
vividhāś ca prthak-ceṣṭā daivaṁ caiv ātra pañcamam ॥14॥

śarīra-vāṅ-manobhir yat karma prārabhate naraḥ ।
nyāyyaṁ vā viparītaṁ vā pañcaite tasya hetavaḥ ॥15॥

O Mighty-Armed, learn form Me now, the five causal factors that decide the attainment of the result in respect of all actions. This was taught by the Sāṁkhya system at the end of the *kṛta* age:

The basis, doer, various instruments and organs, several distinct movements, the chance-element for the fifth.

These five decide the nature of whatever action man undertakes, whether bodily, verbal or mental, either justifiable or not.

Arjuna, *ajñānin*s and *atyāgin*s think they have their own *karma*s. Being the decision-makers, they think their fruits have to be enjoyed or suffered by themselves, here as well as in the hereafter. But the doer alone is not the causal factor of *karma*. Five are such factors as taught by the ancient Sāṁkhya system: a basic substance, the doer, the nature of instruments and organs utilized, the nature of various physical movements, and above all the chance-element.

No action can take place in vacuity. The action of flow takes place in the basic substance water. So too all actions in nature have to have an underlying substance that makes them possible. That substance can be none other than the one that also appears as ourselves, the doers.

A doer (*kartā*) has to be present where there is *karma*. This *kartā*, none else than the "I"-sense in each, needs suitable instuments and bodily organs to perform *karma*s properly. For example, feet are needed to do the *karma* of walking, hands for grasping, eyes for seeing, mind for thinking and so on. Each doer performs a *karma* in the best way he can, utilizing the organs and instruments in his control. Such utilization appears in the form of various physical movements (*ceṣṭā*s) which usually are counted as the actual *karma*s.

A *karma* performed with a specific good intention in mind need not necessarily turn out to be so. Even if done well, the desired result might slip away. The confluence of all favourable factors, being a chance element, is not in any one's control; it is called *daivam* here.

Even those who wrongly think they have their own *karma*s should perceive these five factors that control their performance and end result. The notion that the success of a *karma* depends on the doer alone, is wrong, and it is true with all *karma*s whether worldly or ritualistic, whether bodily, verbal or mental, and whether justifiable or not.

This analysis of the factors involved in *karma*s is a contribution of the very ancient Sāṁkhya philosophy; it is not a teaching of Mine. My teaching in this respect is to be stated in Verse 17 and its goal is liberating one from all bondages of *karma*s and their fruits, through *jñāna* and *tyāga*. My teaching does not aim at keeping the aspirant down in the world of ignorance (*ajñāna*) as *atyāgin*s whose case, as you know, we are dealing with at the moment. *Atyāgin*s are those who in their *ajñāna* (ignorance) think of themselves as *kartā*s and as the only deciding factor in the success of a *karma*. How should such be counted? I shall tell you:

तत्रैवं सति कर्तारमात्मानं केवलं तु यः।
पश्यत्यकृतबुद्धित्वान्न स पश्यति दुर्मतिः ॥१६॥

tatraivaṁ sati kartāram ātmānaṁ kevalaṁ tu yaḥ ।
paśyaty akr̥ta-buddhitvān na sa paśyati durmatiḥ ॥16॥

If one, in spite of being so, thinks of oneself alone as the isolated doer, then he should be counted as of distorted mind. Of an intelligence of no formation, he never perceives what is to be perceived.

Arjuna, even those who know the five causal factors of *karma* are *atyāgī*s, and thus *ajñānins*. Then how much worse is the state of one who thinks of himself alone as the deciding factor of *karma*s? Such are to be treated as the *ajñānin*s among *ajñānins*, of immature or distorted thinking faculty. Though discriminating the five causal factors pertains to *ajñāna,* it serves at least as the first stepping stone towards *jñāna.*

Now I shall tell you what kind of *karma* I recommend in an individual's life:

यस्य नाहङ्कृतो भावो बुद्धिर्यस्य न लिप्यते।
हत्वापि स इमांल्लोकान्न हन्ति न निबध्यते ॥१७॥

yasya nāhaṁkr̥to bhāvo buddhir yasya na lipyate ।
hatvāpi sa imāṁl lokān na hanti na nibadhyate ॥17॥

He whose attitude is not "I am the doer," whose thinking is unsullied by attachments (towards fruits of action), even if he happens to kill all these people, he really is no killer at all, nor is he in bondage.

Arjuna, a *yogī,* as you know, is whom I consider the best among humans. Whosoever experiences his beingness as inseparably one with Me, the ultimate Reality, is to be called a *yogī.* As I assume the form of the cosmos, he sees himself as a minute part of it existing inseparably and ensuring the perfection of the cosmic system. All *karma*s, in his perception, take place in My Cosmic Form which includes himself. He never feels himself to be the doer of any *karma,* even if it happens to be that of killing an entire army. What made you frightened in the beginning was perceiving *karma* as yours and thinking of yourself as the killer, because of the mistaken idea that *karmas* occur depending on the decision of their doers. Even if you think of yourself as the doer, the occurrence of your *karmas* depends not on you alone, but on the five factors detailed earlier.

I shall now tell you how knowledge prompts one to action:

ज्ञानं ज्ञेयं परिज्ञाता त्रिविधा कर्मचोदना।
करणं कर्म कर्तेति त्रिविधः कर्मसंग्रहः ॥१८॥

jñānaṁ jñeyaṁ parijñātā trividhā karma-codanā ।
karaṇam karma karteti trividhaḥ karma-saṁgrahaḥ ॥18॥

Knowledge, object of knowledge and knower — thus three-fold are the factors that incite one to action. Instruments, actual action and the actor — these three are the constituents of a context of action.

Arjuna, that the three-fold factors well known in Vedānta as *tripuṭi,* are inherent in every event of knowing, as we are well aware of. Each aspect of knowledge one gains impels one to do something new or to say something new. What one does depends on the nature and character of each of these three-fold factors. This explains why different people react differently to one and the same situation or idea. A three-foldness could be discerned in the context of action as well: instruments of action, the actual action and the person who acts. I don't have to remind you that both these *tripuṭis* are meaningful only for *ajñānins* or *atyāgins;* never with *jñānins* or *tyāgins.* Of the six factors involved in these two *tripuṭis,* three —*jñāna, karma, kartā* — are directly related to the end result of any *karma,* and these can also be different in nature depending on the three *guṇas* present. Now I shall tell you how are they so:

ज्ञानं कर्म च कर्ता च त्रिधैव गुणभेदतः ।
प्रोच्यते गुणसंख्याने यथावच्छृणु तान्यपि ॥१९॥

jñānaṁ karma ca kartā ca tridhaiva guṇa-bhedataḥ I
procyate guṇa-saṁkhyāne yathāvāc chr̥ṇu tāny api II19 II

Knowledge, action and the person who acts too, as held by the Sāṁkhya system that thinks of *guṇas*, can be of three kinds depending on the difference of *guṇas* in each. Hear from Me now, how do they differ:

सर्वभूतेषु येनैकं भावमव्ययमीक्षते ।
अविभक्तं विभक्तेषु तज्ज्ञानं विद्धि सात्त्विकम् ॥२०॥

sarva-bhūteṣu yenaikaṁ bhāvam avyayam īkṣate I
avibhaktaṁ vibhakteṣu taj jñānaṁ viddhi sāttvikam II20 II

The knowledge by which the one unexpended essence is perceived in all that has come into being, the one undivided in all that appears divided — understand it as *sāttvika.*

Arjuna, *sāttvika* is the type of *jñāna* that leads one to the ultimate goal; it also is the knowledge that enables one to see oneself in full identity with the Cosmic Form. The *vyavasāyātmikā buddhi* (fully convincing and resolute knowledge) I referred to earlier in Chapter II is also none other than this.[1]

पृथक्त्वेन तु यज्ज्ञानं नानाभावान्पृथग्विधान् ।
वेत्ति सर्वेषु भूतेषु तज्ज्ञानं विद्धि राजसम् ॥२१॥

pr̥thaktvena tu yaj jñānaṁ nānā-bhāvān pr̥thag-vidhān I
vetti sarveṣu bhūteṣu taj jñānaṁ viddhi rājasam II21 II

1. This is also what Narayana Guru refers to as the *sama* (same) kind of knowledge.

> The knowledge that sees, in all that has come into being, their multiple apparent forms of different kinds as separately existing realities — understand it as the *rājasa* kind of knowledge.

Arjuna, the many forms assumed by that which really exists are endless. Considering each as separately real is natural to the *rājasa* kind of knowledge. Using the term I referred in Chapter II, it can be characterized as *avyavasāyātmikā buddhi* (unconvincing and irresolute knowledge).[1]

यत्तु कृत्स्नवदेकस्मिन्कार्ये सक्तमहैतुकम् ।
अतत्त्वार्थवदल्पं च तत्तामसमुदाहृतम् ॥२२॥

yat tu kṛtsnavad ekasmin kārye saktam ahaitukam ।
atattvārthavad alpaṁ ca tat tāmasam udāhṛtam ॥22॥

> And that knowledge, clinging as it is to some particular effect for no reason, that treats that particular effect as the whole, based on no principle concerning the real, that takes cognizance only of a little, is said to be *tāmasa*.

Arjuna, people's perception in the usual course takes into account their own existence alone, or at the most that of their family and business. The reality that everyone lives as inseparably one with the whole and hence life has to be perceived holistically, does not strike them. Likewise, the object they have interest in are also thought of as having an existence of its own. The fact that a Reality causal to both oneself and the object exists, is never considered. In short, what they take to be forming the whole of life is in truth only a little part. If what happens within that range goes aganist one's calculations, one thinks life has turned upside down. Such a feeling surges up only because he is incapable of thinking of life properly based on undeniable principles. What I have been trying to do so far, was enabling you to

1. Narayana Guru calls it *anya* (the other).

think properly of life with a holistic perception. Those whose mind never turns to such perception, remain constantly in a darkness — the darkness of *tamoguṇa.*

Now let us see how the nature of one's *karma* varies according to the three *guṇas*:

नियतं सङ्गरहितमरागद्वेषतः कृतम् ।
अफलप्रेप्सुना कर्म यत्तत्सात्त्विकमुच्यते ॥२३॥

niyataṁ saṅga-rahitam arāga-dveṣataḥ kṛtam ।
aphala-prepsunā karma yat tat sāttvikam ucyate ॥23॥

Inevitable actions (*niyata karmas*) done desireless of fruits and attachmentless, with neither love nor hatred, are called *sāttvika karmas.*

Arjuna, I need not remind you that *sāttvika karma* helps one to become a true *yogī.*

यत्तु कामेप्सुना कर्म साहङ्कारेण वा पुनः ।
क्रियते बहुलायासं तद्राजसमुदाहृतम् ॥२४॥

yat tu kāmepsunā karma sāhaṁkāreṇa vā punaḥ ।
kriyate bahulāyāsaṁ tad rājasam udāhṛtam ॥24॥

And the action done motivated by desires or with I-sense, and accomplished with much effort is said to be *rājasa.*

Arjuna, he who does the *rājasa* type of *karma,* by the very act, binds himself to those very *karmas.*

अनुबन्धं क्षयं हिंसामनपेक्ष्य च पौरुषम् ।
मोहादारभ्यते कर्म यत्तत्तामसमुच्यते ॥२५॥

anubandhaṁ kṣayaṁ hiṁsām anapekṣya ca pauruṣam ।
mohād ārabhyate karma yat tat tāmasam ucyate ॥25॥

Actions undertaken with a deluded mind, unmindful of consequential ruin, injury to others and human limitations, are declared to be *tāmasa.*

Arjuna, making one's own life hell-like is what this kind of *karmas* lands us in.

The "I"-sense with which *karmas* are done by an individual, known as *kartṛtva,* or the sense of agency of action, again based on the three *guṇas,* can be of different kinds.

मुक्तसङ्गो ऽनहंवादी धृत्युत्साहसमन्वितः।
सिद्धयसिद्धयोर्निर्विकारः कर्ता सात्त्विक उच्यते ॥२६॥

mukta-saṅgo 'nahaṁ-vādī dhṛty-utsāha-samanvitaḥ ।
siddhy-asiddhyor nirvikāraḥ kartā sāttvika ucyate ॥26॥

The *kartā* (doer of actions) who is free from attachments, who does not refer to himself as the doer, who in the mean time is endowed with firmness and zeal, who remains unmoved by success or failure of the *karma,* is said to be *sāttvika.*

Arjuna, as the *sāttvika karmas* help one become a *karma-yogin,* so too a *sāttvika kartā* naturally becomes a *karma-yogin* himself, or rather, being a *sāttvika kartā* is an external mark of a *karma yogin.*

रागी कर्मफलप्रेप्सुर्लुब्धो हिंसात्मको ऽशुचिः।
हर्षशोकान्वितः कर्ता राजसः परिकीर्तितः ॥२७॥

rāgī karma-phala-prepsur lubdho hiṁsātmako 'śuciḥ ।
harṣa-śokānvitaḥ kartā rājasaḥ parikīrtitaḥ ॥27॥

The doer of actions who is attached to what he does, who is keen on obtaining their fruits, who undertakes harmful and unclean actions, who is subject to exaltation and depression owing to the results of what he does — he is well known as a *rājasa kartā.*

अयुक्तः प्राकृतः स्तब्धः शठो नैकृतिको ऽलसः ।
विषादी दीर्घसूत्री च कर्ता तामस उच्यते ॥२८॥

ayuktaḥ prākrtaḥ stabdhaḥ śaṭho naikṛtiko 'lasaḥ ।
viṣādī dīrgha-sūtrī ca kartā tāmasa ucyate ॥28॥

An *ayukta* (one incapable of perceiving himself, his mind and his actions, as fully in identity with what they really are one with inseparably), who is crude, stubborn, deceitful, malicious, lazy, despondent, procrastinating — such a *kartā* is said to be *tāmasa.*

Arjuna, finding oneself in full identity with the Cosmic Form while remaining active in life by being engaged in activities fit for one's personal traits, requires a discriminative mind and well founded reasoning. After having discerned the vocation and way of life proper to one as part of the whole, what one needs is the firmness of mind (*dhṛti*) to stick to it. The discriminating and reasoning mind (*buddhi*) as well as *dhṛti* can be basically of three types depending on the *guṇa*s predominant.

बुद्धेर्भेदं धृतेश्चैव गुणतस्त्रिविधं शृणु ।
प्रोच्यमानमशेषेण पृथक्त्वेन धनञ्जय ॥२९॥

buddher bhedaṁ dhṛteś caiva guṇatas trividhaṁ śṛṇu ।
procyamānam aśesena pṛthaktvena dhanañjaya ॥29॥

The discriminative and reasoning mind (*buddhi*) and the firmness of mind (*dhṛti*) are also three-fold, each according to the *guṇa*s, O Arjuna. I shall tell you fully and severally how they are so. Do listen to Me.

प्रवृत्तिं च निवृत्तिं च कार्याकार्ये भयाभये ।
बन्धं मोक्षं च या वेत्ति बुद्धिः सा पार्थ सात्त्विकी ॥३०॥

> *pravr̥ttiṁ ca nivr̥ttiṁ ca kāryākārye bhayābhaye* |
> *bandhaṁ mokṣaṁ ca yā vetti buddhiḥ sā pārtha sāttvikī* ||30 ||

> The discriminative and reasoning mind that discerns positive way of action and the negative way of withdrawal from action, what ought to be done and what ought not to be done, what is to be feared and what is absolute fearlessness, binding and liberating actions — such *buddhi,* O Arjuna, is *sāttvika.*

Arjuna, in the positive way of action (*pravr̥tti-mārga*), one eagerly intends to do something with the sense; "I am bound to do it; so I will do it." There are also a few who are well aware that their existence is but part of the existence of the whole, that what they do is nothing but part of the creativity of the whole becoming manifest. Such persons never feel the urge for getting involved in activities intentionally. This natural bent to withdraw oneself from intentional activities is known as *nivr̥tti-mārga.* Well known in Indian spiritual tradition are these two paths, the former going with ritualism and the latter with wisdom. Differentiating these two paths is a mark of having proper *sāttvika buddhi.* What one of *pravr̥tti-mārga* thinks of as *kārya* (what one ought to do) may be *akārya* (what one ought not do) for the other, for the former perceives oneself as the doer, and the latter knows the whole or nature or Myself to be the doer. In the like manner, what one of *nivr̥tti-mārga* does for ensuring the upkeep of the cosmic order, for the coherent existence of the entire life system (*loka saṁgraha*), will be thought of as uncalled for by the other, for no apparent personal benefit is seen there.

Perceiving the all-underlying Reality in oneself, and what is Real in oneself as underlying everything, makes one free of all fears. For this reason, this wisdom is often considered a synonym for fearlessness (*abhaya*). He who sees himself as existing separate, on the other hand, always fears the "other"; indeed he fears everything. His life in effect is a continuous search for security.

Bondage (*bandha*) too is meaningful only when one thinks of oneself as a separately existing entity. If the one Reality alone exists, then who is there to be bonded to? Perceiving one Reality or *paramātmā* alone existing as everything, is what makes one fully Liberated (*mukta*).

Arjuna, one who has this discriminating mind naturally resorts to the way of withdrawal from intentional actions, and lives fearless and liberated. One who lacks this mind, on the other hand, lives engaged in benefit-motivated actions, full of fear. The discriminating reason which can see this distinction is to be called *sāttvika buddhi.*

Now let us look at the *rājasika buddhi.*

यया धर्ममधर्मं च कार्यं चाकार्यमेव च।
अयथावत्प्रजानाति बुद्धिः सा पार्थ राजसी॥३१॥

yayā dharmam adharmaṁ ca kāryaṁ cākāryam eva ca ।
ayathāvat prajānāti buddhiḥ sā pārtha rājasī ॥31 ॥

> That discriminative reasoning mind which understands not the righteous (*dharma*) and the unrighteous (*adharma*), what ought to be done (*kārya*) and what ought not be done (*akārya*), as they should be, is the *rājasa buddhi.*

Arjuna, what *dharma* and *adharma* signify was made clear as early as the very outset of this discourse. A proper understanding of it alone makes one capable of deciding what one should and should not do in particular situations in life. Those who misconceive *dharma* and *adharma* are liable to mix up *kārya* with *akārya* making life a chaotic mess and an aimless excursion. No life of that sort is blissful and blessed in the absolutist sense.

Now let us see what a *tāmasa buddhi* is:

अधर्मं धर्ममिति या मन्यते तमसावृता।
सर्वार्थान्विपरीतांश्च बुद्धिः सा पार्थ तामसी॥३२॥

adharmaṁ dharmam iti yā manyate tamasāvṛtā ।
sarvārthān viparītāṁś ca buddhiḥ sā pārtha tāmasī ॥32 ॥

> That discriminative reasoning mind, enveloped by darkness as it is, that mistakes *adharma* for *dharma* and takes reversely all similar values, O Pārtha, is *tāmasa buddhi*.

The firmness of mind too, according to the dominant *guṇa*s, is of three kinds as follows:

धृत्या यया धारयते मनःप्राणेन्द्रियक्रियाः ।
योगेनाव्यभिचारिण्या धृतिः सा पार्थ सात्त्विकी ॥३३॥

dhṛtyā yayā dhārayate manaḥ-prāṇendriya-kriyāḥ ।
yogenāvyabhicāriṇyā dhṛtiḥ sā pārtha sāttvikī ॥33॥

> The firmness that holds within its ambit the activities of mental faculties, vital functions (*prāṇa*s) and senses, by following the path of *yoga* non-deflectingly, O Pārtha, is the *dhṛti* that is *sāttvika*.

Arjuna, being endowed with a discriminative and proper reasoning mind alone is of no use in making oneself liberated while living as part of this world. An uncompromising firmness of mind to abide by what is discerned as propitious is also a must for a person who is capable of discriminating *dharma* and *adharma*, *kārya* and *akārya* and the like. Many *yoga*-based directions on how this firmness could be achieved were given in the first half of this dialogue. One who follows them willingly is to be counted as a *yogī*. His mind, *prāṇa*s and sense organs never distract him from the chosen path, to render him directionless like a canoe lost mid-stream in turbulent waters. All of these, on the contrary, while functioning naturally, remain within his firm control and he is thus able to transform them into the means for achieving his final goal. Such a firmness of mind (*dhṛti*) is to be characterized as *sāttvika*.

Now I shall tell you which kind of firmness is to be counted as *rājasa*.

यया तु धर्मकामार्थान्धृत्या धारयतेऽर्जुन।
प्रसङ्गेन फलाकाङ्क्षी धृतिः सा पार्थ राजसी ॥३४॥

yayā tu dharma-kāmārthān dhṛtyā dhārayate 'rjuna ।
prasaṅgena phalākāṅkṣī dhṛtiḥ sā pārtha rājasī ॥34॥

The firmness by which one holds *dharma* (righteousness), *kāma* (fulfilment of desires) and *artha* (earning wealth) as values that make life meaningful, always accompanied by strong attachment and the resultant intense desire for enjoying the fruits of action, O Pārtha, such a *dhṛti* is to be termed *rājasa.*

Arjuna, four are the human values (*puruṣārthas*) traditionally held aspirable by Indians — *dharma* (righteousness), *artha* (owning wealth), *kāma* (fulfilment of desires), *mokṣa* (final Liberation). The last one is known as *parama-puruṣārtha* (the supreme human value). The other three are held high by those who are interested in ordinary worldly pleasures, the I-sense and mine-sense never leaving them. Desire for enjoying the results of what they do is naturally very strong. The firmness of mind they have can be considered the *rājasa* type of *dhṛti.*

Now we come to the *tāmasa* kind of *dhṛti.*

यया स्वप्नं भयं शोकं विषादं मदमेव च।
न विमुञ्चति दुर्मेधा धृतिः सा पार्थ तामसी ॥३५॥

yayā svapnaṁ bhayaṁ śokaṁ viṣādaṁ madam eva ca ।
na vimuñcati durmedhā dhṛtiḥ sā pārtha tāmasī ॥35॥

The firmness with which one of perverted mind does not leave behind sleepiness, fear, grief, despondency, as also inebriety, it, O Pārtha, is the *tāmasa* type of *dhṛti.*

Arjuna, the ideal *tyāga* (relinquishment) is the general theme we are dealing with now. As we are concerned with *karmas*, the relinquishment could either be of the fruits of action or of actions themselves; the former to be called *tyāga* and the latter *saṁnyāsa.* In either case, what matters is *karma,* and what we have so far been doing in this chapter is examining the various factors, *sāttvika, rājasa,* or *tāmasa* in kind, that decide the nature of *karma.* All *karmas*, whatever the influencing factors, are aimed at ensuring happiness which also vary in nature depending on the *guṇa* dominant in the doer. Let us now examine how this is:

सुखं त्विदानीं त्रिविधं शृणु मे भरतर्षभ।
अभ्यासाद्रमते यत्र दुःखान्तं च निगच्छति ॥३६॥

sukhaṁ tv idānīṁ trividhaṁ śṛṇu me bharatarṣabha ।
abhyāsād ramate yatra duḥkhāntaṁ ca nigacchati ॥36॥

Happiness in this world too, O Best of Bharatas, is of three types. One, by practising them with understanding, rejoices in life and puts an end to all sorrows.

I shall tell you what the *sāttvika* type of happiness (*sukha*) is:

यत्तदग्रे विषमिव परिणामे ऽमृतोपमम्।
तत्सुखं सात्त्विकं प्रोक्तमात्मबुद्धिप्रसादजम् ॥३७॥

yat tad agre viṣam iva pariṇāme 'mṛtopamam ।
tat sukhaṁ sāttvikaṁ proktam ātma-buddhi-prasādajam ॥37॥

The happiness felt poison-like in the beginning and ambrosia-like at the end, is said to be *sāttvika.* It is born of the Blissfulness of Self-knowledge.

Arjuna, Self-knowledge (*ātma-jñāna*), as you know, means knowing oneself properly and really as the one immortal *ātmā* in essence. The awareness, "I am the eternal *ātmā*" is what is referred to here as *ātma-buddhi.* A Blissfulness arises of this awareness, which can be understood as that awareness itself. This happiness is ceaseless all through life and is signified by the word *ātma-buddhi-prasāda.* This best of all happiness aspirable in life is to be considered the *sāttvika* type. Many may be the obstructions and afflictions one will have to suffer in the search for this happiness, many a momentary pleasure will have to be forsaken. Yet what all these sufferings eventually results in is the eternal Blissfulness of living with a full awareness of who and what one really is, as part of the Cosmic Form.

Now the *rājasa* type of happiness:

विषयेन्द्रियसंयोगाद्यत्तदग्रे ऽमृतोपमम्।
परिणामे विषमिव तत्सुखं राजसं स्मृतम्॥३८॥

viṣayendriya-saṁyogād yat tad agre 'mṛtopamam ।
pariṇāme viṣam iva tat sukhaṁ rājasaṁ smṛtam ॥38॥

The happiness that arises out of the contact of senses with their objects, and felt ambrosia-like at the beginning and poison-like at the end, is understood as the *rājasa* type.

Arjuna, those with the *rajo-guṇa* predominant also live as forming part of My Cosmic Form; their longing too is to live happily. Happiness, as they see it, is derived from external pleasurable objects, the reason why they constantly direct their sense organs to the concerned objects if enjoyable and withdraw them if detestable. Such sense pleasures initially are felt to be exhilarating and nectar-like. The sense objects, after a while, begin to look insipid, and then one begins to keep oneself away from them; if they do not get out of the way they may even be treated as a nuisance. The mind, by then would have become infatuated by another pleasurable object. The pleasure derived from this latter also is no exception. Such enjoyment of pleasures, hopping from one pleasurable object to another, is to be considered *rājasa* in nature.

Now hear from Me what the *tāmasa* kind of happiness is:

यदग्रे चानुबन्धे च सुखं मोहनमात्मनः।
निद्रालस्यप्रमादोत्थं तत्तामसमुदाहृतम्॥३९॥

yad agre cānubandhe ca sukhaṁ mohanam ātmanaḥ ।
nidrālasya-pramādotthaṁ tat tāmasam udāhṛtam ॥39॥

That which originates from a delusion of self-happiness and ends with so, arising from sleepiness, slothfulness and heedlessness as it is, is the *tāmasa* kind of happiness.

Arjuna, the *tāmasa* type of happiness, in fact, is no happiness at all; it originates from some idea of happiness that is illusory, and ends with a delusion of happiness, the real happiness always remaining unexperienced.

Arjuna, you must now have got a clear picture as to how the three *guṇas* make our *karmas*, our life and our experiences of pleasure and pain endlessly diverse. The impact of *guṇas*, in fact, is everywhere in *prakṛti*. Look at how universal it is:

न तदस्ति पृथिव्यां वा दिवि देवेषु वा पुनः।
सत्त्वं प्रकृतिजैर्मुक्तं यदेभिः स्यात्त्रिभिर्गुणैः ॥४०॥

na tad asti pṛthivyāṁ vā divi deveṣu vā punaḥ ।
sattvaṁ prakṛtijair muktaṁ yad ebhiḥ syāt tribhir guṇaiḥ ॥40॥

No entity either in the earth, in heaven or amongst gods, ever remains free of the impact of the three *guṇas* of *prakṛti*.

Arjuna, what you saw earlier as My Cosmic Form has in it all the worlds, heaven and earth included. Whatever appears to be in those worlds is part of My body, is part of *prakṛti*. The three *guṇas* are related to *prakṛti* as are heat and light to fire. No entity is free from these *guṇas*. Only I, the *paramātmā*, the one essential Substance that constitutes the being of all such entities, remains beyond the *guṇas* and hence is *guṇātīta*.

Indescribable and even unthinkable is the variety of the intermingling of *guṇas* in *prakṛti*. What I pointed out are only certain aspects of it related to human activities. Based on this it is possible to explore how the *guṇas* influence other fields of human interest as well. The impact of the *guṇas* already mentioned are only a pointer to its endless realm.

One, guided by this pointer, has to make a self-exploration and find out for oneself which *guṇa* is dominant in oneself and which *guṇa* activates oneself in a particular situation. Then it becomes self-revealed as to what one's inner nature is as part of the total nature. This self-revelation helps one decide for oneself which field of activity or occupation fits in with one's own personal traits, and it is such activities and occupation that one should engage oneself in, in order to ensure a happy and peaceful life, and above all to experience a sense of absolute Freedom. The occupation fit for one need not befit another, and therefore attempts to imitate others renders life miserable. Each person has a different blend of *guṇa*s in him. Nevertheless, based on certain common features, the *guṇa*-and-*karma*-based personal traits of human beings can be classified into four:

ब्राह्मणक्षत्रियविशां शूद्राणां च परंतप ।
कर्माणि प्रविभक्तानि स्वभावप्रभवैर्गुणैः ॥४१॥

brāhmaṇa-kṣatriya-viśāṁ śūdrāṇāṁ ca paraṁtapa ।
karmāṇi pravibhaktāni svabhāva-prabhāvair guṇaiḥ ॥41॥

O Conqueror of Foes (Arjuna), separate are the vocations of brāhmaṇas, kṣatriyas, vaiśyas and śūdras in conformity with the *guṇa*s that emerge as a result of My self-manifestation.

Arjuna, the *karma*s natural with human beings can be classified as those of brāhmaṇas, kṣatriyas, vaiśyas and śūdras. The basis for this classification is simply the three *guṇa*s. I, the one all-underlying Substance, assuming the Cosmic Form, appear as all the entities of countless names and forms, each endowed with a particular blend of the three *guṇa*s, and human beings are no exception. The resultant difference in personal peculiarities is evident in human beings, from bodily features to extremely subtle mental functions and life-interests. This characterization is not based on any social prejudice or the intention of anyone to exploit someone else. *Karma*s natural to one owing to the particular blend of *guṇa*s in one alone is its criterion. All form part of My Cosmic Form, and hence My earlier statement *cāturvarṇyam mayā sṛṣṭam* (the four-fold colouration of human character was created by Myself, IV.13). First I shall detail to you what are the *karmas* natural with the brāhmaṇa type of people.

शमो दमस्तपः शौचं क्षान्तिरार्जवमेव च ।
ज्ञानं विज्ञानमास्तिक्यं ब्रह्मकर्म स्वभावजम् ॥४२ ॥

śamo damas tapaḥ śaucam kṣāntir ārjavam eva ca ।
jñānaṁ vijñānam āstikyaṁ brahma-karma svabhāvajam ॥42 ॥

The *karmas* of the brāhmaṇa type of people are naturally characterized by serenity, self-restraint, austere self-effort for attaining wisdom (*tapas*), purity, forgiveness and straightforwardness. So too are yearning for *jñāna* and *vijñāna,* and a firm belief in Me.

Arjuna, the peculiar human traits mentioned here need no further clarification and as I have shed light on it earlier, though not as the defining characteristics of the brāhmaṇa type. Not that one who practises all these deliberately becomes a brāhmaṇa, but only that these behavioural patterns are natural with brāhmaṇas and they find joy in being so.

Let us now come to the peculiarities of the kṣatriya type of people.

शौर्यं तेजो धृतिर्दाक्ष्यं युद्धे चाप्यपलायनम् ।
दानमीश्वरभावश्च क्षात्रं कर्म स्वभावजम् ॥४३ ॥

śauryaṁ tejo dhṛtir dākṣyaṁ yaddhe cāpy apalāyanam ।
dānam īśvara-bhāvaś ca kṣātraṁ karma svabhāvajam ।43 ॥

Prowess, brightness, firmness, masterliness, never pulling back from battle, generosity, overlordship — these are characteristics apparent in the *karmas* of the *kṣatriya* type of people.

Coming now to the vaiśyas and śūdras:

कृषिगौरक्ष्यवाणिज्यं वैश्यकर्म स्वभावजम्।
परिचर्यात्मकं कर्म शूद्रस्यापि स्वभावजम्॥४४॥

kṛṣi-gaurakṣya-vāṇijyaṁ vaiśya-karma svabhāvajam ।
paricaryātmakaṁ karma śūdrasyāpi svabhāvajam ॥44॥

Farming, rearing cattle and doing business are *karma*s natural with the vaiśya type, and doing service, likewise, is the *karma* natural with the śūdra type.

Arjuna, to be of different colours character-wise, as part of My Cosmic Form, is natural with human beings. I prefer to call these divisible-into-four-human traits as *varṇa*s (colours) and hence the name *cātur-varṇya* given to this classification of psychological types. Given that these *varṇa*s are part of My Cosmic Form, I could be well considered their originator (*kartā*). These *varṇa*s, on the other hand, having no specifiable intending originator — not even Me — I am their non-doer (*akartā*) as well, as was pointed out earlier (IV.13).

Cāturvarṇya as a social phenomenon hierarchically conceived, admittedly is in practice now, and may be so in future as well. Yet it is of no relevance in the context of this discourse, for what it deals with is not sociology, but *brahma-vidyā*. The aspect we give special emphasis to in this context is this: each person while living fully as himself, engaged in activities natural to him, has to find identity with total nature or with My Cosmic Form.

The *cāturvarṇya* that pervails as a social evil admits a hierarchy of social order made up of different castes, whereas the one I refer to here considers all the four *varṇa*s as of equal status. However, it need not be claimed that all the four do feel the same sense of freedom in life. A brāhmaṇa type of person considers knowledge as of high value and hence learning and teaching are the vocations he likes. He is accepted and respected by all those who love knowledge, and, since wisdom makes man free, a brāhmaṇa type always feels free.

A kṣatriya's natural interest is in giving leadership to the state and its people. People give him respect when they feel they get the leadership they are in need of. Such leaders are honoured by those people, never by others. They are respected within their state, not necessarily outside. In a foreign country they are just like anyone else. The sense of freedom they feel, their acceptability, the respect they get — all are within the limits of the state or society concerned, and in no way as universal as the respect for brāhmaṇa types.

To work hard and accumulate wealth is the aim of vaiśyas. The freedom they enjoy is what their money can buy.

Selling their own freedom for the sake of livelihood is what śūdras do. A job of high position in government service or in the service of some business concern, is often thought of as enviable, but such jobs, simply for the reason that they involve forsaking one's freedom, are definitely to be counted as of śūdra type.

I, as a man of wisdom, as a *guru,* love those who love wisdom, but as the one Reality that unfolds itself as everything, all are equal to Me. I love all equally, for all are part of My Cosmic Form. I treat all beings in the same way that everyone treats their own body. As is My attitude towards them equal, so is equal the opportunity for everyone to attain Me. To clarify this point further:

स्वे स्वे कर्मण्यभिरतः संसिद्धिं लभते नरः ।
स्वकर्मनिरतः सिद्धिं यथा विन्दति तच्छृणु ॥४५॥

sve sve karmaṇy abhirataḥ saṁsiddhiṁ labhate naraḥ ।
sva-karma-nirataḥ siddhiṁ yathā vindati tacchr̥ṇu ॥45॥

The man who finds delight in being engaged in activities fit for one's own nature attains perfect life-fulfilment. Now hear from Me how is this fulfilment attained by one who devotes oneself to occupations natural to one.

Arjuna, it must now be clear to you that the occupation fit for one person may not be fitting for another. Being engaged in activities fit for one keeps one happy, so that the passing of time goes unnoticed. The happiness one feels thus is nothing other than Self-Happiness (*ātmānanda*) — the Happiness of perceiving directly what is essential and potential in oneself. The sense of absolute Freedom one experiences thus is the final Liberation or *mukti.* This Blissfulness or *ānanda* experienced by a brāhmaṇa, when engaged in his natural activities, is in no way superior to the one felt by a śūdra when he is engrossed in activities fit for him, for both are the *ānanda* of bringing to fruition what is essential and potential in oneself. In this sense, the four *varṇa*s I mention here are among themselves, neither one inferior nor superior to another. I shall clarify further how everyone, irrespective of the difference in *varṇa*s, can attain the final life-fulfilment.

यतः प्रवृत्तिर्भूतानां येन सर्वमिदं ततम्।
स्वकर्मणा तमभ्यर्च्य सिद्धिं विन्दति मानवः ॥४६॥

yataḥ pravṛttir bhūtānāṁ yena sarvam idaṁ tatam ।
sva-karmaṇā tam abhyarcya siddhiṁ vindati mānavaḥ ॥46॥

The one causal Reality from which do emerge the different activities of all beings, and which also is the Substance that pervades the being of everything — by performing one's natural activities as an offering of worship unto It, a human being attains perfection in life.

Arjuna, as you are well aware, I am the one Reality that unfolds itself as the Cosmic Form and as all the beings in it. The creative urge in Me is what effects this self-unfoldment. The same creative urge pulsates in every being that emerges from Me and exists as inseparably one with Me, the reason for their existence being an active one, and humans are no exception. Only the awareness, "I am active" differentiates human from other beings. This very same awareness is what also implants in a human the sense of agency of actions (*kartṛtva*), and thus he thinks, "I am the doer of these actions." But the enlightenment that it is *paramātmā* or Myself — the Absolute — that subsists as the Reality in every being and pulsates in the form of their *karma*s, transforms all actions into an offering of worship to *paramātmā* or Myself. One then sees only the pulsation of *paramātmā* in all actions. Performing actions with this awareness makes one experience one's inseparable identity with *paramātmā* — the ultimate goal one can attain in life. Only by realizing one's identity with the whole while engaged in activities that are befitting of one's personal traits, can this goal be attained. Such a way of being active in life, is known as *svadharma* and its importance should not be lost sight of.

श्रेयान्स्वधर्मो विगुणः परधर्मात्स्वनुष्ठितात्।
स्वभावनियतं कर्म कुर्वन्नाप्नोति किल्बिषम्॥४७॥

śreyān svadharmo viguṇaḥ para-dharmāt svanuṣṭhitāt ।
svabhāva-niyataṁ karma kurvan nāpnoti kilbiṣam ॥47॥

Much better than actions well-done yet unfit for one's nature (*paradharma*), are actions fit for one's nature (*svadharma*) though ill-done. He who performs actions that are inevitable in the course of events and fit for one's nature, incurs no sin.

Arjuna, what *svadharma* implies must have become sufficiently clear to you. Its opposite is *paradharma,* meaning actions that do not fit in with one's personal traits. Many are often forced by circumstances to do *karmas* that are not in any way befitting their personal peculiarities. Individuals are often forced to opt for jobs foreign to their nature, instigated either by lack of opportunities or by greed. Even such unfit jobs might be executed well, taking into account the financial benefits they offer, yet they are never done with a sense of joy. The longing when in the job will always be to finish with it somehow and to be free of it. And time too drags on while engaged in the job. Continuing this leads to mental stress which may eventually turn pathological, rendering life quite out of balance. Being engaged in *svadharma,* on the other hand, keeps one happy and the passage of time is never felt. The job will be experienced as part of one's life's progress. Such jobs, even if ill-done, not only do not harm one's life, but keeps one happy also.

Arjuna, coming now back to your own case, you by both *guṇa* and *karma,* are a kṣatriya, and this battle offers you, without your desiring it, an opportunity to bring out and activate the immense kṣatriya type of potential held within you, and thus to realize the *ātmānanda* of experiencing directly what you are as part of the whole. Fearing sin, earlier, you even desired to take on a mendicant's role, which is doubtless, a *paradharma* for you. Battling is clearly your *svadharma,* and by being engaged in it, perceiving it as forming an integral part of the overall *kṛti* or *karma* of *prakṛti,* you go beyond the reach of sin and merit, and thus become free from all "sins" connected with battling. Two are the distinguishing features of such *karma*s: one, they should always fully agree with one's personal traits (*svabhāva*) and two, they should become necessary (*niyata*) as an inevitable part of the total flow of *karma*s of *prakṛti.* Such is the *karma* you are now destined to do. You should realize, even as you are engaged in such *karma*s, that you are not their doer (*kartā*). Not being a doer of *karma,* you remain untouched by sin. To state the same as a general principle:

सहजं कर्म कौन्तेय सदोषमपि न त्यजेत्।
सर्वारम्भा हि दोषेण धूमेनाग्निरिवावृताः ॥४८॥

sahajaṁ karma kaunteya sadoṣam api na tyajet ।
sarvārambhā hi doṣeṇa dhūmenāgnir ivāvṛtāḥ ॥48॥

Arjuna, actions natural to one's personal traits, even if they happen to be blameful, should not be given up. All undertakings, in fact, are clouded by some blemish, as is fire by smoke.

Arjuna, the *karma*s one happens to do as part of the total flow of nature, seen with the eye of social conventions and norms of morality, may be adjudged blameful, as in your case now. Still such *karma*s are not to be given up. Arjuna, no endeavour in this world can be entirely blameless; some defect is always present even as smoke always accompanies fire. Remaining unattached is what one can do in this regard. Such an attitude always takes one to *naiṣkarmya siddhi* (the attainment of having to do no *karma* at all). To clarify:

असक्तबुद्धिः सर्वत्र जितात्मा विगतस्पृहः ।
नैष्कर्म्यसिद्धिं परमां संन्यासेनाधिगच्छति ॥४९॥

asakta-buddhiḥ sarvatra jitātmā vigata-spṛhaḥ ।
naiṣkarmya-siddhiṁ paramāṁ saṁnyāsenādhigacchati ॥49॥

Completely unattached to everything, in full self-command, and all-desires-gone, one, through renunciation (*saṁnyāsa*), attains the supreme perfection of transcending actions (*naiṣkarmya-siddhi*).

Arjuna, *naiṣkarmya-siddhi* (the attainment of perfection of transcending actions) is yet another name for the sense of liberatedness, also called *mukti* or *mokṣa,* attainable while living in this world. It is the attainment of a state of mind of not feeling obliged to do any willful action. *Karma*s are the strongest of all forces that cause bondage in life. In your case also, the fear of sin arose from your wrong notion that you were the doer of the *karma* of battling. It could be well said that the sense of sin is the most dreadful eventuality of one's attachment to what one does. Only one way is open to save oneself from this tragic situation: to renounce *karma*s. It is never attained just by remaining inactive. On the other hand, performing all necessary and natural actions with the clear awareness that all *karma*s form part of My Cosmic Form or of *prakṛti,* is the way. Such actions are not prompted by the prospect of enjoying their favourable results in future. Unmotivated actions can be done only by those who are unattached. And only those who are in self-command can remain unattached. Such renounce their actions into the total *prakṛti,* and this act of renouncing is to be called *saṁnyāsa.* A *saṁnyāsin* (one who renounces action thus), while being engaged in activities natural and inevitable, inwardly experiences the attainment of *naiṣkarmya-siddhi.* The definition of *saṁnyāsa* given at the beginning of this chapter is to be understood in the light of this elucidation. What a *saṁnyāsin* gains, in effect, is attaining Me. How is it? I shall tell you:

सिद्धिं प्राप्तो यथा ब्रह्म तथाप्नोति निबोध मे ।
समासेनैव कौन्तेय निष्ठा ज्ञानस्य या परा ॥५०॥

siddhiṁ prāpto yathā brahma tathāpnoti nibodha me ।
samāsenaiva kaunteya niṣṭhā jñānasya yā parā ॥50॥

On gaining this (*naiṣkarmya-*) *siddhi* how one attains *Brahman,* O Arjuna, do hear from Me now in summary. It, in fact, is what constitutes the supreme consummation of wisdom.

Arjuna, those who have attained *naiṣkarmya-siddhi,* as you know, perceive themselves and whatever *karma* they do, as forming part of My Cosmic Form. Such were called *karma-yogin*s earlier in Chapter III. Shifting the emphasis from doing *karma* to the intuitive awareness with which such *karma*s are done, the same attainment becomes *jñāna-yoga* portrayed in Chapter IV. The supreme state of *jñāna* conceived there consists of perceiving all beings in oneself and oneself in Me, the Absolute or *Brahman.* To express the very same essence of wisdom in terms appropriate to the present context: those who perform *karma*s with a sense of detachment, perceiving those *karma*s as forming part of the overall *karma* of My Cosmic Form, attain *naiṣkarmya-siddhi.* To attain Me as conceived in Chapter IV in abstract terms, and what is referred to here with the concrete Cosmic Form taken into account, means the same: to attain *Brahman.*

Now what I am going to state summarily is how a *karma-yogin* or rather an attainer of *naiṣkarmya-siddhi,* becomes a *jñāna-yogin,* fully identified with *Brahman.* What kind of spiritual discipline transforms a *karma-yogin* into a *jñāna-yogin,* making the difference between the two of no relevance, is what I am going to clarify now:

बुद्ध्या विशुद्धया युक्तो धृत्यात्मानं नियम्य च ।
शब्दादीन्विषयांस्त्यक्त्वा रागद्वेषौ व्युदस्य च ॥५१॥
विविक्तसेवी लघ्वाशी यतवाक्कायमानसः ।
ध्यानयोगपरो नित्यं वैराग्यं समुपाश्रितः ॥५२॥

अहङ्कारं बलं दर्पं कामं क्रोधं परिग्रहम्।
विमुच्य निर्ममः शान्तो ब्रह्मभूयाय कल्पते ॥५३॥

buddhyā viśuddhayā yukto dhṛtyātmānaṁ niyamya ca ।
śabdādīn viṣayāṁs tyaktvā rāga-dveṣau vyudasya ca ॥51 ॥

vivikta-sevī laghvāśī yata-vāk-kāya-mānasaḥ ।
dhyāna-yoga-paro nityaṁ vairāgyaṁ sam upāśritaḥ ॥52 ॥

ahaṁkāraṁ balaṁ darpaṁ kāmaṁ krodhaṁ parigraham ।
vimucya nirmamaḥ śānto brahma-bhūyāya kalpate ॥53 ॥

One, endowed with clarity of understanding, should restrain oneself with firmness. Then should one renounce pleasurable objects like sound. So too are to be laid aside both liking and disliking.

One should then have a liking for secluded life, eating little. Speech, body and mind are to be subdued. One should as well be constantly searching for identity with Me in a meditative mood, resorting to passionlessness.

Free from egoism, sense of being powerful, arrogance, desire, anger, covetousness and devoid of mine-sense, one should remain calm and peaceful. He is fit to become *Brahman* and remain as *Brahman*.

Arjuna, how our understanding (*buddhi*) can be *sāttvika, rājasa* or *tāmasa,* we have already noticed. Those endowed with the *sāttvika* type of understanding alone are competent to experience identity with *Brahman.* They should also have the *sāttvika* type of firmness of mind. Momentary pleasures offered by sense objects, as you know, are very forceful in detracting us from our chosen path in life aimed at the Supreme Goal. These have to be kept away from the reach of senses and mind by constant practice. When such a practice becomes well stabilized, one realizes that one's real interest does not lie there. One realizes that eating good food is not the goal for which we live, but that we eat in order to live. One then becomes aware of the fact that eating simple food is good for health as well as for attaining the Supreme Goal of life. Then one likes to resist the temptations of delicious food. The awareness that all *karmas*, whether bodily, verbal or mental, are not one's own but belong to *paramātmā*, relieves one of the zest for engaging in various *karmas*. Any such zest for action, as and when it wells up, should be subdued.

Dhyāna (meditation) means to practise to perceive oneself as inseparable with *paramātmā*, as a wave with ocean. It leads to the state of experiencing *yoga* (the state of identity) and those who practise it constantly are to be called *dhyāna-yoga-paras*. The life-interest of such persons always finds itself rooted in the One or oneness. Any diversion of interest to the many has to be understood as caused by the sense of attachment and passion originating from *rajo-guṇa*. He whose aim is attaining *Brahman* has to subdue these by practising *vairāgya* (sense of non-attachment and passionlessness) while deliberately directing one's interest to attaining *Brahman*.

A wave becoming enlightened, "I am nothing but ocean in essence," wipes out all its egoism (*ahaṁkāra*) or I-sense. Along with the I-sense (*ahaṁkāra*) goes mine-sense (*mamakāra*) as well. I-sense and mine-sense are always absent in a *dhyāna-yoga-parā*. If even a trace remains, it has to be deliberately pushed out. The absence of I-sense and mine-sense ensures ceasing of the sense of power (*bala*), arrogance (*darpa*), desire (*kāma*), anger (*krodha*), covetousness (*parigraha*) and related emotions. One, in whom all these have become well stabilized, alone attains calmness and finds peacefulness, the consummation of the wisdom delineated earlier in Verse IV.35.

I shall now tell you how one of this attainment lives:

ब्रह्मभूतः प्रसन्नात्मा न शोचति न काङ्क्षति।
समः सर्वेषु भूतेषु मद्भक्तिं लभते पराम् ॥५४॥

brahma-bhūtaḥ prasannātmā na śocati na kāṅkṣati ।
samaḥ sarveṣu bhūteṣu mad-bhaktiṁ labhate parām ॥54॥

Having become *Brahman*, he, blissful serenity in essence, neither does grieve in life nor does have any desire to fulfil. Seeing the same in everything that has come into being as he is, he attains the Supreme State of being absorbed in Me.

Arjuna, similar to an ornament knowing, "I am really gold," is one's realization, "I am really *Brahman.*" "I" thereafter will be known not as an individual but the ultimate Reality, *Brahman.* Life's problems, as perceived by one of this realization, are no more "his," but *Brahman's.* This illumination fills one's being with a blissful serenity, and in that state he could be called *prasannātmā.* He experiences his own self-content as of the essence of this serenity. Vagaries of life do not make him grieve, but on the other hand, he faces them firmly with the boldness of being *Brahman.* What guides his life is not aspiration for personal benefits, but the joy of partaking of the overall flow of *karma*s of *prakṛti.*

What the word *sama* (seeing the same) signifies is not mere apparent equality of things among themselves; this sameness is that of the equality of status of everything as various manifestations of one and the same Reality. The cosmos being the sum total of all that has become manifest in Me, seeing Me alone in each and every constituent element of the cosmos is but natural, and it is what the word *sama* means.

Bhaj means the constant process of meditatively perceiving Me, and one who does so is a *bhakta* and one's state of being so is called *bhakti.* As related to the active state of one's existence, it implies perceiving everything one happens to do as part of becoming absorbed in Me.[1]

One who is well aware of the philosophical vision behind *karma-*

1. The *bhakti* and *bhakta* understood here is much different from the ones conceived popularly in various *bhakti* cults. Fully philosophical and visionary in significance, this *bhakta* is defined by Narayana Guru thus:

   ānanda ātmā brahmeti nāmaitasyaiva tanyate
   iti niścita-dhīr yasya sa bhakta iti viśrutaḥ
   — Darśanamālā, VIII.5

   (One who is fully convinced that *ānanda, ātmā* and *Brahman* are three different names of one and the same Reality is well known as a *bhakta.*)

yoga, as you know, becomes a *jñāna-yogin*. In other words, both *karma-yoga* and *jñāna-yoga* become one *yoga* in a real *jñānin*, and this is the state of being *brahma-bhūta* (one who has become *brahman* oneself). The state of a *bhakta* is, in essence, no other. In short, *karma-yoga*, *jñāna-yoga* and *bhakti* are inseparably one in a *jñānin*. A real *karma-yogin* will always be a *jñāna-yogin* and thus a *bhakta;* so too a real *jñāna-yogin* will be a *karma-yogin* who does *karma*s with a sense of complete detachment; a real *bhakta*, likewise, will be a *yogī* who does not differentiate *karma-yoga* and *jñāna-yoga*. I shall tell you now what ultimately happens to such a *bhakta:*

भक्त्या मामभिजानाति यावान्यश्चास्मि तत्त्वतः ।
ततो मां तत्त्वतो ज्ञात्वा विशते तदनन्तरम् ॥५५॥

bhaktyā mām abhijānāti yāvān yaś-cāsmi tattvataḥ ।
tato māṁ tattvato jñātvā viśate tad-anantaram ॥55॥

Such a *bhakta*, through his *bhakti*, appraises truly and correctly of who I am and what sort of Reality I am. Having known Me thus truly and correctly, he then becomes fully settled down in Me.

Arjuna, there are two ways of knowing: one, knowing something as an object external to the knower; and the other, the knower knowing Reality as the essential content of his own being. The latter is the type of knowledge qualified here as *tattvataḥ* (based on *tattva*). The implications of *tattva* we have already examined in detail. On knowing what ocean is, a wave becomes one with it and finds itself settling down in it. Such is the knowledge of the one who knows Me based on *tattva*. The knower, by knowing Me thus, enters Me and finds himself well settled down in Me. There are, of course, many who think of Me and conceive ideas about Me, such ideas need not necessarily be right. No such shortcoming exists in respect of the knowledge one acquires by entering what is to be known, becoming it, and experiencing what it is as one's own essential content. Knowing what ultimately is Real, knowing Me, knowing *Brahman*, in this manner is often referred to as *aparokṣānubhūti* (non-mediate experiential awareness). This intuitive experience is what a *bhakta* feels to be filling his own being.

The statement, "Having known Me thus truly and correctly, he then becomes fully settled down in Me," may seem to imply a temporal sequence, but it is not to be understood so. How the events "knowing Me" and "becoming well settled down in Me" are related is also to be understood based on *tattva.* The two are like two sides of one coin, one meaningless without the other.

Even as one enters Me and settles down in Me, one has to continue doing one's *svadharma.* That *svadharma,* as far as you are concerned, is battling. Being engaged in *svadharma* with the intuitive perception we have just described makes one cross the bounds of sin and merit. What kind of world is it that he reaches then? I shall tell you:

सर्वकर्माण्यपि सदा कुर्वाणो मद्व्यपाश्रयः ।
मत्प्रसादादवाप्नोति शाश्वतं पदमव्ययम् ॥५६ ॥

sarva-karmāny api sadā kurvāṇo mad-vyapāśrayaḥ ।
mat-prsādād avāpnoti śāśvataṁ padam avyayam ॥56 ॥

Though continuing to do all actions, relying in all respects upon Me alone as he is, he attains by My Grace the ever-lasting and undiminishing state of existence.

Arjuna, if one does all *karma*s natural to one in life relying on Me or the Absolute alone, if one has entered Me, has become Myself by seeing himself as part of My Cosmic Form, then what guides his *karma*s are neither Vedic injunctions nor social conventions. He perceives all the *karma*s he happens to do as forming part of the never ending creative unfoldment of the Cosmic Form. He perceives all *karma*s in Me and seeing Myself alone everywhere and in everything, always experiences an ineffable serenity and stability, which is none other than My Grace. I am everlasting; I am undiminishing; My everlasting and undiminishing state becomes his also because of this unitive perception.

Arjuna, let us now go back to the original question you asked me at the very beginning in Verse II.7: "Tell me decisively what is best for me." Now that your mind is well prepared to receive what I mean if I directly answer the question, I do not hesitate to do so.

चेतसा सर्वकर्माणि मयि संन्यस्य मत्परः ।
बुद्धियोगमुपाश्रित्य मच्चित्तः सततं भव ॥५७॥

cetasā sarva-karmāṇi mayi saṁnyasya mat-paraḥ ।
buddhi-yogam upāśritya mac-cittaḥ satataṁ bhava ॥57॥

Mentally renouncing all *karma*s unto Me, regarding Me alone as the lone goal interested in, become one who constantly has My mind, by resorting to the *yoga* of understanding.

Arjuna, it is in one's understanding, to be more precise, in one's intuitive perception, that the state of being in yogic union happens. Since we have gone through its different stages, the details of that perception need not be repeated here. An individual's own unity with Me experienced as an enlightenment could be called *buddhi-yoga.* Once that state is attained, you have nothing of your own; everything is Mine. You have no *karma* of your own, all *karma*s are Mine, for whatever you can think of as yours has all already been renounced unto Me. Neither do you have a mind of your own; your mind is My mind.

You should not hesitate to do the *karma* that forms part of your *svadharma,* which becomes inevitable as part of the course of flow of events in nature. On the other hand, you should perform them with all dexterity with the understanding that what assumes the form of that particular life-situation, the *karma* inevitable in that situation, and its eventual results, are all Myself or *Brahman.* Neither the sense of being the doer of actions (*kartṛtva*) nor that of being the enjoyer of their fruits (*bhoktṛtva*) will then impel you to act. The decision as to what *karma* to do and how, is usually taken by your mind. Now that your mind has become My mind, your decision naturally has to be My decision. You thus become a real *yogī.* You will then perceive all the decisions you take merely as a spark of the function of My mind. Do remain a *yogī* with this illumination; and do perform actions natural to you seeing non-action (*akarma*) in all such action (*karma*). This is what is best for you. No *karma* then will be felt to be hard to accomplish. To clarify this point:

मच्चित्तः सर्वदुर्गाणि मत्प्रसादात्तरिष्यसि ।
अथ चेत्त्वमहङ्कारान्न श्रोष्यसि विनङ्क्ष्यसि ॥५८॥

maccittaḥ sarva-durgāṇi mat-prasādāt tariṣyasi ।
atha cet tvam ahaṅkārān na śroṣyasi vinaṅkṣyasi ॥58॥

Having become of My mind, you will overcome all obstacles by My Grace. On the other hand, if you, owing to the dominance of I-sense, do not take heed of this teaching, what you face will be destruction.

Arjuna, two are the alternatives before you now. The first is to battle with the idea that you are the one who does this *karma,* that it is your obligatory duty to do so and filled with a longing to conquer your foes. The second is to battle with a sense of detachment and the perception that you are merely a fragment of My Cosmic Form, not existing apart from Me, and perceiving your mind and its ideas as Mine, and with the mind of a *yogī,* perceiving this battle as your *svadharma.* Having to face obstacles is natural with all kinds of actions. Such obstacles cause mental stress if you resort to the first alternative, for the reason that you are attached to what you do. If done with the awareness that all *karma*s are *Brahman*'s or *ātmā*'s, then the obstacles also are felt as a part of the creative unfoldment of *Brahman.* The equanimity you feel then could be well considered My Grace.

In case of you resorting to the first alternative, nothing of the valuable teaching I gave so far will be appreciated by you. This teaching will not find its way into the mind of anyone who performs actions with egoism or I-sense. Obstacles that happen incidentally will be taken seriously; supposedly "sinful" *karma*s will make them remorseful; failure to achieve the expected result will make them feel lost; and many such ill-effects will follow their actions. Such could virtually be treated as already lost or doomed to destruction.

Now look back at the state of mind you were in before we started this dialogue:

यदहङ्कारमाश्रित्य न योत्स्य इति मन्यसे ।
मिथ्यैष व्यवसायस्ते प्रकृतिस्त्वां नियोक्ष्यति ॥५९॥

yad ahaṅkāram āśritya na yotsya iti manyase ।
mithyaiṣa vyavasāyas te prakṛtis tvāṁ niyokṣyati ॥59॥

By relying on your "I-sense" was your decision, "I will not fight"; in vain was that decision, for *prakṛti* will ordain you to act.

Arjuna, you were afraid of the sinful act of having to kill your own masters and kith and kin, and this made you decide not to fight. Only those who perform sinful acts become sinners. Only those who perform acts become either sinners or otherwise. Then what about the one who does not do any *karma* at all? Neither sin nor merit is attached to him.

It must be now quite clear to you from what I have been teaching elaborately, that you are not the doer of any *karma*. All *karma*s take place in *prakṛti*, and *prakṛti* is nothing but My own creative urge become self-unfolded. You will realize in the wake of this overall perception of life that your decision not to fight was in vain. *Prakṛti*'s overall activity can never be stopped or controlled by any individual being. Unbridled, it is let loose to take its own course by Me. No individual being can stop it. Being unaware of this reality alone was, what was wrong in your perception of life.

Arjuna, you are a part of My Cosmic Form, and the Cosmic Form is creative on its own. It is ceaselessly active. And as a part of it, you too have to remain active. So it is with everyone everywhere. No one should think of escaping from the *karma*s natural with the Cosmic Form. I shall make this point clearer:

स्वभावजेन कौन्तेय निबद्धः स्वेन कर्मणा।
कर्तुं नेच्छसि यन्मोहात्करिष्यस्यवशो ऽपि तत्॥६०॥

svabhāvajena kaunteya nibaddhaḥ svena karmaṇā ।
kartuṁ necchasi yan mohāt kariṣyasy avaśo 'pi tat ॥60॥

Arjuna, everyone is bound by their own nature-born *karma*. The very same *karma*, that you, deluded as you were, decided not to do, you will perform helplessly.

Arjuna, as you know, it is only as part of My Cosmic Form, creative even in its most atomic component, that any being has existence, and all the *karma*s we do are only a manifestation of this creative urge. That *ātmā*, the *sat*, can never remain unmanifest and thus *bhāva*-less, was made clear as early as in Verse II.16. *Karma* is present wherever manifestaion occurs and thus *bhāva* appears, and those *karmas*, in human beings, assume the form of bodily, verbal and mental actions. Of the numerous mental actions, one is free will (*icchā*), and it decides what one should do and should not do. When applying this free will and taking decisions, human beings, piteously enough, remain completely oblivious of the fact that their free will is not of their making, but is in them as part of *prakṛti*. Applying it in life too is part of *prakṛti*'s *kṛti* or *karma*.

Whatever thus finds expression in an individual being is called *sva-bhāva* (one's own innate disposition). The word *svabhāva* means also "*ātmā*'s own," "My own" manifest form. No one can evade such *karma*s. One type of *karma* alone is worth giving up deliberately: *kāmya-karma*s (motivated actions). Natural *karma*s that find expression in one as the outcome of one's own innate disposition are never to be given up; they, on the other hand, are necessarily to be done as forming part of *prakṛti*'s flow of actions. You should see Me alone even in those actions. Such a natural *karma* was what you wrongly willed not to do; and it was the idea that you were the doer of it that made you take such a wrong decision. You will helplessly have to do such *karma*s even in the case of your deciding not to do them; *prakṛti* will make you do them. As natural and inevitable as the actions of breathing and eating, are those of doing one's *svadharma*. Such is the overall scheme of life, and I am the one who systemizes it. All systemization involves knowledge, and I Myself am pure knowledge or consciousness. And that *cit* manifests itself, simply for the joy of perceiving the endless potential innate within itself; this systemization of life occurs as a part of it. I, *cit* in essence, am the Substance that fills the being of every entity in the entire cosmos, systemizing it as a living whole. He who lives with this enlightenment makes his life fully stabilized in Me, taking it beyond sin and merit. How I hold together the cosmos as a living system, I shall tell you:

ईश्वरः सर्वभूतानां हृद्देशे ऽर्जुन तिष्ठति ।
भ्रामयन्सर्वभूतानि यन्त्रारूढानि मायया ॥६१ ॥

īśvaraḥ sarva-bhūtānāṁ hṛd-deśe 'rjuna tiṣṭhati ।
bhrāmayan sarva-bhūtāni yantrārūḍhāni māyayā ॥61 ॥

The all-controlling one (*Īśvara*) abides in the heart-like region in all that has come into being. He, owing to his own *māyā*, makes all of these revolve as though mounted on a machine.

Arjuna, how I am the all-controlling one (*Īśvara*) has already become quite clear. *Īśvara* is the Sanskrit word for God also. Inexplicable is the way I, pure Cousciousness in essence, assumes the form of everything material and mental, and keep all of them unceasingly active. In fact, it is unwise to desire to logically know the secret of the world and the phenomenon of life. If the secret becomes revealed to someone, he may lose interest in living, for all the novelty of living is lost. Living remains an experience of novelty only as long as the secret of life remains a mystery. A life in which events happen as logically calculated and predicted will be mechanical and therefore lacking novelty. What makes a *jñānin* of one is not one's logical understanding of the constitution and function of the world or his ability to define it, but the contentment of being part of the Great Mystery that the world is. This Mystery consists of the way I unfold Myself as the world and control it from within as *Īśvara* or God. The only explicit answer to the question, "How do I do it?" is this: *māyā*. *Māyā* is what makes Me appear as this world. Everything in the world revolves because of the very same *māyā*, and this revolving is what we call life. This realized, one feels the contentment that nothing more remains to be known. This contentment is what Vedānta considers as its final Goal, as well as the end of knowing, which the word Vedānta means (*veda*, knowledge and *anta*, the end of). Perceiving every moment of life thus as God alone, *Brahman* alone, *paramātmā* alone, *ātmā* alone, oneself alone, constitutes one's taking refuge in God. The wise alone do it, and they alone experience the Grace of God. I shall clarify the nature of this Graceful experience further:

तमेव शरणं गच्छ सर्वभावेन भारत ।
तत्प्रसादात्परां शान्तिं स्थानं प्राप्स्यसि शाश्वतम् ॥६२॥

tam eva śaraṇam gaccha sarva-bhāvena bhārata ।
tat-prasādāt parāṁ śāntiṁ sthānaṁ prāpsyasi śāśvatam ॥62॥

O Bhārata, seek refuge in Him alone in all aspects of your existence. By His Grace will you attain the everlasting abode of Supreme Peacefulness.

Arjuna, there is one Reality alone for you to take refuge in: the one Substance that fills your own being. It is nothing but *Brahman* or *Īśvara*. Relying on anything else makes life infested with problems and conflicting situations. Perceiving one Reality alone, Me alone, in everything, on the other hand, enables experiencing the peacefulness of directly seeing the unpredictable way in which God assumes the Cosmic Form. Living will then be seen to be not a process undergone by the individual, but by God or Myself. This peacefulness is the highest goal a man can attain in life. It liberates one from all sorts of bondage and obligations, it is itself the Supreme Liberation or *mukti*, also called *mokṣa*.

इति ते ज्ञानमाख्यातं गुह्याद्गुह्यतरं मया।
विमृश्यैतदशेषेण यथेच्छसि तथा कुरु ॥63॥

iti te jñānam ākhyātaṁ guhyād guhyataraṁ mayā ।
vimṛśyaitad aśeṣeṇa yathecchasi tathā kuru ॥63॥

Thus I have disclosed to you the wisdom that is the secret of all secrets. You may critically scrutinize it fully, omitting nothing, and then do as you prefer.

Arjuna, you came to Me as a seeker confounded on *dharma*. What I have been teaching you so far is the wisdom that completely dispels your confusions. You need not accept this teaching in the way a believer blindly does. This wisdom is a science — the science of life, the science of *Brahman* (*brahma-vidyā*). No science is meant to be believed in, it is to be critically examined and understood perceptively. Since this teaching is about the supreme secret of life, knowing it gives one the self-confidence of being able to decide on one's own, what to do and what not to do at each moment of life. This explains why I ask you to critically examine what I taught you and then to do as you prefer. Truth makes you liberated. Part of this liberatedness is the freedom you feel in deciding what to do and what not to do, with an intuitive perception of Reality concerning life. That freedom is yours now. At this critical juncture, therefore, you have to freely decide what is righteous (*dharma*) and what is unrighteous (*adharma*) for you. Yet one thing will remain unchanged: enlightened with Truth, one can only live as a replica of that Truth.

The wisdom I taught you is secret in more than one respect. This science concerns life, which has always been a mystery. No one has succeeded in unravelling it, though many banged their heads aganist it. No one expects that it will ever be unravelled either. It will always remain a mystery. If at all it could be made the subject-matter of a scientific study, it is in the way I have just taught you. The Reality still remains a mystery, only the seeker, in his attempts to understand it, becomes merged in it. All zest for knowing, then, gives place to the contentment and peacefulness of being part of the mystery. This is one respect in which this teaching is a secret.

Unlike ordinary sciences that deal with worldly appearances alone, this one looks inward and realizes that what is Real in oneself is what is real in everything else. An integral intuitive awareness, this experiential certitude is incommunicable, and in that respect also it is a secret.

However, this does not mean that the science concerning it is meant to be kept a secret. True seekers should have access to it, for such are able to understand and appreciate its mystery as mystery, and they being part of it. I found such a seeker in you, the reason for My teaching you this wisdom so elaborately.

सर्वगुह्यतमं भूयः शृणु मे परमं वचः ।
इष्टो ऽसि मे दृढमिति ततो वक्ष्यामि ते हितम् ॥६४ ॥

sarva-guhyatamaṁ bhūyaḥ śṛṇu me paramaṁ vacaḥ ।
iṣṭo 'si me dṛḍham iti tato vakṣyāmi te hitam ॥64 ॥

Listen again to My supreme word that constitutes the most secret of all words. I deign to tell you this that is good for you, only because I am sure that you are very dear to Me.

Arjuna, you are now well aware of the secret nature of the wisdom I have just taught you. Though such a secret, I have taught it to you elaborately extending over seventeen chapters. Being so elaborate, at least a few may find it difficult to locate the key-point of the teaching; perhaps you also have missed it. I shall, therefore, point out the crux of the entire teaching:

मन्मना भव मद्भक्तो मद्याजी मां नमस्कुरु ।
मामेवैष्यसि सत्यं ते प्रतिजाने प्रियो ऽसि मे ॥६५ ॥

man-manā bhava mad-bhakto mad-yājī māṁ namas-kuru ।
mām evaiṣyasi satyaṁ te pratijāne priyo 'si me ॥65 ॥

Become one of My mind; become one who meditatively perceives Me alone; become one who offers himself unto Me; bow down before Me alone; then, Me alone you will attain. I declare this Truth to you because you are very dear to Me.

Arjuna, no repeating of the significance of these words is necessary at this point. The connotations of becoming one of My mind, along with its benefits, have just been made clear in the present chapter. What meditative perceiving (*bhaj*) implies was laid bare in all its details, along with showing its various stages, from Chapters XII to XVIII. How one's *karma*s and then oneself are to be offered unto Me, was described earlier in Chapters III and IV. One Reality alone does exist as adorable and worshipable: *Brahman* that unfolds itself as everything, that exists assuming the apparent form of everything. Once that Reality is known, you and that Reality are no longer two. This is the one way, the only practical way, the only direct way, of attaining Me.

I shall now restate the same Truth as a direct solution to the original problem of yours:

सर्वधर्मान्परित्यज्य मामेकं शरणं व्रज।
अहं त्वा सर्वपापेभ्यो मोक्षयिष्यामि मा शुचः ॥६६॥

sarva-dharmān parityajya mām ekaṁ śaraṇaṁ vraja ।
ahaṁ tvā sarva-pāpebhyo mokṣayiṣyāmi mā śucaḥ ॥66॥

Abandon all *dharma*s and take refuge in Me alone. I will liberate you from all sins. You don't have to grieve.

Arjuna, you came to Me with a confounded mind, unable to decide which was *dharma* and which was *adharma*. Helping you avoid all *adharma*s and guiding you to the way of *dharma* — what all religionists do — is not the purpose of My teaching. *Dharma* and *adharma* are meaningful only in relation to *karma*s and they in turn originate from Me. Rely on Me alone by realizing your identity with Me; then you automatically go beyond both *dharma* and *adharma*.

It was a sense of sin that made you grieve. Sin and merit are meaningful only with the doers of *karma;* all *karmas* are Mine alone, and I have no sense of being their doer either. Being so, My *karmas* are neither sinful or meritorious. As you see your identity with Me, the *karmas* you do are also seen to form part of My being. This perception makes you free from both sin and merit, and in this way you become liberated (*mukta*). This liberation is not merely from sin alone, but from *karmas* as well, and this itself is liberatedness (*mukti* or *mokṣa*).

इदं ते नातपस्काय नाभक्ताय कदाचन।
न चाशुश्रूषवे वाच्यं न च मां यो ऽभ्यसूयति ॥६७॥

idaṁ te nātapaskāya nābhaktāya kadācana ।
na cāśuśrūṣave vācyaṁ na ca māṁ yo 'bhyasūyati ॥67॥

This wisdom is never to be spoken about by you to anyone of no *tapas,* nor to one unwilling to meditatively perceive Me, nor to one not eager to listen, nor to one who cavils at Me.

Arjuna, though the wisdom I have imparted to you may be taught to anyone, it may not be understandable to many. Finding life meaningless unless its meaning is known, someone may crave to know Reality, and only such a one will understand this wisdom-teaching. For others it may seem to be high sounding but meaningless words, and this wisdom should not be opened before such people.

Those who crave for wisdom never treat this *Gītā* merely as a collection of holy verses to be learnt by heart, nor as a mere *śāstra* (science) either. For them, this is an embodiment of the Supreme Blissfulness of attaining Liberation. That Blissfulness transcends even the words, verses and meaning of this text. These words and their meaning are merely instrumental in revealing this Blissfulness to a seeker. And a seeker's inner being should remain full of heat to receive this revelation. Along with it comes the real *bhakti* or willingness to meditatively perceive the one Reality or Me alone in everything.

You may also have to do in future what I have done for you now. Nay, it will be your responsibility to impart this wisdom to real seekers. Similarly responsible should be those who attain this Blissful Goal by some other means as well. This wisdom secret should not get lost; it should be handed down from generation to generation through the process of a *guru* imparting it to a real disciple. The responsibility of keeping such a tradition alive is yours, as well as of those like you. By doing so, they not only hand down this wisdom to posterity, but they attain Me as well, thus:

य इदं परमं गुह्यं मद्भक्तेष्वभिधास्यति ।
भक्तिं मयि परां कृत्वा मामेवैष्यत्यसंशयः ॥६८ ॥

ya idaṁ paramaṁ guhyaṁ mad-bhakteṣv abhidhāsyati ।
bhaktiṁ mayi parāṁ kṛtvā mām evaiṣyaty asaṁśayaḥ ॥68 ॥

He who imparts this Supreme Secret unto My *bhakta,* by doing so, actualizes his genuine *bhakti* for Me and thus doubtlessly comes to Me.

And more,

न च तस्मान्मनुष्येषु कश्चिन्मे प्रियकृत्तमः ।
भविता न च मे तस्मादन्यः प्रियतरो भुवि ॥६९ ॥

na ca tasmān manuṣyeṣu kaścin me priya-kṛttamaḥ ।
bhavitā na ca me tasmād anyaḥ priyataro bhuvi ॥69 ॥

Among humans who do things dear to Me, none is there dearer to Me than the one who imparts this wisdom to seekers. Nor will there be in future anyone dearer to Me in this world.

Arjuna, it is not that those who impart this wisdom alone are the ones dearest to Me; those who seek this wisdom, properly taking advantage of this dialogue of ours, are also very dear to Me. Therefore,

अध्येष्यते च य इमं धर्म्यं संवादमावयोः।
ज्ञानयज्ञेन तेनाहमिष्टः स्यामिति मे मतिः ॥७०॥

adhyeṣyate ca ya imaṁ dharmyaṁ saṁvādam āvayoḥ ।
jñāna-yajñena tenāham iṣṭaḥ syām iti me matiḥ ॥70॥

He who attentively studies this support-of-all-wisdom-dialogue of ours, by that very wisdom sacrifice I become propitiated. So is My conclusive stand.

Arjuna, studying this wisdom dialogue with a *yogic* (dialectical) intuitive perception constitutes *jñāna-yajña* (wisdom sacrifice). All *yajña*s in the Vedic context, as you know, are meant to propitiate some deity which, in the present *jñāna-yajña,* is Myself. The deity, on becoming pleased with a sacrifice, no doubt, does favours to the sacrificer; so too I, pleased with the wisdom-sacrifice, become gracious to the seeker. That Grace is none other than the seeker's experiencing the blissful serenity and liberation of finding himself in full identity with Me. This experience is to be gained while living here in this world, the reason for qualifying this dialogue and the wisdom it contains as *dharmya* (the support-of-all), for it always remains a support for life. In the sense that it guides the entire course of practical life also it is *dharmya.* This wisdom is available to all, but not everyone avails of it. Who really attains it, has already been made clear to you. Nevertheless, as a forewarning to those who fortuitously become interested in it, I repeat it:

श्रद्धावाननसूयश्च शृणुयादपि यो नरः।
सोऽपि मुक्तः शुभांल्लोकान्प्राप्नुयात्पुण्यकर्मणाम्॥७१॥

śraddhāvān anasūyaś ca śṛnuyād api yo naraḥ ।
so 'pi muktaḥ śubhāṁ lokān prāpnuyāt puṇya-karmaṇām ॥71॥

Should a person, endowed with *śraddhā* and uncarping, happens to listen to this wisdom-teaching, he too becomes liberated and attains the auspicious worlds of those who perform meritorious deeds.

Arjuna, the implications of *śraddhā* and what its role is in the context of gaining wisdom, have been made clear earlier. A seeker approaching a *guru* faithfully listens to his words, cogitates on them on his own, and then attains the final certitude and goal. The disciple should not listen with the intention of testing the integrity of his wisdom, nor to have an argument with him. Those who approach a *guru* with such intentions were earlier dubbed as *saṁśayātmā*s (the doubting ones). Not only do they not attain wisdom, but their own egoism becomes their enemy causing their peril.

Another sort of devout people also exists who consider this scripture a holy object, and reading it or listening to it as a meritorious deed. Though not helpful in attaining wisdom, their devotion is well acknowledged in ritualism, with the belief that, by performing meritorious deeds, one attains the auspicious world of heaven. Such a belief is not quite out of place even in the context of the *Gītā*. The practice of reading it as a religious ritual helps one attain at least the auspicious worlds aimed at by ritualism. Yet such worlds are not eternal, nor is the happiness of that world everlasting. One who reaches there, on the running out of his merit, necessarily has to come back to this world of sufferings, as was stated earlier in Verse IX.21. Different is the case of the one who studies this scripture with full faith as a wisdom-sacrifice. The world they gain is not heaven, but Myself, the eternal One. Attaining Me, they too become eternal.

Arjuna, I have now imparted to you everything I intended to teach. Now tell Me:

कच्चिदेतच्छ्रुतं पार्थ त्वयैकाग्रेण चेतसा ।
कच्चिदज्ञानसंमोहः प्रनष्टस्ते धनञ्जय ॥७२॥

kaccid etac chrutaṁ pārtha tvayaikāgreṇa cetasā ।
kaccid ajñāna-saṁmohaḥ pranaṣṭas te dhanañjaya ॥72॥

Arjuna, you must have listened to Me with one-pointed attention. O Dhanañjaya, is your ignorance-born delusion destroyed?

अर्जुन उवाच —

नष्टो मोहः स्मृतिर्लब्धा त्वत्प्रसादान्मयाच्युत ।
स्थितो ऽस्मि गतसन्देहः करिष्ये वचनं तव ॥७३॥

arjuna uvāca —

naṣṭo mohaḥ smṛtir labdhā tvat-prasādān mayācyuta ।
sthito 'smi gata-sandehaḥ kariṣye vacanaṁ tava ॥73॥

Arjuna said —

Gone is my delusion and cognizance of myself obtained back again, because, O Acyuta, of your Grace. I stand here firm now with all doubts dispelled. And I'll work to practise your word-wisdom.

Dhṛtarāṣṭra:

Sañjaya, confounding again is the way this dialogue concludes. Look, Kṛṣṇa asked Arjuna, "Do as you please," but Arjuna replies, "I shall work to practise your word-wisdom." Why can't Arjuna do as he thinks good?

Sañjaya:

O King, your internal eye still remains as blind as a your external eye. What Kṛṣṇa has just detailed is the nature of the ultimate Reality that underlies and controls life. Arjuna's words now indicate that he did comprehend it wholly. He says, "Gone is my delusion, and cognizance of myself obtained again, I now stand firm with all doubts dispelled." One of such an enlightenment has no other alternative than living as a perceptible expression of the imperceptible Reality. Such a way of living means, following the teaching of the *guru,* and that alone is what Arjuna says he will do.

I have so far been perceiving directly, as if I were an eye-witness, this sublime wisdom-dialogue and describing it to you as well. I shall now tell you what I personally feel about it.

सञ्जय उवाच -

इत्यहं वासुदेवस्य पार्थस्य च महात्मनः।
संवादमिममश्रौषमद्भुतं रोमहर्षणम् ॥७४॥

sañjaya uvāca —

ity ahaṁ vāsudevasya pārthasya ca mahātmanaḥ ।
saṁvādam imam aśrauṣam adbhutaṁ roma-harṣaṇam ॥74॥

Sañjaya said —

I happened to listen thus, with my hair standing on end, to the astonishing dialogue between Kṛṣṇa and Arjuna the great.

व्यासप्रसादाच्छ्रुतवानेतद्गुह्यमहं परम्।
योगं योगेश्वरात्कृष्णात्साक्षात्कथयतः स्वयम् ॥७५॥

vyāsa-prasādāc chrutavān etad guhyaṁ ahaṁ param ।
yogaṁ yogeśvarāt kṛṣṇāt sākṣāt kathayataḥ svayam ॥75॥

By Vyāsa's Grace is it that I happened to listen to this mysterious and most secret *yoga*-teaching as was elucidated directly by Kṛṣṇa the Lord of *yoga* himself.

O King Dhṛtarāṣṭra, as you know, Vyāsa blessed me with a divine eye to see all that happens on the Battlefield of Kurukṣetra while sitting here in this palace; thus I too got the great fortune of listening to this dialogue and understanding it.

Janmejaya:

O Lord Vyāsa, I was listening to your words intently. I know, this *Gītā* is really your own teaching brought forth as the words of Kṛṣṇa. You and Kṛṣṇa, in principle, are not two at all, for Kṛṣṇa is a character created by you, and the words he speaks are your own. I feel, therefore, that the word *vyāsa-prasādāt* (by the Grace of Vyāsa), put at the end of the text is somewhat like the signature an artist puts at the bottom of a painting. It indicates also that the world had the fortune of having this wisdom-teaching only because of your Grace. Those who take to a serious study of this text too should have the feeling that they get this opportunity only because of your Grace.

राजन्संस्मृत्य संस्मृत्य संवादमिममद्भुतम् ।
केशवार्जुनयोः पुण्यं हृष्यामि च मुहुर्मुहुः ॥७६ ॥
तच्च संस्मृत्य संस्मृत्य रुपमत्यद्भुतं हरेः ।
विस्मयो मे महान्राजन्हृष्यामि च पुनः पुनः ॥७७ ॥

rājan saṁsmṛtya saṁsmṛtya saṁvādam imam adbhutam ।
keśavārjunayoḥ puṇyaṁ hṛṣyāmi ca muhur muhuḥ ॥76 ॥

tac ca saṁsmṛtya saṁsmṛtya rūpam atyadbhutaṁ hareḥ ।
vismayo me mahān rājan hṛṣyāmi ca punaḥ punaḥ ॥77 ॥

O King, ruminating again and again on this wonderful and sacred dialogue between Keśava and Arjuna, I rejoice again and again.

The more I recall again and again the most marvellous (Cosmic) Form of Hari (Viṣṇu or Kṛṣṇa), the greater becomes my astonishment; so I rejoice again and again as well.

Sañjaya:

O King, the core of the teaching conveyed through this dialogue can be ruminated and enjoyed. Even such rumination is always accompanied by an experience of blissfulness. More than that blissfulness, it should be accompanied by perceiving the Cosmic Form of *paramātmā* or Kṛṣṇa. In other words, it has to be a blissful experience of seeing everything as well as oneself, together with all *karmas*, as comprising the Cosmic Form of *Brahman*. Then alone does the grandeur of this wisdom dialogue become fully revealed and experientially appreciated, which is the reason for qualifying this sacred science as *guhya* (secret) and *yoga* at the same time. Its origin also, you know, is from Kṛṣṇa, the Lord of *Yoga* (*yogeśvara*). Therefore,

---

यत्र योगेश्वरः कृष्णो यत्र पार्थो धनुर्धरः।
तत्र श्रीर्विजयो भूतिर्ध्रुवा नीतिर्मतिर्मम ॥७८॥

yatra yogeśvaraḥ kṛṣṇo yatra pārtho dhanurdharaḥ ।
tatra śrīr vijayo bhūtir dhruvā nītir matir mama ॥78॥

Where there is Kṛṣṇa, the Lord of Yoga, where there is Arjuna the Archer, there alone is prosperity, there alone is victory, there alone is progress, there alone is stable justice. This is my conviction.

Janmejaya:

O Lord Vyāsa, we saw Arjuna at the beginning in a confused state of mind, fearful with his bow slipping out of his hands. In contrast, he is now seen holding his bow firmly. It shows Arjuna, by the Grace of Yogeśvara, has become a *yogī* himself. He perceives himself as a forming part of the Cosmic Form of the Yogeśvara. His *karma* of battling, from now on, will be seen only as forming an integral part of the infinite and eternal flow of *karma* natural with the Cosmic Form. Arjuna will no longer feel himself to be the doer of that *karma* or any *karma.* Doubtlessly he will not be benefit-motivated in doing *karmas* either. At the same time he will experience at each moment the Self-Happiness (*ātmānanda*) of fully bringing out all the potentials hidden within himself in his *svadharma* of fighting.

O Lord Vyāsa, this scripture, no doubt, will continue forever to help those who are intent on making their own life fully liberated, meaningful and blissful. May your Grace be on every one of them!

Thus ends Chapter Eighteen entitled Saṁnyāsa-Yoga, of the Bhagavad-Gītā, the essence of the Upaniṣads, that embodies brahma-vidyā as a yoga-śāstra, in the form of a dialogue between Śrī Kṛṣṇa and Arjuna.

॥ ***Thus ends the Bhagavad-Gītā, the essence of the Upaniṣads*** ॥

Glossary

Abhayam : Fearlessness. One of the aspects in which the knowledge of *Brahman* is experienced as a value.

Abhyāsa : Continued practice or repetitively doing something of high value.

Adharma: That which is against *dharma.*

Adhyātma: Loosely translated as spirituality. Strictly, that kind of knowledge which tries to understand the Reality in everything, with one's self-existence as the point of reference. (from *adhi,* "to make a basis," and *ātmā,* "oneself or the self").

Adhyātma-śāstra: Scriptures. The texts that help seekers attain the all-underlying Reality through knowing the Reality that underlies one's own being.

Adhiṣṭhāna: That on which everything rests.

Āgāmi-karma: See *Karma.*

Ahaṁkāra: The I-sense each individual has.

Ahiṁsā : The habit of abstaining from killing or hurting others in thought, word or deed.

Aiśvarya: Supremacy. In ordinary usage, affluence.

Ajñāna: Ignorance. The mistaken notion, concerning oneself and the world, that what appears manifestly is real, completely oblivious of the one all-underlying Reality called *Brahman* or *ātman.*

Ajñānin: The one in *ajñāna* (see *ajñāna* above).

Akarma: Non-action.

Akṣara: The imperishable. Refers to the Ultimate Reality, *Brahman.*

Akṣara-puruṣa: The imperishable person. The personified concept of *Brahman.*

Amṛta: Immortality or the Immortal Reality. Poetically imagined as the elixir in a golden pot that emerged from the Milk-Ocean when the *deva*s and the *asura*s churned it together.

Amṛtattva: The state of being *amṛta* or immortal.

Ānanda: Bliss. To be understood in the context of the 'Good' in Western philosophy as a supreme value. *Sat, cit* and *ānanda* are terms conjointly used to describe the Absolute (*Brahman*) in Vedānta. Concerning an individual being, it is to be understood as the value-consciousness that enables one to evaluate one's own experiences either as pleasant or unpleasant.

Ananya-manas: The state in which one experiences one's mind as fully identified with the cosmic mind.

*Antaḥkaraṇa*s: The common name for the four mental faculties involved in the process of knowing: namely *manas* (questioning), *buddhi* (reasoning), *citta* (memorizing and recalling) and *ahaṁkāra* (relating what is known to oneself in terms of value experience).

Aṇu: Atom. Literally, the indivisible.

Ānvīkṣikī: Logical Philosophy; Metaphysics. One of the three basic human disciplines. The other two are *vārtā* and *daṇḍa* (see).

Aparā: Relativistic; conditional.

Aparokṣānubhūti: Literally, im-mediate experience. The intuitive experience of one's own identity with the Absolute or *Brahman*. The satisfaction or fulfilment of enquiry on one's finding the Reality searched for as oneself.

Aprameya: The unknowable; the inconceivable.

Apūrva: The mysterious factor, according to Mīmāmsakas, that retains the immediate effects of Vedic rituals, enabling the performer to enjoy their results either in this life or hereafter.

Aratī: The psychological disorder in which one becomes interested in nothing.

Arcir-mārga: The path of brightness; another name for *devayāna* (see).

Āścarya: Feeling the mysteriousness of life and the world, oneself being part of it.

Asuras: The opposite of *suras* or *devas* (gods — the fair or bright entities inhabiting the Vedic heaven). Demons. This idea might have come into being with reference to anyone who opposed the Āryan penetration, ideologically or in historical activity. The conflict between the *devas* and *asuras* permeates the whole of the spiritual literature of the Vedic Indians, and has to be understood historically or in pure dialectics according to the requirements of the context. Max-Müller thinks there is an affinity between *Ahura* (*Ahura Mazda*) of the Zoroastrians and *Asura*.

Āsurī-prakṛti: Demonic character of human beings.

Āsurī-sampat: The state of possessing *āsurī-prakṛti* (see).

Anātman: Non-self.

Ātmārāma: One who enjoys being oneself by knowing the real content of oneself.

Avatāra: Incarnation of God, a concept of Vaiṣṇavism that Viṣṇu incarnates from time to time to save the world from evil forces. Ten such incarnations are believed in, nine of the past and one yet to come.

Avidyā: Nescience or ignorance. That function of consciousness because of which the unreal is taken for the real, and the real for the unreal. The root-cause of *ajñāna* (see) and sufferings.

Avyakta: That which is not specific and definable. The opposite of *vyakta*.

Bhagavān: The word denoting God, used in the context of devotion (*bhakti*). Literally, one in possession of brilliant qualities (*bhagas*).

Bhajanā: Popularly, to sing devotional songs. Philosophically, intense contemplation.

Bhakta: See *bhakti.*

Bhakti: Devotedness. Derived from the root *bhaj,* meaning "to meditate constantly on something." It can either be fully supported by wisdom (*jñāna*) or be in the form of full surrender to God with no understanding as such. The latter form is known as *prapatti.* A devotee is called *bhakta.*

Bhāva: Any transient form the eternal Reality (*sat*) assumes. Without a *bhāva, sat* never exists, neither can any *bhāva* be there without *sat* existing.

Bhoktā (*Bhoktṛ*): Enjoyer, the subject who enjoys.

Bhūta: That which has come into being.

Brahman: The Absolute. Derived from the verb root *bṛh,* "to grow constantly." Literally, "that which grows constantly."

Brahmacārin: (From *Brahman,* the Absolute, and *cārin,* he who moves on.) One who is moving on the path of *Brahman.* Name of one who is in the first stage of life as a student in a *gurukula.* Such a way of life is called *brahamacarya.* As a corollary, this kind of life would include such disciplines as continence as helpful to realization. But the abstinence from sex is only one of the implied considerations in the discipline of *brahmacarya.* As evidenced many times in the Upaniṣads, *ṛṣi*s have been married and were still able to walk the path of *Brahman.*

Brahmacarya: The state of being a *brahmacārin* (see).

Brahma-vidyā: The Science of the Absolute. Another name for Vedānta.

Brāhmaṇa: One of the four *varṇa*s in the *cāturvarṇya* (see) concept, referring to those who love to learn and teach.

Brāhmī-sthiti: The state in which one finds oneself well founded in *Brahman.*

Buddhi: Understanding. Also denotes the reasoning faculty of mind.

Cāturvarṇya: The four psychological types or mental colourations as conceived by Indian psychologists. These are brāhmaṇa, kṣatriya, vaiśya, śūdra. Those who are by nature inclined to learning and teaching are brāhmaṇas; those who give leadership to the public with firm mind are kṣatriyas; those who are desirous of becoming wealthy taking to agriculture, rearing cattle, trading and so on are vaiśyas; those who by nature like to live by serving others are śūdras.

Cetanā: The life principle that animates beings. *Cit* in its functional state.

Chandas: Prosody. Regarded as one of the disciplines auxiliary to Vedas. Vedic hymns. Vedic metres.

Cit: Literally, "consciousness." The essential content of the imperishable Reality, pervading all the perishable and visible forms, is pure Consciousness. Hence, *Brahman* is designated as *cit* in essence. See *sat* and *ānanda* also.

Citta: The memorizing and recalling faculty of mind. One of the *antaḥkaraṇa*s (see).

Dakṣiṇā: Free gifts offered to priests and *saṁnyāsins*. It is customary that priests, at the conclusion of all Vedic rituals, should be pleased by the sacrificer with such gifts.

Daivī-prakṛti: Divine nature in human beings, as opposed to *Asurī-prakṛti* (see).

Dāna: Giving, granting, teaching. A gift offered as a religious rite.

Daṇḍa: The science of statecraft and politics. One of the three basic human disciplines. The other two are *ānvīkṣikī* and *vārtā*.

Deha: Physical body. Literally, "that which grows."

Dehī (*dehin*) : The substance that assumes the form of *deha* (see).

Deva: God. Inhabitants of the Vedic heaven.

Devayāna: The path of the gods. One of the two paths through which the departed souls supposedly go to the other world, from where they will not return. Literally, "the bright path." Also called *śukla-gati,* the white path. (See *pitṛyāna*) Another name for *arcir-mārga* (see).

Dharma: Derived from the root *dhṛ* "to support." The universal functional system that sustains world and life. Righteous way of life fully in harmony with the universal order.

Dharmya: That which is in accordance with *dharma;* that which can be practised in actual life as a part of the cosmic order.

Dhṛti: Firmness of mind.

Dhūma mārga: See *pitṛyāna.*

Dhyāna: Meditation.

Dveṣa: Hatred; dislike.

Ekāgratā: One-pointed attention and concern, particularly with regard to the attainment of the final goal of life.

Eṣaṇā: Desire. Most common worldly interests : these are *putreṣaṇā* (interest in one's children), *vitteṣaṇā* (interest in wealth) and *dāreṣaṇā* (interest in wife). These are the strongest binding forces in worldly life.

Guṇas: Qualities or functional peculiarities inherent in nature. These are three: *sattva, rajas* and *tamas.*

Guṇātīta: One who has gone beyond the limitations and impacts of the three *guṇas* (see).

Guru: (from *gu,* "darkness," and *ru,* "to counteract"). The banisher of darkness or ignorance. A spiritual teacher or preceptor.

Guru-bhakti: The devotedness a disciple feels towards his *guru.*

Guru-śiṣya-pārasparya: The intimate bipolar rapport between *guru* and disciple. No effective imparting of wisdom is possible in the absence of this rapport.

Guru-suśrūṣā: Personal services a disciple does willingly to his *guru.*

Gurutva: Respect for *guru*-hood.

Icchā: The power of volition.

Indriya: Sense organs. The five sense organs and the five organs of action (speech, hands, feet, excretory organ, genitals) together.

Īśa: The Sanskrit equivalent to God. Literally, "one who controls." It refers to the principle that controls the integral law that sustains each entity as a particular mode of expression of the universal being.

Iṣṭa-karma: Pious acts such as performing fire-sacrifices, worshipping deities and the like, contrasted with *pūrtta karma*s which are pious acts meant for public benefits, such as digging public wells, building camp-sheds for travellers, planting shade trees and the like.

Īśvara: The Sanskrit equivalent to "God." Literally, "one who controls everything." *Īśa + vara; vara,* means "the highest."

Īśvara-praṇidhāna: Profound meditation on God.

Itihāsa: The Sanskrit word for "Epic." Defined as "the narration of ancient historical events in order to teach the four basic human values," viz., *dharma* (righteousness), *artha* (wealth), *kāma* (desires) and *mokṣa* (final liberation).

Jaṅgama: Anything movable.

Japa: Muttering of sacred formulas. Literally, "to gain clarity both mentally and verbally."

Jāti-dharma: One's obligation on account of the caste system and tribal traditions.

Jitātmā: A person who is fully in his own control.

Jīva: The Sanskrit equivalent to "living organism." Mistaken for the Sanskrit equivalent to "soul." Often confused with *ātman*, the self.

Jīvātmā: Individuated self, as against the universal Self (*paramātman*), in Śaṅkara's school of Vedānta.

Jñāna: Wisdom. In the Vedāntic context, the Wisdom of the non-difference of oneself from the universal Reality. The way of *jñāna* (*jñāna-mārga*) is contrasted with that of rituals and action (*karma-mārga*).

Karma: All actions in general. Philosophically the creative urge inherent in the Imperishable Reality, causing the emergence of all manifest forms from Itself. In the Vedic context, the ritual of burnt-sacrifice enjoined by the Vedas. As a religious belief of the Hindus, the incipient memory factors clinging to the souls as a residue of their past deeds. All are bound to enjoy or suffer the fruits of their deeds, and will have to reincarnate for this purpose. One might be accumulating more *karma*s in the new birth. This vicious chain of actions goes on till one attains final release. Such *karma*s are divided into three categories — *sañcita karma* (the actions accumulated in all the previous births), *āgāmī karma* (fresh actions done in the present lifetime) and *prārabdha karma* (action already initiated but eating of its fruits is not finished with).

Kṣara-puruṣa: The perishable person; referring to the individual soul.

Kṣatriya: The warrior class. One of the four classes of the Indian caste-system. Originally refers to the psychological type which has prowess, brightness, firmness, skill, generosity, dignity and never-absconding as its main characteristics.

Kṣetra: The field. *Kṣetra,* defined as body in the *Bhagavad-Gītā*, includes in it everything that is changeful, both physical and mental. *Kṣetrajña* is the consciousness that witnesses all that happens in the realm of *kṣetra*. The entire Chapter XIII of the *Bhagavad-Gītā* is devoted to a discussion of this, one of the central points of philosophy.

Kṣetrajña: See *kṣetra.*

Kula-dharma: One's obligation to clan traditions.

Kūṭastha: Fully stable like a rock. Referring to *Brahman* or *ātman.*

Loka: The world. Literally, "that which is perceptible."

Loka-saṁgraha: Concern for the overall system of life.

Mahābhārata: One of the two Indian Epics. The *Bhagavad-Gītā* forms part of it.

Maharṣi: Maha + ṛṣi; a great *ṛṣi* or seer.

Mahā-vākyas: Literally, "the great sentences." Applied to the conclusive formula of Vedāntic wisdom, such as *tat-tvam-asi* (That thou art), *aham brahamāsmi* (I am *Brahman*), *prajñānam brahma* (Consciousness is *Brahman*), *ayam ātma brahma* (this self is *Brahman*), *auṁ tat sat* (*auṁ*, that is what is real), *sarvam khalvidam brahma* (everything here indeed is *Brahman*).

Mamakāra: "Mine"-sense that always follows "I"-sense (*ahaṁkāra*).

Manas: Mind. That which is constituted of *manas* is called *manomaya*. *Manas* consists of the questioning and imagining faculties of consciousness.

Manīṣin (*Manīṣī*): A wise person.

Matam: Religion. Literally, "one's confirmed opinion."

Māyā: The mysterious urge inherent in the Absolute (*Brahman or ātman*) to unfold itself as all the worlds and the phenomenon of life. The very appearing of the world caused thus ends up in becoming a sort of veil put over the Absolute, hiding its vision from our view and making the illusory vision that the apparent world is the real.

Moha: Confused or deluded state of mind.

Mukti (*mokṣa*): Final liberation. Literally, "freedom."

Muni: A silent recluse.

Mūrti: Concrete form that an abstract something assumes. Used also to mean any worshippable idol, in this context.

Naimittika-karma: Actions one has to do incidentally in life.

Naiṣkarmya-siddhi : Attaining the state of mind of feeling no obligation to do any action as such.

Nididhyāsana: The last stage of gaining wisdom. *Śravaṇa* (hearing the word of instruction from the *guru*) and *manana* (intense cogitation on what is heard from the *guru*) are the two preceding stages.

Niḥśreyas: The name given to the final goal, by the Nyāya school of thought.

Nirveda: Another word for *vairāgya* (see).

Niṣkāma-karma: Action not motivated by personal benefits, but performed as a part of the creative function of nature with full sense of detachment. Such actions keep their doers always liberated from all bondages.

Nitya-karmas: The action one is bound to do everyday.

Nīti: Justice.

Nivṛtti-mārga: The way of withdrawal. Followed by those who are interested in wisdom. See *Pravṛtti-mārga.*

Niyama: Self-restraint. The second of the eight principal steps for final attainment according to the Yoga school: it consists of cleanliness, contentment, austerity, self-learning and meditation on God.

Pañca-śuddhi: Five kinds of cleanliness to be practised: of mind, words, body, senses and surroundings.

Pañcīkaraṇa: The way the five basic elements supposedly are blended together so as to appear as actual physical elements.

Paṇḍita: Another word for *jñānin*. One who possesses *paṇḍā*, the wisdom represented by the Upaniṣads.

Parā: The transcendental.

Paradharma: Occupation foreign to one's personal traits.

Paramānanda: Supreme Happiness.

Paramātman (*paramātmā*): The Supreme or Transcendental Self.

Pārasparya: Mutual respect and concern between two, as between husband and wife, *guru* and disciple.

Pitṛ: The soul of the departed.

Pitṛ-loka: The world of the departed souls (from *pitṛ*, "manes" or departed souls, and *loka*, "the world").

Pitṛyāna: The path of the manes. One of the two paths through which the departed souls supposedly travel to the other world, from where they would be returning. Also called *kṛṣṇa gati* (the black path) and *dhūma-mārga* (the path of smoke).

Prajā: That which is born. All living beings.

Prajāpati: Literally, "the lord of those who are born." Name applied to the Creator as the progenitor of all living beings, and represents an ontological version of Brahmā the Creator.

Prakṛti: Nature. Literally, "that which is always in an active state." This activeness is inherent in the ultimate Reality or *Brahman*. *Brahman* in its active state is called *prakṛti*.

Pralaya: The Deluge. Literally, "proper dissolution."

Pramāda: Inability to behave as situation demands.

*Pramāṇa*s: Any valid means of certitude (*pramā*). Six of them are acceptable to Vedāntins, and their validity, excepting that of *śabda*, is only in respect of worldly knowledge. They are *pratyakṣa* (perception), *anumāna* (inference), *upamāna* (comparison or analogy), *śabda* (scriptures), *arthāpatti* (presumption) and *anupalabdhi* (non-apprehension).

Pramātṛ: The knower. The subject.

Prameya: Object of knowledge.

Prāṇa: The vital breath. The functions of vital breath are identified as five, namely *prāṇa* (going upward), *apāna* (going downward), *vyāna* (that which takes vitality to every part of the body), *samāna* (that which keeps the balance of the body) and *udāna* (that which leaves the body at death).

Prāṇāyāma: Restraining the breath during the mental recitation of sacred formulas. The fourth of the eight steps for attainment according to the Yoga System.

Prārabdha-karma: See *karma*.

Pravacana: Discourse given by a learned person or *guru*. After completing formal education under a *guru*, a student has to continue his studies at home through self-study (*svādhyāya*) complemented by attending discourses of the learned as and when occasions arise. Eventually, he too will have to give discourses.

Pravṛtti-mārga: The way of active involvement as against *nivṛtti-mārga* (see).

Prayāṇa-kāla: The time of departing from this world, or the moment one gives up identity with the body.

Preyas: The common name for the aggregate of worldly values.

Punar-āvṛtti: Repeated coming back to this world or to worldly life.

Purāṇas: Literally, "the ancient." The collection of legends of antiquity, meant mainly for teaching the common man the philosophy of the Upaniṣads with the help of numerous tales.

Puruṣa: Literally, "person." The word is used both in universal and particular senses. In the universal sense, He is the cosmic person who has the entire cosmos for his body. In this sense He is often called *virāṭ-puruṣa*.

Puruṣottama: The Absolute principle or Godhead as distinct from demigods and divinities of various religious expressions. *Puruṣa*, in the Sāṁkhya Philosophy, is the spiritual principle as contrasted with *prakṛti* or material nature. When Advaita revalues this concept of *puruṣa* in an effort to raise it above all taints of dualistic implications, the idea of *puruṣottama* arises, as in Chapter XV of the *Bhagavad-Gītā*, where there is transcendence of both the eternal and the transient aspects of knowledge.

Rāga: The attachmant one develops towards pleasurable objects.

Rājā: King; literally, "one who brings about harmony."

Rajo-guṇa: See *guṇas*.

Rāmāyaṇa: An epic (like the *Mahābhārata*) composed by Vālmikī centred round the history of Rāma, the king of Ayodhyā, who travelled to the extreme south of India and to Sri Lanka. The *Rāmāyaṇa* brings in juxtaposition the Āryan and the proto-Āryan civilizations of India.

Ṛṣi: Literally, "a seer, a seer of Reality." Name applied to those sages of ancient India who lived generally in the seclusion of forests and wrote holy scriptures of canonical importance and classical value. They were not necessarily monks, and many of them had their wives living with them. *Maharṣi* means a great *ṛṣi.*

Śabda: Literally, any sound or word. In the philosophical context, any scriptural utterance, one of the *pramāṇa*s (see*)*. The only means that leads to transcendental knowledge. Also called *āgama* and *śruti.*

Sādhu: Good, virtuous.

Sāgara: The abode of *amṛta;* ocean.

Sākṣātkāra: Realization.

Samadarśin: One who views everything as one Reality having become manifest differently, and thus seeing one in many.

Samādhi: Finding one's own proper abode and becoming stabilized in it.

Sambhava: Event; the coming into being of something.

Saṁkalpa: Mind's wilful imagining.

Sāṁkhya: One of the six systems of Indian Philosophy.

*Sāṁkhya-buddhi:*Applying properly one's reasoning power to find out the ultimate meaning of life.

Saṁnyāsa: Renouncing in general; renouncing all desire-motivated actions.

Saṁsāra: The world of becoming. Literally, "that which is always changing." A synonym for worldly life, considered full of sufferings.

Saṁśaya: Doubt.

Saṁśayātmā: One who doubts the veracity of one's own *guru*'s teaching.

Sanātana: The eternal.

Sañcita-karma: See *karma.*

Santoṣa: To be happy with what one already possesses.

Saṁtuṣṭa: One in a state of *santoṣa* (see).

Śarīra: Literally, "that which perishes." The physical body or visible form.

Śāstra: Literally, "science." Any basic scripture.

Sat: That which exists always. The subsisting Reality in all the transistory forms of the visible world, even as gold is the subsisting reality in all ornaments. *Brahman,* as this subsisting Reality, is designated as *sat*. See *ānanda* and *cit* also.

Sattva-guṇa: See *guṇa*s.

Sattva-śuddhi: Purity of one's being; mental purity.

Śauca: Cleanliness.

Sāyujya: Experiencing one's own merger in the Absolute.

*Siddha*s: Those of unworldly attainments; those who have attained their final goal.

Siddhi: Unworldly attainments; attainment of one's final goal.

Śiṣya: A disciple; seeker.

*Smṛti*s: Learning or scriptural lore remembered by a student when he applies wisdom-teaching in his practical life. Obligatory conduct and religious duties belong to this category. Also known as *Dharma-Śāstra.* What is taught in them are subject to change in accordance with time and clime.

Soma: Name of a creeper, the most important ingredient in ancient fire sacrifices; its juice.

Śraddhā: One of the prerequisites on the part of a seeker. Willingness to have full faith in the truthfulness of the word of the *guru* and of the scriptures. A necessary stepping stone to *manana.*

Śravaṇa: Intense cogitation on what is directly heard from a *guru* (*śravaṇa*), leading finally to full conviction and realization (*nididhyāsana*).

Śṛeyas: Highest value one can aspire to in life, represented by wisdom, as against *preyas* (see).

Śruti: That which is heard. The words heard from a *guru.* The recorded utterings of the past *guru*s concerning pure wisdom-teaching of eternal value. All the Upaniṣads are considered *śruti*s.

Sthāvara: The immovable, as against *jaṅgama* (see).

Sthita-prajña: One who is fully stabilized in enlightened awareness.

Śuddhi: Purity (see *pañca-śuddhi*).

Śūdras: See *cāturvarṇya.*

Sukham: Another word for *ānanda.*

Śukla-gati: Another name for *devayāna.*

Sukṛtam: Literally, "well-done." In the Vedic sense the meticulous performance of rituals and the merits accrued thereby. Any meritorious deed. The merit achieved through such deeds.

Sukṛti: One who does *sukṛtam.*

*Sura*s: Gods, inhabitants of heaven. Literally, "those who give abundantly."

Svadhā: The offerings made to appease *pitṛ*s.

Svādhyāya: The self-study a student has to continue at home after completing formal education under a *guru* and leaving the *gurukula.*

Tamo-guṇa: See *Guṇa*s.

Tapas: Austere self-discipline. Literally, "heating up."

Tat: That. Stands for the Absolute or *Brahman* as the Reality to be searched for.

Tattva: The state of "that" being "that" pure and simple; basic principle; basic Reality.

Tattva-darśin: A visionary of basic principle or basic Reality, the oneness of *tat* (That) and *tvam* (you or oneself).

Tattva-vit: The knowner of *tattva* (see).

Tyāga: Relinquishment; relinquishing the fruits of action.

Udāsīna: Indifference; the state in which no like or dislike is aroused.

Upāsanā: Worship, adoration; literally, "sitting closely and doing services."

Upaniṣads: When the chapter of *karma* or ritualistic action has been transcended by a religious student or *brahmacārin,* he is ready to receive the posterior philosophical teachings which constitute Vedānta (i.e., the end of the Vedas). The Vedānta is non-theological, concerned with the Absolute or *Brahman.* The word is said to be derived form *upa,* "beside" and *niṣad,* "sitting near," so that it is a teaching received by a disciple when he is allowed to sit and listen to philosophical teachings near or by the side of the *guru.*

Uttama-puruṣa: The same as *puruṣottama* (see).

Vairāgya: Sense of detachment towards everything transient.

Vaiśya: One of the four castes of the Indian caste system. The merchant and the agriculturist class. As a psychological type, those who find life-fulfilment in farming, tending cattle and trade.

Varṇa: Literally, "colour." The four different psychological types recognized by traditional Indian psychologists. They are, brāhmaṇa, kṣatriya, vaiśya, and śūdra. It was confused with *jāti* (see) making it instrumental for social discrimination and exploitation of the weak.

Varṣa: Indian mythologial concept of continents. India, in this context, is known as Bhārata-varṣa.

Vārtā: The science of agriculture and trade; one of the three basic disciplines, the other two being *ānvīkṣikī* and *daṇḍa.*

Vedānta: When the Vedic teaching was revalued in philosophical terms by later *ṛṣis*, a body of literature called Vedānta arose in the history of Indian thought. This often goes contrary to the Vedic tendency of rituals and obligations, announcing freedom and stressing self-realization. Later we find Śaṅkara, Rāmānuja and Madhva, referred to as three typical Vedāntic philosophers, although the *gurus* of the Vedāntic line (*paramparā*) are many.

Vedas: The earliest of the Indian scriptures, collected into four volumes, namely the *Ṛgveda, Yajurveda, Sāmaveda,* and *Atharvaveda.* They praise Indra, Varuṇa, Mitra and other phenomenal gods of nature. They were later overcome by the Upaniṣads. The word Veda means "knowledge." The Vedas generally stand for rituals (*karma*).

Vibhūti: Specific manifest form.

Vidyā: Knowledge. That function of consicousness because of which one understands the Real as the real and unreal as the unreal.

Vijñāna: Any specific or applied form of knowledge or wisdom.

Vikarma: Wrong action.

Vikṛti: Anything that evolves from *prakṛti.*

Virāṭ-puruṣa: See *puruṣa.*

Vyabhicāra: Deviation from the path of *brahmacarya;* also used to mean prostitution.

Vyakta: That which is specific and definable.

Vyakti: An individual; anything that has a specific (*vyakta*) form.

Yajamāna: A person who employs priests to perform fire-sacrifice for his sake.

Yajña: Sacrifice. Vedic fire-sacrifice. To offer what is considered as possessed by an individual back to the universal *prakṛti* to which everything, including ourselves, belongs.

Yajña-śiṣṭa: The remains of a *yajña*, partaken by the participants as symbolizing the grace of God.

Yati: One of self-restraint.

Yoga: (From the root *yuj*). Each finding one's inseparable oneness with the one causal Reality, just as an ornament finds its oneness with gold. As a contemplative method of self-enquiry, the way of expressing an inexpressible reality by showing its two opposite sides and leaving the unitive meaning to be understood by the reader or seeker on his own. For example, attaining immortality and crossing over death are two expressions meaning the same. But these two expressions are opposite in nature. They have in between them a meaning that cannot be expressed as it is. Different systems of *yoga* have been developed in India, each giving emphasis to some particular pair joined together. Patañjali's system is known also as *Rāja-Yoga*. The names such as *Haṭha-Yoga, Karma-Yoga, Jñāna-Yoga, Bhakti-Yoga* are popular. Each of the eighteen chapters of the *Bhagavad-Gītā* is also named a *yoga*. The *Bhagavad-Gītā* itself claims to be a *Yoga-Śāstra* (textbook on the science of *yoga*).

Yoga-bhraṣṭa: He who is thrown out of *yoga*.

Yoga-buddhi: The awareness attained by the method of *yoga* (see).

Yoga-kṣema: The well-being one feels when fully identified with the Total.

Yogārūḍha: The state in which one is fully identified with the Absolute or the Total.

Yogī (*Yogin*): One who is an adept in *yoga*.

Yuga: Mythological concept of the age of the world. The ages are four: *Kṛta* or *Satya*, *Tretā*, *Dvāpara*, and *Kali*, the duration of each is said to the respectively 1,728,000, years, 1,296,000 years, 864,000 years and 432,000 years. Supposedly we are living in the *Kali-yuga* in which 75 per cent of human virtues are lost.

Index